Michael Burgoon
Michael Ruffner

Human Communication

A Revision of
Approaching Speech/Communication

Holt, Rinehart and Winston

New York   Chicago   San Francisco   Atlanta   Dallas
Montreal   Toronto   London   Sydney

Editor	Roth Wilkofsky
Senior Project Editor	Lester A. Sheinis
Copy Editor	Cecil P. Golann
Production Manager	Robert de Villeneuve
Picture Editor	Gina Jackson
Design	Arthur Ritter
Drawings	Rex Lau and Diane Mayo
Indexer	Jane R. Tonero
Typography	Precision Typographers

Other acknowledgments appear on page 524.

Library of Congress Cataloging in Publication Data

Burgoon, Michael.
  Human communication.
  Published in 1974 under title: Approaching
speech/communication.
  Includes bibliographies and index.
  1. Communication. I. Ruffner, Michael, joint
author. II. Title.
P90.B85 1978   808.5   77–17511
ISBN: 0–03–020416–X

Preface

Human Communication is a book designed for the introductory course in speech and communication. It is a fundamentals approach to the basic course in that we have covered a broad spectrum of information about communication. The book is divided into three major sections dealing with (1) the *nature* of human communication and the variables that affect that complex process; (2) the *contexts* in which communication occurs, including the dyad, small-group, public-speaking, and mass-communication contexts; (3) the *functions* of human communication, including persuasion and compliance gain, development of social relationships, and the management of conflict. The scope is intentionally broad; we have attempted to provide only an introductory level treatment of important information about a variety of human communication situations.

Although this is a revised edition of an earlier book, it is not a traditional second edition. Much of the material in this book is new and different from the earlier edition. Moreover, the perspective we have taken mandated a title change; this treatment is more concerned with an examination of the total process of human communication. We still believe that people interested in a public-speaking approach to a basic communication course will find this text useful and informative. A great deal of material on speech anxiety, speech preparation, and public speaking has been added. Those who wish to emphasize interpersonal and small-group approaches to an introductory course will find that this book offers current research and thinking in those areas, presented in a way that we hope students will find useful and interesting. Finally, we have added chapters on the communication process that we feel any

student, regardless of the nature of the course, should be introduced to.

We have had the assistance of about thirty reviews from professionals in the communication disciplines. Those reviews gave us almost thirty suggestions about the "right" way to organize a basic text. The organizational pattern we have evolved may not satisfy everyone, but it does represent our best effort at cogently organizing a vast amount of material in a limited space. We attempt to provide a perspective on the process of human communication and develop the book from that perspective. As the book progresses we feel that more and more substance is provided; we hope that student understanding, consequently, will increase at an ever-accelerating rate.

We think that a major strength of this book is the instructional modules that accompany the chapters. We have used many new and previously unpublished exercises in these modules that we believe illustrate many of the important concepts in the chapters. As instructors, we do not believe that only the instructor should know the "real" purpose of the exercises while the students do not know what is happening. The exercises in this book are there for all to see and use. The student is told what is expected and is asked for analysis, criticism, and reactions to those exercises. These instructional modules are self-contained, and students can pace themselves through definitions, study questions, and exercises. *If a student successfully completes the material in the instructional modules, it is highly probable that he or she has mastered the text material*. We worked diligently to provide exercises that made sense and had potential learning value for the students.

This book is based heavily on current research in human communication, but it is not a research monograph. We have attempted to provide evidence that describes how people communicate and with what effect. It has not been our intent, however, to overwhelm the student and the instructor with technical descriptions of research literature. We have attempted to translate the research into useful statements about the present state of knowledge in our discipline. We have also attempted to suggest applications of that research in everyday communication situations. At times we merely describe what is known about human communication; at other times we have been unafraid to speculate about how one might communicate more effectively. We hope that it is apparent to all when we are describing and when we are speculating. We very much want the student to be able to apply what we have to say in this book to his or her own communication experiences. Throughout the writing of this edition we have taken great care to improve on the format, readability, and language usage of the first edition. Specifically, we have directed our attention toward both the beginning student and the communication scholar. We would hope that each reader of this text bears in mind that others with more or less communication training will also be scrutinizing this material. Some of our critics have accused us of being frivolous, light, irreverent, and yet sometimes pedantic in our approach. The sharp reader or word buff can quickly ascertain that this approach can be summed up as *f-l-i-p*. We must plead guilty to this primarily because we see the world in *f-l-i-p* terms. While we view the world in this fashion, we are quite serious about communication generally and promoting a better understanding of communication specifically.

While we were researching material for this book, two thoughts occurred to us. First, neither of us knew enough about nonverbal communication to provide a thorough synthesis, and, second, we needed a sound ending that would bridge our coverage to communication in the future. So we began a slow, painstaking, and methodical search to find the best authors in the field to write a nonverbal chapter and a commentary on communication in the future. We are pleased to report that this extensive and impartial search turned up for the tasks, respectively, the wife and the former major professor of the first author. We are quite pleased with the results, regardless of the search procedure. We feel that Chapter 5, written by Judee K. Burgoon, is easily one of the best nonverbal communication chapters written to date. Moreover, Gerald Miller's piece on communication in the future, a particularly excellent and timely commentary, is of unquestionable benefit to our perspective of human communication; it serves as the Epilogue of the book.

The writing of a textbook often becomes a long and arduous task owing to the time element, the tedium, and the bulk of material to be covered. Therefore, it is becoming increasingly common to find college textbooks written by two or more authors. While such collaboration often increases the quality and scope of the final product, two temperamental or egotistical writers involved in unproductive conflict or competition may decrease the quality of the work. We were quite fortunate in that with similar temperaments, motivations, and writing skills, we were able to stimulate each other and channel our energies into productive ends. We hope that this thoroughly enjoyable and profitable experience for us is evident in the final product.

Like most college professors, the roots of our academic growth go deep into that bastion of knowledge—the library. Perhaps it is from earlier times when we had the luxury to browse for hours in that library that we chose this calling. We find ourselves with precious little time to browse at length in the library now, and, consequently, many of us have become disenfranchised with that venerable institution. We are grateful that this book has given us the opportunity to reacquaint ourselves with this old friend.

We would like to express our appreciation to the following people, who helped by evaluating the weaknesses of the first edition and/or reviewing the second-edition manuscript: Raymond Beard, State University of New York College at Cortland; Robert Benjamin, San Diego State University; Loretta Blahna, University of Minnesota; Richard Crable, Purdue University; Donald Cushman, Michigan State University; Shirley Gilbert, University of Denver; Dennis Gunderson, University of Alabama; Roger Haney, University of Kentucky; Cal Hylton, San Jose State University; Lynda Lee Kaid, University of Oklahoma; Jerry Koehler, University of South Florida; Al Kowitz, California State University at Sacramento; Charles Larson, Northern Illinois University; Patrick McDermott, University of Wyoming; Gerald Miller, Michigan State University; Michael Moore, University of Maryland; Robert Nofsinger, Jr., Washington State University; Nicholas Rausch, Saint Martin's College; Jerry Reynolds, Hardin-Simmons University; George Rodman, University of New Hampshire; Lawrence Rosenfeld, University of New Mexico; Judith Runkle, University of Delaware; Laura Salazar, Grand Valley State College; William Seiler, University of Nebraska; J. Ted Swindley, Tarleton State University; Dianne Weinand, Loyola University of Chicago; Allen Weiner, University of Southern California.

Many people have provided assistance to me (Michael Ruffner) in one form or another prior to and during the writing of this book. This includes the Harolds, Mamies, Karas, Harrys, and Michaels. To them and others like them I am grateful.

Finally, I (Michael Burgoon) would like to thank several important people. I once again publicly proclaim my huge intellectual debt to Gerry Miller. The Millers have been unwavering friends. Norm Fontes has taught me much about friendship, and sections were written with him in mind. The Heplers and the Hyltons have demonstrated the prospect and promise of long-term dyads; I thank them for the restoration of faith. Roth Wilkofsky and Lester Sheinis of Holt, Rinehart and Winston have been truly an author's editors. Roth believed in this project and allowed us to write our book. Roth and Lester were both there when we needed them, but, more importantly, were not there when we did not need them. I recognize Dr. Robert Bryan, who more than any other person is responsible for the intellectual climate of the University of Florida today, for allowing me to go to Michigan State University, where I was able to finish my writing of this book. To those people at Michigan State University who denied the injunction that "you can't go home again," I thank you for welcoming us and treating us as colleagues. A more personal acknowledgment is to Judee Burgoon, who still is sometimes my student, sometimes my teacher, but now is my full-time companion. I again thank all of those people who care about me and human communication in whichever order.

M.B.
M.R.

Gainesville, Florida
October 1977

Contents

Preface   iii

SECTION 1
THE VARIABLES IN THE COMMUNICATION PROCESS   1

CHAPTER 1   AN INTRODUCTION TO HUMAN COMMUNICATION   3
Assumptions About Human Communication   4
The Nature of the Communication Process   8
   The Transactional Nature of Communication   9
   The Affective Nature of Communication   10
   The Personal Nature of Communication   10
   The Instrumental Nature of Communication   11
   The Consummatory Purpose of Communication   12

Defining the Communication Process   13
Models of Communication   18
   An Information-Centered Model of Communication   20
   The SMCR Model   21
   The Westley-MacLean Model   23

CHAPTER 2   SOURCE VARIABLES   33
Credibility as a Source Variable   34
   The Dimensions of Source Credibility   35
   The Dynamics of Source Credibility   41

Homophily-Heterophily in Communication   43
   Determining Homophily-Heterophily   44
   The Relationship of Homophily-Heterophily to Communication   45
   Compensations for Heterophily   47

Power as a Source Variable   48
   The Components and Types of Power   48
   Conditions That Maximize the Effectiveness of Power   53

CHAPTER 3   RECEIVER VARIABLES   65
Demographic Analysis of an Audience   67
   Age   67
   Sex   68
   Sex Roles   69
   Social and Economic Background   70
   Racial and Ethnic Factors   71
   Intelligence   71

Personality Analysis of a Receiver   72
   Dogmatism   72
   Self-esteem   73
   Aggressiveness and Hostility   74
   Anxiety   75
   Prior Attitudes   75

Machiavellianism   76

Variations in Receiver Listening Ability   77
Barriers to Effective Listening   79

Feedback: The Receiver's Response   81
Interpersonal Trust   84

CHAPTER 4   VARIABLES INHIBITING EFFECTIVE COMMUNICATION   95
Communication as Symbols of Reality   96
Communication and Perception   98
Communication and Selectivity   100
Selective Exposure   100
Selective Attention   101
Selective Perception   103
Selective Retention   105

Inference Versus Observation   107
Intensional Orientations   109
Pointing   110
Blindering   110

Allness   111
Frozen Evaluation   113
Polarization   115
Bypassing   118

CHAPTER 5   NONVERBAL COMMUNICATION   Judee K. Burgoon   129
The Nonverbal Codes   130
Proxemics   130
Chronemics   134
Kinesics   136
Physical Appearance   140
Haptics   141
Paralanguage   143
Artifacts   144

Functions of Nonverbal Communication   146
Symbolic Displays   146
Metamessages   148
Structuring Interaction   152
Self-presentation   153
Manipulating Others   155

SECTION 2
COMMUNICATION CONTEXTS   173

CHAPTER 6   COMMUNICATING WITH ANOTHER   175
Defining Interpersonal Communication   176

Predictions as Defining Characteristics   176
Levels of Knowing as Interpersonal Communication   181
Roles as a Definition of Interpersonal Communication   182
A Developmental View of Interpersonal Communication   185
Form and Function in Interpersonal Communication   187

The Nature of Dyadic Communication   190
Interpersonal Orientations in the Dyad   194
Interpersonal Control in the Dyad   198
Symmetrical Relationships   198
Complementary Relationships   199
Parallel Relationships   201

Self-disclosure   202
Impression Management and Self-disclosing Behavior   202
The Effects of Self-disclosure on the Discloser   203
The Effects of Self-disclosure on the Dyad   205
Risks of Self-disclosure   207

CHAPTER 7   SMALL-GROUP COMMUNICATION   223
The Small Group Defined   224
Characteristics That Make the Small Group Unique   225
Theories for Small-Group Communication   229
Small-Group Structure   231
The Functions of Small Groups   238
Social Relationships   239
Education   239
Persuasion   240
Problem Solving and Decision Making   241
Therapy   245

Discussion in the Small Group   247
Effective Small-Group Discussion   247
Obstacles to Effective Group Discussion   248
Costs and Benefits of Small-Group Discussion   251

Leadership in the Small Group   253
Leadership Styles   255
Leadership and Social Influence   256
Effective Leadership   257

CHAPTER 8   PUBLIC COMMUNICATION: PRIOR ANALYSIS OF THE PUBLIC
SPEAKING SITUATION   269
The Public Communication Context: Some Defining
Characteristics   271
Anxiety About Public Speaking and What to Do About It   275
Assessing Anxiety   275
The Nature of Communication Anxiety   276
What to Do About Your Anxiety   283

Evaluating Public Speeches 287
Initial Planning of the Speech 287
  Deciding the Purpose of the Speech 287
  Analyzing the Audience 287
  Analyzing the Occasion and Location 288
  Choosing the Topic 288

CHAPTER 9 PUBLIC COMMUNICATION: PREPARING AND DELIVERING A
           PUBLIC SPEECH 293
           Preparing a Speech 294
             Invention 294
             Disposition 298
             Style 309
             Delivery 314

           Some Concluding Comments on Effective Public Speaking 316

CHAPTER 10 MASS COMMUNICATION 335
            The Nature of Mass Communication 336
            Theories of Mass Communication 339
              Individual Difference Theory 339
              Social Categories Theory 341
              Social Relationships Theory 341
              Cultural Norms Theory 342
              Environmental Theory 343
              Play Theory 344
              Reflective-Projective Theory 344

            How Mass Communication Works 345
              How Different Media Operate 345
              Transmission of Communication 346
              Opinion Leaders 347
              Gatekeepers 349
              Selectivity in Exposure to Mass Communication 351

            Functions of the Mass Media 352
              Institutional Function 352
              Social Functions 355

            The Impact of Mass Communication 361
              Cognition and Comprehension 362
              Attitude and Value Change 362
              Behavioral Change 363
              The Impact on Children 363
              Forming Expectations 364
              Violence and Aggression 365
              The Report of the Surgeon General's Scientific Advisory Committee on
                Television and Social Behavior 366

Contents

SECTION 3
COMMENTS ON THE FUNCTIONS OF HUMAN COMMUNICATION 375

CHAPTER 11 PERSUASION: APPROACHES TO GAINING COMPLIANCE 377
Defining the Persuasion Process 378
Approaches to Persuasion 381
Learning Theories 383
Consistency Theories 386
Social Judgment Theory 397

CHAPTER 12 PERSUASION: APPLICATIONS AND MESSAGE STRATEGIES 405
The Components of a Persuasive Message 406
Claim 407
Warrant 407
Data 407

Selecting Message Appeals That Are Persuasive 409
Appeals Based on Evidence 410
Appeals Based on Fear 412
Appeals Based on Humor 414
Appeals Varying in Language Intensity 416

Making Strategic Decisions About What to Include in a Persuasive
Message 419
Structuring Effective Persuasive Messages 420
Organizing Supporting Materials 421
Identifying the Source of Evidence 422

Revealing Your Desire to Persuade 422
Presenting Problems and Solutions 423
Stating Points of Agreement and Disagreement 423
Stating Your Conclusions 424

Some Concluding Comments 424

**CHAPTER 13 COMMUNICATION AND THE DEVELOPMENT OF SOCIAL
RELATIONSHIPS** 441
Factors That Promote the Establishment of Social Relationships 442
Rewards as a Determinant of Attraction 443
Similarity and Attraction 446
Proximity and Attraction 447
Self-esteem, Dependence, and Attraction 451
Physical Attraction 452
Phases of Attraction 455
Power and Status as Determinants of Social Relationships 456

Outcomes of Satisfactory Social Relationships 458
Affiliation 459
Affection 460

CONTENTS

Affinity 461
Self-concept 462
Confirmation of Self 464
Reduction of Uncertainty 465
Impression Management 466

Toward Developing Social Relationships, or What Follows *Hello?* 467
Similarity and Attraction 468
Initial Interactions 469
Developing Affinity 471

CHAPTER 14   COMMUNICATION AND CONFLICT   483

Levels of Conflict 484
Intrapersonal Conflict 484
Interpersonal Conflict 485
Intragroup Conflict 486
Intergroup Conflict 487
Institutional Conflict 489

Types of Conflict 490
Real Conflict 490
Artificial Conflict 491
Induced Conflict 491
Violent Versus Nonviolent Conflict 491
Face-to-Face Versus Mediated Conflict 492
Principles and Pragmatics in Conflict 492

Decisions That Promote Conflict 492
Approach-Approach 493
Approach-Avoidance 494
Avoidance-Avoidance 494

Costs and Benefits of Conflict 495
The Costs of Conflict 495
The Benefits of Conflict 496

Strategies for Managing Conflict, or What Follows *Go to Hell?* 499

EPILOGUE
COMMUNICATION IN THE THIRD 100 YEARS: CAN HUMANITY AND TECHNOLOGY COEXIST PEACEFULLY?   Gerald R. Miller   511
The Inevitable Growth of Communication Technology 515
The Debit Side of the Ledger: Possible Harmful Effects of Increased Technology 518
Some Thoughts on Balancing the Scales Between Human Communicators and Mediated Systems 522

Acknowledgments 524
Index 525

Section 1 THE VARIABLES IN THE COMMUNICATION PROCESS

The first section of the book builds the framework for better understanding the complex process of human communication. Several assumptions and misconceptions about the nature of human communication are explored. We suggest that some conceptions of communication are more valuable than others as tools for improving our skills as communicators and for understanding this very complex activity. We also offer several models of communication as well as discuss the use of models as an aid in understanding.

Several important variables that affect human communication will be discussed early in this book. Characteristics of both the source and receiver that affect the likelihood of success in any given communication event and some of the common variables that inhibit effective communication will be explored. Finally the nature and functions of our nonverbal communication will be examined. Throughout, suggestions will be made as to how one goes about managing these important variables in order to be a more effective communicator.

Chapter 1
AN INTRODUCTION TO HUMAN COMMUNICATION

Someone once insightfully said that a fish would be the last to discover the existence of water. What this person probably meant by the statement was that, because water was such a pervasive and important part of a fish's environment, its existence would not even be noticed unless it were absent. In many ways, the manner in which people perceive communication is analogous to a fish's awareness of water. Communication, like water to a fish, surrounds us. We constantly communicate with others; and, except for the biological functions that sustain us, there is no activity more pervasive and critical than communication. Yet people invariably take communication for granted. We have heard many of our students at the beginning of each term question our insistence that communication is a highly complex and difficult process. "After all," the students said, "we have been communicating for nearly twenty years, and we have gotten by without your help so far." We would not be so presumptuous as to suggest that people should read our book—or another like it—to get by. Our purpose is merely to convey to you that there is more to communication than meets the eye.

In so doing, we feel that it is necessary and imperative to dispel some of the more common myths about communication. If we were attempting to write a book about differential calculus, we could be relatively sure of two things: (1) that the majority of our readers would be virtually uninitiated in the subject and (2) that few would dismiss the complexity of the subject on the basis of many years of exposure to it. In short, we are suggesting that just because we are writing about the communication process and just because people have been exposed to it for a number of years, it does not follow that any of us know all there is to know. This process still has many intricacies that go unnoticed without our undivided and complete attention.

In the past we have appealed to our students for that attention to the communication process. We have also attempted to assist them in analyzing it systematically and considering the numerous factors that come to bear in different communication situations. Some came to the conclusion, as we hope you will, that they were communication experts *only* to the extent that they had engaged in the communication process for a number of years. Others, unfortunately, though agreeing that there are many names, terms, processes, approaches, and effects that they had never heard of before, insisted that we were making the process more complex than it is. They felt that they could "get by" simply by getting out there and "relating to people." We do not wish to argue this point. Those who are unmotivated or think that they have all the answers, in terms of communicating with others, will find little of value in this book.

We feel that it is important to step back from the communication process and attempt to analyze it systematically and logically. Through such an analysis people might be better able to recognize, comprehend, and apply many of the principles in the communication process. In so doing, they might actually improve their communication effectiveness instead of just "getting by." Moreover, by increasing communication competencies, people ought to be able to "relate to others" more frequently and more effectively if they choose.

Clearly, no one exists in a vacuum. Everyone belongs to a spiraling hierarchy comprised of interpersonal bonds, family, groups, and organizations. The pervasiveness of communication in this hierarchy is but one indication of the importance of this process in our lives. Through communication, people can exert some control over their physical and social environments. Changes in the social system, the establishment of personal bonds, the successful management of conflict, personal rewards and gratifications, and the accomplishment of mutual goals are possible only through some sort of communication behavior. The social system itself is an accomplishment—or creation—of communication. Communication is pervasive and important; people shape it and it shapes them. It is our assumption that most people will want to learn more about this vital aspect of human behavior, and it is with this thought that we begin.

Assumptions About Human Communication

Perhaps it will be helpful to examine first some of the assumptions that people hold about human communication. Some of these assumptions have been popularized by the media, by business organizations, by some educators, and in some cases by enthusiasts trying to stress the importance of communication skills. We need to let you know what we personally believe from the outset.

All of the problems of this world are not communication problems. Cool Hand Luke in the movie of that name commonly pointed out that "what we have here is a failure to communicate." Others have picked up that slogan and are willing to apply it to any problem area in which two or more human beings seem to find themselves. All problems cannot be traced to some kind of a failure to communicate. People differ in their attitudes, beliefs, and values; and that leads them to behave in different ways. Those patterns of behavior often cause problems in human relationships. We are not willing to concede that people's thinking and behaving differently are necessarily a problem of communication. All of the communication we might be able to produce may leave one unconverted and unconvinced. We doubt that such a state of affairs would constitute a failure to communicate. People can well understand someone's position and reject the validity of it.

All of the problems in this world cannot be solved by more and better communication. Just as all people's problems are not necessarily related to their communication skills, so it must be that they cannot necessarily solve all problems by focusing on communication. It is painfully obvious in this society that more communication does not necessarily solve problems. In fact, people are so saturated with communication and information that they need to learn better when to communicate and when to refrain from communication. Perhaps it is disappointing for those in our profession to realize that everything is not within our domain of expertise; we could certainly become financially independent if it were so. Companies that plan to invest a great deal of money in promoting "better communication" will be sorely disappointed in the results if the basis of their problems is not related to communi-

cation. Educators must know that all of the problems between teacher and student cannot and will not be solved just by improving communication. These kinds of examples are apparent in many situations. There are problems between people and problems inherent in systems that have nothing to do with the ability to communicate and that, therefore, cannot be solved by increasing the amount of communication.

In a recent consulting experience, this point was made very clear to us. A large company had recently developed a product that would lead to a safer consumer product if they could convince manufacturers to use it. This safety product had a number of desirable characteristics, at least from the point of view of the developing company, and it should have been a marketable commodity. However, the manufacturers simply would not purchase it. The executives of this major company were convinced that they obviously had a "communication problem." They truly felt that if they could just convey how important and good their product was, the manufacturers would be eager to purchase large quantities. They retained a communication consultant (one of the authors) to help them devise a communication strategy to solve the problem. It was quickly discovered that there really wasn't a communication problem at all. The manufacturers were actually aware of how much the new product would add to consumer safety and were convinced that this was a real breakthrough in technology. However, they had decided that they just did not want to spend the money required to purchase the item in question because there was not that much importance attached to consumer safety.

Strategies designed to communicate more information to the potential customers about the worth of the product were doomed. People often assume that if others disagree with them or are unwilling to behave as they desire, the others must simply not understand. If they do not understand, it is necessary to communicate some more with them. This is just not how things are. There is no necessary relationship between the amount of communication and anything else. More communication will not always solve the problem and, in fact, sometimes can make it worse. People who dislike each other can often grow to dislike each still more simply by communicating more with each other. They find out how really different and intolerable the other individual is.

We also object to the notion that, although *quantity* of communication is not a predictor of whether a problem will be solved, if somehow the *quality* of that communication can be increased, things will get better. Things do not necessarily happen this way either. In the preceding example, the quality of communication between the product developer and the manufacturers probably had little to do with the final outcome. It would have been impossible to improve much on the quality of communication because the manufacturers were truly convinced of the worth of the product. They understood and even believed everything that was said. They just did not think it important enough to warrant action. To claim that "it is not how much we communicate but what is said" is misleading; some problems will never be solvable through communication attempts.

Communication is not without costs. Many people suggest that it really does not cost anything to communicate; so, therefore, why not try. That is not really true. Attempting to communicate effectively with other people takes a great deal of effort and energy. It is hard work. Organizations must think of costs in terms of dollars, but individuals must actively consider how much time they are willing to invest in any given situation to improve their communication. We have known people who do not know when to give up on attempting to communicate about something. People have to learn to analyze situations to determine when it is worth it to them to spend the energy attempting to communicate. If a person has very different political views from one's own, abhors one's present life-style, or is generally unpleasant to be around, it is well to consider what are the benefits of attempting to communicate with that person compared to the costs involved. Sometimes it is just more productive to communicate with such a person as little as possible. We would hope that this book will help people to be better able to decide for themselves when communication is worth the effort required; clearly, we think it *is* in many circumstances.

Communication does not break down. Machines break down; communication does not. All of us have probably heard someone describe a situation in which he or she felt that "communication had broken down." We don't think so. Communication attempts can be successful or unsuccessful. We can be effective or ineffective in our attempts to communicate, but we simply cannot envision communication breaking down. We will suggest later in this chapter that the very nature of communication makes it an ongoing process in which it is difficult, if not impossible, to identify a beginning and/or end. In fact, it has been suggested that it is "impossible to not communicate."[1] It is more than just a semantic game that leads us to deplore strongly the use of the term *breakdown* to describe communication. We have often heard people revert to the too simple explanation that communication had broken down to describe a situation in which there was a problem. Has communication "broken down" if one cannot convince a person to believe as one does? Obviously, we have already said we do not think that failure to influence is even a communication problem in specific cases. Communication occurred; the outcome was just not what was expected or desired.

The use of the word *breakdown* provides little information. It does not provide any information that would allow people to solve a problem or avoid a similar situation in the future. To the extent that they accept such superficial descriptions of communication problems, people tend to limit their ability to analyze, adapt to, and change communication situations. Therefore, we will not use this term to describe communication problems between people. Maybe our aversion to this term is related to the fact that both authors own sports cars and are used to a more precise, identifiable usage of the term *breakdown*.

[1]See for example, P. Watzlawick, J. Beavin, and D. Jackson, *Pragmatics of Human Communication* (New York: W. W. Norton, 1967), pp. 48–51.

Communication is not good or bad. We will not suggest that communication itself has inherent qualities. We would not even claim that possessing many skills in communicating would satisfy our notion of what is good. Communication must be judged as a tool that can be used for good or bad ends. We shall say more about communication as a tool in this chapter and throughout the book. Let us say here that our suggestions about effective communication are as valuable to the would-be huckster as they are to the sincere individual. People can use communication to become demagogues, to incite riots, and to initiate wars. They can also use it as a tool to serve humanity or to grow and develop as individuals. There are some individuals who we hope will not come to possess more effective communication strategies, for they might not use them for the proper ends. However, that is a decision that is not left for all of us to make. Perhaps there is one comforting thought about this question. If people in general truly understand the process of communication, perhaps they can be effective in using the tool in desirable ways *and* resisting those who use it in ways found to be unacceptable.

The study of communication is not just about producing more effective messages. For too long people have equated effective communication with the ability to *produce* messages that would persuade, entertain, inform, or do a variety of other things. We would not argue with the assertions that effective production of communication is an important attribute and that people can and should be competent at doing this. However, we think that any definition of the competent communicator must also include message *consumption*. A person who is elegant in elocution but does not listen or understand others cannot be called an effective communicator. We must develop skills that emphasize both message production and message consumption. To that end, we have devoted our efforts in this book.[2] But first we must understand the nature of the communication process.

The Nature of the Communication Process

In the first weeks of life an infant begins to learn the complex process of communication. Babies cry when they want food or attention, and they quickly learn that this crying behavior is a way of exerting control over their environment. It is also known that, early in life, infants respond to and are able to discriminate human speech sounds from other forms of noise. Later a child will learn to talk, and verbal communication will be added to his or her repertoire of gestures and sounds. But the process of learning to communicate does not stop in early childhood. People are constantly relearning and redefining their means of communication so that they can adapt to changing circumstances in their personal lives or the world around them. Communication is a constantly changing, dynamic function, involving exchange and interaction. One theorist has suggested that every sentence should begin

and end with the word *and* to make people aware of the ongoing nature of their communication activities.[3] Although such a suggestion was probably not meant to be taken literally, people should be aware of the dynamic properties of the process of human communication.

When we say that communication is a process, we mean that *communication has no easily defined beginning and end; it is dynamic and not static; when one stops the process, communication ceases to exist.* Perhaps it would be helpful to examine a simple biological analogy to underscore these important notions of process. The digestive system can be a useful analogy. To explain digestion, we could list the elements of the digestive process as just the organs involved: the mouth, stomach, small and large intestines, pancreas, and liver. But these elements alone do not constitute the actual process of digestion. For example, the stomach cannot digest meat proteins until the meat has been broken down in the mouth and then worked on by the enzyme pepsin. In turn, pepsin cannot perform its function without the aid of hydrochloric acid. All of the elements of the digestive process must work together, interacting and changing to meet different needs. Like digestion, the process of communication also involves change, interaction, adaptation, and an ongoing function.

Another major consideration of this process notion, as has been mentioned, is that once one stops the process, what is being studied no longer exists. When the biological function of digestion ceases, there is no process to study. Communica-

[2]Although we have seen some of these myths appearing in other books recently, *we* would like to acknowledge our scholarly debt to Dr. Michael Scott, from whom we first heard these enumerated.

[3]D. Fabun, *Communications, The Transfer of Meaning* (Beverly Hills, Calif.: Glenco Press, 1968), p. 4.

tion is a process because when it stops, it no longer exists.[4] Unlike machines that can be disassembled and put back together, communication occurs, or it does not occur. When the process is arrested, it is difficult to analyze communication, for there is little left to study. This, of course, means that communication is ideally studied while it is occurring. The difficulties in actually studying such a process are immense but worthwhile.

THE TRANSACTIONAL NATURE OF COMMUNICATION

Whatever your goals in life, you will eventually find it necessary—and advantageous—to learn to communicate more effectively. If you are interviewed for job, you will have an immediate need to communicate your skills, intelligence, and desire to work. If you are beginning a dating relationship, you may wish to communicate the acceptance or rejection of your partner's actions. If you hold a managerial position in a corporation, you will need to communicate your business ideas to your subordinates and superiors. In short, you will be forced to come to grips with the fact that all communication is transactional in nature. *When we say that communication is transactional, we mean that a change in any one element in the process can alter all elements of communication.*

When one communicates with another person, there must be some relaying or sharing of meaning between the two. The communication affects both source and receiver and can affect future messages that will be produced. If you are trying to com-

[4]G. Cronkhite, *Communication and Awareness* (Menlo Park, Calif.: Cummings, 1976), p. 51.

municate with a friend, you might be called the *source* of communication and the friend might be called the *receiver.* One of the first things that you look for when relaying your message is the reaction of your friend. Is he or she interested in what you are saying? Does he or she seem to understand your message? You look for visual responses (a smile or an eye movement, for example) and then a verbal response to your message. When the receiver reacts to a message sent by a source, the receiver provides cues for the source about the way the message is being received. These cues are known as feedback. Without feedback, it is difficult to judge with any degree of accuracy how effective any communication transaction is. As you can no doubt see, the distinctions between source and receiver are at best arbitrary labels. People are *simultaneously* acting as source and receiver in many communication situations. A person is giving feedback, talking, responding, acting, and reacting continually through a communication event. Each person is constantly *participating* in the communication activity. All of these things can *alter* the other elements in the process and create a completely different communication event. That is what we mean by transaction.

The responses that a receiver makes to a source can change the speaker. Given enough negative feedback about one's beliefs and attitudes, pressure to change is obviously present. The entire relationship between two people can change as a result of but one message. An insensitive or rude comment can severely damage a friendship. Adding or removing one or more persons from a conversation also changes the entire nature of the communication event. When you communicate with another individual, you are adding to the history of the communication relationship. You will be somewhat different as a result of that communication, and it will no doubt affect the way you communicate in the future. Communication cannot be erased, for it affects the participants; the essence of understanding the transactional nature of communication is to understand how any element in the process of communication can alter the entire communication relationship.

THE AFFECTIVE NATURE OF COMMUNICATION

There is an old riddle that asks the question, "If a tree falls in a deserted forest, has sound really been made?" In other words, if no one is around to hear the crash, might it be supposed that the sound did not exist at all? Communication, whether it is nonverbal or verbal, cannot exist if there is no one around to receive the signals. Everything that people are willing to label communication has an impact on someone. Of course, this is obvious from what we said about the transactional nature of communication, and we do not wish to belabor the point. However, we do wish to stress that much of the response to communication is affective and is involved with people's emotions and feelings. People do make subjective evaluations of the communication of others and respond to them on the basis of how they themselves are affected. We must also stress that people have affective or emotional responses to communication from others, and that, too, helps determine the nature of future communication. Communication must have an impact on *someone,* or it simply isn't communication.

THE PERSONAL NATURE OF COMMUNICATION

Words are important to communication because they are convenient symbols by which we can share meaning. A word, however, is not the thing it represents, and a symbol is something that stands for something else. Likewise, the meaning or "message" is not in a word but in the people who use the word. *Meaning* is that which is intended, as by language. Examining a common word such as *chair* illustrates this point. What kind of *chair* do you visualize when you hear this word? Do you see a large, overstuffed living room chair, a hard, wooden dining room chair, or a metal folding chair? If you heard someone say, "They gave him the chair," would you know what is meant? Would the message have the same meaning if the person being talked about was in one case a college professor and in another case a murderer?

Because meanings are in people, communication is as personal as the individuals who use it. It is impossible to separate self from the communication process because all our experiences, attitudes, and emotions are involved and will affect the way we send and interpret messages. According to Kenneth Boulding, every individual has a unique "image" of self—a special way of viewing the world that is the result of all his or her personal experiences since childhood. The image of self that people have affects their communication activities:

. . . our image is in itself resistant to change. When it receives messages which conflict with it, its first impulse is to reject them as in some sense untrue. Suppose, for instance, that somebody tells us something which is inconsistent with our picture of a certain person. Our first impulse is to reject the proffered information as false. As we continue to receive messages which contradict our image, however, we begin to have doubts, and then one day we receive a message which overthrows our previous image and we revise it completely. The person, for instance, whom we saw as a trusted friend is now seen to be a hypocrite and a deceiver.[5]

The purpose of any communication, however, is to achieve shared meanings, but the symbolic nature of communication makes this difficult to accomplish. Not only is language symbolic—each word carrying varied connotations for different people—but language, too, is a process that is constantly changing. Consider, for example, an excerpt from George Washington's inaugural speech in 1789:

All I dare hope is that, if in executing this task I have been too much swayed by a grateful remembrance of former instances, or by an affectionate sensibility to this transcendent proof of the confidence of my fellow-citizens, and have thence too little consulted my incapacity as well as disinclination for the weighty and untried cares before me, my error will be palliated by the motives which misled me, and its consequences be judged by my country with some share of the partiality with which they originated.

Now compare the excerpt with one from President Carter's inaugural speech in

1977, and see how much our use of language has changed:

You have given me a great responsibility—to stay close to you, to be worthy of you and to exemplify what you are. Let us create together a new national spirit of unity and trust. Your strength can compensate for my weakness, and your wisdom can help to minimize my mistakes.

Let us learn together and laugh together and work together and pray together, confident that in the end we will triumph together in the right.

Language is not the only element of communication that is subject to change. It is very doubtful that George Washington would have understood the meaning of the much-used sign of *V* for victory (or for peace). Such signs, gestures, and behavioral cues, all integral parts of nonverbal communication, are also abstractions of reality. Each has different symbolic meanings for different people. Because communication is a personal process, a shared code (or codes) of symbols is required for people to understand each other, and some standardized usages do exist.

THE INSTRUMENTAL NATURE OF COMMUNICATION

We said earlier that communication is a tool that people use to achieve certain ends. That statement underscores the instrumental nature of the process of communication. Communication serves as an instrument by which people gain control over their physical and social environment. People can use communication for a variety of purposes that we will deal with in this textbook. Using the available

[5]K. E. Boulding, *The Image: Knowledge in Life and Society* (Ann Arbor, Mich.: University of Michigan Press, 1956), pp. 8–9.

means of persuasion to gain compliance is one function of communication that has gained considerable attention from antiquity to the present. People often attempt to change the attitudes and/or behaviors of others, and communication becomes the vehicle of change. In fact, Berlo suggests that it is useful to view all communication as persuasive in nature.[6] We understand how such a perspective can be taken. One could suggest that we are trying to "persuade" people to like us, to view us as credible, to accept our point of view, or to do a variety of other things. However, we have taken the position that communication can serve a variety of functions. Looking at everything through the perspective of persuasion limits our understanding of the multifunctioned nature of communication. There are certain communication situations in which an obvious intent to persuade is present, and we believe it useful to view communication as a tool to gain compliance in those specific contexts.

However, in other situations, the conscious intent to persuade is not present. We think communication to develop social relationships and to manage conflicts is not best viewed from an advocacy point of view. We offer other models of analysis of those functions that we find useful. People also enter into situations with an instrumental purpose to make decisions, gain information, entertain, inform, and achieve a number of other outcomes. We treat all of those as separate functions and suggest ways in which communication can serve as an instrument to help us obtain desired outcomes. We do take the position that *instrumental communication is a*

strategic activity. People can plan in advance and adopt strategies that are likely to make them more effective in a variety of contexts. They can also devise strategies to insure that communication will serve a variety of functions for them. Some people eschew the word *manipulation* when describing human communication. We do not share such a strong aversion to the term, for we know that communication can be used to manipulate others. However, we have claimed that manipulation can be for good or bad ends. If people do devise strategies to use communication in an instrumental fashion, we also know, as we have said, that people devise strategies to resist influence and manipulation. Much of this book is devoted to the instrumental purposes of communication.

THE CONSUMMATORY PURPOSE OF COMMUNICATION

The distinctions between the instrumental and consummatory purposes of communication are not always easy to make. McCroskey refers to expressive communication as that communication that is not necessarily meant to affect another person.[7] He suggests that such communication reflects people's feelings whereas instrumental communication may or may not represent true feelings. Berlo suggests that communication with *consummatory purposes has immediate reward value to the communicator*.[8] He suggests that producing a composition may have consummatory values because the communicator enjoys the composition

[6]D. K. Berlo, *The Process of Communication* (New York: Holt, Rinehart and Winston, 1960), pp. 1–17.

[7]J. C. McCroskey, *An Introduction to Rhetorical Communication*, 2d ed. (Englewood Cliffs, N.J.: Prentice-Hall, 1972), pp. 21–22.

[8]D. K. Berlo, 1960, pp. 18–19.

process. However, he further adds that presenting a composition to an audience so that they might share the communicator's satisfaction would also be an example of communication with primarily a consummatory purpose. We do not totally accept either definition of consummatory communication.

We would define consummatory purpose as any communication activity that has the goal of satisfying the communicator without any necessary intent to affect anyone else. People may engage in conversation just because they enjoy talking. Talking satisfies certain felt needs. Others benefit by simply verbalizing ideas and notions with another. Many people enjoy performing, not for the impact it *might* have on an audience, but because they find a certain amount of joy in communicating. We would take exception with the McCroskey definition because we think that people often express "real" feelings and frequently say things that they don't necessarily believe just because it is satisfying. We have a close friend who obviously enjoys telling stories, and he could not care less whether they are "real" or "true." He just likes telling them. We also believe that the Berlo example of affecting an audience in a positive way would not qualify as consummatory communication under our present definition. The intent was obviously to produce a positive impact on others. The act of communicating can provide catharsis and/or be gratifying to the communicator without intent to affect others.

We must now return to our discussion of the transactional nature of communication, for we have said that all communication does affect all elements in the communication process. *Just because there was no intent (that is, purpose) to have an impact does not in any way imply that no impact will occur.* In fact, communication will have impact. A good performance, a well-written composition, or a cathartic conversation will become a part of the communication history of the participants. These will likely affect how others perceive a person and communicate with that person in future encounters. Moreover, it is our feeling that many communication transactions have both instrumental and consummatory goals. However, we think it is useful to examine what the major purpose of the communicator is in a given situation in order to make distinctions concerning whether the communication was primarily intended to be instrumental or consummatory.

Defining the Communication Process

Not surprisingly, there are numerous definitions of communication.[9] However, most people agree with the assumptions that have been stated so far: that communication is a dynamic process, that the communication process is a transaction that will affect both the sender and the receiver, and that communication is a personal, symbolic process requiring a shared code or codes of abstractions. Beyond these basic shared assumptions, communication theorists differ on how they are willing to define communication.

[9]For a list of over 125 such definitions, see F. E. X. Dance and C. E. Larson, *The Functions of Human Communication—A Theoretical Approach* (New York: Holt, Rinehart and Winston, 1976), pp. 171–192.

The basic disagreements revolve around the notion of *intent*. Does communication have to be an intentional behavior designed to produce some effect? People have devised what have been called *source-oriented definitions* that answer this question affirmatively. Such definitions would suggest that communication is all activities in which a person (the source) intentionally transmits stimuli to evoke a response.[10] Miller and Steinberg state this position even more strongly when they say:

> We have chosen to restrict our discussion of communication to intentional symbolic transactions: those in which at least one of the parties transmits a message to another with the purpose of modifying the other's behavior (such as getting him to do or not to do something or to believe or not to believe something). By our definition, intent to communicate and intent to influence are synonymous. If there is no intent, there is no message.[11]

Attaching the concept of intentionality in this manner tends to make one view all communication activities as instrumental in nature; more specifically, it leads one to view all communication as persuasive. Such a view focuses attention on certain variables in the process, such as the content of a speech or message, the way it is delivered, and its persuasiveness. Much of the writing using such a definition focuses on the production of effective messages.

Another way of viewing communica-tion has brought forth what others have called *receiver-oriented definitions* of communication. These definitions view communication as all activities in which a person (the receiver) responds to a stimulus.[12] Cronkhite offers a broad definition of communication that is similar to the preceding one when he suggests that "human communication has occurred when a human being responds to a symbol."[13] He suggests that communication can be produced intentionally or unintentionally and responded to in an intentional or unintentional manner. This definition is so broad that it only rules out nonsymbolic behavior as communication. Cronkhite even suggests that people can communicate with themselves by reading their own writing or listening to their voices on tape.

We do not find these broad definitions of communication to be very useful in our examination of the process. They are sometimes so general that *anything* that one does can be called communication. In this text, we are not going to consider any behavior communication unless it involves two or more people. Some people will obviously find fault with that decision. We find no reason to invent a word called intrapersonal communication or communication with one's self. It is obvious to us that people think, reflect, carry on internal dialogues with themselves, read their own writing, or listen to themselves on tape. But to call these activities communication would violate the assumptions about communication that we

[10]G. R. Miller, "On Defining Communication: Another Stab," *Journal of Communication*, 26 (1966), pp. 88–89.

[11]G. R. Miller and M. Steinberg, *Between People* (Palo Alto, Calif.: Science Research Associates, 1975), p. 35.

[12]S. S. Stevens, "Introduction: A Definition of Communication," *Journal of the Acoustical Society of America*, 22 (1950), p. 687.

[13]G. Cronkhite, 1976, p. 20.

Our behavior is not considered communication unless it involves two or more people. (Photograph: Michael Weisbrot)

hold. Obviously, intrapersonal variables are important factors in how one communicates. We can think things over and convince ourselves, but that is really not how we prefer to use the term *communication*.

However, we do not dismiss definitions that emphasize the receiver out-of-hand. Such definitions place emphasis on how the receiver perceives and interprets symbolic behavior. In fact, we devote a great deal of this text to such an analysis. Source-oriented definitions have been criticized as too narrow because they exclude nonintentional, but nevertheless message-carrying activities. Receiver-oriented definitions have been criticized because they fail to make a distinction between communication and other kinds of behavior. A source-oriented view stresses certain variables, such as effective production, whereas the receiver-oriented definitions stress different variables—the receiver and the meaning a message has for him or her. Surely both approaches can be of value to the student of communication.

An examination of Fig. 1.1 might help in developing our view of communication:

In Fig. 1.1 we have no difficulty in labeling Cell A as communication. Most definitions of communication would agree that when a source intends to direct symbolic behavior toward someone and a receiver perceives that intent was present, we can say that there has been communication. Please note that *this does not mean that either party has to agree on the nature of the intent of the communication.* A source might be attempting to share information (intent) while the receiver might believe that the source was attempting to be coercive (perceived intent). Obviously, there will be communication problems in such an event. However, such a situation would be consistent with our notion of communication.

We also have little trouble dismissing Cell D as communication. If you do not intend to communicate with another and that person does not perceive such an intent on your part, none of the conditions of communication have been met. If you pass someone in the hall and do not in-tend to communicate and that person does not perceive that you intended to communicate, you have simply passed in the hall. Some behavior occurred, but it had no symbolic meaning to either party.

The other two cells in the diagram present more difficulty. In Cell B the communicator does not intend to communicate, but someone else believes such an intent was present. Receiver-oriented approaches would definitely say that such an event was communication. People ascribed meaning to some symbol. The source-oriented people would deny such an assertion. We are not going to argue as to whether or not that such a situation is communication. You can decide for yourself. We do know that such situations are common and can cause problems for people and can alter the nature of their future communication. Many nonverbal behaviors occur below the level of awareness of people; however, other people ascribe meanings to them. If you frown, fail to recognize someone, say things in a strange way, or any number of other things, it can affect the receiver's perceptions of you and your motives. To the

	Source has an intent to communicate	Source does not have an intent to communicate
Receiver perceives an intent to communicate	A. Communication	B. Ascribed Communication
Receiver does not perceive an intent to communicate	C. Communication Attempt	D. Behavior

Fig. 1.1 Communication and intent.

THE VARIABLES IN THE COMMUNICATION PROCESS

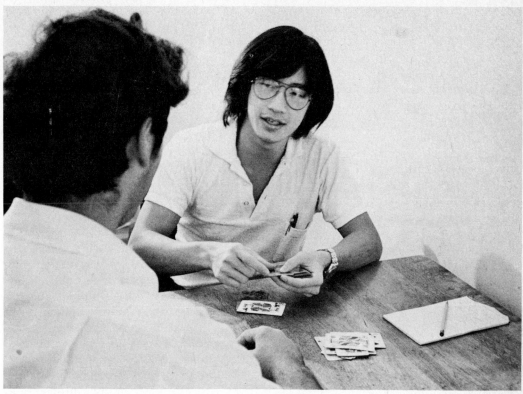

Two people playing cards and talking, an example of dyadic communication. (Photograph: Michael Weisbrot)

extent that you are oblivious to these personal traits, you are likely to have difficulties with people, and those problems can affect the communication relationship. *The problems are a lack of awareness or lack of understanding of how your behaviors affect others.* A person who wishes to be an effective communicator must become more sensitive to the impact of his or her behaviors (whether intentional or not) on other people. A person will want to maximize the behaviors that he knows are effective or live with the negative results of behaviors that tend to be perceived as negative and/or inappropriate.

Cell C also presents a problem for us. Obviously, an attempt to communicate has been made. Whether such an attempt would meet everyone's definition of communication is not all that important to us. Clearly, this area deserves study because prople need to learn strategies for using communication for instrumental purposes. The *problem in this situation is failure to be understood.* We will spend a considerable amount of time, especially in Chapter 6, differentiating between failure to understand and failure to be understood. These failures require different communication strategies to correct the problem. Let us just note that *if* the purpose of the communication event was *purely consummatory* in nature, the source might not care whether the receiver perceived intent even if the source did. The event or the act of communicating itself could satisfy the source. Obviously, such a situation occurs rarely, and receivers are likely to perceive that some intent was there, or no communication would have occurred in their presence.

So, in summary, we think the question of intent and perceived intent is important to the extent that it focuses on problems that can be solved with different communication strategies. We believe situations represented by Cells A, B, and C deserve our attention as we explore the process of effective communication. Perhaps we would be wise to briefly state our definition of communication:

> Communication is symbolic behavior that occurs between two or more participating individuals. It has the characteristics of being a process, it is transactional in nature, and it is affective. It is a purposive, goal-directed behavior that can have instrumental or consummatory ends.

Models of Communication

By this point it should be obvious that even though communication is too often taken for granted as a simple, daily part of the lives of all of us, complexities do emerge. Although communication has been defined and its characteristics described, we still need to suggest *a method for focusing on the analysis* of the structures and functions of human communication.

It will probably be helpful to represent communication in the form of a model, thereby enabling us to visualize and analyze different aspects of the process.

A model, as we will use the term in this book, is a visual representation. Just as a map of the world—a model illustrating the continents, oceans, and mountains—helps us to conceptualize the relationships of one to the other. A communication model can be a helpful, if symbolic, representation of this process.

One of the difficulties involved in constructing and using a model of a process is that we must freeze and isolate the elements involved. In our earlier example of the digestive process, we alluded to the problems of just diagramming the various organs or elements involved in digestion. Such a model does not show the process in action. A model by its nature is a static representation, which arrests a process at one point. A model is also an abstraction, and simplification is inherent in abstracting. This presents another problem: in proposing a model of communication, we are, no doubt, presenting an oversimplified view of a very complex process. We have seen how many elements are involved in some simple communication activity. It would be impossible to represent all of the elements of communication in one model.

Despite the limitations inherent in models and the difficulty involved in using them, there are many good reasons to use models in an analysis of the communication process. First, models help focus one's attention on various aspects of the process. This can be a useful teaching device, for it allows one to consider what specific models include and what others leave out. Models can also be used in practical ways to analyze real problems and prevent the occurrence of future problems. Just as economic models can be used to formulate national policy, communication models can be used to suggest methods of solving or avoiding problems. It is also possible to change various elements in models to test ways that such a change might affect other elements. It is possible to make such predictions and experiment with the relationships between elements in models in ways that are impossible in real situations. A model may also serve as a subjective view of the process, expressing one person's unique way of viewing communication. Moreover, models allow one to visualize and analyze separate parts of the process that may be difficult to analyze in other ways. In fact, the very simplification that we cited as a drawback is also an asset: models are used to clarify and simplify complex systems. Models can use an observer's perspective and, with it, the capacity to understand why communication problems occur and how they can be avoided.

Different models have greater or lesser utility in different situations. One model may be very adequate for studying one function of communication whereas we may find another perspective is better when analyzing another function. In fact, when we were involved with writing Chapter Six in this textbook, we worked with a model, of our own creation, that assisted us in organizing and explaining the material. That visual representation assisted us in conceptualizing what we thought was a complex process. It was useful to us in that the modeling process itself helped us better organize our communication with you.

Many people have provided insights on the nature of communication that provide a beginning point in identifying the necessary elements and provide questions that must be answered in order to develop models of human communication. We will briefly discuss two of those people who obviously made contributions to later attempts to construct communication models.

The Greek philosopher Aristotle was very concerned with communication. He examined and labeled several basic elements of the communication process, which were later expanded into a classical model. For Aristotle, the key elements in the process were simply the speaker, the speech, and the audience.

Aristotle focused on rhetorical communication, or the art of persuasive speaking, because this was a necessary skill in his day, used in the courts, the legislature, and the popular assemblies. Because all these forms of public speaking involved persuasion, Aristotle was interested in discovering the most effective means of persuasion in speech.

According to Aristotle, the factors that played a role in determining the persuasive effects of a speech were the contents of a speech, its arrangement, and the manner in which it was delivered. Aristotle was also aware of the role of the audience. "Persuasion is effected through the audience," he said, "when they are brought by the speech into a state of emotion." [14]

[14] L. Cooper, *Rhetoric of Aristotle* (New York: Appleton-Century-Crofts, 1960), p. 9.

Other elements that effected persuasion included the character (ethos) of the speaker and the arguments he made in the speech.

In 1948, Harold Laswell, a social scientist, proposed a model of communication that analyzed the process in terms of the functions performed by it in human societies.[15] Laswell isolated and defined three definite functions. These were (1) *surveillance* of the environment—alerting members of a community to dangers and opportunities in the environment; (2) *correlation* of the different parts of society in making a response to the environment; and (3) *transmission* of the social heritage from one generation to another.

Laswell maintained that there were groups of specialists who were responsible for carrying out these functions. For example, political leaders and diplomats belong to the first group of surveyors of the environment. Educators, journalists, and speakers help correlate or gather the responses of the people to new information. Family members and school educators pass on the social heritage.

Laswell recognized that not all communication is "two-way," with a smooth flow of information and feedback occurring between sender and receiver. In our complex society, much information is filtered through message controllers—editors, censors, or propagandists—who receive the information and then pass it on to the public with some modifications or distortions. According to Laswell, one vital function of communication is to provide information about other world powers because we as a nation depend on communication as a means of preserving our own strength. Therefore, he concludes, it is essential for an organized society to discover and control any factors that may interfere with efficient communication. He suggested that a simple way to describe the communication process was to answer the following questions:

Who
Says What
In Which Channel
To Whom
With What Effect?

AN INFORMATION-CENTERED MODEL OF COMMUNICATION

Many models of communication have been concerned with how information passes from one point to another. Probably the best known of the models was developed by Shannon and Weaver.[16] Shannon was an engineer at Bell Telephone, and he was concerned with the accurate transmission of messages over the telephone. Weaver extended Shannon's concept to apply to all types of communication.

Perhaps you remember playing a game called Telephone when you were a child. A message was passed from child to child, and the information in the message was usually quite distorted when it arrived at the last person in the chain. The Shannon and Weaver model is concerned with the same problem: accurate message transmission. It envisions a source who encodes or creates a message and transmits it through a channel to a receiver who decodes or recreates the message (See Fig. 1.2).

[15]H. D. Laswell, "The Structure and Function of Communication in Society," in *The Communication of Ideas*, ed. L. Bryson (New York: Harper and Row, 1948), pp. 37–51.

[16]C. E. Shannon and W. Weaver, *The Mathematical Theory of Communication* (Urbana, Ill.: University of Illinois Press, 1949).

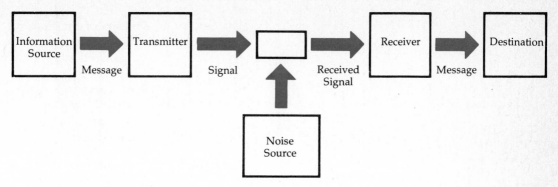

Fig. 1.2 The Shannon and Weaver model.

A key concept introduced in the Shannon and Weaver model is *noise*, that is, any additional and unwanted stimuli that can disrupt the accuracy of the message being transmitted. Noise can be the static interference on a phone call or loud music at a party or a siren outside one's window. According to Shannon and Weaver, noise is always present in the channel to be picked up by the receiver along with the message. Communication experts have extended this concept to include "psychological" as well as physical noise. Psychological noise refers to the interference of a person's own thoughts and feelings that disrupt the accurate reception of a message. We have all experienced moments when our daydreams (psychological noise) have caused us to miss a message completely.

The Shannon-Weaver Model is basically a *linear* model of communication that visualizes communication as a one-way process. Because communication is an interactive process as we have repeatedly said, this model has some problems in application. Even if one were to add *feedback* from receiver to source, this representation still ignores much of the simultaneity and transactive nature of the process of communication. Moreover, this model does not deal with the different contexts in which communication can occur. It probably has some drawbacks in the contexts of the small group, public speaking, and mass communication. Another problem with this model is that it fails to specify attributes of the source, message, channel, and receiver that might be important in the total process of communication.

THE SMCR MODEL

David Berlo proposed a model that emphasized how attributes of the four major elements (source, channel, message, and receiver) affect communication.[17] This SMCR model solves some of the problems of the previously discussed Shannon-Weaver model by such an inclusion.

As defined by Berlo, the source is the creator of the message, that is, some group or person with a reason for engaging in communication. The message is the translation of ideas into a symbolic code, such as language or gestures; the channel is the

[17]D. K. Berlo, 1960, pp. 23–38.

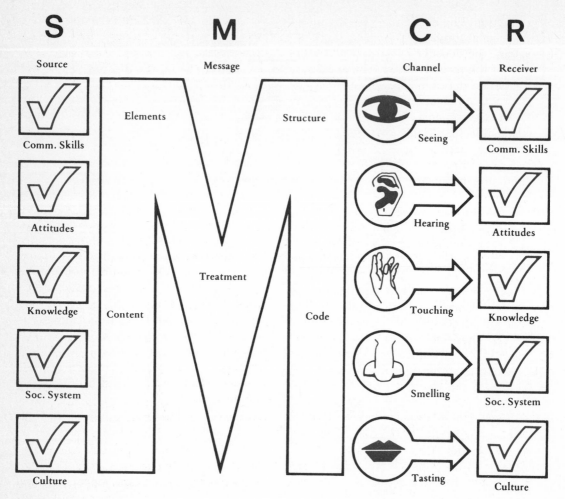

Fig. 1.3 The Berlo model.

medium through which the message is carried; and the receiver is the person (or group) who is the target of communication.

Berlo's model also specifies the need for encoders and decoders in the communication process. The encoder is responsible for expressing the source's purpose in the form of a message. In face-to-face situations, the encoding function is performed by the vocal mechanisms, muscle systems, and other artifacts such as appearance, dress, and environment that produce verbal and nonverbal messages. However, it also is possible to separate the encoder from the source. Although we have been serving as the source of communication in preparing this text, typewriter, typesetters, and a host of other people have assisted in the final encoding or message production. The decoding mechanism operates in a similar manner. In most instances, the decoder is the set of sensory skills of the receiver. However, in certain situations, decoders are present in the process that are not the intended receivers. In large organizations, people can be responsible for decoding messages prior to passing them to executives. Often only message summaries will be sent to people whom one desires to receive a message in its entirety.

In face-to-face, small-group, and public-address situations, the channel is the air through which sound waves travel. In mass communication, there are many channels: television, radio, newspapers, books, and magazines. Berlo's model also describes some personal factors that may have an affect upon the communication process. These elements are the communication skills, attitudes, knowledge, social system, and cultural environment of both the source and the receiver.

The SMCR can be criticized on many of the same grounds that we earlier used to suggest problems with the Shannon-Weaver model. This model again is concerned with transmitting information from one source to a receiver. The effects of feedback are minimized in the model, and the simultaneous behavior of people as sources and receivers is not adequately covered. In fairness to Berlo, he does recognize these notions in his work, but his model fails to account fully for the dynamic nature of communication. This model also has limited utility in dealing with communication in different contexts. However, this model represents a beginning point, and we have chosen to organize the first section of this text around some of the elements contained in this

model. We can examine source and receiver attributes, behaviors, and perceptions and analyze their effects on the process of communication. The next four chapters will do just that. As we move into different contexts and functions, we will apply models that we think are more useful.

THE WESTLEY-MACLEAN MODEL

We want to end our discussion of models by including a model that has been widely used to model communication in different contexts. This model is useful, for it demonstrates the utility of developing more complex models that handle communication in different contexts. This model was important to us in developing the second section of the text, which examines the contextual effects of communication. It provided us with a guide for making distinctions among communication in various levels of complex contexts. Westley and MacLean formulated a model that covered both dyadic and mass communication and also included feedback as an integral part of the communication process.[18] In fact, one of the distinctions that Westley and MacLean make between dyadic (or two people) and mass communication depends primarily on the differences in feedback. In face-to-face communication, there is immediate feedback from the receiver. Many kinds of stimuli pass between the receiver and the source in dyadic communication, and the source has the advantage of learning the receiver's responses almost immediately.

In mass communication, feedback is

[18]B. H. Westley and M. S. MacLean, Jr., "A Conceptual Model for Communication Research," *Journalism Quarterly*, 34 (1957), pp. 31–38.

usually delayed and minimized. This is simple to understand if you picture a typical mass communication situation, such as a televised presidential speech. The president may be successful in delivering his message to thousands of viewers, but he receives no immediate feedback from his listeners, for he can neither see nor hear their reactions. The feedback or reaction of the receivers to this message may be delayed for days or weeks until the general reaction of the public has been recorded. But even this is minimized feedback because each individual's reactions are unknown to the source.

Basically there are five elements in the Westley and MacLean model: objects of orientation, a message, a source, a receiver, and feedback. The source *(A)* focuses on a particular object or event in his (or her) environment *(X)* and creates a message about it *(X')* which he (or she) transmits to a receiver *(B)*. The receiver, in turn, sends feedback $(f_{B A})$ about the message to the source.

In a mass communication situation, Westley and MacLean add another element *C. C* is a "gatekeeper" or opinion leader who receives messages *(X')* from the sources of mass media (A_x) or focuses on objects of orientation (X_3, X_4) in his (or her) environment. Using this information, the gatekeeper then creates his (or her) own message *(X")*, which he (or she) transmits to the receiver *(B)*. This provides a kind of filtering system, for the receivers do not get their information directly from a source, but rather from a person who selects information from many sources. For example, if you had an

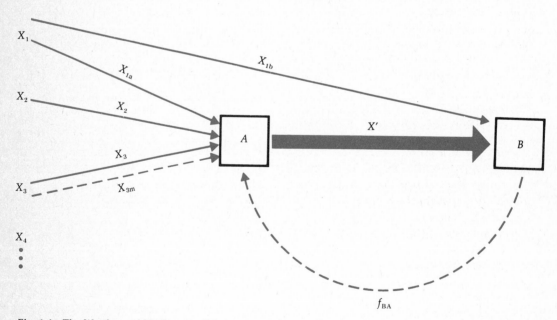

Fig. 1.4 The Westley and MacLean model.

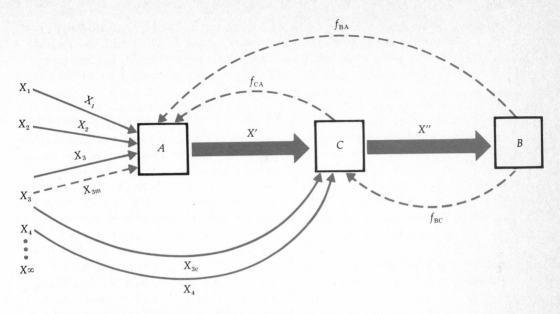

Fig. 1.5 The Westley and MacLean model.

interest in animal communication, you might read several books and watch a few television documentaries about the subject. During a conversation with a friend, you might mention something about an experiment to teach chimpanzees to use sign language. In doing this, you are filtering information. But, more important, you are providing your friend with an extended environment because you are making your friend focus on an object of orientation that was not in his (or her) environment or that was previously unnoticed. In mass communication, feedback may flow in three directions: from the receiver to the gatekeeper, from the receiver to the mass media source, and from the opinion leader to the mass media source.

Westley and MacLean do not confine their model to the level of the individual.

In fact, they stress that the receiver may be a group or social institution. According to Westley and MacLean, any individual, group, or system has a need to send and receive messages as a means of orientation to the enivronment.

The Westley and MacLean model encompasses several important concepts: feedback, the differences and similarities of interpersonal and mass communication, and the importance of opinion leaders as an additional element in mass communication.

All of these models have different levels of utility, depending on the situation. All stress the importance of people and the symbolic behavior they use in the communication process. We now turn to a chapter-by-chapter analysis of the elements of communication.

SUMMARY

1. Communication is a pervasive activity that serves many important functions in a society and in our personal lives. The process of communication enables people to exert control over their environment.

2. There are several common conceptions about communication that we do not believe: (a) we do not believe that all problems are problems of communication, (b) we do not believe that all problems can be solved by more or better communication, (c) communication is not without costs, (d) communication does not break down, (e) communication is not good or bad, and (f) the study of communication is not just about producing more effective messages.

3. Communication is a process that is constantly changing. Moreover, when you stop the process, communication no longer exists.

4. Communication is transactional in that when one element in the process is changed, changes in all elements can occur. The source and receiver are constantly having an impact on each other through symbolic behavior.

5. Communication involves subjective evaluations and is affective. Those emotional responses affect the way we communicate with others and in turn how others communicate with us.

6. Communication is a process that involves a shared code or codes of verbal and nonverbal symbols. The meanings of symbols are in the people who use them, not in the symbols themselves; meanings are in people.

7. Communication is instrumental in that we use it as a tool to affect other people and to control our environment. It is a strategic activity that we use to serve a variety of purposes. Communication can also have a consummatory purpose in that the act of communication itself can provide satisfaction to a communicator. Most communication events can have both consummatory and instrumental purposes.

8. Communication may be defined from either a source or a receiver perspective. Source-oriented definitions include as communication any activity in which a source deliberately transmits stimuli to evoke a response. Receiver-oriented definitions include as communication any activity in which the receiver responds to a stimulus. A source-oriented view focuses on the production of effective messages by the speaker. A receiver-oriented view focuses on the message's meaning to the receiver.

9. The question of whether communication has to be intentional or not is important. When the receiver has an intent to communicate and the receiver perceives such an intent, we have no trouble calling that communication. When there is not an intent to communicate on the part of the source and the receiver perceives no intent, we have no

trouble in calling that noncommunication behavior. It is more difficult to decide in other cases. When a source has no intent to communicate but a receiver perceives there is one, we have ascribed communication and a failure to understand. When a source has intent to communicate that is not perceived by the receiver, we have a communication attempt and a failure to be understood.

10. A model is a visual representation that helps us to conceptualize the relationship of various elements involved in a process such as communication. Models by their nature are simplified abstractions that isolate the elements and freeze the action of a process. Although models present a distorted view of a process, they are helpful because they can clarify complex systems.

11. From Aristotle's writings it is possible to extrapolate a classical model of rhetorical communication that contains three elements: the speaker, the message, and the audience. Aristotle also maintained that the construction of the message and the character of the speaker played an important part in persuading an audience.

12. According to Laswell, communication has three functions: surveillance of the environment, correlation of different social groups, and transmission of the social heritage. Laswell describes communication with the following questions: Who/Says What/In Which Channel/To Whom/With What Effect?

13. The Shannon-Weaver model is concerned with the accurate transmission of a message. This model presents a source who sends a message through a channel to a receiver. Noise is any additional stimuli in the channel that can disrupt the accurate reception of the message.

14. Berlo's SMCR model contains four major elements: source, message, channel, and receiver. This model also focuses on the encoding and decoding functions that take place during communication. It specifies five personal factors that will affect communicators: their communication skills, attitudes, knowledge, social system, and cultural environment.

15. In the Westley and MacLean model, the source (A) creates a message (X') about an object of orientation (X) in his (or her) environment. The source then sends the message to a receiver (B), who transmits feedback (f_{BA}) about the message to the source. This model introduces a filter system in mass communication situations. A gatekeeper (C) selects information from the many sources of mass media (A_s) or from objects in his (or her) environment (X_s), creates a message, and sends it to other people (B_s).

SUGGESTED READING

Berlo, David K. *The Process of Communication.* New York: Holt, Rinehart and Winston, 1960.

Dance, Frank E. X., and Carl E. Larson. *The Functions of Human Communication: A Theoretical Approach.* New York: Holt, Rinehart and Winston, 1976.

Miller, Gerald R., and Mark Steinberg. *Between People.* Palo Alto, Calif.: Science Research Associates, 1975.

Watzlawick, Paul, Janet Beavin; and Don Jackson. *Pragmatics of Human Communication.* New York: W. W. Norton, 1967.

From the Reading

Define the following terms.

communication
communication problems
process
transactional nature
affective nature
personal nature
meaning
symbol
instrumental nature
consummatory nature
intent
source-oriented definition
receiver-oriented definition
purposive behavior
goal-directed behavior
lack of understanding
failure to be understood
model
feedback
gatekeeper
objects of orientation
source
message
channel
receiver
encoder
decoder
noise
extended environment

Study Questions

1. What constitutes a communication problem? How does one distinguish a communication problem from other types of problems?
2. How does one decide whether communication will solve a problem or not?
3. How should one go about deciding whether the benefits of communication outweigh the costs? What are the possible costs involved?
4. Can one really take the position that communication is neither good nor bad? Do you agree with that statement?
5. Why is the usefulness of the term *communication breakdown* limited?
6. What is meant when communication is said to be a process? What are the distinguishing characteristics of a process?
7. What is meant by the statement that communication is transactional.
8. The statement that meanings are in people has a great deal of importance in the study of human communication. How does it affect the way we look at the process of communication?
9. Distinguish between instrumental and consummatory purposes in communication. How do they differ? Does this seem to be a useful way to view communication?
10. The question of intent in communication is of critical importance. What is your view on whether intent has to be present to call any behavior communication? Why?
11. Distinguish among communication, communica-

tion attempts, ascribed communication, and other behavior.

12. Distinguish between failures of understanding and failure to be understood. What different strategies might be used to solve these problems?

13. What are the advantages of using models of communication?

14. What are the problems associated with the use of models?

15. What are the strengths of the Shannon-Weaver model of communication? What problems do you see with this model?

16. What are the elements of the Berlo (SMCR) model? What improvements over the Shannon-Weaver model does the SMCR model offer? What are the weaknesses of the SMCR model?

17. Westley and MacLean have suggested a model that differs from the earlier models in several ways. How does it differ? What are the strong points and weak points of the Westley-MacLean model?

AN EXERCISE IN SELF-ANALYSIS

We believe that the study of communication must involve some self-analysis. It is our hope that you will examine your own goals as a communicator and develop ways to become more effective in your communication relationships. Below are some questions that we would like you to consider:

1. What does "communication" mean to you?

2. How effective are you in face-to-face communication?

3. Describe the situations in which you have the most difficulty communicating with others?

4. What do you consider to be your strengths as a communicator?

5. What aspects of your communication ability would you most like to improve?

6. Are there specific communication situations that make you particularly nervous or anxious?

7. What kind of initial impression do you think you make on other people? Why do you think so?

AN EXERCISE IN APPLYING MODELS TO COMMUNICATION PROBLEMS

All of us have been involved in situations in which we were less than satisfied with the communication. We want each of you to think of such a situation and record what you think were the important characteristics of that event. Now we would like you to use one (or more) of the models suggested in this chapter to see if you can:

1. Identify the elements of communication in the problem situation.
2. Identify the problems involved that made the event unsatisfying or led to a problem.
3. Suggest possible solutions to the problem.

Now form small groups of students, and discuss both the problems of communication and the application of models to those problems. Were there similarities in the nature of the problems? Did people offer different perspectives on the source of the problem and its solution?

AN EXERCISE TO DEVELOP A MODEL OF COMMUNICATION

We have had good luck in suggesting to our students that they develop models of communication. We suggest that you attempt to develop a model that you think will be of use. Think about the following things:

1. What kinds of things do I want the model to do?
2. What kinds of communication events is the model to represent?

3. How complete should a model be?
4. What are the elements of communication that are most important to identify?
5. What are the relationships among the elements?
6. What are the limitations of this model?
7. What are the advantages of this model?

Chapter 2
SOURCE VARIABLES

Henry David Thoreau wrote, "It takes two to speak the truth—one to speak, and another to hear." In emphasizing this view of communication, Thoreau pointed out the interdependence of the participants in the process. Each participant in the process of communication affects and is affected by the other people involved. This chapter and the next are devoted to an analysis of variables that affect people engaged in communication. Because the source and receiver are so interdependent and do mutually affect one another, it might seem to some that devoting one chapter to source variables and the other to receiver variables is at best arbitrary. In most situations, people play a variety of roles and often act as both source and receiver. People are constantly sending messages and, in turn, being bombarded with communication. It is probably not at all clear who might be called a source and who might be called a receiver in many communication transactions. *However, we think it is valuable to attempt to isolate some of the variables that operate when we judge the attributes of a communicator.* Even if the distinction between source and receiver is somewhat artificial, it is useful to consider how other people judge us when we attempt to communicate with them. No communicator speaks well unless the receivers judge it to be so.

At first glance, the situation seems a dispiriting one. A speaker can certainly work to improve the content and delivery of a public speech: a careful outline can be prepared, research on the accuracy and completeness of the facts can be accomplished, and one can practice on the words that will be spoken. People in dyadic and small-group communication situations can spend time and effort being concerned and informed communicators. People in mass media institutions can spend millions of dollars attempting to communicate effectively. But what can people do to insure that listeners will believe that they are speaking well? Can a source alter the way the receivers of communication perceive him or her?

A careful study of the source variables in communication indicates that there are steps that a speaker can take (short of plastic surgery and complete personality rehabilitation) to enhance other people's perceptions of him or her as an effective communicator. People can adapt their communication strategies in ways that will increase the likelihood of their being perceived more positively by their intended receivers. The kind of situation in which a source is communicating obviously is an important determinant of the kinds of behavior required on the part of the source to be perceived as an effective communicator. People must behave differently when talking with one person or a few people as compared to their behavior when making a speech. Moreover, the kind of function that the source wishes his or her communication to serve affects strategies designed to impress receivers positively. Strategies involved in persuading someone obviously differ from those used in making new friends. Though there are many different things that will affect perceptions of the source of communication, there are also many regularities in the way people judge communicators. Certain judgments are made about communicators regardless of the context or function of communication. This chapter will examine some of the common judgments that are made about communicators.

This examination of source variables reveals the problems that people face going into a communication situation. Yet, at the same time, it suggests some solutions to these problems, setting out guidelines to achieve effective communication. We will examine how people judge the credibility of a communicator and make some suggestions as to how one can be perceived as more credible and, therefore, more effective as a communicator in a variety of contexts. We will also examine in a general way how judgments of similarity and dissimilarity affect the communication process. Suggestions on how optimal levels of perceived similarity can positively affect communication will be offered. Finally, we will examine the effects of power in communication relationships and the sources of power that people have over other people as an important predictor of what will be communicated and with what effect.

Credibility as a Source Variable

We are all aware that some people are more effective communicators than others. Many times the reasons for this effectiveness are not readily apparent to the people involved in a communication situation. When people tend to persuade us or are naturally likable or are able to enter situations and settle difficulties, they are usually held in high esteem by others. When we cannot explain why these people have the impact they do, we often claim they simply possess "charisma." However, the use of a word like *charisma* is not very helpful to those of us who wish to obtain greater understanding of human communication. Because it is hard to identify those variables that make one person a charismatic leader and another person not, it is also difficult to help someone else be a more charismatic and thus a more effective communicator. Therefore, we must look for specific attributes of a source, including his or her communication behavior, to understand the real meaning of this ambiguous term.

From antiquity to the present, scholars have recognized that people make certain decisions about a source that promote effective communication. Aristotle claimed that *ethos,* or the quality we call credibility, is the most potent means of persuasion. Plato, Cicero, and Quintilian all wrote of the importance of source ethos or credibility but differed somewhat in their definitions of that quality.

A considerable amount of experimental research attests to the importance of source credibility in the communication transaction. The source with high credibility is more effective in producing a variety of desired outcomes than one with low credibility. In fact, the credibility of a communicator may be the best single predictor of the course or direction of most communication transactions. Of course, no communicator possesses an inherent quality called credibility. Source credibility is something that exists "in the eye of the beholder." *The receiver must confer credibility on a speaker, or it does not exist.* Because credibility is a perceived phenomenon, suggestions for establishing or enhancing this quality depend on many situational and personal variables.

In any communication transaction, there are personal variables that the source brings to the situation. These include such qualities as sex, age, ethnic origin, and speech disorders. Some of these characteristics—or at least the way they are projected—may not be within the source's control. As each receiver is a unique individual, the way he or she perceives the source is based on past experience. For example, a racially prejudiced person may be incapable of perceiving former Black Panther leader Bobby Seale as highly credible. Mickey Rooney may see John Wayne as tall, whereas Bill Walton may not share this perception. In other words, two people, when talking to the same person, may respond to that person quite differently as a result of their prior experience and individual perceptions. Nevertheless, research has demonstrated that a speaker can, to some extent, control these factors and thereby become a more effective communicator. Knowledge of the way a receiver perceives a speaker's credibility can provide helpful insights into the communication process.

THE DIMENSIONS OF SOURCE CREDIBILITY

Contemporary communication scholars have systematically analyzed what constitutes a "credible speaker." The results of their analysis indicate that people tend to evaluate a communication source on at least five specific dimensions.[1] Two of these dimensions, *competence,* or the source's knowledge of the subject, and *character,* or the apparent trustworthiness of the source, were identified by early writers and have withstood the test of time. Recent research supports the importance of these two dimensions and also suggests that people evaluate a speaker's credibility on the basis of his or her *composure, sociability, and extroversion.*

[1]J. C. McCroskey, T. Jensen, and C. Valencia, *Measurement of the Credibility of Peers and Spouses,* Paper presented at the International Communication Association Convention, Montreal, 1973.

Each of these dimensions acts independently to influence the source's effectiveness as a communicator. For example, you can decide a person has great expertise on a particular topic but nevertheless believe he is untrustworthy. Similarly, a person can be very likable and composed but be judged by others as having little competence on a specific subject. In any given situation, one decision may be more important than the others and, therefore, be a better predictor of communication effectiveness. In a social situation, you may not care whether a person is extremely knowledgeable about Elizabethan drama so long as you enjoy talking with the person. However, if you are injured, it may matter little if your doctor is sociable and outgoing; you simply want someone who is competent to treat your broken arm.

The dimension of competence. It is common in most communication situations for a receiver to judge a source's competence on the subject being discussed. In fact, research indicates that perceptions of competence may be the single most important predictor of how people differentiate between credible and noncredible sources.[2] This is probably especially true in those situations in which the function of communication is to persuade or inform. If a speaker is not perceived to be competent or knowledgeable on a topic, it makes little difference how trustworthy, composed, sociable, or extroverted he or she happens to be; people will remain unpersuaded and uninformed. If the func-

[2] See McCroskey, Jensen, and Valencia, 1973, and D. K. Berlo, J. B. Lemert, and R. Mertz, "Dimensions for Evaluating the Acceptability of Message Sources," *Public Opinion Quarterly*, 33 (1969), pp. 563–576.

tion of communication happens to be the development of social relationships, the perceived competence of the source may be less important. However, there is evidence to suggest that generally knowledgeable people are often sought out for interactions. People make competence judgments on such variables as level of education, accessibility to current or pertinent information, or direct experience with the subject under discussion. Whether or not the receivers are themselves competent to judge the source's competence seems to make little difference; they make a judgment, and it affects their communication. Overall, the speaker who is perceived as competent has a higher probability of being effective in a variety of communication situations.

There are several things a source may do to increase his or her perceived competence. In public speaking situations, it is common for a speaker to be introduced to the audience by another person. If the person making the introduction refers to the speaker's title, such as doctor or professor, or even labels him or her as "a leading expert," this may enhance the audience's perception of the source's competence. The speaker may indicate expertise on the topic by referring to previous experience with the subject, by mentioning other highly competent people with whom he or she is associated, by careful preparation, or by skillful use of evidence.

If the receivers perceive a source to be low in competence, there is little likelihood that the speaker will be effective, regardless of his actual expertise on the subject being discussed. A good example of this involves a group of students who were invited to hear a lecture on life among the Ashanti. The speaker, a white woman, was given an introduction specifically designed to ensure that she was perceived as competent; the audience was told that the source was born in Africa and raised among the Ashanti. Nevertheless, the predominantly black American audience was extremely unreceptive. The speaker was thoroughly familiar with the African experience of the Ashanti. She could converse easily and at length with the Ashanti people about shared cultural experiences; in fact, the native Africans perceived her to be "one of them" despite her skin color. But the audience of black students had a very different perception of her competence to speak on what *they perceived to be the* "black experience." Communication was difficult because although the speaker knew what it was like to be an Ashanti, she did not know what it was like to be an American black, and her audience doubted her competence to speak on the announced topic.

Clearly, the woman's skin color was not in her control, but she could have taken steps to change the audience's perceptions. For example, she might have been perceived as more competent if she had directly confronted the situation and admitted to the audience that she did not understand the black American experience but could provide information about Africa that might be of interest. Sometimes an admission of lack of competence in one area is perceived as an indication of other kinds of competence.

Many research studies have demonstrated the importance of perceived competence. A great deal of that research has been done on the persuasion function of communication, and we will discuss that research in detail later in the text. However, suffice it to say that when people attribute messages to sources that they consider highly credible, more attitude change will occur. In classic studies, the same voice and the same persuasive message have been attributed to a highly competent source (for example, the surgeon general, a doctor, a research professor) or to a lowly competent source (for example, a high school student, a convict, and so on). In these studies, the message has been considerably more persuasive when the people believed it was from a highly competent source. In other situations, it has been shown that people direct more communication toward people they perceive to be competent and are more willing to receive communication from such a person. Moreover, people who are perceived as competent are likely to emerge as leaders in group situations. Obviously, perceived competence is an important variable that affects communication situations.

In most situations, a source cannot be perceived as "too competent"; an ideal source would be one who is highly competent to discuss the topic under consideration. However, the perception of competence is itself a multidimensional process involving several variables. For example, a nuclear physicist heading a research project may be so brilliant that he cannot effectively express his ideas to his subordinates. In such an instance, his research assistants may perceive him as highly competent on one dimension (mastery of subject matter) but incompetent on another (ability to express himself). On the basis of this example, one might caution speakers to determine carefully those variables most important to their audiences if they are to be effective.

The dimension of character. The popular rejoinder "You're a good man, Charlie Brown," is an estimate of character perceived as goodness, decency, or trustworthiness. The dimension of character has a strong influence on the receiver's perception of source credibility. The term credibility gap, popularized in the early 1960s, refers almost solely to this dimension. The government was saying one thing, and later press accounts indicated it was doing the opposite. Recent problems in government have made people generally skeptical about the character of our national leaders. Political leaders have had to adapt their communication strategies to put more stress on the character dimension, and much political rhetoric is aimed at changing peoples' images of the trustworthiness of elected leaders.

When people believe a communicator to be low in character or trustworthiness, they are less likely even to listen, let alone be influenced by, the message. Many people will simply terminate conversations or avoid situations in which they might be forced to communicate with someone who does not meet their personal standards of character. To some extent, we judge competence on the basis of objective qualifications (education, work experience, and other credentials), but perceptions of character are most often highly personal judgments about the nature of a source. Those judgments can be based upon firsthand experience with the source, but often judgments about people are made by others prior to any direct contact.

In a Gallup poll, the CBS newscaster Walter Cronkite was found to be the most trusted man in the United States. One can only speculate as to the reasons for these findings. People obviously feel that he is an honest reporter who does not bias the news with his own feelings and who cannot be compromised. Therefore, if Cronkite said one thing and the government said another, the position advocated by Cronkite would probably be believed by the majority of people who heard both messages. Another former network newscaster created some controversy when he appeared in a commercial for an airline. The decision makers at the airline probably did not believe the newsman would be seen as competent to discuss the construction of airplanes; however, they were betting that the American people believed him to be of high character and would, therefore, be persuaded by the commercials. Other newscasters criticized this arrangement, claiming that his lack of objectivity concerning the airline would damage the perceived objectivity of all newsmen. In fact, newsmen have turned down lucrative assignments to avoid having to do commercials as part of their duties.

The question of how one establishes and maintains perceptions of high character is a difficult one. Obviously, any past experience that questions a person's integrity reduces perceived character. People who change positions over time can be seen as less trustworthy, even if the change itself is a good one. It is doubtful that an ideal source would be anything other than high in character. The best advice for insuring perceptions of high character is to be consistently honest. To the extent that persons are perceived to be of

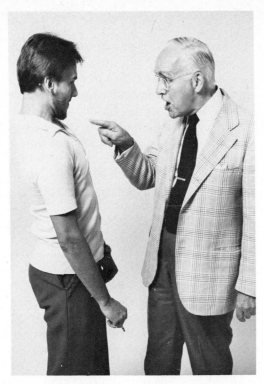

Very often, an authority figure will easily intimidate another person. A person who is composed, especially under conditions of considerable stress, is perceived to be more credible than a person who is not composed. (Photograph: Maury Englander)

high character, they will be able to facilitate more effective communication. It is certainly a goal worth seeking.

The dimension of composure. A person who is composed, especially under conditions of considerable stress, is perceived to be more credible than a person who is not composed. Research indicates that a speaker who is nervous or produces a number of nonfluencies (stammering and "uhs" and "ers") is less credible and less able to persuade others.[3] Some speech students are immediately perceived as more credible in the early part of the course because they can keep composed during the stress-producing first speeches. Many people we call "good public speakers" are not more competent or of higher character, but more composed.

To increase one's perceived composure, the beginning public speaker can practice delivery to reduce nonfluencies and apparent nervousness. Fidgeting, shuffling of papers, and other distracting behavior often reduce a speaker's perceived composure. In American culture, extreme displays of emotion are also perceived as lack of poise. Many political commentators attribute Senator Muskie's defeat in the presidential primaries of 1972 to a moment when he lost his composure and publicly cried because of newspaper attacks on his wife. However, it is hard to predict the effect that an individual instance of lack of composure will have. The environment in which these events occur may greatly alter the outcome. In two different instances, Walter Cronkite lost his composure. During the 1968 Democratic Convention, he became visibly angry when a floor reporter was accosted. When the first man landed on the moon, he was clearly elated and used emotional language unusual for him. Certainly the Gallup poll mentioned earlier indicates that Cronkite did not suffer any loss of credibility because of his behavior on these occasions, but few of us enjoy the status that Walter

[3]G. R. Miller and M. A. Hewgill, "The Effects of Variations in Nonfluency on Audience Ratings of Source Credibility," *Quarterly Journal of Speech, 50* (1964), pp. 36–44.

Cronkite has in the eyes of the American public.

What may be true for a public figure or for a person delivering a speech may not be true for people in other communication situations. We obviously do not expect our friends to be totally composed at all times, nor do they necessarily become less credible to us because they occasionally emote instead of reason. In fact, few of us would be attracted to someone who was totally composed under various kinds of stress. However, we probably would not be happy with a person who could not retain some composure when the situation called for such behavior. Much research suggests that we value the ability to remain composed and that in many, but not all, communication situations the composed communicator is perceived to be more effective.

The dimension of sociability. Sources that project likableness to their receivers are regarded as sociable. People who like each other tend to spend more time communicating with each other and are influenced by each other. Research indicates that our interpersonal communication contacts are very influential in shaping and changing our attitudes on a variety of issues. Peers influence our political behavior, help determine the products we consume, and shape our thinking in numerous ways. The recent trends in advertising try to present advocates of consumer products as likable people; much of the "image advertising" in politics is also designed tó do just this. We tend to like people who give us the feeling that they like and respect us, and we avoid those who do not. Therefore, we are more likely to attend to and be influenced by those whom we perceive as sociable.

There is more to sociability than just interpersonal liking. Although we may not have a friendship with—or a deep liking for—a person, if one is cooperative and friendly in task situations, he or she will be perceived as more sociable. The person who goes about his work in a cheerful, friendly manner is likely to be a preferred co-worker. All of these things combine to make a person appear to be more approachable and communicative. In all likelihood, those we consider unsociable will not be a part of our communication activities and will have little influence on us.

Many people expect more than just platitudes about being friendly and sociable as ways to be more effective communicators. Most of us would sincerely desire to improve our social relationships and, in effect, be perceived as sociable persons. We think that this function of communication is an extremely important one and have devoted an entire chapter to this in the last section of the book. This brief discussion of the dimension of sociability is offered only to stress that it is an important part of how people judge sources of communication.

The dimension of extroversion. The outgoing personality who engages readily in communication situations is considered an extrovert. The person who is talkative and not timid in communication activities is sometimes said to be a dynamic speaker; he or she *may* be an effective communicator. However, a person who is too extroverted may talk too much and take over conversations. We have all been

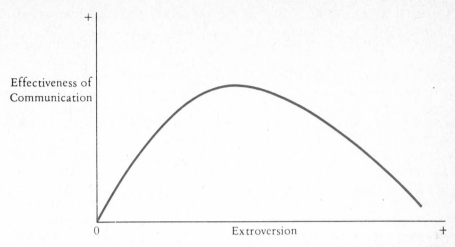

Fig. 2.1 Relationship of extroversion and communicating effectiveness.

in situations in which very dynamic, extroverted people so dominated the scene that we felt like an unnecessary part of the conversation (few who know the authors of this text will believe such a statement). Although the optimum amount of source extroversion varies from receiver to receiver, people generally prefer to communicate with people who possess this attribute in moderation.[4]

A person who is too introverted may make communication so tedious and effortful that we simply give up. It is hard work communicating with a person who has little to say. On the other hand, people who show no sensitivity to our need to participate in the communication and are enamored only with the sound of their own voices are not likely to be preferred. We like people who can strike a balance. In most social situations, there is a fine

[4]J. K. Burgoon, "The Ideal Source: A Reexamination of Source Credibility Measurement," *Central States Speech Journal*, 27 (1976), pp. 200–206.

line between being "the life of the party" and "a smashing bore." Figure 2.1 may help clarify the relationship between extroversion and effective communication.

As extroversion increases, people enjoy talking with, and listening to, a dynamic person. An extroverted person holds their attention and is generally interesting. However, at some point—and this point varies with people and situations—increased extroversion annoys people and makes them either dislike the person or withdraw from the situation.

THE DYNAMICS OF SOURCE CREDIBILITY

Perceptions of a source's credibility are subject to change. Often a source comes to the communication situation with some degree of credibility already established. The degree of credibility perceived in the source prior to any specific communication event is called *initial credibility*. When we say of a speaker that "his reputation preceded him," we are commenting on his initial credibility. For example, a world-famous Arctic explorer talking before a group of professional geographers could expect to have a high degree of initial credibility with his audience. The speaker with a high degree of initial credibility is likely to use a very different communication strategy from that of persons who are seeking to establish or enhance their credibility.

During any communication event, the source's credibility may be reevaluated and either heightened or lowered in the receiver's mind. This assessment or modification of initial credibility is called *transactional credibility*. People continually assess a speaker and make evaluative changes during a communication transaction, because they react to many kinds of verbal and nonverbal behavior. For example, if the Arctic explorer told his audience of geographers that he had a poor sense of direction and had to rely on a hired guide, the audience members would probably reduce their initial perceptions of his credibility. A source may also improve his or her credibility during a transaction by not behaving as expected. Civil behavior on the part of a very militant person may be so unexpected that it catches an audience by surprise and makes the person appear to be very "reasonable" or credible and, therefore, persuasive. What a speaker says and does is continually being processed and evaluated by the people with whom he or she is communicating. If a source is aware of the criteria by which he or she is being judged, better decisions can be made about what must be done to insure continued perceptions of high credibility.

Terminal credibility is the receiver's perception of a source at the completion of a communication event. For example, if the militant person continued to behave in a polite manner throughout his or her speech, the audience would probably have a higher evaluation of that person at the end than at the beginning. All of us have, at one time or another, entered a conversation with low regard for someone and ended the communication with a completely altered perception. Terminal credibility is important because it will influence a person's initial credibility if that person should communicate again with the same receiver.

People's perceptions of others change between communication events. A receiver might change his or her attitude or values and, therefore, be less receptive to a given source the next time they communicate. It is also possible that external variables will cause a receiver to change the evaluation of a source between communication events. We learn about people by receiving new and different information from other sources; this information may, in turn, alter our perceptions. Sometimes this change is positive and allows us to make more valid judgments, but sometimes we allow rumor and innuendo to alter our perceptions. Therefore, it is important to evaluate the sources of information about other people as well as the people with whom we communicate.

Other things may change a receiver's perception of a source's credibility. A person may have a high terminal credibility in a previous encounter because the topic of conversation was one that he or she was competent to discuss. In the next communication transaction, this same source may discuss a subject about which he or she has little knowledge. This may affect the receiver's perception of the speaker's competence in a negative way. However, a source who had high terminal credibility at an earlier time on a completely different topic may be held in high esteem on unrelated topics. This "halo effect" operates in a variety of situations. For example, a student who writes a good first examination paper may have an easier time in the rest of the course because of the early establishment of credibility. Clearly, credibility is ever-changing between and within communication events, topics, and people. But even though this variable is subject to change, it deserves serious attention from those wishing to be effective communicators.

Homophily-Heterophily in Communication

Do opposites attract, or does like attract like? This age-old question is related to another basis of perceptions that people have of communicators. We spent some time thinking about what we were going to call this basis of judgment in this edition of our book for we fear that social scientists have been overzealous in using and sometimes inventing "fifty-cent words" to replace more commonly used terms. *Homophily* refers to the degree to which interacting individuals are similar in certain attributes. Like others, we plead guilty to using this term in our first edition and find with some amusement that the term is more properly spelled with a *y* instead of an *i*. However we decided to retain the use of the term in this edition, because this concept (and spelling) is widely

Because homophily-heterophily involves a variety of attributes, we can be both homophilous and heterophilous with another person at the same time. The above two people are homophilous in their political philosophies and general life-styles but heterophilous in their physical dimensions. (Photograph: Maury Englander)

used by educators in our discipline, and we think you might run into it in other places.

Attributes that lead to homophily may include demographic characteristics such as age, education, and socioeconomic status; or they may include attitudes, beliefs, and values. If another person were completely identical to you (which is, of course, an impossibility), he or she would be completely homophilous with you. Some twins might come close to meeting this definition. At the opposite end of the similarity continuum is *heterophily*, or dissimilarity. The degree to which someone differs from us in various attributes is the degree of heterophily between us.

Because homophily-heterophily involves a variety of attributes, we can be both homophilous and heterophilous with another person at the same time. An electrician and a physician are heterophilous along the dimension of occupation, but homophilous on political attitudes if they both vote Republican and oppose higher taxes. Two college students may be highly homophilous in terms of age, race, education, status, and background but heterophilous in beliefs, if one is convinced that marijuana is physically harmful and the other believes it is completely safe. Their heterophily may involve only one belief or it may involve several; the homophily-heterophily relationship of any two people is highly complex. Knowing their level of similarity on one attribute does not necessarily make it possible to predict their similarity on another.

It is important to recognize that the homophilous or heterophilous relationship between a source and a receiver is just that —a relationship. Homophily, like credibility, is not something inherent in a source or receiver. It can only be measured by the relationship of the two people involved. The perceptive communicator will understand the need to determine on what attributes a person or people are similar or dissimilar. In the next chapter and in Chapter 6, we spend a considerable amount of time discussing methods of such analysis and make suggestions for adapting communication strategies based on those differences. The context in which communication occurs is obviously an important determinant of how much information can be obtained about similarity-dissimilarity. In the dyadic context, it is easier to assess the one other person involved. In the public speaking and mass communication contexts, it may be impossible to recognize degrees of likeness and difference on several dimensions with *each* of the receivers.

DETERMINING HOMOPHILY-HETEROPHILY

If the source is to identify his or her homophily or heterophily relationships with receivers, there must be some way to determine the similarity or dissimilarity between and among them. There are two ways of measuring homophily-heterophily: one objective and one subjective. An objective measure is the amount of similarity or dissimilarity that is apparent to an impartial observer. The same IQ score or the same yearly income would be two objective measures of homophily. Subjective measures, on the other hand, are those based on the perceptions of the participants. In any communication transaction, both source and receiver act in the light of their perceptions of each other rather than of some objective indicator of their heterophily level. If a source believes that he or she has much higher status than his or her receiver, no amount of objective measures and observations revealing equality will make the communication relationship homophilous.

This is not to suggest that subjective and objective measures of homophily are totally unrelated. In many cases, there is a great deal of agreement between the similarity perceived by an impartial observer and that of the participants in the communication transaction. However, in other cases there are significant differences between subjective and objective measures. People often overestimate similarity between themselves and people they like. People engaged in conflict situations may overestimate the amount of difference between them and the person with whom they are having problems. An impartial observer is often valuable in pointing out that the differences between the combatants is not as marked as the participants perceive them to be.

THE RELATIONSHIP OF HOMOPHILY-HETEROPHILY TO COMMUNICATION

The homophily-heterophily relationship between the source and receiver will affect their communication transactions in two important ways: it determines who will communicate with whom and also how successful that communication will be. When a person has a choice of whom he or she will communicate with, he or she will tend to choose someone like himself or herself.[5] People of the same status who live close to each other or who work together will interact more.[6] Iowa farmers talk about agricultural innovation to persons who share similar interests and attitudes,[7] whereas ghetto residents discuss family planning with persons of the same age, family size, and status.[8] This tendency for voluntary communication patterns to be homophilous makes sense. People who are similar share common interests that provide the subjects for communication.

As might be expected, homophily may lead to more effective communication.[9] The effectiveness, of course, depends on the degree of homophily. Total homophily produces a static state; people who are in agreement may have little to talk about. Conversely, people who are highly heterophilous may lack the common experiences or vocabulary necessary for understanding and effective communication. The Hindu and the American will have difficulty discussing the nutritive value of beef because of their different attitudes toward cows. The industrial executive may be unable to discuss company business with a local plant worker owing to a lack of a common vocabulary, background, or perspective. The best degree of similarity is, therefore, what has been labeled *optimal heterophily*.[10] Optimal heterophily is slight dissimilarity. If two people are homophilous on several attributes but optimally heterophilous on the subject

[5]E. M. Rogers and D. K. Bhowmik, "Homophily-Heterophily: Relational Concepts for Communication Research," in *Speech Communication Behavior,* ed. Larry L. Barker and Robert J. Kibler (Englewood Cliffs, N.J.: Prentice-Hall, 1971), p. 212.

[6]B. E. Collins and H. Guetzkow, *A Social Psychology of Group Processes for Decision Making* (New York: John Wiley and Sons, 1964), p. 178.

[7]R. H. Warland, "Personal Influence: The Degree of Similarity of Those Who Interact" (Master's thesis, Iowa State University, 1970).

[8]J. Palmore, "The Chicago Snowball: A Study of the Flow and Diffusion of Family Planning Information," in *Sociological Contributions to Family Planning Research,* ed. Donald J. Bogue (Chicago: University of Chicago Community and Family Study Center, 1972).

[9]E. M. Rogers and F. F. Shoemaker, *Communication of Innovations: A Cross-Cultural Approach* (New York: Free Press, 1971), p. 14.

[10]Rogers and Shoemaker, 1971, p. 15.

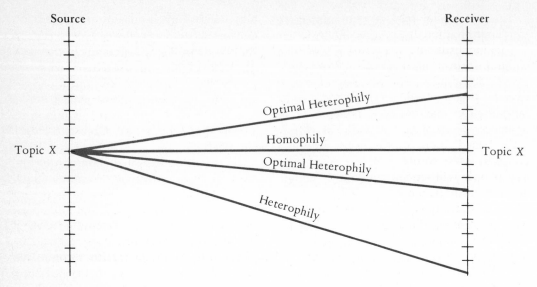

Fig. 2.2 Model of homophily-heterophily between source and receiver.

of discussion, they will be more likely to communicate effectively. They will have the common ground for understanding with enough difference to produce a dynamic, beneficial interaction. Figure 2.2 illustrates the different possible combinations of homophily.

Another consideration related to optimal heterophily is the relevance of the homophilous or heterophilous attributes. Homophily or optimal heterophily need only exist on those attributes that are relevant to the issue of concern. A receiver's age may be a very important characteristic for the source discussing political views, but a dissimilarity in age is unlikely to affect a discussion of the best types of fishing lures. To insure effective communication, a source should identify the relevant attributes and emphasize similarities on these dimensions. This is not a simple task, for what is relevant to one person may be irrelevant to another.

Our perceptions of homophily-heterophily can also affect our perceptions of the credibility of the source. For example, if we perceive a person to be very heterophilous in terms of amount of knowledge possessed on a topic, we are likely to rate that person very high on the competence dimension of credibility. Under such conditions, a heterophilous relationship between source and receiver may be acceptable, even desirable. Heterophilous sources are often consulted for information because of their perceived competence. In many cases, this increased perception of competence based upon differences in sources and receivers facilitates learning and increases the influence of the source. Therefore, any notion of what constitutes optimal heterophily must take into account what the function of communication is meant to serve.

We will discuss the relationship between similarity and the development of satisfactory social relationships in detail in a later chapter. In the case of developing friendships and social relationships, communication is more effective when people are similar. There are a variety of reasons that we will discuss later about how one can maximize the probability of developing satisfactory social relationships based upon communication strategies that stress similarities. We also know that people will tend to view people who are homophilous more positively on some of the other dimensions of source credibility. For example, it makes sense to suggest that most people are more likely to see people who are similar as more sociable and probably more trustworthy.

In summary, heterophily and homophily must be considered in terms of what purpose the communication is to serve. At times, heterophily between source and receiver will lead to desirable outcomes such as learning and persuasion. In other cases, people will have more effective communication transactions when interacting with homophilous individuals.

It appears that if people begin with a homophilous (or optimally heterophilous) relationship, communication has a high probability of success. But what about the situations in which the initial relationship is heterophilous? Heterophilous communication cannot be avoided. In fact, many of our daily communication activities can be classified as heterophilous: teacher to student, parent to child, and employer to employee. The problem of heterophilous relationships has long confronted agencies, such as the Peace Corps, that are attempting to bring about social change. How does a clearly heterophilous source convince a Peruvian peasant to adopt water-boiling techniques or Pakistanis to adopt

birth control methods? How do you gain acceptance of your grading proposals by a faculty committee or persuade your employer to give you a raise?

COMPENSATIONS FOR HETEROPHILY

There are several ways of compensating for or overcoming heterophily. One of the most effective is frequent interaction, which can increase attraction and homophily. For example, students living on the same dormitory floor can overcome initial dissimilarities through frequent conversation. However, if the initial dissimilarities are too severe, communication attempts may not only be unrewarding but may discourage future communication. The Indonesian visitor who condemns Americans for the wastefulness and excessive use of pollution-causing disposable paper products will probably be too heterophilous with the owner of a paper products company for effective communication to take place.

Another way to compensate for heterophily is for a source to develop empathy, or the ability to project himself (or herself) into another person's role—in this case, the role of the receiver. Developing empathy is a difficult task in a heterophilous relationship, for the existence of heterophily suggests that each person has had little experience with the other's role. If people can actually place themselves in some of the same circumstances as the others, they may better develop empathy. This is why Peace Corps volunteers undergo extensive training in the customs and language of the country in which they are to live. To be effective communicators in such a situation, they must live like the natives.

A source may compensate for heterophily in a communication situation by paying close attention to the feedback of his or her receivers.[11] Of course, feedback may be necessary just to indicate to the source that heterophily does exist; people tend to assume that others are homophilous with them until it is proved otherwise. When dissimilarities do exist, these need to be recognized so that misunderstandings do not develop. Thus, feedback provides the source with the necessary information about his or her receivers. By attending closely to feedback, the source can better understand the receiver's language patterns, norms, beliefs, and behavior and also can develop more empathy. Social workers in the ghetto or on the Indian reservation must be especially attuned to the unique vocabulary and habits of their clientele, if they are to communicate with these people in any helpful way.

Homophily, then, is an important consideration for a source. The degree of one's homophily with others will affect his or her choice of receivers, the effectiveness of the communication, and the receivers' perception of his or her credibility. We must stress that no one statement can be made on strategies to alter perceptions of homophily-heterophily. In some cases, it will serve the purpose of the source to be perceived as heterophilous with intended receivers. In fact, it may be necessary to be so perceived in order to achieve the desired outcomes of the interaction. Communication strategies designed to highlight these differences are advised. In other cases, homophily between source and receiver will lead to desirable outcomes. In several later chapters, we will discuss how adaptations can be

[11]Rogers and Bhowmik, 1971, p. 222.

made that will alter perceptions of similarity to serve different functions.

Power as a Source Variable

Although power is often ignored in discussions of human relationships, it does affect many of our daily communication activities. The fact that teachers can assign passing or failing grades, that parents can give or withhold support money, or that employers can promote or dismiss workers will influence the nature of the communication that takes place between each group of interactants. Power, like credibility and homophily, is a perceived phenomenon; it exists in a source to the extent that a receiver perceives it to be there. When a receiver does perceive that a source possesses some sort of power, specific patterns of communication behavior can be predicted. There are several types of power that can be attributed to a source.

THE COMPONENTS AND TYPES OF POWER

A source brings to a communication situation certain personal resources that may be perceived as power elements by the receiver. Among these resources of power are such personal qualities as wealth, prestige, skill, information, and physical strength. Thus, if the mayor of a city asked a resident to head an antilitter campaign, the citizen might accept the mayor's offer because he or she perceives the official to have power by virtue of prestige and position. A complete list of the resources of power available to a source in a communication situation cannot be constructed because any particular quality may be perceived (or not perceived) as a power element by the receiver. Thus, a person who earns $10,000 a year may be so "impressed" by a president of a corporation who earns $100,000 a year that he might follow the president's advice to invest his life savings in a particular stock. However, a person of considerable wealth may not be very impressed by the same person and will not follow the advice. The resources of power available to a source are relative to the receiver's perception in a particular communication situation.

In any communication interaction, a receiver has certain unique physical, psychological, and social needs. The source's potential for satisfying the needs of the receiver provides the motive bases for power to operate in a communication situation. The motive bases are the reasons we have for allowing people to exert control over us; they are the needs we desire to have satisfied by the source of communication. Thus, the citizen who agrees to head the antilitter campaign may be satisfying his or her need to be a community leader. A need to be held in favor might also influence the citizen to answer the mayor in an affirmative fashion. The worker who agrees to invest savings may be satisfying a need to be associated with people of higher status or to make a "fast buck." Clearly, the resources of power are contingent upon the needs of a particular receiver or group of receivers. Indeed, these two components of power (resources and needs or motive bases) may combine to create five distinct types of power in a communication transaction.

Reward power. The ability of a source to provide positive sanctions if the receiver complies with the source's request is called reward power.[12] The actual sanctions administered by the source may take the form of concrete rewards, such as money and other physical objects, or they may be intangible rewards, such as praise and affection. An employer who gives his salesmen bonuses based on their performance is exercising reward power. Of course, the actual reward offered must be perceived by the receiver as worthwhile, or it will have little impact. To one salesman, a week's vacation in the Bahamas may not be worth the extra effort needed to secure the bonus. To another salesman, simply being "Number One" may be sufficient reward for working the extra hours necessary to top the other members of the sales force. Thus, to a great extent, the exercise of reward power is dependent on the source's ability to perceive the needs of the receiver accurately.

In addition to perceiving the reward as worthwhile, the receiver must see the potential reward as being within the source's power to bestow. For example, a person seeking public office who offers another person a position in his (or her) administration in return for campaign work must be perceived by the receiver as having a chance to fulfill the promise. If the receiver thinks there is no possibility that the candidate will win (and if winning is the only base of power the source might have), it is unlikely that he or she will comply with the candidate's request to work in the campaign. In other words, an empty promise is not likely to motivate a receiver if it is perceived as such.

[12]See J. R. P. French, Jr., and B. Raven, "The Bases of Social Power," in *Group Dynamics* D. Cartwright and A. Zander, eds. (New York: Harper and Row, 1968), pp. 259–268, for a review of types of power.

As one would expect, the ability of the source to induce compliance increases as the magnitude of the reward increases. The sales manager who offers the position of assistant manager as a reward to the best salesman is likely to have more power than one who offers a week's salary as a reward. (This is dependent on each salesman's perception of the reward as worthwhile and within the sales manager's power to bestow.) The successful use of reward power may further increase the source's power, for the receiver is likely to attach more significance to promises of future rewards. Therefore, if the sales manager does, in fact, promote the best salesman to the position of assistant manager, other salesmen are likely to perceive future promises of rewards as highly probable. In other words, the manager's credibility along the character dimension will be enhanced, making him or her more effective. Conversely, if the sales manager fails to live up to the promise, his or her credibility will probably be diminished, and ability to exercise reward power over the sales force is likely to be decreased.

Coercive power. Coercive power refers to the ability of a source to administer negative sanctions[13] (punishment) if the receiver does not comply with the source's request. For example, American prisoners of war in North Vietnam were forced to make "confessions" and "repudiations" through the threat of torture and even death. From this perspective, coercive power may be seen as a negative form of reward power. However, coercive power may also involve the threat to withhold reward, as in the case of a manager who threatens to withhold the raise of a salesman who does not maintain a minimal level of performance.

The fact that the source in many communication situations may exert either reward or coercive power leads to an inevitable question: Which is more effective? Studies have shown that positive and negative sanctions are equally effective in inducing overt compliance to the source's request.[14] It is important to note, however, that the use of either kind of power may have profound impact on other variables in the communication interaction. For example, the use of reward power is likely to increase the attraction of a receiver to a source, whereas the use of coercive power tends to decrease this attraction. Thus the manager who administers only negative sanctions to staff members will probably be disliked and may very well find it difficult to retain the employees. As the use of negative sanctions requires more surveillance or scrutiny by an administrator, the manager who employs coercive power may find that he or she must devote a great deal of time to "catching" the workers. Needless to say, this can have a detrimental effect on morale and may affect the manager's ability to perform other functions that support his or her role relationship with subordinates. A receiver may also react negatively to the use of reward power if it is perceived to be bribery or is seen as compromising one's integrity. We have probably all been in situations in which we came to resent people trying to force our com-

[13]W. T. McGuire, "The Nature of Attitudes and Attitude Change," in *The Handbook of Social Psychology,* ed. G. Lindsey and E. Aronson, 2d ed., vol. 3 (Reading, Mass.: Addison-Wesley, 1969), pp. 194–196.

[14]W. T. McGuire, 1969, p. 194.

pliance by "buying" us. Even with these potential problems of reward power, most people will still find this type of power far superior to relying on coercion.

Referent power. If the source in a communication situation makes an appeal to a receiver to "do this for me," the source is exercising referent power. In such an instance, the source is appealing to the receiver's wish to please him or her or to be like the source. At the basis of referent power is the feeling of oneness or identification that the receiver perceives in his or her relationship to the source. For referent power to exist, the receiver must want to be like the source. Most people have, at one time or another, imitated the behavior or "parroted" the beliefs or attitudes of someone whom they found attractive. Most parents can attest to the existence of referent power. For example, when the leader of a group of teen-agers adopts a new style of clothing, the other members of the group are likely to conform.

Referent power differs from reward power and coercive power in the motive for compliance. For example, a musician in an orchestra may "play his heart out" to please his conductor and get a raise in pay. The conductor in such a situation is exercising reward power over the musician. Then too, the musician may play well after the conductor has noted that his or her technique is rusty and needs improvement if he or she is to keep a job in the orchestra. In this situation, the conductor is exercising coercive power. However, if the musician plays his or her best because he wants to be liked by the orchestra leader, then the conductor is exercising referent power.

The use of referent power in a highly structured organization such as a corporation may cause long-term problems. The manager who is well liked by his or her subordinates may be able to get them to perform well by asking them "to do this for me." However, the manager's success may result in his/her promotion to a different position. In such a case, the new administrator may find his or her subordinates difficult to manage because he or she does not have referent power over them.

Expert power. The concept of expert power is closely related to the competence dimension of source credibility discussed earlier in this chapter. A person in a communication situation may be accorded power because the receiver *perceives* the source as having superior knowledge or expertise on a particular subject. At this point we must make a clear distinction between expert power and *informational influence.* Influence may result simply from information provided by a source. Information may be presented that is logical, rational, and consistent with the receiver's prior beliefs. The information itself may motivate the receiver to act. However, expert power derives from the reputation of the source whereas in informational influence "it is the content of the communication that is important, not the nature of the influencing agent." [15] We will devote two chapters later in the text to influence processes, but this distinction is important in our present discussion. An exam-

[15] B. H. Raven, "Social Influence and Power," in *Current Studies in Social Psychology,* ed. I. D. Steiner and M. Fishbein (New York: Holt, Rinehart and Winston, 1965), p. 372.

ple of expert power should make this distinction clear. A patient is likely to accept a doctor's diagnosis and follow instructions even though the patient is not given any more information about the nature of the illness or the treatment. Thus, expert power can bring about compliance without affecting a receiver's understanding, attitudes, or beliefs. Vesting expert power in a person can drastically alter our communication with people. Many people are afraid to question a doctor (or other expert source) for fear of appearing to be unintelligent. Such unchallenged acceptance is not always in the best interest of the receiver.

A receiver tends to perceive a source's expertise in relation to his or her own knowledge of the subject being discussed.[16] For example, a person who perceives himself as the best player in his or her golf club is more likely to accept advice from Arnold Palmer than from a caddy—even though both say exactly the same thing, "Keep your head down!" The power accorded an expert source varies from topic to topic. Although millions of parents may consider Dr. Benjamin Spock an expert on baby care, he is not considered an expert on politics and is, therefore, likely to have little influence on people's choice of a presidential candidate. In fact, it has been shown that a source's ability to exert expert power may be diminished by a source's attempt to influence receivers on a topic outside his or her area of expertise. Some people may reject Spock's recommendations on child rearing because of his political affiliations.

Like referent power, expert power is vested in a specific individual. This may

[16] J. R. P. French and B. Raven, 1968, p. 267.

cause problems within an organization that relies heavily on an expert's judgment without questioning or understanding the content of the communication. For example, the staff of an engineering department of a manufacturer may rely on the expertise of a single person to solve technical problems. The rest of the staff may merely accept orders because the person has the reputation of being bright and right; this would be deference to expert power. If the expert should leave, they would be unable to carry on without him or her because they were not in the habit of asking the expert's reasons for giving certain orders. Another problem associated with heavy reliance on expert power is that the experts are not always right. Unquestioning acceptance of communication without regard to content can be full of peril.

Legitimate power. Legitimate power stems from the internalized values of the receiver that affirm that the source has a "right" to influence him or her. When irate parents tell their recalcitrant child to come inside "because we said so," they are exercising legitimate power. The child is likely to comply because values that have been reinforced for many years tell him that his mother or father has the right to command him to do this. Similarly, if persons are practicing Roman Catholics or Jews, they will feel "obliged" to comply with the advice of their priest or rabbi on religious matters, because this person has legitimate power over them.

Persons holding certain positions within highly structured organizations or social institutions may be accorded the right to prescribe other people's behavior.

Thus, a judge has the right to place a prisoner on probation, a teacher has the right to assign homework, and a supervisor has the right to request an employee to perform certain tasks. In such instances, the receiver—the prisoner, student, or worker—is obliged to comply with the source, not by virtue of the source's personality, but by virtue of the office the source holds.

To some extent, the use of legitimate power may direct the nature and flow of communication between people. Thus, in the military, each person may prescribe certain behavior for his or her subordinates, but no subordinate may prescribe the behavior of a superior. Likewise, the statement "The Cabots speak only to the Lowells and the Lowells speak only to God" defines the communication lines within a particular social structure—that of upper-class Bostonians.

The range of legitimate power that a source can exert over a receiver varies from situation to situation and may change over time. When legitimate power is based on mutually shared cultural values, the source's influence is usually broad. Thus, for many years, a husband was able to prescribe his wife's behavior in practically every area of her life. He could tell her whom to talk to, where she could and could not go, and what she should wear. This was possible because both shared the cultural belief that the wife was subordinate to the husband. Parents have broad legitimate power over their children, for children are still perceived as extensions of their parents. In most instances, however, legitimate power is rather narrowly defined by the context of the communication situation. A supervisor has the right to tell his or her employees what work tasks to perform, but does not have the right to tell them which candidates to vote for in an election. In fact, if a source attempts to exert influence in an area in which he or she does not have legitimate power, the source may decrease the ability to influence in all areas, including those in which he or she has the right to influence.

Legitimate power may involve the exercise of other types of power. Thus, a judge may be perceived as having legitimate power to exercise coercive power over a prisoner. An employer may be perceived as having the right to exercise reward power over employees. Of course, a receiver may also perceive a source's power to be illegitimate. Thus, a student in a required course may resent a professor's attempt to use referent power, for the student feels "forced" to take the course. However, a student may perceive the professor's attempt to use referent power in an elective course as acceptable.

CONDITIONS THAT MAXIMIZE THE EFFECTIVENESS OF POWER

The receiver makes at least three separate decisions that affect whether a source can effectively exert power in a relationship;[17] all three of these decisions are based upon receiver perceptions. The first decision is *perceived control*, or the receiver's decision as to whether the source can apply positive sanctions (rewards) or negative sanctions (punishments) if the request of the source is not followed by compliance. For example, if a stranger in street clothes tells you and your friends

[17]W. T. McGuire, 1969, pp. 194–196.

not to stand on the corner talking, you will probably ignore the request unless the stranger pulls out a police badge and accuses you of loitering. Even though you might perceive the request to be an exercise in illegitimate power, you still might comply because you perceive the person to have control of the possible punishments. Conversely, if a receiver perceives a source to have power (even if the source does not), the receiver is likely to comply with the request. Thus, if you and your friends *thought* the stranger to be a plainclothes detective, you would probably comply with the request to "move along" without a challenge.

The notion of perceived control is obviously very important when a source attempts to exercise reward or coercive power because these two types of power are based solely on the ability to control behavior based upon possible sanctions. People will engage in ingratiating communication to avoid punishment or receive rewards, but the moment that the source loses the resources to control and/or the needs of the receiver change, the communication patterns will change markedly. Relationships built solely on control rarely continue when ability to control is lost.

The second decision is *perceived concern*, or the receiver's decision as to whether the source really cares if the receiver complies with the request. Many times people make requests of others that they do not really expect to be fulfilled; often they could not care less whether the receiver complies or not. There are many rules in colleges and universities that seem to have no basis in rationality. However, we are often forced to tell our students that they must obey those rules; we

obviously cannot take the daring step of telling them that they do not have to follow the administrator's dicta. However, in many cases we really do not care what behaviors follow. When the receiver perceives a lack of concern, there is little likelihood that compliance will occur. However, if there is perceived concern, the receiver will likely carefully consider a decision not to comply. If a person has control of rewards and punishments and is concerned about compliance, the receiver is likely to respond as requested. If a person asks another person to behave in a certain way "for him" or "for her" (referent power) and it is obviously important to the source, a receiver will probably comply if he or she values the relationship.

A final decision of the receiver is based upon *perceived scrutiny*. The receiver must decide if the source has the ability to scrutinize whether he or she has complied with the source's request. Suppose, for instance, an English professor assigns a novel, stating that the students will not be tested on content of the book but that the class will discuss it at the next meeting. A student who planned to attend the next class might well read the book for a variety of reasons. One of those reasons might be the fact that the professor would have a chance to see if the assignment was fulfilled. However, a student who had no intention of attending the next class might not read the text because the professor would have no way of ever knowing whether the assignment was completed or not. We learned with some amusement that students at the University of Florida have been simply ignoring the required three courses in physical education because they know that the college offices did not have the manpower to check on whether the requirement had been fulfilled. The college administrators obviously have the power to control the situation because they can hold up graduation. They at least profess to be concerned that students meet the course requirements, but they were not surveying the situation to see that compliance occurred. As we stated earlier, one of the main problems in using reward or coercive power is the need for constant surveillance. If we do not communicate with people and give them good reasons for behaving in a certain way but instead rely simply on rewards or threats, we cannot expect the desired behaviors to continue unless we are constantly watching and scrutinizing the situation. This need for surveillance leads to an unfortunate self-fulfilling prophecy in many instances. We have often heard supervisors say that their employees are lazy and the threat of unemployment is the only basis of power that was effective. They cite as evidence the fact that unless the workers are watched constantly, they will not perform their duties. Obviously, if people have no internal reasons for compliance and are simply going along to avoid punishment, we cannot reasonably expect them to continue working when the threat of punishment no longer exists. The giving of good reasons for compliance may be as important a power base as any we know.

SUMMARY

1. An important variable in any communication situation is source credibility. Receivers make judgments about sources that can have an important impact on what is communicated and how it is received. Credibility is a perceptual phenomenon. A source is only credible if the receiver believes it to be so.

2. There are five decisions that a receiver makes about a source; these are known as the dimensions of credibility. These decision points are: competence, or the source's perceived knowledge of the subject; character, or the apparent trustworthiness of the source; composure, or the extent to which the communicator tends to be in control in situations that produce stress; sociability, or the degree to which the source seems likable and friendly; extroversion, or an outgoing personality. Each of these dimensions acts independently to influence the source's effectiveness as a communicator.

3. A wise communicator will try to appear very competent, composed, sociable, and of good character. Research indicates that people who are moderately extroverted are more positively evaluated than people who are extremely high or low in this dimension.

4. Because source credibility is attributed by receivers, it is subject to change over time. At the beginning of a communication transaction, the receiver assesses the source's initial credibility. During the com-

munication transaction, a receiver may modify his or her initial impression; we have called this transactional credibility. After the communication has ended, the receiver is left with a final perception of the source, which is called terminal credibility. To emphasize the process nature of communication, we might point out that terminal credibility acts as initial credibility the next time the participants interact.

5. Another variable in the communication transaction is homophily, or the degree of perceived similarity between source and receiver. Heterophily refers to the degree of perceived dissimilarity between the interactants. The nature of the relationship and the function of communication determine the optimal degree of homophily-heterophily. In some conditions, where the function of communication is persuasion or information acquisition, heterophily may serve the source. In social relationships, people who are homophilous tend to spend more time communicating. Frequent interaction, the development of empathy, and close attention to feedback help overcome problems associated with great degrees of dissimilarity.

6. A third important variable is power. If a receiver perceives a source to have power, the nature of communication will change. The components of power are the resources possessed by a source that will satisfy some felt need of the receiver.

7. A source may be perceived to have at least five different types of power. Reward power is the ability of the source to apply positive sanctions. Coercive power is the ability to deliver negative sanctions. Referent power is the ability to appeal to a receiver's wish to please or be like the source. Expert power is accorded to a source when the receiver believes that he or she has superior knowledge on a topic. This is distinguished from informational influence in that a source with expert power gains compliance not because of the content of the communication but rather because of his or her reputation. Legitimate power stems from the internalized values of the receiver that affirms the source's right to exert control of the situation.

8. The receiver makes three decisions about the source that affect the use of power in communication situation. The first is perceived control that is, whether or not the source has the ability to apply sanctions. If the source has no ability to deliver sanctions, certain types of power-based appeals will be ineffective. If there is no perceived concern (that is, the receiver's decision as to whether the source really cares if the request is complied with or not), the source will not influence behavior. Finally, there is perceived scrutiny, or the receiver's decision whether the source has the ability to determine if the request has been fulfilled.

SUGGESTED READING

French, John R. P., and Bertram Raven. "The Bases of Social Power," in *Group Dynamics*. Edited by D. Cartwright and A. Zander. New York: Harper and Row, 1968, pp. 259–268.

Jacobson, Wally D. *Power and Interpersonal Relationships*. Belmont, Calif.: Wadsworth, 1972.

McCroskey, James C. "Ethos, A Dominant Factor in Persuasive Communication," in *Introduction to Rhetorical Communication*. Englewood Cliffs, N.J.: Prentice-Hall, 1972, pp. 63–81.

————"Scales for the Measurement of Ethos," *Speech Monographs, 33* (1966), pp. 65–72.

Rogers, Everett M., and Dilip K. Bhowmik. "Homophily-Heterophily: Relational Concepts for Communication Research," in *Speech Communication Behavior*. Edited by L. Barker and R. Kibler. Englewood Cliffs, N.J.: Prentice-Hall, 1971, pp. 206–225.

From the Reading

Define the following terms.

perceptual phenomenon
credibility
competence
character
composure
sociability
extroversion
initial credibility
transactional credibility
terminal credibility
homophily
heterophily
optimal heterophily
objective and
  subjective measures
power
resources
motive bases
reward power
coercive power
referent power
expert power
legitimate power

Study Questions

1. What does it mean to suggest that no source inherently possesses credibility?
2. What are the possible determinants of source credibility?
3. What does it mean to say that the five dimensions of source credibility are independent?
4. What are the steps that a person can take to improve perceptions of his or her competence?
5. How would an "ideal" source be rated on the dimension of competence? Can a person be too competent?
6. What are the steps that can be taken to improve perceptions of character? Can a person possess too much character?
7. How do we judge people on the dimension of composure? Does the nature of the communication relationship alter how composed we expect people to be? How?
8. What is a sociable person? How can we change people's impression of our sociability?
9. How extroverted should one be if he or she wishes to be positively evaluated? How do judgments on this dimension differ from the other dimensions of credibility?

10. What are the possible effects of credibility on the communication process?
11. What are homophily and heterophily? How do they affect communication?
12. How does one decide what level of heterophily is desirable?
13. What are the components of power?
14. How can one effectively use reward power? What are the potential problems associated with the use of this type of power?
15. The use of coercive power can cause problems in a relationship. What are the possible negative outcomes?
16. How does one go about using referent power? What are the problems that often occur when referent power is used?
17. Expert power is something that affects all of us. What are the possible negative and positive outcomes associated with the use of the base of power?
18. Distinguish between legitimate and illegitimate power.
19. What three decisions will the receiver make about the source's use of power that will influence outcomes?

AN EXERCISE IN ASSESSING CREDIBILITY

Credibility Rating Scale

Instructions

1. Place a circle around the number that *you* think would best describe an "ideal" rating for a communicator. How would a source you consider to be very credible be marked on each adjective pair? A *4* indicates that you think both adjectives describe the person equally well.

expert	1 2 3 4 5 6 7	inexpert
unintelligent	1 2 3 4 5 6 7	intelligent
intellectual	1 2 3 4 5 6 7	narrow
poised	1 2 3 4 5 6 7	nervous
tense	1 2 3 4 5 6 7	relaxed
calm	1 2 3 4 5 6 7	anxious

good-natured	1 2 3 4 5 6 7	irritable
cheerful	1 2 3 4 5 6 7	gloomy
unfriendly	1 2 3 4 5 6 7	friendly
timid	1 2 3 4 5 6 7	bold
verbal	1 2 3 4 5 6 7	quiet
talkative	1 2 3 4 5 6 7	silent
dishonest	1 2 3 4 5 6 7	honest
unsympathetic	1 2 3 4 5 6 7	sympathetic
good	1 2 3 4 5 6 7	bad

2. Now go back and place an X through each number by each adjective pair that best describes how you think most of your acquaintances rate *you*.
3. Finally place brackets ([ ]) around the number by each adjective pair that represents *you as you see yourself*.

Questions to Consider

1. What items are meant to represent perceived competence, composure, sociability, extroversion, and character?
2. What are the general patterns that emerge for an "ideal" source? What is an ideal source like?
3. How do numbers 2 and 3 differ from number 1? As a class, do you find similar patterns that develop in doing this evaluation? Why do they exist?

AN EXERCISE TO DEVELOP A CAMPAIGN TO CHANGE THE CREDIBILITY OF AN INDIVIDUAL

Three people are running for the same student government office. You are to design a campaign to change the credibility of each one. Please concentrate on how one might go about changing or developing perceptions of credibility.

Donn Winslow has been active in student government for the past three years. He is a member of the "establishment student groups" and has worked his way up in student politics. He is often quoted in the student newspaper on campus issues. His grades are acceptable. He has been very active on committees and is well known. He is a member of the most powerful political party on campus.

Melissa Parsley is a newcomer to student politics and is a resident of a local dormitory. Her major interests have been in a campus academic honor society. Her grades are excellent. She is not well known in student politics.

Thomas Stampps is the leader of the opposition party and is running at the head of their ticket. Although he has been active in student government, charges have been made that he made errors in disbursing student funds when he was treasurer of an organization. He is well known on campus and has had a powerful political base.

1. How would the communication strategies of each candidate differ?
2. What facets of credibility deserve special attention for each? Are there similarities? What are the differences?
3. Would you suggest a strategy of attempting to decrease the credibility of the opposing candidates? If so, on what dimensions of credibility would you center your attention?
4. What are the differences that might be used to develop credibility as opposed to changing it?
5. Would you try to concentrate on all of the dimensions of credibility for each candidate?

AN EXERCISE TO RANK WELL-KNOWN PEOPLE ON CREDIBILITY

Directions: Each class member, as an individual, should rank all the following persons in the order of his or her regard for that person as a source of communication. (The ranking #1 designates the source you most respect, whereas a ranking of #15 denotes that source you least respect in this particular group of persons.) After you have completed your rankings, join the remainder of the class, and attempt to *determine why* people ranked the sources in the manner and order they did.

Rank	*Name*
_____	Muhammed Ali
_____	Bella Abzug
_____	Johnny Carson
_____	Jimmy Carter
_____	Betty Ford
_____	Gerald Ford
_____	Germaine Greer
_____	your university president
_____	Henry Kissinger
_____	your state governor
_____	Joe Namath
_____	Richard Nixon
_____	Ronald Reagan
_____	Walter Cronkite
_____	George Wallace

(*Note:* All persons must be ranked. Two ties are allowed.)

AN EXERCISE TO ANALYZE THE OCCURRENCE OF THE USE OF DIFFERENT TYPES OF POWER

Power Log

Purpose

As the text points out, power is a variable that is frequently ignored in discussions of interpersonal relationships. All of us can cite many instances of the use (or abuse) of power by corporations, government, and university administrators. What we often are unaware of is the extent of our *own* daily utilization of power on our friends, acquaintances, and even strangers. The purpose of this exercise is to illustrate the frequency of this usage and to bring about a better understanding of the dimensions and types of interpersonal power.

Instructions

You are to keep a "log" or record of all the times you use (regardless of how successful the attempt) some type of power for at *least* one full day. It should include a brief description of the situation, the type of power used, and the way each dimension of power relates to this particular situation.

Although you might think that you don't use power very often, when you keep the log, try to focus on the "little" things that occur. For example, why did your date agree to go to the ballgame when he/she really wanted to go to the beach? Why do your roommates turn down the stereo when you try to study? Or, for that matter, what dimensions of power are lacking when they won't turn it down?

Questions you might consider for class discussion could include: Should a relationship exist between homophily and the effectiveness of referent power? How is credibility related to the effectiveness of power? Would the use of coercive power change perceptions of credibility?

AN EXERCISE TO USE POWER TO GAIN COMPLIANCE

We have had some success in experimenting with power in nonclassroom situations. Form groups of three or more, and choose a situation in which you attempt to use *one* type of power. Groups should select different types of power for this experiment. One group might use reward power, another coercive, and so on.

Select a behavior that you want to experiment with. We have had groups attempt to get people not to use an elevator in a campus building.

1. Devise a strategy to get people to comply with your wishes. Base that communication on one type of power.
2. How did people respond?

3. What type of power brought the most compliance?
4. Did the behavior that each group chose make a difference in what type of power was most effective? How?
5. Was there any difficulty involved in making people believe that you had control, concern, and scrutiny? How did you try to establish the perception that these variables were present?

AN EXERCISE TO DEFINE OPTIMAL LEVELS OF HOMOPHILY-HETEROPHILY

We want you to consider four different communication situations (and list the characteristics in each situation) in which you would desire to have the receiver perceive you as homophilous. Now list the attributes on which you would desire to be seen as homophilous.

Table 2.1

An Attempt to Persuade		An Attempt to Inform		An Attempt to Develop a Friendship		An Attempt to Get a Date	
Homophilous	Heterophilous	Homophilous	Heterophilous	Homophilous	Heterophilous	Homophilous	Heterophilous

1. What attributes were most likely to be placed in the homophilous column in each communication situation? How about the heterophilous column?
2. Did the communication situation make an important difference in what attributes were placed in what category?
3. Compare your attributes with those chosen by other people in the class. Do people generally list the same attributes in the same column?
4. As a class, consider why certain choices were made.

Chapter 3
RECEIVER VARIABLES

Message reception is unfortunately often thought of as a passive activity. People frequently equate physical presence with message reception. Educators, to some extent, may be responsible for this notion because they place an inordinate amount of emphasis on speaker characteristics and effective message construction. However, common sense and theory would dictate that the receiver is just as important as the source in the communication process. Even the most dynamic speaker using the most eloquent logic will be rendered ineffective if there is no one to receive this message. Although no thoughtful person is willing to contest the idea that the decoding or receiving of a message is a different process from constructing or transmitting it, most people overlook the fact that both activities are precisely that—they are processes; they are active.

Face-to-face communication situations provide a good perspective for viewing this transactional relationship between source and receiver. As we said in the last chapter, during the course of any conversation, the participants frequently change communication roles. One may initiate the conversation, acting as the original source of the communication, but may become the receiver in responding to another participant's comments. A similar exchange occurs in small-group situations, where a number of individuals engage in group discussion, sending messages and receiving them in rapid succession. The participants in public communication situations also share these two roles when the audience is encouraged to ask questions immediately after the presentation.

In this chapter we will focus on the receiver as an important force in the communication process. The receiver exerts definite control over the communication situation by the nature of his or her reactions or response to the speaker and the message. Whereas the initiator of some communication can determine the level of interaction or the topic of conversation, the receiver participates in the initial decision as to whether the interaction will proceed any further. The receiver can also structure the situation by deciding how much attention will be given to the source or the message. It is not uncommon for a receiver to set the tone of an entire conversation by choosing to "hear" only certain elements of the message. Andy Capp, the cartoon character, is notorious for determining the level of interaction between his wife and assorted cronies while maintaining his primary role of communication receiver. Andy very seldom initiates conversation, but he successfully controls it either by refusing to talk or by deftly changing the topic. He is not a very accommodating communication partner unless the activity includes drinking, soccer, or darts.

Unlike Andy Capp and his friends, real-life communication situations must be accompanied by accommodation between the source and receiver if the interaction is to be effective and worthwhile. Just as the receiver adjusts to the source, the source must also adjust his or her messages to the receiver. Each receiver is unique in terms of age, sex, personality, intelligence, skills, and experiences. These characteristics, which are brought into every communication situation, will have some impact upon the source and the message. The accommodation of the source to these

receiver characteristics can foster feelings of trust and mutual sharing between the interactants, which, in turn, might make the communication more effective.

Owing to the numerous and diverse personal attributes of both the source and the receiver, this accommodation is not always easy to establish. Because, in our view, the receiver plays such an integral role in communication transactions, the effective speaker or communicator must attempt to gather knowledge about these unique receiver characteristics. This is often easier said than done, however. One cannot always preface a conversation with an interrogation of the other participant concerning his or her personal attributes any more than one can pass out a questionnaire to an audience to assess their backgrounds and interests prior to delivering a speech. The best one can do is to make certain *predictions* and *generalizations* about the receiver or audience based upon one's past knowledge. Though these may not always be effective or accurate, it is the only recourse in most situations.

Forming generalizations and making predictions about a given receiver or audience constitute making an *audience analysis*. One confounding factor in analyzing an audience is that as the size of the audience increases, the more unlikely one is to make valid and predictable generalizations about one's listeners. In other words, the more people one has, the more potential for error one has. Nonetheless, most communication scholars are in agreement as to the necessity for relying upon generalizations:

As soon as a speaker attempts to influence the thoughts and actions of two or more people simultaneously, he faces a dilemma. Although he realizes that acceptance of his viewpoint is a personal and singular process, the speaker cannot consider independently and at the same time each listener in his audience. The communicator has no choice but to draw general conclusions about the similarities and differences in alignment of the separate auditors who collectively form his audience.[1]

Obviously, a skilled analysis of the audience is one for which the predictions and generalizations are sufficient in number and are accurate in describing the audience. We have devoted a great deal of time in Chapter 6 to describing the different levels of analysis that might be employed in assessing participants in the communication process. For our purposes here we will limit our discussion to demographic and personality analyses of the audience.

Demographic Analysis of an Audience

When a communicator is aware of the characteristics of his or her audience and understands how these characteristics may affect its reception of a message, he or she is better able to structure that message and alter his or her delivery to the particular needs of the audience members. The audience may consist of just one or a few receivers in face-to-face and small-group situations, or the audience can number in the thousands or even millions in the mass communication experience. Because of the vast number of receivers who re-

spond in a mass communication or large-group situation, the audience in such instances can best be analyzed according to demographic characteristics. These are vital statistics such as age, sex, race, and social and economic background.

AGE

The familiar expression "You can't teach an old dog new tricks" sums up, to some extent, our knowledge of the impact of age on the persuasibility of the receiver. Indeed, communication research on the subject is almost nonexistent. Two early studies do seem to confirm the idea that as age increases, a person's susceptibility to persuasion decreases.[2] Psychological research on the relationship between age and suggestibility to hypnosis provides some tangential support for this hypothesis.[3]

One can only speculate as to the reasons for this seemingly inverse relationship between age and persuasibility. From casual observation, it does seem evident that young people tend to be more idealistic, optimistic, and flexible in their views than older people. Older adults tend to be more pragmatic and cautious, perhaps as a result of having experienced more discour-

[1]H. M. Martin and C. W. Colburn, *Communication and Consensus* (San Francisco: Harcourt Brace Jovanovich, 1972), p. 71.

[2]C. Marple, "The Comparative Susceptibility of Three Age Levels to the Suggestion of Group Versus Expert Opinion," *Journal of Social Psychology*, 4 (1933), pp. 176–186, and I. L. Janis and D. Rife, "Persuasibility and Emotional Disorder," in *Personality and Persuasibility*, ed. C. I. Howland and I. L. Janis (New Haven: Yale University Press, 1959), pp. 121–137.

[3]W. J. McGuire, "The Nature of Attitudes and Attitude Change," in *The Handbook of Social Psychology*, ed. G. Lindsey and E. Aronson, 2d ed., vol. 3 (Reading, Mass.: Addison-Wesley, 1969), pp. 248–249.

agements and rejections in life. Certainly, the middle-aged and elderly may have a greater stake in our society, for they earn more money and own more property and possessions than young people. The fact that they have more to lose may explain their reluctance to accept change.

Regardless of the exact relationship between age and persuasibility and the reasons for this relationship, it is clear that the age of an audience is a demographic characteristic that the source should assess. Obviously, different age groups will show an interest in different subject matter. A group of high school students may be vitally interested in a panel discussion on the merits of a liberal arts versus a business education, but the subject is likely to have little appeal to forty-five-year-old executives. Politicians have often considered the age of their audience when deciding which campaign issue to talk about. A smart politician is likely to campaign for better housing and medical care for the elderly when addressing a group of senior citizens, whereas he may switch his topic to federal assistance for education when speaking on a college campus.

There is also considerable evidence that the rewarding or inhibiting effects of simple verbal expressions of approval or disapproval vary with age and other related factors.[4] The effectiveness of praise and approval diminishes with maturity, and the information value of social reinforcement becomes more important with age.[5]

The effective communicator might wish to keep these factors in mind when interacting in either interpersonal, small-group, or public communication settings.

SEX

Sex is a variable that involves both biological and social factors. Some scientists argue that women are psychologically different from men because of differences in their biological characteristics—especially their ability to bear children. Regardless of the validity of this theory, people often attribute certain qualities to women on the basis of sexual stereotypes: softness or femininity, maternal instincts, emotionality, and greater persuasibility. Many communication researchers have tested the hypothesis that women are easier to persuade than men. In one study, a group of college students at the University of Washington listened to a short persuasive speech opposing further expansion of federal government power in health and education. They were then tested for the degree of attitude change caused by the speeches. The results showed that the female students were persuaded by the speech to a greater degree than the male students. In addition, the women transferred the effects of the persuasive appeal to general and nonrelevant items more than men did. Specifically, the female subjects showed more attitude change on statements such as "Government power has already been expanded too far," and "Government price control would result in unfair discrimination."[6]

A considerable number of other experiments support the claim that women are generally more persuasible than men.

[4]H. W. Stevenson, "Social Reinforcement of Children's Behavior," in *Advances in Child Development*, ed. L. P. Pipsitt and C. C. Spiker, vol. 2 (New York: Academic Press, 1965).

[5]J. Gerwirtz, "Three Determinants of Attention Seeking in Young Children," *Monographs for the Society for Research in Child Development*, 19, No. 2 (1954).

[6]T. M. Scheidel, "Sex and Persuadability," *Speech Monographs*, 30 (1963), pp. 353–358.

However, when other variables are introduced, the results are not as clear-cut. One study with college students focused on the relationship between frustration, sex, and persuasibility. The subjects in the "frustrated" group were told that they were inferior students; those in the "ego-satisfied" group were told that they were superior students. The subjects were then tested to determine the degree of attitude change toward the topics of the persuasive messages. The results show that frustrated females change attitudes more than frustrated males. However, in the "ego-satisfied" group, no significant differences appeared between male and female subjects.[7] In another experiment, there was no difference in persuasibility between male and female receivers when the speaker was a woman.[8]

Analysis of the sex variable is particularly complex because of the role of social conditioning in the formation of male and female attitudes. From an early age, girls are taught that agreeableness and yielding are desirable behaviors for women in our society, whereas males are reinforced for aggressive behavior. Research has shown that there is no difference in persuasibility between preadolescent boys and girls. Other research has shown that aggressive people tend to be more resistant to persuasion than submissive people. These findings tangentially support the notion that differences in persuasibility may be caused by social factors. If this line of reasoning is correct, we might expect the women's liberation movement and new child-rearing patterns to have a tremendous impact on the difference in persuasibility between men and women.

Still another explanation for greater persuasibility among women is that they may be more verbal than men. Girls usually learn to talk and read earlier than boys. Some experts contend that women are better message receivers than men; they attend to and comprehend the spoken and written word more carefully.[9] This may also explain the greater attitude change observed in women after listening to a persuasive appeal.

SEX ROLES

Along with any social changes comes a reexamination of traditional roles. The social forces that have been operating in this country for the past decade have forced a close examination of the sex roles people play and the stereotypes that accompany these roles. People are reevaluating what is acceptable for males *and* females. We need not dwell on inequality between the sexes, which has persisted for many years. That is an obvious fact. What is not so obvious is that a sizable portion of the population is unconcerned with rigid sex-typed roles. Bem was one of the first to investigate the *androgynous* personality, that is, the personality of one who is able to assume both masculine and feminine roles.[10] This study and other research are attempts to debunk the myth of "fluffy women and chesty men." However, we could easily argue that a need also exists to debunk the myth of "fluffy men and

[7]C. W. Carmichael, "Frustration, Sex and Persuadability," *Western Speech, 34,* No. 4 (1970), pp. 300–307.

[8]F. H. Knower, "Experimental Studies of Change in Attitudes: A Study of the Effect of Oral Argument on Changes of Attitude," *Journal of Social Psychology, 6* (1935), pp. 315–344.

[9]McGuire, p. 251.

[10]S. L. Bem, "Androgyny vs. the Tight Little Lives of Fluffy Women and Chesty Men," *Psychology Today, 9* (1975), pp. 58–62.

chesty women." It suggests that certain personality types will not conform to rigidly defined roles of how men or women "should" behave.

In spite of less rigidity in what men and women can do, traditional sex-determined role standards still persist in terms of sex stereotypes. We "expect" emotional women and rational men. Many writers and educators believe that such sex-role standards produce unnecessary internal conflicts, are incompatible with both individual and societal interests because they are unnecessarily restrictive, and lead to the reinforcement of these stereotypes. Some current research has indicated a general disapproval of traditional sex-determined role standards.[11] People are now more willing to accept less rigidly defined roles. The views that people have on the roles of men and women will, no doubt, affect our communication with them.

We can apply information concerning sex roles to make finer discriminations about our audience. Research on androgyny indicates that many people are able to take on the best characteristics of both sexes and are not bound to traditional sex roles. Women are not necessarily persuasible, and men are not always rational. Therefore, the wise communicator will consider people's views of sex roles in determining the most appropriate communication strategy.

SOCIAL AND ECONOMIC BACKGROUND

Studies in the field of communication have indicated that the social and economic background of the audience will have a significant impact upon their responses to a speaker and his or her message.[12] A poor person and a wealthy person are likely to be so heterophilous on such a wide range of attributes that effective communication may be hampered. Each interactant in such a situation comes from a different culture; each has had different experiences; each holds different attitudes, values, and goals. In short, the lack of a common frame of reference may make communication between the two extremely difficult.

The communication problems that arise when people of different social and economic backgrounds interact become evident upon a consideration of a hypothetical, though not unrealistic, communication situation. Suppose a well-meaning (and well-dressed) social worker comes to a ghetto neighborhood once a week to talk to teen-agers about career guidance. The social worker is white, well educated, and from an upper middle-class neighborhood. The teen-agers are Puerto Rican, high school dropouts, or indifferent students, and they live in a run-down neighborhood. Before the social worker even opens his or her mouth, he or she is at a disadvantage. First, the social worker is probably unfamiliar with the verbal and nonverbal dialect and customs of the group; to them, he or she is an outsider. Secondly, the social worker's values are not the same as theirs. He or she was raised in a culture that favored education and rewarded good marks in school. The teen-agers grew up in a culture that rein-

---

[11]L. J. Ellis and P. M. Bentler, "Traditional Sex-Determined Role Standards and Sex Stereotypes," *Journal of Personality and Social Psychology*, 25 (1973), pp. 28–34.

[12]For an especially good discussion of this problem, see Jack Daniels, "The Poor: Aliens in an Affluent Society: Cross-Cultural Communications," *Today's Speech*, 18, No. 1 (1970), pp. 15–21.

forced the importance of living for the moment—after all, who knows what tomorrow may bring, especially to the poor. The teen-agers are also likely to be hostile and mistrusting of the social worker, for to them it may seem as if everything had been handed to him or her.

Clearly, the differences in the social and economic backgrounds of the social worker and the teen-agers will cause communication problems. Conversely, if the communicator and receivers are homophilous in their social and economic backgrounds, and if they share common life experiences, more communication is likely to occur, and the communication attempts will probably be more successful. This is one reason why many programs in poor neighborhoods have had greater success when using community members as leaders.

RACIAL AND ETHNIC FACTORS

It would seem logical that communication between interactants of the same race or ethnic group would be more effective than communication between people of different races or ethnic groups. Prejudice and hostility between the different groups may account for some of the communication problems. In addition, members of different races and ethnic groups are often from different social and economic background. Cultural differences are an inherent part of racial and ethnic differences.

Once again the principles of homophily and heterophily come into play. People are more attracted to those who are like themselves than to those who are different. People perceive blacks to be different from whites, Puerto Ricans to be different from WASPs, and Chicanos to be different from Italians. The fact that members of different racial and ethnic groups are less likely to interact facilitates misunderstanding and the maintenance of stereotypes. A Jewish teacher in a public school in New York City was once observed scolding a young Puerto Rican boy. "Look at me when I talk to you," the angry woman shouted. The boy lowered his head even more; his eyes stared at the ground. "Did you hear me?" said the teacher. "Look at me!" The boy shook his head to acknowledge that he had indeed heard the teacher's words, but his head remained down. "You're absolutely impossible," the teacher said in exasperation. Unfortunately, the teacher did not realize that in his culture it would have been a sign of disrespect for the boy to look at her while she was scolding him. He was already in trouble and was instinctively trying to avoid more. His exasperation was probably as great as the teacher's when he was dragged off to the principal's office.

INTELLIGENCE

Many of the studies that have attempted to determine the relationship between intelligence and persuasibility have been beset by measurement problems. In one early study, unsupported propaganda statements effected less attitude change in people with high intelligence than in people with low intelligence.[13] In another study conducted among army recruits, it was found that educated subjects were more persuasible than subjects with little education when the speech was a logical

[13]H. J. Wegrocki, "The Effect of Prestige Suggestibility on Emotional Attitude," *Journal of Social Psychology*, 5 (1934), pp. 384–394.

one.[14] However, one must question the validity of using formal education as a measurement of intelligence. In general, there seems to be no evidence to support the hypothesis that intelligence and persuasibility are related in either a positive or negative way.

Members of a well-educated audience may possess many advantages as receivers: they are usually knowledgeable on a wide range of topics, their vocabulary is good, and their message comprehension is also likely to be good. Since well-educated people tend to be knowledgeable, they also tend to be critical of unsupported messages. However, one cannot assume that there is any relationship between a person's critical ability and his or her persuasibility.

Personality Analysis of a Receiver

Demographic analysis of an audience may be useful to a source in some situations, but it is also beneficial to view receivers as individuals possessing a unique personality that will affect their response to a message. For example, outgoingness, shyness, hostility, or anxiety are characteristics of one's personality that remain fairly stable from situation to situation. It, therefore, seemed logical to a number of communication theorists that one should be able to predict a person's response to a message on the basis of a particular per-

sonality trait. Indeed, a considerable amount of time and effort has been devoted to determining the relationships between certain personality traits and persuasibility. The findings may be of use to a source because they provide some insights into the nature of the decoding process.

DOGMATISM

Dogmatism has been defined as a relatively closed system of beliefs or disbeliefs about reality.[15] A dogmatic person is authoritarian, narrow, self-opinionated, and close-minded. Such people are unbending in their beliefs and slow to accept new ideas or concepts. Because they believe they are always right, dogmatic individuals have low tolerance for others they perceive as wrong—that is, those who do not agree with them. The television character Archie Bunker is a perfect example of a dogmatic person. Archie is steadfast in his beliefs; he "knows" he is right, and, therefore, anyone who has a diverse opinion is wrong. For instance, if Archie's son-in-law, Michael, tries to persuade Archie to believe that President Nixon was wrong to impound funds appropriated by Congress for day care centers, Archie is likely to argue that this cutback must have been necessary because the president is always right. Of course, dogmatism is not a personality trait limited to political conservatives. Michael himself is equally as dogmatic as Archie and would probably automatically disapprove of any conservative political action.

[14]C. I. Hovland, A. A. Lumsdaine, and F. D. Sheffield, "The Effects of Presenting 'One Side' Versus 'Both Sides' in Changing Opinions on a Controversial Subject," in *Experiments in Mass Communication*, Volume 3 of *Social Psychology of World War II.* (Princeton, N.J.: Princeton University Press, 1949), pp. 201–227.

[15]M. Rokeach, "The Nature and Meaning of Dogmatism," *Psychology Review,* 61, No. 3 (1954), p. 195.

Dogmatic people are definitely not free-thinkers; they are likely to place great emphasis on authority figures. In fact, research indicates that dogmatic people may be more persuasible than open-minded people when they consider the source of the message to be authoritative.[16] Thus, Archie probably changed his attitudes about those "Commies" after President Nixon's trips to Russia and China. Dogmatic people also tend to have difficulty discriminating between the content of a message and its source.[17] Highly dogmatic receivers who are extremely patriotic are likely to perceive a patriotic speech by a person they know to be an antiwar leader as anti-American because of their difficulty in separating the message from the source.

SELF-ESTEEM

Every individual has a personal concept of self, formed partially from his or her own perceptions and partially from the feedback received from others in social situations. The evaluation a person makes of himself or herself provides the basis for concepts of self-esteem. Individuals with high self-esteem generally consider themselves to be superior to others on a number of counts. Research has consistently shown that high self-esteem individuals will be less influenced by a failure experience, owing to their tendency to use avoidance defenses, whereas low self-esteem individuals will be more influenced by failure experiences.[18] This finding clearly points to the caution that must be exercised in delivering negative feedback to another person.

Self-esteem is a personality variable that will greatly affect the way a person receives and reacts to a message. Individuals with low self-esteem are generally easier to persuade than those with high self-esteem.[19] Low self-esteem persons are conformists by nature; they have little confidence in their own opinions and so are easily persuaded by someone else's ideas. Individuals with high self-esteem have greater confidence in their opinions and find it easier to challenge the ideas of others. This makes them less susceptible to persuasion.

Relationships between self-esteem and persuasibility may also be discussed in terms of defensive behavior. One experimenter found that persons high in self-esteem use avoidance mechanisms that lead them to reject threatening persuasive appeals.[20] In the study, a group of Yale students with high self-esteem rejected a persuasive communication that presented very negative statements about army life because the topic was threatening to their concept of self and their life-style. Students with high self-esteem were influenced more by an optimistic message that enhanced their self-image by present-

[16]M. F. Hunt and G. R. Miller, "Open- and Closed-Mindedness, Belief-Discrepant Communication, and Tolerance for Cognitive Inconsistency," *Journal of Personality and Social Psychology, 8* (1968), pp. 35–37.

[17]R. Vacchiano, P. Strauss, and L. Hockman, "The Open and Closed Mind: A Review of Dogmatism," *Psychological Bulletin, 71*, No. 4 (1969), p. 261.

[18]R. E. Nesbitt and A. Gordon, "Self-esteem and Susceptibility to Social Influence," *Journal of Personality and Social Psychology, 5* (1967), pp. 268–276.

[19]I. L. Janis and P. B. Field, "A Behavioral Assessment of Persuasibility," in Hovland and Janis, pp. 29–54.

[20]H. Leventhal and S. I. Perloe, "A Relationship Between Self-Esteem and Persuasibility," *Journal of Abnormal and Social Psychology, 64* (1962), pp. 385–388.

ing favorable attitudes about army life. On the other hand, subjects with low self-esteem used defense mechanisms that led them to reject the optimistic appeal and accept the threatening one. On the basis of these findings, it would seem likely that a student with low self-esteem would reject a professor's optimistic statement that the student will be able to pass the next examination if he studies. Conversely, a student with high self-esteem is likely to reject the same professor's pessimistic statement that the student will probably fail the examination.

In several experiments, the self-esteem of subjects has been manipulated to determine the effects that changes in this variable have on a person's resistance to persuasion. Studies have shown that increasing a person's self-esteem before the person listens to a persuasive appeal makes him or her less persuasible.[21] This seems to be true even if the success experience prior to the persuasive appeal had nothing to do with the content of the message. These findings seem logical and consistent with others, because providing people with a success experience is likely to increase their confidence, thereby making them less vulnerable to the persuasive attempts of others. However, these results seem applicable only when the persuasive message is a simple one. When the message is complex, it is difficult to make predictions about the persuasibility of receivers.

AGGRESSIVENESS AND HOSTILITY

The personality dimension of aggressiveness is closely related to self-esteem.

An aggressive individual tends to be outgoing, self-assertive, forceful in his or her interactions with others, and generally quite confident in terms of general abilities. Logically, aggressive individuals also tend to be high in self-esteem. This has led some communication theorists to speculate that aggressive people are probably less persuadable than unaggressive people. Several research investigations have supported this hypothesis.[22]

When an aggressive person is frustrated, he or she is likely to become hostile. A hostile receiver is one who is antagonistic and unfriendly toward the source. The relation among aggression, frustration, and hostility leads some communication researchers to suggest that raising a receiver's level of hostility by abusive treatment prior to a persuasive appeal will make the receiver less persuasible. The results of several experiments demonstrate that the relationship between the receiver's hostility level and his (or her) persuasibility is not quite that simple. A receiver who has been annoyed prior to hearing a persuasive appeal is more receptive to appeals that call for harsh actions and less receptive to appeals that call for neutral or good actions. In other words, the content of the message seems to affect the persuasibility of a hostile receiver. Thus, a student protester who has just been jostled by police in a campus demonstration is likely to be more persuaded by an appeal to occupy the administration office forcibly than by one that suggests that the protester and the other demonstrators go home.

[21]For a complete discussion, see G. R. Miller and M. Burgoon, *New Techniques of Persuasion* (New York: Harper and Row, 1973), pp. 21–23.

[22]See R. P. Abelson and G. S. Lesser, "The Developmental Theory of Persuadability," and I. L. Janis and D. Rife, "Persuadability and Emotional Disorder," in Hovland and Janis, pp. 121–166.

ANXIETY

Anxiety level will affect one's need to interact or affiliate with others. In a classic experiment, Schachter demonstrated that anxiety-producing situations can increase an individual's need to affiliate with others and can alter preexisting criteria for choosing companions.[23] Increased affiliative behavior will lead to alterations in communication behavior and will affect the degree of persuasibility. Anxiety is a state of worriedness, tension, and apprehension about the unknown. Early studies that focused on the question of whether or not anxiety affected the receiver's persuasibility resulted in confusing and contradictory findings. One study showed receivers with high anxiety to be more persuasible than receivers with low anxiety.[24] Another study found the opposite to be true.[25] As in the case of hostility, anxiety and persuasibility seem related to the content of the persuasive appeal.[26]

When receivers with chronically high anxiety are exposed to an anxiety-producing message, they tend to become less persuasible.[27] This behavior is probably defensive. Highly anxious people seem to have a threshold of anxiety beyond which they block out messages they are unable to cope with. Thus, smokers who are very anxious about their health are likely to reject a strong fear appeal that attempts to persuade them to stop smoking. On the other hand, when receivers with low anxiety are exposed to anxiety-producing messages, they tend to become more persuasible. In such cases, the message stimulates the receiver, causing him or her to pay more attention to its content and thereby enhancing the possibility of attitude change. If a receiver with low anxiety hears the same strong fear appeal to stop smoking, he or she will probably be persuaded by it.

PRIOR ATTITUDES

Every receiver brings to the communication situation a set of prior attitudes, or preconceived notions, that are the result of past learning experiences. Suppose a white Southerner was raised on the theory that blacks are intellectually inferior to whites. If he or she hears a speech given by Julian Bond, a black congressman from Georgia, his or her prior attitudes about blacks will probably interfere with accurate message perception. No matter how intelligently Representative Bond speaks, the listener may still see the speech as further evidence of black inferiority because of his or her prior attitudes.

Research in the fields of psychology and communication clearly demonstrates that people who have strong attitudes and beliefs on a particular topic behave in ways that reinforce their opinions.[28] They may do this by seeking out messages that confirm their beliefs and avoiding messages that challenge their opinions; they may misperceive messages that are discrepant, or different from their own views; or they may disparage the source of the message

[23]S. Schachter, *The Psychology of Affiliation* (Stanford, Calif.: Stanford University Press, 1959), pp. 17–19.

[24]J. Nunnally and H. Bobren, "Variables Influencing the Willingness to Receive Communications on Mental Health," *Journal of Personality, 27* (1959), pp. 38–46.

[25]I. L. Janis and S. Feshbach, "Effects of Fear-Arousing Communications," *Journal of Personality and Social Psychology, 1* (1965), pp. 17–27.

[26]Miller and Burgoon, pp. 24–27.

[27]Ibid., pp. 23–24.

[28]J. M. Levine and G. Murphy, "The Learning and Forgetting of Controversial Material," *Journal of Abnormal and Social Psychology, 34* (1943), pp. 507–517.

or the message itself. In other words, people with strong prior attitudes on a topic are difficult to persuade, and the more extreme their attitudes, the less persuasible they become.

The extent to which a receiver is involved in or committed to his prior opinions will influence his persuasibility. In one study, a group of boys and girls were exposed to two messages.[29] One message argued for stricter school rules for boys; the other argued for more school control over the type of clothing girls could wear. The boys in the experiment disparaged the relevant message (stricter school rules for boys) and the speaker more than the girls did; the girls disparaged the message they were involved in more than the boys did. Similarly, people who have made a public commitment to a position are more difficult to persuade than those who have not made such a commitment.[30] Thus the wise communicator avoids pushing his receivers into a situation in which they feel compelled to take a strong stand on the issue under debate.

Directly related to the prior attitudes of receivers is the degree of attitude similarity between them and the source. Receivers will favor a source they see as having similar attitudes to their own. They will view that source as more intelligent, better informed, and better adjusted than one with dissimilar attitudes.[31] Simply speaking, we like people who have similar views to our own and are generally more responsive to a message from a source we perceive as similar to ourselves. This is often the case among friends and may help to explain why people find it easier to communicate with their friends than with strangers.

MACHIAVELLIANISM

Since Niccolò Machiavelli wrote *The Prince* in 1532, the term *Machiavellianism* has come to connote the use of guile, deceit, and opportunism in interpersonal relations. The Machiavellian, or Mach, is an individual who manipulates others for his or her own purposes.[32] The high Mach, according to Christie and Geis, has a personality devoid of interest in interpersonal relationships, unconcerned with group morality, limited commitment to anything other than self, and possessing a distorted perception of reality due to the influence of personal needs.[33] The low Mach has opposite attributes, although these persons have a tendency to sway to communicating about irrelevant topics.

Cristie and Geis have found that high Machs are consistent in behaving manipulatively in interactions with peers when studied in the laboratory, and they assume that most of the interpersonal manipulation that occurs outside of the laboratory is verbally mediated.[34] As far as low Machs are concerned, they appear to be more susceptible to emotional involvement in interactions on an interpersonal

[29]A. H. Eagly and M. Manus, "Evaluation of Message and Communicator as a Function of Involvement," *Journal of Personality and Social Psychology, 3* (1966), pp. 483–485.

[30]H. B. Gerard, "Conformity and Commitment to the Group," *Journal of Abnormal and Social Psychology, 68* (1964), pp. 209–211.

[31]Don Byrne, "Interpersonal Attraction and Attitude Similarity," *Journal of Abnormal and Social Psychology, 62*, No. 3 (1961), pp. 713–715.

[32]For an excellent discussion, see R. Christie and F. Geis, *Studies In Machiavellianism* (New York: Academic Press, 1970).

[33]Christie and Geis, pp. 36–37.

[34]Ibid., p. 90.

level and tend to be somewhat easily manipulated.

In game situations, the high Mach does not assume that the other members in the game will be loyal, nor does he or she feel betrayed when they are not. If the stakes are high enough, the high Mach has little difficulty advocating a position contrary to his or her beliefs, as long as this will insure success in the game.[35] In another study, Burgoon found that high Machs are more successful in unstructured groups where face-to-face communication with other group members is possible.[36] In other words, the high Mach has a superior talent for improvisation in terms of thinking on his or her feet when others are present. Thus, the high Mach will usually perform in a more persuasive manner than low Machs in dyadic and small-group communication contexts. The Mach is persuaded less but persuades more. Adapting to such a personality trait is important for a communicator.

Variations in Receiver Listening Ability

As we have stressed throughout this chapter, message reception is a vital and active link in the communication chain. Listening is the essential receiver skill in any communication situation, and no two receivers possess the same listening skills.

[35]M. Burgoon, G. R. Miller, and S. L. Tubbs, "Machiavellianism, Justification, and Attitude Change Following Counterattitudinal Advocacy," *Journal of Personality and Social Psychology*, 22 (1972), pp. 366–371.

[36]M. Burgoon, "The Relationship Between Willingness to Manipulate Others and Success in Two Different Types of Speech Communication Courses," *The Speech Teacher*, 20 (1971), pp. 178–183.

Perhaps the most obvious factor that might influence communication accuracy is the *physical and psychological capability* of both the sender and receiver to discharge their functions in the communication encounter. We will concentrate here on the physical and psychological factors affecting audience or receiver abilities to *hear, comprehend,* and *retain* communication messages. In other words, we are concerned with differences in receiver listening abilities.

Hearing, the first component of listening, is the physical ability to receive sounds. We will not belabor the point that a physical impairment will make it difficult, if not impossible, for a receiver to hear the spoken word. There are many physical maladies affecting an individuals' hearing ability. The allied disciplines of speech audiology and pathology concern themselves with these physical impairments to hearing. In terms of an interpersonal communication perspective, we suggest that the speaker keep in mind that a considerable number of people have some difficulty with their auditory apparatus. In fact, speech clinicians are the first to point out that many people with hearing disorders don't even know that they have an auditory impairment. Although one may not be able to ascertain whether or not a receiver suffers from such a problem, some knowledge of the incidence of this problem may explain some receiver behavior.

Comprehension, the ability to interpret and understand the spoken word, is the next component of listening. Obviously, a person who cannot hear a verbal message will also be unable to comprehend it. A receiver will be limited in his or her ability to comprehend a verbal message if the message variables are too complex, if the receiver has a limited vocabulary or intelligence level, or if the speaker has some difficulty with the articulatory mechanisms. Attention to the demographic and personality variables we just discussed should be sufficient to compensate for vocabulary, complexity, and intelligence. The receiver should keep in mind that articulatory difficulties may be either chronic or temporary. It is not uncommon for physical exhaustion, high anxiety level, or prolonged speaking to impair temporarily a communicator's speaking ability. All of these factors will have some effect on the receiver's comprehension level and ultimately, will detract from communication accuracy. The receiver can adjust to factors such as poor *vocal quality* (hoarseness, harshness, nasality, breathiness), poor *pitch patterns*, and other *nonfluencies*. With the exception of extreme cases, there is an initial period of getting used to such sounds. After this period of adjustment, listening comprehension does not seem to be significantly affected. Stuttering by the speaker has even been sufficiently adapted to by receivers such that message comprehension was not significantly impaired.[37]

The third component of listening, retention, is the ability to remember what has been said. Good listening habits, particularly the ability to recall information, are especially critical to college students, who depend on lectures and discussions for a great deal of their information. Only recently has listening been recognized as a

skill that can be taught. Studies at the University of Minnesota have revealed that students often recall better than they understand. To discover the reasons why recall is often superior to comprehension in students, experimenters hypothesized that if students anticipated what they were looking for in a speech, their comprehension and retention of the material would be increased. During the experiment, two groups of freshmen listened to the same speech and were then questioned on its content. In one group, however, the material was prefaced by anticipatory or goal-setting comments that directed the students to look for certain items in the material. The results confirmed the hypothesis that anticipation is an important part of effective listening.[38]

Experiments such as these point up a need for specific training in listening. They are helpful in isolating variables that contribute to good listening skills. For many years educators thought that improving reading ability automatically improved listening ability. On the basis of continued research, today we know there is no necessary direct relationship between reading ability and listening skills.

Everyone enjoys listening to a clever and entertaining speaker discussing an interesting topic, but what happens when the speaker is humorless, the topic boring, and the vocabulary difficult? In such a situation, the inexperienced listener is likely to turn off all listening powers and begin daydreaming or napping. This is an effective escape mechanism, but not very helpful in increasing a person's knowledge or improving listening skills. Practi-

[37]C. Petrie, "Informative Speaking: A Summary and Bibliography of Related Research," *Speech Monographs*, 30 (1963), pp. 79–91.

[38]C. T. Brown, "Studies in Listening Comprehension," *Speech Monographs*, 126 (1959), pp. 288–294.

cally every student has on at least one occasion been startled into reality by a direct question by the teacher when he or she was faking attention. In addition to helping one to avoid embarrassment, knowledge of some of the common barriers to effective listening will prove to be invaluable to most college students.

BARRIERS TO EFFECTIVE LISTENING

Most people have developed poor listening habits owing to a lack of formalized training in listening. A necessary first step in correcting deficient listening habits is recognition of the common barriers to effective listening. This recognition must be accompanied by a conscious intent to improve listening skills and a great deal of hard work in overcoming these obstacles. We will provide an aggregation of some of the common barriers to effective listening, but we will leave the desire and diligence to your own devices.

1. *Physical Impairments.* Some physical impairment on the part of either the sender or the receiver can hinder effective communication. Communication participants can compensate for these deficiencies, and speech clinicians can help to alleviate or lessen the effects of such impairments.

2. *Disinterest.* Poor listeners frequently excuse themselves from reception of verbal messages because they are uninterested in the discussion. Although the effective listener may feel the same way about the topic, he or she will attempt to ferret out the necessary information. College students, particularly, do not have the luxury of being uninterested, unless, of course, their purpose of being college students serves a social rather than an academic end.

3. *Distracting Speaker Characteristics.* Individual differences are such that most of us will encounter communicators who simply annoy us. We will not like the way they dress, their particular style of delivery, the tone or pitch of their voice, or their gestures or mannerisms. In short, many people look for excuses not to listen. The good listener will ignore such factors and concentrate on the material.

4. *Inflammatory Language.* Although profanity is the most common type of inflammatory language, it is by no means the only type of language that throws listening behaviors into a frenzy. Suggestive terms; racial, ethnic, or sexual slurs; and unpopular or unfamiliar slang expressions may also raise objections in the receiver. Try to ignore such language, and concentrate on the essence of the material, even though your objections may be considerable. Remember that people operate with differing sets of moral and ethical codes, not to mention different levels of common sense.

5. *Verbal Battle.* It is a common fault of the poor listener to debate silently with the spoken ideas of the speaker. It is difficult to listen when one is attempting to pick apart a speaker's comments or think up a terribly witty or clever reply. Don't try to argue with a message—listen to it.

6. *Physical and Psychological Distractions.* There are many physical distractions that impede effective listening. Noise, room temperature, lighting, furnishings, and the presence of others are but a few. Similarly, psychological factors such as tension, anxiety, fatigue, and excessive emotion can impede listening. Although we often have little control over environmental factors, we can prepare ourselves in advance when we know that our full attention is required for some listening situation. The good listener will also insure that distractions from other inattentive listeners do not interfere with his or her ability to receive a verbal message. College students who pay to attend class should *never* permit others to disrupt their education by talking or creating distractions.

7. *Note taking.* Students especially are conditioned to take notes on everything said in a lecture. Many important points are lost in asking the person beside you what was just said. Moreover, many speakers are not even outlinable. The effective listener will jot down *major points* and perhaps will emphasize other points with a parenthetical reference to some familiar experience or fact. The poor listener will try to take down every word that was spo-

In note taking, the effective listener will jot down major points. The poor listener will try to take down every word that was spoken. (Photograph: German Information Center)

ken. An effective form of note taking is to fill in an outline of the major points *immediately* after the lecture or discussion.

8. *Fact Hunting.* Some people are conditioned to listen only for facts. A well-organized speech (see the public speaking chapters) uses facts to provide evidence for major themes or claims. By attending to facts only, you may miss the major points of the address. The wise listener will concentrate on major points and will leave the facts for later.

9. *False Security.* Americans, on the average, speak at approximately 125 words per minute, whereas the average thought process can accommodate many more words per minute. Roughly, the receiver can take in information nearly four times faster than the speaker can put it out. Without realizing it consciously, most of us sense that we can let our mind wander for a brief, few seconds and still turn our attention back to the speaker in time to capture the next idea or topic. Unfortunately, or fortunately, depending on the speaker or the source of our inattention, we frequently do not return to the discussion in time to catch the next point. The good listener will use this speech-thought differential wisely to recapitulate or preview the verbal content.

10. *Effort Expended.* Listening effectively is hard work and requires an expenditure of effort commensurate with the difficulty of the material. The type of listening patterns appropriate for bull sessions or for talk shows like that of Johnny Carson will hardly prepare one for a difficult physics lecture or a political debate. The effective listener must practice his or her listening skills on some difficult material.

As we stated earlier, effective listening can be possible only when the receiver is motivated to listen to the communication. Listening is a difficult task requiring attention, energy, and skill. An effective listener must adjust to the vagaries of the speaker as well as to the physical surroundings in which the communication transaction takes place. It is easy for a person to focus his or her attention on a speaker's physical appearance, a nearby conversation, or distracting environmental factors. But all of these distractions interfere with effective listening and accurate communication. The rewards of improved listening are many and varied. A good listener is not only a better student, but will probably be a better employee, a more informed voter, and a generally well-liked individual.

Feedback: The Receiver's Response

Rarely when in sound mind do we find ourselves conversing with a chair or a coffee table. The reason seems obvious: these are inanimate objects. Yet a computer is an inanimate object, and we can engage in a kind of communication with it. The fundamental difference between a chair and a computer is that the latter can respond to us. This response of a receiver to the source's message is called *feedback*, and it is a vital part of the communication process.

Human feedback differs greatly from the feedback provided by a machine. A machine such as a computer is coded to answer certain questions in a specific manner, providing such information as "correct," "incorrect," or "insufficient input." When a human receiver provides feedback for a source, he or she engages in a complex series of verbal and nonverbal behavior. The receiver may smile, frown, sigh, yawn, wiggle, nod the head in agreement or disagreement, and make a variety of verbal answers. These cues let the source know whether his or her message is being accurately received; they are one of the most powerful means of control the receiver has.

Feedback enables the source to correct and adjust his or her message to fit the needs of the receiver. Suppose a college professor is demonstrating a difficult principle to a class. Midway through the lecture he or she notices a negative response from the students. Some yawn, others look confused, and several classmates are whispering and comparing notes. From the feedback he or she is receiving, the professor concludes that his or her message is not getting through to the students. So the professor changes his or her words and gestures in an attempt to improve the message. The receivers in this situation have exercised control over the source through feedback; consequently, the feedback was useful to the source by providing information that helped the source accomplish his or her objectives.

The significance of feedback in the communication process cannot be exaggerated. Feedback is the link between source and receiver that gives communication its transactional nature; just as the receiver provides feedback for the source, the source responds and emits cues back to the receiver. The speaker adjusts to the receiver, but the receiver also adjusts to the speaker in a simultaneous process. All the persons involved in communication send messages and emit feedback, so that they are linked together in a dynamic transaction.

The greatest advantage of face-to-face or small-group communication lies in the amount and type of feedback provided. Face-to-face communication provides a continuous flow of immediate feedback. The source can easily see and hear the responses of the receiver, which help him or her evaluate the effectiveness of his or her message. If the feedback indicates that the message is not coming through, the communicator has the opportunity of immediately changing his or her tactics.

In mass communication situations, however, feedback is often delayed because of the separation of source and receiver. Consider the writer, TV performer, or political candidate who records a speech for radio. Each is a source with a message to get across to the public, and each is concerned about the way that message will be received. Yet these sources can neither see nor hear the reactions of their listeners; they may not even be sure that they actually have an audience. Any feedback they may receive is delayed; so they do not have the opportunity to adjust and retransmit their message immediately to the audience.

When feedback is delayed, the receiver's ability to respond to a message—

and to create an impact through his or her responses—is minimized. The receiver may write a letter to the source or even call the TV or radio station, but he or she will never be sure that his or her message is noted by the source. Nor can the source rely on the few random samples of feedback he or she receives as being indicative of the reaction of the entire audience.

The effects of feedback on learning situations were tested in a classic study by two communication experimenters, Harold Leavitt and Ronald Mueller.[39] In the experiment, specific material was communicated to four groups of students under different feedback conditions. In the *zero feedback* condition, the teacher sat behind a blackboard and allowed no questions from the students. In the *visual audience* condition, the students could see the teacher, but no verbal feedback was allowed. In the *yes-no* condition, the students were allowed to respond with only "Yes" or "No." Finally, in *free feedback,* the students were permitted to ask questions and make comments as often as they wished. The results confirmed the beneficial effects of feedback in learning situations. Scores indicating how well students learned the material increased steadily from zero to free feedback conditions.

Not all feedback is perceived as good or helpful to the source. Every receiver has the ability to emit positive or negative feedback, and we have all consciously used this power to exert control over a source. If a man approaches a woman at a party and begins talking to her, the woman may emit positive feedback by smiling, using direct eye contact, and participating in the conversation. Negative feedback might consist of yawning in the man's face, glancing around the room, and answering only direct questions in monosyllables. Positive feedback is encouraging and rewarding to the source. If a source receives positive feedback, he or she is likely to repeat the actions that produced the feedback. Negative feedback is unpleasant or punishing to the source and will probably cause the source to change his or her tactics.

Studies have shown that positive and negative feedback may have a tremendous impact on the delivery of a speaker.[40] Negative feedback tends to make a speaker less fluent than positive feedback. The communicator's rate of speaking has been found to increase with positive feedback and decrease with negative feedback. In one study, negative feedback produced a significant increase in the loudness of the speaker's voice, but positive feedback had no effect on volume. Negative feedback causes speakers to shorten their presentation, whereas positive feedback causes speakers to perceive their presentations as longer than they actually are. Negative feedback generally inhibits the delivery of a speaker.

Feedback may even affect the source's attitude toward the subject he or she is discussing.[41] It has been demonstrated that if a person receives positive feedback when defending a belief that is discrepant from his or her own, that person is likely to change his or her attitude about the

[39]H. J. Leavitt and R. A. Mueller, "Some Effects of Feedback on Communication," *Human Relations, 4* (1951), pp. 401–410.

[40]J. C. Gardiner, "A Synthesis of Experimental Studies on Speech Communication Feedback," *Journal of Communication, 21* (1971), pp. 17–20.
[41]Ibid., pp. 20–24.

Receiver Variables

topic. For example, suppose a student in a social problems course is required to make a speech on the legalization of marijuana. The student knows that the professor is against its legalization, and so the student decides to argue this position, even though he or she believes marijuana should be legalized. If the student receives praise from his or her classmates and a good grade from the professor, the student is likely to change his or her own attitude and favor the position that marijuana should not be legalized. However, if a speaker receives negative feedback when arguing a position in which he or she does not believe, the speaker probably will not change his opinion. When a speaker argues from a position that is consistent with his or her own beliefs, both very positive and very negative feedback will strengthen his or her attitude.

The way people perceive the feedback they receive depends on their personality, feelings, and experiences. For example, a person may hear only what he or she wants to hear. Selective attention is the ability to attend closely to messages that are consistent with one's attitudes while attending less closely or ignoring messages that are inconsistent. A dogmatic person often uses selective attention to avoid coping with conflicting ideas. A parent may attend a lecture on the pros and cons of legalizing marijuana and "hear" only the cons because he or she wants these ideas reinforced.

Another problem exists when a person tries to interpret nonverbal cues, which may not be consistent with another person's true inner feelings. A frown may not mean displeasure but concentration; a smile can be sarcastic and not a sign of approval. Interpreting a receiver's responses to a message is a difficult and complex task and one that unfortunately carries a high margin of error.

People are dependent on communication for their very survival, and feedback is the essence of the communication process. Without feedback, we could never exchange ideas, test new theories, or even learn about each other. Our dependence on feedback is most poignantly illustrated when a former prisoner of war speaks of his years in isolation as the cruelest experience of all. Feedback also plays a vital role in our development, for our concept of self is formed and constantly challenged by our perception of the way others see us. Vital personal needs are also met by feedback. Each of us has the need to feel significant, worthwhile, and loved; and these needs can be met by positive supportive feedback.

Interpersonal Trust

We thought it proper and fitting to close our discussion of the source and receiver in the communication process with interpersonal trust. Although we will constantly refer to interpersonal trust throughout the remainder of this text, we chose to present an extended discussion of this source/receiver relationship here to emphasize the tremendous impact interpersonal trust has on dyadic, small group, public, and mass communication contexts.

Interpersonal trust can be thought of as an expectancy that the word, promise, or verbal or written statement of another can be relied upon. In order to understand the way trust influences the effectiveness of communication and to become aware of the dysfunctions created by lack of interpersonal trust, we must first understand the dynamics of a trusting relationship. There are three variables that are operative in any such relationship: an individual's concept of self, perceptions about the behavior of another, and the resulting effect of a person's own demonstration of trust on the overall relationship.[42]

An individual's self-concept will undoubtedly affect the degree of confidence, spontaneity, and openness in his or her personal relationship. An individual with a favorable self-concept is more likely to be confident that his or her ideas are worthy of public disclosure, whereas an individual with a low self-concept might be threatened by the ideas or opinions of others. Those who are confident of themselves and their ideas will usually be more spontaneous in their responses to communication messages. Many students suffering from poor self-concept seldom contribute to class discussions because they feel disposed to think out every word lest they say something "wrong or stupid." In other words, they lack the confidence and the resulting spontaneity to make their ideas public. The individual who bases his or her identity on a deep personal trust of self-worth, rather than seeking this identity in the reflection in the eyes of others, will be more open about public disclosures regardless of whether he or she initially trusts in others.

[42]For an excellent discussion of interpersonal trust, see J. Gibb, "Defensive Communication," *Journal of Communication*, 11 (1964), pp. 141–148, and K. Giffin, "Interpersonal Trust in Small Group Communication," *Quarterly Journal of Speech*, 53 (1967), pp. 224–234.

We do not mean to imply that perceptions of the behavior of others are not important. This second variable of interpersonal trust will assist the source in modifying or reinforcing initial impressions of the trust relationship. For example, an individual who makes personal feelings and attitudes known to another will be influenced by the reactions or behaviors of the receiver. If the receiver behaves with genuine warmth and receptiveness and also responds to the message in the appropriate manner, the interpersonal trust that led the source to divulge certain information will be reinforced. On the other hand, if the receiver behaves in such a way as to create doubt in the source as to his or her honesty, openness, or concern, the source will modify future communication. Behavior that ridicules or pokes fun at the communication of a source, even though the intent was not malicious, tends to weaken interpersonal trust. This behavior might conflict with the source's self-concept, and the source might perceive this receiver behavior as cruel and harsh instead of in good fun.

When others respond with genuine warmth and concern, an individual will usually invest increasingly greater efforts into communicating more accurately and, in turn, responding favorably to the communications of others. The effect of mutual trust on the communication process will be the growth of mutual confidence and respect, as well as a lessening of defensive behavior and suspicion. In such an atmosphere, the incidence of misunderstanding each other is lessened, and when misunderstandings do occur, more effort will be directed toward resolving them. A climate of mutual interpersonal trust is more likely to make all concerned parties more objective and favorable to perceptions of the others' behavior.

This brief examination of the favorable effects of a trusting relationship suggests several factors that can impede or seriously impair the effectiveness of communication. One of these factors is criticism or *negative feedback*. We cannot overemphasize the necessity for interpersonal trust when negative feedback is necessary. Criticism or an unfavorable evaluation of the ideas or behaviors of another must be carried out in a climate of mutual trust. Most people cannot and will not react favorably to criticism unless they trust the veracity, objectivity, and good intentions of another. It is difficult to say negative things to someone you care about. Decisions about whether or not to deliver negative feedback should be tempered with the level of interpersonal trust that exists. If a person does not trust you on an interpersonal level, it is highly unlikely that he or she will respond as you desire to your negative evaluation; so you might as well save your breath.

The behavior of others can reinforce initial feelings of distrust or increase the likelihood of conflict and defensive behavior as easily as it can confirm feelings of initial trust. Persuasion or obvious attempts to influence the emotions or attitudes of the listener, an attempt to *vindicate one's own position* rather than an attempt to

achieve understanding of another's views, an attitude of *superiority regarding one's own views* coupled with ridicule for the other's ideas—all of these behaviors can create suspicion, decrease the receptivity of the listener, and impede the growth of mutual trust and respect.

The cycle of distrust is very difficult to break once such defensive behavior has become the dominant element in the communication pattern. Neither party receives enough support or acceptance for his or her communication to warrant openness and understanding. At this point, one of the few ways to salvage the situation is to introduce the views of a disinterested third party. By expressing empathy with both positions, by attempting to clarify the problems that have emerged rather than supporting one position or the other, and by introducing new information that may resolve the misunderstanding, a third person can create an atmosphere of trust within which the original communication can be effectively reevaluated and discussed.

We will provide a more complete discussion of interpersonal trust within the contexts of social relationships and conflict in the last two chapters. For the remaining chapters in between, we urge that you keep in mind that most communication situations will be mediated to some extent by mutual trust between the source and receiver.

SUMMARY   1. The receiver is often considered the passive person in the communication process, although without the receiver there would be no transfer of meaning. To some extent, the receiver exerts a degree of control over the source, and both receiver and source must accommodate each other in the communication transaction.

2. A source must make certain generalizations and predictions about the audience. A demographic analysis of the audience can provide information with which to make such generalizations and predictions. Six demographic variables will aid in making these assumptions: age, sex, sex role, social and economic background, racial and ethnic factors, and intelligence. Although generalizations and predictions based on these variables may not always be accurate, sometimes they are all a source has available.

3. It is often beneficial to view a receiver as an individual who possesses unique personality dimensions. An individual's personality usually remains fairly stable over time and may, therefore, affect the way a receiver responds to a message. A personality analysis of the receivers can improve predictions concerning audience reaction, and it can assist in making communications more effective with given receivers. When dogmatic people are confronted with a persuasive message from a source whom they consider to be authoritative, they are generally more persuadable than open-minded individuals. People with high self-esteem are generally less persuasible than people with low self-esteem. Aggressive people are generally less persuadable than unaggressive people. The anxiety level of a receiver tends to interact with the content of the message, thereby affecting the receiver's persuadability. Receivers with high anxiety tend to be less persuaded by anxiety-producing messages, whereas receivers with low anxiety tend to be more persuaded by anxiety-producing messages. Receivers with strong prior attitudes on a topic are less persuadable than receivers with neutral attitudes. Finally, a high degree of involvement in or commitment to an idea will make a receiver less receptive to a message that argues counter to the receiver's prior attitudes.

4. Machiavellianism has come to connote the use of guile, deceit, and opportunism in interpersonal relationships. The Machiavellian (Mach) is a person who manipulates others for some self-interest. This individual can have a significant effect on the communication situation. High Machs tend to be more successful and create more of an impact in face-to-face communication situations than do their less manipulative counterparts.

5. Listening, the essential receiver skill in any communication situation, involves hearing, comprehension, and retention. Most people have developed poor listening habits owing to a lack of formal training in listening. The source may effectively increase audience reception of the message by prefacing the speech or communication with goal-setting statements.

6. Feedback is the response of the receiver to the communication mes-

sage of the source. It serves as the link between the interactants, giving communication a spontaneous and transactional nature. Feedback enables the source to judge the impact of his or her message and to adjust the message to meet the needs of the receiver or audience. Feedback may also affect the source's delivery and the attitudes concerning the topic being discussed. Feedback is much more prevalent in face-to-face and small-group situations than in public or mass communication settings, where it is usually minimal or delayed. The effectiveness of communication generally increases as the amount of feedback increases.

7. Interpersonal trust is the expectancy that the word, promise, or verbal or written statement of another can be relied upon. Three factors seem to operate in the development of trust in interpersonal communication situations: an individual's concept of self, perceptions about the behavior of others, and the resulting effect of a person's own demonstration of trust in the overall relationship. Negative feedback, obvious persuasive attempts, and superiority regarding one's own opinion are common deterrents to interpersonal trust. The development of mutual trust is likely to reduce the possibility of defensive behavior, thereby increasing the effectiveness of the communication between the source and receiver.

SUGGESTED READING

Clevenger, Theodore, Jr. *Audience Analysis.* Indianapolis: Bobbs-Merrill Company, 1971.

Giffin, Kim, and Bobby R. Patton. "Personal Trust in Human Interaction," in *Basic Readings in Interpersonal Communication.* New York: Harper and Row, 1971.

Hovland, Carl I., and Irving L. Janis, eds. *Personality and Persuasibility.* New Haven: Yale University Press, 1959.

Maccoby, Eleanor E., and Carol N. Jacklin. *The Psychology of Sex Differences.* Stanford: Stanford University Press, 1974.

Weaver, Carl H. *Human Listening Processes and Behavior.* Indianapolis: Bobbs-Merrill, 1972.

From the Reading	Study Questions
Define the following terms. message reception transactional	1. Why is message reception an active process? 2. In what ways does the receiver exert control over the communication situation?

accommodation
auditors
generalization
demographic analysis
sex role
androgyny
stereotyping
dogmatic
negative feedback
self-assertive
anxiety state
chronic syndrome
Mach
listening ability
nonfluencies
physical impairment
inflammatory language
feedback
zero feedback condition
delivery
interpersonal trust
defensive behavior
individual differences

3. How do the source and receiver accommodate each other in communication transactions?
4. What inferences does the source have to make about the receiver or audience?
5. What factors would you consider in making a demographic assessment of the audience? Will these factors hold for all members of the audience? Why or why not?
6. How can a knowledge of sex roles assist in structuring oral communication? Explain how androgyny will affect the transfer of meaning?
7. How can a speaker take the individual differences of the receiver into account when delivering an oral presentation?
8. What do we know about the persuasibility of highly dogmatic individuals?
9. How are individuals with high self-esteem as opposed to those with low self-esteem likely to influence face-to-face communication?
10. How might you plan a speech to minimize audience members who are very anxious? Hostile and aggressive?
11. How do high Machs differ from low Machs in interpersonal communication contexts? In mass communication situations?
12. What factors constitute listening behavior?
13. What are ten barriers that have come to be recognized as impeding effective listening?
14. Explain how listening can be learned. Why do so many people have difficulty listening?
15. How does feedback mediate the communication process? Is feedback more important to the source or to the receiver?
16. What is interpersonal trust? What are the three components of trust?
17. How can one recognize when a trusting relationship exists?
18. What factors will most likely break down or impede interpersonal trust?

AN EXERCISE DESIGNED TO ANALYZE WILLINGNESS TO MANIPULATE

Complete the Mach IV Scale, which measures an individual's willingness to manipulate others in interpersonal communication situations that follow.

Scoring: The ten items marked (*) are scored as indicated (that is, 1=1, 2=2, 3=3, and so on). The ten items marked (#) are scored in the opposite direction (that is, 1=7, 2=6, 3=5, and so on). Simply add the twenty circled items according to this format. Because a scoring constant of 20 is added to each individual's score, the sum of these twenty items should fall somewhere between 40 and 160.

Interpretation: The average score, or theoretical neutral point, on this scale is 100. This means that the average person's willingness to manipulate others will be approximately 100 on the Mach IV scale. The average person also will deviate 20 points above or below the theoretical neutral point of 100. Locate your score on the following chart:

Table 3.1

Score	Willingness to Manipulate	Unwillingness to Manipulate
160–141	High	
140–121	Moderate	
120–101	Average	
100–81		Average
80–61		Moderate
60–41		High

Instructions: Indicate the degree to which you agree with the statements below by circling whether you (1) strongly agree, (2) agree, (3) slightly agree, (4) neither agree or disagree, (5) slightly disagree, (6) disagree, or (7) strongly disagree. Work quickly and record your first impressions.

1 2 3 4 5 6 7 Never tell anyone the real reason you did something unless it is useful to do so. (1)#

1 2 3 4 5 6 7 The best way to handle people is to tell them what they want to hear. (2)#

1 2 3 4 5 6 7 One should take action only when sure it is morally right. (3)*

1 2 3 4 5 6 7 Most people are basically good and kind. (4)*

1 2 3 4 5 6 7 It is safest to assume that all people have a vicious streak and that it will come out when they are given a chance. (5)#

1 2 3 4 5 6 7 Honesty is the best policy in all cases. (6)*

1 2 3 4 5 6 7 There is no excuse for lying to someone else. (7)*

1 2 3 4 5 6 7 Generally speaking, men won't work hard unless they're forced to do so. (8) #

1 2 3 4 5 6 7 All in all, it is better to be humble and honest than important and dishonest. (9) *

1 2 3 4 5 6 7 When you ask someone to do something for you, it is best to give the real reasons for wanting it rather than giving reasons that might carry more weight. (10) *

1 2 3 4 5 6 7 Most people who get ahead in the world lead clean moral lives. (11) *

1 2 3 4 5 6 7 Anyone who completely trusts anyone else is asking for trouble. (12) #

1 2 3 4 5 6 7 The biggest difference between most criminals and other people is that criminals are stupid enough to get caught. (13) #

1 2 3 4 5 6 7 Most men are brave. (14) *

1 2 3 4 5 6 7 It is wise to flatter important people. (15) #

1 2 3 4 5 6 7 It is possible to be good in all respects. (16) *

1 2 3 4 5 6 7 Barnum was very wrong when he said there's a sucker born every minute. (17) *

1 2 3 4 5 6 7 It is hard to get ahead without cutting corners here and there. (18) #

1 2 3 4 5 6 7 People suffering from incurable diseases should have the choice of being put painlessly to death. (19) #

1 2 3 4 5 6 7 Most men forget more easily the death of their father than the loss of their property. (20) #

Questions to Consider

1. On the basis of your score on the Mach IV Scale, how effective do you think you are in interpersonal communication situations? Does your score accurately reflect the way you perceive yourself?
2. In looking at some of the scores of your classmates, how might knowledge of their willingness to manipulate others assist you in communicating with them more effectively?
3. Select several of your classmates, and try to estimate their Mach IV score based on previous interactions with them. Is your estimate close to their actual score? How might you estimate a person's willingness to manipulate others without the benefit of a Mach scale?
4. Is a willingness to manipulate others in interpersonal communication situations a desirable or undesirable trait? Why?

AN EXERCISE DESIGNED TO ANALYZE YOUR AUDIENCE

Each member of the class will prepare a short speech on any topic of his or her choice. Prior to delivering the address, give the instructor a written analysis of the audience and a statement of how you think the audience will react to both you and your address. After each speech the instructor and the class will provide feedback about how accurately you analyzed the audience and how close the audience reaction was to your anticipated reaction.

Questions to Consider

1. How might your audience analysis have been different if your address had been intended for a different purpose (that is, a persuasive speech instead of speech to inform)?
2. What are some factors you should consider in anticipating audience reaction to your speech? Will these same factors still apply for communication on a face-to-face basis? Why or why not?
3. What are the possible ways to obtain demographic and personality data for an intended audience? For a single receiver?

EXERCISES DESIGNED TO EXAMINE THE EFFECTS OF FEEDBACK

1. Select a professor who teaches a course other than your present speech communication course. Arrange with the other students in the class to provide the professor with positive feedback (verbal agreement, head nodding in the affirmative, looks of agreement or excitement, or a spontaneous outbreak of applause) every time he or she walks to the right side of the classroom for one week. Did you notice any changes in the professor's behavior during this week? What is the connection between feedback and the professor's behavior?
2. Form three groups approximately equal in size. Prepare a personal note for each member of your group, telling him or her of some trait or quality for which you admire him (or her). These notes may be signed or unsigned. Place each person's notes containing positive feedback in a separate pile, and have each person read his or her notes. As a group, discuss the impact of these positive feedback conditions on the communication climate of your group. Note how each of you reacts to this positive feedback. Replicate this procedure, using notes conveying negative feedback. Do you notice any difference in the attitudes of your group?

EXERCISES DESIGNED TO INCREASE EFFECTIVE LISTENING SKILLS

1. As a class or in smaller groups, attempt to construct a test for measuring an individual's listening ability. Have the class agree on an approach, and develop the instru-

ment. Form several groups, and have each group administer this measure to subjects outside of class. Each group will report in class the results of their testing. Make any refinements to this listening test that seem appropriate.

2. The class should select a passage from a book or prepare a statement on any topic of their choice. These should be typed and no longer than two pages. Form pairs, and duplicate either a passage or a prepared statement, so that each pair has a copy of the identical information. Half of the pairs will have selected individuals outside of class to listen to a reading of this information and will question them about the contents after they have listened to the oral presentation. *Do not* forewarn the subjects that you will ask them questions after they listen to the reading. The other pairs will follow this same procedure, but they will forewarn the subjects that they will be questioned after the oral presentation. Each pair should report its findings to the class, and a record should be kept of the results. Do people listen more effectively when they have been forewarned that they will be held responsible for oral information? What differences can you notice in these two types of listening behavior?

Chapter 4
VARIABLES INHIBITING EFFECTIVE COMMUNICATION

We believe that it is appropriate to extend our discussion of source and receiver variables in the communication process with mention of some other variables that inhibit effective communication between communicators. It is not uncommon, particularly after one reads about the dynamic and transactional interface between the source and the receiver, to assume that communication will occur smoothly if one takes into account the various source and receiver factors that we just discussed. This is not the case at all, and we do not intend to convey this impression. We humans probably fail in communicating accurate reflections of our thoughts and feelings more often than we convey precise meanings for our cognitive and behavioral faculties.

As you will recall from our introductory remarks, our plan for this book is to follow the present discussion of communication variables with a section on communication contexts and a final section on the various functions that communication may serve. In discussing the different contexts in which communication may occur —the dyad, small-group, public speaking, and mass communication settings—we feel that it is more appropriate to discuss first the variables that inhibit those particular types of communication in those contexts. It also makes more sense to us to reserve discussion of inhibiting factors that arise when one is attempting to persuade, to facilitate social relationships, or to manage conflict for a more detailed analysis of these communication functions. Given this particular rationale, we will focus our attention in this chapter on some of the more common and general factors that inhibit communication regardless of the context or purpose of that communication. We urge the reader to keep in mind that these obstacles, as well as those that we will introduce in later chapters, can and will inhibit all communication attempts to one degree or another.

Communication, as we have emphasized earlier in the text, is a highly personal and individualized process, and, to some extent, we can trace most communication problems back to this fact. If we probe into the attitudes, perceptions, and psychological predispositions of any communication participants and into the way they use language to express themselves, it sometimes seems implausible that communication can succeed on anything but the most elementary of levels. For even when people share a common and cultural background, they are ultimately isolated from each other's reality by individual differences involving experiential factors, personality, morality, and philosophical orientations and also by the feelings and expectations they associate with words, the symbols of this reality. Each person is a unique organism who responds to unique stimuli in his or her unique environment in a unique manner. These qualifications may seem a bit overwhelming and pessimistic, but they point to what we consider a sobering fact of life: communication, at the very best, involves a compromise of meaning between individuals.

Communication as Symbols of Reality

Fundamental to any understanding of the inhibiting factors in the communication process is a thorough awareness of the symbolic nature of communication and language. Several factors are critical to this particular approach. First, we will draw a *distinction between language and speech.* Language is the most important aspect of and in a sense the cause of speech; but it is not identical with speech. Our language is not simply the sum total of all the speech sounds made by speakers of English, although most of these speech sounds are determined by the language in some way or another. Ferdinand de Saussure (1857–1913), the French linguist, made what is perhaps the most famous distinction between language and speech. He distinguished between "*la langue,*" which is both the grammatic and semantic system that makes speech possible, and "*la parole,*" which is the actual vocal output of the speaker. He drew a parallel between the performance of a symphony orchestra and the spoken sentences used in any language. A symphony is both an abstract musical structure and an actual performance. Performances differ from each other and also in important ways from the original structure perceived by the composer. Musicians make mistakes and conductors impose their idiosyncrasies on the musical composition. It is the same with speech and language. There is an abstract structure that conforms to the system of the language, but a particular speaker deviates from that actual structure in actually speaking. Deviations occur in terms of the way words are employed or the type of words employed.

A second important factor is that the *words* enabling a language to be communicated to members of a particular social system are *symbols of abstract ideas or things.* Symbols have no meaning in themselves. They require some type of interpretation, and they are arbitrary. For common meaning to be reached in communication, common meanings must be ascribed to symbols or words. People must be sensitive to the meanings that other people give to specific symbols. However, when people forget that words are symbols and require interpretation, they play roles out of Alice in Wonderland in assuming, "when I use a word, it means just what I choose it to mean—neither more nor less." This obviously ignores the role of the other people involved in communication.

We make our world meaningful by interpreting symbols, that is, by creating meaning for words. As one philosopher observed:

> Man lives in a symbolic universe. . . . He does not confront reality immediately; he cannot see it, as it were, face to face . . . instead of dealing with things themselves man is in a sense constantly conversing with himself. He has so enveloped himself in linguistic (symbolic) forms that he cannot see or know anything except by the interposition of this artificial medium.[1]

Communication, then, requires that people become familiar with a particular language or code. The process of learning any language is a matter of acquiring an increasingly larger repertoire of shared interpretations for symbols. Because words have no meaning in themselves—but only in the interpretations we create for them—we must resist the tendency to view communication in terms of "right" and "wrong" symbols. Communication involves sharing symbols of reality, and one person's *interpretation* of reality may be quite different from our own.

A third factor involves the *nature of language*. Various aspects of the environment are given names through language. In other words, language orders reality. It is the principal vehicle for social communication, it influences the human social structure, and it is ultimately influenced by social forces. Many have even suggested that a society is a product of its language. Language separates and specifies certain features of the environment that are relevant to a particular society's mutual concerns and interests. For example, the Eskimo employs many different words to draw minute distinctions for snow, whereas Arabs are said to have thousands of words in their language connected in some way with the camel. Inhabitants of the Solomon Islands have nine different names for the coconut, but no name corresponding to our general word for coconut. However, they have only one word for the different meals of the day, whereas we employ several.[2]

We believe that you will be better able to appreciate some of the variables inhibiting effective communication if you can view the communication process as composed of symbols of reality. Many of the factors that impede effective communication are a result of both misperceptions and interpretations about symbols, as well as the fact that communication is a very selective process in terms of what people expose themselves to and how they use this information.

[1] E. Cassirer, *An Essay on Man* (New Haven, Conn.: Yale University Press, 1944), p. 25.

[2] M. Lewis, *Language in Society* (New York: Social Science Research Council, 1948).

Communication and Perception

Communication is inexplicably tied to perceptions people have about their world and the other people inhabiting their world. It has also been suggested that both communication and perceptions are inextricably tied to language. One of the most persistent and influential notions of language and society is the *Whorf-Sapir hypothesis*. The basic premise of this theory is that our modes of thinking as well as the artifacts of our culture are at the mercy of the language we speak.[3] For example, we can probably not even perceive seven different types of snow because we have no labels to attach to such differences. This notion grew out of early anthropological studies of the languages of the American Indians, often called Amerind languages. Whorf argued that our whole perceptions of the world are at the mercy of the language we speak and, particularly, of the grammar of that language. For example, he argued that the Hopi Indians could never perceive the world in terms of Aristotelian philosophy because that philosophy, as well as the whole of European philosophy, demands a separation between objects (existence) and action (motion or events). This distinction cannot be easily expressed in the Hopi language. On the other hand, the Hopi perception of this object-event relationship is difficult for Indo-Europeans to comprehend. Whorf argued that in English, verbs are used to denote action, whereas in Hopi the distinction between nouns and verbs is a distinction based en-

[3] B. L. Whorf, *Language, Thought and Reality* (New York: Wiley, 1957).

tirely on duration instead of being a distinction between action and things. If the Whorf-Sapir hypothesis is correct, the basic perception of nature is determined by our language.

The perceptions that people bring into communication situations have also been linked to *psychological dispositions*. Psychological research abounds with examples that logical or analytical thinking does not occur as the prevalent mode of human response, but as a limited reaction under conditions of need. People often respond according to the law of least effort. In terms of communication behavior, this appears at the most fundamental level in the tendency to confuse words or language with the things or processes they name. This inability to grasp the difference between a symbol and its referent causes differing perceptions due to a failure to check back from language to experience and reality constantly. One would expect to be able to establish enough common symbols or perceptions to suit any communication situation. But people are not governed by objective and immutable laws of logic, and they are not a community of computerized minds. People are psychologically different beings who often do not know exactly what they think or believe, and so their communication attempts may inaccurately represent their own feelings and perceptions. If we acknowledge that thinking is integral to communicating, we can readily see how people create their own barriers in the communication process.

Closely related to differing psychological dispositions in forming perceptions is the *limited experience factor*. Owing to the fact that language is symbolic in nature, it can only evoke meaning in a receiver if that receiver has experiences corresponding to that symbol. Even if people could all speak the same language, it would not alleviate the problem if their experiential backgrounds were different. Each individual lives in a private world of his or her own perceptions, emotions, and attitudes. To the extent that these perceptions arise from similar contacts with similar aspects of reality as experienced by others, communication can share more than a common language. But language itself, even if very exact and precise, is a very limited device for producing mutual understanding when it has no basis in common experience. On the basis of some of these perceptions, then, people will employ differing degrees of selectivity in their communication behavior.

Most people are unaware that communication is a very selective process, and they are unaware that selectivity greatly affects the nature of their communication activities. In tuning in a specific television program, a person is making a selective choice that will influence his or her communication behavior. (Photograph: Michael Weisbrot)

Communication and Selectivity

Most people are unaware that communication is a very selective process, and they are unaware that selectivity greatly affects the nature of their communication activities. The significance of selectivity becomes apparent when we consider a common communication situation, such as watching the evening news.

For the sake of clarification, let us focus for a while on a hypothetical man, Mr. Smith, at home on a Tuesday evening at 7 P.M. Having finished dinner, Mr. Smith decides to relax and turn on the evening news. Of course, he has a choice among several networks, but, like most of us, he prefers one over all the others. In making his decision, Mr. Smith is selectively exposing himself to just one of a number of possible news programs. Having selected which station to watch, Mr. Smith may pay attention only to certain news stories. He may, for example, attend to only the political and economic news of the day, avoiding sports, entertainment, and the weather—all of which bore him. Of those messages to which Mr. Smith pays attention, he will perceive and interpret each in a very personal way. For instance, being a liberal Democrat, he may interpret a story about a Republican-sponsored bill to increase federal expenditures for highway construction as just another indication of Republican insensitivity to the needs of the city dweller. Mr. Smith's selectivity does not stop here. On the next day and those that follow, he will retain just a few of the messages that he received during the news program.

While highlighting the importance of selectivity in communication, the example of Mr. Smith also points out the stop-gate nature of these selective processes. In short, we cannot pay attention to a message to which we are not exposed; we cannot perceive and interpret a message to which we have not attended; and we cannot retain a message that we have not perceived. Clearly, the subject of selectivity deserves careful consideration in any discussion of effective ways to communicate. Fortunately, experimental research has provided some helpful insights into the processes of selective exposure, attention, perception, and retention.

SELECTIVE EXPOSURE

It appears that people tend to choose from the variety of communication experiences available to them so that they are exposed to ideas and attitudes that reaffirm their own, thereby bolstering their image of themselves and what they "know." Such behavior is founded on a basic aspect of human nature: the rationale behind almost all human activity is the strong need to protect, maintain, and enhance one's self-concept or image. In a study conducted during the 1940 presidential election, it was determined that more Republicans than Democrats exposed themselves to the campaign messages of Willkie (the Republican candidate) and that more Democrats than Republicans followed Roosevelt's campaign.[4] Another study showed that the people who followed a media campaign designed to enhance attitudes toward the United Nations already had favorable opinions about the organization and its operation.[5] Similarly, a series of radio

[4]J. T. Klapper, *The Effects of Mass Communication* (New York: The Free Press, 1960), p. 20.
[5]Ibid., p. 21.

programs intended to teach tolerance of other nationalities by discussing the cultural contributions of different ethnic groups was listened to mainly by people of the particular ethnic group being praised.[6]

Because research clearly demonstrates that people tend to expose themselves selectively to messages that support their self-image, we would expect the converse of this principle also to be true—that is, people tend to avoid messages that challenge their preconceptions. For example, we would expect a person who has very traditional attitudes about the roles of men and women to avoid listening to the messages of feminist supporters because they are a threat to a self-concept that has been reinforced since childhood. Some evidence from experiments does confirm this idea. For instance, in the 1940 presidential study previously mentioned, the researchers found that very partisan Republican and Democratic voters tended to insulate themselves from the messages of the opposition candidate, more so than less partisan voters. However, some experts challenge the idea that people intentionally avoid exposure to messages that are unfavorable to their self-image. Indeed, evidence is scant, and, for the moment, *all that can be said with certainty is that people selectively expose themselves to messages that reinforce their already existing attitudes.*

SELECTIVE ATTENTION

Information theorists tell us that although the eye can handle about five million bits of data per second, the brain is able to "compute" the information at a

[6]Ibid., p. 21.

much lower rate. Obviously, at any given time, a person must select the information to which he or she will give active attention, or else nothing will make sense.

The information received is usually held for a short time in what may be called "short-term sensory storage"—something like a short-term memory bank—from which the person draws according to his or her capacity to process sensory input. When one does draw from it, the person may either respond to the data immediately or transfer the information to a more permanent memory bank.[7] For example, let us say that you are reading a newspaper and have focused almost all your attention on an article that interests you a great deal. If a friend sitting nearby happens to say a few words to you, you will probably continue to focus on the article. However, the stimulus provided by your friend's voice has not been totally neglected; it may simply have been transferred by your sensory receptors to the memory bank. Minutes later, when you have completed the article, you will have the capacity to draw the message (simply that "someone" said "something" to you) out of storage and attend to whatever your friend had been trying to convey. Clearly, a person can give attention only to a limited number of stimuli at one particular time.

There are several factors that may interfere with a person's ability to attend to stimuli in the environment. The most obvious obstacles are caused by certain physiological impairments, such as poor eyesight, poor hearing, or color blindness. A person with normal vision, for example, turns his attention to the color of the traf-

[7]H. Egeth, "Selective Attention," *Psychological Bulletin*, 67 (1967), pp. 41–57.

fic light before crossing a street. A person who is color-blind, however, will attend to different stimuli in the same situation. In all likelihood, he or she will check to see which light is the brightest—the top or the bottom. If it is the top light, it will be concluded that the light is red.

Certain physiological needs can also interfere with interpersonal communication. Suppose you are having an extremely busy day at the office, with no time for anything but a few quick coffee breaks. Immediately after work, you are required to attend a seminar featuring several speakers discussing their view on modern business management. The topics may be of interest to you; in fact, you may be seeking specific information that you know they can provide. But try as you will to listen to what is being said, you can think of nothing but the dinner that is to follow. In such a case your physiological need (hunger) has forced you to selectively focus on "food" as the most important stimulus in your environment. This need has imparied your ability to attend to other desirable stimuli. To some extent, training facilitates our ability to attend to certain stimuli that we know we will need at a particular moment. An aeronautical engineer at the Kennedy Space Center is faced with an awesome array of dials, graphs, buttons, toggle switches, and computer readouts. Unless he or she knows what to look for—that is, unless he or she consciously selects certain stimuli (a process of selective attention that seems impossible to the untrained observer)—effective communication with co-workers will be impaired. On a less sophisticated level, a key-punch operator who works for a department store may be trained to at-tend to certain facts, such as the customer's name and address, his or her account number, the price of items purchased, the amount of payments made, and the date.

Sometimes our past experience forces us to focus our attention on certain stimuli in our environment. This is fortunate for us, or, like Nero, we might be fiddling while our own house burns. Stimuli that imply an immediate danger often narrow our attention in this way. If someone shouts, "Watch out for that car," we would not consciously have to choose to attend to that warning rather than choose to watch the dog dig up the lawn across the street or to look at an attractive sunset on the horizon. Through past experience and familiarity with similar information, we automatically select the warning as the most important of all stimuli available to us.

Sometimes, however, familiarity with certain information tends to make a person negligent in his or her conscious selection of data. If a student is familiar with the material being discussed in a lecture, that student might be less attentive to the professor's words than if he or she had no knowledge of the subject. The professor's attempt to communicate is thus foiled by the student's assumption that he or she already knows what the professor intends to say; the student's attention to the professor's message is limited to "one-ear listening."

A sender may employ various techniques to gain a receiver's attention. For many years, the volume level of television commercials was markedly higher than the volume of regular programming. To some extent, this focused viewer's attention on the advertiser's message. Consequently, the FCC outlawed this practice. Sometimes breaking the flow of one communication with another sender's message may mitigate the effectiveness of either message. Consider, for example, a television documentary on poverty that is interrupted by a commercial that urges the viewer to "live the good life" by vacationing on some Caribbean island. The airline's message may permanently disrupt the viewer's thoughts about the documentary message, and this may annoy the viewer to the point that he or she refuses to focus his or her attention on the commercial message. There are, of course, some viewers whose attention may wane after the first five minutes of a program. In such cases, a commercial break may serve to draw back their attention from incidental stimuli—family, friends, a snack, or a beer—to the electronic messages on the television.

Some communicators also create obstacles by focusing our attention on some things to the exclusion of others. For example, when a salesperson emphasizes the solid construction of a car, its 2,000-cc overhead cam engine, fully synchronized four-speed transmission, rack-and-pinion steering, and award-winning design, that salesperson is riveting attention on what he or she considers the most important—and salesworthy—features of the car. However, in doing so, the salesperson is diverting attention from what may be the most practical consideration: will the car fit the garage? If not, the customer who buys it may regard the salesperson's message as a failure because it did not provide him or her with an essential bit of information. From the salesperson's perspective, the communication will be viewed as

a great success, unless, of course, the customer returns to the showroom with an angry complaint.

Sometimes noise will affect our attention in a communication situation. Experiments in which subjects were orally instructed to attend to only certain stimuli in the environment confirm this fact. In one series of tests, subjects simultaneously received two or more auditory messages. It was found that a message can be most easily heard in noise when the message and the noise come from two different locations.[8] It was also demonstrated that the differences in the intensity of sounds aid in selectively attending to one message among several—even if the relevant message is softer.[9]

Some of these data are borne out by our everyday experiences. For instance, two messages produced very close to each other and of equal volume intensity usually cancel each other out. One example is the mother who is trying to decipher the screams and protests of her two children, each of whom is accusing the other of spilling a glass of milk. In moments of high debate when the voices of two opposing groups are spiraling to an incredible noise level, it is oten the softer words of some less emotional person that pierce through the noise and hold our attention.

SELECTIVE PERCEPTION

Perhaps the most workable definition of perception is that it is "the process of

[8]I. J. Hirsch, "The Relation Between Localization and Intelligibility," *Journal of the Accoustical Society of America,* 22 (1950), pp. 196–200.

[9]J. P. Egan, E. C. Carterette, and E. J. Thoring, "Some Factors Affecting Multichannel Listening," *Journal of the Acoustical Society of America,* 26 (1954), pp. 774–782.

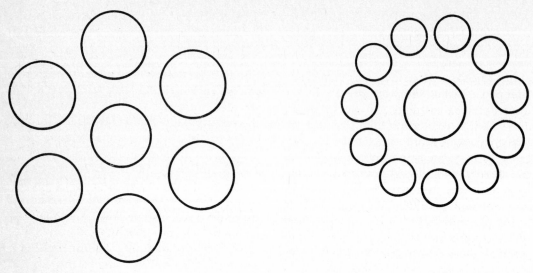

Fig. 4.1 Environmental factors may affect a person's perception of stimuli. Do the center circles in these figures appear to be the same size?

making sense out of experience—the imputing of meaning to experience."[10] However, the process of perception is not as simple as this definition may at first seem. To begin with, different people do not experience the same stimuli in exactly the same way. Differences in environment; differences in sensory receptors; differences in internalized values, goals, and attitudes—all contribute to differences in the way a person perceives reality. Furthermore, language—the process by which we impute meaning—compounds the problems caused by these physiological and psychological differences. No two people invest a particular word with exactly the same meaning. To one person, the word *happy* may mean not being depressed; to another person, it may mean being overjoyed at some won-

[10]W. V. Haney, *Communication and Organizational Behavior* (Homewood, Illinois: Richard D. Irwin, Inc., 1967), p. 52.

drous event that has taken place. The communication problems that result from these individual differences are often intensified by the fact that people tend to be unaware that differences do, in fact, exist. In short, we think that what we perceive is reality—how can there be differences?

Most people have experienced moments when their perceptions of a particular person or situation or object differed greatly from the perceptions of other people. For example, Dr. William Jones may be perceived as an excellent surgeon by a man whose life was saved by a delicate heart operation that the doctor performed. The husband of a woman who died under Dr. Jones's scalpel may perceive the doctor as a quack whose license should be revoked. Dr. Jones's wife perceives him as a sensitive and dedicated professional and a loving husband. His children view him as a strict father whose gaze makes them uncomfortable. Will the real Dr. Jones please stand up? Of course, the point is that there is no real Dr. Jones. Each person thinks his or her private perception of Dr. Jones is the real man.

A person's past experiences and expectations will affect the way he or she perceives stimuli in his or her environment. For example, if a critic you respect writes a brilliant review of a new film, the review is likely to create a favorable image of the movie in your mind. More important, this favorable impression will affect your actual perception of the film—if you expect to like the movie, you probably will like it. Many experimental studies have confirmed the powerful impact that past experiences and expectations have on a person's perception of a message. In one study, people who were exposed to a neutral statement on school bussing tended to perceive it as antibussing when the message was attributed to George Wallace and probussing when it was attributed to Martin Luther King.[11] Ninety-five percent of the subjects in another test judged "cookies" excellent to good until they found out the cookies were made of dog biscuits.

People often forget that words, which function to define, label, or categorize, restrict our perceptions of other people, things, and situations. For example, in one study two groups of subjects were shown identical drawings of ambiguous shapes, and each group was given a different "label" for the same drawing. When asked to reproduce the shapes, the subjects consistently drew the shapes more in accordance with the words used to describe them than with the actual shapes they saw (see Fig. 4.2). William

Haney, in his book *Communication and Organizational Behavior*, has commented on the way words narrow people's perception of reality.

> One cannot help wondering how long progress has been retarded by the assignation of inappropriate names. How much time was lost and how many lives were squandered by the term *malaria*? Contracted from the Italian words *mala aria* ('bad air'), it perpetuated the erroneous notion that the disease was caused by the bad air of the swamps. . . . And how many bright and willing scientists were inhibited from even dreaming of the possibility that the *atom* (from the Greek for *indivisible*) *could* be split largely because its *name* said it could *not* be divided?[12]

SELECTIVE RETENTION

The principle of selective retention states that people more accurately remember messages that are favorable to their self-image than messages that are unfavorable. In short, people remember the good times and forget the bad. An amazing example of this can be seen in the fact that former inmates of Auschwitz actually hold reunions, during which they grow sentimental over remembered jokes, sounding just like old fraternity brothers at the annual class dinner. A few experimental studies have also confirmed this hypothesis. In one study, a pro-Communist message and an anti-Communist message were both presented to two groups of college students.[13] One group had favorable attitudes toward communism, and the other group had unfavorable

[11]J. W. Koehler, J. C. McCroskey, and W. E. Arnold, *The Effects of Receiver's Constancy-Expectation in Communication*, Research Monograph, Department of Speech, Pennsylvania State University, 1966.

[12]W. V. Haney, 1967, p. 143.

[13]J. M. Levine and G. Murphy, "The Learning and Forgetting of Controversial Statements," *Journal of Abnormal and Social Psychology*, 38 (1948), pp. 507 –517.

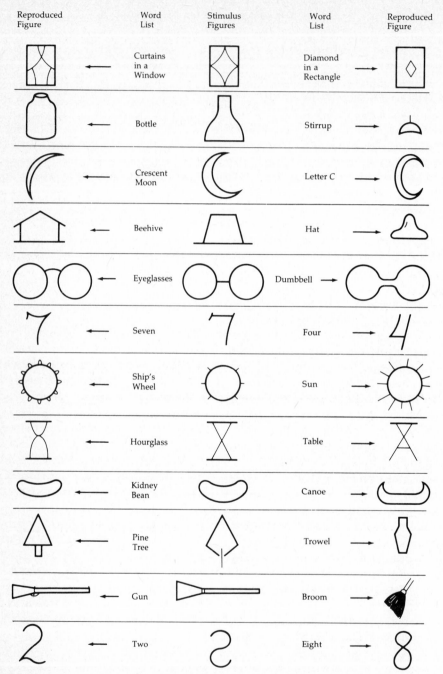

Reproduced Figure	Word List	Stimulus Figures	Word List	Reproduced Figure
	← Curtains in a Window		Diamond in a Rectangle →	
	← Bottle		Stirrup →	
	← Crescent Moon		Letter C →	
	← Beehive		Hat →	
	← Eyeglasses		Dumbbell →	
	← Seven		Four →	
	← Ship's Wheel		Sun →	
	← Hourglass		Table →	
	← Kidney Bean		Canoe →	
	← Pine Tree		Trowel →	
	← Gun		Broom →	
	← Two		Eight →	

Fig. 4.2 These figures drawn by subjects in an experiment demonstrate that language may affect a person's perception of stimuli.

THE VARIABLES IN THE COMMUNICATION PROCESS

attitudes. Not surprisingly, the members of each group more accurately retained the message that was in agreement with their attitudes than the message that challenged their attitudes. Likewise, each group forgot the unfavorable message more quickly than the favorable one.

It is rather difficult to discuss selective retention apart from attention and perception, for all are functions of the same basic process. In fact, sometimes it is virtually impossible to assign degrees of importance to each function. For instance, let us say a person is exposed to a political message and shortly thereafter presents an incomplete or distorted report on what he or she has heard. Were the "data" themselves incorrectly perceived, or was the retention incomplete or distorted? Or were both perception and retention inaccurate? If the time lapse between the perception and the report is lengthy, it becomes even more difficult to answer these questions.

The available research makes it difficult to make many conclusive statements about the retention process. It does seem that retention of at least part of a message is improved if intense sensory stimuli accompany the message. Teachers, for example, often use visual aids to help their students remember the message they are listening to. Sometimes increasing the motivation for retention is helpful. Thus, if a professor tells his or her students that remembering that day's lecture will assure them of passing the next exam, the students will probably be more mentally receptive, will concentrate more deeply, and thus will remember the lecture more fully and accurately. However, if the lecture seemed confusing to the students or involved material with which they had no prior contact, the degree and accuracy of

the students' retention (and the success of the professor's communication) will be limited.

It would seem that retention in conjunction with other selective processes can be quite detrimental to effective communication. Our perceptions, as we have said, are, in part, influenced by our memory of past experiences and messages. If we do not retain messages that conflict with our basic self-image or if these messages become distorted in memory with the passage of time, our future perceptions will be narrowed or distorted. The cycle of behavior that results may be a difficult one to break, and consequently our communication efforts may be greatly hampered.

Inference Versus Observation

One important factor that may inhibit communication is the failure by people and language to distinguish between statements of inference and statements of observation. Observational and inferential statements are often very difficult to distinguish, especially because our language provides no grammatical, syntactical, or pronunciational distinctions between them. Thus, it is not surprising that our failure to distinguish on these verbal levels contributes appreciably to the difficulty we have on cognitive levels. In short, we find it exceedingly easy to make inferences about reality as we perceive it and to utter inferential statements with the false assurance that we are dealing with facts as we observed them.

An early, classic study concerned with the effect of this inference-observation confusion on the taking of legal testimony will demonstrate this point.[14] An instructor at the University of Wisconsin arranged with four of his seventy-five students before class to disrupt the class in the following manner. While the instructor was collecting papers from students in the front row, two students in the rear began to fight and throw fists and books at each other in wild disarray. Simultaneously, another student in the front row threw two silver dollars into the air, permitted them to fall to the floor, and raced after them. The instructor ordered the three students from the room, and immediately after he did this, the fourth student stood up and walked slowly out of the room. As all four students were exiting the room, he wrote the time on the blackboard, erased it, and wrote it on the board again. The instructor asked the class to write out an account of this incident for future testimony. This was not unusual because many universities in 1918 were on a student self-governing basis.

The results of these student testimonies is a classic example of the inference-observation confusion. The instructor was reported to be standing at the front, middle, back, and side of the room. Even though all had seen him writing the time on the board as the four were exiting the room, he was reported to be sitting at his desk hanging his head in embarrassment, holding the door open for the four, and standing in the middle of the room threatening to break up the disturbance. Many students reported that they had "seen" the two combatants break a desk and shatter it and that it was part of the desk that the

[14]M. C. Otto, "Testimony and Human Behavior," *Journal of Criminal Law and Criminology*, 9 (1918), pp. 98–104.

third student rushed to retrieve. Ironically, it was the student sitting beside the boy who threw two silver dollars into the air who reported this "observation." Finally, though most did not even see the fourth student walk from the room, he reportedly ran from the room in order to avoid the fighting.

The inference-observation dilemma also involves a degree of risk taking. Everyone is, of course, aware of taking a calculated risk. People frequently observe a situation —like the amount of material to be covered on the final exam—and decide not to study much of the material because it *may not* be on the final examination. They are inferring that the exam questions will be limited and that they can get away with not studying much of the material. Whether their hunch or inference is right or wrong, they are still aware of the potential outcomes of such behavior. Unfortunately, when we fail to recognize that we have made an inference (or conclusion from facts or premises) instead of an observation (or noting the occurrence of some observable phenomenon), we are not aware of the possible outcomes, which can sometimes prove costly, dangerous, or even fatal. During the Vietnam conflict a helicopter crew was returning to their base camp after a long mission. About an hour's flying time away from their base camp one hungry crewman spotted a group of soldiers sitting around a campfire in an open field and suggested that the chopper drop down for a couple of minutes so they could grab some much needed nourishment and relief from a grueling day. The rest of the crew agreed with the *inference* that the enemy would not be sitting in an open field with an

American gunship approaching quickly. When the helicopter descended low enough to see the soldiers, the crew made the frantic *observation* that the soldiers were, in fact, not their own. This confusion between observation and inference caused one death and one serious injury, not to mention the tremendous grief and embarrassment that would haunt the other crew members for the rest of their lives.

As we stated earlier, our language does not necessarily discern between inference and observation, and people are frequently unprepared or unwilling to make this distinction. The following table lists some of the characteristics between statements of observation and statements of inference:

Table 4.1

Statements of Observation

1. Can be made only after actually observing some behavior or occurence.
2. Must stay within the parameters of the observation.
3. Are appropriate only for the actual observer.
4. Approach certainty or sureness.

Statements of Inference

1. Can be made at any time.
2. Goes beyond the parameters of actual observation. An inference can be made to the limits of one's imagination.
3. Can be made by anyone, not just by the observer.
4. State only degrees of probability or likelihood.

We are not implying that inferences should not be made. Quite the contrary, inferences are at times the only recourse we have available. We are suggesting that inferences be *labeled* as inferences with a certain degree of probability associated with them. When inferences, especially incorrect ones, are considered to be actual observations, effective communication will surely suffer.

Intensional Orientations

Intensional orientation is the situation in which people are more concerned with their feelings, emotions, inferences, attitudes, evaluations, and perceptions than they are with the objects, people, and relationships that occur outside of their minds in the real world. In other words, an individual behaves intensionally when he or she responds to these feelings, inferences, evaluations, and perceptions as if he or she were responding to the people, objects, and relationships in reality. It has been reported that a significant number of Americans experience some fear of flying. It is not uncommon to see airport bathrooms filled with people nervously relieving themselves a dozen or more times within a half hour of flight time or to see otherwise relaxed and confident individuals clutching bottles of motion sickness tablets passionately in their hands. It is also not uncommon to see people upheave before the plane even takes off. (At least one of the authors must admit to all of these behaviors). These are classic symptoms of intensional orientation, in which people may be reacting to their fears and misconceptions about the term *flying* rather than to the actual flying experience. (At least one of the authors must admit that thinking about flying is far worse than the actual flight.)

With this general notion of intensional orientation in mind, we will discuss several specific instances in which intensional orientation impedes effective communication.

POINTING

It should be obvious to everyone that the words that we use to define objects can significantly affect the manner in which we react to the actual objects. The words we use in language point or call attention to something. Again we remind you that words have no meaning in themselves; so this pointing function that words have is determined by the people using the words. Stated simply, people, not words, point or call attention to other things. The problem is the same word will invariably call attention to different things for different people, but people fail to take this fact into account. This leads a couple to experience differing feelings with the term *love,* office mates to disagree sharply over exactly what constitutes "quiet," and two countries to stall negotiations over disputes involving "reconciliation."

Words, in pointing to other concepts or perceptions, will also conjure up certain associations in our minds. The story is told about the manager of a department store who once received a shipment of quality handkerchiefs and placed half of them on a table marked "Fine Irish Linen" and the other identical handkerchiefs on another table marked "Nose Rags—Three for a Quarter." As the story goes, the "Irish Linens" outsold the "Nose Rags" five to one. Apparently, the use of the term *Irish Linens* pointed to a certain qual-

ity product and enabled people to associate use of this merchandise with culture and refinement. Similarly, the use of the word *sporty* in car advertisements seems to elicit notions of a quick, responsive machine associated with the wild life of the Grand Prix racing circuit, even if the term is used to describe a Ford Pinto with a racing stripe and chrome wheel covers added. Of course, people will differ in the pointing and associating functions that they assign to particular words.

BLINDERING

In a similar sense, the words we use to define situations or problems may act as blinders in our approach to the situation or problem. Blindering may lead to undesirable solutions or approaches, or it may significantly delay or impede action or resolution. For example, we have found that when we have alerted our students on occasion that some lecture material is somewhat "difficult," we were trying to indicate that the material would require some thought and attention, not that the material was "impossible" to grasp. Some reacted as if we had suggested that they become experts in quantum physics. Owing to the use of the word *difficult,* some of these students defined the situation as much too strenuous and demanding of them. In other words, the word *difficult* acted as a blinder in preventing them from evaluating our discussion accurately.

Benjamin Lee Whorf, the noted language expert whom we cited earlier, provides an example of an undesirable solution due to blindering from his early employment as a fire insurance adjuster.[15] In one investigation, he observed that

[15]B. L. Whorf, 1957, p. 135.

people tended to be very cautious around what they called "gasoline drums." Great care was taken to prevent smoking or striking matches in their vicinity. But when the drums were emptied and then labeled "empty gasoline drums," caution was thrown to the wind. Employees smoked cigarettes with abandon around the drums, and some even tossed lighted cigarette butts into these "empty drums." They were blindered by the term *empty drums,* and did not even stop to think that it is the fumes remaining in a gasoline can that are more dangerous than the gasoline itself. The resulting fire was attributed indirectly to the words used to define this particular situation.

When blindering does occur, there are several courses of action that might prove useful. A first step might be to consult someone outside of the immediate area of concentration. Labor and management frequently rely on neutral third parties who have a fresh approach and who are not blindered by hours or even days of tedious rhetoric. Next one should begin a task at once and not dwell on the perfect solution or approach. Some students seem to have much difficulty beginning papers or projects, but, once started, they usually progress rapidly. The important point is to start a task. Start anywhere—the middle, the end, or the beginning if possible —but start. Finally, tension is often responsible for blindering. When people become stale or frustrated in some activity, it is not uncommon for words to create mental blocks. Shifting to an unrelated task or trying to relax physically may break the tension cycle.

Intensional orientations are caused both by the nature of our language and by the nature of ourselves. We will discuss more

fully in several chapters to follow the individual differences of the communication participants as they impede effective communication.

We will now turn our attention to four communication phenomena that inhibit effective communication in a variety of contexts.

Allness

People frequently operate under two faulty assumptions. The first is that it is possible to know everything about something. For that matter, it is questionable whether it is possible to know everything about anything, but people sometimes act as if they do. The second erroneous assertion is that whatever people happen to be communicating about a topic includes all that is important about that subject. When one considers that a significant proportion of communication is based upon these faulty assumptions, it is not hard to understand why so much of our communication behavior falls short of the intended goal.

Our knowledge of reality can be neither total nor infallible. The selectivity processes that we discussed earlier indicate that our knowledge of anything at any given time can only be partial. The nervous system responds to a limited number of stimuli from any particular environment; the sensory receptors, which vary in sensitivity from person to person, modify those stimuli that are perceived; and past experiences and recollections shape our reactions to the stimuli. Our perspective of a particular event or idea further modifies our knowledge of them. The students who viewed the altercation in our earlier example all arrived at different impressions of the situation. Their "knowledge" of this particular reality was far from total or infallible. Finally, there is the time factor. We cannot know all that a thing was or all that it will be, nor can we know the entire pattern of its relationship to other things in the world. Our observations are limited to the present tense.

The problem of allness arises when people fail to remember that their responses to reality are simply abstractions. Irving Lee, an important figure in the field of general semantics, stated the point most lucidly:

> Whenever we respond we abstract some details from a total situation, so that some others must be left out. Every way of looking brings with it some areas of blindness.[16]

An old story that has circulated for years will illustrate this point. Two American women, a matronly grandmother with her young and attractive granddaughter, were seated in a railroad compartment with a German and an Italian officer. As the train entered a long and dark mountain tunnel, all that was heard was a loud kiss and the resounding slap. When the train emerged from the tunnel, all four occupants of the compartment stole quick glances at one another, but no one spoke. The grandmother, thinking to herself, reflected on what a fine granddaughter she had. She would never have to worry about her taking care of herself. The granddaughter marveled at what a hard wallop her grandmother packed and felt pleased with the older woman's spunk. The German officer mused pensively, "How clever these Italians are. They steal a kiss and have the

other fellow slapped." The Italian officer chuckled to himself, "How clever I am. I kissed my own hand and slapped the German."

The process of abstracting is not only characteristic of nervous system responses but also of the structure of our language. Even if an individual perceives a multitude of details, his or her description will necessarily focus attention on only a limited number of them. When we say that a "Porsche Turbo Carrerra is the fastest, the best, and the most sophisticated sports car in production today," we are creating a picture that focuses on only certain details about this object. It is an *abstract* picture that neglects many important factors that also constitute a "Porsche Turbo Carrerra." For instance, it costs thirty thousand dollars, it is inordinately expensive to operate and maintain, and it is too much machine for normal driving conditions. People cannot help abstracting when they use language, and in fact; it assists them in ordering their thoughts. The danger is that people often regard abstractions—and the labels they affix to people and objects—as all that can be known, or is important to know, about the things they are describing.

The assumption of allness or totality can create substantial barriers to effective communication. When a young woman says that an aspiring suitor is a "nerd," she is basing her statement on a limited perception of the young man. Yet her judgment will probably prevent her from viewing the young man in any light other than that of a "nerd." The woman, in all likelihood, will deny the young suitor any opportunity of expressing other aspects of his personality. Furthermore, through

---

[16]I. J. Lee, *Language Habits in Human Affairs* (New York: Harper and Brothers, 1941), p. 57.

these allness comments, she may persuade others also to limit interaction with the young man. Clearly, allness can have a devastating effect on communication.

The problem of allness is not limited to dyadic communication. It may affect any social organization or institution. If government leaders regard their nation's way of life as the final word rather than as abstractions from a multiplicity of possible life-styles, ideologies, or orientations; or if they permit labels such as "Socialist" or "Communist" to represent all that is important to know about the people from other nations—then communication becomes an exercise in futility. Nations have fought in the past and will continue to fight in the future under assumptions of allness.

Frozen Evaluation

People often feel most comfortable when they can slip their perceptions beneath a label or into a category. Language, of course, facilitates this process. Furthermore, once an evaluation has been made, people do not like to modify it. It is easier for a person to perceive no changes, to believe that once another person or situation or thing is "pigeonholed," it is forever. A consideration of a simple word such as *river* illustrates the pervasiveness of our frozen conception of reality. The word itself does not suggest the fact that the river is in a state of constant change. Instead, the word makes us perceive the river as a static, changeless object. Nothing—not even a brick—is changeless, and no description applies forever. Each thing has an unfolding history, and our descriptions

of things should reflect this fact. Yet consciously and unconsciously, in our language and in our thinking (which affects and is affected by language), we often disregard change and the fact that all things are in process. The assumption of "nonchange" can have more serious implications and be more detrimental to our ability to communicate than the example of a river may suggest.

Frozen evaluations may have devastating effects on other people's lives. For example, criminals who have served their prison sentences and seek to begin a new life often find themselves imprisoned once again—this time within the frozen evaluations of friends, relatives, and employers who think "once a crook, always a crook." Many officials who control penal institutions also disregard the potential for change. Prison conditions perpetuate the image of being a criminal rather than helping to create a new image for the prisoner's future life. In some cases, a prisoner's acceptance of this frozen evaluation of himself causes him to live up to the term "hardened criminal" in an almost self-fulfilling prophecy. Indeed, the label is libel.

When words are confused with reality, they become burdensome weights that anchor past evaluations within our minds. They can, in fact, lend support to the rationale for preserving such evaluations. Women, for example, were formerly referred to as "weak-minded," "fragile," "emotional," "passive," and "immature." Certainly that was good enough reason to consider them inferior! In the nineteenth century the word *woman* suggested about as much of process and change as the word *table*. Men could *become*—states-

Frozen evaluations may have devastating effects on people's lives. The truck driver in the illustration above is an example of how today's women are trying to escape from frozen evaluations and the stereotyped roles of the past. (Photograph: Michael Weisbrot)

men, lawyers, philosophers, and doctors; women simply were—women. Members of one-half the population reveled in the language of change while members of the other half remained suspended within a frozen evaluation.

For women, the momentum of past evaluations proved an irresistible force, one that was impervious to the contradictions of experience. Women who had actually changed their lives still remained trapped within the assumption of non-change; and the discrepancy between new experience and inherited evaluations created a strain that was physically and mentally disruptive. The momentum was halted, finally, when women stopped compiling evidence of equality and simply assumed it. The insight that opened a new level of communication between women was quite simple: women's old image was "ersatz" reality, a man-made product; women could not deny this past reality; but they could reevaluate it, discard the language biases that supported it, and thus create a whole new reality for both men and women.

The why of frozen evaluations, the reason for holding onto assumptions that no longer mesh with experience, is rather difficult to pinpoint. The passage of time often invests these evaluations with the authority of tradition to which people consciously and unconsciously yield control of their lives. Frozen evaluations can make our world seem more stable, more secure; but they can also make it seem dismally fated. We would despair of solving the social, economic, and political problems we face if we communicated solely on the basis of past assumptions about reality.

Polarization

Communication and problem solving are obstructed not only by frozen evaluations but also by too few evaluations. The complexity of experience and the inevitable process of change require us to make more subtle and more numerous distinctions than are found in simple "either-or" evaluations. Perceiving the world in terms of contradictory opposites, or *polarities*, saves time and certainly simplifies life; but it is an illusory and potentially dangerous simplification that can create lines of battle and destroy lines of communication.

Polarization occurs when a person fails to distinguish between a true dichotomy and an artificial one. A true dichotomy exists when there are in fact only two alternatives, or two values, to describe a situation. Something that is *A* cannot at the same time be *not-A*; if you are thirty years old, you cannot at the same time be forty years old. There is, in other words, no middle ground. Artificial dichotomies, however, imply the existence of only two alternatives or values, when, in fact, there may be several alternatives or gradations

between polarized values. We refer to someone as being either sane or insane, happy or unhappy, a success or a failure, assuming there is no middle ground. We arbitrarily polarize values and create either-or situations when, in fact, the experiences of our lives suggest a multitude of "in-betweens."

Polarization implies a limitation of choices: if you regard your way of handling a problem as the "right" way, then another person's way of handling the problem must be the "wrong" way. Your delusion of only two alternatives is the real limitation, for there can be many ways of handling a problem. Even if your way seems absolutely right for you, that is no justification for self-righteously polarizing yourself from another person's method. Furthermore, people's methods may intersect or overlap at some point, suggesting a synthesis of values rather than a polarization.

Perceiving the world in terms of polarities can lead to many types of negative behavior, detrimental to ourselves and others. By suggesting an unbridgeable gap between any two values, rather than an unbroken continuum of values connecting people with different ideas and experiences, polarization creates unnatural rifts between people and may foster antagonism and irrational hostilities. History has shown us the devastating effects of such polarizations; yet they are still allowed to control much of our behavior as the following news items demonstrate:

James Michener, one of the most successful and popular novelists of our times, interviewed a mother who lived near the Kent State campus for his book *"Kent State: What Happened and Why,"* published in 1971 by Random House.

In it Michener records the following dialogue:

Mother: Anyone who appears on the streets of a city like Kent with long hair, dirty clothes or bare feet deserves to be shot . . . it would have been a lot better if the guards had shot the whole lot of them.

Michener: But you had three sons there.

Mother: If they didn't do what the guards told them they should have been mowed down.

Professor of psychology: Is long hair a justification for shooting someone?

Mother: Yes. We have got to clean up this nation. And we'll start with the long hairs.

Professor: Would you permit one of your sons to be shot simply because he went barefooted?

Mother: Yes.

Professor: Where do you get such ideas?

Mother: I teach at the local high school.

Professor: Do you mean that you are teaching your students such things?

Mother: Yes. I teach them the truth. That the lazy, the dirty, the ones you see walking the streets and doing nothing ought all to be shot.[17]

If they are not for us, then they are against us; if they are against us (meaning "different" from us in one or several of their values and beliefs), they are against all that is "right" and "good"—and, therefore, any action taken against them is justified.

Sometimes polarizations are not inadvertently, but deliberately, used to bend the thinking of an audience, to affect emotions, and to direct behavior. In fact, polarizations are one of the most common affective elements in writing and speaking. One way that a speaker may polarize "his" or "her" side from "theirs" is by arbitrarily assigning different values to

[17]From "Keeping Up," *Parade Magazine*, Long Island Press, Sunday, November 21, 1971.

equivalent or similar behavior. This type of polarization occurs not only on a national or political level, but also in daily interpersonal communication. Mother does not approve of Sharon's boyfriend José, but she thinks that Barry is just fine. So when José phones Sharon, Mother says, "Why does that boy always tie up our phone? He's so annoying. Doesn't he have any work to do? He talks on and on like an old housewife!" But when Barry calls, Mother says, "Isn't that nice? He's so attentive. Probably taking time out from his studies to see how you are. I'll bet he's interesting to talk to!"

Mother's attempt to sway Sharon's emotions is a comparatively harmless use of polarization, although Sharon might disagree. But in the *wrong* hands (excuse the implicit polarization) this manipulation of emotions can be dangerous. People are not inherently weak-willed or stupid, nor will they normally accept the exhortations of just any street-corner reformer. But life's problems can seem dreadfully complex, and so it is sometimes difficult to resist the communicator (especially an authoritative one) who simplifies it. Fortunately, many speakers have the integrity and respect for truth to qualify poliarzations by pointing out, for example, what is wrong with their side. Others, however, are blinded by their own polarizations and their desire to control.

Some scientists have suggested that man's biological composition causes people to think in either-or terms. Although this hypothesis has not been in any way confirmed, it is clear that language plays a role in creating polarizations. For one thing, the grammatical structure of our language does not distinguish between true and artificial dichotomies. Both types of statements use the either-or form. For example, an employer tends to rate his employees as either "good" workers or "bad" workers. Few are willing to say that an employee is sometimes good at one task and sometimes bad at other tasks. Linguistically, people are encouraged to simplify their thinking into such terms because there is a lack of quantifying substantive words in our language to express the degrees between polar words such as "good" and "bad." It is almost second nature, linguistically speaking, to opt for the polar word rather than to use adjectival and adverbial modifiers or descriptive phrases.

The pace and style of life in our society also condition us to polarized behavior and thinking. Business transactions often require immediate either-or decisions, and the "philosopher-businessman" who muses over the infinite complexity of any situation may find himself a full-time unemployed philosopher. Careful contemplation and reflection, even in areas involving complex social problems, are not highly valued commodities. Action, not thought, receives the praise in an industrial society, and action often demands clear-cut polar decisions. The Good Products Company will either market a new toothpaste or it will not. Of course, this is not to imply that all such decisions are detrimental. If the alternatives for any action are consistently updated to accommodate changing conditions, polar decisions actually facilitate progress. But if the polarizations blind us to new sets of alternatives, we may simply shuttle back and forth within the same two-valued response.

Social conditioning unfortunately tends to reinforce the same polar values system

Commercial advertising reinforces the polar self-image with products that imply "success," "happy," "rich," and "young"; if we are unsure at which end of the pole we are hanging, a purchase (a lifetime of them) may insure us of being at the "right" end. (Photograph: Michael Weisbrot)

that constricts individual development. Not long after children learn the basic tools of communication, they are taught the basic polarities such as success-failure, happy-unhappy, rich-poor, young-old. Commercial advertising reinforces the polar self-image with products that imply "success," "happy," "rich," and "young"; if we are unsure at which end of the pole we are hanging, a purchase (a lifetime of them) may insure us of being at the "right" end. Pop culture also steps in with its own polar trap: "where-it's-at" versus "nowhere."

Bypassing

Many times, in the process of communication, words are like "ships passing in the night." Or, to use another trite expression, the meaning a sender intended his words to have "goes right over the head" of the receiver. Effective communication does not take place when sender and receiver are at different levels of understanding. Perhaps the people involved are using the same words to mean different things, in which case they may believe they agree about the meaning intended when, in fact, they do not. Or perhaps they are using different words to represent the same thing—which may lead people to believe they disagree about meaning when, in fact, they do not. In both cases, communication problems occur because the receivers assume that their word uses are also the word uses of the sender of the message. Communication fails because word meanings bypass each other.

At the root of the problem of bypassing is the assumption (consciously or unconsciously made) that words themselves have meaning—that if I, for example, say the word *cat* to you, it is somehow equivalent to handing you the concrete thing itself. But the words are not the things themselves; they are symbols of things. It is people who create these symbols and invest them with meaning. Thus, if I say, "Cat," there is no guarantee that the word alone will convey the exact image of a green-eyed tiger-striped cat that I have in mind. You may have learned the word under different conditions from those under which I learned the word; so the symbol evokes for you the picture of a large, fluffy, white Persian cat. The word itself has no fixed meaning; its meaning lies in the way I use it and you perceive it.

Words also have no fixed usage. As there are only a finite number of words to represent an infinite number of "things" (objects, facts, experiences), the same word may be used in a variety of ways and thus may be interpreted in a variety of ways. Bypassing is often the result of failing to consider this multiple usage of words in the process of communication. A classic example of this involves two producers, one American and one British, who jointly financed a new play. When the drama opened in London, it received rave reviews, and the British producer quickly sent a telegram to his American counterpart. The telegram read "Posting notices tomorrow." The American was very disappointed, for to him the phrase meant the show was closing the next day. To the British producer, the message meant that he was sending the reviews by mail in the morning.

Word usage is dependent on several other factors. One is simply the passage of time. Some words drop out of popular usage: *icebox* and *parlor*, for example, have been replaced in most people's vocabularies by *refrigerator* and *living room*. A person may, of course, still use the older terms; but many people will not understand what that person is talking about, for they have had no experience with these symbols. Other words, such as *cool*, have not only remained a part of working vocabularies but have acquired several new usages with the passing of the years. For this reason, a communicator must indicate the usage intended by the context in which he or she places the word.

Another factor in multiple usage is the regional variation given to certain words. A pizza at the Staten Island ferry terminal in Manhattan means a thin crust of dough, with heaps of tomato sauce, plenty of cheese and unconscionable amounts of olive oil. A pizza at Hamptom Beach, New Hampshire, means a thick hunk of bread with an almost negligible layer of tomato sauce on top. The word is the same, but, depending on the location, it represents very different realities.

A third factor that increases the potential for word bypassing is the common and technical interpretations given to the same words. To a composer, the word *bridge* means a transitional passage between two musical movements; to a dentist, it means a replacement for one or more (but not all) a person's natural teeth; to a sailor, the word refers to the steering platform above the main deck of a ship; and to an electrician, it represents a special kind of circuit. If specialists are working together in the same field, communication problems are minimal because word usages are already agreed upon. But if specialists in different areas are required to work together, there must be some prior orientation to each other's vocabularies if communication is to be effective. Misunderstanding is even more likely when a specialist speaks to a layman, for many technical terms have very different meanings in common usage.

All the problems of usage can be dealt with if the parties involved genuinely desire to perceive each other's meanings. But we cannot dismiss the idea that bypassing may be intentional. In politics, for example, the person running for election wishes to attract as many votes as possible. For this reason he may limit his statements on controversial subjects to broad or ambiguous terms that can be interpreted in several ways. The candidate becomes "all things to all men." Advertisers also count on misinterpretation by the public. When a commercial claims that nine out of ten doctors recommend Aunt Mary's Nose Drops, the advertiser may literally mean nine out of a single group of ten doctors. But he (or she) expects that the audience will bypass this meaning and perceive it as "nine out of *every* ten doctors."

Words can be manipulated to represent whatever a person wishes. The motivations for this intentional bypassing are varied. They are not necessarily completely honorable or completely dishonorable, but the result is the same: words become further divorced from the reality for which they stand. The problem of bypassing on the national level inspired the novelist Norman Mailer to propose a "fifth estate"—a group of people who would test the statements made by our government to see if they corresponded to the reality of the government's actions and policies. But the idea was considered unrealistic, if for no other reason than that people often prefer to be bypassed rather than risk confrontation with an unpleasant reality.

SUMMARY

1. All communication involves a compromise of meaning between people because each individual responds to communication, symbols of reality, in unique and personal ways. Although language provides a shared system for interpreting symbols, each person invests a word with different meaning. Language may also facilitate misunderstanding, for it leads us to view words as reality instead of as abstract symbols of reality.

2. Much of communication depends upon the particular language of the participants. The Whorf-Sapir hypothesis asserts that people's perception of the world is at the mercy of the language they speak. Language, as well as psychological disposition and previous experience, affect the perceptions that people bring into communication situations.

3. The process of selectivity in communication operates such that a person must be exposed to a message or cannot attend to it; a person must attend to a message or cannot perceive it; a person must perceive a message or cannot retain it. Various factors such as physiological impairments, psychological and physical needs, cultural background, and prior attitudes will affect each stage of this selectivity process.

4. Receivers selectively attend to only a limited number of stimuli at any one time. Physiological factors, psychological needs, and past experiences affect a person's ability to attend to stimuli in the environment. Other variables that affect attention are the quantity and difficulty of incoming stimuli.

5. Perception is the process of imputing meaning to experience. Physiological, psychological, experiential, and semantic factors all impinge on people's perceptions. No two people will perceive the same stimuli in exactly the same way.

6. Individuals more accurately retain messages that are favorable to their self-image. A person also tends to forget unfavorable messages more quickly than favorable ones. The retention of at least part of a message seems to be improved if intense sensory stimuli accompany the message. Selective retention thus reinforces one's self-image.

7. An important factor inhibiting effective communication is the tendency of people to fail in distinguishing between statements of inference and statements of observation. Risk taking is also at stake in the inference-observation confusion. Though people often take calculated risks, when people make inferences and take them for actual observations, they may not even be aware of the potential undesirable consequences. This can often lead to unpleasant or even fatal results.

8. Intensional orientations take place when people are less concerned with the people, objects, situations, and relationships that occur in the real world than they are with their feelings, perceptions, inferences, and evaluations. Specific types of intensional orientations are pointing and blindering. Pointing happens when the words we use in communicating with others point to or call our attention to something. Similar words will point to different things in different people. Blindering occurs when the words we use to define or describe situations act as blinders to our approach to a problem.

9. Allness involves two faulty assumptions: it is possible to know everything there is to know about something, and whatever people say about something includes all that is important about the subject. A person's knowledge of reality can never be complete or infallible, but people many times behave as if it were so. Every way of looking at something brings with it some areas of blindness.

10. People often treat words as if they were reality instead of symbols of that reality. Language enables us to pigeonhole experiences and, to some extent, facilitates our perception of the world as a "frozen" reality. When people assume nonchange in a world that is constantly changing direction, frozen evaluations occur.

11. Polarization occurs when people fail to distinguish between true and artificial dichotomies. A true dichotomy is a situation in which only two alternatives exist. An artificial dichotomy implies the existence of only two alternatives, when, in fact, several may exist. Polarization is often inadvertent, but sometimes polarities are used to influence another's thinking. Because our language does not distinguish between true and artificial dichotomies, it facilitates the polarization process. Perceiving the world in terms of polarities is a convenient process, but it is one that may create obstacles to effective communication, for most situations offer a wide range of viable possibilities rather than only two.

12. Bypassing occurs when the source and receiver impute different meaning to the words of a communication message. The assumption that words themselves have meaning is also at the heart of the bypassing dilemma. Multiple usage based on cultural, regional, temporal, and technical factors contribute to the problem of bypassing and result in less than effective communications.

SUGGESTED READING

Brown, Roger. *Psycholinguistics.* New York: Free Press, 1970.

Haney, William V. *Communication and Organizational Behavior.* 2d Ed. Homewood, Illinois: Richard B. Irwin, Inc., 1967.

Katz, Daniel. "Psychological Barriers to Communication," in *Messages: A Reader in Human Communication*. Edited by Jean Civikly. New York: Random House, 1974.

Lee, Irving J. *Language Habits in Human Affairs*. New York: Harper Brothers, 1941.

Vernon, Magdalene D. *The Psychology of Perception*. Baltimore: Penguin Books, 1963.

Whorf, Benjamin L. *Language, Thought and Reality*. New York: Wiley, 1957.

From the Reading	Study Questions
Define the following terms. language speech symbols abstraction perception experiential factor selectivity inference observation probability certainty intensional orientation pointing blindering allness frozen evaluation polarization bypassing true dichotomy artificial dichotomy retention meaning interpretation labeling	1. Why is a distinction between language and speech important? 2. What factors support the notion that communication is an expression of symbols reflecting reality? 3. Explain the Whorf-Sapir hypothesis. How does this provide one explanation of inaccuracy in communication? 4. In what different ways do general perceptions inhibit effective communication? 5. What factors influence an individual's constructions or interpretations of reality? 6. How does the selectivity process work in communication situations? 7. How does selective exposure affect communication? Selective attention? Selective perception? Selective retention? 8. What factors contribute to people's confusing observations with inferences? 9. How can you recognize statements of observation? Statements of inference? 10. What are intensional orientations? Name and define two specific instances of intensional orientation. 11. How can people guard against intensional orientations? What effect do they have on the communication process? 12. How would you counteract the two faulty assumptions that lead to allness? 13. How does frozen evaluation lead to differences in perceptions?

THE VARIABLES IN THE COMMUNICATION PROCESS

14. List five instances of artificial dichotomies and as many instances of true dichotomies as you can. How would you aid people in recognizing these differences?
15. How do individual differences in the source and receiver cause bypassing?
16. How many other variables that inhibit effective communication can you cite?

AN EXERCISE DESIGNED TO SHOW THE EXTENT TO WHICH WE BASE JUDGMENTS ON INFERENCE RATHER THAN FACT OR OBSERVATION

Read the following account, and answer the twelve statements *before* you look at the correct answers.

Bennett Beamer, energetic product manager for a balloon manufacturing firm, decided to develop a new process for creating puncture-proof balloons. He authorized three of his executives to spend up to $20,000 each without consulting him. He also transferred one of his brightest employees, Baggins, to the East Coast plant to conduct independent research on the process. Within four days, Baggins developed an ingenious new approach to the balloon problem.

Statements

1. Beamer transferred one of his brightest men to the East Coast.   ? T F
2. Beamer overvalued Baggins's ability.   ? T F
3. Baggins "bombed out"—that is, did not develop anything new!   ? T F
4. Baggins was not authorized to spend money without consulting Beamer.   ? T F
5. Only three executives were authorized to spend money without consulting Beamer.   ? T F
6. The product manager transferred one of his brightest employees to the East Coast plant.   ? T F
7. Three men were authorized to spend up to $20,000 each without consulting Beamer.   ? T F
8. Beamer's opinion of Baggins was that he was a brilliant executive.   ? T F
9. The story makes reference to five people.   ? T F
10. Beamer was the product manager of a balloon manufacturing firm.   ? T F
11. Baggins's newly developed approach solved the balloon problem.   ? T F
12. The executives authorized to spend $20,000 each were working on the new balloon-making process.   ? T F

Discussion

1. Discuss the answer to each question with the student.
    (1.) ?—Baggins might have been a woman.

(2.) ?—story does not provide this information.

(3.) F—story claims that he did develop something new.

(4.) ?—story does not provide this information.

(5.) ?—story does not state conclusively that only three were authorized to spend $20,000.

(6.) T—concurs with information given in the story.

(7.) ?—the term *executive* does not indicate gender.

(8.) ?—may or may not be true; it is possible that someone in authority over Beamer recommended Baggins as a "brilliant" employee.

(9.) ?—If Baggins was not one of the executives given authority to use $20,000, this would be true, but the story does not provide this information.

(10.) T—concurs with information given in the story.

(11.) ?—story does not provide this information; there is simply the implication that Baggins's approach provided a solution.

(12.) ?—We can only infer this, but the story does not provide conclusive proof.

2. Ask the students to think of personal instances when they acted upon inference rather than fact and to describe the consequences of their having failed to make the distinction.

AN EXERCISE DESIGNED TO ILLUSTRATE THE EFFECT OF INTENSIONAL ORIENTATION

Objective: Draw through all nine dots.

Restrictions: 1. Start with your pen or pencil on any one of the dots.

2. Draw four straight lines without removing your pen or pencil from the paper.

3. You may cross over lines, but you may not retrace any line.

Hint: Most people have difficulty with this problem because the dots impose an unnecessary fourth restriction.

● ● ●
● ● ●
● ● ●

Questions to Consider

1. What is the self-imposed fourth restriction?
2. Why do people invariably add this restriction?
3. What specific type of intensional orientation does this problem represent?
4. What are some suggestions for eliminating this type of orientation?

AN EXERCISE DESIGNED TO SHOW THE TENDENCY TO RESPOND TO WORDS AND SYMBOLS AS IF THEY HAD A FIXED MEANING*

Procedure

1. The mathematical symbols for the words *addition, subtraction, multiplication,* and *division* are introduced and studied at a very early stage in our schooling; and, therefore, most of us respond automatically to them. In fact, changing our interpretation of these symbols would require a conscious and consistent effort. To illustrate this fact, set the students in groups of four, and supply each student with a copy of Test *X* and Test *Y.* Allow ten minutes for completion of the exercises.

2. Have each group correct their tests and compare their experiences with changed symbols.

Changed Symbol Test X

Code:
- $(+)$ multiply
- $(\div)$ add
- $(-)$ divide
- $(\times)$ subtract

$5 + 4 =$	$30 - 5 =$
$7 \times 3 =$	$18 - 9 =$
$12 - 3 =$	$13 \times 2 =$
$11 + 11 =$	$4 - 1 =$
$10 \div 5 =$	$10 + 10 =$
$14 - 7 =$	$20 - 4 =$
$4 \times 4 =$	$19 + 1 =$
$36 - 6 =$	$6 \times 2 =$
$17 + 2 =$	$12 - 4 =$

Changed Symbol Test Y

To complete this test, use the code given in Text *X* in addition to the numerical values assigned to the letter symbols below. Express your answers in terms of the letter symbols.

*Adapted from Karen R. Krupar, *Communication Games* (New York: The Free Press, 1973).

Variables Inhibiting Effective Communication

a	*b*	*c*	*d*	*e*	*f*	*g*	*h*	*i*	*j*	*k*	*l*	*m*	*n*	*o*	*p*	*q*	*r*	*s*	*t*
1	2	3	4	5	6	7	8	9	10	11	12	13	14	15	16	17	18	19	20

u	*v*	*w*	*x*	*y*	*z*
21	22	23	24	25	26

$$o \div u =$$ $$l + b =$$
$$k + c =$$ $$n \times h =$$
$$j - e =$$ $$y \div q =$$
$$g \times b =$$ $$k \times g =$$
$$s \div m =$$ $$j \times a =$$
$$x - f =$$ $$r + e =$$
$$z - m =$$ $$m + i =$$
$$l \times i =$$ $$n - g =$$
$$w \div p =$$ $$t \times d =$$

Discussion

1. Was it difficult to complete the test within the time limit?
2. Did you find it necessary to refer back to the code given in Text *X*, or did you find it comparatively easy to reorient yourself to (and memorize) the new meanings assigned to the symbols?
3. Did any in your group learn one changed symbol at a time and then work out all the problems in the test involving that symbol? If not, did you use any other specific method of working out the problems?
4. Do you think that with continued practice on similar exercises your facility with changed symbols would increase? Or do you think that your present level of inflexibility toward new symbol meanings is virtually unalterable because of the strength of past conditioning?
5. Do certain words—such as *policeman* and *housewife*—evoke in your mind a set of images just as mathematical symbols elicit certain automatic responses? What are the consequences if we do not reevaluate the meanings suggested by such words or if we allow reflex thinking to dominate our responses to symbols?
6. If we fail to acknowledge the multiple meanings a single word can have for different people—that is, if we use a word as though it had only one meaning, the one we associate with it—what problems in communication might result?

AN EXERCISE IN SERIAL MESSAGE TRANSMISSION

Select a minimum of four people to leave the classroom. Have another student give a brief description of some event to the rest of the class. You can make up a story or describe something that really happened. Make the story as brief as you can and as clear as possible.

Bring one person back into the room, and tell the story to him or her. You may decide to allow the person to ask questions or not. Communicate as effectively as you can with that person. Now bring in another person, and have the first receiver tell the story to the second person; then have the second person tell the story to the third person, and so on, until the last person outside of the room has heard the story. Now have the last person tell the story to the class.

Questions to Consider

1. What happened to the story? Does the final story resemble the first story?
2. If there was distortion, where did it occur?
3. What selectivity processes operated in this exercise?
4. What communication principles are involved in this exercise?

Chapter 5
NONVERBAL COMMUNICATION
Judee K. Burgoon

A local graffiti board carries the inscription "You hear my words but you miss my meaning." This statement, which reflects the notion that there is more to meaning than just words themselves, is really a plea for awareness of nonverbal communication—those messages that take a form other than words. Such messages are a frequently overlooked aspect of communication; yet they are very powerful. They are our first and only means of communication in infancy. Even when we have mastered the verbal language systems, we continue to rely on such things as gestures, glances, touches, and voice qualities to carry much of the meaning in our transactions with others. In fact, one estimate is that 65 percent of the social meaning in interpersonal interchange is transmitted nonverbally. When someone says, "I could tell from his eyes that he was angry" or "Her voice made it clear that we were finished talking," they are actually responding to nonverbal communication.

Despite the important role that nonverbal messages play in our day-to-day interactions, few people are conscious of the ways in which they use such messages or how they respond to the nonverbal cues of others. It is ironic that people spend twelve years of school systematically studying verbal language, but almost no time is devoted to the study of the syntax or vocabulary of nonverbal behavior. The result is that our ability to send and interpret nonverbal messages is generally inadequate. The authors hope that this chapter will begin to remedy that deficit by bringing more nonverbal behaviors into conscious awareness. Once people become aware of such behaviors, they are usually better able to bring them under conscious control.

One word of advice, however. Before you jump to the conclusion that much of what we know about nonverbal communication is intuitive, think twice. It is true that some of it is intuitive, but many aspects only seem so with the benefit of hindsight. Take, for example, posture and liking. When students read that people typically have the most relaxed posture around individuals they dislike, that seems plausible because a person doesn't feel the need to appear interested or maintain an attractive posture around disliked others. But before knowing that relationship, most students predict that people will be most relaxed with those they like. This is just one example of the many nonintuitive and counterintuitive ways in which nonverbal cues operate. It should underscore for you the fact that all nonverbal communication is not readily and easily understood. Many behaviors have the same meaning, some behaviors have several different meanings, and some behaviors have no meaning. All of this indicates that nonverbal communication is a rather complex enterprise. Contrary to popular belief, it is not possible to "read another person like a book." But it is possible to become more observant of one's own nonverbal discourse and more attuned to the meanings of others.

The Nonverbal Codes

Nonverbal communication has many modes of expression. Research suggests that there are seven commonly used "codes" or mediums for conveying messages. Each of these codes has some unique properties that influence the com-

munication roles it performs. We will examine these properties first, then turn to the various communication functions the nonverbal codes serve.

PROXEMICS

Proxemics, or the ways in which people structure and use space in their daily lives, is one of the key dimensions of nonverbal communication. The distances we maintain between ourselves and others and our reactions to inappropriate spacing have a potent impact on the communication process. A well-known example that illustrates the importance of proxemics comes from an embassy cocktail party. A newly arrived American diplomat was carrying on a conversation with his Arab host. As was the custom in his country, the Arab moved up very close to the American. This made the American very uncomfortable; so he retreated a few feet. Not used to such a distance, the Arab moved in again, and again the American retreated. This comedy of advance and retreat continued until the Arab had literally chased the American across the length of the room. The American's impression of the Arab was that he was pushy, whereas the Arab regarded the American as cold and aloof. Clearly, each person had sent unintentional messages through his use of space.

Dimensions of proxemics. This example highlights one of the underlying concepts of proxemics: the human need for certain amounts of space. People seem to have two different types of spatial needs, the first of which is *territoriality*, which consists of a need for and defense of territory.

Like animals, humans apparently carve out territories. A father's workshop is his territory, just as the kitchen is generally perceived as the mother's territory. Likewise, a family's home and property are its territory, which means that these are not openly accessible to strangers or intruders. Some people and some cultures demand more territory than others. For instance, the Japanese seem to be satisfied with very little space for their homes, whereas in other cultures, such as our own, people feel hemmed in if they do not have large living space. Perhaps the key variable is not so much the actual amount of space available as it is the individual's perception of the adequacy of that space.

The physical and social effects of inadequate territory are illuminated by various studies of overcrowded conditions. A classic study with rats found that even when there was plenty of food and water available in their environment, the rats became aggressive, neurotic, sexually deviant, and ill when their territory was reduced by overpopulation.[1] Sociological studies have found similar results among inhabitants of heavily populated urban areas.[2] The avoidance of communication and the heated confrontations that characterize residents of particularly congested areas may be partially attributable to inadequate territory.

The other human spatial need is for *personal space*. Personal space differs from territory in that it is not a fixed geographic area. Rather, it is an invisible "bubble" of

space that the individual carries with him. Depending on the situation, a person's need for space may expand or contract; personal space has no rigid boundary. If a person is in a formal situation, he or she will probably feel much more need for personal space than if the situation is an intimate one. A multitude of factors combine to determine a person's needs or preferences for space. These preferences are responsible for cultural proxemic norms, which are the standards of behavior that society considers correct.

Personal space preferences and norms. A person's *gender* will partly determine his or her choice of distance in an interaction. In general, two females will sit or stand closer to each other than they will to males; males, in turn, will sit or stand closer to the opposite sex than they will to each other. The *race* of the interactants may also affect distance. Not surprisingly, whites and blacks usually maintain greater distance from each other than from people of their own race.

A third factor is *status*. As a sign of respect, we generally stand further away from people who are of higher status. It is easy to tell by watching subordinates approach a seated business executive just what their status relationship is; those who stand in the doorway are likely to be of much lower status than those who walk up to the edge of the desk. Or notice the degree of deference students show professors in the distance they maintain. Closely related to status is the effect of *age*. We often stand closer to our peers than to persons who are older or younger.

Another determinant of our use of space is *personality*. Persons who are extro-

---

[1]J. B. Calhoun, "Population Density and Social Pathology," *Scientific American, 206* (February 1962), pp. 139–146.

[2]D. E. Davis, "Physiological Effects of Continued Crowding," in *Behavior and Environment*, ed. A. H. Esser (New York: Plenum Press, 1971).

verted and outgoing are willing to be closer to others than those who are shy and introverted. A recent interesting finding suggests that aggession may be connected to personal space needs. In a prison study, two groups of men were tested on their reactions to people closing in on them. One group of prisoners had histories of violent behavior; the other group did not. The men were told to stand in the middle of a room while a person slowly walked toward them. The prisoners were instructed to say, "Stop" when they felt that the invader was too close. The men in the violent group kept the invader twice as far away as the men in the nonviolent group. In terms of volume, the violent men required personal space zones that were four times the size of the space zones needed by men in the nonviolent group.[3]

Yet another factor determining spatial preference is *ethnic and cultural background.* Anthropological observations suggest that standards of spatial use vary greatly in different societies. For most Americans, the average conversational distance when they are standing ranges from 18 to 28 inches; distances closer than 18 inches are presumably reserved for intimate interactions.[4] In comparison to people in other cultures, Americans tend to maintain greater distances from one another. This difference has created some embarrassing situations in the past for the American travelers in Italy and Latin America, who misinterpreted the friendly advances of the natives. There is some evidence now, however, that these cultural

differences are becoming less noticeable.[5] It is possible that international travel and the mass media are helping to standardize personal distance practices.

Overriding many of the above variables is *personal attraction.* As would be expected, people approach much closer to someone they find attractive; people are also much more willing to tolerate the approach of someone they find attractive. Similar to the effect of attraction is the degree of acquaintanceship. People maintain a greater distance from strangers than from acquaintances, and they come closest to friends.[6] This makes sense, for if we are not attracted to a person, that person remains only an acquaintance or even a stranger. If we are attracted to someone, a friendship usually develops.

Other influences on personal distance are such situational variables as the *topic,* the *social situation,* and a person's *psychological state.* All of these factors affect a person's spatial needs at a given moment. For example, students expecting to receive praise will sit closer to a professor than students who expect to receive an unfavorable report of their class progress.[7] Similarly, people are likely to stand closer in an informal situation than in a formal one because the nature of the social event has altered their personal space needs. Most people have experienced moments when they were so upset that they preferred others, even intimate friends, to keep their distance. Of course, in many

[3]A. F. Kinzel, "Towards an Understanding of Violence," *Attitude,* 1, No. 1 (1969).

[4]F. N. Willis, "Initial Speaking Distance as a Function of the Speaker's Relationship," *Psychomemetric Science,* 5 (1966), pp. 221–222.

[5]R. F. Forston and C. U. Larson, "The Dynamics of Space: An Experimental Study in Proxemic Behavior Among Latin Americans and North Americans," *Journal of Communication,* 18 (1968), pp. 109–116.

[6]K. B. Little, "Personal Space," *Journal of Experimental Social Psychology,* 1 (1965), pp. 237–247.

[7]W. E. Leipold, "Psychological Distance in a Dyadic Interview" (Ph.D. diss. University of South Dakota, 1963).

THE VARIABLES IN THE COMMUNICATION PROCESS

situations an individual may feel that his or her personal space has been invaded, that is, he or she has less space than is needed. To cope with such situations, a person may communicate his or her discomfort in a variety of ways. Experts have determined that there are several patterns of response to the invasion of personal space.

Responses to personal space invasion. You can discover some responses to personal space invasion by conducting a simple experiment: find a fellow student seated alone at a large library table; then sit down in the seat immediately next to him or her. Chances are that the person will first try to counteract your intrusion by avoiding eye contact, shifting body orientation away from you, and creating "barriers" with such objects as books or coats. If that fails, he or she may glare at you or perhaps even subject you to verbal abuse. If all else fails, the person may take flight. Responses will differ from individual to individual, but nearly all will show signs of discomfort.[8]

In such places as a crowded elevator or bus, a different response pattern is likely to occur. People have learned that in such instances, invasion of their personal space is necessary. They cope with the situation by treating other people around them as nonpersons or objects. The next time you find yourself in such a place, notice the absence of eye contact and the rigid posture of the other people. This behavior

People have learned that in such places as a crowded elevator or bus, invasion of their personal space is necessary. They cope with the situation by treating other people around them as nonpersons or objects. (Photograph: Maury Englander)

helps to reduce some of the tension created by strangers who are in a space zone usually reserved for intimates. As explained by Robert Sommer, an expert in proxemics:

A nonperson cannot invade someone's personal space anymore than a tree or chair can. It is common under certain conditions for one person to react to another as an object or part of the background.[9]

[8]M. L. Patterson, S. Mullens and J. Romano, "Compensatory Reactions to Spatial Intrusion," *Sociometry, 34* (1971), pp. 114–121; N. J. Felipe and R. Sommer, "Invasions of Personal Space," *Social Problems, 14* (1966), pp. 206–214; and J. C. Baxter and B. F. Deanovitch, "Anxiety Effects of Inappropriate Crowding," *Journal of Consulting and Clinical Psychology, 35* (1970), pp. 174–178.

[9]R. Sommer, *Personal Space* (Englewood Cliffs, N.J.: Prentice-Hall, 1969), p. 24.

It is clear that people have strong spatial needs and strong reactions to violations of their personal space or territory. As a result, proxemic variations can serve as a very powerful communication vehicle. The ways in which people define and defend territories, the distances they adopt from others, and the arrangements of space that they create can all act as messages.

CHRONEMICS

An interesting but often overlooked dimension of nonverbal communication is *chronemics*, or our use of time. Our music gives strong evidence of the meanings conveyed by time. Our notions of time, how we "use" it, the timing of events, our emotional responses to time, even the length of our pauses—all of these contribute to the communicative effect of time. Just recall a few phrases from some musical favorites: "Time, oh good, good time, where did you go," "Time won't let me," and "I'll stay until it's time for you to go." Or consider such expressions as "dead time," "time on our hands," "lead time," and "making time." Clearly, we are time-conscious and conscious of the meanings conveyed by the way we deal with time.

Our sensitivity to time is partly revealed through our reliance on clocks. Notice how few people you meet in a single day who do not wear a watch. We are so obsessed with time, in fact, that we become genuinely disturbed if a few minutes are "wasted." After all, "time is money." We view time as a commodity to be spent, earned, saved, or wasted. We also divide time into small increments; we are even conscious of passing seconds.

In contrast, other cultures have less concrete notions of time. In them, time is a vague sense of the present. It is "here and now," and punctuality is not valued. The Sioux Indians have this orientation. In their language, there are no words for "late" and "waiting." Among the Pueblo Indians, things take place "when the time is right," whenever that may be. Such cultural differences in peoples' attitudes toward time have caused many problems for government officials and businessmen at home and abroad. The federal government lost thousands of dollars on construction projects because the Hopi Indians did not have a concept of a "fixed date" by which a house or road would be completed. Many American businessmen have told angry tales of having to wait a half hour or longer to see an Arab or a Latin-American associate. To Americans, a waiting period of this length is an insult, but in other cultures it is appropriate.

Cultural time systems. The ways in which Americans use time can be divided into three sets: technical, formal, and informal.[10] *Technical time* is used in certain professions such as astronomy, but the terminology (solar, sidereal, and anamolistic year) carries little meaning for the layman. *Formal time* is our traditional, conscious time structure. It includes our division of time into days, months, years, and seasons. Our uses of cycles of time, such as day and night; our valuation of time; our perceptions of its depth, duration, and tangibility—these are all part of our formal time system. Edward Hall has commented on the importance of formal time patterns to Americans:

The American never questions the fact that time should be planned and future events

[10]E. T. Hall, *Silent Language* (New York: Doubleday, 1959).

fitted into a schedule. He thinks that people should look forward to the future and not dwell too much in the past. His future is not very far ahead of him. Results must be obtained in the foreseeable future—one or two years or, at most, five or ten. Promises to meet deadlines and appointments are taken very seriously. There are real penalties for being late and for not keeping commitments in time.[11]

The third system, *informal time*, is the one that causes us the most difficulty because it is our loosely defined and out-of-consciousness time system. Whereas the vocabulary of informal time is generally the same as that of formal time, its meaning is less clear because it is dependent on the context rather than on clear-cut definitions. Moreover, the informal manner in which it is learned means that we are usually not consciously aware of it. It is the features of our informal time system that typically function as message elements.

Message elements. One message element is urgency. Nowhere is it spelled out what it means to be "urgent" in our culture. But if you received a phone call at two in the morning, you would undoubtedly assume that the call was urgent, whereas a call received at two in the afternoon would be routine. How we use time signals the importance of something.

Another element of our informal time system is *duration*, a particularly potent element in our culture. Each person has his or her own definition of what is a short, long, or impossibly long period of time. With Americans' heightened sensitivity to the passage of time, "forever"

[11]Ibid., p. 134.

may actually be a relatively short period, technically speaking. Five minutes may be impossibly long if a person is waiting to see the dentist. Because we attribute meanings to the amount of time we have to wait to see someone, it is possible nonverbally to tell someone what we think of him or her through this mode.

The *timing* and *sequencing* of activities and statements are two additional chronemic variables that have message potential. When something takes place and what order things follow are important. A hostess may plan a dinner party on a Saturday night, when she knows no one will have to work the next day, or she may plan it for a week night, when she knows everyone will have to leave early in the evening. Each choice carries a different meaning. Similarly, with dating situations, the timing and order of events may be critical: When do you first kiss? How far in advance do you call for a date? How late do you stay out on a second date? In our verbal communication, the placement of pauses and climaxes is of equal importance. The success of comedians such as Jack Benny and Bob Hope has been partly due to their excellent sense of timing.

A final consideration is the time pattern that an individual generally follows. Americans seem to follow one of two patterns. Some people habitually operate in a *diffused point pattern:* they arrive somewhere around the appointed time. They may be early or late, but they have some built-in maximum range of acceptability and are usually consistent in either their early or late arrival pattern. In contrast, those who operate on the *displaced point pattern* see the appointed time as a fixed boundary that cannot be violated. These are the people who usually come at the scheduled time or earlier. Whereas people have tendencies to follow either the diffused or the displaced point pattern, the nature of an event may also determine which pattern is used. The diffused point pattern is perfectly acceptable for a shopping trip; but, for a business appointment, it is appropriate to arrive early or on time but never late (five minutes beyond the scheduled time being considered late). Conversely, if one is invited to a cocktail party at 6:00, one often isn't really expected until 7:00 or later. However, if dinner is to be served, it is required that one arrive promptly at 6:00 or, at the very latest, 6:15.

Misjudgments and misuses of these informal time systems can lead others to interpret our nonverbal behavior inaccurately. The person who is habitually late on the job expresses lack of interest, disorganization, and disrespect for the employer. The party guest who stays long after the others have departed may communicate insensitivity and selfishness by dallying. We know of one instance where, instead of staying late, a couple arrived two hours early for a party and could not be dissuaded by their hosts, who were in the throes of last-minute cleanup, that they were not welcome. Obviously, such violations of the informal "rules" for our culture are bound to carry strong messages, whether intended or not. It is just this feature of time—the fact that we do not openly identify or discuss the rules and the meanings attached to them—that permits chronemics to operate as a subtle but powerful code.

KINESICS

A more traditionally studied dimension of nonverbal communication is *kinesics*, or the visual aspects of behavior. Included under this heading are movement and posture, gestures, facial expressions, and eye behavior. These modes of behavior have long been recognized as carrying meaning in an interaction. At the turn of the century, a movement even developed —the elocutionary movement—to teach people how to convey emotions through various body positions, facial expressions, and gestures. For instance, the upturned palms signified supplication; the outturned hand at the brow showed distress or fear. These artificial behaviors can be seen in the old silent movies. Although people may ridicule such overdramatizing, kinesic behaviors are still being prescribed in speech classes today. Consider a few excerpts from a contemporary public speaking text:

> Stand with the feet no more than six inches apart, with one foot somewhat behind the other. . . .
> Keep the shoulders on a level, and avoid the sailor's roll. . . .
> Keep a hand on the lectern, even though in this maneuver you will be shifting hands at the back corner of the stand as you turn. . . .
> [When gesturing] start the movement by letting the *wrist* lead; the hand *follows* at first and gradually catches up by the time the stroke is reached. . . .
> Keep your eyes on your hearers.[12]

These recommendations underline the belief that kinesic behavior is important. This is a fair assumption, for research has demonstrated that, when compared to other nonverbal codes or to the verbal code, kinesic cues usually carry the greater

[12]D. C. Bryant and K. R. Wallace, *Oral Communication* (New York: Appleton-Century-Crofts, 1962).

portion of the meaning being transmitted.[13]

Message elements. One of the reasons kinesic cues carry so much information is because there are so many different features that can be varied as message elements. Every part of the body—from the eyebrows and eyes to the legs and feet—can be manipulated, and this gives rise to endless possible combinations of features. One person has even estimated that there are 250,000 expressions possible in the face region alone.

Fortunately, not all of these minute differences in expressions are meaningful. It appears from the research to date that kinesic cues are used in rather systematic ways. Some experts even believe that kinesic patterns follow rules, much like our verbal language system does. Hence, it is possible to reduce the vast number of kinesic cues to a smaller, more manageable set of meaningful behaviors. Altogether there seem to be fifty or sixty distinguishable body movements, with thirty-three of them in the head and face region alone.[14]

Interpretation of such cues is further aided by the fact that kinesic cues are norm-governed; that is, people follow consistent patterns in their use of kinesic cues.

Kinesic norms. As with proxemics, there is a wide range of factors determining kinesic norms. Perhaps the most noticeable one is *gender.* Men and women differ in their kinesic usage in a number of ways. For instance, men walk differently and even carry books differently from the way women do. Males and females also have characteristically different ways of sitting. Notice, for instance, differences in the way men and women cross their legs. In general, women use fewer gestures than men but engage in more eye contact.[15] People have strong stereotypes of masculine and feminine behavior. As a result, the man who deviates from the norm may be regarded as effeminate or homosexual, when his kinesic behaviors may actually have been learned because they were appropriate for his ethnic background or because they were comfortable. Similarly, women who deviate may be considered unattractive or domineering.

A second consideration is *race.* K. R. Johnson in his examination of kinesic patterns among blacks has commented on the unique walk adopted by some young blacks to signal masculinity and sensuality:

The young Black males' walk is different. First of all, it's much slower—it's more of a stroll. The head is sometimes slightly elevated and casually tipped to the side. Only one arm swings at the side with the hand slightly cupped. The other arm hangs limply to the side or it's tucked in the pocket. The gait is slow, casual and rhythmic. The gait is almost a walking dance, with all parts of the body moving in rhythmic harmony. This

---

[13]A. Mehrabian and S. Ferris, "Inference of Attitudes from Nonverbal Communication in Two Channels," *Journal of Consulting Psychology, 31* (1967), pp. 248–252.

[14]R. L. Birdwhistell, *Kinesics and Context* (Philadelphia: University of Pennsylvania Press, 1970).

[15]For an extended discussion of gestures, see P. Ekman and W. V. Friesen, "Hand Movements," *Journal of Communication, 22* (1972), pp. 353–374. For an extended discussion of eye behavior, see P. C. Elisworth and L. M. Ludwig, "Visual Behavior in Social Interaction," *Journal of Communication, 22* (1972), pp. 375–401.

Men and women have characteristically different ways of sitting. Notice, for instance, differences in the way they cross their legs. (Photographs: Maury Englander)

THE VARIABLES IN THE COMMUNICATION PROCESS

walk is . . . referred to as "walking that walk."[16]

Ethnic and cultural background also make a difference. For example, Italian-Americans use different gestures from those used by Mexican-Americans. Sitting and standing patterns in the United States vary radically from those used in many African and Middle Eastern countries. Cultures may dictate different behavioral patterns that are appropriate for various types of situations. For instance, in Ireland great displays of grief are expected at funerals, whereas in Japan, widows are expected to maintain a stoic smile.

Cultures also differ in the meanings they assign to the same behavior. One vice-president learned this when he traveled through Latin America on a goodwill tour. As he stepped off the plane in one country, he held up his hand in the A-O.K. sign (thumb and forefinger touching to form a circle) to show that he was happy to be there. To his dismay, the crowd booed him. They were equally dismayed by his behavior. He had made what was considered in their country an obscene gesture.

A fifth consideration is *social class.* Working-class women tend to use more "masculine" gestures, as do working-class men.[17]

Beyond these basic patterns of kinesic behavior, people do develop their own unique patterns, which remain fairly consistent over time. Each person has his or her own characteristic head and shoulder

Note the kinesic cues in the hand and facial expression and eye movement of this flirting couple. (Photograph: Maury Englander)

movements, gestures, and gaze patterns. For example, the amount of time a person spends in directly gazing at another may range from 28 percent to 70 percent of the total time of the interaction. Because of wide variations in individuals, it is possible to misinterpret idiosyncratic behavior. A person who yawns when he's anxious may be perceived as tired or uninterested.

Despite the considerable confusion and

[16]K. R. Johnson, "Black Kinesics: Some Non-verbal Communication Patterns in the Black Culture," in *Intercultural Communication: A Reader,* ed. L. A. Samovar and R. E. Porter (Belmont, Calif.: Wadsworth, 1972), pp. 181–189.

[17]L. Hamalian, "Communication by Gesture in the Middle East," *ETC,* 22 (1965), pp. 43–49.

misunderstanding that is possible with kinesic cues, they still remain one of the most effective and heavily relied on nonverbal codes, in part because they are so noticeable, in part because people trust visual information, and in part because there is an infinite number of cues that can be combined to produce precise messages. Kinesic behaviors will, therefore, play a dominant role in all the communication functions to be discussed.

PHYSICAL APPEARANCE

Another visual dimension of nonverbal communication is the *physical appearance* of the human body. Our preoccupation with appearance was insightfully noted by the earl of Chesterfield in the late eighteenth century:

> Women who are either indisputably beautiful, or indisputably ugly, are best flattered upon the score of their understandings; but those who are in a state of mediocrity are best flattered upon their beauty, or at least their graces; for every woman who is not absolutely ugly thinks herself handsome.[18]

Men and women are both very conscious of their own appearance and that of others. In fact, physical attractiveness is often the key determinant of whether people will choose to become acquainted. One study found that the biggest predictor of whether people were satisfied with a computer date was the physical attractiveness of their partner.[19]

Dimensions of physical appearance. A number of appearance features may be used as communication vehicles. The first is *body shape, height, and weight.* Our bodies may be categorized as one of three general types: (1) the endomorph, which is soft, round, and fat; (2) the mesomorph, which is bony, muscular, and athletic; and (3) the ectomorph, which is tall, thin, and fragile. Research has clearly shown that people stereotype our personality on the basis of our body types. Some personality attitudes connected with the endomorph are sluggishness, tolerance, affability, warmth, affection, generosity, complacency, and kindness. Adjectives applicable to the mesomorph are dominant, cheerful, reckless, argumentative, hot-tempered, optimistic, enthusiastic, confident, and efficient. The ectomorph is characterized as detached, introspective, serious, cautious, meticulous, thoughtful, sensitive, tactful, shy, and suspicious.

Body shape, height, and weight have a definite impact on others. For example, endomorphs are frequently discriminated against in seeking jobs, whereas tall men seem to win out consistently over short men for jobs.[20] In fact, a University of Pittsburgh survey of graduates found men over six feet two inches in height receiving higher starting salaries than men under six feet. The reason these bodily features create such reactions may be a function of physical attractiveness. Our stereotyped image of the hero is someone who is tall and athletic rather than short and fat. The stereotyped heroine is moderately tall and sleek. These stereotypes are perpetuated by the mass media in

[18]P. D. Stanhope, earl of Chesterfield, in a letter, September 5, 1780.

[19]E. Walster, V. Aronson, D. Abrahams, and L. Rottman, "Importance of Physical Attractiveness in Dating Behavior," *Journal of Personality and Social Psychology,* 4 (1966), pp. 508–516.

[20]M. L. Knapp, *Nonverbal Communication in Human Interaction* (New York: Holt, Rinehart and Winston, 1972), p. 73.

THE VARIABLES IN THE COMMUNICATION PROCESS

their selection of people who fit the "image" of a movie or TV star. Persons who deviate from these images may, therefore, be perceived as less attractive.

A second relevant dimension is *skin*. Skin color, texture, and the presence of such things as wrinkles, blemishes, scars, and freckles can all have an effect on our impressions of others and our interest in interacting with them. *Hair*—its color, length, style, texture, and cleanliness— has similar effects. Most bearded, long-haired men can testify to experiences of discrimination because of their appearance. Whether or not such an appearance is intended as defiance or rejection of society's values, it is interpreted as such by older generations. The reaction to long hair has been so strong that at times violent incidents have been known to occur.

Three other important dimensions are *clothing, accessories,* and *cosmetics.* Numerous studies have examined the various features of dress that have some communication value. Everything from the texture, color, and design of fabrics used to the stylishness and neatness of a garment or outfit can make a difference. Peoples' preferences for and uses of these features are related to their personality and social background. Observers apparently recognize this fact because a person's typical dress is interpreted as a message about his or her life-style, values, personality, and attitudes toward others. An employer is likely to perceive signals of disrespect from the employee who always shows up in jeans or signals of availability from the female secretary who wears short skirts and tight-fitting sweaters. Accessories may also carry meaning. The presence or absence of jewelry and its style may indicate age, wealth, and status. Just the

wearing of glasses has its effects: persons with glasses are rated more intelligent, dependable, industrious, conventional, shy, and religious but less attractive and sophisticated. Similarly with makeup. A 1959 study found that women who wore lipstick were perceived as more frivolous, less talkative, more placid, more conscientious, and, surprisingly, less interested in the opposite sex.[21] Today it is more likely that lipstick and other makeup would be a sign of greater interest in the opposite sex.

Physical appearance as communication. Although it should be clear that physical appearance cues produce strong reactions in others, physical appearance as a code is more limited than some of the other nonverbal codes. This is because during any interaction it cannot be altered easily and because across the history of any relationship it has its major impact in the early stages of the relationship. Once people become acquainted, they tend to rely less on the external information supplied by physical appearance and more on firsthand personal knowledge. Thus physical appearance is mostly effective at the beginnings—of both conversations and long-term relationships. But as we shall see, those first impression effects can still be important.

HAPTICS

Haptics, or our use of touch in the communication process, is just beginning to receive attention from serious researchers.

[21]W. McKeachie, "Lipstick as a Determiner of First Impressions of Personality: An Experiment for the General Psychology Course," *Journal of Social Psychology,* 36 (1952), pp. 241–244.

Physical appearance cues often produce strong reactions in others. Once people become acquainted, however, they tend to rely less on the external information supplied by physical appearance and more on first-hand personal knowledge. (Photograph: Maury Englander)

Our need for touch seems to be powerful. We know, for instance, that monkeys raised without any contact with other monkeys will spend hours clinging to a cloth-covered wire figure, preferring it to an uncovered figure that supplies food. This need for contact can also be seen in babies raised in orphanages and institutions. In many orphanages, babies are left for hours by themselves, lying in their beds in an environment with almost no sensory stimulation. They are rarely touched or held for any length of time. Such babies first become apathetic and lifeless, then develop bizarre behaviors; many even die. If human contact is so essential in early life, it seems reasonable to conclude that touch can have significant communicative value.

Touch in the American culture. Despite the apparent value and utility of touch, it is discouraged as a mode of communication. Our clothing styles and taboos about revealing our bodies reflects our inhibited view of touch. Boys learn at an early age that touching is not masculine, especially among males. This may explain the great attraction of contact sports for boys; it is one of the few situations in which body contact is condoned. The rituals of huddling in close contact and slapping on the basketball court demonstrate the recognized value of touch in communicating solidarity, supportiveness, and enthusiasm.

For girls, touching is more acceptable. A girl may hug her father or mother without disapproval. It is permissible (though uncommon) for girls to hold hands or put their arms around one another, but unfavorable insinuations would be made about boys who did the same thing. It is possible that all findings on proxemic preferences, especially on sex differences, really indicate our fear and avoidance of touch. Thus males sit the farthest apart from each other because touching would be inappropriate.

This avoidance of touch is taught at an early age. As children, we are frequently told not to touch other objects, "improper" parts of Mommy's or Daddy's body, and even parts of our own body. To

THE VARIABLES IN THE COMMUNICATION PROCESS

compensate for reduced tactile stimulation, we formalize acceptable forms of tactile interaction. The handshake, social dancing, the perfunctory kiss: all of these are acceptable means of communicating by touch. Touching certain parts of the body is also acceptable, if the touches are not prolonged. Brushing an arm or putting a hand on someone's shoulder is permissible, but touching the abdomen or thigh is not, except in overtly sexual situations.

Many of our touching taboos have evolved out of our sexual mores or moral attitudes. Touching in our culture carries with it sexual overtones. Because ours is not a sexually free society, touching is frowned upon. Adolescents are taught not to touch their dates. Parents frequently avoid intimate contact in front of their children for fear of providing a "permissive" model of interpersonal behavior.

Touch as communication. As a result of our disapproval of intimate behavior, we deny ourselves a meaningful avenue of communication. Touch can be an effective means of expressing understanding, sympathy, affection, and interest. In one hospital, nurses who touched their patients found the patients had better attitudes toward them and increased their verbal output.[22] Encounter groups emphasize touching as a way of breaking down communication barriers. Through touch, members become more aware of each other and supposedly more sensitive to each other's needs. By allowing others to

touch them, they make themselves vulnerable, which is a prerequisite to building trust.

If touch is so potent, why has it been so suppressed in our society? One explanation is that as societies progress, they substitute for touch other signs and symbols, such as language. From this perspective, touch, like drums, is regarded as a sign of a primitive society; refinement and "sophistication" thus dictate a reduction in such personal, ambiguous forms of communication as touch.

But our society is not likely to eliminate haptic communication totally. The recognition by clinical psychologists of the value of touching, the impact of the encounter movement, and the changing sexual mores of young people may instead contribute to an increasing acceptance of touching behavior. It may become possible for men openly to display affection through touch, as is already done in other cultures. And perhaps even the phrase "a touching scene" will take on a new meaning.

PARALANGUAGE

Paralanguage is concerned with the use of the voice in communication. It focuses on how we say something rather than what we say. It is, therefore, referred to as the *vocal* element of speech, as opposed to the *verbal* element, which is the words and their meanings. Actually, our vocal behavior is often critical to understanding the meanings of words. Consider the following sentence: "How could she do it?" Depending on whether the emphasis is on *how, could, she,* or *do,* the sentence carries different meaning. Thus paralanguage

[22]D. C. Agulera, "Relationships Between Physical Contact and Verbal Interaction Between Nurses and Patients," *Journal of Psychiatric Nursing,* 5 (1967), pp. 5–21.

means an accessory to, or subsidiary of, language. Our vocal behavior is instrumental to understanding our language.

Dimensions of paralanguage. Paralanguage can be broken down into several categories. *Voice quality* is the characteristic tonal quality of the voice, based on such factors as resonance, articulation, lip control, and rhythm control. *Intensity*, or the pressure of sound waves that are perceived as loud or soft, is another area of vocal behavior. *Rate and timing* refer to the speed at which a person speaks and the length and location of pauses. *Pitch*, another element of paralanguage, is the fundamental frequency and range of the voice. *Vocal segregates* are nonfluencies or irregularities (*ers* and *ums*) in our speech patterns. *Fluency* is the term used to describe the absence of distractions such as repetitions, hesitations, stuttering, vocal segregates, and false starts. *Vocal patterns* include inflectional patterns, dialects, and other combinations of vocal elements that form identifiable patterns. The final area of paralanguage focuses on *vocal characterizers*, such things as crying, laughing, yelling, sneezing, sighing, and snorting.

The combination of all these elements should produce in each of us a unique voice. Who could question the uniqueness of the voices of Everett Dirksen, Marlene Dietrich, or Howard Cosell? The fact that the FBI has begun using voice prints along with fingerprints to identify criminals confirms the singularity of our vocal behavior.

The voice as a code. Because each voice has distinctive properties, people view the voice much as they do a written signature—it is presumed to reveal a great deal about the speaker. From the voice, people glean information about a person's physical and psychological makeup, his or her educational and social background, and a whole host of other characteristics. Like physical appearance, vocal cues are an important contributor to our first impressions of others and our expectations about their communication behavior.

But the voice performs a much wider range of communication functions than this. The innumerable combinations of paralanguage features, coupled with the tremendous capacity of the human ear to detect subtle differences, make it possible for paralanguage to be a very flexible, multipurpose code. The voice is a key carrier of emotional messages. It reflects our attitudes toward others and our relationships with them. We use vocal cues to create certain impressions and influence the actions of others. And besides clarifying verbal messages, paralinguistic cues may actually regulate the flow of verbal communication. Thus paralanguage is a very powerful nonverbal code. It probably ranks second only to kinesics in terms of its significance in interactions.

ARTIFACTS

The last nonverbal code that deserves mention is *artifacts*, which is the use of the environment and objects within it. A person's office or home and its furnishings carry messages about him or her. Furthermore, surroundings can significantly affect verbal interactions. The lighting, temperature, ventilation, size, and architectural style, color, furnishings, and attractiveness of the environment are all important factors.

Consider some different settings. A bar

or restaurant is dimly lit, with subdued colors. It features comfortable, intimately arranged chairs and tables to encourage its customers to linger. An office is usually brightly lit, properly ventilated, kept at a slightly cool temperature, painted in neutral (nondistracting and nonirritating) colors, and furnished with functional chairs and desks that are not conducive to relaxation. A church sanctuary has lofty inspiring ceilings, subdued colors that set an atmosphere of peace and reflection, or reds and purples that are rich in religious symbolism, and stiff uncomfortable pews to force attention to the minister. Each setting conveys a message about the kind of activity and interaction that is acceptable in that atmosphere. The owners or designers can thus manipulate settings to suit their preferences. The restaurant owner who wants quick turnover in clientele will raise the lights and purchase less comfortable furniture. One businessman has been designing chairs explicitly intended to discourage people from sitting too long. A famous hotel replaced all its comfortable lobby furniture with hard benches and chairs to encourage people to circulate among its shops rather than sit. The same principle is employed in airports.

In this manner, the environment we control becomes an extension of ourselves. Our furnishings reflect our personalities and tastes. Persons who decorate in green say something different about themselves from what persons who decorate in pink say. The memorabilia that populate people's desks or rooms, even their stationery, give clues about themselves. Status can be clearly communicated by the elegance of a person's office and its location. For instance, offices in corners with windows and those with their own private door have more status than those located in the middle of a large room. Employees with large wooden desks clearly have more status than those with small metal ones. Business executives who recognize this can use office location and furnishings to motivate their workers.

Placement of furniture within a room may also carry a message. Notice, for example, where professors place their desks within their offices. Those who have their desks between themselves and the doorway have established a barrier that reduced their accessibility to students. The placement of furniture in a public setting can do much to increase or decrease interaction. Studies in hospitals and other public institutions, where chairs have been lined up along the walls for the convenience of janitors, have found very little interaction. Similarly, in a classroom with fixed rows of chairs, there is less overall interaction than with a circular arrangement. Conversely, in bars, where people are seated at tables in close proximity and in intimate arrangements, interaction is frequent and personal.

Other features of the environment that have an impact are its attractiveness and the degree of sensory stimulation it provides. In one study, subjects rated photographs of people's faces significantly higher in attractiveness when the subjects were in a "beautiful" room than when they were in an "ugly" room.[23] Unattractive rooms are seen as fatiguing and displeasing, whereas attractive rooms tend to create feelings of well-being. The degree

[23]N. L. Mintz, "Effects of Esthetic Surroundings: II. Prolonged and Repeated Experience in a 'Beautiful' and 'Ugly' Room," *Journal of Psychology, 41* (1956), pp. 459–466.

of sensory stimulation can further contribute or detract from the atmosphere of a setting. There is a good deal of evidence to suggest that both understimulation and overstimulation are undesirable.

Our environment both communicates and impinges upon the communication process. The way we design and use the elements in our environment transmits messages about ourselves and dictates the nature of the communication that will occur. Thus artifacts are responsible for defining the communication context. They help to determine how all the other nonverbal codes are to be interpreted.

Functions of Nonverbal Communication

It would be a mistake to assume that the nonverbal codes operate independently of one another or that they have distinctly different purposes. Rather, they are frequently dependent on one another to create the total meaning of a message. Although some of the codes are more specialized than others in what communication roles they fulfill, most of them perform the same communication functions and they act in combination to perform those functions. The functions can be grouped into five general categories: symbolic displays, metamessages, structuring interaction, self-presentation, and manipulating others.

SYMBOLIC DISPLAYS

Much of nonverbal communication occurs in the form of specific cues or patterns of cues that are symbolic in nature;

There are displays of emotions that are universally recognized across cultures. (Photograph: Michael Weisbrot)

that is, they have conventionally recognized meaning for receivers. Like verbal communication, cues have shared meaning among the users. For example, flags, armbands, and campaign buttons have all been used as symbolic communication. The associations and reactions they are intended to create are clear. A particularly good example is the story of a frustrated Californian who had tried in vain to receive compensation for his faulty new automobile. The dealer and the manufacturer both failed to respond satisfactorily to his claims. Realizing the futility of his efforts, he resorted to symbolic communication to protest his treatment; he painted big yellow lemons on the sides of his car and parked it in front of the dealer's office.

Symbolic displays may be either universal or culture-specific.

Universal displays. Universal displays are those that are universally recognized across cultures. They might even be regarded as species-specific displays, by which is meant displays unique to the human species, except for the fact that many similarities between human behavior and that of lower primates or other species have been uncovered. For instance, such behaviors as smiling and sticking out the tongue occur among apes as well as humans.

Regardless of how unique they are to humans, such displays are an important facet of communication because they act as a universal language where verbal communication fails. They capture the commonality in human needs and activities. The most extensively studied cross-cultural displays are expressions of emotions. Our emotional states are usually revealed through the body, face, and eyes. Body positions typically indicate a person's general mood or gross affective state, whereas the face gives clues to specific feelings. Researchers have discovered that Western cultures and primitive tribes alike use the same basic facial displays for certain primary emotions such as anger, disgust, happiness, sadness, and fear.[24] Most people are also fairly accurate in de-

ciding whether a person feels pleasant or unpleasant, relaxed or aroused. Beyond that, however, it becomes more difficult to make accurate judgments. For instance, a person may have difficulty distinguishing between rage and resentment, happiness and amusement, or pride and confidence. Thus only certain kinesic displays may act as universal messages.

Kinesic cues are not the only indicators of emotions. A person's vocal behavior may provide clues to his or her emotional state. For instance, a loud, high-pitched, irregular, clipped voice may communicate anger, whereas a slow, slurred, soft voice with irregular pauses and downward inflections may signal sadness.[25] Yet many individual differences exist in communicating the same emotion. Moreover, the same emotion can be expressed in different ways at different times. A person may shout one time when angry and whisper intensely another time. Persons also differ in their sensitivity and accuracy in judging vocal cues. Consequently, no firm statements can be made about which vocal behaviors are universally symbolic, except perhaps laughing and crying.

Beyond emotional displays, there are many other kinds of displays that are common to all humans. The prime example is gender displays. As noted under the codes, there are sex differences in the ways various codes are used. These differences may serve to identify our gender. Thus males learn "masculine" stances, and women learn "feminine" sitting positions. Other behaviors, such as the way we walk, the gestures we use, the way we touch others, our voice qualities, and even

[24]P. Ekman and W. V. Friesen, "Constants Across Cultures in the Face and Emotion," *Journal of Personality and Social Psychology*, 17 (1971), pp. 124–129.

[25]J. R. Davitz, *The Communication of Emotional Meaning* (New York: McGraw-Hill, 1964).

the distances we adopt, may all signal our sex. Similarly, we may use nonverbal behaviors to signal other kinds of displays that are common to most species, including play behavior, aggression, and escape.

Culture-specific displays. According to anthropologists, each culture uses a number of gestures and expressions that have direct verbal equivalents. These behaviors, called *emblems,* have clearly understood meaning within the culture and are often substituted for verbal expressions. For instance, a waving hand means hello or good-bye, and a finger pressed to the temple like a gun means suicide. Lowered eyes, a shake of the head, and a frown may all signal "No."

Although all cultures seem to use emblems for similar purposes—things like greetings, insults, and giving directions—they do not use the same behaviors for any given meaning. Americans point directions with their fingers; some Africans point with their lips. Cultures may also use the same behaviors as emblems but assign them different meanings. This leads to a lot of confusion when people travel in foreign countries and are not familiar with the different symbol systems, as the Nixon incident with the A-O.K. sign illustrates. Another example that undoubtedly gives Americans trouble is the eyebrow flash. This probably began as a universal display. It is a quick, often unnoticed raising of the eyebrows that in most countries is a greeting signal. In the United States, we have expanded the meanings of the display to include friendliness, interest, and approval. Consequently, Americans are very accustomed

to using this behavior in conversation. Unfortunately, in many countries the eyebrow flash is a flirtation signal, and in Japan and China specifically it is considered impolite and even rude. One wonders how many American tourists have invited advances or insulted the natives without ever knowing it.

METAMESSAGES

Metamessages are, strictly speaking, messages about messages. In terms of nonverbal communication, they are those messages that comment upon or clarify the interpretation of other nonverbal messages or the verbal message. Three important ways in which nonverbal cues function as metacommunication are as verbal complements, as relational messages, and as attitudinal messages.

Verbal complements. One of the clearly recognized purposes of nonverbal cues is to strengthen understanding of the verbal message that they accompany. There are at least five ways in which nonverbal cues work in conjunction with the verbal message. One is *redundancy.* Nonverbal behavior frequently repeats what is being said verbally. For example, if an instructor tells you that you have five minutes to finish a test and simultaneously holds up five fingers, he or she is providing nonverbal redundancy.

A second function of nonverbal behavior is *accentuation,* the highlighting or emphasizing of a verbal message. When Nikita Khrushchev pounded a desk top with his shoe during a speech at the United Nations, he was rather strongly accenting a point in his message. On a less dramatic level, moving closer to someone who has expressed interest in you highlights the message of friendliness that may have first been signaled with the eyes.

Elaboration is a third way in which non-verbal cues aid the verbal message. By modifying or expanding upon the verbal message, such cues clarify the total meaning. The smiles and gestures of the returning traveler discussing his or her trip provide added information. The lingering touch after a fight may carry a much stronger plea for reconciliation than the difficult words of apology preceding this nonverbal behavior.

Fourth, nonverbal behaviors may provide *contradiction* of the verbal message. A woman who says "No" verbally may actually have "Yes" in her eyes. Such contradictions may be intentional or unintentional. If a person sarcastically says, "That is the most brilliant performance I have ever seen," he or she is intentionally contradicting the verbal statement through the tone of voice. Such contradictions may add intensity to the overall meaning. However, many times the contradictions are actually accidental betrayals of true feelings, as in the case of the person who unconvincingly raves about an unwanted gift. When the verbal communication is contradicted by the nonverbal behavior, people tend to believe the nonverbal message.[26]

26M. Argyle, F. Alkema, and R. Gilmour, "The Communication of Friendly and Hostile Attitudes by Verbal and Nonverbal Signals," *European Journal of Social Psychology*, 1 (1971), pp. 385–402; E. K. Fujimoto, "The Comparative Power of Verbal and Nonverbal Symbols," (Diss.: Ohio State University, 1971); A. Mehrabian and M. Wiener, "Decoding of Inconsistent Communications," *Journal of Personality and Social Psychology*, 6 (1967), pp. 108–114.

Finally, nonverbal cues may at times be used in *substitution* for portions of the verbal message. Typically, emblems are used for this purpose. Nonverbal substitution may be used when the verbal channel is restricted, as in the case of trying to communicate across a noisy room. Substituion may occur when the verbal channel seems less capable of expressing the meaning, as in the case of showing disapproval of what someone is saying. Nonverbal cues can also heighten attention to the verbal message through contrast. A stern glance following the verbal statement, "Is that clear?" may be all that is necessary to make the point.

Relational messages. Relational messages are messages that reveal the nature of the relationship between two or more people. Any communication may have two levels to it, the "content" level—the information and ideas being exchanged—and the "relational" level—the indications of how the parties involved feel about each other and the relationship. When people signal their intentions and expectations toward others, when they reveal the degree to which they like someone or grant that person status and power, they are communicating at the relational level.

The nonverbal codes are constantly in use expressing relational messages while the verbal band is being used for other purposes. It is often easier and less risky to define relationships through nonverbal messages than to commit ourselves verbally. Thus we rely heavily on the combined nonverbal codes to send and receive messages of liking, approval, trust, dominance, and so forth.

One category of relational messages that

has received considerable attention in the nonverbal literature is *liking and attraction.* Our bodies communicate much about our feelings toward others. If we lean forward or face a person directly, we probably like the person; conversely, if we lean back or turn our face away, we probably dislike the person. People often mirror the sitting or standing positions of someone they like or agree wtih. Long gazes and less frequent glances are interpreted as liking. A person's degree of muscular relaxation further connotes liking; people are moderately relaxed with those they like.

Our liking of others is additionally reflected in the way we include them within a communication circle. When we wish to affiliate with others, we often use our body to form an inclusive unit. We may cross our legs and orient our bodies toward the person we wish to include. While doing this, we may also use our arms and legs as barriers to others we want to exclude from the interaction. Most people use direct eye contact to cement the bond further. They avoid eye contact with those who attempt to intrude, or they alternatively glare at them. As with other dimensions of nonverbal behavior, cultural differences may change the kinesic pattern associated with liking or disliking other people. Some blacks have developed their own effective means of communicating dislike or disapproval: they roll their eyes. Although such behavior may not be noticed by whites, other blacks are usually very aware of it, and the meaning of the behavior is clear.

Yet another way in which attraction may be communicated is through the use of courtship rituals. In a series of interesting studies, A. E. Scheflen, a psychologist, has demonstrated that there are consistent patterns of human courtship behavior.[27] The term *quasi-courtship behavior* refers to the flirting games that go on between men and women, whether or not they are interested in each other. In many instances, it is merely a ritual in which both parties agree implicitly that it will not go beyond an understood point. They simply engage in the behavior to assert their own sexual attractiveness. In other instances, it serves as a prelude to more intimate relations. Quasi-courtship behavior then becomes a means of determining another's availability and approachability.

The ritual frequently begins with extended, penetrating eye contact, which creates emotional arousal. Women hold their thighs together, walk with the upper arms against their body, and tilt their pelvises slightly forward. Men stand with their thighs apart, hold their arms away from their body, swing them as they walk, and carry their pelvises slightly back. Attraction is further evidenced by heightened muscle tone and erect postures. Men pull their stomachs in, whereas women throw their chests out to emphasize their breasts. Both sexes engage in preening behavior: tugging at socks, rearranging clothes and makeup, stroking hair, and glancing in mirrors. If women are open to a man's advances, they may cross their legs to expose a thigh, unfold their arms, engage in flirting glances, and roll their hips. Both men and women may open more buttons on their shirt or blouse than they usually do.

[27]A. E. Scheflen, "Quasi-Courtship Behavior in Psychotherapy," *Psychiatry, 28* (1965), pp. 245–257, and "The Significance of Posture in Communicative Systems," *Psychiatry, 27* (1964), pp. 316–331.

In the advanced stages, men and women may invade each other's personal space. This also has an arousing effect. If seated, they will close others out by their shoulder and leg positions. Once an intimate distance has been established, touching is likely to occur. Men may brush a woman's arm; women may touch a man's thigh. If contact progresses beyond this stage, chances are it is no longer "quasi" courtship behavior.

A second type of relational message that may be effectively communicated nonverbally is *credibilty*. Our judgments of another person's trustworthiness, competence, friendliness, and so forth are influenced by the nonverbal behaviors they use. The white-coated doctor who walks briskly and speaks with an "air of authority" is attempting to inspire confidence in us. The politician who uses energetic, expansive gestures may be trying to convince us that he or she is both dynamic and insightful. Even such a seemingly minor feature such as dialect may affect our evaluation of someone's credibility. For example, the female New Yorker is seen as more dynamic but less sociable in comparison with the female Southerner who is seen as the least composed of any of five regional speakers. The New York and General American dialects are perceived as indicators of more competence than the Northeastern, Southeastern, and Southern dialects.[28] This may explain why radio broadcasters work hard to achieve General American (dialect-free) speech.

A final type of relational message for

which nonverbal cues are enlisted is the communication of status and power. Artifacts and clothing are frequently called upon to signal status and power. Plush offices, luxury automobiles, and custom-tailored clothes are taken as measures of a person's importance. Eye contact may reveal a person's position in a group. The individual who receives the most eye contact from others is usually the one with the most power. Yet another code that may be used in a subtle way to communicate status is chronemics. One person who had a keen understanding of this use of time was Harry Truman. When he was president, an important editor who came to see him was kept waiting 45 minutes. When an aide informed Truman that the editor was becoming impatient, Truman replied that when he was junior senator from Missouri, that same editor had kept him "cooling his heels" in the outer office for an hour and a half. As far as he was concerned, the SOB had 45 minutes to go.

Attitudinal messages. Attitudinal messages reveal a person's attitude toward some issue. At times they may serve as verbal complements by clarifying the emotions underlying a person's verbal statement. A good example of this is the use of gestures. When we are demoralized or unenthusiastic about some topic, we use fewer gestures than when we are excited or angered. At other times attitudinal messages may also have a relational component in that the attitude expressed applies to both issues and people. J. Horton offers a good example of this in his essay "Time and Cool People." He notes that many young blacks today have a different sense of time, which they use to

[28]J. K. Toomb, J. Quiggins, D. L. Moore, J. B. MacNeill, and C. M. Liddell, "The Effects of Regional Dialects on Initial Source Credibility," paper presented at the International Communication Association Convention, Atlanta, April 1972.

communicate both their values and their attitudes toward white society:

> Negro street time is built around the irrelevance of clock time, white man's time, and the relevance of street values and activities. Like anyone else, a street dude is on time by the standard clock whenever he wants to be, not on time when he does not want to be and does not have to be.
>
> When the women in school hit the street at the lunch hour and he wants to throw them a rap, he will be there then and not one hour after they have left. But he may be kicked out of high school for truancy or lose his job for being late and unreliable. . . .
>
> In the street, watches have a special and specific meaning. Watches are for pawning and not for telling time. . . .
>
> Personal time as expressed in parties and other street activities is not simply deficient knowledge and use of standard time. It is a positive adaptation to generations of living whenever and wherever possible outside of the sound of the white man's clock. The personal clock is an adaptation to the chance and accidental character of events on the street and to the very positive value placed on emotion and feeling.[29]

STRUCTURING INTERACTION

A third major function of nonverbal communication is defining communication contexts and regulating the flow of interaction within those contexts. Probably the primary code responsible for defining the context is artifacts. The way in which an environment is designed, arranged, and furnished will set the general tone for communication. A formal environment will produce formal communication. A small, dimly lit space with comfortable furniture will produce more casual and intimate communication. The environment may also provide clues about what roles people are expected to take. A friend reports that when she went to see the president of her university about an affirmative action matter, she found herself ushered to a seat twenty feet from the president, who ensconced himself behind an enormous desk. It was clear to her that she was to take a subordinate role and he, the dominant one. Similarly, the presence of a silver tea service at a meeting between foreign diplomats means that any negotiations will be conducted in a very formal, polite fashion and only after the social amenities have been satisfied.

Nonverbal cues may also be used to regulate the flow of an interaction. Kinesics is the predominant code used for this purpose. People have several means of indicating when they are willing to listen and when they want to talk. Leaning back may signal that a person is listening, whereas leaning forward signals that he or she wants to talk. When we use eye contact and a head movement, we tell another person that he or she may begin speaking. Conversely, looking away or filling a pause with a gesture is a way of preventing an interruption and maintaining control of the conversation. One other way a person may indirectly control an interaction is by using direct, continuous eye contact to signal his or her desire for feedback and to demand attention. As the face is such a good indicator of the way someone feels about us, it is natural that we look at the face frequently when we want feedback. This tends to force the other

[29]J. Horton, "Time and Cool People," in *Intercultural Communication: A Reader,* ed. L. A. Samovar and R. E. Porter (Belmont, Calif.: Wadsworth, 1972), pp. 84–96.

person's attention on ourselves and to induce nonverbal or verbal feedback.

Beyond kinesic behaviors, proxemics and vocalics may have a regulatory affect on interaction. Such things as shifts in distance, changes in vocal rate, and changes in volume can encourage or discourage another person from speaking.

SELF-PRESENTATION

A fourth way in which nonverbal cues serve a communication is in the presentation of self, or the image that we present to others. It is Erving Goffman's contention that human behavior can be viewed as a drama. Much of our behavior is a matter of playing roles for others, just as actors play roles. When we are "on stage," we create a front for others. That front may change from audience to audience. We may have one set of behaviors that fit the role of friend and another set of behaviors that are appropriate for the role of lover. You, no doubt, show different facets of your personality to your family from the facets you show to an employer.

Nonverbal behaviors are relevant to self-presentation in that successful performances of our roles are dependent on the degree to which nonverbal messages are well coordinated with each other and with the verbal level of interaction. Nonverbal cues are also responsible for creating someone's initial expectations of what roles we are likely to play. Research has demonstrated that nonverbal information heavily colors first impressions. Those first impressions may lead to a successful or unsuccessful self-presentation, depending on whether the sender intends to create those perceptions or not.

The two nonverbal codes that are most responsible for initial perceptions are physical appearance and paralanguage. The relationship between body type and personality has already been noted earlier. People judge our personality from body type alone. Our body shape is one feature over which we have little control when it comes to managing an impression. But we do have control over apparel, which is a major influence on first impressions when people are previously unacquainted. Clothing has been found to be significantly related to the perceived status and social roles of others. An executive who wears a two-hundred-dollar designer suit to the office is likely to be perceived as high in status. However, a clerk wearing the same suit may be seen as status-seeking instead. Clothing is also seen as an indicant of personality. Women rated high on good appearance are seen as more sociable and more intelligent.[30] Dress may even influence perceptions of the political philosophy of the wearer. In a study limited to college students, persons dressed "less conventionally" have been classified as radical, problack, left-wing, and prone to marijuana use. Conversely, figures dressed "conventionally" have been perceived as career-oriented and favoring the traditional "fun and football" culture.[31]

Vocal cues lead to the same kinds of judgments. Listeners make judgments of a person's socioeconomic status, education,

[30]S. S. Silverman, *Clothing and Appearance; Their Psychological Meaning for Teen-age Girls*, Research monograph, Bureau of Publications, Teachers College, Columbia University, 1945.

[31]J. Kelley, "Dress and Non-Verbal Communication," paper presented at the Annual Conference of the American Association for Public Opinion Research, May 1969.

and occupation from voice cues alone and often with high accuracy.[32] Even when a person tries to disguise his or her status, vocally the true status is often detected. Paralanguage also contributes to impressions of personality, although these may be more stereotypical than accurate. A slow, low-pitched voice creates an impression of the speaker as kind and good-natured. Males and females with flat voices are both perceived as cold, sluggish, withdrawn, and masculine. Persons with nasal voices are seen as whining, nagging, and unpleasant. Males with a breathy voice are perceived as young and artistic; breathy females are seen as feminine, petite, pretty, high strung, shallow, and not very intelligent.[33]

Once people move beyond the initial stages of acquaintanceship, physical appearance cues become less important to the impression being created, and greater reliance is placed on the other codes. Dress may still act to identify the role a person is performing, but other codes that have the potential of being varied during an interaction become much more useful. Depending on what kind of impression a person is trying to manage, all the cues that are used as relational messages may be brought into play to manipulate that image consciously. Thus the student who wants to communicate friendliness and interest in class may sit closer to the front,

lean forward during lectures, engage in frequent eye contact, and smile a lot. Of course, the performance may fail if done to excess, for excessive behaviors are seen as insincere.

Sometimes performances may be designed actually to deceive others. When such performances take place, the body may give off totally unconscious clues that betray true feelings or intent. For highly perceptive observers, small changes in facial expressions can provide clues to a person's actual feelings.[34] But these are often difficult to observe because people try to disguise their attitudes by controlling facial expression. Easier to read indicators are hand, leg, and foot movements. People are less careful to control these parts of their bodies because they do not expect them to be noticed. Consequently nonverbal behavior can leak information about the real state of affairs. Jiggling feet and legs unconsciously reveal anxiety, nervousness, and fear. When there is an increase in fidgety, anxiety-revealing gestures, there is also generally a reduction in illustrative gestures. An increase in hand shrugs (a gesture of helplessness) has also been found to occur when people are induced to lie.[35] Deception may further be suggested through a person's eye contact. Because direct eye contact connotes honesty, the person who is lying may avoid eye contact for fear that his eyes will give him away. Others may attempt to main-

[32]D. S. Ellis, "Speech and Social Status in America," *Social Forces, 45* (1967), pp. 431–451; L. S. Harms, "Listener Judgments of Status Cues in Speech," *Quarterly Journal of Speech, 47* (1961), pp. 164–168; T. H. Pear, *Voice and Personality* (London: Chapman and Hall, 1931).

[33]D. W. Addington, "The Relationship of Selected Vocal Characteristics to Personality Perception," *Speech Monographs, 35* (1968), pp. 492–503.

[34]E. A. Haggard and K. S. Issacs, "Micromomentary Facial Expressions as Indicators of Ego Mechanisms in Psychotherapy," in *Methods of Research on Psychotherapy,* ed. L. A. Gottschalk and A. H. Auerback (New York: Appleton-Century-Crofts, 1966).

[35]P. Ekman and W. V. Friesen, "Hand Movements," *Journal of Communication, 22* (1972), pp. 353–374.

THE VARIABLES IN THE COMMUNICATION PROCESS

tain a direct gaze, but they are likely to overcompensate. The result is that many efforts to deceive others are unsuccessful because the audience recognizes that something is amiss. A successful performance truly depends on consistency among the nonverbal and verbal codes; lying usually produces inconsistency. Thus, although nonverbal behaviors may be enlisted to create various fronts, they may also be used by observers to peak behind the facade.

MANIPULATING OTHERS

From the label, manipulating others, this last function of nonverbal communication, may sound like an extension of the previous one. In one respect it is because it concerns the intentional use of nonverbal messages by a source. But it differs from self-presentation in that it is concerned with the ways nonverbal behaviors can be used to alter how others think and act rather than how they view the source. Much of our communication is designed to produce learning, attitude change, and/or behavioral change. Nonverbal behaviors can be instrumental in producing those outcomes. Hence nonverbal communication "manipulates" others.

The learning process is one that has received substantial attention from educators and researchers; yet little is known about the specific ways in which nonverbal cues can be used to enhance comprehension and retention. We do know that learning can be reinforced through the presentation of rewards. It seems reasonable to think that things like smiling, nodding, and other approval cues, which are interpersonally rewarding, might also foster greater acquisition of knowledge. Shows of warmth have been found to heighten learning among children.[36] Just what constitutes warmth, however, is not clear.

Another nonverbal feature that seems to be relevant is the environment. The location in which learning takes place can either arouse attention or distract it, depending on such things as the colors used, the comfort level of furniture, the temperature, the lighting, and the noise level. Bright colors lead people to be more alert intellectually, whereas dark colors lead to duller reactions. Extremely comfortable chairs, warm temperatures, dim lighting, and soothing music may lead to too much relaxation, whereas their opposites may create such discomfort and fatigue that they are also distracting. Some intermediate degree of stimulation appears to be the best for heightening attention, but again exactly what is the proper intermediate level has yet to be determined. At least the person who wants his or her verbal message understood can avoid environmental extremes. Hospitals training doctors in difficult transplant techniques will maximize accurate learning by avoiding both highly sterile and highly distracting locales for the instruction.

One other nonverbal code that has received some investigation is paralanguage. It has generally been presumed that rapid speech, poor vocal quality, and nonfluencies interfere with comprehension of what a person is saying. Studies on intelligibility have found that highly intelligible speakers use longer syllable dura-

[36]J. S. Kleinfeld, "Effects of Nonverbal Warmth on the Learning of Eskimo and White Students," *Journal of Social Psychology,* 92 (1974), pp. 3–9.

tion, greater intensity, less pause time, and more pitch variety.[37] Nevertheless, research has also shown that listeners are highly adaptable to differences in vocal presentations. For example, a rapid rate of speaking with little pause time does not seriously hurt comprehension.[38] In fact, as long as a speaker is understandable, poor vocal quality, pitch variety, and fluency do not reduce comprehension in a receiver. Surprisingly, it has been found that stutterers may be more effective speakers because people pay closer attention to what they are saying.

Though the learning process has been somewhat slighted in the nonverbal literature, persuasion as an outcome has not. A variety of nonverbal strategies has been found to be effective in encouraging attitude change, ranging from affiliation and credibility cues to attractiveness appeals and violations of expectations. It is known that voices with more intonation, more volume, faster rate, and more fluency are perceived as more persuasive. Such cues communicate confidence and credibility. Similarly, a somewhat erect posture and rhythmic, forceful gestures can contribute to the same impression, thereby heightening persuasiveness. Facial expressions that show liking and approval also seem to have the same effect.[39]

Another nonverbal feature that adds to persuasiveness is physical attractiveness. One study dressed a female speaker in rather unattractive clothing and gave her an oily, unkempt appearance. Not surprisingly, she was much less persuasive with her audience than when she wore attractive clothing, makeup, and a flattering hair style.[40] Physical appearance cues may operate in yet another way. They may lead to a violation of expectations. A "hippie-looking" speaker who argues for tax reform may actually be more convincing than a conservatively dressed speaker. The appearance cues may lead a receiver to expect either unintelligent or radical views from such a speaker. A rational presentation on a "conservative" topic, therefore, comes as a pleasant surprise. If this interpretation is correct, it is possible that students may actually be more influential with peers and teachers alike by dressing in a deviant fashion, so long as what is said then counters the expectations set up by the dress.

A final communication outcome in which nonverbal cues play a significant role is the modification of others' behavior. Nonverbal cues can be used in a variety of ways to manipulate the way others communicate and act. Some of the strategies that produce an impact are threat cues, appeals to power and status, and violations of expectations. Some very interesting studies have been conducted on the power of staring as a threat. Drivers who receive stares from a pedestrian on a street corner will actually cross the intersection faster than those who don't receive stares.[41] Stares are threatening, and people

[37]N. W. Heimstra and V. S. Ellingstad, *Human Behavior: A Systems Approach* (Monterey, Calif.: Brooks/Cole Publishing, 1972).

[38]D. B. Orr, "Time Compressed Speech—A Perspective," *Journal of Communication, 18* (1968), pp. 288–292.

[39]A. Mehrabian and M. Williams, "Nonverbal Concomitants of Perceived and Intended Persuasiveness," *Journal of Personality and Social Psychology, 13* (1969), pp. 37–58.

[40]J. Mills and E. Aronson, "Opinion Change as a Function of the Communicator's Attractiveness and Desire to Influence," *Journal of Personality and Social Psychology, 1* (1965), pp. 73–77.

[41]P. C. Ellsworth, J. M. Carlsmith, and A. Henson, "The Stare as a Stimulus to Flight in Human Subjects," *Journal of Personality and Social Psychology, 21* (1972), pp. 302–311.

THE VARIABLES IN THE COMMUNICATION PROCESS

will take actions to avoid them. Uniforms may implicitly suggest a threat as well, although uniforms also carry connotations of status. People typically comply with the requests of a uniformed individual, even when the requests are illegitimate. For instance, a person dressed in a nondescript uniform asked pedestrians to put a dime in a parking meter for a stranger's car. The vast majority complied.[42] Even when uniforms aren't used, clothing so effectively communicates status that it can influence the actions of others. Notice the differences in treatment that well-dressed and casually dressed customers receive from waiters or salespeople.

On a more positive note, nonverbal affiliation and liking cues can effectively alter the way others behave. Such cues may encourage another person to acquire a new skill, to volunteer assistance when help is needed, and even to become more intimate in his or her communication. For instance, touching usually leads to more disclosure of intimate information.

One last way in which nonverbal behaviors may modify the actions of others is through violations of norms and expectations. It was noted earlier that proxemic behavior is highly norm-governed. People develop expectations about what distances others will adopt. A violation of the normative distance can, therefore, have some interesting effects. If you invade your neighbor's space, he or she may become more active nonverbally, use more vocalized pauses (*ums* and *ers*), and become more verbose and less flexible in verbal statements.[43] Violations of dress expectations can also have some detrimental consequences. One study done by two college students tested the effects of hair and dress on people's willingness to sign a harmless petition. In one situation, the male student had long hair and a beard, and the female experimenter wore long hair; both had on "hippie" clothing. On the second occasion the male cut his hair and was clean shaven, the female wore her hair up, and both dressed "conservatively." Not surprisingly, significantly fewer people signed the petition of the "long hairs." The conclusion to be drawn is that violating expectations can have either positive or negative effects, depending on what kind of violation it is and what your purpose is. Positive violations may increase persuasion and lead to desired behavioral changes; negative violations may produce undesirable outcomes. In this area and many others, we are only beginning to understand the ways in which nonverbal communication operates and the power that it holds.

SUMMARY

1. Nonverbal messages are a powerful part of the communication process. Because so much of nonverbal behavior operates outside of conscious awareness, most people fail to recognize the wide range of roles that such messages play. Misinterpretation is common.

2. Nonverbal communication may be classified according to the different codes or modes of expression that are used. The seven primary

[42]L. Bickman, "The Social Power of a Uniform," *Journal of Applied Social Psychology*, 4 (1974), pp. 47–61.

[43]P. Garner, "The Effects of Personal Space on Interpersonal Communication" (Master's thesis, Illinois State University, 1972).

ones are proxemics, chronemics, kinesics, physical appearance, haptics, paralanguage, and artifacts.

3. Proxemics is the study of the ways in which human beings structure and use space to communicate. People have two spatial needs: territoriality and personal space. Sex, race, status, age, personality variables, cultural norms, personal attraction, and situational variables all affect an individual's space needs. People resent invasions of their personal space and have developed several response patterns to deal with such invasions.

4. Chronemics is the study of the way human beings use time. The American use of time falls into three categories or sets: technical time, or scientific breakdowns that have little bearing on nonverbal communication; formal time, or the traditional, conscious divisions of time such as years, months, and days: and informal time, which is dependent on the context of a communication situation for its definition. The American use of informal time follows two patterns: the diffused point pattern, in which people arrive somewhere around the appointed time, and the displaced point pattern, in which people arrive at or before the appointed time.

5. Kinesics, or the visual aspects of behavior, has long been recognized as carrying meaning in a communication interaction. Sex, race, culture, and social status often influence kinesic behavior; however, every individual develops his or her own unique kinesic patterns. A person uses the body to communicate much about his or her feelings toward others. A person's emotional state may be revealed through the body, face, eye movements and gestures. Kinesic behavior may also provide clues to an individual's status and background.

6. Our physical appearance may also carry messages to another person. People tend to stereotype our personalities on the basis of our body type. Research indicates that people may perceive our weight and height as indicators of our personality. In addition, hair, dress, accessories, and cosmetics are often used as indicators of certain traits. Dress is most typically seen as a message about a person's life-style and status. Physical appearance as a nonverbal code is primarily important in first impressions.

7. Haptics is the study of man's use of touch. Touch has significant communicative value, but in our society it has been discouraged as a mode of communication except in intimate relationships.

8. Paralanguage is the study of the vocal (as opposed to verbal) aspects of speech. Because there are so many features of the voice that can be varied, paralanguage fulfills a broad range of communication functions. It is relevant to such things as the way people signal the

nature of their relationship to one another, the regulation of interactions, the impressions that people try to create, and the learning and persuasion processes.

9. Artifacts are a final nonverbal code that may both serve as a message vehicle and influence the communication transmitted through other codes. The design of an environment reflects the interests and personalities of the designer and the users of the space. Features such as linear perspective, lighting, temperature, color, and furniture arrangement help to dictate the kind of communication that will take place. Objects may also carry messages.

10. The nonverbal codes, taken together, perform a number of communication functions. They may act as symbolic messages and metamessages. They may structure interactions. They may be used to manipulate one's self-presentation and the behaviors of others.

11. Nonverbal symbolic messages may be universal, as in the case of emotional displays and gender displays, or they may be culture-specific, as in the case of emblems. Kinesics, artifacts, and physical appearance are the codes most likely to be used for symbolic purposes.

12. The nonverbal codes act as metamessages by clarifying verbal statements through redundancy, accentuation, elaboration, contradiction, and substitution. They also function as metacommunication by supplying relational messages and attitudinal messages. Kinesics, paralanguage, physical appearance, haptics, proxemics, artifacts, and chronemics may all signal such relational considerations as liking, attraction, credibility, and status, as well as attitudes toward what is being said.

13. Yet another major function of nonverbal communication is the structuring of interactions. Environmental features are an important source of clues as to what roles people are expected to perform in any situation. Kinesic, vocalic, proxemic, and haptic cues are used to regulate the flow of interaction. They determine whose turn it is to speak, how long each person will speak, and sometimes even what the people will talk about.

14. A fourth communication role that nonverbal behaviors perform is self-presentation, the impressions people attempt to create for others. Much of interaction can be viewed as a drama, with each person performing a role for an audience. Nonverbal cues are important in determining whether the front that is presented is successful or not. Often people leak unintended information about themselves through their nonverbal behaviors that is counter to the image they are trying to project. This is especially true when deception is attempted. Thus nonverbal cues may either confirm or disconfirm a performance.

15. Finally, nonverbal cues may be enlisted in efforts to enhance learning, attitude change, and behavior change. A number of strategies involving nonverbal behaviors can be used to manipulate the actions of others. Liking and approval cues, credibility appeals, power and status appeals, threat cues, attractiveness manipulations, attention arousal or distraction manipulations, and violations of expectations have all been found effective as modification techniques.

SUGGESTED READING

Burgoon, Judee K., and Thomas J. Saine. *The Unspoken Dialogue*. Boston: Houghton Mifflin Co., 1978.

Hall, Edward T. *The Silent Language*. New York: Doubleday, 1959.

Knapp, Mark L. *Nonverbal Communication in Human Interaction*. 2nd Ed. New York: Holt, Rinehart and Winston, 1978.

Leathers, Dale G. *Nonverbal Communication Systems*. Boston: Allyn and Bacon, 1976.

Montagu, Ashley. *Touching: The Human Significance of Skin*. New York: Columbia University Press, 1971.

Rosenfeld, Lawrence B., and Jean M. Civikly. *With Words Unspoken*. New York: Holt, Rinehart and Winston, 1976.

From the Reading	Study Questions
Define the following terms. code proxemics territoriality personal space chronemics formal time informal time diffused point pattern displaced point pattern kinesics haptics paralanguage pitch voice quality vocal intensity fluency vocal segregates	1. What are the seven primary nonverbal codes? 2. How does territoriality differ from personal space? To what degree do humans have a need for territory and personal space? 3. What are some factors influencing personal space norms? How do people respond when those norms are violated? 4. How is time regarded in the American culture? What patterns do we follow? 5. What features of time can serve as message elements? 6. How does the kinesic code compare to other codes in terms of its communication potential? How many different kinesic features can be varied? 7. What are some factors influencing kinesic norms? 8. What role does physical appearance play as a communication code? What are some of the features that can be varied as message elements? 9. How important is touch to human development?

vocal characterizers
artifacts
displays
emblem
metamessage
relational message
quasi-courtship
regulation
self-presentation

What are some of the effects of touch deprivation?

10. How does the American culture view touch? How does this influence the use of touch as communication?

11. How does paralanguage compare to other codes in terms of communication potential? What are some of the features that can be varied as message elements?

12. In what ways do environmental features and objects function as communication? What dimensions are relevant as communication vehicles or influences?

13. What are symbolic displays? What is the difference between universal and culture-specific displays?

14. What are some examples of universal displays? Of culture-specific displays? Which nonverbal codes are most often used for these purposes?

15. What kinds of nonverbal messages qualify as metamessages? In what ways can verbal messages be complemented?

16. Which nonverbal codes function as relational messages? What are some examples of nonverbal cues that signal liking and attraction? Credibility? Status and power?

17. What are attitudinal messages? Give some examples.

18. What nonverbal codes play a role in structuring interaction? What are some ways in which the flow of conversation is controlled nonverbally?

19. How do nonverbal behaviors play a part in self-presentation? Are deception performances typically successful? Why or why not?

20. What are some nonverbal strategies that can be used to modify the learning, attitudes, and actions of others?

AN EXERCISE DESIGNED TO IDENTIFY PROXEMIC NORMS AND REACTIONS TO VIOLATIONS OF THOSE NORMS

The purpose of this exercise is to give you an opportunity to observe firsthand the proxemic norms in your immediate environment and the ways in which people respond to violations of those norms. Below are a series of suggested norms and norm violations that can be examined. Divide the class into small teams, and have each team select a different option. Those who observe the norms will simply select a number of places in which to make the observations and then make careful records of what occurs. Those who violate the norms will have to decide who is going to be the violator and how the violation is going to be carried out. After all observations have been made, compare the results in class.

Questions to consider: How similar are the results to what was reported in the text? What factors seemed to influence the normative distances adopted? Were there any special factors that influenced the types of responses people made to violations? What conclusions can be drawn about the role of proxemics as communication?

Suggestions for Observing Norms

1. Observe the most frequent seating pattern of pairs in a restaurant, bar, or library for same sex or mixed sex pairs.
2. Measure the distance that peers initially maintain from you in a standing conversation.
3. Observe the distance that strangers maintain when approached (sex, race, age, or status differences can be observed).
4. Measure (or estimate) the distance that students maintain from a faculty member.
5. Observe the seating pattern in a bus, restaurant, or bar and the order in which seats fill.
6. Observe differences in conversational distance for two different age, status, or ethnic groups.
7. Observe "territorial markers" (barriers, and so on) in a restaurant, library, dorm room, or office.

Suggestions for Violating Norms

1. Sit directly next to a person at an empty table in the library, restaurant, or bar (or in the seat next to a person in an empty theater or bus).
2. Face the people in an elevator (rather than the elevator door).
3. Stand closer than normal to a person in an empty elevator.
4. Take someone else's chair in a restaurant or the library.
5. Follow too closely behind persons walking in a building or on the street.
6. Invade the space of the same person (a stranger) for several successive days in a class.
7. Sit too close to strangers in a specific environment (for example, class).
8. Maintain a greater distance than normal from a close friend for several days.

AN EXERCISE DESIGNED TO ILLUSTRATE THE RELATIONSHIP OF BODY TYPE TO PERSONALITY

Before reading any further, complete the Self-description of Temperament on page 163. Complete it as accurately and honestly as you can.

Because the research suggests that body type and personality are strongly related, this is an opportunity for you to see how well your body type and personality match up.

1. Make a list of the answers you gave to the Self-description of Temperament.

2. Assign yourself a score on body type. This involves giving yourself three scores, ranging from 1 to 7, on the degrees to which your body has endomorphic, mesomorphic, and ectomorphic features. Suppose you are the tall, skinny, fragile type. Then you would score a 1 (the lowest score) on endomorphy, a 1 on mesomorphy, and a 7 (the highest score) on ectomorphy. If, instead, you are rather athletic but are getting a little heavy around the middle, you might assign yourself a score of 3/7/1 for endomorphy, mesomorphy, and ectomorphy, respectively. As a guideline, Muhammad Ali is roughly a 2/7/1, Abraham Lincoln was a 1/5/6, and Raquel Welch is close to a 1/7/2.

3. To compare your personality to that of others with your personality type, look at the list of adjectives following the Self-description of Temperament. Circle the ones you used to describe yourself. They should be approximately proportional under the three headings to the proportions you assigned yourself on body type. For example, if you scored yourself 1/4/4 on body type, you should have few adjectives in the endomorphic column and about an equal number in both the mesomorphic and ectomorphic columns. If you scored yourself a 7/1/1, almost all the adjectives should fall in the endomorphic column. If you have sometime in your life undergone a significant weight change, it is possible that the adjectives will partly fit your former body type.

Questions to Consider: How well did your body type match the personality characteristics? How well did the class match up as a whole? Do you think the personality traits are more a matter of stereotypes, or do they seem to have a real correspondence to body type? What explanations are possible for the way the results turned out in your class? How important do you think these personality associations of body type are to communication?

Self-description of Temperament

Instructions: Fill in each blank with a word from the suggested list following each statement. For any blank, three in each statement, you may select any word from the list of twelve immediately following. An exact word to fit you may not be in the list, but select the words that seem to fit *most closely* the way you are.

1. I feel most of the time ——————, —————, and —————.

calm	relaxed	complacent
anxious	confident	reticent
cheerful	tense	energetic
contented	impetuous	self-conscious

2. When I study or work, I seem to be —————, —————, and —————.

efficient	sluggish	precise
enthusiastic	competitive	determined

| reflective | leisurely | thoughtful |
| placid | meticulous | cooperative |

3. Socially I am _____, _____, and _____.

outgoing	considerate	argumentative
affable	awkward	shy
tolerant	affected	talkative
gentle-tempered	soft-tempered	hot-tempered

4. I am rather _____, _____, and _____.

active	forgiving	sympathetic
warm	courageous	serious
domineering	suspicious	softhearted
introspective	cool	enterprising

5. Other people consider me rather _____, _____, and _____.

generous	optimistic	sensitive
adventurous	affectionate	kind
withdrawn	reckless	cautious
dominant	detached	dependent

6. Underline *one* word out of three in each of the following lines that most closely describes the way you are.

   a. assertive, relaxed, tense
   b. hot-tempered, cool, warm
   c. withdrawn, sociable, active
   d. confident, tactful, kind
   e. dependent, dominant, detached
   f. enterprising, affable, anxious

Personality Traits Associated with Body Type

Endomorphic (soft, round, fat)	*Mesomorphic* (bony, muscular, athletic)	*Ectomorphic* (tall, thin, fragile)
dependent	dominant	detached
calm	cheerful	tense
relaxed	confident	anxious
complacent	energetic	reticent
contented	impetuous	self-conscious
sluggish	efficient	meticulous
placid	enthusiastic	reflective
leisurely	competitive	precise
cooperative	determined	thoughtful
affable	outgoing	considerate
tolerant	argumentative	shy
affected	talkative	awkward
warm	active	cool

forgiving	domineering	suspicious
sympathetic	courageous	introspective
softhearted	enterprising	serious
generous	adventurous	cautious
affectionate	reckless	tactful
kind	assertive	sensitive
sociable	optimistic	withdrawn
soft-tempered	hot-tempered	gentle-tempered

AN EXERCISE DESIGNED TO EXAMINE THE EMBLEMS USED IN THE AMERICAN CULTURE

This exercise is a good way to determine how much agreement exists on the meanings of various emblems in this culture and the number of emblems that can be used to express the same meaning. The exercise is a modified version of Charades.

A series of verbal statements follows, for which emblems exist in our culture. These should be copied on separate slips of paper, with at least two or three copies made of each. All the slips are then placed facedown in a box.

The class is then divided into two teams. The teams alternate having one member draw a verbal statement and encode that statement via an emblem for the team. The team has ten seconds to guess the correct emblem. A correct guess earns the team *one point*. If no correct guess is made within the time limit, the opposite team may have a member attempt the same emblem for an extra point before the team takes its regular turn.

Three rules

1. Once a verbal statement has been encoded with one emblem, a new emblem must be used the next time that statement is drawn. If the person taking the turn cannot think of a way to express the statement, the team forfeits the turn.
2. Within any one turn, only one emblem can be attempted. The encoder may take some time (within reason) to decide which gesture to use, but once he or she begins, the same behavior must be used during the ten-second guessing period. The behavior may be repeated as many times as the encoder chooses.
3. Each member of a team must take a turn before any member can take a second turn (that is, turns must rotate).

Verbal Equivalents of Emblems

Stop.	(S)he's dead.	I need a ride.	I don't know.
Go.	(S)he's finished.	Come forward.	(S)he's something else!
Yes.	I can't hear you.	Go away.	(S)he's crazy.
No.	Well done!	Not now.	Peace.

1.   (German Information Center)   2.   (Maury Englander)   3.   (Maury Englander)

5.   6.   (Maury Englander)

4.   (Maury Englander)   7.   (Maury Englander)

8.   (Maury Englander)   9.   (Maury Englander)   10.   (Maury Englander)

THE VARIABLES IN THE COMMUNICATION PROCESS

To the right.	Not acceptable.	Glad to meet you.	Victory.
To the left.	You stupid idiot!	That stinks!	Not good—not bad.
Hello.	(S)he killed himself.	I don't trust him (her).	How stupid of me.
Good-bye.	I'm fed up.	Not bad! (or Great!)	I can't remember.
Up.	Down.	I don't believe that.	Time's up.
Here's what I think of you (insult).		I'm warning you.	I refuse to listen.

AN EXERCISE DESIGNED TO EXAMINE EMOTIONAL DISPLAYS

Some emotional displays are easy to interpret; others are more difficult and lead to high variability in interpretation among receivers. See how well you can match the pictures on the opposite page to the list of emotions below. Each number can only be used once. There are more emotions listed than pictures.

Questions to consider: Which photographs were most easy to judge? Most difficult? How did your answers compare to those of the rest of the class? Would you consider yourself a highly accurate decoder of emotions? In what ways could the judging of these emotions be made easier?

Anger	_____	Surprise	_____
Wrath	_____	Fear	_____
Indignation	_____	Loneliness	_____
Happiness	_____	Contentment	_____
Joy	_____	Love	_____
Sadness	_____	Sympathy	_____
Despair	_____	Disgust	_____
Resentment	_____	Frustration	_____
Boredom	_____	Irritation	_____
Pain	_____	Confusion	_____
Amusement	_____	Disbelief	_____

AN EXERCISE DESIGNED TO ILLUSTRATE HOW STATUS RELATIONSHIPS ARE COMMUNICATED

Following is a series of situations involving different messages and different status relationships. Choose pairs of students to role play these situations (or create other situations); then discuss after each the vocalic, spatial, and kinesic cues that were used, whether the dramatization was realistic, whether it was appropriate, and what might have resulted had either person altered specific behaviors.

1. A child (A) must tell his/her father (B) that he/she was caught cheating on a test and that the father must see the school principal.
2. A woman (A) tells her husband (B) that they are going to have a baby.

3. An employee (A) has come to see the boss (B) about taking a week off work during a very busy time.
4. A student (A) visits a classmate (B) to encourage him/her to join a fraternity/sorority.
5. A businessman (A) tells his secretary (B) that she has made a serious error.
6. An adult (A) expresses sympathy to a close friend (B) who has had a death in the family.
7. A teen-age girl (A) tells another teen-age girl (B) about a very exciting date.
8. A young man (A) tells another young man (B) about his intentions to marry.
9. A female superintendent (A) chastises a male teacher (B) for lying about his absences from school.
10. A stockbroker (A) informs his client (B) that his stocks have seriously dropped in value.

AN EXERCISE DESIGNED TO TEST THE EFFECTS OF NONVERBAL BEHAVIORS ON THE ACTIONS OF OTHERS

This is an experiment that must be conducted outside of class. An entire class can participate, or any smaller number of students can conduct it. It is designed to see how various nonverbal behaviors affect helping responses.

1. Divide up into pairs. Each member of a pair will take turns serving as an observer and an experimenter.
2. Decide what kind of request for help you want to make. One that works well is to approach people outside some public place and ask them if they can give you change for a quarter or a quarter in return for your change. Another one is to ask people to write down directions to some place (the place must require complicated directions). If you have several people conducting the experiment, you may want to try several different kinds of requests.
3. Choose which nonverbal behaviors you want to examine. For each behavior, you will need two conditions, one in which the behavior of interest is present and one in which it is not. Some possible comparisons are the following:
Sloppy dress to neat dress.
Attractive appearance (including makeup, hair, and clothing) to unattractive appearance.
Staring to not staring (the stare would precede the request).
Smiling to no smiling.
Unpleasant voice to pleasant voice.
Touch to no touch (touch would take the form of touching the arm or elbow).
Direct eye contact to averted eye contact.
Again, the more people working on the experiment, the more nonverbal behaviors can be tested.

4. Carefully plan your procedures. Determine where you are going to conduct the experiment (for example, outside a grocery store or department store), what times of day you are going to do it, how you are actually going to engage in the nonverbal behavior, where the observer is going to stand, what you are going to count as a helping versus a nonhelping response, and how you are going to record the responses.
5. When you actually conduct the experiment, you should take turns being the experimenter and being the observer. Each person should also do both forms of the nonverbal behavior. If it is dress, for example, one person may be dressed formally and the other informally, and both take turns approaching subjects during a given time period. Then reverse the dress roles, and repeat the procedures during a second time period.
6. While conducting the experiment, the observer should watch the experimenter to see that the behavior is uniform each time. For instance, if the behavior being tested is eye contact, then the amount of smiling should be constant across all situations. The observer can also keep the record of the responses and take note of any unexpected reactions.
7. Things to consider when analyzing the data: how much of a difference was there between the two experimental conditions? Did reactions differ from experimenter to experimenter? Were there any sex differences in responses? If more than one nonverbal behavior was tested or more than one type of request used, what differences across nonverbal cues and types of request were there? In what ways could the methods used be improved or modified to produce different results?

POSSIBLE NONVERBAL EXERCISES

1. The next time you are engaged in a conversation, move as far as you can from the other person. Observe and later record the other person's reaction to your behavior. In what ways did the other person indicate his or her discomfort?
2. Recall a personal incident in which you used time to convey a message to someone or one in which another person used time to convey a message to you. Compare the experiences with other members of the class.
3. Choose a newscaster whom you consider to be an excellent speaker. What vocal elements contribute to his or her excellence? Contrast the newscaster's vocal qualities with those of a person whom you consider to be a poor speaker.
4. During the course of a week, observe several of your professors to determine how they use kinesics to emphasize, clarify, or contradict their verbal messages. Record two examples of each of these functions of kinesic behavior; then compare the kinesic patterns of your professors.

5. For a week keep a record of how many times you touch others and they touch you. In what way do sex differences contribute to the amount and type of touching behavior?
6. During a conversation, stare directly at the eyes of the other person for a long time. What reaction does your behavior produce in the other person?
7. Select someone with whom you are friendly, and observe that person's living quarters. What furnishings, objects, or features of the environment reveal something about your friend's personality?

Section 2 COMMUNICATION CONTEXTS

In the first section of this book, we attempted to elaborate on the nature of human communication and identify some of the important variables in that process. We now turn to the task of analyzing the contexts in which communication occurs. It is obvious that many of the important verbal, nonverbal, and human variables that we have already discussed operate similarly across the many contexts. For example, we would expect people to wish to be considered credible whether they were communicating with one or many. We would expect a certain amount of analysis of the receiver or the audience to be present in any communication situation. There are, however, important differences in the kind and amount of communication in one context as compared with another. The situation prescribes rules of interaction, imposes constraints, and provides opportunities for differing kinds of communication transactions to occur.

This section will examine contextual variables that tend to mediate human communication. We will provide the defining characteristics of each communication context and discuss different kinds of communication patterns that are both likely and possible in each situation. Finally, we will examine the ways people might operate more effectively in each context.

Chapter 6
COMMUNICATING WITH ANOTHER

In the first edition of this textbook, the use of the term *interpersonal communication* was regularly avoided. At that time we were concerned with how "loosely" people were using the concept of communicating interpersonally with others. To some people, interpersonal communication was *any* communication that occurred between two people in a nonmediated way. Usually, people in face-to-face communication situations were said to be communicating interpersonally regardless of the nature of that communication. However, it was less clear whether two close friends talking on the telephone would be engaged in interpersonal communication or not. Two lovers writing very intimate letters would probably not be engaged in interpersonal communication because they were not interacting face-to-face. Some suggested that interpersonal communication must be distinguished from public speaking and small-group communication because it was "different." The clear specification of the differences was not all that apparent to us at the time. Others suggested that only communication that expressed warmth, openness, and support of another should be classified as interpersonal in nature. Finally, we were perplexed by a commonly accepted notion that any communication "between people" was interpersonal. This meant to us that everything and nothing could be called interpersonal communication. Therefore, we opted not to use the term very much in the first edition, but an interesting thing happened. When the first edition of this text was reviewed by communication instructors at a variety of schools, they continually referred to the chapter on dyadic communication as the "interpersonal communication chapter." Therefore, we decided to present some of our assumptions about interpersonal and noninterpersonal communication before proceeding with our discussion of communication among dyads.

The first thing that we should say is that, from our perspective, all dyadic communication is not necessarily interpersonal in nature. Because people are interacting on a face-to-face basis with only one other individual, it does not mean, in our opinion, that they have an interpersonal relationship with that person, nor does it mean that their communication is interpersonal. We will suggest later in this chapter that the dyad is a highly likely context for the development of interpersonal communication. Here we are suggesting that two people merely talking does not qualify as interpersonal communication. The second assumption we make is that interpersonal communication can occur in a variety of contexts. Some communication in small groups is interpersonal in nature, and some is not. Some communication in public speaking contexts should definitely be called interpersonal. In other words, the defining characteristics of interpersonal communication are not context-bound; rather, it is the nature of the communication that makes it interpersonal or noninterpersonal.

Defining Interpersonal Communication

There are several approaches that we can use to define interpersonal communication as separate and distinct from other forms of communication. It has been our assumption throughout this textbook that communication is a means of controlling one's environment. We have also suggested that people use communication strategically to manipulate situations and gain control for a variety of purposes. To gain control of one's environment so as to realize certain physical, economic, or social rewards from it has been called the basic function of all communication.[1] If people are to use communication to gain control, they must constantly make predictions about people. We must learn to anticipate how we will react to other people and, importantly, how other people will react to us and to our communication. It is then possible to begin to offer a definition of interpersonal communication based on the kinds of predictions we use in interactions with others.

PREDICTIONS AS DEFINING CHARACTERISTICS

Gerald Miller and Mark Steinberg have made some very important and insightful contributions to our understanding of human communication by offering a new way to conceptualize interpersonal communication.[2] They share our assumption that people strategically select communication strategies that will maximize their probability of being successful in their communication attempt. Moreover, they suggest that "when people communicate,

[1]G. R. Miller and M. Steinberg, *Between People—A New Analysis of Interpersonal Communication* (Palo Alto, Calif.: Science Research Associates, 1975), pp. 33–58.
[2]Miller and Steinberg, 1975, have provided this conceptualization, and it has influenced our thinking in this entire section. We gratefully acknowledge our intellectual debt to them.

they make predictions about the effects, or outcomes, of their communication behavior."[3] The importance of their contributions to our understanding of interpersonal communication lies in their identification of three different levels of analysis used in making predictions.

Cultural-level data. Culture has been thought of as the collection of regularities, norms, social institutions, habits, accepted practices, and a variety of other ideas and artifacts shared by some collection of people. There have been a variety of attempts by anthropologists and sociologists to set the boundaries of cultures and study the unique and identifying characteristics of cultures. Sometimes cultures are defined in terms of geographical location, ethnic and religious patterns, or a variety of other ways. We usually suggest that people belong to the same cultural grouping when they share common methods of behaving and seem to hold similar attitudes and values. Cultures then hold power over their members even if that power is not so obvious to the members of that specific culture.

We develop norms of what is appropriate and inappropriate conduct based upon culturally dictated ideas. Our values of what is good and bad are influenced by the culture in which we live. An American in Spain often finds himself dining alone in a restaurant because he has arrived at what he considers to be an appropriate time to have dinner. The Spanish, on the other hand, tend to have their evening meal at ten or eleven. Some societies give their elderly a great deal of power to con-

[3]G. R. Miller and M. Steinberg, 1975, p. 7.

trol family affairs, whereas other cultures tend to ignore the old. There are norms of conduct that give regularities and, therefore, predictability to the behaviors of people that share the same cultural heritage. We can predict with some level of confidence that people will behave in certain ways because from childhood they have been taught appropriate modes of conduct as determined by their culture.

We also know that cultural heritage can be a significant predictor of how people will communicate with each other. In the chapter on nonverbal communication, we discussed many of the regularities that exist in this culture while also comparing and contrasting those norms with the norms of other cultures. There are also verbal behaviors such as choice and use of language that are culturally determined. Obviously, there are cultural groups within any given society, and behaviors vary across those large collections of people. What all of this says is that *we* communicate in relatively predictable ways, and people can usually make predictions about how we will behave based upon cultural-level data. Moreover, we can make predictions both about how other people will communicate with us and how they will respond to our communication on the basis of the same kind of data.

However, there are some obvious problems associated with basing predictions about other people solely on cultural-level data that have probably not escaped the reader. The first possible problem is that one is often wrong when cultural-level data form the only basis of prediction. When dealing with any specific individual, we must be careful as to just how much we will trust cultural-level predictions. All Orientals are not inscrutable; they are individuals with differing personalities. A former secretary of agriculture, Earl Butz, paid the price for sharing cultural-level predictions about the wants and desires of black Americans in a much-publicized racial slur. Mexican-Americans have recently objected to advertisements that project the image of this cultural group as larcenous and lazy. Often very offensive and incorrect stereotypes are used to describe cultural groups. We, on a very personal level, deplore such stereotypes. However, we are not willing to go so far as to say that all stereotypes are unuseful. To the extent that we are forced to make judgments about large groups of individuals about which we do not have individual data, we are in some part forced to gather cultural-level data and base our communication strategies on those data. In later chapters, we will discuss how people speaking to large groups or people making decisions in the mass media must focus on cultural-level data if they are to make predictions at all. Such predictions assist us, but we must never forget that to err in the individual case is not only possible but likely.

Obviously, when we base our communication strategies strictly on cultural-level data, we are not communicating interpersonally. We are in the process of generalizing from data based on collections of individuals while not discriminating and adapting our communication to the specific individuals, or people with whom we are communicating. So this first level of analysis does not meet what we would call the minimum standards to be called communication at an interpersonal level.

Sociological-level data. We also make predictions about other people based upon data at a less broad-based level than we just discussed. Miller and Steinberg suggest that this next level of analysis is based upon judgments we make about people just by knowing what groups they belong to. Most of us have heard judgments being made about people because they were fraternity or sorority members, members of a civic or social club, or members in some group that we are willing to judge. President Carter's Attorney General Bell faced some difficulty with Senate approval of his appointment because of his membership in clubs that had discriminatory membership policies. The inference was being made that Judge Bell must also hold racist views if he is a member of a group known to have such beliefs. In the end, Griffin Bell resigned those memberships rather than have the Senate and the public make such sociological predictions.

Although the groups previously discussed represent social collections in which membership is usually, if not always, voluntary, there are other group memberships over which people have little control. One cannot choose to belong to a group called the elderly, middle-aged, or young. However, whether we belong to groups by choice or not, membership can be used as a basis of making predictions about behavior. We make predictions based upon such affiliation because we generalize from knowing the attributes of a few group members to inferences about all members of the group. If you "know" a small number of fraternity or sorority members, you might be able to make inferences and predictions about the kinds of people who would be likely to join such a social group. This level of analysis is like basing predictions about people on cultural-level data in that we generalize from knowing something about small numbers of people to making statements about larger collections of individuals.

As is the case with cultural-level data, there are some inherent problems associated with making predictions on sociological-level data. All members of any given group will most definitely differ in ways that could not be explained by some group label. Basing predictions on a sociological-level analysis in order to try to predict how students will respond to a basic communication group is difficult. Obviously, some readers will not be amused by what we think is funny. Whenever we make predictions based upon group characteristics, we have error built into that prediction. We will likely not be accurate about a number or maybe even all of the individuals in that group. In other words, there may be no one individual in the group who actually possesses all of the characteristics we ascribe to people who belong to the group.

However, we must at times resort to sociological-level data because we have no other options. As we are writing this text, we are making predictions about what the group of people labeled college students will find acceptable and useful. Obviously, we know only a few representatives of the entire class called students; so we must generalize what we know about the few to make predictions about the many. However, we are reasonably sure that all of the material will not be useful to every reader. Moreover, it is possible that

not one single student will be impressed by *everything* we have to say. In other words, we will make errors about what the group of people we are writing for will find interesting and useful. We really do not have much choice but to guide our communication behavior on some sort of generalization about what we know about students. We would never have the ability to collect data on the individual needs of all of our potential readers; so we do the best we can to maximize positive response. In a later chapter, we suggest that the public speaker must rely on sociological-level data to make predictions about how specific groups might respond to his or her speech. One cannot predict on the basis of data from every member of the audience in those situations. Obviously, the mass media make attempts to gather information on the kinds of groupings that expose themselves to particular media so that communication can be targeted at the interests of those groups. Be cautious when trying to apply sociological-level data to any specific individual, for applying it to an individual may result in error. However, do not discount the value of making reasoned predictions based upon what you know of group membership. It at times represents the best, if not the only, data available for your use.

As you can probably guess, we would not be willing to call communication based only on sociological-level data interpersonal in nature. You are still generalizing from knowledge of a few and planning strategies based upon that collective judgment. Strategies are not necessarily being adapted to the people directly involved in the communication transaction.

Obviously, discriminating among different individuals and relying on those discriminations to plan communication strategies require another level of analysis.

Psychological-level data. The level of analysis of psychological-level data requires "knowing" the person or people involved in the communication transaction. Although we may have a great deal of cultural and sociological data, we might not be very comfortable about predicting what specific behaviors a person we are talking with might exhibit. Let us think of how one goes about gaining psychological-level data. Much of our communication behavior in initial encounters is designed to provide us with more information about the person or people with whom we are talking. As we will discuss in detail in the later chapter on developing social relationships, much of what goes on in the first few minutes of interaction between strangers is some kind of information sharing about the participants. Obviously, the information shared cannot usually be called intimate revelations, but we do usually give people some information about ourselves and seek the same in return from them.

Obviously, as we interact with people over time, we gain more psychological-level data about that person. *However, we think that it is important to stress that time spent in interacting alone will not insure the development of interpersonal relationships.* We can all think of situations in which we have spent a great deal of time interacting with other people and still felt that we had little data about them as individuals. Some college professors practice the deliberate strategy of attempting to limit the amount of psychological data that students may obtain about them. They feel—and we are not suggesting this is necessarily wrong—that students should not be allowed to be on personal terms with them, or they will be less effective as professionals. Others have less strong feelings and provide a great deal of psychological-level data because they are equally convinced that this strategy makes them more effective teachers.

In most communication transactions, we are using some combination of cultural, sociological, and psychological data. Obviously, as we develop relationships with other people, we tend to use more and more psychological data. When we discriminate the reactions of specific individuals and predict how they will react to us and, in turn, how we will react to them, we are strategically communicating in an interpersonal manner. In other words, our communication strategies are based upon our knowledge of individual differences of the people we are interacting with. We are now actively discriminating one person from another on the basis of the persons' unique characteristics rather than generalizing from our knowledge of only a few.

There are some problems that we should briefly mention in deciding whether communication is interpersonal or not based upon these levels of prediction. First, the two or more participants in any transaction may not be operating at the same level of prediction. For example, many skilled manipulators will do everything possible to get on an interpersonal basis with another, but use every possible communication strategy to deny the other person any psychological data about themselves. In that way, they can find out what will work with the other person and what will fail. They can then adapt their communication to that person's needs. Encyclopedia salesmen, used-car dealers, and panhandlers are notorious for having mastered these kinds of communication skills.

Sometimes, too, people will be in situations in which they are making predictions about others based on data different from what others use to judge them. We recently encouraged counselors to make sure that they maintained a *mixed-level* relationship with their clients. Obviously, clients are there to discuss their problems, not learn of the problems of the therapist.[4] To the extent that people in the counseling relationship establish interpersonal relationships with the therapist, it may be dysfunctional in terms of solving their problems. Many people become very dependent on the friendship of the counselor and lose track of the reasons that they sought counseling, which was to correct a problem or change behaviors. In other communication transactions a person might deal with people who are very unwilling to provide psychological data about themselves, whereas the person in question might feel very willing and comfortable with that kind of communication. That again will lead to a mixed-level relationship. At the close of this present chapter we will discuss some of the benefits and risks of such self-disclosure, but suf-

fice it to say at this point that people differ in their willingness to provide and use psychological-level data.

In other communication contexts, it is quite possible that you will have to interact with several people simultaneously. In those cases you might find yourself engaging in conversations that varied across levels of prediction because you were trying to adapt to several people at once. Some people in a small-group communication situation may be on an interpersonal level with you whereas others may have provided you with mostly sociological-level data. Still others may have provided you with little except for cultural identification. Obviously, the communication strategies will have to be adapted to recognize those different levels between people. All in all, this way of viewing interpersonal communication is of real value to us, for it forces us to use rather precise ways of determining whether communication can be classified as interpersonal. There are some other perspectives that we wish to explore in defining interpersonal communication.

LEVELS OF KNOWING AS INTERPERSONAL COMMUNICATION

We might accept that the more we know about other people, the more interpersonal our communication is likely to be with them. Certainly, that is the assumption that we have operated with in the preceding discussion involving our levels of prediction scheme. However, the question of what it means to know someone can be useful in our attempt to define interpersonal communication more systematically. The preceding material would

[4]D. Vaughn and M. Burgoon, "Interpersonal Communication in the Therapeutic Setting: Mariah or Messiah?" in *Explorations in Interpersonal Communication,* ed. G. R. Miller (Beverly Hills, Calif.: Sage Publications, 1976), pp. 255–275.

suggest that we know someone when we can adapt our communication strategies to account for individual differences. We know someone when we can predict how we will respond to that person's communication and when we know how he or she will react to our communication. We also think we know a person when we can predict how the person will behave in different situations. All of those conceptions of knowing revolve around prediction. In one sense, *to know is to be able to predict*.

Although we have no particular quarrel with that conception of knowing, we think that there are other indicants of knowing some other person. We can predict that people will behave in certain ways and be both reliable and accurate. However, we still might have trouble explaining *why* they do as they do. Just being able to predict does not mean that one can explain the behaviors of others. When we know people well enough to be able to explain the underlying causes of their reactions to our communication and why they choose to communicate as they do, we are more able to adapt our communication to be effective with them. If we understand what appears to motivate them, we can be persuasive, informative, develop close social relationships, or fulfill whatever function of communication we so desire. The authors have a colleague whom they find very predictable in his reactions to any administrative edict, suggestion, or policy. We know that he will react in a predictably negative way. However, even after spending a great deal of time communicating with the man, the authors still do not have a clear understanding of the explanation for these behaviors. Even though they can predict in advance what the reaction will be, they are not prepared to adapt their communi-

cation in such a way as to cope with the problem. However, they might have a higher probability of successfully dealing with this situation if they understood why these reactions were forthcoming.

Just as the main purpose of science is to explain and predict, so is the purpose of interpersonal communication. Let us again say that just being able to predict a person's behavior does not mean that one can explain it. However, *if one can explain behavior, then one should be able to predict it*. Therefore, we would suggest that communication that attempts to seek reasons and to understand why people communicate as they do is communication aimed at establishing a *more* interpersonal relationship.

ROLES AS A DEFINITION OF INTERPERSONAL COMMUNICATION

A final useful device for analyzing communication transactions in terms of their interpersonal nature is to look at the roles participants play. Roles are the patterns of behavior and kinds of communication strategies adopted that are seen as appropriate to a given social situation. We obviously play a variety of roles in our daily lives, and those roles change from interaction to interaction and from situation to situation.

In communication transactions that we would tend to call noninterpersonal, *prescribed roles* are dominant. Prescribed roles are usually determined by norms and rules that are external to the communication transaction. There is also a tendency for role prescriptions to *limit* the kinds of behaviors that are acceptable in any given situation. There are role prescriptions that are culturally determined, and there are roles that are socially defined in terms of group pressure. Perhaps an example of role prescriptions would help. We definitely, as a culture, have role prescriptions that determine how we expect the president of the United States to behave. Simply stated, there are patterns of behavior that are acceptable, and there are other patterns that are seen as inappropriate. For example, President Carter carries his own luggage. People have learned to accept this as a personal preference rather than a failure to carry out his prescribed role. However, at first, concern was expressed by many that he was somehow debasing the office by not conforming to prescriptions of appropriate behavior. Almost every position, occupation, or activity carries with it some prescribed role behaviors.

We also have prescribed role behaviors that help dictate what kinds of communication behaviors are appropriate across situations. For years, we have prescribed how a "lady" or a "gentleman" must act if they are to continue to be called by those terms. We also have some fairly rigid prescriptions about how one goes about making acquaintances or initiating interaction. We do not disclose too much too soon about ourselves, nor do we press other people to become instantly intimate in their communication behavior. These prescribed role behaviors are not usually negotiated by the people involved in the communication transaction. That is what we mean when we say that prescribed roles are an *external locus of control* or are imposed by outside factors. They tend to limit the kinds of communication that we will engage in. We focus our efforts on avoiding inappropriate forms of communication.

This external locus of control can be imposed by cultural considerations, as in the case of society's determining the kinds of behavior appropriate for President Carter. We have a variety of protocols that determine what is appropriate and when it is appropriate. However, not all role prescriptions are culturally determined. The groups that we belong to also impose specific sanctions that give us notions of proper communication roles. Social organizations have very prescriptive sanctions about how members are to behave. You are probably aware of organizations, clubs, and other groups that spend considerable efforts dictating how members *should* behave. As professors, we know that the university and the community offer several prescriptions on appropriate behavior that we consciously and unconsciously carry with us. Those role prescriptions often affect how we will communicate with our students and colleagues.

In initial interactions, we rely on prescriptions to assist us in initiating conversation, gathering information, and controlling interactions. Prescriptions of how people ought to behave give us a certain level of predictability. We make those predictions and "follow the rules" in many cases without even thinking about what the rules are or why they exist. However, as we gain more information about the people we communicate with, prescribed roles tend to be less dominant in controlling interactions. *Negotiated roles* take on added importance, and at least a part of the behaviors is directly controlled by the participants in the communication transactions. Some externally imposed rules of conduct are replaced by roles agreed to or negotiated as appropriate by the participants. Sometimes these negotiated roles are explicitly agreed to, and in other cases a more implicit bargain is reached on what constitutes appropriate communication behavior.

We talked about Carter's violation of the prescribed role of presidents not carrying their own luggage. He was no doubt, at that time, attempting to negotiate with the public a new role for himself and for the presidency. He at least has claimed to want to do away with prescriptive behaviors that give the notion of an "imperial presidency." By not following certain prescriptions, he was attempting a negotiation. Most relationships that exist over any reasonable length of time evolve some pattern of negotiated roles between and among the participants. We then develop expectancies based more on what has been negotiated than on externally imposed rules. The expected roles then become an *internal locus of control* whereby people can then negotiate rules or conduct and make decisions about the appropriateness of communication on the basis of whatever considerations they think important. People can still negotiate roles based upon what one or more of them think is culturally appropriate. A more powerful person in the transaction can use coercive means to force negotiated roles to be accepted by another person or other people. To the extent that participation in the negotiation or ability to influence outcomes is based on power and not subject to change, the relationships tend to be less interpersonal. Negotiated roles can either restrict or expand the range of allowable behaviors in a relationship. For example, an authoritarian manager can negotiate much more restrictive rules than the organization as a whole prescribes; this, in effect, limits the acceptable behavior. In other kinds of situations, people may agree to ignore certain prescriptions and

actually allow more freedom for participants. Finally, just the presence of a negotiated set of rules does not mean that the relationship is or will be interpersonal in nature. Just because we have negotiated with our students to call us by our first names instead of the prescribed "doctor" does not mean that we are on an interpersonal basis with them. All we are saying is that negotiated roles differ from prescribed roles in that expectations of communication behavior are based upon internal rather than external controls.

People who wish to establish interpersonal communication with others can use negotiated roles as a method of reaching that level. As we gain more psychological-level data and gain more ability to explain why people communicate as they do, we have the ability to change our views of role conduct. We tend to rely more and more on negotiated roles, and prescriptive roles become less important. However, the interpersonal relationship must also be one that allows people to play a variety of roles. It must also establish a consensus concerning the need for the introduction of new roles as the relationship progresses. For example, one can accept the fact that a wife plays the roles of professional, lover, mother, intelligent and independent person, and a number of others simultaneously. Obviously, in our society not everyone accepts that women should play all of those roles. Many people revert to what have to be strictly prescribed roles about the "woman's place being in the kitchen." However, many are willing to negotiate new roles of marriage and/or male-female roles. That is a necessary second step. The final step is one of accepting and understanding *enacted roles*. When we learn of the complexity of

The prescribed role of "woman's place being in the kitchen" has given way to negotiated roles as women seek personal fulfillment in the modern world. (Photograph: German Information Center)

people, we understand that they are capable of playing a variety of roles. We come to understand that they behave very differently *on the basis of what they see as appropriate for them.* Our judgments of them need not be dictated by what is prescribed or what we have negotiated in a direct sense with them. We accept their complexity, but more importantly we understand why they play specific roles. A significant characteristic of the interpersonal communication relationship is the facility with which new role behaviors can be added to a relationship. Actually, rules

about rules are generated by the people involved in the communication relationship. If people understand that one of the rules of the relationship is to be considerate of others' feelings and to do others no harm, they can feel free to add new roles and explore communication behaviors that do not violate the basic relationship. They are more free to experiment and test new communication behaviors.

Our basis of judgment becomes enacted roles. We are less concerned with rules of conduct that control and more concerned with people developing roles that are complex and varied but satisfying. Our concerns are much less directed toward satisfying either external or internal concerns than with directly determined rules. Our attention is on understanding. So we would claim that most initial interactions rely on prescribed roles. As people communicate, they negotiate roles that are acceptable and that may or may not conform to external prescriptions. People on an interpersonal level are more concerned with understanding enacted roles.

A DEVELOPMENTAL VIEW OF INTERPERSONAL COMMUNICATION

It is our hope that the extended discussion of factors that can be used to judge whether interpersonal communication is part of a relationship will lead to a useful model. We have obviously placed some very severe constraints on what we are willling to call interpersonal communication, and several things should be obvious from what we have said:

1. Interpersonal communication is a developmental process. Most initial encounters would not qualify as

what we would call interpersonal in nature. It takes time and effort to develop a communication style with people that allows development of an interpersonal relationship.

2. We do not believe that the channel of communication is an important determinant of whether communication is interpersonal or not. People can obviously communicate orally, nonverbally, in a written form, or through a variety of mediated forms in an interpersonal manner.

3. Interpersonal communication as we have defined it occurs rather infrequently and with only a few people for most of us. We have neither the time nor the energy to make sure that all of our relationships with others reach this level.

4. Part of what determines whether a relationship is interpersonal in nature is the level of prediction that we use to devise communication strategies. Cultural and sociological data can be very useful in making predictions, and we use these data constantly. However, strategies based on psychological-level data are called interpersonal communication.

5. When one generalizes from the few to the many to devise strategies, that is noninterpersonal communication. Discrimination of strategies to fit individuals is a characteristic of interpersonal communication.

6. The basis that people use to enact and evaluate the appropriateness of roles also distinguishes interpersonal communication from noninterpersonal communication. Prescribed roles that limit acceptable

behaviors are noninterpersonal in nature. Negotiated roles can either limit behavior or expand freedom. The existence of negotiated roles does not necessarily insure that the relationship will be interpersonal. However, the process of negotiation can be used to develop an interpersonal relationship. When people accept and understand the enacted roles of people, they are behaving in an interpersonal manner. Such acceptance expands the potential communication behaviors that are acceptable in the relationship.

7. The level of knowing also determines whether a relationship is interpersonal or not. We start an initial communication relationship, knowing very little. As we gain information, we can make predictions about how we will behave and how others will react. However, just because we can accurately predict behavior does not mean that we can explain why people behave as they do. Interpersonal communication is characterized by being able to explain.

All of the preceding summary can be visually represented in the model of Interpersonal Communication presented in Fig. 6.1. We have attempted to model the process in such a way as to incorporate the important variables we have discussed. Perhaps other things should be added to this model as one considers communication in the various contexts. It should also be said that the reader may better understand how models aid our thinking if they recognize that we developed this model prior to writing this chapter. The visualization of the model along with its assistance in focusing, directing, and sharpening our thinking helped us better understand the process of interpersonal communication as we struggled to come to grips with it. It may not have been as apparent as we would like to have made it earlier in the book just how important models can be to the person interested in communication. It at least helped us in our attempt to understand and explain a complex process.

FORM AND FUNCTION IN INTERPERSONAL COMMUNICATION

Although we have spent considerable time discussing the attributes of interpersonal communication, it is important that we briefly examine the arenas in which people use interpersonal communication. Moreover, we wish to discuss the functions that interpersonal approaches might serve. The remainder of this book is devoted to an analysis of the communication contexts and functions. In this section, we examine dyadic, small-group, public, and mass communication. Obviously, these contexts vary in complexity, and we will be devoting a great deal of effort to analyzing how these contexts differ and how they are similar. However, it is important for you to understand that the conceptualization we have offered of interpersonal communication is *potentially important in planning communication strategies in each of these contexts*. We emphatically reject the notion that interpersonal communication is limited to only certain contexts.

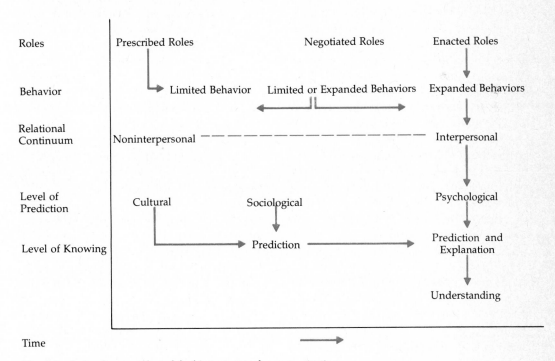

Fig. 6.1 A developmental model of interpersonal communication.

We hope that you consider in each of the contexts—as we discuss the important defining characteristics, crucial variables, and strategies of communication—how our notions of communicating interpersonally might be used. We obviously have to make decisions as to how much energy we are willing to devote to gathering data, making predictions, and offering explanations based upon psychological-level data. It is obviously easier to collect such data and make adaptations to only one other person; the dyadic communication situation is one in which communicating at the interpersonal level is most probable. Friends, spouses, co-workers, and others who spend great amounts of time communicating one-to-one are the most likely people to establish close interpersonal relationships.

The dyadic situation is not the only context in which interpersonal communication can occur. In small-group situations, people do gain tremendous amounts of data about other group members. In task-oriented groups that exist for long periods of time, it is quite likely that several interpersonal relationships will develop. Using interpersonal strategies in the small-group context can lead to several positive outcomes. To the extent that people can accurately predict and explain the communication behavior of others, it is possible that better decisions can be made in efficient ways. It is likely that each and every member of a given group will not choose to develop interpersonal relationships with everyone else; in fact, it might not even be possible to do so. However, one should consider just how much effort he or she is willing to give to using the suggested techniques of establishing interpersonal communication.

As more people get involved in the communication transaction, it is obviously more difficult to use interpersonal strategies. Many public speakers do not see the audience as individuals but imagine some collective group as an entity. In most public speaking situations, speakers have to rely on cultural- and sociological-level data and adapt strategies based upon that kind of generalization. However, when a speaker can use interpersonal strategies with even a very small segment of the audience, it can greatly enhance his or her effectiveness. Often speakers will direct their attention to one person in the audience whom they know and communicate directly with that person for often very brief periods. Demonstrating interpersonal skills even in the public speaking situation can increase the audience's estimation of the person's credibility and effectiveness. President Kennedy was very adept at "personalizing" his press conferences by bantering with specific individuals in the press corps. He could obviously predict and probably explain the behaviors of specific reporters because he had taken the time and made the effort to collect data on them. In 1977, President Carter seemed to be at least "breaking even" in his encounters with the press, and the public at large was responding favorably.

People responsible for making decisions in the mass communication context can rarely make decisions or adapt strategies in ways that we suggested were appropriate for interpersonal communication. By definition, these media institutions serve a large audience, and most of the programming decisions are based upon notions of what most of the people desire and need. It would be stretching a point to suggest that much of any interpersonal communication occurs through mass channels. However, *there are people who certainly perceive that mass media are on an interpersonal basis with them.* Soap opera characters and their problems become real, newscasters become the most trusted people in the culture, and great amounts of trust are placed in media institutions. Columns in newspapers designed to help people solve their problems, advice from Dear Abby and Ann Landers, and call-in radio shows are but a few examples of how the media have attempted to adapt to individual needs. However, few of the needs that can be solved by direct interaction can really be expected to be satisfied by the media. It is fair to suggest that most media institutions are acutely aware that individual differences exist in audience members and are aware that decisions made on cultural- and sociological-level data are error-prone. Such an awareness is important, and we will discuss how media adapt strategies to compensate for that error. At this point, it might be interesting at least to speculate how media institutions might change to become more interpersonal in the not-too-distant future. As we develop interactive cable systems that reach offices and homes, we will have to face new problems. How will interpersonal relationships change as the media become more and more pervasive? Can the media adapt to satisfy the conditions we suggested for calling communication interpersonal?

As we said earlier in this chapter, we think that interpersonal communication can serve a variety of functions. Other writers have taken a more limited view of the operation of interpersonal communication. One recent article suggested that the only function that interpersonal communication served was the development of self-concept.[5] Other people have suggested that interpersonal communication is basically a helping relationship.[6] People who are on an interpersonal basis are seen as supportive, warm, and open. To say the least, these positions are different from ours. It should be obvious that there is great potential for control of other human beings when you can explain and predict their behavior. It is, at least for us, frightening to think of the potential control that people have over other people when they possess a great deal of psychological data about them. However, control can be used for good or bad ends. When we are operating in a situation in which each participant is on an interpersonal level, *reciprocal control* is present. Although the other person or people can predict and explain your behavior and thereby have control over you, it is possible for you to also exert control because of your knowledge of them. Interpersonal communication strategies can be used to serve each of the functions discussed in the final section of this text. Control can be exercised to gain compliance and persuade others. Those people we know intimately are likely targets for communication designed to convert them to beliefs and attitudes we desire them to hold. In a similar way, we can use interpersonal strategies to manage conflicts. If we can explain the source of conflict, we have completed the first step in resolving or managing it. We also know that strategies can be used to make friends

[5]D. P. Cushman and R. T. Craig, "Communication System: Interpersonal Implications" in *Explorations in Interpersonal Communication*, ed. G. R. Miller (Beverly Hills, Calif.: Sage Publications, 1976), pp. 37–58.

[6]R. W. Pace and R. R. Boren, *The Human Transaction* (Glenview, Ill.: Scott, Foresman and Company, 1973), pp. 309–315.

and develop effective social relationships. Interpersonal communication strategies allow us to control our environment and affords us control over other people. However, the other side of the coin must be stressed. Interpersonal strategies can allow us to resist the control of others. More will be said of this later, but suffice it to say that interpersonal communication serves us in many ways and that service is rendered in a variety of contexts.

We suggest that you use the following format in examining the contexts that we will discuss in this section. The following questions might provide useful insights in how you wish to adapt your communication strategies:

1. How might this context afford possibilities for using cultural-, sociological-, and psychological-level data?
2. How would interpersonal approaches in these contexts differ from noninterpersonal approaches?
3. What approaches are the most likely to be adopted in each context?
4. How would the outcomes differ if an interpersonal or noninterpersonal approach were adopted?
5. What is the probability of success of an interpersonal approach?
6. Is it really even worth the effort involved to attempt an interpersonal approach in this situation? What are the costs? What are the benefits?

The Nature of Dyadic Communication

There are several factors that make dyadic communication somewhat unique as compared to the small-group, public speaking, or mass communication contexts that we discuss in this section. The first of those factors is *degree of perceived privacy*. When people have total privacy, they are generally able to give free reign to their thoughts and emotions. Their thinking is spontaneous and largely uncontrolled by outside forces. As one would expect, this interior monologue is quite different from what we have called communication throughout this book. As soon as another person arrives on the scene, people normally modify their thoughts and responses to accommodate the demands of dyadic communication. It is not surprising that any one-to-one interaction is going to be modified either by the actual presence of a third person (or group of people) or by the implication that anything one says in the dyadic context will eventually be revealed to others.

In special instances, both these threats to privacy are precluded. For example, in the confessional booth, the church member assumes that disclosures to the priest will not be overheard and also that the priest will not relate them to anyone else. This physical degree of perceived privacy —based on both actual physical isolation and the sacrosanct status of confession— contribute to a proportionately high degree of honesty.

Sometimes two people share a degree of privacy even in the midst of a large group. The "barriers" between those in the one-to-one interaction and the rest of the crowd are noise level and other interfering stimuli. At a party or similar social gathering, the noise level is usually high enough so that any message exchanged between a dyad in close proximity will probably be insulated from those outside the conversation. Furthermore, at such gatherings there are usually a number of distracting stimuli that reduce the chance of being overheard. Nevertheless, the content of the communication is usually less personal than it might be in a situation in which privacy was assured. The uniqueness of the dyadic context is that the participants can take actions to create private communication. They can simply arrange to have privacy by being alone, closing an office door, or simply not communicating until they are alone. Such private communication is usually not possible in other contexts.

In other dyadic situations, privacy is assured, even though others may be present. It is based on trust in the discretion of those who overhear the conversation or in a specific (though sometimes unspoken) code of behavior that governs those who are present. For example, the privacy of interactions between diplomats and statesmen is strictly maintained until it has been determined that public disclosure will not deter the progress of negotiations. A similar code of ethics has protected the interactions of all high-ranking government officials. In mass communication contexts, the privacy of communication between source and reporter has, at least until recently, received governmental sanction. However, devious invasions of protected one-to-one interactions, the most flagrant example of which is "bugging," have more or less made a joke of perceived privacy—and have made part-time paranoiacs of some public officials and private citizens.

When privacy is desired, the dyadic communication context offers an opportunity for such communication. Communication that could not or would not be carried on in other contexts can be reserved for those situations in which only one other is present. This perceived privacy is linked to a second characteristic of dyadic communication, which is the *potential for intimacy*. Much of the structure of our society is built upon intimacy between dyads. The institution of marriage is but one dyadic relationship in which intimacy is maintained for long periods of time. People have a sense of immediacy and involvement when involved in face-to-face interactions with one other person that is seldom perceived in other contexts. As they gain more psychological-level data and establish interpersonal relationships, the probability of intimate communication developing is increased. Obviously, not all dyadic relationships will take on the characteristics of interpersonal relationships. But when such relationships do develop, there is a sense of perceived intimacy with the other person that changes the nature of the communication.

Communication behaviors that occur within dyads that are intimate and usually private are sometimes considered inappropriate in any other context. For example, the display of affection between two people might be very natural and appropriate in the dyadic context. However, the "public display of affection" that is likely the same as a private display with at least one other person present is less probably to be considered appropriate conduct.

Even if the dyadic communication situation happens to be one that is not completely private or an extremely intimate one, there are condiitions that make communication unique in comparison to other contexts. First, there is the possibility of *utilizing feedback.* In general, feedback is more available in the dyad than in any other communication situation. Feedback contributes to and sustains the dynamic nature of face-to-face interaction. Because this feedback is usually more specific than in other situations, it enables two people to "zero in" on confusion or misunderstandings and guides them in modifying or redefining their messages until each other's meanings are better understood. Feedback in the dyadic context is also specifically directed at one person. Often, in other contexts, the intended target of feedback is ambiguous. A person in such a context may finally get to participate and vent anger or express disagreement with what one person has said; however, the group members may not be aware at all to whom that feedback is being directed. Often comments are intentionally vague so as not to offend any one person. In other situations, there is less opportunity to provide immediate and direct feedback. Often a public speaker is not sure if feedback is directed at him or her or if the person is reacting to other audience members, the surroundings, or the situation. Because, in the dyad, we only have two people involved, targets of feedback are usually not ambiguous. However, as there are numerous types of dyadic situations, it would be unwise to treat the level of feedback as a constant.

In face-to-face interaction, the two people are provided with both verbal and nonverbal feedback, so that it is *comparatively* easy to make a variety of judgments about the other person's emotions, attitudes, and comprehension *while the conversation is in progress; the feedback is immediate.* If the nonverbal and verbal feedback are conflicting, a person can adapt the communication to determine which reflects the other person's true feelings. Immediate feedback can indicate lack of comprehension and/or disagreement, and a person can change tactics in midstream.

The visual element is missing in one-to-one communication over the telephone, but this form of dyadic interaction may have distinct advantages. It is obvious that using the phone is often simpler than having to meet, and most of us use this mediated form of dyadic communication simply for the sake of efficiency. Moreover, some people find that over the phone, with no visual information involved, they can be more intimate in their conversations or more easily sustain a train of thought. Many friends stay on the telephone for hours, yet find that when they meet, they have nothing to say to each other. Perhaps in "live" confrontation some people feel too shy to express themselves, or perhaps the personality or physical bearing of one person overshadows or intimidates the other member of the dyad. Furthermore, superfluous visual stimuli may distract from the verbal interaction.

Both audio and many visual elements are missing in written interactions, but, like the telephone, this form of communication has special advantages. Some people simply find it easier to express themselves in writing. Distracting stimuli can be reduced until one is left with unencumbered thoughts, and there is no pressure to "think on one's feet" or keep up with a conversation. People will often say things in writing that they would never consider saying in face-to-face interaction. Often people use written memos to protect themselves and maintain a record of dyadic communication that would not be present in an interaction. The main disadvantages of writing are lack of spontaneity in adapting the communication and lack of immediate feedback. Though a writer may intend one meaning in tone and structure of a message, a receiver often reads in very different meanings; the delay in feedback may simply enhance the misunderstanding and further obstruct effective communication.

Dyadic communication is more *spontaneous* in most cases than communication occurring in other contexts. People easily adapt and change their communication styles and adjust content to meet the needs of the situation. There is usually *more direct participation* in the interaction in this context than in any other. In a small-group communication situation, one or more members of the group can simply not participate and in many cases may not even be involved. By definition, the public speaking and mass communication contexts limit the ability of all people involved to participate in the communication. It is more difficult for one part of a dyad not to be involved and active in some sort of dialogue; it is, of course, possible, but that kind of interaction is likely to be short-lived. People are *coactive, and the situation is transactional.* By *coactive* is meant the fact that people are simultaneously acting as both sources and receivers of communication. They are sending messages and giving and receiving during the communication event. They are changing and being changed as things progress. Because people are coactive, there is not a tendency to develop specialized communication roles as in other contexts. We rarely find designated leaders, information givers-only, or a variety of other specialized roles that are often found in small groups. Seldom do we have someone just

listening and someone speaking as in the public communication context. The specialized nature of communicators in the mass media cannot even be compared to communication in a dyadic conversation. In the dyad, people play a variety of roles that are ever-changing.

The dyadic communication context *can be a prime place for collecting and using psychological-level data.* In other situations we are often forced to rely on conceptions of a "group or audience" and generalize from our knowledge of few to a notion of the many. *If* we choose, we can use the dyadic communication situation to collect data on the other person and adapt our communication strategy to discriminate that person from others. As we have repeatedly stressed, the dyad does not insure that this process will occur. However, if people desire to adopt communication strategies based upon psychological-level data, this context affords a prime opportunity.

The dyad is often characterized by *less formality*, and a wider variety of behaviors are often acceptable. Language choice and usage are less constrained; and we tend to use more slang, colloquialisms, in-words, and other language-related variables in these situations. Rules of interaction tend to be negotiated very quickly by the participants, and there is a tendency to rely less on external loci of control. We experiment, test, and take risks in evaluating plans, objectives, and courses of actions that we might be unwilling to do in other situations. Most of us probably tend to feel less threatened and anxious about communicating in this context than in other more formal situations.[7]

One final consideration seems in order

[7]We will fully discuss communication anxiety and public speaking in Chapter 8.

Communicating with Another

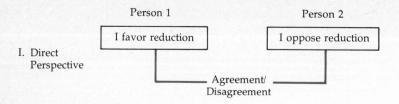

I. Direct
Perspective

Fig. 6.2   Assessing agreement in a dyad.

in discussing the characteristics of dyadic communication. We think that William Wilmot made an insightful comment when he suggested that the dyad cannot rely on "majority rule" and appeal to others to put pressure on the other person to accept one's own point of view.[8] This, of course, happens in other contexts, and the communication can be centered more on achieving that workable majority than on arriving at consensus. The other person in a dyad is all you have. Ways other than pressure are often mandated because each person possesses the power to "influence a decision by withdrawal or veto." Such a withdrawal ends the relationship. There is no other context in which losing just one member can have such an impact. Group members come and go; substitutes can be found for public speakers; mass media personalities constantly change. The dyad has no such organizational life that exists beyond the willingness of *each* member of the pair to continue.

Interpersonal Orientations in the Dyad

It is useful to analyze communication in the dyadic context from several different perspectives. First, *content* is being communicated. We express our feelings about ideas, objects, and issues. We desire people to believe as we believe, and we attempt to share information. We also communicate in ways designed to determine the *beliefs* of the other person in the dyad. We also tend to seek information about the other person's *perceptions and beliefs* about ourselves and our ideas.[9]

The content approach can be used to determine if people in a dyad agree or disagree on the topic being discussed. Much communication is designed to share with the other person what our beliefs and attitudes are on a range of issues. People evaluate objects and ideas differently, and this difference can range from very slight to very great. For example, two people might want to determine how the other feels about reduced criminal penalties for possession of certain controlled substances. Their first task is *assessment of agreement* (see Fig. 6.2.)

The feelings that each person has about the topic of communication is called the *direct perspective*. Much communication, especially in initial stages of interaction, is aimed at determining what direct perspective on a range of issues each partici-

[8]W. W. Wilmot, *Dyadic Communication: A Transactional Perspective* (Reading, Mass.: Addison-Wesley, 1975), pp. 16–17.

[9]See·R. D. Laing, H. Phillipson, and A. R. Lee, *Interpersonal Perception* (Baltimore: Perennial Library, 1966) for a complete discussion of these levels of analysis.

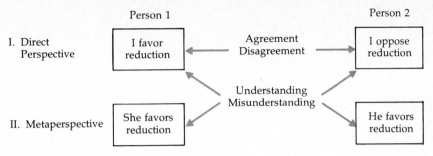

Fig. 6.3 Assessment of agreement/disagreement.

pant holds. People assess the degree to which agreement and disagreement are present in the dyad and often plan communication strategies aimed at changing the other person.

The belief approach is aimed at assessing *understanding and misunderstanding* in the dyad. It adds the metaperspective, which is our perception of what the other person feels or believes about the content of communication (see Fig. 6.3).

In this example we have disagreement on the direct perspective; Persons 1 and 2 do not have similar beliefs. However, there is a case of *both* understanding and misunderstanding present in this dyad. He misunderstands her position on reduction of penalties. His metaperspective is not at all consistent with her direct perspective. But her metaperspective is consistent with his direct perspective. In other words, she understands him on this issue. As one can see, there can either be understanding or misunderstanding regardless of whether people agree or disagree on issues. It is possible wrongly to ignore this important level of analysis in dyadic communication. If Person 1 just assumes that he is correct about the attitudes of the second person, he will, of course, commit errors. One common error in communication is to assume that we know a great deal about the other people's attitudes and beliefs. There is also a tendency for us to believe that people we know are more similar to us than they really are.[10] The person wishing to be more effective in dyadic communication will strive to assess just what the other person thinks and feels. Moreover, one should constantly remember that it is important to attempt to gain understanding even if one is not in agreement with the direct perspectives of the other person. Misunderstanding of the other's position can only cause problems.

The third approach, perceptions and beliefs about ourselves and our ideas, is concerned with *realization or failure of realization*. This approach is concerned with an analysis of what you think the other person thinks you think.

In our example (see Fig. 6.4) there is both a realization and a failure of realization. In this case, he should have a feeling of being understood (realization). Her situation is different in that she has evidence that he does not understand her direct perspective (failure of realization). He fa-

[10]See, for example, D. Byrne and B. Blaylock, "Similarity and Assumed Similarity Between Husbands and Wives," *Journal of Abnormal and Social Psychology*, 67 (1963), pp. 636–640.

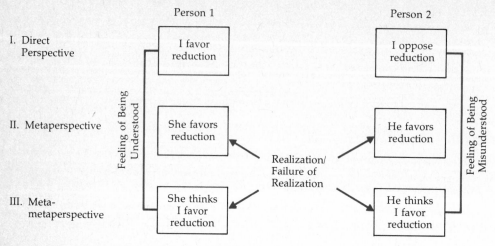

Fig. 6.4 Assessing realization or failure of realization.

vors reduction, and it is his belief that she thinks he favors reduction. Therefore, his meta-metaperspective is consistent with his direct perspective. It is likely that he feels satisfied that at least he has communicated effectively enough so that she understands what he believes.

She cannot help but feel misunderstood, and she is likely to be very frustrated with this communication transaction. She actually opposes reducing penalties, but he thinks she favors reduction. If they have spent time communicating and this occurs, she is likely to be less than satisfied with this communication outcome. Perhaps it would help to summarize just what happens in terms of understanding at each level.

1. *Understanding.* Understanding happens when the metaperspective of one person corresponds with the direct perspective of the other individual. This happens when the person correctly identifies your beliefs (see Fig. 6.5).
2. *Being Understood.* Being understood occurs when the meta-metaperspective of one individual is the same as the metaperspective of the other person. Person 1 understands what Person 2 thinks (see Fig. 6.6).
3. *The Feeling of Being Understood.* One has the feeling of being understood when one's own meta-metaperspective corresponds with his or her own direct perspective (see Fig. 6.7).

Fig. 6.5

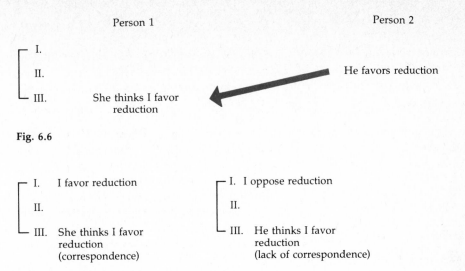

Person 1

Person 2

I.

II.

III.   She thinks I favor
            reduction

He favors reduction

Fig. 6.6

I.   I favor reduction

II.

III.   She thinks I favor
       reduction
       (correspondence)

I.   I oppose reduction

II.

III.   He thinks I favor
       reduction
       (lack of correspondence)

Fig. 6.7

There is some satisfaction involved in feeling that one understands another person and in feeling that one has been understood.[11] When there is a lack of correspondence between levels in the dyad, communication strategies are likely to be used to gain understanding. As we have said, people will spend great efforts to insure agreement at the first level. However, there are times when people also just agree to disagree. This probably comes when people clearly understand the position of the other and accept that it is not worth the effort required to change it.

It is interesting to pose the question of whether people prefer to understand or be understood. As we have pointed out, those are two very separate outcomes of dyadic communication. People who are constantly trying to make themselves understood often come away from the communication transaction with little understanding of the other person. We also

[11]R. D. Laing, H. Phillipson and A. R. Lee, 1966.

assume that people do not understand us when in fact they disagree with us. We have had students who were unhappy with their grades come and argue forcefully for a change in our evaluations. After listening to their appeals, we have often felt that we just could not agree with their position. More than once, a student has responded that we just did not understand. Actually, we did understand rather clearly the case that was being advanced. However, the student was so involved with *being understood* that he or she failed to *understand* what we were saying in response. There is a difference between agreeing and disagreeing, understanding and being understood.

Clearly, some people may not understand each other or really care to invest much effort in reaching understanding. People also have more understanding concerning some issues than on others. It is possible, too, as in the example we used, for one person in the dyad to have a great deal of understanding whereas the other

Communicating with Another

one completely misunderstands everything that is happening.

This model of analysis can be valuable for locating communication problems between two people. It can suggest the proper levels to center attention on, and it can locate sources of misunderstanding. Perhaps it would be useful to suggest some questions that can be asked about dyadic communication:

1. Do we agree or disagree on the content of what we are talking about?
2. Is a communication strategy going to be adopted that attempts to produce agreement, or are we going to agree to disagree?
3. Do I understand the position that the other person holds? How sure am I that I understand? What am I basing this on?
4. Does the other person understand how I feel about the issue? What has the other person done to indicate understanding/misunderstanding.
5. Is my communication strategy more designed to make sure I am being understood, or am I investing as much energy in understanding?
6. Does the other person believe that I understand her/him?

The answers to these questions must dictate communication strategy. There is little use in stressing agreement/disagreement if lack of understanding is the problem. You can use feedback to indicate that you do not *understand* the other person, or you can come right to the point and suggest to the other person that you do not believe that *you are being understood*. Directing the communication to the proper level can lead to correspondence between levels of understanding.

Interpersonal Control in the Dyad

Control of the situation in dyadic communication is always an issue. Communication will be developed to establish rules of control, and this will affect all of the behavior of the participants in dyadic communication. In any situation, there should be no question of whether control exists or not; the appropriate questions are who controls what and under what conditions. People develop patterns of interaction that help in answering those questions. We will discuss three such relationships: symmetrical, complementary, and parallel.[12]

SYMMETRICAL RELATIONSHIPS

Symmetrical relationships are based upon notions of equality. In symmetrical relationships, both participants believe that they have an equal right to define the relationship. Both individuals believe that they are free to exercise control, and the options available to one are available to the other. In the symmetrical relationships, *the differences between the participants are minimized.*[13]

Most of us would probably suggest that symmetrical relationships are, in fact, very desirable states. We at least pay homage to the notion of equality, and many of us do not like to think in terms of control, dominance, and submission. However, the question of dominance is not necessarily settled even if both people agree that their relationship is symmetrical. The communication between the two might

[12]Symmetrical and complementary relationships are discussed in a very cogent manner in P. Watzlawick, J. H. Beavin and D. D. Jackson, *Pragmatics of Human Communication* (New York: W. W. Norton, 1967).
[13]Ibid., pp. 67–70.

become very competitive. Dominance does not become an ignored issue; people simply compete for it.[14] We have all been in conversations in which one participant will mention something that he or she has done only to have the other person immediately come back with a report of an equally (or more) impressive accomplishment that he or she has obtained. These kinds of communication patterns attempting to maintain equality rigidly and to resist dominance by one participant can escalate into real conflict in the dyad.

Although one might think that symmetrical relationships in which both people agreed on the right of equal control would be stable and enduring, the opposite sometimes tends to be the case. These relationships are often very unstable because everything has to be negotiated. If a person cannot take an action without negotiating the right to take that action, problems are bound to erupt. In a marriage situation, problems that threaten the existence of the relationship often occur over each spouse's demand to be equal. To negotiate in every instance who has the right to do what, to whom, and how often would be tedious and require great amounts of patience.

As you can see, the symmetrical relationship is just not workable in many contexts. The inefficiency associated with negotiating every action could cripple work pairs. A co-worker would probably not wish to have to discuss every action with a partner. When the objective of the pair is some sort of efficient productivity, a completely symmetical relationship will probably prove unsatisfactory.

In the last section, we discussed the seeking of understanding and attempts to be understood. The symmetrical relationship is one in which understanding may be inhibited. Much of the communication activity is *not* centered on the understanding processes. Neither person is really as concerned with interpreting what the other is saying. Little effort is directed either at understanding the direct perspective or in assessing metaperspectives. *We tend to look at how the other person is viewing our equality* and not at what is being understood. Communication aimed at defining status is recurrent, and hostility is frequent. When two people with large egos communicate, attempts to maintain symmetry are assured. When Mark Twain first met the painter James Whistler, Twain approached one of the paintings in progress and nearly touched it with his gloved hand. Whistler exclaimed, "For the love of God, be careful, Clemens! You don't seem to realize that the paint is fresh." "That's all right," responded Twain, "I have my gloves on." Symmetry was maintained.

COMPLEMENTARY RELATIONSHIPS

In complementary relationships, differences between the two communicators are maximized. One person is usually dominant, and one person is primarily submissive in the relationship. *The behavior of one must be mutually complementary to the other.* When one person attempts to initiate plans, the other person is accepting. Many superior-subordinate relationships are complementary. The parent-child relationship is complementary in that to be a

[14]D. D. Jackson, "Family Interaction, Family Homeostasis and Some Implications for Conjoint Family Psychotherapy" in *Individual and Familial Dynamics*, ed. J. H. Masserman (New York: Grune and Stratton, 1959), pp. 122–141.

parent, a person must have a child. They are mutually complementary, and one usually initiates action and is in charge. Some marital relationships are rigidly complementary with one spouse being in charge and the other willingly following. One partner occupies the superior, primary, or "one-up" position, whereas the other is subordinate, secondary, or "one-down."[15]

This brief description makes this relationship sound very undesirable and may lead us to reject this kind of communication pattern prematurely. Complementary relationships are not necessarily dysfunctional. This kind of arrangement is often harmonious, and coordination of activities is easier. People in submissive positions can often learn a great deal by listening to the dominant person and doing as that person says. This is especially true if the dominant person has control based upon his or her expert power. In such cases, we would probably not desire to be on an equal basis with the person possessing immense expertise. Our relationships with our doctors are usually complementary. We do not seek medical advice (usually) to assert our equality to the physician. We willingly follow orders and do as we are told. The bases of power that we discussed earlier in the book all provide reasons why people accept complementary relationships. The power to reward or punish, expertise, and many other factors combine to make us willing followers at times. We also accept complementary relationships because they can be efficient. Sometimes it just isn't worth hassling

about power to control; it is easier to do as expected.

The marriage situation is an interesting arena to examine complementary relationships. Many people would suggest that traditional values would hold that the male is the master of the house, sets agendas, and controls activities. The female is seen as submissive and one-down, and she reacts rather than makes suggestions. Some very interesting research has turned up some intriguing findings.[16] Only about 25 percent of the couples reported complementary relationships with the male being dominant. Over 50 percent of the couples reported reversing the traditional concept with the female being dominant. The females in these relationships controlled the conversations, whereas the male tended to smooth over rough spots. Millar suggests that the dominating-husband/submissive-wife relationships may be a myth that needs to be dispelled.

Rigidly complementary relationships are not without their problems. If the same person always controls and dictates, there is a real danger in the relationships becoming stagnant. When one person is dominant in all cases, the other does not grow and develop new competencies. The dominant person feels that he or she must provide protection in exchange for compliance.[17] People tend to become resentful of doing things because they perceive no choice. Actually *both* people can get trapped into roles that they really do not wish to play. If anything happens to the

[15]P. Watzlawick, J. H. Beavin, and D. D. Jackson, 1967, pp. 67–70.

[16]F. E. Millar, "A Transactional Analysis of Marital Communication," Ph.D. diss., Michigan State University, 1973.

[17]T. E. Mills, *The Sociology of Small Groups* (Englewood Cliffs, N.J.: Prentice-Hall, 1967), p. 123.

relationship, the people involved can actually be incompetent to carry on. A person used to being dominated totally may have little ability to make decisions. Perhaps one solution to this problem would be to consider roles that are neither rigidly symmetrical nor complementary.

PARALLEL RELATIONSHIPS

A pattern of communication that might prove satisfactory in a variety of dyadic encounters has been labeled parallelism.[18] Instead of holding to rigidly symmetrical relationships that can promote competition and/or hostility or relying just on complementary relationships that produce stagnation and inhibit growth, people can develop a more flexible style.

A parallel relationship allows each participant to have some areas of control, and each person plays the dominant or one-up role at times and then plays the submissive or one-down role at other times. On certain kinds of decisions, they can agree to equality and concede that each has the right to control, suggest, and direct. There is actually a crossover of symmetrical and complementary roles. This kind of relationship often occurs in informal dyads in which frequent topic shifts lead to different people taking control. In many cases, the nature of the topic and whether there is agreement or disagreement will determine who happens to be controlling the communication at any one time. Even though there is a pattern of interchangeable complementary relationships, there

[18]See, W. J. Lederer and D. D. Jackson, *The Mirages of Marriage* (New York: W. W. Norton, 1968), p. 169.

can be areas in which people concede the right to determine direction mutually, and the communication can instantly become symmetrical.

In more enduring relationships such as marriage, friendship, and family dyads, this pattern can be very workable. A husband and wife may concede different areas of control based upon mutual interest and competence. They might also agree to rotate tasks that neither particularly enjoys. They then form a series of complementary decision-making units. However, they can still agree that they must be symmetrical when it comes to major decisions like taking a new job or relocating to a new geographical region. The communication is not based upon appeals to doing things in the same way "because they have always been done that way" or believing that things "should be the way they have been." The flexible pattern allows changes and can prevent some of the problems we discussed earlier with rigidly complementary relationships.

The parallel structure also allows the dyad to avoid the constant competition associated with rigidly symmetrical roles. They do not have to "win" on every issue and can accept that understanding and negotiation can be as important to the long-run health of a relationship as anything else. There is a tendency for such dyads to avoid all-or-nothing statements or absolute demands. This does not mean that each person must be *totally flexible*. A person might still define limits of what is tolerable but do so in a way that does not threaten the other. There is usually a great deal of emphasis placed on metaperspectives. It is incumbent on each to understand the feelings of the other person because those feelings become the basis for negotiating appropriate behaviors. When the power base of each individual is roughly equivalent and when the association is voluntary, a parallel relationship is likely to be beneficial. There can be acceptance of the fact that they will at times be one-up or one-down. They are also aware of the kinds of situations in which they will find it necessary to be one-across. The nature of the dyad and the reasons for maintaining the relationship will take precedence over rigidity as a method of definition.

Self-disclosure

Feedback is helpful in any communication situation only if the people involved know the way to use it, and they can know the way to use it only if they gain understanding of themselves and others. Dyadic interaction probably offers the best opportunity for increasing such understanding. Casual interactions (ones that are unplanned or nonpurposive or that at least seem so to the people involved) provide an outlet for the natural and strong desire to share ideas, feelings, and problems, and they create an ambience favorable to the growth of interpersonal trust and mutual receptivity. However, as we also noted earlier, there are no guarantees implicit in the design of dyadic interaction. Consciously or unconsciously, people may work against intimate communication and disclosing the self in even the most private dyadic communication. We think it is important to examine self-disclosure in dyadic communication. That examination will include an examination of the kinds of communication that can be

appropriately called self-disclosive as well as a discussion of the effects of disclosive communication on the dyad. Finally, we will point out some of the risks and benefits of self-disclosure.

IMPRESSION MANAGEMENT AND SELF-DISCLOSING BEHAVIOR

People from a variety of academic disciplines have become interested in self-disclosure. One of the problems that they have faced is defining just what kind of communication is disclosive. Unfortunately, many of the definitions have proved to be less than useful. For example, one definition suggests that "self-disclosure is any *message* about the self that a person communicates to another."[19] We think this definition is so inclusive that it is of limited use. Any communication that intentionally or unintentionally gives another person information about oneself would be called self-disclosure. All verbal and nonverbal messages could then be called self-disclosive. We believe that the distinction that Culbert offers is very valuable in our analysis:

> Self disclosure refers to an individual's explicitly communicating to one or more persons information that he believes these others would be unlikely to acquire unless he himself discloses it."[20]

Culbert distinguishes self-disclosure from self-description in that he claims self-description is self-data that an individual

[19]L. R. Wheeless and J. Grotz, "Conceptualization and Measurement of Self Disclosure," *Human Communication Research,* 2, (1976), p. 338.
[20]S. A. Culbert, *Interpersonal Process of Self Disclosure: It Takes Two to See One* (Washington, D. C.: NTL Institute for Applied Behavioral Science, 1967), p. 160.

feels comfortable in describing or revealing to *most* others. There are certain things about ourselves that we would be willing under most circumstances to reveal to most people. That would not be properly called self-disclosure. There are two critical variables present in disclosive communication: the data are revealed *intentionally*, and these data can only be obtained if the person wishes to reveal them.

There are other distinctions that are also important for us to consider. It is quite possible to reveal a great deal of information about oneself that may be very manipulative in intent. Some people manipulate their lives in order to achieve popularity, power, and success; they often treat themselves as objects by masquerading in roles that are designed to benefit them in some way. The selective revealing of data about oneself in order to persuade, coerce, or in other ways benefit the communicator is *impression management*. There are many communication situations in which impression management is an effective and workable technique, and we do not intend to offer indictments of this form of communication; all of us work very hard to manage impressions. In many persuasion attempts, it is important to reveal personal characteristics to reach desired ends. Many of us carefully manage impressions in social situations. This is as it should be. Miller and Steinberg distinguish between "genuine" and "apparent" self-disclosure in a similar way.[21] Genuine self-disclosure is a private act as evidenced by reluctance to share the information with most other persons; when it is revealed, it usually strengthens a bond between two people and leads to increased trust.[22] On the other hand, apparent self-disclosure is a tactic used to share information that is not really private. There is some risk involved with genuine self-disclosure, whereas the only risk involved in apparent self-disclosure is that the manipulative strategy will not prove successful. We have devoted several later chapters to impression management, for we all desire to manage impressions for a variety of communication functions.

Self-disclosure is intentional communication that reveals the self to another person as one sees oneself. The data are usually considered very private and would not be revealed to most people. It is information about oneself that could only come from the person in question. The purpose of that communication is one of sharing rather than managing how another views oneself. People usually feel some risk involved in genuinely self-disclosing.

THE EFFECTS OF SELF-DISCLOSURE ON THE DISCLOSER

One of the people who has done a great deal of work in self-disclosure, Sidney Jourard, has made great claims about the positive effects of self-disclosure on the person doing the revealing. He claims that an accurate portrayal of the self to others is a prerequisite for self-knowledge. Jourard also claims that "no man can come to know himself except as an outcome of disclosing himself to another person."[23] He believes, too, that a person must actively and consistently work at expressing his or

[21]G. R. Miller and M. Steinberg, 1975, pp. 309–323.

[22]Ibid., p. 324.

[23]S. Jourard, *The Transparent Self* (New York: Van Nostrand, 1971), p. 6.

her thoughts and feelings in order to strengthen and sustain self-identity or to avoid self-alienation. He further says:

> Through my self-disclosure, I let others know my soul. They can know it, really know it, only as I make it known. In fact, I am beginning to suspect that I can't even know *my own soul* except as I disclose it. I suspect that I will know myself "for real" at the exact moment that I have succeeded in making it known through my disclosure to another person.[24]

Many people claim that when one is isolated from meaningful interactions with others, he or she can become prey to delusions and fantasies about himself or herself in relation to the rest of the world. This results because knowledge is fed by a single and certainly not infallible source —one's own perceptions. Through interactions with others, a person can become aware of the multifaceted and multivalued nature of reality; one can then modify self-images so that they more truly correspond to real (not imagined) capacities and limitations.

Jourard has even claimed that the ability to self-disclosure is an indication of psychological health. He claims that remaining mentally healthy is dependent on the intimacy of one's communication. He further states that "every maladjusted person is a person who has not made himself known to another human being and in consequence does not know himself."[25] These are some very far-reaching claims and deserve to be examined.

Frankly, we have a hard time accepting everything that is said about the value of self-disclosure. We think that though it may be true that *others will not come to know you unless you know yourself*, we are not convinced that everyone must be highly self-disclosive if he or she is to come to know himself or herself. Introspection, self-reflection, and a variety of other techniques can be used to come to know oneself at least a bit better. People also learn about themselves by participating in a variety of communication contexts. It seems to us that a skilled communicator can gain a great deal of information about the self by simply analyzing his or her behavior and considering how people respond. We come to know ourselves by how people react to us. However, that knowledge is gained in a variety of situations.

Self-disclosure can benefit many people, but we are unwilling, on the basis of our examination of the research data and our experiences in living, to suggest that it is a universal panacea for all human problems. Some people have little desire to reveal much about themselves. Those people seem to function quite well in a variety of situations, and we would not be willing to call them "maladjusted." There are a number of people who are comfortable with what they are and what they are not and find very little need to communicate that to others. Other people express little desire to "know" themselves any better, and we are quite content to let them make that decision.

Other people do express a need to be very intimate with others and are willing and able to disclose a variety of private things. There is no doubt that these people feel that they are growing and learning from such communication. That is obviously a healthy condition for them. To the extent that people benefit from self-

[24]Ibid., p. 184.
[25]Ibid., p. 32.

disclosive acts, we condone that kind of communication. Most of us do develop relationships in which we are willing to disclose private information. In some interesting research, Gilbert found that with highly intimate information, the target of the disclosure (whom you are communicating with) is an important determinant of willingness to self-disclose.[26] The likelihood of disclosing specific intimate items was 31 percent for strangers, 42 percent for acquaintances, 64 percent for parents, 89 percent for friends, and 91 percent for spouses. She asked people whether they would be willing to disclose certain things (see the instructional module at the end of this chapter) to specific targets. Interestingly, there is a "privateness" factor that indicates areas wherein we just are unwilling to disclose some things. This obviously varies from person to person, but it would be interesting for you to see how willing you are to disclose intimate information to different people. Obviously, as information becomes less intimate, willingness to disclose becomes higher with all targets. Differential willingness to disclose is an important factor. Judgments about the overall worth of self-disclosive communication must be seen as highly dependent on the needs it serves for each individual.

THE EFFECTS OF SELF-DISCLOSURE ON THE DYAD

Although the effects of disclosive communication on the communicator are highly variable, there are some rather consistent effects that such communication will have on the dyad.

Appropriateness. At times, self-disclosure in a dyad might seem very appropriate or suitable and serve to heighten satisfaction by the participants. Increased self-disclosure can lead to increased interpersonal attraction but that findings must be mediated by the context. We have often suffered on airplanes with the misfortune of being seated next to a person who desired to reveal the most intimate details that we did not care to hear. Often, we have been "put off" by this situation and desired some way to escape. Culbert found that people report a preference for low-disclosing people in stranger-to-stranger dyads.[27] Obviously, in conditions of initial interaction, immediate, intimate self-disclosure can be seen as very inappropriate and even be considered an indication of maladjustment. We do have norms of communication conduct that work against self-disclosure early in a relationship.

Another measure of appropriateness has to be the relevance of the communication to the situation. Even if people have been engaged in dyadic communication for a long period of time, self-disclosure is not always relevant. The person who must constantly self-disclose regardless of the content of communication quickly becomes a bore. Sometimes we engage in dyadic communication only to solve a problem or complete a task. Disclosing of one's feelings, if constant, may prove to be a barrier to that function. A supervisor who continually tells you how hard he or

[26]S. J. Gilbert, "Empirical and Theoretical Extensions of Self-Disclosure" in *Explorations in Interpersonal Communication*, ed. G. R. Miller (Beverly Hills, Calif.: Sage Publishers, 1976), pp. 197–214.

[27]S. A. Culbert, "Trainer Self-Disclosure and Member Growth in T-Groups," *Journal of Applied Behavioral Science*, 4 (1968), pp. 47–73.

she works and how oppressive his or her job is can become an interpersonal burden you do not wish to bear. Termination of the relationship or withdrawal from future interactions is possible.

Valence. Many people have just assumed that to self-disclose is to reveal negative things about the self.[28] It probably does not make much sense to conceptualize the process in this way, for at times we are much more reluctant to disclose positive things about us than we are willing to be self-deprecating. The valence (positive or negative) aspects of self-disclosure can produce different outcomes in the dyad. There is research to indicate that people generally prefer others who positively self-disclose. We prefer to communicate with people who are positive about themselves.[29] This is especially true in initial interactions.[30] People who initially disclose very negative things about themselves are likely to convince us that they are not worth communicating with further.

As the nature of the relationship changes, the likelihood of different kinds of self-disclosure increases. When we develop close friendships, it is seen as more appropriate to disclose negative characteristics. In fact, with people with whom we are extremely close, negative disclosures are not seen as inappropriate. In fact, a

willingness to disclose such things can be seen as an indicant of trust and respect. When that is the case, attraction for the discloser can be increased.

Reciprocity. Evidence suggests that to some extent self-disclosure begets self-disclosure. As people begin to disclose to us, we are more willing to share our feelings with them. A spiral of self-disclosure occurs at least for a period of time. The pattern of disclosure becomes somewhat symmetrical, and, in long-term dyads, people have usually disclosed a relatively equal amount about themselves. If one person in the dyad is unwilling to reciprocate disclosive communication, it usually serves to inhibit the other from continuing to be more disclosive.[31] It is reasoned that this reciprocity occurs because people disclose only when they feel safe and that disclosure by one person makes the person feel trusted and respected and, therefore, more safe to self-disclose.

The best evidence is also that self-disclosure is incremental. It usually increases slowly as the relationship becomes more stable and permanent.[32] Initial interactions seldom have high disclosure, but disclosure increases gradually as trust and respect increase. Let us say that all of this probably reaches a point in which further self-disclosure is unlikely. There are points beyond which one or more people will not go (area of privateness), and when that point is reached, the reciprocity and incremental increase in self-disclosure ter-

[28]L. R. Wheeless, "Self Disclosure and Interpersonal Solidarity," *Human Communication Research, 3* (1976), pp. 47–61.

[29]S. J. Gilbert and D. Horenstein, "The Communication of Self-Disclosure: Level Versus Valence," *Human Communication Research, 1* (1975), pp. 316–322.

[30]P. M. Blau, *Exchange and Power in Social Life* (New York: Wiley, 1964), p. 49.

[31]See W. B. Pearce and S. M. Sharp, "Self-Disclosing Communication," *Journal of Communication, 23* (1973), pp. 418–419.

[32]Ibid., p. 421.

minate. If one person does not recognize that this has occurred, that person's continued pressure for more self-disclosure can lead to disruption or even termination of the dyadic relationship.

RISKS OF SELF-DISCLOSURE

As we have repeatedly stated, self-disclosure does not always lead to positive outcomes. There are certain risks inherent in these attempts. There are several reasons why people choose not to be highly self-disclosive. First, our society has not placed a high premium on this kind of communication. For many years, we considered the need to self-disclose as a sign of weakness. Men have traditionally been less willing to disclose than have women, although this is changing.[33] One possible explanation of this is that males are expected to be strong, and any attempt to reveal one's self is seen as a weakness. We think that this conception of the proper role of males and females is changing, and we are not displeased with that.

There are also inherent risks. When we do reveal ourselves to another, we risk being embarrassed or disconfirmed. People may reject our attempts, and we may suffer greatly from that rejection. This fear of rejection is a source of resistance to self-disclosure. This risk is recognized by everyone concerned with the effects of self-disclosure. As we have said, inappropriate, irrelevant, and unwanted self-disclosure can disrupt the dyad. There is a risk that our self-disclosure will change or

terminate important dyadic relationships. As Rubin suggests:

> When we reveal to another person something of our true self, we must be prepared for the possibility that he will examine what we have revealed and find it wanting.[34]

Perhaps an elegant statement by Powell sums all of this up nicely: "If I tell you who I am, you may not like who I am and it is all that I have."[35]

Although there are many inherent risks involved in self-disclosive communication, the potentials for positive outcomes are great. We are going to make no dicta about how you should go about deciding whether the risks outweigh the benefits. That is a very personal matter, and the decision will not be the same for all people. However, we have tried to point out that many people need and desire relationships that afford the opportunity for self-disclosure. When such a relationship does develop, we do grow and flourish as people. Most of us have developed such relationships and desire to continue them. The authors have also tried to point out some of the effects of self-disclosure on the discloser and on the people to whom we reveal ourselves. All outcomes are not positive, and there are attendant risks in communicating in this manner. It will never be truer of anything said in this book than to close by saying that it is your move and your choice.

[33]For more complete discussions of the literature on self-disclosure, see the previously cited articles by Shirley J. Gilbert.

[34]Z. Rubin, *Liking and Loving* (New York: Holt, Rinehart and Winston, 1973), p. 160.

[35]J. Powell, *Why I Am Afraid to Tell You Who I Am: Insights on Self-Awareness, Personal Growth and Interpersonal Communication* (Niles, Ill.: Argus Communications, 1969), p. 12.

SUMMARY

1. All communication between two people is not what should be called interpersonal communication. More useful ways of viewing interpersonal communication are based upon levels of prediction, levels of knowing, and roles played in the dyadic interaction. Interpersonal communication, as we define it, occurs in a variety of contexts, including the dyad, small-group, public speaking, and mass communication situations.

2. When people communicate, they make predictions about the effects, or outcomes, of their communication behavior. The first level of data that people make predictions from is the cultural level. We can predict how people will behave on the basis of a knowledge of the culture from which they come. Because people develop norms of behavior based upon culturally determined rules, regularities in behavior can be expected. We come to base our communication with others on those expected behaviors to some extent. We generalize from our knowledge of a few people in the culture to make predictions on how people will behave. Interactions based only on cultural-level data do not qualify as interpersonal in nature.

3. The second level of data that we use to make predictions is called the sociological level. We base predictions about the behavior of people on what we know about their group memberships. Some group memberships are voluntary whereas we have no choice about being classified as members of other groups. The groups we belong to usually have some influence on our behavior, and we can make predictions based on that notion. Sometimes we simply cannot gather data on individuals, and using sociological data can be useful. This process also generalizes from knowledge about the few to make predictions about the entire group. A relationship using only sociological data would not be properly called an interpersonal one.

4. Communication strategies that discriminate among individuals and make predictions based on individual differences operate on psychological-level data and are interpersonal in nature. It takes time and effort to gather psychological-level data, and this is not possible in all situations. In most communication transactions we use some combination of cultural-, sociological-, and psychological-level data to make predictions.

5. The second way of analyzing communication is based upon levels of knowing. The first level is predicition, which we have discussed. The second level of knowing requires being able to explain why people behave as they do. When one can explain behavior, he or she can also predict future actions.

6. The kinds of roles that we use are also ways of differentiating inter-

personal from noninterpersonal interactions. In initial communication relationships, much of the interaction is based on prescribed rules. There is an external locus of control that dictates the kinds of behaviors that are and are not appropriate. As we develop relationships, negotiated roles become more common. People jointly determine in some cases, and in other cases one person uses some power base to develop roles. Negotiated roles can either expand or restrict the freedom people have in a dyadic relationship. Just because people have negotiated roles does not mean that they have an interpersonal relationship. When the basis of judgment is on an understanding of enacted roles, the relationship is more interpersonal. We attempt to understand that each person is capable of playing a variety of roles. We come to understand why certain roles are performed.

7. There are several characteristics that make the dyadic communication context unique. There is a high degree of perceived privacy, potential for intimacy, and a great possibility for using feedback. Feedback is especially important, for it is spontaneous, directed, and immediate. Dyadic communication is also more spontaneous and less formal than communication in other contexts. People can adapt communication strategies to fit the situation. There is usually more direct participation, and the situation is one in which the participants are coactive, that is, simultaneously acting as a source and receiver. The dyadic context is a prime arena for collecting and using psychological-level data. We cannot appeal to majority rule in the dyad. Communication must be directed at consensus.

8. We can approach the dyads by understanding different levels of communication. At the first level (direct perspective), people communicate about their agreement/disagreement on issues. The second level (metaperspective) is communication about our understanding of the other's position. A third level involves whether we feel that we are being understood. There is a difference between understanding and being understood. This analysis can help locate problems in dyads. There is no sense pretending that disagreement is an issue if, in fact, misunderstanding is a problem. In a similar way, we can agree to disagree and then work on understanding and being understood.

9. People develop patterns of interaction that exert control of the dyadic communication. In symmetrical relationships the differences between people are minimized. Both individuals believe that they have an equal right to exercise control and that the options available to one are available to both. Such a relationship can be very competitive, and hostility is frequent. People are consistently trying to determine

how the other person views his or her equality. Almost every situation requires negotiation prior to taking any action. Complementary relationships maximize the differences between people. One person is one-up (superior), and the other is one-down (subordinate). One initiates and plans activities, and the other agrees. These relationships are often harmonious, and the coordination of activities is relatively easy. Often complementary relationships can stagnate, and people fail to grow and develop as individuals. The dominant person tends to provide protection in exchange for compliance. Parallel relationships allow each person to have areas of control while still allowing for equal participation in some areas. This flexible pattern allows changes in roles and can prevent some of the problems associated with rigidly complementary or rigidly symmetrical relationships.

10. Self-disclosure communication is information that is willingly given to another individual that is private and usually involves some risk. That information is not generally available unless the discloser wishes it to be known. Apparent self-disclosure is associated with impression management that is manipulative and designed to serve a purpose other than revealing the self.

11. Some people argue that we only come to know our own self by disclosing that self to others. That people are more healthy to the extent that they self disclose is one view. Maladjustment is seen as the inability to disclose. People do differ in their desire and need to self-disclose. Though self-disclosure may be valuable for some, there is little evidence to suggest that it is a panacea for all human problems.

12. Self-disclosive communication has a pronounced impact on dyads. Self-disclosure that is seen as inappropriate or irrelevant to the situation can make the discloser appear to be less worthwhile to communicate with in future encounters. In initial interactions, positive self-disclosures make the person appear as more attractive than do negative self-disclosures. As the relationship develops, more negative self-disclosure is seen as more appropriate, and such communication can actually increase trust. There is a norm of reciprocity such that self-disclosure by one person increases the disclosive communication of the other. People are presumed to feel safer with people who trust them enough to reveal private information. That prompts them to also be more intimate in their communication. There is probably a point beyond which more self-disclosure by one person will not increase the self-disclosure of the other. We have a point of privacy that we tend to protect. Failure by one person to recognize this point can lead to problems in the dyadic relationships.

13. There are definite risks associated with self-disclosure. Each individ-

ual should weigh these risks along with the potential benefits to decide the kinds of self-disclosure he or she is willing to offer. No dicta should be made about the need or worth of self-disclosure for the individual; it is a private matter that is best decided by the person involved.

SUGGESTED READING

Jourard, Sidney M. *Self-Disclosure—An Experimental Analysis of the Transparent Self*. New York: Wiley-Interscience, 1971.

Millar, Dan P., and Frank E. Millar. *Messages and Myths*. New York: Alfred Publishing, 1976.

Miller, Gerald R. ed. *Explorations in Interpersonal Communication*. Beverly Hills, Calif.: Sage Publishing, 1976.

———and Mark Steinberg. *Between People*. Palo Alto, Calif.: Science Research Associates, 1975.

Watzlawick, Paul; Janet Beavin; and Don D. Jackson. *Pragmatics of Human Communication*. New York: W. W. Norton, 1967.

Wilmot, William W. *Dyadic Communication: A Transactional Perspective*. Reading, Mass.: Addison-Wesley, 1975.

From the Reading

Define the following terms.

interpersonal communication
cultural, sociological, and psychological data
stereotypes
mixed-level relationships
prediction
explanation
prescribed role
negotiated role
enacted role
external locus of control
internal locus of control
perceived privacy
perceived intimacy
direct feedback
specific feedback
coactive

Study Questions

1. Why is it important to distinguish between interpersonal and noninterpersonal communication?
2. How does the way of distinguishing interpersonal communication offered in this chapter differ from past approaches?
3. What are the primary differences in cultural-, sociological-, and psychological-level data?
4. How do we use each level of data in dyadic relationships?
5. What are the problems associated with using each level of data?
6. Distinguish between the ability to predict and the ability to explain. Why can we predict if we can explain? Can we always explain if we can predict?
7. Distinguish between prescribed, negotiated, and enacted roles. How do we use each in communication transactions? How does the development of relationships change these roles? How can we distin-

direct perspective
metaperspective
meta-metaperspective
understanding
being understood
realization
symmetrical relationship
complementary relationship
parallel relationship
self-disclosure
self-description
impression management
privateness factor
appropriateness
valence
reciprocity

guish interpersonal from noninterpersonal situations on the basis of roles?

8. How does the locus of control affect freedom of behavior in the dyad?

9. Distinguish among direct perspectives and other levels of analysis (metaperspectives and meta-metaperspectives). How do we use different communication strategies at each level? How do problems emerge in dyads where people are operating at different levels of understanding?

10. How do communication strategies aimed at being understood differ from those seeking to understand?

11. How do dyadic communication contexts differ from other contexts? What are the advantages of communicating in a dyad?

12. How do we distinguish among symmetrical, complementary, and parallel relationships?

13. What are the advantages and disadvantages of each kind of relationship?

14. What are the primary communication strategies apparent in each relationship?

15. How do we distinguish among self-disclosure, self-description, and impression management? What is the difference between apparent and genuine disclosure?

16. How does self-disclosure affect the discloser? What are the different views on this question?

17. How might self-disclosure affect the dyad? What factors should be considered?

18. What are the risks and benefits of self-disclosure?

AN EXERCISE DESIGNED TO USE DIFFERENT LEVELS OF DATA ANALYSIS

1. Form groups of three (or more) people from your class. It is important that these groups be comprised of people who have not interacted with each other a great deal in the past.

2. Rate each person on the following items. Use the following scale to answer each item. Place the appropriate number to the right of the word in Column A.

Disagree ___1___ ___2___ ___3___ ___4___ ___5___ Agree

	A	B
Tall	_____	_____
Intelligent	_____	_____
Serious	_____	_____
Humorous	_____	_____
Sexy	_____	_____
Easygoing	_____	_____
Compulsive	_____	_____
Old	_____	_____
Athletic	_____	_____
Political	_____	_____
Romantic	_____	_____
Wealthy	_____	_____
Conservative	_____	_____
Liberal	_____	_____
Outspoken	_____	_____
Opinionated	_____	_____
Shy	_____	_____
Attractive	_____	_____
Interesting	_____	_____
Religious	_____	_____
Friendly	_____	_____

No one will see your evaluations but you.

3. Which of your evaluations were based primarily on nonverbal factors?

_____

Which of your evaluations were based primarily on verbal behaviors?

_____

Which of your evaluations were based on cultural-level data? _____
_____ . Which were based upon sociological-
level data? _____ .
Which were based on psychological-level data? _____
_____

4. Now we would like you to communicate with people you have just evaluated to get better acquainted. Feel free to interact in any manner you deem appropriate.

5. After you have finished your discussion, please go back and reevaluate the people by placing the appropriate numbers in column B.

6. Which items changed? _____

   Which items remained the same? _____
   _____

7. Did you use different levels of data as the discussion progressed?
8. It might be interesting to consider how other people evaluated you both before and after this exercise. How do you think the communication changed things?

An Exercise in Self-disclosure

We would like you to form dyads based on any kind of criteria the group wishes to use.

Directions: Select five questions from the list that follows that you and your partner will ask each other. Explore the question at any level of intimacy you choose, until one of you declines an "invitation" to disclose further information. At this point you should move on to another question. For *each* question indicate how much information you, yourself, would be willing to tell your partner. Mark as follows: 0 for each question you would be unwilling to talk about with your partner. Mark a 1 if you would be willing to talk about that question in general terms with your partner, but would not be willing to reveal any extremely personal information about yourself. Mark a 2 only on those questions that you would be willing to confide completely and very personally with your partner. Notice on your score sheet there is also a section marked as follows: 2. My invitation was refused by the other person. When the exercise begins, mark those questions on which your "invitation" to disclose was refused by your partner. Also note if your partner accepted your invitation and answered your question.

1. What are your usual ways of dealing with depression, anxiety, and anger?
2. What are your personal religious views and the nature of your religious participation, if any?
3. What are the actions you have most regretted doing in your life? Why?
4. What are the ways in which you feel most maladjusted or immature?
5. What are your views on politics?
6. What are your personal goals for the next ten years or so?
7. What are the habits and reactions of yours that bother you at present?
8. What are the sources of strain and dissatisfaction in your relationships with the opposite sex?
9. What are your hobbies? How do you like to spend your spare time?
10. What are the occasions in your life on which you were happiest?
11. What are the aspects of your daily work that satisfy and bother you?
12. What characteristics of yourself give you cause for pride and satisfaction?
13. Who are the persons in your life whom you most resent? Why?
14. What are the unhappiest moments in your life? Why?

15. What are your preferences and dislikes in music?
16. What are the circumstances under which you become depressed and when your feelings are hurt?
17. What are your guiltiest secrets?

---

1. Questions I intend to ask my partner.
   a ____ b ____ c ____ d ____ e ____
2. My invitation was refused by the other person.
   a ____ b ____ c ____ d ____ e ____

Questions to Consider

1. Were there differences in the kinds of questions that each of you were willing to disclose? What were the differences?
2. What items were people most willing to disclose about themselves? Least willing?
3. Were there answers that seemed to be self-descriptions more than self-disclosures?
4. Did most of the answers seem to be genuine or apparent?

An Exercise Designed to Analyze the Effects of Self-disclosure

Would you please consider each of the following items listed. They are separated by their degree of intimateness and their valence. Please use the following scale to rank each item:

Unwilling to disclose ___1___ ___2___ ___3___ ___4___ ___5___ Willing to disclose

Would you please answer each item on this scale for each of the following people: stranger, acquaintance, friend, parent, spouse or lover.

Table 6.1

	Stranger	Acquaintance	Friend	Parent	Spouse/Lover
Nonintimate Kinds of group activity I enjoy	_____	_____	_____	_____	_____
+ How much I like traveling with others	_____	_____	_____	_____	_____
My strong admiration for professionals	_____	_____	_____	_____	_____

Table 6.1 (continued)

		Stranger	Acquaintance	Friend	Parent	Spouse/Lover
Neutral	Whether or not I laugh at dirty jokes	_____	_____	_____	_____	_____
	Whether or not I enjoy the excitement of a crowd	_____	_____	_____	_____	_____
	The amount I drink at parties	_____	_____	_____	_____	_____
−	My aversion to crowds	_____	_____	_____	_____	_____
	My strong aversion to another's snoring	_____	_____	_____	_____	_____
	My problems with liquor	_____	_____	_____	_____	_____
	Moderately Intimate					
+	The kind of people I find it easy to talk to	_____	_____	_____	_____	_____
	My expectations for others	_____	_____	_____	_____	_____
	My ability to support others	_____	_____	_____	_____	_____
Neutral	Which I value more: friendship or money	_____	_____	_____	_____	_____
	Whether or not I like being the center of attention	_____	_____	_____	_____	_____
	My feelings about people who are different from me	_____	_____	_____	_____	_____
−	Things that bug me about others	_____	_____	_____	_____	_____
	Lies that I have told my friends	_____	_____	_____	_____	_____
	My tendencies to get even with people I dislike	_____	_____	_____	_____	_____
	Intimate					
+	My good reputation with others	_____	_____	_____	_____	_____
	My sexual prowess and fulfillment	_____	_____	_____	_____	_____
	My capacity to be open with others	_____	_____	_____	_____	_____
Neutral	Things I don't like to talk about with others	_____	_____	_____	_____	_____
	My problems in interpersonal relationships	_____	_____	_____	_____	_____
	My tendency to keep a distance between myself and others	_____	_____	_____	_____	_____

Table 6.1 (continued)

	Stranger	Acquaintance	Friend	Parent	Spouse/Lover
Things that would cause me to break up a friendship	_____	_____	_____	_____	_____
How I feel when someone doesn't accept friendship	_____	_____	_____	_____	_____
Times when others have made me feel uncomfortable	_____	_____	_____	_____	_____

Questions to Consider

1. How do the targets of disclosure affect your willingness to disclose?
2. Does the valence and intimacy help determine to whom you would disclose information? In what ways?
3. How does your self-disclosure profile compare to the percentages and patterns discussed in this chapter?

An Exercize Designed to Analyze Relational Communication

This exercise can be accomplished in several ways. The first requirement is to have at least one dyad communicating. One pair can be observed by the entire class, or, if video tape equipment is available, several dyads can be taped and then observed by everyone.

Another way that might make the communication more informal is to create triads in class. Have two people discuss issues or make a decision or solve a problem. Have the other person observe the conversation

Answer the following questions:

1. What things were done to make the communication symmetrical (you might want to record specific comments)?_____
   _____
   _____
   _____
   _____

2. What things were done that indicated a complementary reaction? _____
   _____
   _____
   _____
   _____
   _____

3. Were there instances in which the communication patterns indicated a parallel relationship? _____

_____
_____
_____
_____

This exercise can be adapted to be useful to friends and spouses. You might want to consider analyzing (in private) a communication transaction between you and some significant other.

Was the communication complementary, symmetrical, parallel? What kinds of events led you to this judgment? What is the nature of that relationship? Are you satisfied with it?

RELATIONAL COMMUNICATION IN THE MASS MEDIA

It seems to us that many television shows use notions of relational communication as humor and drama. Select some television show and analyze the relationships between two (or more) of the characters. Try the following scheme by simply marking an instance of the following:

Table 6.2

Character 1					Character 2
One-Up	One-Down	One-Across	One-Up	One-Down	One-Across

1. What patterns emerged?
2. What are the intended effects of this relational communication?
3. How prevalent is one-up/one-down communication? How is it used effectively as humor?
4. Did you have difficulty in analyzing the communication from this relational perspective?

AN EXERCISE TO ANALYZE AGREEMENT, UNDERSTANDING, AND BEING UNDERSTOOD

We think it would be useful to form triads and determine if we can assess people's level of understanding on several issues.

Agree to discuss five issues about which you have attitudes of beliefs:

1.

2.

3.

4.

5.

Have two people agree to participate in this interaction, and have the other observe. Try to make the person understand and, if possible, accept your point of view.

The observer should record the following:

Issue # _____

Person_____(A)
Direct Perspective_____

_____
_____

What does person A understand
Person B to believe about this
topic (metaperspective)?_____
_____
_____

What does Person A think that
Person B believes that he or she
(Person A) believes about this
topic?_____
_____
_____

Person_____(B)
Direct Perspective_____

_____
_____

What does Person B understand Person
A to believe about this topic? _____
_____
_____

What does Person B think that Person A
believes that he or she (Person B)
believes about the topic? _____
_____
_____

Is Person A concentrating more effort on understanding or being understood?_____

_____

_____

Is Person B concentrating more effort on understanding or being understood?_____

_____

_____

Each participant should answer the following:
My direct perspective_____

_____ .

What the other person thinks I believe_____

_____ .

What I think the other person believes_____

_____ .

Did I spend more time trying to be understood or attempting to understand? _____

_____

_____ .

Now each participant should compare his or her perceptions with the other person and the observer. Where did differences occur? Do people better understand the positions of each after sharing this information?

Now select another issue, and have the person who was the observer become a participant and another member of the triad observe the discussion. Repeat the process.

Chapter 7
SMALL-GROUP COMMUNICATION

Rarely does any society encourage or teach its members to be alone. Groups intrude on every facet of modern society. Shortly after birth we join the most primary of groups—the family—and the majority of us seldom relinquish membership in some type of group for the duration of our lives. The presence of others can reassure or motivate us to greater accomplishments, or it can make us anxious and interfere with the quality of our performance. Isolation from other members of society is normally an involuntary gesture reserved for members of penal institutions or prisoners of war. When individuals do choose to isolate themselves from others, society usually refers to them as loners, misanthropes, or antisocials.

During the early 1970s American moviegoers were treated—or mistreated, as the case may be—to a series of movies stressing societies' loners, misanthropes, and antisocials. Notable among these were Richard Harris in *Man in the Wilderness* and Robert Redford in *Jeremiah Johnson*. Both films were a marked departure from the usually volatile and gregarious fare produced by the film industry. Richard Harris spent the majority of the film grimacing, muttering to himself, or chatting with a white snow rabbit. Robert Redford, on the other hand, was afforded a brief group encounter, but the Indian maiden could not speak English, and the young boy could not even speak. The audiences that we were exposed to seemed to react less to the physical hardships endured by Harris and Redford than to their social isolation and lack of communication outlets. If nothing else, these films depict the tremendous dependence society places on group involvement and the emphasis individuals place on communication with others. They also suggest to us that small-group communication is a truly unique and distinctive phenomenon.

It is not unreasonable to suggest that there are probably more small groups than people in this country. If for no other reason then, small-group communication is a necessary and vital part of our communication repertoire. As people spend a significant portion of their lives in groups—family, work, church, social, political, school, recreation, and special interest groups—it makes sense that they also spend a significant portion of their lives communicating in the small-group context. Though we believe that small-group communication is unique and distinctive, we do not maintain that it is unusual or infrequent. If anything, it is the norm, for most people communicate as much or more in small groups than in dyadic, public address, or mass communication contexts. Although we will devote our attention in this chapter to the unique features of small-group communication, the reader should keep in mind that many of the variables that we have discussed earlier will also come to bear in the small-group setting.

The Small Group Defined

Small-group communication is *unique* because the group setting provides great potential for producing highly complex and quality outcomes that cannot be associated with any other type of human communication. A task too difficult for one might be easily handled by several. Small-group communication is *distinctive* because the interactions of individual personalities, the group personality, and the various communication skills or lack of skills representative of groups will generate pressures or forces that do not operate in any other environment.

There have been an almost inexhaustible number of definitions suggested for small groups. We feel that a useful way of defining the small group, borrowing elements from many previous definitions, is the following: *the face-to-face interaction of three or more individuals, for a recognized purpose such as information sharing, self-maintenance, or problem solving, such that the members are able to recall personal characteristics of the other members accurately.*

The term *face-to-face* means that the members of the small group must be able to see and hear each other and also must be able to adjust behaviors to the verbal and nonverbal feedback of fellow members. This definition excludes aggregates of individuals who are not in close proximity, such as members of the International Communication Association who correspond only through the mail. It also excludes collections of individuals who do not communicate with each other, such as five individuals who happen to stop by a construction site momentarily to watch the erection of a new building. This situation refers to the *interaction* element of the definition. We are reserving the small-group context for *three to approximately twenty* interactants. We choose to call communication encounters between two individuals dyadic, whereas encounters of more than twenty persons are really more large-scale than the small-group setting. This is a relatively common distinction.

The next key element is that of a *recognized purpose*, which provides some type of group identity of group personality. When the purpose of the group is information sharing, the communication is intended to impart knowledge. The Senate Armed Services Committee meets frequently to share information that is needed by various agencies within the government to make subsequent decisions. Small groups concerned with self-maintenance usually focus attention on the group members or the structure of the group itself. The communication resulting is normally reflective of situations affecting one group member to another or one group member with respect to the entire group. The purpose can be satisfaction of personal needs, satisfaction of collective needs, or even survival of the group itself. Graduate students usually form small groups to combat real or imagined threats to their status, to provide moral support, and to insure that all members of the group "make it" or get their degree. The final recognized purpose of the small group is to solve some problem. This process usually involves some type of decision making prior to alleviating some pragmatic difficulty. This is the case where many heads are better than one. A group of students is more likely to solve a difficult chemistry problem than one student, and, in the same sense, a group of school board members is more apt to reach an equitable solution to racial disturbances in a high school than is the principal working alone.

The last key element is that the members are able to *recall the personal characteristics of the other members accurately.* This implies that each member of the group relates to every other member in such a way that the existence and purpose of the group is clear and that the identification of each member with the group is relatively stable and permanent. A small group clearly exists if the relationships of the group members are significant enough to draw the attention and recollection of the group. For example, if a group of students waiting in line to pay their fees communicated long enough and could recollect the personal characteristics of the other persons waiting in line at a later time, they would have many, if not all, the characteristics of a small group.

Our purpose in providing this definition of a small group is to distinguish it from the dyadic, public address, and mass communication contexts discussed elsewhere in the text. Our definition, of course, implies that small-group communication is an ongoing and frequent activity and is marked by less privacy than in dyadic communication. Moreover, as there are more people involved, small groups are obviously more structured than these two other communication situations. On the other hand, more feedback is present in the small-group setting than in either public or mass communication.

In addition to these essentials, there are still other characteristics of small groups that further distinguish them from other communication contexts. We have synthesized from a wide variety of sources in order to provide a detailed accounting of unique small-group variables.

Characteristics That Make the Small Group Unique

One of the earliest laboratory investigations was an 1897 study by Triplett concerning social facilitation.[1] Triplett was interested in the effects of competition on individual behavior, and he began collecting data from the official records of bicycle races maintained by the Racing Board of the League of American Wheelmen. He compared unpaced races, in which a single rider attempted to beat an established time; paced races, in which a lone rider also attempted to beat an established time, but with a swift multicycle setting the pace; and competitions, where several riders competed in an ordinary race. Triplett determined that times were fastest for competition, next fastest for paced events, and slowest for unpaced events. Other research has also demonstrated that small groups have a facilitating effect on individual members such that motivation is increased under social conditions. Many professional tennis players have indicated that their level of play is higher when a crowd is present, despite the boisterous and distracting nature of fans sitting courtside. This phenomenon is referred to as the dynamogenic effect, which holds that the presence of others releases latent energy that the individual is unable to release on his own.

Small groups take on a *group personality* or identity of their own. Rather than a conglomerate of all the individual personalities, the group personality is a singular and separate entity. The group may be characterized as a highly rigid and traditional entity, whereas all of the individual members might be very flexible and extroverted. The presence of others can calm even the most enthusiastic of individuals,

and it can also turn the most passive of individuals into a mass of energy. Groups develop their own modes of behavior and particular orientations just as individuals do. All of us have probably done something at one time or another in a group that we wouldn't dream of doing as individuals. The group personality can transform upstanding citizens into an ugly mob, or it can turn shiftless and unskilled individuals into a productive unit.

A third characteristic of small groups is the establishment of *group norms* or a shared acceptance of rules. Group norms identify the ways in which members of the group behave and ways that are considered by them to be correct and proper. Each group establishes its own system of values and concepts of normative behavior. In time these group norms become individual norms, for the individual members value the group and want to be like it. Group norms are believed to emerge in two ways.[2] When individuals seek to validate their beliefs and cannot check these beliefs personally, they accept what the rest of the group believes to be true. Male political groups traditionally believed females were unfit for public office. In the absence of verifiable evidence, individual male members accepted the group consensus that females were unfit for public office. In recent years national women's groups have provided support that women are indeed capable of holding public office, and males no longer have to depend on the opinions of others in their group for information regarding the female role. The second way in which group

[1] N. Triplett, "The Dynamogenic Factors in Pacemaking and Competition, *American Journal of Psychology,* 9 (1897), pp. 507–533.

[2] L. Festinger, "Informal Social Communication" in *Group Dynamics,* ed. D. Cartwright and A. Zander (New York: Harper and Row, 1968), pp. 182–191.

norms emerge is out of necessity for the survival and effectiveness of the group. Interactions of group members must be coordinated in order to have the group satisfy its goals.

Group *cohesiveness* refers to the overall attraction of group members to each other and the forces that impel them to remain in the group. Most theorists are in agreement that cohesiveness refers to the degree to which members of a group desire to remain within the group.[3] Group cohesiveness is determined for the most part by two factors. First, normative behavior tends to be strong when members are attracted to and identify with the group. College students who are highly attracted to a particular social fraternity have been known to comply with bizarre behaviors during pledge initiations so as to identify with the fraternity. The second factor is the length of group membership. Group members tend to develop more similar values the longer the continued interaction with the group. The level of group cohesiveness can have a significant impact on normative behavior. Members of highly cohesive groups have been shown to be cooperative and friendly and generally to behave in ways designed to promote group solidarity, whereas low cohesive group members behave much more independently, with little concern for other group members.[4]

A fifth characteristic of small groups is *commitment* to the task. As we have already stated, groups exist for some purpose. Therefore, the small group is unique in that there will be certain levels of commitment on the part of the groups as a whole and on the part of individual members. The possibility always exists that the aspiration level set by an individual member is inconsistent with the level of aspiration for that individual set by the group. Disparity between individual goals and group requirements is usually less when a member's task is relevant to the group goal, when the goal is moderate rather than intensely difficult, and when other group members pressure the individual strongly to perform at a certain level.[5] Commitment to the group goal usually carries with it two interrelated motives: the desire for group success and the desire to avoid group failure. A high level of commitment to group goals can overcome apathy, hostility, and seemingly insurmountable obstacles, whereas a low level of commitment can render even the most superlative coalition useless or ineffective.

Interdependency exists to a large degree in groups because the individual members must subordinate their individual desires and goals so that the group goal will be accomplished. A typical example involves class projects where a group of students is expected to produce some outcome. Invariably, one or more of the group members is not willing to contribute his or her fair share. As the group will receive a joint grade, either the recalcitrant members will have to subordinate their desires to the group goal, or all will suffer. Whatever the outcome, we can all agree that this type of interdependency is unique to the small-group context.

Group *size* simply refers to the number

[3]D. Cartwright, "The Nature of Group Cohesiveness," in *Group Dynamics* ed. D. Cartwright and A. Zander (New York: Harper and Row, 1968), p. 91.

[4]M. Shaw, *Group Dynamics,* 2d ed. (New York: McGraw-Hill, 1976), pp. 206-207.

[5]A. Zander, *Motives and Goals in Groups* (New York: Academic Press, 1971), p. 174.

of individuals who constitute the group. It is frequently a vitally important factor in determining the quality of communication and productivity within the group. Although ten opinions may be superior to five, there is also twice the potential for conflict or disagreement. One way to look at this variable is that too many individuals may get in each other's way or may simply insist on bringing their own biases to bear on the situation. An increase in group size may augment potential early productivity without creating a corresponding increase in actual productivity.[6] Early research has shown that as group size increases, the quality of interaction also increases because the consequences of alienating other group members becomes less severe;[7] and productivity increases with size up to a point, with the more aggressive members of large groups tending to stifle contributions of the more reticent individuals.[8] As we mentioned earlier, the group differs from the dyad in that alienating one (or more) individuals will not necessarily terminate the relationship. The effects of group size are quite tentative and unclear. A great deal depends on the individual members, the leadership patterns, and the group goals. We will discuss group size as it relates to organizational structure later in this chapter.

An eighth characteristic, which is limited strictly to the group setting, is the *risky shift*. Research has consistently found that decisions made by groups were riskier than prediscussion decisions made by the individual members of the group.[9] Many have argued that this phenomenon is due to the diffusion of responsibility that occurs in the group decision-making process, whereas others insist that it is due to influence by the individual who has the riskiest opinion or simply a cultural value. We will discuss the risky shift in respect to group conflict in Chapter 14.

The final characteristic of small groups is the *assembly effect bonus*. Burgoon and Burgoon refer to this as the extra productivity that is caused specifically by the nature of groups or, more specifically, productivity in excess of the combined product of the same individuals working independently.[10] This is more or less a chain reaction in which some contribution or inspiration by one group member triggers further inspiration or productivity in the other members. The extra productivity results from division of labor, coordination of effort, specialization, and less physical and psychological tension that can take place only within the group. It is hoped that the writing of this textbook will result in some pedagogical merit due to the assembly effect bonus. In working closely with each other and in consulting with our colleagues and publishers, we hope that we have provided a readable and complete compilation of the pertinent factors and concerns affecting human communication. We will discuss this topic further in the section dealing with problem solving and decision making.

It should be obvious that these nine

[6]I. D. Steiner, *Group Process and Productivity* (New York: Academic Press, 1972), p. 78.

[7]P. E. Slater, "Contrasting Correlates of Group Size," *Sociometry*, 21 (1958), pp. 129–139.

[8]C. A. Gibb, "The Effects of Group Size and of Threat Reduction upon Creativity in a Problem-Solving Situation," *American Psychologist*, 6 (1951), p. 324 (abstract).

[9]A review of the research on the risky shift phenomenon is reported in M. Shaw, *Group Dynamics* (New York: McGraw-Hill, 1971), pp. 73–76.

[10]M. Burgoon, J. Heston, and J. McCroskey, *Small Group Communication: A Functional Approach* (New York: Holt, Rinehart and Winston, 1974), p. 5.

characteristics distinguishing small-group contexts from other communication situations may serve as either facilitators or inhibitors of communication in the small group and of outcomes associated with group efforts. A better understanding of why these factors may either inhibit or facilitate communication in the small group will be possible within some theoretical framework. Toward that end we will briefly discuss several theoretical formulations that have been used by group communication specialists to explain communication processes in the small group.

Theories for Small-Group Communication

Theoretical approaches are important to the study of group communication processes. A concern for theory gradually emerged when group communication specialists began to view themselves as scholars engaged in inquiry about group communication processes and concerned with more than just improving the group discussion skills of their students. We agree that some knowledge of the theoretical bases of small-group interactions is both necessary and prudent for the development of more effective group discussion skills.

Social comparison theory. In this approach, group communication is thought to occur because of the need individuals have to compare their attitudes, opinions, and abilities with those of others.[11] According to this theory, the pressure one feels to communicate with other group members increases when it becomes apparent that disagreement concerning the event is present, when the event increases in importance and when group cohesiveness increases. In addition to these conformity pressures, the desire to change position within the group's social structure or to change groups will motivate group communication. Moreover, after a group decision is made, group members may communicate to obtain information that bolsters or makes them more comfortable with that decision. This theory attempts to explain why communication increases or decreases between group members.

Group syntality theory. The group syntality theory approaches the study of group interaction on the basis of the dimensions of the group and the dynamics of syntality, which is the personality of the group or any effect that the group has as a totality.[12] The dimensions of the group refer to population traits or individual characteristics such as age, intelligence, and so on; syntality traits or any effect that the group has acting as a whole; and internal structure, which refers to specific roles, cliques, status positions, and the like. The dynamics of syntality are measured by synergy, or the degree of energy each individual brings into the group to apply to group goals. Much of the group synergy or energy must be expended toward maintaining group harmony and cohesion. Group structure, syntality, and individual characteristics can be used to predict specific group behaviors.

[11]L. Festinger, "Informal Social Communication," *Psychological Review,* 57 (1950), pp. 271–282.

[12]R. Cattell, "Concepts and Methods in the Measurement of Group Syntality," *Psychological Review,* 55 (1948), pp. 48–63.

Social exchange theory. The social exchange theory is predicated on the notion that one can obtain an understanding of the complex nature of groups by examining the dyadic relationship.[13] The group is considered to be a collection of dyads. This formulation assumes that human interaction involves goods and services for exchange and that costs and rewards perceived in situations will serve to elicit responses from individuals during social interaction. If the rewards are either insufficient or outweighed by the costs, group interaction will be terminated, or the individuals involved will modify their behavior to secure whatever rewards they seek. The group structure will help in defining the exact nature of costs and rewards. This theory is important because it attempts to explain the group phenomenon in terms of the economic and behavioral concepts of cost and reward.

Group achievement theory. The group achievement theory is mainly concerned with group productivity or achievement through the examination of member inputs, mediating variables, and group outputs. Member inputs can be identified as individual performance, interaction, and expectations. The mediating variables are the formal and role structures of the group such as status, norms, goals, and so on. The group output is the achievement or accomplishment of the task or group purpose. The productivity of any group can be explained by the consequences of performances, interactions, and expectations mediated through group structure.[14] In other words, performances, interactions, and expectations (input variables) lead to formal structure and role structure (mediating variables), which, in turn, lead to productivity, morale, and cohesion (group achievement).

Sociometric theory. The sociometric theory is an early theory that was concerned with the attractions and repulsions that individuals feel toward one another and with the implications of such feelings for group structure and formation. Sociometry is a psychological construct referring to a methodological and theoretical approach to groups.[15] The assumption here is that individuals within the group who are attracted to each other will communicate more, whereas individuals who are repulsed will communicate less. The level of attraction and repulsion can be measured by means of a sociometric test, where group members are asked to rank each other in terms of interpersonal attractiveness and task effectiveness. By analyzing these sociometric structures of the group, one can determine how cohesive and productive the group is likely to be.

Though some of these theories are more comprehensive and employ more precision in the definition and measurement of variables than others, each can provide a different perspective for viewing the small-group process. There is no right or wrong theory. All can be useful guides for understanding group interaction because all of these theories take a slightly different approach to this phenomenon. Keeping some of these distinctions and possi-

[13]J. Thibaut and H. Kelly, *The Social Psychology of Groups* (New York: Wiley, 1959).

[14]R. Stogdill, *Individual Behavior and Group Achievement* (New York: Oxford University Press, 1959).

[15]J. L. Moreno, *Who Shall Survive? A New Approach to the Problem of Human Interrelations* (Washington, D.C.: Nervous and Mental Disease Publishing Co., 1934).

ble theoretical approaches concerning small-group processes in mind, we will now turn toward some of the variables within group structure.

Small-Group Structure

The structure of a small group is determined by the inputs into the group. These inputs will then determine the structure of group communication, much as the different types of materials will determine the brand name of a particular automobile. Inputs are generally categorized as to *individual characteristics, group characteristics,* and *external factors*. It must be remembered that these inputs are not constant and will vary from individual to individual, group to group, and situation to situation. Therefore, explanation or prediction of group outcomes must be based on examination of the inputs or variables specific to that particular group.

Individual characteristics are the unique differences attributable to the individual members of the group. We normally think of individual characteristics in terms of the differences among group members in the ways they think and behave. Though the potential list of individual differences is infinite, we will select some of the key variables for examination. Personality is probably the most fundamental of individual differences. A group composed entirely of highly structured and dogmatic individuals is surely expected to behave in a different way from a group made up of confident and flexible individuals. Attitudes, values, and individual beliefs are also very important individual differences. Individuals differ in their orientations to the world, their perceptions of

themselves and others, and their system for evaluating other people and events. People with differing value systems will see the world differently. These differences will sometimes add variety and interest to a group, but they will also contribute to the overall group structure. Another major individual difference is general ability or intelligence, quickness, aptitude, and verbal facility. A person's general abilities will usually determine his or her initial status within the group, as well as determine final position within the governing hierarchy. Moreover, these general abilities will ultimately determine patterns of communication interaction among the group members. It is not difficult to identify the members within a group who make the greatest impact, for the discussion usually centers around them. Closely related to these variables are the individual areas of experience. Educational level, exposure to certain ideas and behaviors, socioeconomic status, geographic location, prior employment, areas of interest, and family patterns will affect an individual's ability to relate to other group members and will determine an individual's relative contribution to the group.

Group characteristics are normally considered in terms of group size, the type of group, and the frequency and duration of interaction. In addition, the demographic features of the group can be used to make predictions prior to any interaction. Group size is a very important variable in making such determinations. The interaction of persons in a small group is more complex in some ways than in other communication situations because of the number of people who are actually communicating at one time or another. Each

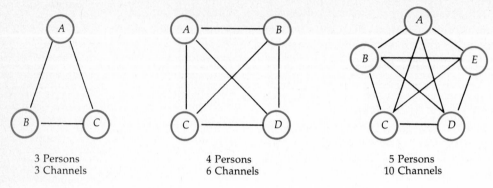

3 Persons
3 Channels

4 Persons
6 Channels

5 Persons
10 Channels

Fig. 7.1 Channels of communication.

person added to the group multiplies the number of channels along which communication can travel. In a group with three people, there are three channels. In a group of four persons, there are six channels. In a five person group, there are ten channels. See Fig. 7.1.

As the number of channels increases, so does the potential for error and conflict. Just as each group member has his or her own needs, goals, attitudes, language habits, and idiosyncrasies, so must he or she cope with all the varied characteristics of all the other members of the group. At the same time, added channels of communication work in a synergistic fashion; the range of inputs and opportunities for problem solving are likely to be increased. Five persons working together are likely to produce more solutions to a problem than seven persons working individually. Thus, in small-group situations, there seems to be a trade-off; what is lost in terms of communication accuracy may be balanced by an increase in the amount and quality of inputs. The ultimate goal of any group is to maximize communication effectiveness while obtaining the optimum range of differences. A group that is too small and whose members are too ho-

mogeneous may breed stagnation, whereas a group that is too large and whose members are too dissimilar may breed conflict and confusion. The optimum size of a group and the optimum dissimilarity among its members must be dictated by the group's purposes or functions.

The type of group is also an important group characteristic for determining structure. Groups could be primarily social or problem-oriented, members could be voluntary or assigned to the group, the group could be continuous or temporary, and, finally, the group could have specific goals or general goals. The communication patterns can differ according to the type of group or the nature of the task(s) relevant to the group. A socially oriented group will engage in different types of communication from those of a task-oriented group. Similar considerations regarding time limitations, the relationship of the group members and the complexity of the group tasks can also provide insights into group structure.

External factors affecting groups may be classified as to environmental factors and externally imposed restrictions. Environmental factors are elements in the immediate locus of the group that have some impact on its functioning. Factors such as temperature, lighting, seating arrangement, furnishings, coloring of the room, amount of noise, windows, and general attractiveness of the environment are all environmental variables that are likely to make a difference in the interaction of a group. Most students are painfully aware of the effects on communication and attention of an overcrowded classroom that is too warm, too noisy and has paint peeling from the walls and an absence of windows. Externally imposed restrictions include any normative rules or procedures governing the group that are imposed by a source outside the group. Often a leader will be designated by a higher authority, such as a teacher or instructor, and placed in charge of an existing group. In addition, time, size, content, or location restrictions may be imposed on a group such that interaction patterns and structure will be altered.

In order to understand why a small group functions as it does, one must understand and recognize these major individual and group characteristics, as well as the external factors affecting the group. Ultimately related to the structure of the group are the communication networks existing between the interactants within the group.

Communication networks. Communication networks are the patterns or channels of communication between participants in the small group. Certain channels may be open to some individuals but closed to others. Knowledge of these channel linkages will indicate who can transmit and receive messages to and from each other, how the messages are transmitted and received, and the sequence of messages. The content of the message is not of importance here, for it is not a primary concern in the establishment of group structure. Communication networks should not be confused with seating arrangement, which simply refers to the physical arrangement of the interactants. Seating arrangement may have an effect on communication networks, however. Some of the more common networks are represented in Fig. 7.2.

Organizations normally refer to the formal legitimate network of communication as going through channels, or utilizing the channels formally recognized as the primary communication network of the organizaton. The system of networks is most readily seen in the military. There are established channels for seeking information, obtaining authority, and expressing grievances. Individuals are discouraged from venturing outside these established channels. For example, a recruit who wishes to ask for permission to go on leave for the holidays must first communicate this desire to the platoon sergeant, who then communicates with the platoon leader, who, in turn, seeks the approval of the company commander. Even though the recruit might be eating lunch beside the company commander, he or she must still maintain the communication channels or network that has been established.

Centrality and distance are the most frequently employed concepts for distinguishing between networks. The communication distance from one individual in the network to another is the sum of the communication links required for the message to be transmitted and received along the shortest possible route. The rela-

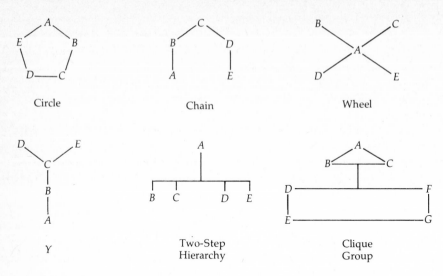

Fig. 7.2 Communication networks in groups.

tive centrality of any interactant's position is the sum of distances between that position and all other positions in the network. Obviously, the most central position in any network is the position with the lowest number representing centrality. As illustrated in Fig. 7.2, the shortest distance between A and C in the circle network is two, whereas the maximum distance is three. In terms of centrality, A's position in the wheel network needs only four communication links to communicate with all members of the group, whereas each other member of the group in his or her present position requires six links to accomplish the same purpose.

There are a number of differences regarding the different networks using a variety of points for comparison. Centralized networks such as the wheel and chain are superior to decentralized networks such as the circle in terms of speed and accuracy of information exchange. For accu-

racy of problem solving, centralized networks are considered more accurate, except for problems involving complex problems. In this case decentralized networks have been found to be superior. Members of decentralized networks have shown greater morale and satisfaction with their group experiences than members employing centralized networks. In general, centralized networks are considered superior for accomplishing simple tasks, whereas decentralized networks foster more cohesive groups and appear to hold a slight advantage in the performance of complex tasks. Greater leadership control has been found with networks like the wheel and two-step hierarchy, but morale might suffer. Circle members send more information, give more answers, provide more feedback, and correct more errors. The formation of cliques or subgroups creates a hierarchy with the majority of communication occurring within subgroups rather than between subgroups.

Obviously, we cannot advocate one particular network over another. The group task and the desired outcome should dictate which network will likely achieve the best results. In addition, many times the group will not have the opportunity of establishing its own network, because in many groups the communication network exists prior to formation of the group. This is frequently the case when some outgroup authority establishes the network to be used in the newly formed group. Our earlier examples of organizations and the hierarchy within the military reflect such a situation.

Group interaction. The structure of a group is related to the ways in which the individual members of the group interact. In order to understand the effect that interaction of the group members has on structure, and the resulting flow of communication, we must first analyze the interactions and behaviors of the group. We will discuss two procedures for analyzing the interaction process or interaction behaviors in the small group.

Bales's Interaction Process Analysis (IPA) is a category system for analyzing the overt interactions of group members developed in 1950 by Robert F. Bales.[16] The IPA is probably the most well known and widely employed guide for the systematic observation of small-group interaction, and Bales devoted much of his professional career toward development and

refinement of this system. Verbal as well as nonverbal behaviors may be recorded with this technique. Although the IPA has undergone several revisions, the early version is more readily understood by students and easier to apply to the classroom; so we will present this version here.

The frequencies of each group member's contributions are placed into one of twelve mutually exclusive categories of either task-related or socioemotional behaviors. Behaviors falling into these twelve categories are generally grouped into positive reactions, answers, questions, or negative reactions. The IPA categories are as follows:

Socioemotional Area: Positive Reactions

1. Shows solidarity, raises other's status, gives help, rewards.
2. Shows tension release, jokes, laughs, shows satisfaction.
3. Agrees, shows passive acceptance, understands, concurs, complies.

Task Area: Answers

4. Gives suggestions, direction, implying autonomy for others.
5. Gives opinions, evaluation, analysis; expresses feelings, wishes.
6. Gives orientation, information; repeats, clarifies, confirms.

Task Area: Questions

7. Asks for orientation, information, repetition, clarification, confirmation.
8. Asks for opinion, evaluation, analysis, expression of feeling.
9. Asks for suggestion, direction, possible ways of action.

---

[16]R. F. Bales, *Interaction Process Analysis: A Method for the Study of Small Groups* (Cambridge, Mass.: Addison-Wesley, 1950).

Socioemotional Area: Negative Reactions

10. Disagrees; shows passive rejection, formality; withholds help.
11. Shows tension, asks for help, withdraws out of field.
12. Shows antagonism, deflates other's status, defends or asserts self.

Interacting groups are assumed to encounter and attempt to resolve problems in six general areas: (1) problems of communication involved in arriving at common definitions and mutual understanding of the situation, (2) problems of evaluation involved in identifying or developing a shared set of criteria or values by means of which alternative solutions are evaluated, (3) problems of control involved with members influencing each other, (4) problems of decision involved with arriving at a collective judgment or decision, (5) problems of tension reduction involved in dealing with group tensions generated during interaction, and (6) problems of reintegration involved in maintaining integration within the group. Behavior classification corresponding to these problems are shown as follows:

Table 7.1

Problem	Corresponding Categories
Communication	6 and 7
Evaluation	5 and 8
Control	4 and 9
Decision	3 and 10
Tension Reduction	2 and 11
Reintegration	1 and 12

The behaviors corresponding to the twelve behaviors can simply be entered on a tally sheet by marking the frequencies with which each group member engages in one of the twelve behavioral categories. A sample tally sheet for the IPA is provided in Table 7.2.

This type of analysis can provide a great deal of information about the interaction processes of small groups. For example, on the basis of behavior frequencies from the sample tally sheet in Table 7.2, we can deduce that member #4 is assuming a leadership role toward the group task and member #2 is providing a disruptive influence in the group. Member #1 seems to be generating the most communication and appears instrumental in controlling the overall behavior of the group. This form of analysis can also be used to examine which types of group outcomes result from which kinds of interaction patterns, whether task or socioemotional behaviors are evenly balanced, whether the group progresses through certain phases of problem solving, whether certain members communicate disproportionately with certain other members, and whether group interaction seems to be following a certain pattern. Knowledge of these elements can prove useful in determining the exact structure of a small group. Keep in mind that closely interrelated with group structure are such factors as whether or not the group will be cohesive and accomplish its goals and whether or not communication within the group will be effective.

Another technique designed for measuring small-group interaction is the Interaction Behavior Measure (IBM).[17] The

[17] J. McCroskey and D. Wright, "The Development of an Instrument for Measuring Interaction Behavior in Small Groups," *Speech Monographs, 38* (1971), pp. 335–340.

Table 7.2 Sample IPA tally sheet

	Group Members				
	#1	*#2*	*#3*	*#4*	*Totals*
1. Shows solidarity	//		///		5
2. Shows tension release	///		//		5
3. Agrees	LHT		/		6
4. Gives suggestions	////			LHT	9
5. Gives opinions	LHT			LHT ///	13
6. Gives orientation	LHT /		//	///	11
7. Asks for orientation	///			///	6
8. Asks for opinion	///		/		4
9. Asks for suggestion	LHT				5
10. Disagrees	//	LHT ///	//	////	14
11. Shows tension		////	/		5
12. Shows antagonism		LHT //	/		8
Totals	39	19	13	23	81

IBM employs six dimensions of group behavior, which serve as the basis upon which group interaction is evaluated. Each of these six dimensions is accompanied by two sets of polar adjectives on a seven-item continuum (semantic differential type scale with bipolar adjectives). The dimensions are relevance, flexibility, tension, orientation, interest, and verbosity. Group behavior is rated periodically at specified intervals, such as every three or five minutes, by marking one of the seven spaces in the continuum that best represents how closely one of the adjectives describes the observed behavior. The IBM scale is shown in Fig. 7.3.

The IBM is designed such that two or more raters should be used to observe and record the group interaction. In fact, the more raters, the better the measurement. Each rater, then, will record his or her observations on each of the twelve items at the prescribed interval (every three or five minutes is normal). *Every rater* fills out an IBM scale for *every member* of the group for each prescribed *time interval*. For example, if five raters observed a ten-member group for thirty minutes at five-minute intervals, a total of 300 IBM scales would be completed.

The most common method for analyzing the results is to average each mem-

Relevance	Relevant	:____:____:____:____:____:____:____:	Irrelevant
	Related	:____:____:____:____:____:____:____:	Unrelated
Flexibility	Flexible	:____:____:____:____:____:____:____:	Inflexible
	Changeable	:____:____:____:____:____:____:____:	Unchangeable
Tension	Bothered	:____:____:____:____:____:____:____:	Cool
	Tense	:____:____:____:____:____:____:____:	Relaxed
Orientation	Task-Oriented	:____:____:____:____:____:____:____:	Socially Oriented
	Ideational	:____:____:____:____:____:____:____:	Personal
Interest	Interested	:____:____:____:____:____:____:____:	Apathetic
	Involved	:____:____:____:____:____:____:____:	Withdrawn
Verbosity	Wordy	:____:____:____:____:____:____:____:	Short
	Brief	:____:____:____:____:____:____:____:	Lengthy

Fig. 7.3 IBM scale.

ber's rating on each dimension and compare the results to the averages of the other members on each of the twelve dimensions. One could then pick out relevant personality traits such as a high degree of dogmatism, a high degree of anxiety, and so on, and compare them on the twelve dimensions of group behavior. A different approach would be to combine all of the group members' scores on a given dimension and see if there was an overall effect on the group as a whole. Finally, a comparison of these interaction patterns could be made to various group outcomes such as achievement, efficacy of decision, problem solving, member satisfaction, and time of solution.

We have discussed the structure of small groups in terms of the number of group members, the communication networks existing between group members, and the interaction of group members. We feel that these interrelated elements work together in determining the structure or

posture of small groups. We are not suggesting that any one word can be used to describe a specific group structure. It is a far too complex process for such parsimony. Group structure is best approached and understood by examining how many people are interacting through communication patterns in what manner. We might add that we could just as easily have discussed group interaction in terms of group size, group structure, and communication networks. At any rate, understanding small-group communication necessitates a thorough knowledge and understanding of all of these interrelated variables.

The Functions of Small Groups

Groups exist in society because they serve some function for society, for the group, or for the individual members of the group. Many times a group will serve more than one of these functions and may fulfill all three simultaneously at times. For example, a jazz quartet may contribute to the cultural life of society, accrue publicity and status for the group itself, and benefit the individual musicians with financial and esthetic rewards. In most instances, however, one function will predominate. Of course, each function satisfies particular needs and has particular effects on the nature of communication within the group. Although there are many specific purposes a group may serve, we will discuss the four major functions that small groups normally serve.

SOCIAL RELATIONSHIPS

Sometimes small groups are primarily concerned with the establishment and maintenance of social relationships. Four individuals who meet once a week to play bridge and stay in touch with each other's lives represent this type of a group. Likewise, a ski group that follows the snow to major ski resorts during the winter months is primarily concerned with social relationships. However, other kinds of groups provide social relationships as secondary functions. Even the most task-oriented group, such as a secretarial pool, may provide its individual members with opportunities for relaxation, rewarding interpersonal relationships, conversation, and entertainment—if only during the lunch hour.

The development of social relationships is a vital area to most people in society. We will defer additional remarks concerning social relationships until later in the text, where we have devoted an entire chapter to this topic. We will concentrate here on the other four functions of small

groups—education, persuasion, problem solving and decision making, and therapy.

EDUCATION

Another function of groups is education. Groups may formally or informally work to achieve and exchange knowledge. A college class is formally and almost exclusively devoted to this function. However, among members of a bridge club or a bird watchers' group, learning may be an accident, a by-product, or a preliminary to the group's main purpose.

Education fulfills individual, group, and societal needs. For individuals, it satisfies curiosity—clearly a potent human drive, as the behavior of children shows. Education may also satisfy a person's desire for competence, or the achievement of expertise and knowledge in a particular area. For the group, certain levels of knowledge may be essential if the group's tasks are to be adequately performed. Thus, the members of an environmental group must first determine the effects that construction of a highway will have on the ecology of an area. Only then will the group be able to complete its task: to decide whether or not to oppose the project. Education is not restricted to task-oriented groups; even the members of a socially oriented group learn from each other. At the societal level, the values of education are overwhelming. Individuals and groups must learn the ways to create and run the basic machinery of society— they must learn to produce goods and services—if the society is to continue functioning and benefiting its members.

Whether or not education is successful

within a small group depends on several of the same communication factors operating in other situations. For example, the processes of selective attention, perception, and retention will affect a receiver when he or she is in a face-to-face, small-group, public address, or mass communication situation. The clarity, meaningfulness, familiarity, and vividness of information presented will also determine how much a receiver understands and learns, as will the amount of redundancy built into the message he hears.[18]

There are, however, three factors unique to the small-group situation that may facilitate or inhibit learning within it. These are the amount of new information contributed, the number of persons in a group, and the frequency of interaction between group members. Group learning can be very effective if each member brings useful knowledge to the group. If none of the members has new knowledge to contribute, nothing is gained.

The size of a group can make a difference to the learning that takes place in it. The larger the group, the greater the potential for a diversity of ideas and knowledge. However, the group may become so large as to be unwieldy. Each person will have less of a chance to participate and receive feedback. Some ideas will necessarily be overlooked and some people ignored.

If each member brings something to the group and the group is of optimum size, then the degree of interaction becomes important. Members in such a group can correct each other's errors, add much in-

[18]M. Daniel Smith, *Theoretical Foundations of Learning and Teaching* (Waltham, Mass.: Xerox College Publishing, 1971).

formation, and create an energetic atmosphere that stimulates learning. Many businessmen recognize this principle by placing employees in task forces to study a problem or by holding "brainstorming" sessions, which often result in fresh insights that one individual could not have developed on his or her own. That is why the degree of interaction among group members is so important. If all members participate, then the group can weed out and integrate the mass of information that results. A small group functioning in this way is an effective instrument for education.

PERSUASION

In many situations, it is not easy to separate persuasion from education. A tennis pro teaching a novice how best to grip the racket may use some persuasion in the form of mild fear—for instance, "If you don't do it the way I'm telling you, you'll get a sore wrist." And a door-to-door salesman trying to persuade a customer to buy a broom may use education as part of his appeal—"Electric vacuum cleaners contribute to the energy crisis by using unnecessary electricity." The thin line separating education from persuasion is probably thinnest in a small-group setting, where members rarely state the exact purpose of their communication.

A person who engages in persuasive attempts in a small-group situation may have much to gain, but he or she may also have much to lose. The satisfactions and risks of using persuasion in a small group are illustrated by the "backroom" discussions that go on when a presidential nominee must select his (or her) running mate. An adviser to the nominee may satisfy his or her own need for dominance and achievement by persuading other advisers to back the vice-presidential candidate of his or her choice. But a group member who advocates attitudes and behavior that deviate significantly from the group's norms will find himself subjected to pressures to conform.[19] A Southerner who advocates the selection of a Southern governor to run with a Southern senator picked as the presidential nominee will undoubtedly find himself pressured to conform to the group's desire for a more "balanced" ticket. If the Southern adviser has high status and is likely to make bad publicity for the party by denouncing the group's proceedings to the press, he or she will receive increased communication as the group attempts to keep him or her within the fold. But if the Southern adviser has low status or maintains his or her deviant position for a long time, he or she may receive less communication and eventually be isolated or rejected.

Whether or not a group member chooses the role of advocate for a single position depends, to some extent, on how much information he or she has.[20] If group members have an abundance of information and alternatives to offer, they will be more likely to adopt neutral roles and simply present all the alternatives. A member who has little information will probably choose one position to defend—perhaps because limited knowledge has made it easier for him or her to make a choice prior to the group discussion. For

instance, the presidential nominee's campaign manager will probably investigate all vice-presidential possibilities and draw up a list, noting the advantages and drawbacks of each. Special interest advisers, however, such as a feminist, a labor leader, a civil rights worker, or a campaign aide who has been spening all his (or her) time analyzing public opinion polls from major cities, will be more likely to advocate a particular candidate because of limited information.

As research indicates, persuasion in a small group setting can be risky. The group member who attempts to persuade must realize that his or her position will probably not be accepted without qualification. If a group member's persuasive attempts are too discrepant from the group's values, he or she may create conflict, thereby jeopardizing his or her own position within the group. A clear understanding of problem solving and decision making in small groups can help a persuader to maximize the results of his efforts.

PROBLEM SOLVING AND DECISION MAKING

Many groups function in order to solve problems and make decisions. These functions are really two parts of a single, continuous process. Problem solving involves discovering previously unknown alternatives or solutions, whereas decision making involves choosing between two or more solutions. Thus, problem solving generates the material on which decisions are based. For instance, a chess club may study all the possible responses that White can make in response to a move by Black in order to find out which

[19]B. Collins and H. Guetzkow, *A Social Psychology of Group Processes for Decision-Making* (New York: Wiley, 1964).
[20]Ibid.

moves lead to a winning position. That is problem solving. The choice of White's best response from all the possibilities is decision making. Sometimes only the first part of the process is necessary; the chess club may discover that there is only one response that will not lead to disaster for White.

Problem solving and decision making address rather obvious individual, group, and societal needs. People and institutions continually face questions that need answers, problems that need solutions, and conflicts that need resolution. Often a group effort is the most efficient, creative, and satisfying way to meet these needs. For instance, the Bobby Fischer-Boris Spassky chess match sent an unprecedented number of experienced and beginning players flocking to chess clubs, where they could work together to anticipate the moves and develop the best strategies for their favorite player. The group sessions often came up with correct lines of play long before the two individual players did.

This greater productivity of group effort is called the assembly effect bonus, which we mentioned earlier. If a group's product is greater than the combined product of the same number of people working alone, the extra product is the bonus. Take, for example, the task of listing uses for brown paper bags. One would not expect an immense bonus of creativity to burst forth during this particular challenge. But, in fact, if five people working alone came up with a total of eighty uses, the same five people working in a group might generate a list of two hundred uses, and the chances are that their list would be more creative as well as longer. One

member might mention that he had seen paper bags used as masks by players in a children's theater in San Francisco that might remind a second member that a paper bag over the head can stop hiccups. This might lead a third member to free-associate to other household uses—say, degreasing chicken stock. The spontaneity, creativity, and diversity of small group interaction make it an excellent tool for problem solving and decision making.

Stages in problem solving and decision making. The movement from problem solving to decision making does not occur in one single, swift jump. In his theory of reflective thinking, John Dewey, suggested that rational thinking involves six phases.[21] These stages have traditionally been regarded as the most logical and orderly process for individual or group problem solving and decision making. The first phase is recognition of a difficulty; the individual or group confronts some problem or uncertainty that is causing frustration. In phase two, the person or group defines or clarifies the exact nature of the problem that he (or she) or it faces. This phase leads to the third: developing criteria for solutions. In phase four, possible solutions are suggested and rationally explored. After adequately studying the possibilities, the individual or group enters phase five: selection of the optimum solution. This is followed by the sixth phase: putting the plan into action.

Research into group problem solving and decision making has shown that at least three stages, roughly corresponding

[21] For an extended discussion on the reflective thinking process, see John Dewey, *How We Think* (New York: Basic Books, 1910).

to those of Dewey, occur.[22] The first phase is called the orientation stage: members ask for and exchange information; they then classify, confirm, and repeat it among themselves. In the second stage called evaluation, group members seek out and discuss their opinions, analyses, and personal feelings concerning the problem. In the third phase, known as the control stage, members ask for and exchange suggestions, directions, solutions, and possible plans for action.

From Dewey's work and that of his followers, a standard agenda has evolved; it is the most commonly used order for analyzing problems in groups and can be adapted to any problem-solving situation.

ing the problem as an open-ended, unbiased policy question. A good example would be, "Should the government regulate marijuana?" If the question were worded, "How can the government eliminate marijuana?" the discussion would be biased by the untested assumption that marijuana is harmful to the public. Similarly, the question, "Should marijuana be legalized or not?" builds in bias, allowing an either-or answer, with no possibility for exploring other policies, such as penalizing dealers but not people who grow marijuana only for personal use or allowing sale but not advertising. Either-or questions close off alternatives rather than encourage a free-flowing discussion.

Standard agenda
I. Definition of the problem.
   A. Definition of terms
   B. Definition of scope
II. Analysis of the problem
   A. History and causes
   B. Effects and extent
III. Criteria for solutions
   A. Generation of Criteria
   B. Ordering of criteria according to priority
IV. Possible solutions
   A. Generation of possible solutions
   B. Evaluation according to criteria
V. Selection of the optimum solution
VI. Plan for action

This agenda approach requires the group to define at the outset the exact nature of the problem it is confronting. Usually, the group should begin by stat-

Once a group has clearly stated its problem, it must define all terms in the question and any other terms likely to turn up in discussion. This step is needed so that group members do not hold widely varying assumptions about what the terms mean. For example, in the marijuana

[22]R. Bales and F. Strodtbeck, "Phases in Group Problem Solving," *The Journal of Abnormal and Social Psychology, 46* (1951), pp. 485–495.

question, does "government" mean federal, local, or state government? Does "regulation" mean only outlawing, or does it encompass a spectrum of controls? Does "marijuana" include hashish, a derivative of cannabis resin, or only cannabis leaves?

While the group is defining terms, the scope of the problem must be narrowed to manageable proportions. The question, "What should be done about drugs?" would include too many divergent subjects to allow an orderly discussion. A better strategy for group problem solving of complex problems is to break them down into smaller segments that can be dealt with one by one.

Before a group tries to analyze a problem, it must gather enough information so that it can fully discuss the causes and effects of the problem and its past and present extent. A decision based on inadequate knowledge is no better—and may be even worse—than no knowledge at all. Furthermore, uninformed people tend to cling to one position instead of being neutral, thus causing conflict and dead-end discussion. For instance, the National Commission on Marijuana and Drug Abuse hired scores of experts to research different aspects of drug use and regulation. If it had not, the commission's members would certainly have become bogged down in ideological arguments; instead, presented with the researcher's information, many of them realized how little they had understood the issues and developed objective, open-minded attitudes.

Once the problem has been fully analyzed, the group moves into a stage that is crucial to decision making—the development of criteria, or standards, for judging possible solutions. These criteria might be based on such factors as time, money and other resources, ethical and value judgments, and any other considerations that the group feels are important. In developing criteria for proposed action on marijuana regulation, one group might decide: Any action must be implemented at once, it must cost less than present regulatory programs, it must not encourage the use of marijuana by minors, and it must not create a profit motive for black marketeers. Another group might choose different criteria: Cost is no object, any solution must discourage marijuana use while clearly differentiating between marijuana and narcotics, and action must not expand the federal drug-regulatory bureaucracy or further crowd the courts. The group must then weigh the importance of each criterion and decide which ones have priority. In this way, alternatives that meet different criteria can be compared according to how well they rank in priority.

After the criteria have been chosen and ordered, all the possible alternatives are explored. Each is evaluated according to how well it meets the criteria. Its benefits are compared to its costs and disadvantages. If no proposed solutions satisfy the criteria, the group must look for more solutions or revise its criteria. The solution or combination of solutions that best meets the criteria is chosen. Thus, the first group in the marijuana example might choose to allow the possession and sale of marijuana under regulations similar to those for alcohol. The second group, using different criteria, might decide against direct control of marijuana and, instead, call for a national program to educate people about transcendental meditation and other alternatives to drugs as means of altering consciousness.

In the last stage of decision making,

group members must determine the best way to implement the proposal. The group must decide what resources are needed, who will take responsibility for putting the plan into action, when it will begin, and so on. Once the plan has been implemented, its effects must be observed and evaluated. If it is a success, with no undesirable side effects, the process is complete. If the plan is not working, however, the group must revert to earlier stages of the problem-solving process, reanalyzing the problem, generating new criteria or solutions, or finding new ways to implement the original solution. Long-range plans generally require continued observation and revision.

The agenda outlined above has been advocated by many as the most effective, but there are many other strategies. One technique that looks especially promising is derived from computer science and is called Backtrack Programming.[23] A group using this method must first set up rigid criteria for the solution. Then the major problem is broken down into subproblems, each of which is solved before the next is considered. For example, if too many airplanes are landing and taking off at an airport, causing congestion and delays, Backtrack Programming would break down this problem into subproblems based on the sources of the traffic and availability of other landing and takeoff sites. Subproblem One might be: Different airlines schedule flights to the same places at the same times and do not fully load their planes. Subproblem Two might

be: There are no other airports within a radius of five hundred miles. This process continues until the group has defined all the subproblems at work in this particular situation. The group considers the subproblems one at a time, beginning with whichever seems to be the most logical starting point. Solutions to the first subproblem are compared to the criteria. The best is chosen, and the group moves on to the next subproblem, building solutions to it based on the solution to the first subproblem. If at any point the group cannot find a solution to meet the criteria, it backtracks to the previous subproblem and changes the solution that is causing the trouble. Backtrack Programming forces consideration of the criteria at each stage in the process, thereby producing an ultimate solution that deals consistently with all the subproblems. Such a systematic, deliberate approach is especially helpful for groups facing complex issues.

THERAPY

In recent years, therapy groups have skyrocketed in popularity. Husbands and wives can join marriage counseling groups to work out problems in their relationships. Drug addicts can seek treatment in a variety of groups such as Daytop and Synanon. Smokers and compulsive eaters can attend group sessions that provide them with emotional support to "quit the habit." Policemen, teachers, and business executives can participate in role-playing groups designed to increase their sensitivity to the needs of ghetto dwellers, students, and subordinates. Underlining all these purposes are the assumptions that it is acceptable for an individual to admit needs and problems to

[23] For a brief description, see M. Scott and E. Bodaken, "Backtrack Programming: A Computer-Based Approach to Group Problem-Solving," Contributed Paper, International Communication Association, Montreal, Quebec, April, 1973.

Underlining the purposes of therapy groups are the assumptions that it is acceptable for an individual to admit needs and problems to others and that empathy may increase the effectiveness of communication among people. (Photograph: Maury Englander)

change knowledge, or spend a socially satisfying evening—although all those things may occur during therapy.

Communication in therapy groups, most typically, involves self-disclosure. In a supportive climate, each member is encouraged to talk openly about his or her feelings. If conflict arises, it may be encouraged or regulated by the therapist or leader, according to his or her understanding of each member's ability to cope with it. Feedback helps the individual learn more about the way he or she responds in certain situations and helps the therapist see the way the individual behaves with others. The group setting provides an opportunity for interaction that could never occur in a one-to-one relationship in the therapist's office. Thus, emphasis in a therapy group is usually on the communication process rather than on the content of the communication. The question to be answered is not, "Can this group agree that John is a hostile person?" but "How does being in a group influence John's behavior?"

Some therapy groups emphasize total release of inhibitions in intense "encounters" or "marathons," where members are supposed to express feelings with no holds barred except for physical violence. Other groups are more long-range and unfocused, such as the therapeutic live-in communities begun in England by R. D. Laing to treat schizophrenics without making them feel institutionalized or cut off from society. And still other groups are highly structured or focused on quite specific personal goals, such as desensitizing phobic people to a particularly fearsome phenomenon—dogs, airplanes, tall buildings, and so on.

others and that empathy may increase the effectiveness of communication among people.

A therapy group differs from other small-group situations in that there is no group goal; instead, the object of the therapy group is to help each individual achieve personal change. Certainly, he or she must interact with other group members in order to benefit, but his or her main effort is to help himself or herself, not help the group reach consensus, exchange

Although participants in a therapy group often testify to its helpfulness, evidence about the value of such groups is at best tentative. Although authorities may disagree vehemently about the benefits, they concur that any therapy group ought to be run by a person who has proper training and knows the histories of the individuals involved. Groups that undertake such emotionally volatile activities without the guidance of a trained leader may do more harm than good.[24]

Discussion in the Small Group

Effective discussion within the small group setting requires close attention to several factors. Individual members must realize that they now constitute a distinct entity and no longer have the luxury of basking in self-serving gratification. Primary among these factors is recognition by all members of the *exact purpose* or goals of the group. Although a group may meet regularly to solve some problem, many of the individual members may have differing interpretations as to the goals of the group or how the problem should be solved. A group concerned with increased recognition of homosexual preferences might attempt to educate the public regarding sex role behavior. This purpose will not be accomplished if some of the members interpret the goal as simply placating members of the gay faction, whereas other members focus on establishing tolerance by the larger heterosexual community. Recognition of common

goals not only increases the chances of meeting the goal, but it also generates *group identity*, another factor for effective group participation. A sense of group identity helps insure relevant and pertinent discussion regarding any goal the group chooses. Relevant discussion is also closely related to *well-defined roles* for individual group members. Of particular importance is the leadership role, for this role exerts influence on the communication transactions in such a way as to promote pertinent discussion. Lack of effective leadership can significantly impede discussion attempts. We will discuss various types of leadership roles and their effect on group interaction later in the chapter. A final consideration of efective group discussion is that every member must have an accurate understanding of the *specific communication situation*. For effective group discussion, each member must know when to speak and when to listen. In addition, each member must accept the communications of others as discussion, not as final opinions or solutions.

EFFECTIVE SMALL-GROUP DISCUSSION

Effective concomitants of discussion have been formally investigated by numerous researchers. One approach suggests a model consisting of six components considered to be essential for maximum goal attainment.[25] Some of these components reflect our previous remarks; so we will mention them but briefly.

Individual members must subordinate their goals for the accomplishment of the

[24]See M. Liberman, I. Yalom, and M. Miles, *Encounter Groups: First Facts* (New York: Basic Books, 1973).

[25]M. Anderson, "A Model of Group Discussion," *Southern Speech Journal* Summer, 30 (1965), pp. 279–293.

group goal. The importance of having every member of the group recognize and accept the group goal or purpose cannot be overemphasized. Second, the group must be in possession of all available *facts and evidence* relating to a specific topic if they are to solve a problem in that content area. Moreover, inputs from various group members must be weighed against the relative credibility and expertise attributed to a particular group member. In other words, group members must defer to superior knowledge or experience of another member when appropriate. Third, the group must employ a *systematic thought process* for any joint discussion. Some individuals seem to display a marked absence of cognitive structure or common sense. Decision making and problem solving, in particular, must be approached in a logical and systematic fashion. Systematic thinking will prevent a social group from gathering at the park on Sunday afternoon with no provisions for softball equipment or a business meeting from taking place with portfolios missing for half the members. The fourth component is *group structure*. As we indicated earlier, group structure in terms of size, communication networks, and group interaction will mediate the nature and quality of discussion within a small group. Next, effective group discussion is characterized by a common *perceptual framework*. This means that communications between group members must have a common frame of reference in that each member must ascribe the same meanings to the communication. *Leadership*, the sixth component, is vital to insuring equality of participation, quality outcomes, and group harmony. We will discuss this dimension in more detail in a later section of this chapter.

OBSTACLES TO EFFECTIVE GROUP DISCUSSION

We provided a lengthy discussion in Chapter 5 regarding some common obstacles to effective communication. In so doing, we defined the selectivity process as selective exposure, attention, perception, and retention of communication stimuli. As in other communication contexts, the *selectivity processes* are a source of frustration to effective small-group discussion. This process prohibits group members from acquiring the necessary communication to relate to other members of the group, to approach problems in an organized and systematic fashion, to assume the proper role within the group, and to recognize the exact nature of the group's purpose. On the basis of selective exposure, group members may support other members of the group simply because their attitudes or values are consonant rather than because they are viable for the group or accurate. Similarly, a group member may selectively pay less attention to opinions from other group members when this information is inconsistent with his or her views on a particular matter. Although these two processes may or may not be conscious on the part of a group member, selectivity of perceptions and retention are out of the control of the group member. Effective discussion or problem solving rarely takes place when group members perceive fundamental issues differently or have forgotten crucial bits of information. These selectivity processes are unavoidable in all forms of human interaction. They can be compensated for by a climate of openness, honesty, and tolerance.

Another obstacle to effective group discussion is provided by *blockers*, or individuals who talk too much, talk too little, or engage in defensive behavior. Individuals who talk too much and too frequently not only block group goals, but also provide a source of frustration and exasperation for the other members of the group. These types of individuals are all too common in the classroom. There are many plausible reasons for this type of communication behavior. Some people talk simply to hear themselves talk, whereas others say in ten words what could just as easily be said in two words. Also, some people are suffering from delusions that they are more knowledgeable and erudite than they actually are and attempt to impart this "knowledge" on the nearest captive audience. Remedies for this type of blocking range from a sharp blow to the mouth to skillfully directing the discussion to other group members.

The individual who talks too little can deprive the group of a valuable source of potential information, as well as take up space that could be used by a more active contributor. If the group members continue to ignore such a recalcitrant participant, he or she will surely persist in withdrawing from the group. In addition, such an individual might discourage other members from participating by generating a climate of nonparticipation. A supportive climate by the group, gentle coaxing, or posing direct questions at this individual could provide the necessary catalyst for group involvement.

Group participants normally engage in defensive behavior under certain circumstances. The presence of an extremely aggressive and dynamic group member can threaten the rest of the group in such a way that they will defend every contribution or idea to the death in order to gain comparable prestige. Directly attacking the ideas or opinions of another in a sarcastic or insulting manner, even when these opinions have marginal utility, will surely create a defensive air. In a similar vein, defensive behavior usually results when personalities enter into a discussion. Contributions can be gently rejected without calling someone fat, stupid, or juvenile. Care must be taken to acknowledge someone's effort, even if the contribution is lacking. The best way to avoid defensive behavior in a group discussion is to avoid the types of behavior that we have discussed.

The *hidden agenda* is another source of frustration to effective group discussion. A hidden agenda exists when the group goal or the goals of one or more of the individual members differs from the stated purpose of the group. It is not uncommon for individuals to join certain groups solely to meet other people. These individuals will direct more energy toward cultivating social relationships than to accomplishing group goals or tasks. Hidden agendas often lead to behaviors and patterns of interaction that are detrimental to the group purpose. Awareness of a hidden agenda by group members can also lead to disruption of the group. A common example is that of college professors who conduct their own research under the guise of having the class do "research." More than one class has rebelled when the true purpose of their work was discovered. Though the use of hidden agenda can be an effective persuasive device, it also raises ethical and moral issues. We will leave you to your own conscience in terms of using hidden agendas.

Another obstacle involves the distinction between *ideal and practical solutions*. Group discussion may focus on the ideal resolution to a problem that is far too complex and difficult for solution. Instead of concentrating on discussions that may result in some practical outcomes, the group shoots for all or nothing. These types of discussions can waste a lot of time, create tension and conflict, and usually result in nonproductive consequences. The usual discussion involving politics, religion, or sex generally results in these types of negative outcomes. As we will discuss in the mass communication chapter, television violence has been the focus of an infinite number of discussions in the past quarter century. One cannot help but think that such discussions have concentrated too much in the past on the ideal solution instead of a practical solution.

Group interaction is characterized by a *tendency toward conformity*, which has an obvious impact on the effectiveness of discussion. People have been shown to conform in judgments about the lengths of lines even when individual perceptions differed significantly from the consensus opinion.[26] This tendency toward conformity also operates in other areas such as stated opinions or discussions. Many people will agree to anything if they become tired, bored, or frustrated enough. It is

also not uncommon for individuals to conform when they are disinterested in the agenda or feel inadequate concerning their abilities or contributions to the group. This concept is similar to the risky shift that we have discussed earlier and will examine in further detail in Chapter 14.

Effective discussion will also be impeded in the small group when group members rely on *stereotype and tradition*. We have earlier stressed the problems of relying only on cultural- and sociological-level data. Methods, procedures, and ideas that were relevant and cogent in the past may not be operable any longer. Introduction of these dated concepts into the group discussion can create intense conflict and render group discussion ineffective. Likewise, stereotyping or generalizing introduces these same disruptive elements into the discussion. Discussions have raged for years at our own university over the feasibility of co-ed dormitories. The majority of the students were obviously in favor of this practice, whereas the administration balked. One frequently heard opinion focused on the traditional aspect of separate housing facilities for men and women living on campus. This approach more or less boiled down to saying, "If God meant us to have co-ed dorms, He or She would have created them from the very beginning." Another tacit assumption was based on the stereotype that mixed genders cohabitating out of wedlock would surely be considered immoral. The university now has co-ed dorms, but many of the discussions leading up to this outcome could hardly be called effective.

Interpersonal conflict may at times be an-

[26]S. E. Asch, "Effects of Group Pressure Upon the Modification and Distortion of Judgements," in *Groups, Leadership, and Men,* ed. H. Guetzkow (Pittsburgh: Carnegie Press, 1951).

other obstacle to group discussion. Any time a group of individuals gets together, there will be a certain amount of conflict between ideas, personalities, and methods. This problem can be more intensified in small-group interaction than in dyadic contexts owing to the larger number of sources of potential conflict. We provided an in-depth discussion of interpersonal conflict in the last chapter; so we will not dwell on it unnecessarily at this point. We will simply add that much of the communication energy of the group can be dissipated by attempts to manage the interpersonal conflict rather than discuss topics pertinent to the accomplishment of group goals or beneficial for the harmony and satisfaction of group members.

A final obstacle to effective small-group discussion is *improper logic*. As we mentioned earlier, there is a difference between observation and inference. One can observe an event and necessarily draw the proper conclusion from it. Group discussions that attempt to solve a problem or arrive at an equitable decision must employ proper cause and effect analyses. They must decide whether positive outcomes will follow from such and such a procedure or whether additional factors must be taken into account. For example, the presence of one outspoken member in the group does not necessarily mean that dissension that the group is experiencing is attributable to that individual and that immediate expulsion from the group will ease the tension. There could easily be other reasons for the dissension.

These are the obstacles that we believe are most common to the disruption of effective small-group discussion. Of course, there are many more potential obstacles that might impede group discussion in particular situations. Recognition of these obstacles is a necessary first step in evaluating the effectiveness of group discussions. Unfortunately, group discussion does not always have positive consequences. There are both advantages and disadvantages to the small-group discussion context.

COSTS AND BENEFITS OF SMALL-GROUP DISCUSSION

Research has shown that discussion techniques have a number of advantages and disadvantages that accrue from employing small-group communication practices. This is particularly appropriate when the discussion results in a solution to some problem. These considerations will not apply in situations where the ultimate authority of the group lies with one individual and the rest of the group members are excluded from discussions where group policy or action is decided.

One of the advantages of group discussion is that *quality outcomes* are likely to result. Research has demonstrated that group decisions through discussion are frequently superior to those of individuals working alone because of the interaction and corrective feedback among members working conjointly.[27] The assumption here is that the group members possess sufficient expertise to render a viable solution and produce informative and constructive communication. Another advantage is that *acceptance* of ideas and procedures is more likely when group dis-

---

[27]W. Thompson, *Quantitative Research in Public Address and Communication* (New York: Random House, 1967), pp. 97–104.

cussion precedes some outcome. Again, research has demonstrated that decisions made by subordinate group members will experience greater acceptance simply because they played an integral part in the decision-making process.[28] Group members will also be *more committed* to the group task and to the implementation of some negotiated decision when they have been directly involved in analyzing problems and selecting solutions through discussion. Another positive aspect of group discussion techniques is the potential for *increased status*. Some scholars maintain that the responsibility and interaction involved in group decision making engenders a sense of status and recognition for the participants.[29] This is roughly akin to the pride and accomplishment one feels when one has contributed something to the accomplishment of some goal. These positive consequences of group discussion may be offset by the structure of the specific group under consideration, however.

One of the most basic costs involved with group discussion is *time expenditure*. The voicing of many opinions or recommendations for action can take a great deal of time. If the purpose of the group is vocational or recreational in nature, this is no problem. However, if some problem is to be solved or some decision made, an inordinate amount of time can be spent over matters that might just as easily be handled by one individual, especially if this individual is in a power position. Group discussion will also require advance preparation in some cases. This is additional time expended. The time factor must be evaluated in terms of group outcome or the quality of some decision. Monetary expenditure is another potential factor closely related to time expenditures. If the discussion is scheduled during school or working hours, participants will have to leave their jobs or classroom, representing a monetary loss of some sort. Discussions by small groups also frequently necessitate having various materials readily available for the group. These materials cost money. Students wishing to participate in group discussions with notable speakers brought to their campus frequently have to buy literature written by the speaker so that they can familiarize themselves with the speaker's philosophies prior to the discussion session. *Conformity* and the *risky shift* are additional costs to small-group discussion. We have already discussed conformity in this chapter, and we will reserve further comment about the risky shift for a later chapter. A final cost of group discussion is *groupthink*. Irving Janis analyzed a set of important government decisions on foreign policy and found that longstanding, cohesive groups tend to arrive at decisions in a characteristic way, which he termed groupthink. This small-group phenomenon will affect the communication patterns of the group, and any group discussion that meets the criteria set forth by Janis is likely to be affected by groupthink. Janis has compiled a list of symptoms of the groupthink syndrome:[30]

1. An illusion of invulnerability, shared by most or all members,

[28]H. Martin, "Communication Settings," in *Speech Communication: Analysis and Readings*, ed. H. Martin and K. Anderson (Boston: Allyn and Bacon, 1968), pp. 70–74.

[29]Ibid.

[30]I. L. Janis, *Victims of Groupthink* (Boston: Houghton-Mifflin, 1972), pp. 197–198.

which creates excessive optimism and encourages taking extreme risks.

2. Collective efforts to rationalize in order to discount warnings that lead other members to reconsider their assumptions before they recommit themselves to their last policy decisions.

3. An unquestioned belief in the group's inherent morality, inclining the members to ignore the ethical or moral consequences of their decisions.

4. Stereotyped views of enemy leaders as too evil to warrant genuine attempts to negotiate or as too weak or stupid to counter whatever risky attempts are made to defeat their purposes.

5. Direct pressure on any member who expresses strong arguments against any of the group's stereotypes, illusions, or commitments, making clear that this type of dissent is contrary to what is expected of all loyal members.

6. Self-censorship of deviations from apparent group consensus, reflecting each member's inclination to minimize to himself or herself the importance of his doubts and counterarguments.

7. A shared illusion of unanimity concerning judgments conforming to the majority view (partly resulting from self-censorship of deviations, augmented by the false assumption that silence means consent).

8. The emergence of self-appointed mindguards—members who protect the group from adverse information that might shatter their complacency about the effectiveness and the morality of their decisions.

Leadership in the Small Group

Leadership is one of the most crucial roles in small-group interaction. This role will ultimately determine the quantity and quality of communication within the group, the outcome of the group purpose, and the harmony within the group. An individual becomes a leader either by *formal designation* or appointment, or an individual becomes prominent in the group over time and is an *emergent* leader.

It has been assumed that the majority of people would rather be leaders than followers. To this end there has been a virtual avalanche of information concerned with the qualities of leadership appearing in both scholarly and lay publications. In addition, parents tell their children to study hard so that they can become leaders someday, drill sergeants tell recruits to "stand tall and look sharp" so that they can become leaders, and various commercial advertisements tell the consumer how to dress, eat, and smell like a leader.

One of the more useful ways of looking at leadership traits is in terms of the behaviors that should accompany group leadership. Burgoon, Heston, and McCroskey suggest the following leadership functions:[31]

1. *Initiation:* The leader should and does originate and facilitate new

[31]M. Burgoon, J. Heston, and J. McCroskey, *Small Group Communication: A Functional Approach* (New York: Holt, Rinehart and Winston, 1974), pp. 143 –154.

ideas and practices. It is also his or her duty to resist new ideas when he or she feels that they are inappropriate.

2. *Membership Function:* Part of the behaviors of a leader are aimed at making sure that he or she is also a member of the group. This is done by mixing with the group, stressing informal interaction, and taking care of socioemotional needs.

3. *Representation Function:* Often a leader has to defend group members from external threats or act as their spokesman to outside groups.

4. *Organization Function:* A leader is often asked to structure his or her own work and that of others. He or she can be responsible for some things we have discussed earlier, like agenda setting.

5. *Integration Function:* This function requires conflict resolution or management and is concerned with creating an atmosphere conducive to individual happiness.

6. *Internal Information Management:* The leader must, at times, facilitate information exchange among the group members and seek feedback about how well the group is doing. And he or she must often inhibit the free flow of information to protect specific individuals. You will recall in the section on therapy that we suggested that one leadership function in laboratory groups is insuring that people are not personally harmed by information from other people. When information is not needed by all members, the leader functions to insure that those who need to know are informed.

7. *Gatekeeping Function:* When a group has to deal with other groups or organizational units, the leader functions as a filter and manager of information entering and leaving the group. This is a somewhat different function from monitoring the internal communication. If too much information is present, conflict can result as we have already said; this filtering process can reduce that possibility. Sometimes a group wants to say things that they do not wish other people to hear. Gripe sessions often provide cathartic benefits to group members, and the leader reports to others while protecting member anonymity. These two information control functions are of increasing importance in contemporary society. In fact, one principal activity of a decision maker in organizations is controlling the flow of information. We are sure that the discerning reader is already aware that this function is one that can be a positive aspect of group life or a source of problems.

8. *Reward Function:* The leader performs evaluative functions and expresses approval or disapproval of group members. This can be done by material rewards such as pay increases or by conferring status, praise, or recognition. Many group members are extremely sensitive to the leader's reward power, and much of their behavior, verbal and nonverbal communication, and work output is designed to bring them rewards from the leader.

9. *Production Function:* When the leader is responsible for getting a

task accomplished, much of his or her communication behavior is designed to elicit more effort and achievement. Of course, all the other functions we have discussed can lead to more production, although there is no necessary causal link. Happy workers are not necessarily more productive; so a task orientation is necessary to some degree in task groups.

LEADERSHIP STYLES

Another approach to leadership involves examining the effects of various leadership styles of group outcomes. Leadership style refers to the degree of control a leader exercises and his attitudes toward group members. Five distinct styles of leadership have been identified: authoritarian, bureaucratic or supervisory, diplomatic, democratic, and laissez-faire or group-centered.[32]

The authoritarian leader is a controller. His or her word is law and is inflexible. His or her motivation to lead may derive from strong dominance and achievement needs. An authoritarian leader usually relies heavily on rules and order, monopolizes communication, and discourages feedback. His or her group may be well organized and productive, but at the expense of interpersonal relationships, for group members tend to be tense and antagonistic toward each other. Former FBI Director J. Edgar Hoover is a good example of the authoritarian leader. He ran the FBI like a machine, brooked no interference, resented any criticism, and was accountable to no one.

The bureaucratic leader operates as a

[32]Ibid., pp. 143–154.

supervisor, impersonally overseeing and coordinating the group's activity. His god is not himself but The Organization. Rules and agendas make him feel that things are going well. He sees social relationships as unwelcome intrusions into efficiency; so he remains personally aloof and unsympathetic to interpersonal problems among members. He likes to communicate in memos peppered with officialese: disorderly discussions, however creative they may be, give him a feeling that anarchy lurks around the corner. His group may be productive because it is organized, but members tend to be apathetic and stifled. Factory workers often complain that they are treated this way by foremen whose only concern is the number of items that roll off the assembly line.

The diplomatic leader is a manipulator. Like the authoritarian, he or she is motivated by recognition and dominance needs and uses leadership to put himself or herself in the spotlight. The diplomatic leader tends to exert less control (or is at least more subtle about it) and to be more flexible than the authoritarian leader. Unlike the authoritarian, the diplomat is not committed to a particular ideology; this provides him or her with more freedom to adopt strategies to manipulate others. Thus, though he or she may appear to welcome suggestions and feedback democratically, he or she secretly tries to direct and control group outcomes. Talk show hosts often use this leadership style to keep control of the discussion without seeming authoritarian to the audience.

The democratic leader exercises much less control than the other three types of leaders. Such leaders want all the members to share responsibility and develop their own leadership potential. They encourage open participation and feedback and are concerned with both interpersonal and task relationships among group members. Although a democratic leader's group seems less organized and efficient than one that is strong-armed or manipulated into action, it works in a more relaxed atmosphere that tends to breed productivity, originality, and creativity because it makes maximum use of each member's abilities.

The laissez-faire or group-centered leader is highly nondirective. Ask such a leader if he or she *is* the leader, and he or she may deny it; he or she is "just one of the group." The laissez-faire leader wants to get all members to participate without asserting any of his or her authority. His or her communication behavior tends to serve as a link or transition that connects the contributions of group members. If no other group member attempts to exert more control than the laissez-faire leader, the group may be disorganized, unproductive, and apathetic because members feel the group lacks purpose. However, in certain situations, particularly in therapy groups, laissez-faire leadership is the most appropriate and effective of all five leadership styles.

In examining the effects of various styles of leadership, there is no mention of the way people become leaders, the role communication plays in establishing and maintaining leadership or how leadership roles change over time. A consideration of social influence and power recognizes these dynamic aspects of leadership in small groups.

LEADERSHIP AND SOCIAL INFLUENCE

A member may enter a group with externally derived power. For example, a small gourmet cooking class in French cuisine might be headed by a person with well-known credentials, such as Julia Child, or even some lesser known individual who happens to be the chef at a local restaurant. Both teachers, regardless of fame or anonymity, possess externally derived power. It is also possible for a member to build power within the group by establishing his or her credibility and status and engaging in campaigning behavior. For instance, if Julia Child's pastry is surpassed by that of an unsung member, that member's ability to influence other group members in this area is likely to be enhanced. As group tasks change and different members emerge as more competent for given tasks, power shifts. However, a person's power at any time also depends on how well he or she conforms to the group's standards and handles conflict. A potential leader who usually conforms can build up freedom to deviate, if he or she does so infrequently. The chef who proves himself or herself superior to Julia Child in *haute cuisine* may acquire the authority to promote a few eccentric variations on classic recipes. Sometimes a member who is good at resolving interpersonal conflict becomes the group's socioemotional leader. A group may have both a socioemotional leader and a task leader at the same time, although they are unlikely to be the same person.

Communication is received and sent most by those who have the power—that is, the leaders. Also, leaders are more successful at influencing other group members. But if leaders interact primarily with other high status group members, cliques or subgroups may form, low status members may feel threatened, and conflict may result. When subgroups form, feedback between them is frequently reduced, thereby diminishing one of the primary advantages of group interaction. Furthermore, competition and conflict among group members can reduce productivity, group cohesion, and the satisfaction of individual members.[33]

EFFECTIVE LEADERSHIP

Many different attempts have been made to identify the leadership orientations that are the most effective. One such attempt to compile effective leadership traits has led to the Contingency Model of Leadership Effectiveness.[34] In this model the *authoritarian leader* is considered most effective when he or she has power and good relations with group members and when the task is clearly structured. The authoritarian leader is also effective when unfavorable conditions exist, such as little power or group confidence and a poorly defined task. In other words, authoritar-

ian leadership is most effective in controlling conflict and getting the task accomplished, as well as when power and good relations are present and the group task is well structured. The *democratic leader* is most effective in moderately favorable situations where the group faces an unstructured task or where the leader/member relations are tenuous.

We would like to emphasize that probably no leader operates exclusively with just one of these orientations. All leaders behave in ways that fit into each of our five styles of leadership; so our comments are intended to represent effective modes of leadership with respect to general tendencies or most frequent behaviors. All of these orientations have obvious strengths and weaknesses, and the most effective mode of leading a group depends largely on the individual characteristics of both the leader and the group.

SUMMARY

1. Small-group communication may be defined as face-to-face interaction between three or more individuals for a recognized purpose such as information sharing, self-maintenance, or problem solving, such that the members are able to recall personal characteristics of the other members accurately. Small-group communication is more spontaneous and dynamic than public or mass communication, but it is more structured than dyadic communication.

2. The small group is a unique communication context owing to factors such as social facilitation, group personality, group norms, cohesion, commitment, interdependency, the risky shift, and the assembly effect bonus.

3. Theoretical formulations regarding groups have focused on the comparison of attitudes and values with others and on any effects the group has as an aggregate by generalizing the dyadic situation to larger groups, the amount of productivity or achievement of the

[33]M. Deutsch, ''The Effects of Cooperation and Competition upon Group Process,'' in *Group Dynamics*, ed. D. Cartwright and A. Zanders (New York: Harper and Row, 1968).

[34]F. Fiedler, ''The Contingency Model: A Theory of Leadership Effectiveness,'' in *Basic Studies in Social Psychology*, ed. H. Proshansky and B. Seidenbert (New York: Holt, Rinehart and Winston, 1965), pp. 538–551.

group, and the degree of interpersonal attraction between group members.

4. Individual characteristics, group characteristics, and external factors all interact to comprise group structure. Also related to group structure are communication networks, or the channels of communication that exist between members within the group. Finally, group interaction is closely related to group structure. Group structure is best approached and understood by examining how many people are interacting through communication and in what manner.

5. A group may serve some function for the individual member, for the group itself, or for society. Groups may provide members with an opportunity for social relationships, education, persuasion, decision making or problem solving, or therapy.

6. A group may formally or informally work to obtain and exchange information. Whether or not the small group is successful in educating its members depends on several factors. Three factors that are unique to the small group context that may affect learning are amount of new information, group size, and frequency of interaction between group members.

7. Small groups are common and ideal forums for persuasive attempts. A member of a small group who advocates positions that deviate from the group's norms may be subjected to pressures to conform. To some extent, the amount of information a group member possesses may affect his or her choice of positions.

8. Small groups are particularly adept at problem solving and decision making. Small group interaction seems to produce an assembly effect bonus; that is, the group's product is greater than the combined product of the same number of individuals working individually. The reflective thinking theory suggests that there are six steps in problem solving and decision making: recognizing the difficulty, defining and clarifying the problem, developing criteria for resolution, suggesting solutions, selecting the optimum solution, and implementing the plan. Another approach is Backtrack Programming. This method divides the group problem into subproblems, each of which is solved according to rigid criteria established for the overall problem.

9. Unlike other types of groups, a therapy group usually has no group goal. The object of most therapy groups is to assist members in obtaining personal change. Therapy groups should be run only by persons with adequate training and who know the personal case history of each individual member.

10. Effective group discussion requires that all members recognize the

exact purpose of the group, well-defined roles, a group identity, and a knowledge by all of the specific communication situation. In addition, members must subordinate personal goals for the group goal, have all the facts and evidence available and employ systematic thought processes, work from a common perceptual framework, and have effective leadership.

11. The selectivity process, hidden agendas, the tendency toward conformity, employing ideal solutions, relying on stereotype and tradition, interpersonal conflict, and the use of improper logic are all factors that impede small-group discussion.

12. Group discussion may result in positive outcomes such as quality output, more acceptance of ideas or procedures, more commitment by group members, or increased status for individual members. On the other hand, negative consequences such as time and monetary expenditures, risky decisions, and groupthink (the tendency for longstanding, cohesive groups to arrive at decisions in a characteristic way) may result from small-group discussion.

13. Five types of leaders, who are formally appointed or emerge to positions or prominence over time, have been identified: authoritarian, bureaucratic, diplomatic, democratic, and laissez-faire. Each style produces different effects on communication within the group, and specific leadership modes must be geared to the individual group and leader.

SUGGESTED READING

Burgoon, Michael; Judee K. Heston; and James C. McCroskey. *Small Group Communication: A Functional Approach.* New York: Holt, Rinehart and Winston, 1974.

Fisher, B. Aubrey. *Small Group Decision Making: Communication and the Group Process.* New York: McGraw-Hill, 1974.

Gulley, Halbert E., and Dale G. Leathers. *Communication and Group Process: Techniques for Improving the Quality of Small-Group Communication.* 3d ed. New York: Holt, Rinehart and Winston, 1977.

Janis, Irving L. *Victims of Groupthink.* Boston: Houghton-Mifflin, 1972.

Rosenfeld, Lawrence B. *Human Interaction in the Small Group Setting.* Columbus, Ohio: Charles E. Merrill, 1973.

Shaw, Marvin E. *Group Dynamics: The Psychology of Small Group Behavior.* New York: McGraw-Hill, 1971.

From the Reading

Define the following terms.

interaction
social facilitation
norm
risky shift
assembly effect bonus
syntality
centrality
channel
network
interaction process analysis
group personality
reflective thinker
agenda
group structure
hidden agenda
groupthink
conformity
emergent leader
laissez-faire
authoritarian
discussion
defensive behavior
task-oriented

Study Questions

1. What is small-group communication? How does it differ from public or mass communication?
2. What are the unique characteristics of small-group communication? Why are they unique?
3. Explain the assembly effect bonus. When will a group function more efficiently than the sum of individual contributors? Why?
4. What are some of the theoretical approaches to small-group communication? How do they differ? What are their contributions to the knowledge concerning group dynamics?
5. What factors determine the structure of a small group?
6. How does group size affect interaction within the group? Diagram the effect of group size on communication channels.
7. What are communication networks? Explain and diagram some of the more common networks. How do these representations differ from your diagram of the effects of group size on communication channels?
8. Explain one system for analyzing group interaction. What kinds of information are available from such an analysis?
9. What are the major functions that small groups serve? Can you identify any additional functions?
10. What is the reflexive thinking approach to problem solving and decision making? Outline the standard agenda for this approach.
11. What factors affect the small-group discussion?
12. What are the relative advantages and disadvantages of discussion? Under what conditions are they relevant?
13. What variables will determine whether or not small-group discussion is effective. How can you tell when a group discussion has been effective?
14. What are some common obstacles to effective group discussion?
15. Explain the groupthink syndrome. What are three symptoms of this phenomenon?

16. What are the specific types of behaviors that should accompany effective leadership?
17. List the five leadership orientations. How do these types of leaders differ from one another?
18. How would you decide which mode of leadership to employ if you were placed in charge of a group? If you were selected as the group leader by the majority?

An Exercise Designed to Demonstrate Group Versus Individual Productivity

1. Divide the class in half, with half of the students working alone and the remaining half divided into two equal groups.
2. Give both the individuals who are working alone and the two groups who are working collectively the task of generating as many creative uses for the paper clip as they can in a ten-minute period.
3. After five minutes, obtain a progress report from both groups and the individuals as to how many different uses they have generated, and record the results. At the end of the ten-minute period, again record the group and individual averages. Now place the individuals into two groups of approximate size to the original groups, and have them integrate their lists into a group list. Be sure to eliminate all duplications.
4. Have the original groups and the collections of individuals report their final counts. The average across groups will invariably be higher than the averages for the two collections of individuals.
5. Compare the counts for the first five minutes with the final five minutes for both the two groups and the individuals. This will usually show

that the individuals produce very few additional solutions during the second five minutes—they peak early—whereas the group productivity continues at a higher rate during the second five-minute period.
6. Why do groups have higher productivity than the same number of individuals working alone?_____
_____
_____
7. Why is the group more productive than even the combined individual solutions? _____
_____
_____
8. Compare the group lists with the individual lists and the integrated lists. Which solutions are the most creative? _____
_____
_____
9. What are some possible circumstances in which group productivity *would not* be more productive than a collection of individual efforts? ____
_____
_____
10. Why does the group continue to be more creative longer than individuals? _____
_____

An Exercise Designed to Promote Reflective Thinking in Problem Solving and Decision Making

Form groups of five or six, and consider the question of whether or not college students should be given a voice in hiring faculty members. Each group will structure their approach to this issue by completing the skeleton standard agenda outline presented below. Assume that the administration opposes this practice whereas most students are in favor of it.

    I. How should this issue be defined?
       A. What do the terms in question mean?
         1.
         2.
         3.
       B. What limitations should be placed on the discussion?
         1.
         2.
         3.
   II. What is the nature of this problem?
       A. What are the causes of the administration's reluctance?
         1.
         2.
         3.
       B. What effects does this have on the college or university?
         1.
         2.
         3.
  III. What are the criteria that should be used to judge possible solutions?
       A. Which considerations should be applied to these criteria?
         1.
         2.
         3.
       B. Which considerations are the most important?
         1.
         2.
       C. Which criteria are the least important?
         1.
         2.
  IV. What are the possible solutions?
       A.
       B.
       C.

      D.

      E.

  V. Which solutions are best?

     A. Administrative point of view:

        1.

        2.

        3.

     B. Student point of view:

        1.

        2.

        3.

 VI. Which is the best overall solution?_____

_____

VII. How will you implement this plan?_____

_____

After each group has completed their outline, compare the outlines to determine how they differ. It might be interesting to discuss some of the possible reasons why the outlines are different or to generate a class outline.

An Exercise Designed to Solve a Problem in the Small Group

A nuclear holocaust has occurred. The following eleven persons are the only human beings on earth to survive this holocaust. All of them are in a survival shelter with provisions to sustain only seven individuals at a low level for two weeks. It will take two weeks for the external radiation to drop to a safe level. Only seven of the eleven people can remain in the shelter and survive. Which seven should survive? (Form groups of five or six, and decide this issue.)

1. Dr. Dane: Thirty-seven; white; no religious affiliation; Ph.D. in history; college professor; good health; married; one child (Marshall); active; enjoys politics.
2. Mrs. Dane: Thirty-eight; white; Jewish; A.B. and M.A. in psychology; counselor in mental health clinic; good health; married; one child (Marshall); active in community.
3. Marshall Mal Dane: Ten; white; Jewish; special education classes for four years; mentally retarded; I.Q. 70; good health; enjoys his pet dogs.
4. Mrs. Sanchez: Thirty-three; Spanish-American; Catholic, ninth grade education; cocktail waitress; prostitute, good health; abandoned as a child; in foster home as a youth; attacked by foster father at age twelve; ran away from home; returned to reformatory; stayed until sixteen; married at sixteen; divorced eighteen; one child three weeks old (Gerald).
5. Gerald Sanchez: three weeks old; Spanish-American; good health; still nursing.
6. Mary Evans: Eight, black; Protestant; third grade; good health.

7. Babs Armword: Twenty-five; black; atheist; starting last year of nursing school; suspected homosexual activity; good health; seems bitter concerning racial problems; wears hippie clothes.
8. Mrs. Clark: Twenty-eight; black; Protestant; college graduate; electronics engineer; married; no children; good health; enjoys sports; grew up in ghetto.
9. Mr. Blake: Fifty-one; white; Mormon; B.S. in mechanics; very handy; married; four children; good health; enjoys outdoors and working in his shop.
10. Father Jensen: Thirty-seven; white; Catholic; college plus seminary; active in civil rights; criticized for liberal views; good health; former college athlete.
11. Dr. Gonzales: Sixty-six; Spanish-American; Catholic; doctor in general practice; two heart attacks in past five years, but continues to practice.

Questions to Consider

1. Which of the eleven individuals did each group generally wish to exclude from the shelter? Why do you think they were chosen?
2. What were the criteria used by each group for arriving at a decision? Were any personal biases noted in arriving at these criteria? If so, what were they?
3. Did the males and females in the groups differ significantly in their solutions? Did different ethnic or religious orientations produce different opinions?

An Exercise Designed to Assess Discussion in the Small Group

Form several groups, some of which have four members and some of which have seven or eight members. Discuss the following situation:

   A group of local businessmen have demanded reparations from the local university for damage inflicted by students during a demonstration. The university is to some extent dependent on the goodwill and financial support of the business community. The university has chosen to add a special $1.00 fee to the tuition of each student at the university and to deduct the same amount from the salary of each professor.

1. Is the university justified in taking this action?
2. Should the students and faculty accept this policy?
3. Assuming both do not accept this policy, what is the best alternative course of action?
4. If your group has decided that the university's original policy is undesirable, what is a more desirable policy?
5. What should be the university's course of action if the damage could be attributed directly to members of a specific club or organization at the university?
6. How would the situation change if the damage was caused by arson?
7. What would the best course of action be for the university if the cost was in excess of one million dollars?

Some Questions to Consider

1. From the university's point of view, what are some of the advantages and disadvantages of discussing this issue in groups?
2. Did the discussion go more smoothly in the smaller groups of four or in the larger groups of seven or eight? Why?
3. Which individual in your group appeared to exert the most influence? What are some behaviors that caused you to choose this individual as the most influential during this discussion?
4. List five reasons why you felt your discussion group performed effectively, or list five reasons why your discussion group performed inadequately. How did you arrive at a decision regarding the quality of discussion in your group?
5. Do you think the presence of an appointed discussion leader would have altered the discussion within your group? If so, how?

An Exercise Designed to Analyze Small-Group Interaction

Have the class form three approximately equal groups, and have them sit as a group anywhere in the classroom at their discretion. Each group will select three individuals to serve as observers while the group discusses any topic of their choice for fifteen minutes (the observers will insure that the discussion takes place for exactly fifteen minutes). Each observer will complete an Interaction Behavior Measure (IBM) scale for each group member at each five-minute interval.

Relevance	Relevant :____:____:____:____:____:____:____: Irrelevant
	Related :____:____:____:____:____:____:____: Unrelated
Flexibility	Flexible :____:____:____:____:____:____:____: Inflexible
	Changeable :____:____:____:____:____:____:____: Unchangeable
Tension	Bothered :____:____:____:____:____:____:____: Cool
	Tense :____:____:____:____:____:____:____: Relaxed
Orientation	Task-Oriented :____:____:____:____:____:____:____: Socially Oriented
	Ideational :____:____:____:____:____:____:____: Personal
Interest	Interested :____:____:____:____:____:____:____: Apathetic
	Involved :____:____:____:____:____:____:____: Withdrawn
Verbosity	Wordy :____:____:____:____:____:____:____: Short
	Brief :____:____:____:____:____:____:____: Lengthy

Fig. 7.4 IBM scale.

1. Average each individual's ratings on the six dimensions of relevance, flexibility, tension, orientation, interest, and verbosity. Compare the ratings on these six dimensions among the three groups. How do they differ? Why?
2. Combine each individual's scores within each group on the six dimensions separately. Can you identify some overall effect of some phenomenon on the group as a whole?
3. Select the individual in each group who exerted the most influence. How does his or her IBM scale differ from those of other group members?
4. The class might try this exercise again, giving different class members the opportunity of serving as observers and recording the different types of communication networks that the three groups form. After the IBM scales have been completed and the group interactions analyzed, compare the results to the different networks (wheel, chain, circle, and so on) that the groups may form. Will the IBM ratings differ for different communication networks?

Chapter 8

PUBLIC COMMUNICATION: PRIOR ANALYSIS OF THE PUBLIC SPEAKING SITUATION

At one time or another almost everyone has been bored by a tedious public speaker—at a graduation ceremony, at a political meeting, or even in a classroom, where a teacher's droning, singsong delivery seems likely to put everyone to sleep.

Some people, however, are fortunate enough to find themselves in the presence of a real orator: someone who can amuse, entertain, enlighten, or persuade; someone who can move an audience to tears, immerse them in helpless laughter, or bring them roaring to their feet with shouts of approval. A really effective speaker can have an incredible effect on an audience. In fact, the Athenians of the Golden Age thought very highly of the oratorical arts and expected every educated person to have some skill in public speaking. However, they also had a healthy fear of the power of a good speaker to sway people's minds and arouse their passions. In fact, the Athenians invented a name for a speaker who influenced crowds of people in such a way as to enhance his or her own power; such a speaker was called a demagogue or a leader of the mob. Throughout history there have been many demagogues such as Adolf Hitler, whose passionate speeches at mass rallies helped the Nazi party come to power in modern Germany. American politicians regularly accuse their opponents of being guilty of varying degrees of demagoguery in their public speeches.

It is both obvious and fortunate that most public speakers do not use their skills as means to antisocial ends. Some of the most effective modern orators, such as Dr. Martin Luther King, Jr., or the Reverend Billy Graham, have used their skills in the service of people. However, most public speakers are neither demagogues nor missionaries, and their reasons for speaking are far more prosaic: a government official announces that energy costs are continuing to increase; the newly elected president of a service club has to make an acceptance speech; a person is asked to give a technical presentation in a business meeting; a father with some reluctance lectures a scout troop on the art of tying knots.

Most people in this society will be called upon at some time to make a public presentation. Whether they be teacher, business executive, or member of some social club, they are likely at some point in time to be asked to speak to a group. Obviously, we think a knowledge of skills and techniques of public speaking is valuable. However, we do not think that a justification for studying the public communication context should be solely based upon just the consideration that someday you might have to give a public speech. There are many things that you will probably have to do in your life that most likely do not deserve attention in a college classroom. It is our contention that there is a great deal more to be gained from studying public communication than just rehearsing you for some future speech situation that may or may not occur in *your* future.

We hold several assumptions about the value of acquiring knowledge about and participating in public communication. First, we think the ability to organize your communication in such a way as to be effective in presenting information or persuading others has value in situations other than the public speaking context.

Such an ability to organize and present your ideas is highly likely to generalize to other communication situations. How many people could not benefit from knowing more about such organization and presentation in such situations as job interviews, speaking with a superior in an organization, or a variety of everyday occurrences? It is our belief that practice in public speaking does have great transfer and will benefit you in other situations.

There is another major reason for studying public speaking that few, if any of you, might agree with at this point in time. Public speaking can be fun. Many of our students have indicated a willingness to commit acts up to and including certain felonies to avoid having to give a public speech. Some of this feeling is based upon anxiety, and some is based upon lack of knowledge about the public speaking situation. However, we think there is a little ham in most of us, and standing in front of an audience as the center of attention is something that many people find irresistible (many of you probably find it quite resistible at this moment). To work hard on a public speech; to use one's speaking skills; to entertain, persuade, or enlighten an audience—all these offer a special kind of satisfaction, a small sense of power and accomplishment, that is often reward enough for the long hours spent in learning the techniques of public speaking and putting them into practice.

It has been our experience that most people would like to improve their skills in public speaking. However, many people think being an effective speaker is simply beyond their ability. Although it is probably not within the ability of many people to become extremely gifted orators capable of moving the masses, there is no reason to believe that they cannot become at least adequate in public speaking with diligent effort and some practice. Probably, most of us would be satisfied with being adequate. There are some common rules and principles that can be suggested in planning and preparing speeches that might help those people who desire to improve their ability in public speaking. In the next two chapters, we will attempt to provide some general guidelines that are meant to assist in making you a more effective speaker. We hope that in the process we will also give you more appreciation for public communication as an important and enjoyable context in which to participate.

The Public Communication Context: Some Defining Characteristics

We have previously discussed the dyadic and small-group communication contexts and suggested that they were characterized by a great deal of verbal interaction between people, that they allowed immediate and spontaneous feedback, and that they afforded people the opportunity to make more predictions about the other people in the communication transaction based upon psychological-level data. Although there are varied rules of interaction that operated in the interpersonal and small-group communication contexts, many of those rules are subject to constant renegotiation by the parties involved in the transaction. There are several important differences in the characteristics of the public communication context that make it a unique situation.

Because, by the very nature of the communication transaction, speeches are "public" events, there are rules of conduct that conform to cultural-level expectations about what is acceptable. It has been said of the public speaking situation that the "order, rules, and communicative jobs are all well laid out ahead of time . . ."[1] Given that the formal public speaking situation carries with it certain prescriptions, it is well for the speaker to consider and adapt to the unique characteristics of public speaking.

First the speaker must realize that feedback is more restricted in most public speaking situations than in dyadic and small-group communication situations. Although you will get both negative and positive feedback in most audience situations, it will not be of the same kind or quantity that you might receive in other situations. In many situations in which a speech is being delivered, feedback is limited to subtle nonverbal cues. At other times, questions and comments are, by the rules of the situation, discouraged except at the end of a presentation. In other words, the speaker can expect little verbal assessment of how well he or she is doing with an *audience until he or she has already finished doing it.*

The public speaking situation is further characterized by both physical and psychological distance between the audience and the speaker. Because of this distance, the speaker usually perceives less intimacy and maybe even empathy with an audience that he or she might in more interpersonal situations. There is also evidence to suggest that many speakers actually perceive the audience as some

[1]R. P. Hart, G. W. Friedrich, and W. D. Brooks, *Public Communication* (New York: Harper and Row, 1975), p. 24.

"unified whole" rather than as a collection of individuals. Some textbooks urge beginning speakers to think of the audience as an entity rather than as people in attempts to reduce their anxiety about the public speaking situation. This, of course, tends to depersonalize the situation, but this kind of thinking is often very necessary, especially with large audiences. The best data we have are cultural- and sociological-level data, without which it would be impossible to make predictions and adapt our communication behavior to individuals. It is also true that audiences tend to respond as one unit or entity. What all of these together suggests is that the communicator must understand which elements are under his or her control and which elements are not under direct control. It is only through such an understanding that the person can minimize the problems associated with communicating with an audience.

In a public speaking situation, the speaker generally has complete control over the speech itself. One can prepare and rehearse the speech in advance and can usually present it uninterrupted to its conclusion. Control over content, organization, and delivery of a speech is in the hands of the speaker. Some people find that this kind of control can work to their advantage. Many people can be very effective in the public speaking context where they do have these unique controls and yet be relatively ineffective in other contexts that do not allow advanced preparation and a chance at an uninterrupted presentation of ideas. Bernstein and Woodward report that former President Nixon was very comfortable in making speeches, especially from his oval office, but was very reticent about meeting the press for question-and-answer sessions in which he was not as prepared to control the communication.[2] What we are saying is that the public speaking situation can offer people a chance to prepare themselves and communicate in ways that are denied them in other contexts. We have been associated with professors who, given the time, could prepare brilliant lectures that were profound, insightful, and clear; however, in more informal situations they were unable to be influential or informative simply because they could not so easily control the communication.

Yet there are other factors over which the speaker has little or no control in a public speaking situation. One such factor is the environment. The speaker can rarely choose the location in which he or she speaks; control over the physical appearance of the surroundings, lighting, temperature, insulation against noise, and seating arrangements—all of which can influence the effectiveness of the speech—is generally not held by the speaker. Unpleasant surroundings, glaring or dim lighting, high temperatures, poor soundproofing, and uncomfortable seating can all distract listeners and undermine a speech.

A second way in which the speaker lacks control is in the inability to adapt to individual differences in the audience. First, the speaker is not likely to be familiar with the unique characteristics of the individuals making up the audience. Even if such an awareness were present, the speaker could hardly adjust the message to appeal simultaneously to every member

[2]B. Woodward and C. Bernstein, *The Final Days* (New York: Avon, 1976), pp. 138–139.

of the audience. This problem is con pounded, as we said, by the lack of verbal feedback and the ambiguity of much of the nonverbal communication that occurs. For instance, does a completely silent audience indicate courteous attention or disapproval? Obviously, the speaker is most likely to respond to collective audience feedback rather than the feedback from individual listeners.

Another aspect of limited control for a speaker is the effect audience members have on each other. Most public speakers have observed that an audience creates a *contagion:* listeners can emotionally stimulate one another, thus intensifying the effect of the speech. This social facilitation was described somewhat cynically by Quintilian centuries ago:

> The listener's judgment is often swept away by his preference for a particular speaker, or by the applause of an enthusiastic audience. For we are ashamed to disagree with them, and an unconscious modesty prevents us from ranking our own opinions above theirs, though all the time the taste of the

Most public speakers have observed that an audience creates a contagion: listeners can emotionally stimulate one another, thus intensifying the effect of the speech. (Photograph: Michael Weisbrot)

majority is vicious, and the claque may praise even what does not really deserve approval.[3]

Recent research has confirmed the effects of what Hylton has called *observable audience response* on reactions to both the communicator and the speech. People in an audience communicating their approval or disapproval can persuade the rest of the audience to see the speaker or the speech as they see them.[4] The somewhat frightening aspect of this sword has two edges. First, the speaker can rarely control the observable audience response, and, second, it takes very few people to have an impact on the audience at large. However, speakers can sometimes use audience response to serve their own ends. In recent political campaigns, it has been alleged that some candidates have actually placed hecklers in the audience so that they could use them to gain approval from the rest of the audience. When the speaker can turn the negative feedback into a rallying point for his or her own benefit, it is useful. Defending the right of everyone to be heard while making sure the hecklers are not listened to has been an effective rhetorical device of late.

Finally, a speaker has limited control over audience influence. By their feedback, members of the audience can affect the fluency, utterance rate, vocal amplitude, anxiety, eye contact, and body movement of the speaker. Changes in these variables can and do affect the evaluation of the speaker and the speech. Positive feedback can increase the accuracy of message transmission, reinforce certain message characteristics, strengthen the speaker's self-confidence, and reinforce his or her beliefs. Give some speakers just a little positive reinforcement, and they will be transformed from seemingly nervous amateurs into rather accomplished speakers. Negative feedback can seriously affect the speaker's delivery and self-confidence and the clarity of the message. Audience feedback can be a powerful force, whereas a restless, bored, or obviously disapproving audience can demoralize even an experienced speaker.

Perhaps it would be helpful to summarize some of the important characteristics of public communication that bring pitfalls and promise to the public speaker. Hart, Friedrich, and Brooks have suggested the following contrasts between public communication and other more interpersonal context, which are worth repeating here:[5]

1. The message must be relevant to the group as a whole—not merely to one or a few individuals in that group. In public communications, the "common denominator" must be constantly searched for by the speaker.
2. *"Public" language is more restricted,* that is, it is less flexible, uses a more familiar code, is less personal in phrasing, and is filled with fewer connotations than is "private" talk.
3. *Feedback is more restricted* since it is limited to subtle nonverbal responses in many instances.

[3]Quintilian, *Institutio Oratoria*, XI, 1–47.

[4]C. Hylton, "Intra-Audience Effects: Observable Audience Response," *Journal of Communication, 21* (1971), pp. 253–265.

[5]R. P. Hart, G. W. Friedrich, and W. D. Brooks, *Public Communication* (New York: Harper and Row, 1975), p. 25. Used with permission of the publisher.

4. *There is greater audience diversity* to deal with. In public communication we face the difficulty of entering *many* "perceptual worlds" simultaneously.

5. As the size of the audience increases, there is a greater chance of *misinterpreting feedback,* since there's so much to look for.

6. The speaker must do a more *complete job of speech preparation* since there is so little direct moment-to-moment feedback by which he can guide his remarks.

7. The *problem of adaptation* becomes paramount since one message must suffice for many different people.

8. *Audience analysis* is more difficult and necessarily more inaccurate when many people are interacted with simultaneously.

9. It is sometimes *difficult to focus attention* on the message because of the great number of distractions a public situation can entail.

10. A *greater amount of change* is possible in public communicative settings since the message reaches more people in a given unit of time.

Obviously, an awareness of the characteristics of the public speaking situation and knowledge about the problems associated with public communication is an important first step in helping people become more effective public speakers. However, there is another problem that many people experience *when they even think about the possibility of having to give a speech in a public situation.* They get uptight, scared, anxious, or whatever else you might want to label the panic that strikes them when the words *public speech* are used. We think that prior to even considering suggestions for planning, preparing, and delivering a public speech, we ought to turn to some considerations of the causes and effects of this rather widespread phenomenon: *communication anxiety.*

Anxiety About Public Speaking and What to Do About It

ASSESSING ANXIETY

When we told a colleague that we planned to devote a section in this edition of our text to anxiety about public speaking, we were somewhat surprised by the response. He suggested that we ought to reconsider that decision, for pointing out that such anxiety is a problem will only make it worse. In other words, if we focus your attention on this problem, you are likely to become more anxious just thinking about your anxiety. We decided to forgo his sage advice because we think an awareness of the problem of speech anxiety is the first step in controlling it. Upon reviewing the books in communication, we were somewhat surprised to see how little attention has been given recently to this syndrome by other writers. It seems that everyone knows it is there but would just prefer not to talk about it. However, we know that our students have real apprehensions about speaking in public, especially when they are just beginning a public speaking experience. Therefore, we want to examine the nature of speech anxiety as well as look at some other conceptualizations of communication anxiety that transcend the public speaking context, suggest some possible negative outcomes that can result from uncontrolled anxiety, and, finally, offer some practical suggestions about how to reduce your level of anxiety. It is our assumption that such reduction of anxiety will not only assist you in being a more effective speaker, but it will also make the experience more enjoyable for you.

THE NATURE OF COMMUNICATION ANXIETY

Most of you have probably heard the term *stage fright* used to describe anxiety associated with having to communicate or perform something in a public situation. It is probably safe to assume that most people experience some sort of anxiety attack when they are coerced, persuaded, or cajoled into a public performance. Experienced entertainers report that they still feel attacks of stage fright or other mild forms of anxiety prior to performance. Teachers who have been in front of classes for years are often anxious on the first day of class. There is nothing abnormal about experiencing some level of anxiety about public communication; in fact, if you do have such an anxiety, you are like the vast majority of people in this culture. There is also evidence to suggest that public speaking does produce more anxiety than other kinds of communication transactions such as interacting in a small group or with another person.[6]

We have said that some anxiety is normal and to be expected in the public communication context. It is also probably somewhat healthy in that anxiety can motivate people to make sure they are prepared, and it can encourage them to spend extra effort to do a good job. However, too much anxiety about speaking in public can be dysfunctional when it inhibits a person from performing up to his or her capacity. It is very important to us as teachers to look at problems in our students that result from inhibitions rather than inability.

There have been instruments developed specifically to measure people's apprehension about public speaking. We think that the use of these instruments can be a useful device in allowing you to assess just how anxious you are about the prospect of speaking in public. It should also be useful to assess changes in your anxiety as you gain more experience in public speaking. We hope that you will answer the following questions as honestly as you can and really examine your feelings about communicating with people in a public speaking situation.[7]

To obtain your score on this measure, simply add up all of the numbers you marked in the agree/disagree columns. Obviously this self-report measure is only a guide that you may or may not find useful. You probably found some of the questions more difficult than others to answer, especially if you have had no public speaking experience. Perhaps it would be useful to talk about how large numbers of college students have scored on this measure of anxiety about the public speaking situation. The theoretical neutral point on this instrument is a score of 102. You can determine whether you tend to be more

[6]J. C. McCroskey, "Measures of Communication-Bound Anxiety," *Speech Monographs, 37* (1970), p. 277.

[7]Ibid., p. 276.

Table 8.1 Personal report of public speaking anxiety

This instrument is composed of 34 statements concerning feelings about communicating with other people.

Indicate the degree to which the statements apply to you by marking whether you (1) strongly agree, (2) agree, (3) are undecided, (4) disagree, or (5) strongly disagree on each statement. Work quickly; just record your first impression.

	SA	A	UN	D	SD
1. While preparing for a speech, I feel tense and nervous.	5	4	3	2	1
2. I feel tense when I see the words *speech* and *public speech* on a course outline when studying.	5	4	3	2	1
3. My thoughts become confused and jumbled when I am giving a speech.	5	4	3	2	1
4. Right after giving a speech I feel that I have had a pleasant experience.	1	2	3	4	5
5. I get anxious when I think about a speech coming up.	5	4	3	2	1
6. I have no fear of giving a speech.	1	2	3	4	5
7. Although I am nervous just before starting a speech, I soon settle down after starting and feel calm and comfortable.	1	2	3	4	5
8. I look forward to giving a speech.	1	2	3	4	5
9. When the instructor announces a speaking assignment in class, I can feel myself getting tense.	5	4	3	2	1
10. My hands tremble when I am giving a speech.	5	4	3	2	1
11. I feel relaxed when giving a speech.	1	2	3	4	5
12. I enjoy preparing a speech.	1	2	3	4	5
13. I am in constant fear of forgetting what I am prepared to say.	5	4	3	2	1
14. I get anxious when someone asks me something about my topic that I do not know.	5	4	3	2	1
15. I face the prospect of giving a speech with confidence.	1	2	3	4	5
16. I feel I am in complete possession of myself while giving a speech.	1	2	3	4	5
17. My mind is clear when giving a speech.	1	2	3	4	5
18. I do not dread giving a speech.	1	2	3	4	5
19. I perspire just before starting a speech.	5	4	3	2	1
20. My heart beats very fast just as I start a speech.	5	4	3	2	1
21. I experience considerable anxiety while sitting in the room just before my speech starts.	5	4	3	2	1
22. Certain parts of my body feel very tense and rigid before my speech starts.	5	4	3	2	1
23. Realizing that only a little time remains in a speech makes me very tense and anxious.	5	4	3	2	1

Table 8.1 (continued)

24. While giving a speech I know I can control my feelings of tension and stress.	1	2	3	4	5
25. I breathe faster just before starting a speech.	5	4	3	2	1
26. I feel comfortable and relaxed in the hour or so just before giving a speech.	1	2	3	4	5
27. I do poorly on speeches because I am anxious.	5	4	3	2	1
28. I feel anxious when the teacher announces the date of a speaking assignment.	5	4	3	2	1
29. When I make a mistake while giving a speech, I find it hard to concentrate on the parts that follow.	5	4	3	2	1
30. During an important speech I experience a feeling of helplessness building up inside me.	5	4	3	2	1
31. I have trouble falling asleep the night before a speech.	5	4	3	2	1
32. My heart beats very fast while I present my speech.	5	4	3	2	1
33. I feel anxious while waiting to give my speech.	5	4	3	2	1
34. While giving a speech I get so nervous I forget facts I really know.	5	4	3	2	1

My score on this test   First time   _____
Second time   _____
Third time   _____

anxious (a score of 102 to 170) or less anxious (34 to 101) than most people in your class. Let us say that when this was tested on hundreds of college students, the average score tended to be greater than the theoretical neutral point. One reported mean was 115, and approximately 70 percent of the people studied scored between 85 and 149.[8] This would all suggest that many people report being anxious about the public speaking context.

We suggest you use this instrument over time to determine if your anxiety about public speaking changes. We would hope that some of the material in this book would encourage you to view public speaking as an enjoyable and less threat-

[8]Ibid.

ening activity, although we are aware that simply reading about such things has less impact than we as authors might desire. However, we would hope that if you followed some of the suggestions at the end of this chapter for reducing anxiety and, in fact, had the opportunity to participate in speeches in class, then your feelings of anxiety would significantly decrease. At any rate, you have the opportunity to observe yourself over time, and we encourage you to do just that.

Although this instrument provides valuable information in measuring anxiety about public speaking, it does not provide us with very much insight about the causes of this phenomenon. Toward this end we will next attempt to explore some

Table 8.2 Personal report of communication anxiety
College test

This instrument is composed of twenty statements concerning feelings about communicating with other people.

Indicate the degree to which the statements apply to you by marking whether you (1) strongly agree, (2) agree, (3) are undecided, (4) disagree, or (5) strongly disagree with each statement. Work quickly; just record your first impression.

	SA	A	UN	D	SD
1. While participating in a conversation with a new acquaintance, I feel very nervous.	5	4	3	2	1
2. I have no fear of facing an audience.	1	2	3	4	5
3. I look forward to expressing my opinion at meetings.	1	2	3	4	5
4. I look forward to an opportunity to speak in public.	1	2	3	4	5
5. I find the prospect of speaking mildly pleasant.	1	2	3	4	5
6. When communicating, my posture feels strained and unnatural.	5	4	3	2	1
7. I am tense and nervous while participating in group discussions.	5	4	3	2	1
8. Although I talk fluently with friends, I am at a loss for words on the platform.	5	4	3	2	1
9. My hands tremble when I try to handle objects on the platform.	5	4	3	2	1
10. I always avoid speaking in public if possible.	5	4	3	2	1
11. I feel that I am more fluent when talking to people than most other people are.	1	2	3	4	5
12. I am fearful and tense all the while I am speaking before a group of people.	5	4	3	2	1
13. My thoughts become confused and jumbled when I speak before an audience.	5	4	3	2	1
14. Although I am nervous just before getting up, I soon forget my fears and enjoy the experience.	1	2	3	4	5
15. Conversing with people who hold positions of authority causes me to be fearful and tense.	5	4	3	2	1
16. I dislike to use my body and voice expressively.	5	4	3	2	1
17. I feel relaxed and comfortable while speaking.	1	2	3	4	5
18. I feel self-conscious when I am called upon to answer a question or give an opinion in class.	5	4	3	2	1
19. I face the prospect of making a speech with complete confidence.	1	2	3	4	5
20. I would enjoy presenting a speech on a local television show.	1	2	3	4	5

My score on this test _____

Public Communication: Prior Analysis of the Public Speaking Situation of the reasons why people report such anxiety. One possible reason that people report feeling anxious about public speaking is that *they are generally anxious in a variety of communication contexts;* the public speaking situation might just make anxieties that are present in other contexts more apparent. Some have suggested that the term *communication apprehension* is an appropriate label for a more broad-based negative reaction to any real or anticipated communication experience, either public or private, with any number of other people. Though more communication apprehension may be present in large-group settings than in more intimate interpersonal contexts, the distinction that is made between communication apprehension and anxiety about public speaking is that the person who is high in communication apprehension will have negative responses to communication in the variety of contexts that we have already discussed in this section of the book. The person who has anxiety about public speaking will not necessarily be apprehensive in other communication situations. However, the person who has generalized communication apprehension is likely to be extremely anxious about giving a public speech.

As we said earlier, anxiety about public speaking is relatively widespread, and a majority of people have expressed this kind of anxiety at some time or other. Communication apprehension is less pervasive, and fewer people experience it. Most estimates suggest that somewhere between 10 and 20 percent of the population of the United States suffer from extreme communication apprehension, and maybe as many as another 20 percent suffer a moderately high level of communica-

tion anxiety.[9] It might be interesting and useful to allow you to compare your scores on a generalized scale of communication apprehension with your scores on the anxiety toward public speaking measure that we just discussed. The measure of communication apprehension on page 279 was developed for use by college students.

The theoretical neutral point on this scale is 60, and a score higher than that indicates a tendency to report more communication apprehension; a score lower than 60 would indicate lack of communication apprehension. This test has been used to measure the communication anxiety of many college students, and it has been reported that the mean score was 60, which is identical to the theoretical neutral point. From these data we can conclude that unlike the Personal Report of Public Speaking Anxiety test, people do not tend generally to report high apprehension on this measure.[10] However, this instrument deserves special scrutiny for it to be useful to you.

As you probably noticed, many of the items on this scale are very similar to the items on the other scale and are undoubtedly measuring anxiety about public speaking. You should examine your score to determine if you exhibited marking behavior on those items that were concerned with nonpublic speaking situations that was different from the marking behavior on the items that tapped your perceptions of the public speaking situation. For example, you might have marked each public speaking item with a score that indicated you were extremely apprehensive

[9]J. C. McCroskey, "Problems of Communication Anxiety in the Classroom," *The Florida Speech Communication Journal,* 4 (1976), pp. 1–12.

[10]McCroskey, 1970, p. 272.

yet marked all of the other items with scores indicating that you were quite comfortable in other communication contexts. In other words, your score might be artificially high on this generalized scale just because you happen to be anxious about one communication context. You should examine your score carefully item-by-item to determine what led to your final score. You may find that you report communication apprehension across communication contexts and that this generalized anxiety causes you to be extremely negative about the prospect of giving public speeches. That is one possible explanation. This instrument is also limited in giving us insight into what causes anxiety if your marking behavior does not follow this pattern. Moreover, even if a generalized anxiety is responsible for your fear of public speaking, this instrument alone does not tell us enough about the causes of that general perception of communication apprehension.

Although it may seem as if we are barraging you with an endless stream of scales that all measure the same thing, we think it important to consider one final scale that may offer some explanation as to why people are reluctant to communicate

Table 8.3 Scale for unwillingness to communicate

This instrument is composed of fourteen items concerning feelings about communication.

There is no right or wrong answer. Indicate the degree to which each statement applies to you by circling whether you strongly agree, agree, are undecided, disagree, or strongly disagree with each statement.

	SA	A	UN	D	SD
1. I avoid group discussion	5	4	3	2	1
2. I feel self-conscious when talking to others.	5	4	3	2	1
3. I consider myself the quiet type when it comes to talking.	5	4	3	2	1
4. I am good at making conversation.	1	2	3	4	5
5. I feel I am an effective speaker.	1	2	3	4	5
6. I'm afraid to speak up in conversation.	5	4	3	2	1
7. I have no fear about expressing myself in a group.	1	2	3	4	5
8. I think my friends are truthful with me.	1	2	3	4	5
9. Other people are friendly only because they want something out of me.	5	4	3	2	1
10. People only pretend to listen when I talk.	5	4	3	2	1
11. You can generally trust what other people say.	1	2	3	4	5
12. Talking to other people is just a waste of time.	5	4	3	2	1
13. People don't include me in their conversation.	5	4	3	2	1
14. My family doesn't enjoy discussing my interests and activities with me.	5	4	3	2	1

Total score on items 1–7 _____

Total score on items 8–14 _____

in a variety of situations. This scale is more broad-based than the two previous scales and attempts to measure a general unwillingness to communicate. This scale was developed because it was reasoned that there may be reasons other than anxiety or fear that prompt people to avoid communicating in a variety of contexts. It seeks both perceptions of people's feelings about communication and also attempts to determine their perceptions of other people and their role in the communication event.[11]

This scale is actually two different scales in one. The first seven items are designed as a measure of anxiety, introversion, and frequency of participation in various communication contexts. There is evidence to suggest that these items are reliable predictors of how likely a person is to approach and participate in communication situations. Obviously, these items measure more than just your reactions to the public speaking situation. However, we would expect people who have a high score on this dimension to be generally negative about the prospect of speaking in public. The theoretical neutral point on this dimension is 21; scores higher than that indicate a tendency to avoid communication situations when possible. We suggest you compare your scores on this dimension with the scores on the previously discussed instruments. If they are different, you should give some thought to the kinds of communication situations

you are most likely to avoid and those you are likely to approach. One of the important contributions that this scale makes is the recognition that variables other than anxiety make people reluctant to participate in certain communication transactions.

The second set of seven items measures a very different kind of perception from what we have discussed thus far in this chapter. This dimension measures peoples' perceptions of the rewards or lack of rewards attendant upon communicating with other people. It has been suggested that one possible reason that people are anxious about or avoid communication situations is that they have not been rewarded for participating in the past. The score on items 8–14 should give some indication of whether you tend to view communication as generally rewarding or not. These items attempt to tap perceptions of whether a person finds communication rewarding—because others listen, understand, and are honest—or unrewarding because they ignore or try to use him or her. Again, the theoretical neutral point is 21, and a higher score tends to suggest that communication is not seen as rewarding.

The public speaking situation is but one context in which people may have had past experiences that lead them to believe that the effort expended to be an effective speaker is simply not worth it. If people have had bad experiences in this arena or are generally skeptical about the rewards involved, we cannot expect them to approach this situation with any great joy. However, we think it useful to consider at this point how you feel about contexts other than the public speaking situation.

[11]J. K. Burgoon, "The Unwillingness to Communicate Scale: Development and Validation," *Communication Monographs, 43* (1976), pp. 60–69; J. K. Burgoon and M. Burgoon, "Unwillingness to Communicate, Anomia-Alienation, and Communication Apprehension as Predictors of Small Group Communication," *Journal of Psychology, 88* (1974), pp. 31–38.

How rewarding do you find communicating to be? Another interesting question is how your notions of reward relate to your level of anxiety. It is not necessarily true that people who are extremely anxious about communicating in specific contexts also find that they view communication in general as unrewarding. We think it would be useful to compare your scores on this scale with the other instruments we have presented. It may be that you are anxious about certain communication situations because they have been unrewarding in the past. If that is the case, perhaps as you learn more about this public speaking context and other communication situations, you will tend to view them as more rewarding and less threatening.

Perhaps it would be wise to close this section with a comment on the use of these scales. We selected these instruments for inclusion in the chapter because we thought they had been carefully developed and offered a reliable and valid way to measure various forms of communication apprehension. In all cases, they have been used to measure the perceptions of hundreds of students, and they have been validated in differing experimental contexts. However, the main reason that we wanted to include them was to provide tools *useful to you as individuals*. These findings based on large groups of other people may have limited utility to you, but at least the instruments can be used as a beginning in assessing your perceptions of different communication events. You may have only confirmed the obvious with these scales. Some of you may have confirmed that you are not anxious and to you we say, "Great!" Others may have learned something about themselves that

they did not know. We think that if you use the scales provided in this section to assess your feelings before a speech, after gaining experience, and at the end of the course, you might learn more about how things can change. In any case, they are yours to use as you see fit.

WHAT TO DO ABOUT YOUR ANXIETY

We have spent a considerable amount of time discussing how one might go about using the available instruments to measure anxiety about communication and have suggested ways of applying this information to the public speaking context. However, the question that is probably most important to the person who is anxious and wishes to reduce that anxiety is, Just what should be done? Although there have been many suggestions offered for reducing stage fright and/or anxiety about public speaking, there is little solid evidence on which we can make suggestions. However, we do know about some things that have proved effective, and we can draw on our experiences as teachers to try to offer some practical suggestions.

There is considerable evidence to suggest that just practicing public speaking tends to improve confidence levels. It is probably safe to assume that speaking in public is not as bad as the anxious person might believe. When a person is given an opportunity to practice this form of communication, there is less of a tendency to feel inadequate and anxious. When students have been asked about the important reasons that they changed their attitudes toward public speaking, the majority have cited the ability to practice as the most important. Students also attribute the ability to practice communicating in this context as the primary reason for their own improvement. It is also probably true that people who have ample time to prepare speeches can overcome some of their anxiety. The more prepared you feel to speak on a topic, the more confidence you should have. Remember that we are not suggesting that anxiety will go away with preparation and practice. We are simply saying that students indicate that it certainly helps.

There have been other studies that have given more specific suggestions on various aspects of the speaking task that might be useful to review. The type of audience is one factor that has been shown to make a difference. Students tended to improve when they gave speeches to live audiences and to absent audiences such as a television audience. However, when they gave speeches only to absent audiences, there was little decrease in anxiety or improvement in performance reported. Practicing before a live audience is obviously important.[12] The nature of the audience might also affect the level of anxiety a speaker experiences. For those people who are extremely anxious, it might be wise to practice before a small audience of people with whom they are comfortable and who they think might provide useful feedback. Many a suffering spouse hears speeches over and over until the would-be-speaker mate is satisfied that he or she is really ready to perform. Practice can help and should be considered as one way to reduce unmanageable anxiety. Another study has suggested that the use of video tape does not increase anxiety above initial levels.[13] Therefore, the highly anxious person might consider using video and/or audio tape as a means of storing the speeches. In that way, the speaker can become his or her own audience and receive feedback on the speech prior to facing a live group.

Other types of methods have been used to help people who experience severe anxiety. One such method used at a number of colleges and universities is *systematic desensitization*. Basically, this involves the anxious person's learning relaxation techniques and then pairing relaxation responses with anxiety-producing situations (for example, public speaking). If your university has such a program and you feel your anxiety is a problem, perhaps you should consider this technique. Everyone can use the principles of relaxation to some degree in overcoming anxiety. Simply attempting to relax and pairing your thoughts of anxiety with more pleasant thoughts can help. It certainly does not help to make yourself more anxious by dwelling on aspects of the speaking situation that will further agitate you. For those that find that these suggestions are of little help, we suggest that you discuss this problem with your instructor. Perhaps there are some other remedies available that your instructor can suggest for you. One thing we can offer is that even if you are anxious, you are probably going to get better with practice. Just doing it will help. We have also worked with enough groups of college students to know that they are generally supportive and understanding.

[12]J. W. Welke, "The Effects of Intensional and Extensional Audiences on Communicator Anxiety," *Central States Speech Journal,* 19 (1968), pp. 14–18.

[13]J. D. Bush, J. R. Bittner, and W. D. Brooks, "The Effects of the Video-Tape Recorder on Levels of Anxiety, Exhibitionism, and Reticence," *Speech Teacher,* 21 (1972), pp. 127–130.

COMMUNICATION CONTEXTS

Table 8.4

Speech Evaluation Form (Sample)		
Speaker _____ Date _____		
Subject _____ Assignment _____		
Factors	**Evaluation***	**Comments**

Purpose of Speech
  Clear and Concise
  Appropriate to Audience
  Appropriate to Occasion		

Topic of Speech
  Suitable to Speaker
  Relevant to Audience
  Conciseness		

Organization of Speech
  Arrangement of Ideas
  Subordination of Ideas
  Main Points Emphasized
  Main Points Supported
  Purpose of Speech Fulfilled
  Introduction Effective
  Body Effective
  Conclusion Effective
  Transitions
  Internal Summaries
  Use of Evidence		

Analysis
  Approach to Subject
  Interesting?
  Original?
  Central Ideas of
    Speech Supported		

Language and Style
  Conversational
  Vivid
  Redundant Enough
  Brevity
  Parallel Structure
  Variety and Originality
  Personal		

* Often people assign numerical values to each of the factors. For example they select a range of 1 (ineffective) to 5 (effective) and rate people in this way.

Table 8.4 (continued)

Delivery
  Poised
  Anxious
  Vocal Clarity
  Rate of Speech
  Volume
  Pitch Variety
  Fluency
  Voice Quality
  Body Movement
  Gestures
  Posture
  Facial Expression
  Eye Contact

Additional Items

_____
_____
_____
_____
_____
_____
_____
_____
_____

Evaluations of Overall Effectiveness:
_____
_____
_____
_____

Suggestions for Improvement:
_____
_____
_____
_____
_____

One possible source of anxiety is evaluation apprehension. You know you are going to be graded or evaluated on some performance, and this makes you even more anxious. Perhaps one way to overcome this anxiety is to discuss how people go about evaluating public speeches. Knowledge of what to prepare for should be useful.

Evaluating Public Speeches

There are several different ways that people go about the task of evaluating public speeches. We have decided to provide you with the format we normally employ. Included are some of the typical items that we have found to be important in making judgments about the effectiveness of a public speech. These factors represent the kinds of judgments we think people make about speeches whether they occur in the classroom or in any other public context. Although the outline suggested may have little meaning to you at this point in time, we think it will be valuable to keep this form in mind as you read the remainder of this chapter and the one that follows. We will make suggestions about how one plans and prepares a speech so that the probability of being evaluated positively on each of these factors increases. We urge you to use this outline as you read each section of the following material and suggest "comments" to yourself about how you might use the text material to create better speeches. You might also want to consider what items should be added to make this form more complete.

Initial Planning of the Speech

The first steps a speaker must take in planning a speech include deciding the purpose of the speech, analyzing the prospective audience, analyzing the location and occasion of the speech, and choosing a topic. Carelessness in any of these early planning stages can have drastic consequences on the completed speech; thus, even a technically superb speech could be counted a failure if delivered to the wrong audience or at an inappropriate time or if it introduces unfortunate topics.

DECIDING THE PURPOSE OF THE SPEECH

The first question a speaker must ask while preparing a speech is why he or she is making the speech. Is the intent to entertain the audience? To inform them? To persuade them to some course of action? Sometimes the speaker's overriding concern may be to improve his or her reputation with an audience. Politicians, for example, may seek to build credibility, selling themselves as honest, sincere, capable people. In other instances, the situation may dictate whether a speaker is to inform, entertain, or persuade a given audience. An after-dinner speech usually is expected to be entertaining; a freshman orientation speech would probably be mostly informative; a speech at a political rally would be persuasive. The speaker must clarify the purpose in his or her own mind at the outset so that the presentation can be carefully and strategically tailored to meet the goals of the speaker or the goals of those who issue the invitation to speak.

ANALYZING THE AUDIENCE

The second element that a speaker must consider is the nature of the audience. The difficulty of identifying the personal characteristics of the audience is a serious one. We urge the student to review the discussion in Chapter 3 on analyzing variables relating to others in the communication transaction. There are several steps that can be taken to help in defining the audience. One can study the demographic features of the audience: their ages, sex, socioeconomic status, occupations, and geographic background. He or she can try to assess their special interests, values, attitudes, and beliefs that are relevant to the intended topic. Unfortunatley, this preliminary research is often overlooked. The practiced speaker does not ignore such information; he or she critically analyzes the audience and adapts the speech to take advantage of the information that has been obtained. A great deal has been said about how Barry Goldwater failied to analyze his audiences adequately during the 1964 presidential campaign. He told groups of aged individuals about his desire to cut social security benefits and lectured to a group in Texas about the need to curtail a specific defense project when most of them were, in fact, employed on that very project. Though some people might have praised his integrity for saying what he believed regardless of what the audience wanted to hear, many would be reluctant to suggest this strategy as a way of persuading people to support a candidacy. On the basis of careful audience analysis, a speaker can decide if the audience being confronted is friendly, hostile, neutral, apathetic, or mixed. Such information can determine the types of arguments, evidence, and examples that will be used; the emphasis one needs to place on establishing credibility; and the choice of language and delivery style that should be employed.

ANALYZING THE OCCASION AND LOCATION

The time and location of a speech are important considerations, for they can impose restraints on a speaker. A special occasion—such as the Fourth of July or a retirement dinner—may dictate the topic for the speech. If the speaker is one of a number of speakers on a given occasion, he or she will probably want to limit the duration of the speech. A humorous speech would be inappropriate for a solemn occasion, and a solemn one inappropriate for an informal party. A speech before a small indoor gathering and a speech to a large crowd out-of-doors have different requirements in terms of content and delivery. The experienced speaker takes care to ascertain any limitations due to the occasion or location and adapts the speech to take advantage of this knowledge.

A speaker can also effectively utilize the nature of the occasion and location to intensify the impact of his or her message. A somber setting can highlight a serious speech; gay surroundings and a festive occasion can make an audience more responsive to an entertaining speech; a crisis can make the audience more susceptible to an emotionally persuasive speech. By adapting the speech to fit the occasion, the speaker can use both the physical and the psychological circumstances of the situation to enhance the effectiveness of a speech.

CHOOSING THE TOPIC

Even when the speaker is compeltely free to choose the topic for a speech, there are several guidelines that should be considered in order to select the best topic.

Suitability to the speaker. A common error of beginning public speakers is to select a topic that interests them, but about which they know very little. A speaker may find it very difficult to gather authoritative information about an unfamiliar subject; lack of extensive knowledge may make the communicator vulnerable if a mental block should be developed while speaking or if the train of thought is lost. If a familiar topic is chosen, recovery under stress is much easier, and the speaker should also be more prepared to answer questions from the audience. A speaker is often asked to speak precisely because of the special knowledge he or she possesses. If the members of a group invite a foreign policy expert to address them, they would probably be most disappointed to hear a speech about some topic on which the speaker knew very little. This is not to suggest that a speaker should avoid venturing into new areas and learning something; it is merely a warning that speaking on unfamiliar topics has some risk and mandates more thorough preparation.

Relevance to the audience. Some topics are simply not suitable to the audience being addressed. A speaker would be unwise to talk about a technical subject in which the intended audience has no background. If such a topic is necessary, the speaker must be very careful to adapt the explanations and the presentation to the level of the audience's understanding. The speech should also be adapted to the beliefs and values of the audience as we said earlier. The topic chosen should also be adapted so as to make it more meaningful to the audience. A speech on air pollution, for example, will be more meaningful if it includes information on how pollution affects the lives of individual members of the audience. The more meaningful and involving a topic is, the more successful a speech is likely to be.

Conciseness. Another error that speakers often make is to attempt to do too much in the time they have available. The result is either excessively general speeches or terribly long ones. Thomas Jefferson once observed that speeches measured by the hour die by the hour. The mark of a good speaker is succinctness—be clear, specific, and brief. A teacher cannot thoroughly cover the causes and effects of World War II in one class; a politician cannot present all of his or her policies in one speech. The complex topics of drug addiction, growing crime rates, or industrial pollution cannot adequately be covered in a five-minute class presentation. Given time constraints, the speaker must decide how far to narrow a topic and which aspects to emphasize, so that it can be sufficiently discussed and substantiated without resorting to broad generalities. Prudent judgment and careful consideration of the topic prior to beginning to prepare a speech are mandated if one is to be effective.

Appropriateness to intermediate and ultimate goals. There are times when a speaker cannot achieve the ultimate goal of a speech in a single attempt. At other times, it is not even wise to direct a speech toward that ultimate goal. For example, a member of the Peace Corps in a developing country may find that the first task at hand is to convince the audience that his or her desire is to help; considerable effort may have to be expended just to establish the trustworthiness of the communicator. Later speeches can be aimed at persuading people to adopt new ideas and techniques. A speaker facing a hostile audience may take a gradual approach to reaching some final goal. Thus, a speaker who advocates socialized medicine might be smart to begin by acknowledging awareness of the listeners' fears about socialism in general and reassuring them that the whole structure of free enterprise is not being attacked. Then arguments, statistics, and other evidence supporting socialized medicine can be introduced with more likelihood of being accepted.

We cannot state too strongly our feeling that prior analysis of the entire speech situation is important and necessary. It is only through the kinds of prior planning that we have suggested throughout this chapter that people can increase their probability of preparing and delivering effective speeches.

SUMMARY

1. There are several assumptions about the nature of training in public communication that should be emphasized. An ability to organize and present ideas generalizes to other types of communication contexts. Public speaking can also be an enjoyable activity, and most people can master the necessary skills to communicate effectively in this context.

2. The public communication context has several defining characteristics. The communicator has little control over several factors in this situation. Among the things that he or she has limited control over are the environment, adapting to individual differences in the audience, and the effect the audience has on the speaker. However, the speaker has more control over other factors in this context as compared to other communication situations. The communicator can be well prepared and control interruptions so that his or her ideas can be fully developed.

3. The public communication context differs from other contexts in that the message must be relevant to the group as a whole rather than just to individuals, there are prescribed differences in language used, and the speaker must adapt to audience diversity. The speaker must be careful not to interpret vague feedback and is obligated to be well prepared in advance. However, there is also a greater amount of change possible in this context given that the message will reach more people.

4. Anxiety about speaking in public is very common, and a majority of people express concern about having to address a large number of people. There is evidence to suggest that public speaking does produce more anxiety than other communication contexts.

5. We can measure just anxiety about public speaking, or we can look at anxiety about communication in general. Some people are also generally unwilling to communicate because they are reluctant to approach new communication situations or find communication unrewarding.

6. There are several techniques that can be used to overcome this anxiety. The evidence suggests that practice in public speaking is effective in reducing anxiety. A person who is well prepared in advance can also feel less anxiety. Selecting smaller supportive audiences to practice on has been very useful for many anxious communicators. Practice with video tape equipment also allows the speaker to act as his or her own audience and might be useful in reducing anxiety.

7. The first steps in planning a speech include deciding the purpose of the speech; analyzing the audience, location, and occasion of the address; and choosing the topic.

8. There are several guidelines for choosing a topic: suitability to the speaker, relevance to the audience, conciseness, and appropriateness to the intermediate and ultimate goals of the speaker.

9. Without careful initial planning, even the most technically perfect speech can be ineffective.

Chapter 9

PUBLIC COMMUNICATION: PREPARING AND DELIVERING A PUBLIC SPEECH

As this book attempts to discuss communication in a variety of contexts, we are somewhat limited in our ability to discuss all of the different kinds of speeches and different kinds of occasions on which one might be called upon to speak in public. However, we do think that there are some important considerations that ought to be discussed in preparing, organizing, and delivering speeches in the public context. Many of these factors are relevant to the person who wishes to become a more effective speaker regardless of the specific purpose of the speech, the audience it is being delivered to, or the occasion on which the speech is to be given. As we have repeatedly said, speeches are given for a variety of reasons. Sometimes we use the speech as a method of informing people of things we consider important for them to know. At other times we are advocating a position or policy, and it is our desire to have our audience be persuaded and come to believe as we believe. On occasion we might just be introducing someone, attempting to entertain a group, or speaking for a variety of reasons in special situations. The public speech can serve many functions, and the authors have devoted several chapters in the last section of this book to the many functions that communication can serve. *The reader of this book would do well to rely on the information presented in those later chapters when trying to prepare a speech that serves a specific function.*

For the person who wishes to develop a speech that is persuasive, we urge that Chapters 11 and 12 on approaches to persuasion and structuring persuasive messages be used in conjunction with this chapter. For the person who is most concerned with establishing a good relationship with an audience and appearing to be an attractive person, we urge you to consider the information presented in Chapter 13 on developing effective social relationships. Many times people have to take positions in public that are controversial and conflict-producing; at other times the main purpose of speaking is to resolve a conflict that is present. The information presented on conflict management in the last chapter would be useful material to consider. The point we are trying to make is that communication in the public context is used for a variety of reasons. The material we will present in this chapter offers some general principles for organizing and delivering a public speech. However, those principles should not be considered in isolation; the function you wish the speech to serve is important, and we urge you not to forget the factors we discussed in the last chapter on structuring the speech to suit the purpose, audience, and occasion.

Preparing a Speech

In the last chapter, we presented an overview of the kinds of initial planning that should be done prior to the actual preparation of a public speech. Once the speaker has decided what the topic will be, we can consider the question of how the topic will be presented. Traditional studies of rhetoric prescribes five different concepts to be considered in preparing and presenting a speech. The five concepts are invention, disposition, style, memory, and delivery. *Invention* has been defined as the process of investigating and analyzing the subject of the speech. It is during this stage that arguments or ideas are generated. James McCroskey has said about invention:

> Assuming that thorough investigation has uncovered what is knowable about the subject, invention is the process of discovering what among the knowables are sayable by the particular source to the particular audience on the particular occasion to accomplish a particular purpose.[1]

The second concept, *disposition*, concerns the selection, apportionment (emphasis), and arrangement of material. These decisions are interrelated with the process of invention and may occur simultaneously. Once the actual content of the speech has been selected and ordered, the third concept, *style*, becomes important. Stylistic decisions involve language choices to express the ideas. The fourth concept, *memory*, is less important today because most speakers speak from a written text or notes. In times past, however, orators were expected to deliver their speeches entirely from memory. The fifth and final concept, *delivery*, concerns the nonverbal elements of the actual presentation.

INVENTION

The first step in actual preparation of the speech is generating potential ideas. This step demands that the speaker consider all possible aspects of his or her topic and the beliefs, values, and attitudes that might be important to the intended audience.

[1]J. C. McCroskey, *An Introduction to Rhetorical Communication* (Englewood Cliffs, N.J.: Prentice-Hall, 1972), p. 141.

Generating ideas. Several lists of general appeals have been developed that may aid the speaker in discovering all the available lines of argument he or she may use on a given topic. These classification systems should provoke the speaker to think about his or her topic from a variety of perspectives. One such list is known as *stock issues*. These are the general arguments pertinent to any message advocating a policy or policies. These stock issues may take the form of six questions that any speech arguing for a policy should answer.

Is there a compelling need? A speech should establish not only that a need for the policy exists, but also that the problem is significant and widespread. This provides the rationale for adoption of a new policy.

Is the need inherent? This question asks whether the problem can be solved without a major change in the present system or whether indeed a basic policy change is needed. If the problem will solve itself or can be rectified through minor changes in the present system, then the need is not inherent, and the justification for a new policy is minimized. For example, many people have recently called for basic reforms in the financing of political campaigns to reduce corruption in government. If it could be shown that the trouble lies in the fact that present campaign financing laws are not rigorously enforced, the argument for new laws would be seriously weakened.

Is the plan workable? In advocating a new policy, a speaker should demonstrate that his or her ideas will actually work. A policy that does not take into account the political, social, and economic realities of a given situation is unworkable in that sit-

uation. For instance, the idea of establishing a world government is attractive for many reasons, but the proposal is unworkable at present because of differing national goals and international conflicts; very few national governments would consider giving up any of their powers in favor of a single world government.

Is the plan practical? Another issue is whether the proposed plan is practical. Questions of efficiency, time, costs, and availability of resources are involved in the issue of practicality. Some people have suggested that colonizing other planets of our solar system might relieve the problem of overpopulation on earth. Given the present stage of human technology, the costs of such an enterprise and the rate of population expansion, however, such a plan is wholly impractical.

Does the plan meet the need? Even if a plan is practical and workable, it may not satisfy the need. Underlying this issue is the question of the true causes of the problem. Harsher laws and stricter law enforcement, for example, have been offered as solutions to growing crime rates. Such policies would probably put more people in jail, but many experts believe that the only real solutions to the problem involve attacking some of the root causes of crime, such as poverty, unemployment, and social alienation.

What advantages and/or disadvantages will result? In addition to analyzing the problem that the policy is designed to correct, the speaker should evaluate the side effects that will result from his or her proposals. For example, locating a new industrial plant in an economically depressed community may bring increased employment and prosperity, but the new plant may also create pollution or harm the quality of life in other ways. In defending a proposal on the basis of its advantages, the speaker must be able to show that the advantages outweigh any disadvantages that might result. Clearly, any proposal that generates more disadvantages than advantages will be indefensible.

Though the above plan for generating ideas has been most often associated with speeches that are designed to persuade, it also has applications to speaking situations in which people are simply trying to inform others of plans that have already been adopted. If, in a job situation, a person was charged with informing others about company policies, audiences might well want to know what kinds of effects would result from the new policy or plan. A teacher who tries to inform a class on a perspective toward the subject matter might well have to defend that perspective by comparing it to others and showing that there are advantages and practical applications in viewing the subject in this manner.

Assessing effects on the audience. To make a successful speech, the speaker must discover arguments that will make the issue relevant to his or her audience, relating the arguments to the listeners' needs, desires, and values. In a persuasive speech, this is important in order to arouse interest and concern. In an informative speech, an understanding of the audience's needs, beliefs, and values is essential, so that the speaker can predict what they will find believable and useful.

Issues that are likely to arouse audience concern include basic physical needs such as food, water, and shelter; emotional needs such as affection, security, and self-fulfillment; common human desires, such as wealth, material possessions, power, reputation, and beauty; abstract virtues, such as courage, honor, generosity, and patriotism; and conditions or systems upon which people place greater or lesser value, such as peace, order, justice, equality, freedom, democracy, free enterprise, states' rights, and socialism.

Obviously, not all people share the same needs, desires, or values; nor do they place them in the same hierarchy of importance. One individual may place great value on job security, a steadily increasing income, the acquisition of material goods, and a safe and comfortable life in the suburbs. Another individual might find such a life stultifying, placing a much greater value on the freedom, adventure, and variety of a less "stable" existence. Many Americans place a very high value on patriotism, whereas others want no part of what they see as chauvinistic "flag-waving."

The job of the speaker is to assess the needs, desires, and values of his or her particular audience and generate lines of argument that are consistent with or appeal to them. A speech urging people to save money is misdirected if its audience can barely stretch their incomes to cover basic needs of food and shelter; a luxury car salesman's pitch would be wasted on a group of monks whose desires do not include material wealth. A speech on the "wonders of socialism" would have little appeal to a group of small-town businessmen with conservative values; a speech advocating government censorship of newspapers would be inappropriate for a group of civil libertarians.

In the selection of the information that one might include in a speech, it is important to assess the kinds of information the audience is likely to reject and/or accept. As we pointed out in Chapter 4, the selectivity processes tend to make people disregard information that is not consistent with their beliefs, values, and attitudes. We must be careful to include information that is not so discrepant with their beliefs that they will selectively attend to only that part of the speech that gives information that confirms what they know. Also if we include only information that contradicts what they know or believe, they might retain little of what we are trying to inform them.

Investigating and analyzing arguments. In preparing a message, a speaker often compiles a variety of arguments and information before beginning to analyze and reject them; without an initially extensive list, the investigation process may be narrow and stunted. The speaker should explore all possible avenues in order to achieve a complete analysis and to make sure arguments and information that would strengthen the speech are not neglected.

The investigation of a topic should take advantage of all available resources, including personal experience, books, periodicals, journals, abstracts, pamphlets, unpublished professional papers, and persons with special knowledge or related experience. The facts, statistics, opinions, examples, analogies, and anecdotes gathered by the speaker will be used as background knowledge in constructing the speech and as supportive material within the speech itself. There are several principles that can be used as guides in collecting material.

The material should be fresh and interest- *ing to the audience.* Speeches based on facts that are common knowledge, familiar examples, trite analogies, and tired jokes will only bore an audience.

The material should be current. Outdated examples or information may harm the speech. This does not mean that only recent publications should be consulted or that only recent anecdotes and examples should be used. But where conflicting information exists, more credence should generally be given to the more recent findings. Thus, citing research findings on cancer of the 1950s or 1970 estimates of pollution costs may produce inaccurate conclusions. Failure to use recent evidence may leave the speaker vulnerable to attack or rejection by his or her more "current" listeners. Moreover, outdated materials may seem uninteresting and irrelevant to an audience who will not feel more informed or be persuaded.

The material should be authoritative. Unless the speaker is himself or herself an authority on a given subject, any data used to support the subject should be taken from a competent, reputable source and from a source appropriate to the subject. Quoting a history professor on a controversial historical question would be appropriate, but quoting him on a psychological theory would not. The authorities quoted should also be chosen with reference to the nature of the audience. Thus, a certain senator's opinion on international trade might be quite acceptable to one audience, but totally unacceptable to another audience. The important decision is whether the source is competent in the eyes of the audience. The sources of opinions, facts, and statistics should usually be documented within the speech (which makes it particularly important that they be accepted authorities). Sources of examples, analogies, and comparisons need not be cited, but these should still be taken from reliable sources.

The material should be valid. There are two tests of validity the material should pass: internal and external. Internal validity means that the material is consistent within itself or within the context of the speech. It is also known as face validity. To argue that "all politicians are fools or liars" and then to support your argument with a quote from a politician is an obvious example of an internally inconsistent argument. External validity concerns the consistency of material with other known evidence. A businessman who tries to attract new investors by stressing his efficiency and business sense, when it is well known that he has filed for bankruptcy several times, will have a hard time convincing his audience.

The material should be reliable. In other words, the evidence given by one authority should be confirmed by other authorities. The scientist who reports a miracle cure for cancer that cannot be duplicated by other scientists using the same methods cannot be considered a reliable source. Similarly, the authority who says that world starvation is an impossibility may be regarded as unreliable if five of his colleagues have concluded from the same data that it is an imminent danger.

The material should be relevant to the point it is supporting. To cite the charitable act of a businessman as evidence of his honesty would be to present irrelevant material. Similarly, a presidential candidate who takes credit for lowering crime rates during his or her administration or blames rising crime rates on an oppo-nent's administration is usually indulging in wishful thinking, because policies at the presidential level rarely have any effect on local crime. Unless a direct connection between given policies and crime rates can be proved, the evidence is irrelevant.

Finally, there should be sufficient supporting material. It is not enough to give one example or one statistic to defend an argument. If a communicator is going to be convincing, he or she should develop arguments fully in terms of evidence, authoritative opinions, anecdotes, and examples.

The speaker must provide enough accurate evidence to support the arguments or make the information being presented seem credible enough that people will accept and retain it. However, care must be taken not to "overload" a speech with statistics, citations, and other material, or it is likely that audience interest will be lost. If this happens, the end result will be less persuasion, information acceptance, and retention. This, of course, will probably be the opposite of the desired outcome of the speaker. Attention to the above ideas about selecting materials is likely to increase the probability of a speaker's being successful regardless of the nature or purpose of the speech.

DISPOSITION

Concurrently with the invention process, the speaker must consider the dispositional features of the message: the selection, apportionment, and arrangement of materials.

During the investigation stage, the speaker should have uncovered enough information and generated enough arguments to make selection necessary. In addition to the guidelines already offered on choosing content, audience identification should also be considered in the selection process. *Identification* is the process of establishing a common ground, or shared position, with one's audience; obviously, this involves consideration of the needs, desires, and values of the audience. Where choices exist, the communicator should choose those arguments and materials that have the most meaning and impact for the specific audience to be addressed. A psychologist addressing a parents' club, for example, might use the example of parent-child conflict to illustrate a point about human behavior.

Another consideration in selecting arguments is the number to be used, and this, of course, depends partly on the emphasis the speaker wants to give each point. A successful speech usually develops no more than two or three main points, for additional material can lead to audience confusion and boredom. Just as too much evidence in the form of statistics and examples can harm a speech, too many arguments or main points can lessen the speech's impact.

A final consideration in selection and apportionment is the emphasis the speaker wants to place on *ethos*, *logos*, and *pathos*. These are the three traditional forms of proof. Ethos refers to the speaker's credibility; logos refers to logical proof; pathos refers to emotional proof. The emphasis placed on each will be determined primarily by the speaker's goals. If one is most concerned with establishing credibility with the audience, he or she will use arguments that will show him or her in the best light, including references to accomplishments and experience, expressions of praise from others, and statements about the speaker's own ideals and beliefs that are designed to convince the audience he or she is trustworthy and competent.

If the communicators want to stress logos, they will use arguments that appeal to reason and an abundance of evidence. This choice of materials will produce a dispassionate, rational, well-documented message. If the desire is to emphasize pathos, they will select arguments, anecdotes, and examples that appeal to the emotions. We attempt to arouse emotion by playing upon needs, fears, desires, and values. Because differing goals necessitate different choices of material and different amounts of emphasis, it is essential that the communicators predetermine their goals.

The next series of decisions a speaker must make concerns the organization of the message. One decision does not have to be made: all messages must have an introduction, body, and conclusion. Without an adequate introduction and conclusion, a speech would seem incomplete and unpolished. Preparation of the introduction and conclusion is usually left until last, so that these can be properly integrated into the main body of the speech. The speaker's first concern, then, is organization of the body of the speech. In many instances, the nature of the material will suggest the appropriate organizational pattern. A speech on a historical event, for instance, might be organized largely in chronological order.

Where choices exist, though, the speaker should be aware of the possible patterns that can be used. The available patterns fall into two categories: logical arrangements and psychological arrangements. The former are those organizational patterns that inherently make sense, that are logical extensions of the material with which they deal. Psychological patterns, on the other hand, are designed to create a psychological effect. These patterns are intended to elicit those audience reactions desired by the speaker.

Although the remainder of this chapter will discuss both logical and psychological factors that are likely to make a difference in speech organization, *we urge the reader to read the section on psychological organizational variables that affect persuasion that appears in Chapter 12*. If one wants to persuade others, it is critical that the research evidence cited in that chapter be considered in organizing a speech to persuade. Because this material appears later in the book, we will devote most of our efforts in this chapter to organizational patterns that appear in the more formal public speaking situation. The later material is appropriate in the public speaking situation on many occasions, but it is applicable to the interpersonal and small-group situations as well. The following patterns of organization are common methods of structuring a speech.

Deductive organization. One of the most fundamental logical patterns is deductive reasoning. From a major premise or general law a specific conclusion is deduced. There are formally three parts to a deductive argument: the major premise (all-inclusive generalization), the minor premise (or specific statement of fact), and the conclusion drawn from the two premises.

Deductive reasoning may be used to organize the arguments of the speech in order to bring the audience to the desired conclusion. Thus, a speaker might argue that because all American children deserve a quality education (major premise) and because Johnny is an American child (minor premise), Johnny deserves a quality education (conclusion). The speaker might then argue that quality education requires competent teachers (major premise), that Johnny's school lacks competent teachers (minor premise that would require proof), and that, therefore, Johnny's school does not provide quality education. Continuing the line of argument, the speaker may eventually arrive at the conclusion that taxes must be increased to pay for more competent teachers.

Deductive Reasoning

Major premise: All men are mortal.
Minor premise: John is a man.
Conclusion: John is mortal.

In the actual speech, the speaker may easily omit mentioning some of the logical steps because they are obvious (for example, the minor premise that Johnny is an American child). But whether the steps are explicitly stated or only implied, the reasoning is based on the deductive patterns, which moves from general premises to specific conclusions.

Inductive organization. In that it moves from the specific to the general, inductive reasoning is the opposite of deductive reasoning. The speaker who uses this pattern presents several examples or pieces of evidence and from these draws a general conclusion. Thus, a speaker might describe local air pollution laws, cite figures showing that air pollution is increasing, give evidence that few industries have been prosecuted under the laws, and conclude inductively from those three pieces of evidence that local pollution-control laws are not being adequately enforced.

Inductive Reasoning

Evidence: Country X has copper, but no iron.
Evidence: Country Y has iron, but no copper.
Evidence: Country X wants iron; country Y wants copper.
Conclusion: Countries X and Y should trade iron for copper.

Inductive reasoning may be particularly appropriate in a speech before a hostile audience, when the speaker wishes to use a gradual approach to his or her final argument. Stating the argument at the beginning may make a hostile audience even more resistant; the inductive pattern allows the speaker to present first an abundant amount of evidence that may help soften the resistance of the audience.

Cause-effect organization. Another common reasoning pattern is cause-effect reasoning. This pattern may actually take four forms: cause-effect, effect-cause, cause-cause, or effect-effect. In arguments that are ordered from cause to effect, the causes or sources of a given problem are discussed, followed by a discussion of the effects. In the effect-cause pattern, the existing situation is discussed, followed by an analysis of the factors that produced it.

Thus, a history professor speaking about World War I might first discuss its effects. For dramatic effect, however, he or she might prefer to begin with graphic descriptions of the war's effects and then discuss its causes.

Cause-Effect Reasoning

Cause: John has five apples.
Cause: Mary has no apples.
Cause: Mary is greedy, aggressive and stronger than John.
Effect: Mary takes John's apples.

Effect-Cause Reasoning

Effect: Man bites child.
Cause: Child bites man.
Cause: Child laughs at man's lecture on human bites.
Cause: Child bites man again.

If the speaker is dealing with an accepted and understood problem, he or she may be more interested in the relationship of the causes to one another. For instance, the speaker on World War I may discuss the relationship between nationalism and the European arms race, both causes of the war. However, he or she may be more interested in the interrelationship between effects such as the war reparations demanded of Germany and the bitterness felt by the German people.

Chronological organization. Materials frequently require an arrangement that is chronological, or in order of time. At least parts of a history lecture are most logically presented chronologically, moving either forward or backward in time. Similarly, a speaker may wish to use chronological order in explaining a series of events leading up to some current situation.

Chronological Order

Jan. 5: Independent investigator pinpoints waste in government operations.

Jan. 6: Newspaper editorials call for action.

Jan. 9: Congressmen call on President, demand action.

Jan. 10: 5,000 telegrams to White House, demanding action.

Jan. 15: President appoints commission to study problem.

Feb. 22: Commission issues preliminary report: situation serious.

Aug. 13: Commission presents report to President.

Aug. 14: Newspaper headlines on report; news of multiple murder pushes it off front pages for second editions.

Aug. 17: President publicly thanks commission; files report without reading.

Chronological order should be used whenever it is important for the audience to understand the time-order relationship of several events.

Hierarchical organization. Many arguments or concepts can be explained in a hierarchical pattern; that is, each element builds upon, or is intrinsically related to, the next.

A speaker may wish to argue from the simple to the complex, from the parts to the whole, from the whole to the parts, or from basic needs to higher order needs—all examples of hierarchical organization.

Spatial organization. Another pattern of organization is based on the spatial relationship between objects, persons, or places. The relationships are commonly discussed in an order of left-to-right, front-to-back, top-to-bottom, inside-to-outside, or the reverse.

A speaker may wish to include in a speech information on geographical relationships, a description of a room, or an account of an accident in terms of relative locations.

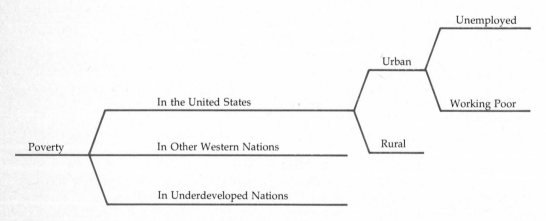

Fig. 9.1 Hierarchical order.

A common

form of
business letter

locates

the date at the top right margin,
the address and salutation below
the date and at the left margin,
the body of the letter two spaces
below the salutation, the complimentary close two spaces under
the body either at left margin or
under the date, and the

complimentary close

with the signature
four spaces below.

Fig. 9.2 Spatial order.

Process organization. In explaining a process or activity, the logical pattern for presentation is according to the process order. Thus, the turning of iron ore into finished steel would be best described by discussing in turn each step of the process. The injunction to "begin at the beginning" is applicable to this pattern.

Fig. 9.3 Structure function.

Process Order
1. Bait hook.
2. Cast line.
3. Wait.
4. Land fish.
5. Cook over open fire.
6. Eat.

Structure-function organization. A common organizational pattern consists of describing a structure and then explaining how it functions. The structure-function method of organization may actually be an elaboration of the process model.

For example, an instructor in auto mechanics would probably first describe each element in the structure of the vehicle, then explain the function or purpose of each part and the interrelationship of parts, and finally explain how the parts combine to make the vehicle move.

Comparison-contrast organization. Two elements of a speech often need to be compared for similarities and contrasted with regard to dissimilarities. The process of comparing and contrasting may take several forms. All aspects of Element A may be described first and then followed by a comparison along the same dimensions for Element B. Or each single dimension of similarity or dissimilarity may be discussed in sequence.

The comparison-contrast organization may also be combined with other patterns. For example, Candidate A may contrast his voting record with Candidate B's voting record and list the votes in chronological order. Or two washing machines may be compared and contrasted by describing their structure and function.

Classification organization. Some subjects lend themselves to a topical or classification order: the material is ordered by classes or categories. The arrangement of chapters in this book partially follows this pattern. Each of the first several chapters concerns a different variable in the communication process. Whenever ideas, people, or objects are grouped and discussed according to their groupings, the classification pattern is being used.

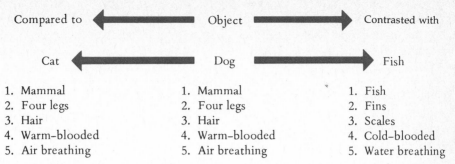

Compared to	Object	Contrasted with
Cat	Dog	Fish
1. Mammal	1. Mammal	1. Fish
2. Four legs	2. Four legs	2. Fins
3. Hair	3. Hair	3. Scales
4. Warm–blooded	4. Warm–blooded	4. Cold–blooded
5. Air breathing	5. Air breathing	5. Water breathing

Fig. 9.4 Comparison contrast.

Table 9.1. Classification order

Opinions of Undergraduates on Coed Dorms

	Yes	No	Don't know
Men	38%	40%	22%
Women	45%	41%	14%
Freshmen	34%	38%	28%
Sophomores	48%	36%	16%
Juniors	53%	45%	2%
Seniors	67%	30%	3%

Opinions of Parents on Coed Dorms

Yes	No	Don't Know
23%	68%	9%

Reflective thinking organization. The organizational pattern known as reflective thinking was described in Chapter 7 on small-group communication. It is essentially an expansion of the problem-solution pattern and is appropriate only for a policy speech. Its advantage is that each stage logically evolves out of the prior stage and criteria are clearly specified, thus guiding the listeners through the decision-making process. The pattern is appropriate both for informative speeches that describe the reasoning behind an existing solution and for persuasive speeches that advocate adoption of a new solution.

Reflective Thinking Organization

My candidate for mayor is a successful businessman.
Therefore, he is efficient and resourceful.
Therefore, he would manage the city efficiently and resourcefully.
Therefore, taxes could be lowered and better services provided.
Therefore, my candidate should be elected.

In addition to these organizational patterns based on logical arrangements or arguments and materials, there are also organizational patterns that have been suggested for speeches based upon motivating audiences to accept information and be persuaded by arguments.

Monroe's motivated sequence. This organizational pattern, developed by Alan Monroe,[2] is designed to motivate the audience to some action advocated by the speaker, although it may be used for informative speeches as well. It is a pattern

[2]A. H. Monroe and D. Ehninger, *Principles of Speech Communication*, 7th brief ed. (Glenview, Ill.: Scott, Foresman and Company, 1975), pp. 243–265.

to be used for an entire speech, from introduction to conclusion. There are five steps: attention, need, satisfaction, visualization, and action.

The speech should begin by vividly drawing the attention of the audience to some problem. This is followed by an in-depth analysis of the need or problem. The speaker then offers a solution to the problem and demonstrates its superiority over alternative proposals. In the fourth step, visualization, the speaker tries to make each listener identify with the problem by projecting himself into the future and visualizing what will happen if he or she does not accept the speaker's proposal. The last step in the sequence is the conclusion, which is a direct appeal to action. A speaker might begin by graphically describing a recent fire in a new skyscraper in which several people died. Then he or she analyzes the problem: outmoded building codes and fire safety regulations in the construction of new skyscrapers. After reminding his or her listeners that they or those close to them could easily be trapped in such a fire unless reforms are made, the speaker calls for action: political pressure to change building codes and fire regulations.

Climactic, anticlimactic, and pyramidal organization. The climactic, anticlimactic, and pyramidal arrangement patterns need to be considered in combination, for only one of the three can be used at one point in time. In any speech, there is usually one point that is stronger, more important, or more interesting than the rest. Climax order places the most important point last, whereas anticlimax order places the most important point first. When the most important point is placed in the middle, pyramidal order is being used.

In a speech intended to inform, the anti-climax order might be preferable if the audience is apathetic and sees no need to pay attention to your comments. The use of an interesting main point in the first part of the speech might well motivate them to attend to the remaining information. If you are trying to persuade an audience that is initially favorable or apathetic to the issue, the use of strong arguments first may sustain them through the weaker or less important arguments that follow. If the audience is hostile toward you or the position being advocated, it might be wise to begin with minor points to gain their favor prior to using your strongest arguments, which come as the climax. The pyramidal structure is rarely advised because both the opening and closing are weak or less interesting points. We usually advise making the speech as a whole strong enough so that one can use some combination of climactic and anticlimactic organization. Open with a relatively strong and interesting, but inoffensive, argument or point, and make sure thay you close with a very strong argument or an important point. Adapting to the audience and insuring that you have more than one strong argument or point make the decisions somewhat easier.

Outlining. The process of selecting and arranging the contents of the speech should implicitly generate a speech outline. The effective speaker turns this implicit outline into a complete written outline. Writing an outline forces the communicator to be certain that his or her speech flows smoothly and includes all the points he or she wants to cover and also that the arrangement is both logical and effective. This same outline can also serve as notes during the delivery of the speech.

The communicator can determine whether a complete-sentence outline or an outline of brief phrases only best suits his needs. Some speakers find that a detailed, full-sentence outline helps them prepare in advance the best wording for main points and makes specific points easier to recall. Others find such outlines cumbersome.

Introductions, conclusions, previews, and summaries. The last stage in the disposition process is preparing the introduction, conclusion, and summaries. The introduction should serve four functions: gaining the listeners' attention, revealing the purpose or topic of the speech, establishing identification, and serving as a transition into the body of the speech. The communicator can gain the audience's attention in a variety of ways. One may begin, for example, with a startling fact, a joke, a hypothetical question, an example, an anec-

---

Basic Speech Outline

  I. Introduction (often written out in full)
 II. Body
    A. First Main Point
      1. Supporting argument
        a. Further subpoint or supporting material
          (1) Evidence, examples, and so on
          (2) Evidence, examples, and so on
        b. Further subpoint or supporting material
      2. Supporting argument
      3. Supporting argument
    B. Second main point
      1. Supporting argument
      2. Supporting argument
    C. Third main point
      1. Supporting argument
      2. Supporting argument
      3. Supporting argument
III. Conclusion (usually written out in full)

The general outline for a speech is given above. The number of main points, subpoints, and amount of supporting material will of course vary with the chosen topic.

dote, or a quotation. The communicator should be able to determine intuitively what has interest value and what does not. Consider this introduction to a speech by Four Guns, an Oglala Sioux Indian judge, at a dinner given for him by a white anthropologist in 1891:

> I have visited the Great Father in Washington, I have attended dinners among white people. Their ways are not our ways. We eat in silence, quietly smoke a pipe and depart. Thus is our host honored. This is not the way of the white man. After his food has been eaten, one is expected to say foolish things. Then the host feels honored. Many of the white man's ways are past our understanding, but now that we have eaten at the white man's table, it is fitting that we honor our host according to the ways of his people.[3]

This introduction immediately captures attention with its startling and mildly humorous look at the white man's custom of after-dinner speeches through an Indian's eyes. It is a graceful and subtle introduction to the body of the speech, which discusses the difference between white ways and Indian ways (a subject of particular interest to the anthropologists in the audience). But Four Guns also has a harsh message for his white audience. In the body of the speech, he will remind them that white men put great trust in written words; yet they have made many treaties with the Indians and then broken the treaties. The Indian, he says, has no need of written promises, for he carries truth in his heart and acts on it. In his introduction, however, Four Guns has prepared the way for his harsh message. By presenting himself initially as the rather simple Indian (he was not) who finds the ways of white men strange, he has flattered his listeners as "sophisticated" white men and encouraged them to feel

patronizing and sympathetic toward him.

At all costs the speaker should avoid the clichés of introductory material, such as "My speech is about . . ." or "Today I'm going to talk to you about . . ." Such introductions are not only dull; they are the sure sign of the amateur. If the speaker is going to try complimenting or flattering his audience, it must be subtly done. Except on certain occasions, such as college reunions, reminiscing or telling the audience "how happy I am to be here" should be avoided. Finally, the introduction should flow smoothly into the body of the speech. It should seem an integrated part of the whole rather than a disjointed, discrete element. Speakers who begin with an effective, attention-getting anecdote and then follow it with "my topic is . . . ," have not yet mastered the art of smooth transition.

Like the introduction, the conclusion is intended to serve as a transition, out of the body of the speech into the final statement. It should articulate smoothly with the body, creating a feeling of completion. There are several ways to conclude a speech. Some possible methods are (1) a summary of the main points; (2) a final quotation; (3) a repetition of the introduction, with a new or more meaningful interpretation; (4) a closing example or anecdote; (5) a projection into the future; (6) a thought-provoking question; and (7) an appeal to action (as in Monroe's motivated sequence). The conclusion should receive special attention from the communicator, as it is responsible for the final impression made on the audience.

Nothing has been said yet about previews and internal summaries. These are minor introductions and conclusions,

[3]Delivered by Four Guns, Oglala Sioux Indian judge, in 1891. Reprinted in C. Wissler, *Indian Cavalcade* (New York: Sheridan House, 1938), p. 171.

which may precede and follow main points or subpoints. For example, after the main point, the communicator might say, "The important things to remember about no-fault automobile insurance are first that it costs the insurance buyer less and second that it lightens the burdensome caseload of the courts." This might then be followed by a preview of the second main point: "No-fault automobile insurance is workable as has been demonstrated by other states that have adopted the program." The preview alerts the audience to what to expect next; the internal summary clarifies the speaker's point for the audience, as well as reviews the subpoints in its development, so that the audience is more likely to remember them. The combination of internal summaries and previews also makes transitions easier from one main point to the next. Because they serve such useful functions, they need not be used sparingly. In fact, common advice to debaters in their message preparation is to "tell them what you're going to do, do it, and then tell them what you've done."

STYLE

When the communicator has completed the invention and disposition stages in preparing his speech, he or she can turn attention to the style. Style refers to the manner in which we express our ideas. Style is a deciding factor in whether a potentially good speech has impact. The style of a speech adds embellishment, but it is not just "icing." Different styles can have decidedly different effects on an audience.

Three basic goals of any speech are that the material be perceived accurately, that

it gain attention, and that it be remembered. These are also the goals of good style. The elements of good style to be discussed below are intended to achieve clarity, interest, or better recall. These factors may, in turn, improve the persuasiveness of a speech.

Conversational speech. An important stylistic consideration is the difference between oral and written communication. Because there are major differences in the way we use language orally and in written form, many of the principles of good writing style are inapplicable to speech. Oral communication is less formal and uses fewer unfamiliar words, shorter words and shorter sentences, more contractions, more superlatives and interjections, more nonstandard words, and more self-references. If a speech is to sound natural, therefore, it should resemble normal spoken communication rather than written discourse. This is what is meant by the recommendation that speeches be informal and conversational. Of course, certain situations demand more formal speech, such as inaugural addresses or government policy statements. But, in the majority of situations, a more conversational approach is preferable. It is one means of establishing rapport with the audience and conveying an image of poise. There follows part of a politician's speech in which he attempts the conversational approach in a radio and television address. Shortly before the speech, he has been accused of using political funds for his personal use:

My fellow Americans, I come before you tonight as a candidate for the vice-presidency and as a man whose honesty and integrity has been questioned . . .

The taxpayers should not be required to finance items which are not official business but which are primarily political business . . .

Well, then, the question arises, you say, well, how do you pay for these and how can you do it legally? . . .

The first way is to be a rich man. I don't happen to be a rich man. So I couldn't use that.

Another way that is used is to put your wife on the payroll. Let me say, incidentally, that my opponent, my opposite number for the vice presidency of the Democratic ticket, does have his wife on the payroll and has had her on the payroll for the past ten years.

Now just let me say this. That is his business, and I am not critical for him for doing that. You will have to pass judgment on that particular point. . . .

I have found that there are so many deserving stenographers in Washington that needed work that I just didn't feel it was right to put my wife on the payroll. My wife sitting over here.[4]

Vividness. Another desirable feature of public speaking style is vivid language. Vividly expressed ideas gain attention and are more easily recalled later. The use of striking words, phrases, comparisons, or examples can heighten the impact of a speech. Often metaphors, similes, and hyperboles can achieve this effect. Vivid language can be used to create interest and maintain the attention of the audience.

The following example of vivid language is from the inaugural speech of President Lyndon Johnson:

Think of our world as it looks from that rocket that is heading toward Mars. It is like a child's globe, hanging in space, the conti-

nents stuck to its side like colored maps. We are all fellow passengers on a dot of earth. And each of us, in the span of time, has really only a moment among our companions . . .

For this is what America is all about. It is the uncrossed desert and the unclimbed ridge. It is the star that is not reached and the harvest that is sleeping in the unplowed ground.

Is our world gone? We say farewell. Is a new world coming? We welcome it—and we bend it to the hopes of man.[5]

Redundancy and brevity. Two somewhat conflicting elements of good style are redundancy and brevity. Redundancy refers to repetition of both expressions and ideas. Such repetition can reinforce a particularly strong point, as well as increase clarity. A common practice of experienced speakers is to repeat key phrases so that they become catchwords for the audience. Consider the use of ''I have a dream'' in this speech by the Reverend Martin Luther King, Jr.:

. . . I still have a dream. It is a dream deeply rooted in the American dream.

I have a dream that one day this nation will rise up and live out the true meaning of its creed: ''. . . that all men are created equal.''

I have a dream that one day on the red hills of Georgia the sons of former slaves and the sons of former slaveholders will be able to sit down together at the table of brotherhood; I have a dream— . . .

That my four little children will one day live in a nation where they will not be judged by the color of their skin but by the

[4]Delivered by Richard M. Nixon on September 23, 1952. Reprinted in McCroskey, 1972, p. 301.

[5]Delivered by Lyndon B. Johnson on January 20, 1965. Reprinted in J. A. Frost, R. A. Adams, D. M. Ellis, and W. B. Fink, *A History of the United States* (Chicago: Follett Education Corp. 1968), p. 659.

Speakers vary in their ability to attract and hold the attention of their audiences. (Photographs: Jane Hamilton-Merritt)

content of their character; I have a dream today.

I have a dream that one day in Alabama . . . little black boys and black girls will be able to join hands with little white boys and white girls as sisters and brothers; I have a dream today.

I have a dream that one day every valley shall be exalted, every hill and mountain shall be made low, and rough places will be made plane and crooked places will be made straight, and the glory of the Lord shall be revealed, and all flesh shall see it together.[6]

When used judiciously, redundancy is a valuable rhetorical device. However, when it is carried to the extreme, it becomes counterproductive. Speakers who are verbose, who use more words and sentences than necessary, bore their audiences. Communicators who can express

[6]Delivered by Martin Luther King, Jr., on August 28, 1963. Reprinted in McCroskey, 1972, p. 288.

themselves succinctly are easier to listen to and generally more persuasive. To achieve clarity and interest, the communicator, therefore, must seek the proper balance between brevity and redundancy.

Parallel structure. An element related to reduncancy is parallel structure, which is the use of the same phrasing or sentence structure to express several related ideas. The following speech, a good example of the use of parallel structure, is from the inaugural address of President John F. Kennedy:

Let both sides explore what problems unite us instead of belaboring these problems which divide us.

Let both sides, for the first time, formulate serious and precise proposals for the inspection and control of arms—and bring the absolute power to destroy other nations under the absolute control of all nations.

Let both sides join to invoke the wonders of science instead of its terrors. Together let us explore the stars, conquer the deserts, eradicate disease, tap the ocean depths, and encourage the arts and commerce.

Let both sides unite to heed in all corners of the earth the command of Isaiah—to "undo the heavy burden . . . [and] let the oppressed go free."[7]

This stylistic device not only has aesthetic appeal; it adds organization, clarity, and unity. It also improves recall of a message. Parallel structure may be used in expressing main points or subpoints or in paralleling elements of a single idea.

Variety and originality. The use of varied language and original expressions can add color and distinction to a speech. Clichés and all-too-familiar ideas are the mark of the commonplace speaker. Speeches are more interesting that use fresh and original expressions and vary the language patterns. Consider this excerpt from an 1854 speech by Seattle, a Dwamish Indian chief:

> Every part of this soil is sacred in the estimation of my people. Every hillside, every valley, every plain and grove, has been hallowed by some sad or happy event in days long vanished. The very dust upon which you now stand because it is rich with the blood of our ancestors and our bare feet are conscious of the sympathetic touch. Even the little children who lived here and rejoiced here for a brief season will love these somber solitudes and at even tide they greet shadowy returning spirits. And when the last Red Man shall have perished, and the memory of my tribe shall have become a myth among White Men, these shores will swarm with the invisible dead of my tribe, and when your children's children think themselves alone in the field, the store, the shop, upon the highway, or in the silence of the pathless woods, they will not be alone. At night when the streets of your cities and villages are silent and you think them deserted, they will throng with the returning hosts that once filled and still love this beautiful land. The White Man will never be alone.[8]

Emphasis. An obvious element of a good speech is the effective use of emphasis, which results from the combination of stylistic emphasis and delivery emphasis. An extremely well-designed and supported speech can still fail if the speaker fails to focus attention on major points. Striking words or expressions, revered grammatical structure, redundancy, hypothetical or rhetorical question, imperative statements, and explicit references to the importance of a point can all add emphasis.

The use of emphasis is finely demonstrated in the following, from an 1876 speech by Frederick Douglass:

> Had Abraham Lincoln died from any of the numerous ills to which flesh is heir—had he reached that good old age of which his vigorous constitution and his temperate habits gave promise—had he been permitted to see the end of this great work—had the solemn curtain of death come down but gradually, we should still have been smitten with a heavy grief, and treasured his name lovingly. But, dying as he did die, by the red hand of violence, killed, assassinated, taken off without warning, not because of personal

---

[7]Delivered by John F. Kennedy on January 20, 1961. Reprinted in McCroskey, 1972, p. 284.

[8]Delivered by Seattle, Dwamish chief in 1854. Reprinted A. Binns, *Northwest Gateway: The Story of the Port of Seattle* (New York: Doubleday and Company, 1941), pp. 103–104.

hate—for no man who knew Abraham Lincoln could hate him—but because of his fidelity to union, he is doubly dear to us, and his memory will be precious forever.[9]

Personalization. Through the process of personalization a communicator allows his or her personality to be revealed. This is accomplished by abundant use of self-references. Through expressions of personal beliefs, feelings, and experiences, the communicator may increase his or her rapport with the audience. Personalization seems to appeal to our curiosity and sense of relatedness with others, thus creating interest value.

The speech from which the following was taken was delivered by Barry Goldwater in accepting the Republican presidential nomination in July 1964:

> Our task would be too great for any man, did he not have with him the hearts and hands of this great Republican party . . .
>
> I do not intend to let peace or freedom be torn from our grasp because of lack of strength or lack of will. *That* I promise you . . .
>
> I pledge that the America I envision in the years ahead will extend its hand in help . . . so that all new nations will at least be *encouraged* to go *our* way—so that they will not wander down the dark alleys of tyranny, or the dead-end streets of collectivism.
>
> Our Republican cause is not to level out the world or make its people conform in computer-regimented sameness.
>
> Our Republican cause is to free our people and light the way for liberty throughout the world.

Ours is a very human cause for very *humane* goals.[10]

Humor. The effects of humor on persuasion are discussed in detail in Chapter 12. There is little evidence to suggest that funny people are more persuasive. However, people often find the use of humor in public speaking situations to be useful. Most of us like to laugh. Few people would deny that they enjoy a really funny speech or a touch of humor in even the most serious of topics. If nothing else, humor can increase the listener's enjoyment and at times gain his or her attention. Humor may take several forms in a speech: a joke, a humorous anecdote, witticisms, insults, or satire.

Let us caution the inexperienced speaker about the possible negative outcomes associated with including humor in a speech. First, it is often difficult really to be funny or to tell a joke properly. Many people do not use humor well, and there is nothing more terrifying for a speaker than attempting to be funny and having the audience not respond. A speaker who attempts to use humor and fails often detracts significantly from an otherwise adequate speech. There is also a time and a place for humor. Prudent judgment will tell you that there are times in which any attempt at humor would be inappropriate. Such ill-timed attempts at humor may have very negative outcomes in terms of audience evaluation. Finally, one must be very careful in the use of satire and insults. We cannot all be Don Rickles, and we should carefully analyze the audience prior to using these forms of humor. Peo-

[9]Delivered by Frederick Douglass in 1876. Reprinted in Frederick Douglass, *The Life and Times of Frederick Douglass* (New York: Reprinted by Crowell-Collier, Inc., 1962), p. 492.

[10]Delivered by Barry Goldwater in July 1964. Reprinted in McCroskey, 1972, p. 292.

ple often do not recognize satire when they hear it, and insults delivered in jest may offend. Good judgment is the key to selecting humor.

Following some of the suggestions on style contained in this section, the inexperienced speaker can produce an impressively effective speech. It is appropriate to conclude this section with an introduction from a speech made by a college freshman. We think you will agree that style and language were very well used here. The speech was delivered by Charles Schalliol on the subject of air pollution:

> The strangler struck in Donora, Pennsylvania, in October of 1948. A thick fog bellowed through the streets enveloping everything in thick sheets of dirty moisture and a greasy black coating. As Tuesday faded into Saturday, the fumes from the big steel mills shrouded the outlines on the landscape. One could barely see across the narrow streets. Traffic stopped. Men lost their way returning from the mills. Walking through the streets, even for a few moments, caused eyes to water and burn. The thick fumes grabbed at the throat and created a choking sensation. The air acquired a sickening bittersweet smell, nearly a taste. Death was in the air.
>
> Before the clouds of fog lifted from Donora, twenty had died, and 6,000 or half of the population were bedridden. Donora was the site of America's first major air pollution disaster.[11]

DELIVERY

The final stage in message preparation is rehearsal of the speech. The speech

[11]First place speech delivered by Charles Schalliol in the men's division of the Intercollegiate Indiana Oratorical Association Contest, Hanover College, March 1967. Reprinted in *Winning Orations, 1967* (Detroit: The Interstate Oratorical Association, 1967), pp. 54–57.

should be rehearsed just as it is going to be presented. Except for formal occasions when a manuscript is necessary, speeches should not be memorized or read from a text. Memorized speeches often sound stilted and monotonous, and the speaker is in danger of drying up if he or she should forget a key section. Rather, the speech should be extemporaneous.

Extemporaneous speech is fluent, natural, and largely spontaneous. It has been rehearsed enough so that the speaker is familiar with it and need not rely heavily on notes, but not so rehearsed that major portions of it are memorized. To discourage overuse of notes or memorization, speakers use only key-word or key-phrase outlines for notes, with only statistics or quotations written out in full. This forces the communicator to be extemporaneous in the presentation and to be conscious of each point he or she is about to make. Extemporaneous style does not preclude careful selection of language, and a speech may still incorporate all the stylistic elements discussed earlier. Repeated rehearsals can insure that these are included, but the speaker should allow enough flexibility in the actual delivery to sound natural and enthusiastic and to adapt to feedback from his or her audience. A completely memorized speech leaves no room for such adaptation.

Other considerations in the actual delivery of a speech include the use of the voice, body movement, posture and gestures, facial expressions, and eye contact. These elements of delivery will be discussed independently. Although we have spent considerable time discussing research findings on nonverbal communication in Chapter 5, we think it is appropriate to offer some practical suggestions for good delivery based on accepted public speaking principles.

The voice. No matter how well a speech has been prepared, the speaker will lose the audience if they cannot hear and understand him or her. *Clear articulation* has always been considered one of the primary elements of good delivery. Demosthenes, one of the most famous speakers of ancient time, is said to have overcome a speech defect by long hours of practice at the seashore. Filling his mouth with pebbles, he would deliver his speeches over the roar of the ocean waves. Countless others have used similar exercises to improve the clarity of their speech. It is doubtful, however, that many people beyond childhood years need extensive practice with tongue twisters or other articulation exercises or that such practice will make noticeable improvements. For those who do have problems with articulation, recognition of the problem and a conscious attempt to solve it will probably produce better results than the practice of artificial exercises. Speakers may be able to pinpoint vocal faults and improve their speech by recording their voices on a tape recorder and playing it back.

Equally as important as vocal clarity is the *rate of speech*. The rate should be varied, but should not be so fast as to be unintelligible or so slow that it drags. Pauses should be used to vary rate, to draw attention, and to add emphasis. Speakers can learn to adjust their rate by listening to themselves on tape and by carefully observing audience feedback.

To be understandable, the *volume of a speech* must also be adequate. The ability to project one's voice to the back of a large room often requires practice. Again, audience feedback is a good clue as to whether they can hear the speaker adequately. Speakers must learn to adapt their volume to the size of the room they are speaking in. Volume can also be varied to emphasize important points. Sudden loudness can startle; sudden softness can cause the audience to listen more attentively.

Another quality of good vocal delivery is *pitch variety*. A monotonous pitch can destroy the effectiveness of any speech. Every individual has a characteristic pitch level and a range of pitches generally used. To achieve variety, your speech pattern should typically include both high and low pitches that are several steps removed from your normal pitch level. Persons with narrow ranges can increase their vocal variety by practicing speaking at high and low pitch levels. Individuals who have an unpleasant pitch level can also change it through conscious effort, as witnessed by the ability of aspiring radio announcers to develop deep-pitched voices. Generally, lower pitch levels are more pleasant for both males and females and, as noted earlier, create a better image.

A pleasant *voice quality* is also important to good vocal delivery. Persons with irritating, unpleasant voices are stereotyped in negative ways. Like pitch, voice quality can be altered through concerted practice.

The final standard element of good vocal delivery is fluency. Although research demonstrates that lack of fluency does not necessarily have a serious negative effect, a fluent speech is easier to listen to and creates the impression of confidence and competence.

Body movement, posture, and gestures. The most useful advice about body movement, posture, and gesture is to avoid distracting behavior. No single pattern of body movement is preferable; it depends on the style that is most comfortable for the speaker. The important consideration is that the speaker not engage in meaningless movements such as nervous pacing, rocking back and forth on the heels, or shifting weight from one foot to the other. Such behavior draws attention away from the speech itself. Similarly, posture should be whatever is comfortable for the speaker as long as it is not so rigid as to appear unnatural or so relaxed and slouched as to appear disinterested or slovenly. One admonition generally given to beginning speakers is not to drape themselves over the podium or to use it as a crutch.

Much of the traditional advice on gestures is artificial and contradictory. It used to be fashionable for men to place one hand in a pocket; now public speaking teachers advise against it. Some texts recommend keeping one hand on the podium at all times; others recommend moving away from it and even in front of it. The best advice seems to be to make gestures natural, varied, meaningful, and large enough to be visible.

Facial expression and eye contact. Like gestures, facial expressions can add clarity and interest to a speech. To be effective, facial expressions should be natural, varied, meaningful, and visible. Idiosyncratic and repetitive expressions can be distracting. Thus, the overriding consideration becomes one of avoiding distracting behavior.

Eye contact is an important element of good delivery. One of the distinguishing features of effective public speakers is the extensive use of eye contact. (A frequent complaint about President Lyndon B. Johnson's speeches was that he seldom looked up from his manuscript, which lowered his audience's attentiveness.) By using continuous eye contact and looking at each member of the audience, the communicator secures their attention, appears to be speaking directly to them, and can better recognize audience feedback. Moreover, direct eye contact conveys an image of honesty and conern, which can boost the speaker's credibility. The values of direct eye contact are a further argument against manuscript speeches and overreliance on notes.

Some Concluding Comments on Effective Public Speaking

This chapter has been somewhat different from the earlier chapters in this book in that we have departed from our tendency merely to describe the results of specific communication behaviors. In this chapter, we have attempted to be prescriptive about the creation of effective public speeches. We have also attempted to provide practical examples of what we thought was effective speech preparation. Obviously, there are other ways to approach speechmaking. One cannot assume that by just following our suggestions in this chapter that he or she will now be able to be effective in any speaking situation. Being an effective public speaker requires work and practice. We do hope that our suggestions, which are based on the best advice we could gather from people interested in teaching public speaking, will increase the probability of people being able to operate as they wish to in the public speaking context. There is obviously room for you to experiment with different organizational structures, choose different kinds and qualities of language, and vary delivery characteristics so that you may find what is most comfortable and effective *for you as a public speaker*.

We urge you to keep in mind that much of your effectiveness will be determined by the audiences you speak to. A willingness to adapt to their needs and desires is the first rule of a successful public speaker. You must be attuned to their feedback and constantly use their reactions to guide you in altering and adjusting your speech. We further urge you not to consider this chapter in isolation from the rest of the book. Throughout this chapter we have suggested material that might be useful in specific public speaking situations. However, we think that much of the material we have discussed in this text must be kept in mind when delivering a speech. The material on credibility, obstacles to communication, nonverbal communication, and many other communication variables will help the person who finds the need to deliver a public speech. Perhaps one final word from one of the earliest rhetoricians, Dionysius the Elder, is a most appropriate way to close this chapter: "Let thy speech be better than silence, or be silent."

SUMMARY

1. Preparing a speech requires consideration of several organizational and delivery variables. The kind of speech to be given, the intended audience, and the occasion mandate different strategies for the public speaker. However, there are some general principles that can be suggested in preparing and delivering speeches.

2. There are five concepts that should be considered in preparing an effective speech: invention, disposition, style, memory, and delivery.

3. Invention is the process of investigating and analyzing the subject of a speech. Invention involves generating ideas for the speech and the investigating and analyzing of arguments and information. It also involves assessing the needs of the audience members and trying to predict the effects of the speech's arguments and information on the audience.

4. Disposition involves the selection, apportionment, and arrangement of materials within the speech. All speeches should have an introduction, body, and conclusion. The speaker may arrange materials in one of two basic organizational patterns: logical and psychological.

5. Logical patterns of organization are those that inherently make sense and follow some preset rules. There are several logical patterns that can be followed depending on the nature of the speech. Deductive, inductive, cause-effect, and chronological arrangements are examples of logical patterns available to the speaker.

6. Psychological patterns are intended to elicit from the audience certain reactions that are desired by the speaker. Monroe's motivated sequence is designed to motivate the audience to some action advocated by the speaker although it may be used for informative speeches as well. There are five steps: attention, need, satisfaction, visualization, and action. Another psychological pattern is climactic, anticlimactic, and pyramidal organization.

7. Style refers to the way the ideas in a speech are expressed. Obviously, the requirements for good oral and written communication are different. The careful use of conversational speech; vivid, varied, and original language; some redundancy combined with brevity; parallel structure; emphasis; personalization; and humor are all stylistic considerations that can enhance the effectiveness of even an inexperienced speaker.

8. A speech should be well rehearsed; the speaker should be familiar enough with the content so that a heavy reliance on notes is unnecessary. However, speeches delivered entirely from memory frequently sound stilted and monotonous. The effective speaker will often have to adapt his or her presentation in reaction to feedback from the audience. The more flexible and prepared the speaker, the more likely that such adaptations can be made.

9. When a speaker is delivering the speech, the qualities of his or her voice are very important. Vocal characteristics include the speaker's articulation, rate of speech, volume, pitch variety, and fluency.

10. Other nonverbal communication variables also affect perceptions of the speaker and the speech. Distracting gestures and facial expressions should be avoided. Frequent and direct eye contact with the audience is likely to make the speaker more effective.

SUGGESTED READING

Barrett, Harold. *Practical Methods in Speech.* 4th ed. New York: Holt, Rinehart and Winston, 1977.

Bryant, Donald C., and Karl R. Wallace. *Fundamentals of Public Speaking.* 5th ed. Englewood Cliffs, N.J.: Prentice-Hall, 1976.

Hart, Roderick P.; Gustav W. Friedrich; and William D. Brooks. *Public Communication.* New York: Harper and Row, 1975.

Monroe, Alan H., and Douglas Ehninger. *Principles of Speech Communication.* 7th brief ed. Glenview, Ill.: Scott, Foresman and Company, 1975.

Phillips, Gerald M., and J. Jerome Zolten. *Structuring Speech—A How to-Do-It Book About Public Speaking.* Indianapolis: Bobbs-Merrill, 1976.

Rogge, Edward, and James C. Ching. *Advanced Public Speaking.* New York: Holt, Rinehart and Winston, 1966.

From the Reading

Define the following terms:

environment
public communication
contagion
communication anxiety
communication apprehension
systematic desensitization
audience demographics
personality analysis
communication reticence
invention
disposition
style
memory
delivery
deduction
induction
chronological
hierarchical
spatial
reflective thinking
climactic
anticlimactic
pyramidal

Study Questions

1. What are the five elements that should be considered when preparing any speech?
2. What are stock issues? What kinds of questions should any policy speech answer?
3. When collecting material for a speech, what are the accepted principles you should take into account?
4. What are the major components of deductive organization. Inductive organization? How do these two types of organization differ?
5. List several other methods of organizing a speech. When might these approaches be useful?
6. How does Monroe's motivated sequence serve to stir the audience to some action advocated by the speaker?
7. Draw a basic speech outline, using deductive organization. What are some advantages to making an outline? Using an outline rather then a prepared text during delivery?
8. What purposes should the introduction, conclusion, and summary serve in any speech?
9. What are some of the relevant factors associated with the style of a public speech?
10. What effect does humor have in the public speaking context?
11. How can articulation, volume, and pitch affect the delivery of a speech? What effect can these factors have on the audience?
12. What types of nonverbal behaviors will influence the effectiveness of a speech?
13. Why is it important to have some knowledge and expertise in the public speaking field?
14. What factors make public communication difficult for many?
15. How would you determine the level of your communication anxiety? The anxiety level of others? Your general unwillingness to communicate?
16. How can communication anxiety or unwillingness to communicate be controlled?
17. What are some specific factors that you can use to determine if a speech is effective?

18. How do you analyze an audience according to demographic factors? Personality factors?
19. What are the generally prescribed guidelines to consider when selecting a topic for a speech?
20. As a speaker, how far will you go in attempts to persuade an audience?

ORGANIZING AND ANALYZING A SPEECH

The inaugural address of John Fitzgerald Kennedy was well received around the world. This speech has been criticized, praised and analyzed by a variety of people since that time. The entire text of that speech is presented, and we would like you to read that speech carefully:

John F. Kennedy
Inaugural Address, January 20, 1961*

Mr. Chief Justice, President Eisenhower, Vice President Nixon, President Truman, reverend clergy, fellow citizens, we observe today not a victory of party, but a celebration of freedom—symbolizing an end, as well as a beginning—signifying renewal, as well as change. For I have sworn before you and Almighty God the same solemn oath our forebears prescribed nearly a century and three quarters ago.

The world is very different now. For man holds in his mortal hands the power to abolish all forms of human poverty and all forms of human life. And yet the same revolutionary beliefs for which our forebears fought are still at issue around the globe—the belief that the rights of man come not from the generosity of the state, but from the hand of God.

We dare not forget today that we are the heirs of that first revolution. Let the word go forth from this time and place, to friend and foe alike, that the torch has been passed to a new generation of Americans—born in this century, tempered by war, disciplined by a hard and bitter peace, proud of our ancient heritage—and unwilling to witness or permit the slow undoing of those human rights to which this Nation has always been committed, and to which we are committed today at home and around the world.

Let every nation know, whether it wishes us well or ill, that we shall pay any price, bear any burden, meet any hardship, support any friend, oppose any foe, in order to assure the survival and the success of liberty.

This much we pledge—and more.

To those old allies whose cultural and spiritual origins we share, we pledge the loyalty of faithful friends. United, there is little we cannot do in a host of cooperative ventures. Divided, there is little we can do—for we dare not meet a powerful challenge at odds and split asunder.

To those new States whom we welcome to the ranks of the free, we pledge our words that one form of colonial control shall not have passed away merely to be replaced by a far greater iron tyranny. We shall not always expect to find them supporting our view. But we shall always hope to find them strongly supporting their own freedom—and to remember that, in the past, those who foolishly sought power by riding the back of the tiger ended up inside.

---

* Inaugural Addresses of Presidents of the United States from George Washington, 1789, to Lyndon Baines Johnson, 1965 (Washington, D.C.: U.S. Government Printing Office, 1965), pp. 267-270.

To those peoples in the huts and villages across the globe struggling to break the bonds of mass misery, we pledge our best efforts to help them help themselves, for whatever period is required—not because the Communists may be doing it, not because we seek their votes, but because it is right. If a free society cannot help the many who are poor, it cannot save the few who are rich.

To our sister republics south of the border, we offer a special pledge—to convert our good words into good deeds, in a new alliance for progress, but assist free men and free governments in casting off the chains of poverty. But this peaceful revolution of hope cannot become the prey of hostile powers. Let all our neighbors know that we shall join with them to oppose aggression or subversion anywhere in the Americas. And let every other power know that this hemisphere intends to reamin the master of its own house.

To that world assembly of sovereign states, the United Nations, our last best hope in an age where the instruments of war have far outpaced the instruments of peace, we renew our pledge of support—to prevent it from becoming merely a forum for invective—to strengthen its shield of the new and the weak—and to enlarge the area in which its writ may run.

Finally, to those nations who would make themselves our adversary, we offer not a pledge but a request: that both sides begin anew the quest for peace, before the dark powers of destruction unleashed by science engulf all humanity in planned or accidental self-destruction.

We dare not tempt them with weakness. For only when our arms are sufficient beyond doubt can we be certain beyond doubt that they will never be employed.

But neither can two great and powerful groups of nations take comfort from our present course —both sides overburdened by the cost of modern weapons, both rightly alarmed by the steady spread of the deadly atom, yet both racing to alter that uncertain balance of terror that stays the hand of mankind's final war.

So let us begin anew—remembering on both sides that civility is not a sign of weakness, and sincerity is always subject to proof. *Let us never negotiate out of fear. But let us never fear to negotiate.*

Let both sides explore what problems unite us instead of laboring those problems which divide us.

Let both sides, for the first time, formulate serious and precise proposals for the inspection and control of arms—and bring the absolute power to destroy other nations under the absolute control of all nations.

Let both sides seek to invoke the wonders of science instead of its terrors. Together let us explore the stars, conquer the deserts, eradicate disease, tap the ocean depths, and encourage the arts and commerce.

Let both sides unite to heed in all corners of the earth the command of Isaiah—to "undo the heavy burdens and to let the oppressed go free."

And if a beachhead of cooperation may push back the jungle of suspicion, let both sides join in creating a new endeavor, not a new balance of power, but a new world of law, where the strong are just and the weak secure and the peace preserved.

All this will not be finished in the first 100 days. Nor will it be finished in the first 1,000 days, nor in the life of this administration, nor even perhaps in our lifetime on this planet. But let us begin.

In your hands, my fellow citizens, more than in mine, will rest the final success or failure of our course. Since this country was founded, each generation of Americans has been summoned to give testimony to its national loyalty. The graves of young Americans who answered the call to service surround the globe.

Now the trumpet summons us again—not as a call to bear arms, though arms we need; not as a call to battle, though embattled we are; but a call to bear the burden of a long twilight struggle, year in, and year out, "rejoicing in hope, patient in tribulation"—a struggle against the common enemies of man: tyranny, poverty, disease, and war itself.

Can we forge against these enemies a grand and global alliance, North and South, East and West, that can assure a more fruitful life for all mankind? Will you join in that historic effort?

In the long history of the world, only a few generations have been granted the role of defending freedom in its hour of maximum danger. I do not shrink from this responsibility—I welcome it. I do not believe that any of us would exchange places with any other people or any other generation. The energy, the faith, the devotion which we bring to this endeavor will light our country and all who serve it—and the glow from that fire can truly light the world.

And so, my fellow Americans, ask not what your country can do for you: Ask what you can do for your country.

My felllow citizens of the world: Ask not what America will do for you, but what together we can do for the freedom of man.

Finally, whether you are citizens of America or citizens of the world, ask of us the same high standards of strength and sacrifice which we ask of you. With a good conscience our only sure reward, with history the final judge of our deeds, let us go forth to lead the land we love, asking His blessing and His help, but knowing that here on earth God's work must truly be our own.

One speech scholar, Donald C. Bryant, has outlined the speech and suggests that the speech follows a clear organizational pattern that allowed Kennedy to speak effectively for his ideas and aspirations. Professor Bryant has suggested that the speech was organized in the following manner:*

Introduction

A. Today we observe, not a party victory, but a celebration of freedom in renewal of the past and realization of change.
  1. From the past I have taken an oath prescribed by our distance forebears.
  2. The world is different now.
     a. Man can abolish all poverty.
     b. He can also destroy all life.
  3. Our forebears' revolutionary belief in human rights under God is still the same. We still believe that these rights do not come from the generosity of the state but from the hand of God.
B. A new generation of Americans is ready to reestablish at home and in the world the human rights to which this nation has always been committed and is still committed.
  1. It is a generation born in this century, tempered by war, and disciplined by a hard and bitter peace.
  2. It is a generation proud of our ancient heritage.
C. We are ready to do anything it takes to assure the survival and success of liberty.

* From Donald C. Bryant and Karl R. Wallace, *Fundamentals of Public Speaking*, 5th ed. (Englewood Cliffs, N.J.: Prentice-Hall, 1976), pp. 445–446.

Development

Proposition: [The new Administration commits itself and the United States to a renewal of our traditional quest for freedom, peace, and human welfare at home and abroad.]

I. We pledge our cooperation and support to the free world.
   A. To our old allies in the North Atlantic Community we pledge the loyalty of faithful friends in new cooperative ventures.
      1. United there is little we cannot do.
      2. Divided we dare not meet a powerful challenge.
   B. To the emerging nations we pledge our support in their efforts for their own true freedom.
      1. Old colonialism must not become tyranny.
      2. We do not expect them always to agree with us.
      3. We warn them against riding the back of the tiger.
   C. To those peoples still struggling with poverty and oppression, we pledge our best efforts to help them help themselves.
      1. We will do so as long as necessary.
      2. We will do so because it is right.
         a. Not because the Communists are doing it.
         b. Not because we want their votes.
         c. If a free society cannot help the many who are poor, it cannot save the few who are rich.
   D. To Latin America we offer a special pledge—to convert good words to good deeds in a new alliance for progress.
      1. We will assist them to eliminate poverty.
      2. We will protect them from foreign aggression and subversion [in a new Monroe Doctrine].
   E. To the United Nations we renew our pledge of support.
      1. To keep it from becoming a "forum of invective."
      2. To strengthen its protection of new and weak nations.
      3. To enlarge its useful scope.

II. To our adversaries we propose that together we begin anew the quest for peace.
   A. We will remain strong enough to discourage aggression against us, but
   A'. We cannot accept the armaments race as satisfactory to either side.
   B. We urge that neither side ever fear to negotiate.
      1. To explore problems which unite us instead of belaboring those that divide us.
      2. To proceed seriously to reveal arms control and inspection.
      3. To use science cooperatively for peaceful purposes.
         a. Develop the exploration of space.
         b. Irrigate the deserts.
         c. Eradicate disease.
         d. Tap the ocean depths.
         e. Encourage the arts and commerce.

4. To relieve misery and oppression in the world.
5. To create, not a new balance of power in the world, but a new rule of law.

III. Though the task is long and hard, we must begin it.

   A. It will not be done in the first hundred days, or a thousand days, or the life of this Administration or perhaps in our lifetime.

   B. Like other generations of Americans, we are summoned to demonstrate our national loyalty.

   1. Young Americans in graves all over the world have demonstrated theirs.
   2. Our success depends more on you than on me.
   3. We are called to struggle against the common enemies of man—tyranny, poverty, disease, and war itself.

      a. We are not called to arms, though we need them.
      b. We are not called to battle, though we are embattled.

IV. I challenge you to join me in the historic task of forging a global alliance to assure a more fruitful life for all mankind.

   A. Few generations, like ours, have been granted the role of defending freedom in its hour of maximum danger.

   B. I welcome the responsibility.

   1. To Americans I say: "Ask not what your country can do for you—ask what you can do for your country."
   2. To the rest of the world I say: "Ask not what America will do for you, but what together we can do for the freedom of man."
   3. To all I say, "Ask of us the same high standards of strength and sacrifice which we ask of you."

   Conclusion

   Let us be assured that God's work on earth must be done by us.

Questions to Consider

1. Does the organization suggested by Professor Bryant seem to fit the speech as you read it?
2. Would you make any changes in the outline?
3. Would such a working outline be sufficient for delivering such an address?

Please use our suggested speech rating instrument to rate the Kennedy speech. You will obviously have to omit all items relating to delivery; but the invention, disposition, style, and so on, can be evaluated by analysis of the text.

1. What do you consider the strong points of the speech?
2. Do you have any criticisms to offer?

Now, we will turn to the most recent inaugural address, delivered by Jimmy Carter on January 20, 1977. The entire text of that speech follows, and we would like to have you read that speech very carefully.

Jimmy Carter
Inaugural Address, January 20, 1977

For myself and for our nation, I want to thank my predecessor for all he has done to heal our land. In this outward and physical ceremony we attest once again to the inner and spiritual strength of our nation.

As my high school teacher, Miss Julia Coleman, used to say, "We must adjust to changing times and still hold to unchanging principles."

Here before me is the Bible used in the inauguration of our first President in 1789, and I have just taken the oath of office on the Bible my mother gave me just a few years ago, opened to a timeless admonition from the ancient prophet Micah:

"He hath showed thee, O man, what is good; and what doth the Lord require of thee, but to do justly, and to love mercy, and to walk humbly with thy God." (Micah 6:8)

This inauguration ceremony marks a new beginning, a new dedication within our Government, and a new spirit among us all. A President may sense and proclaim that new spirit, but only a people can provide it.

Two centuries ago our nation's birth was a milestone in the long quest for freedom, but the bold and brilliant dream which excited the founders of this nation still awaits its consummation. I have no new dream to set forth today, but rather urge a fresh faith in the old dream.

Ours was the first society openly to define itself in terms of both spirituality and human liberty. It is that unique self-definition which has given us an exceptional appeal—but it also imposes on us a special obligation, to take on those moral duties which, when assumed, seem invariably to be in our own best interests.

The world itself is now dominated by a new spirit. Peoples more numerous and more politically aware are craving and now demanding their place in the sun—not just for the benefit of their own physical condition, but for basic human rights.

The passion for freedom is on the rise. Tapping this new spirit, there can be no nobler nor more ambitious task for America to undertake on this day of a new beginning than to help shape a just and peaceful world that is truly humane.

We are a strong nation and we will maintain strength so sufficient that it need not be proven in combat—a quiet strength based not merely on the size of an arsenal, but on the nobility of ideas.

We will be ever vigilant and never vulnerable, and will fight our wars against poverty, ignorance and injustice, for those are the enemies against which our forces can be honorably marshaled.

We are a proudly idealistic nation, but let no one confuse our idealism with weakness.

Because we are free we can never be indifferent to the fate of freedom elsewhere. Our moral sense dictates a clearcut preference for those societies which share with us an abiding respect for individual human rights. We do not seek to intimidate, but it is clear that a world which others can dominate with impunity would be inhospitable to decency and a threat to the well-being of all people.

The world is still engaged in a massive armaments race designed to insure continuing equivalent strength among potential adversaries. We pledge perseverance and wisdom in our efforts to limit the world's armaments to those necessary for each nation's own domestic safety. We will move this year a step toward our ultimate goal—the elimination of all nuclear weapons from this earth.

You have given me a great responsibility—to stay close to you, to be worthy of you and to exemplify what you are. Let us create together a new national spirit of unity and trust. Your strength can compensate for my weakness, and your wisdom can help to minimize my mistakes.

Let us learn together and laugh together and work together and pray together, confident that in the end we will triumph together in the right.

The American dream endures. We must once again have faith in our country—and in one another. I believe America can be better. We can be even stronger than before.

Let our recent mistakes bring a resurgent commitment to the basic principles of our nation, for we know that if we despise our own Government we have no future. We recall in special times when we have stood briefly, but magnificently, united; in those times no prize was beyond our grasp.

But we cannot dwell upon remembered glory. We cannot afford to drift. We reject the prospect of failure or mediocrity or an inferior quality of life for any person.

Our Government must at the same time be both competent and compassionate.

We have already found a high degree of personal liberty, and we are now struggling to enhance equality of opportunity. Our commitment to human rights must be absolute, our laws fair, our natural beauty preserved; the powerful must not persecute the weak, and human dignity must be enhanced.

We have learned that "more" is not necessarily "better," that even our great nation has its recognized limits and that we can neither answer all questions nor solve all problems. We cannot afford to do everything, nor can we afford to lack boldness as we meet the future. So together, in a spirit of individual sacrifice for our common good, we must simply do our best.

Our nation can be strong abroad only if it is strong at home, and we know that the best way to enhance freedom in other lands is to demonstrate here that our democratic system is worthy of emulation.

We urge all other people to join us, for success can mean life instead of death.

Within us, the people of the United States, there is evident a serious and purposeful rekindling of confidence, and I join in the hope that when my time as your President has ended, people might say this about our nation:

That we had remembered the words of Micah and renewed our search for humility, mercy and justice;

That we had torn down the barriers that separated those of different race and region and religion, and where there had been mistrust, built unity, with a respect for diversity;

That we had found productive work for those able to perform it;

That we had strengthened the American family, which is the basis of our society;

That we had ensured respect for the law, and equal treatment under the law, for the weak and the powerful, for the rich and the poor;

And that we had enabled our people to be proud of their own Government once again.

I would hope that the nations of the world might say that we had built a lasting peace, based not on weapons of war but on international policies which reflect our own most previous values.

These are not just my goals. And they will not be my accomplishments, but the affirmation of our nation's continuing moral strength and our belief in an undiminished, ever-expanding American dream.

Now your task is to impose an outline on the Carter address that reflects the way you think it was organized. You might want to use a format similar to the one suggested by Professor Bryant for the Kennedy speech.

Introduction

Development

Conclusion

Questions to Consider

1. How would you analyze the invention, disposition, and style of the Carter address?
2. Are there similarities in this speech and the Kennedy speech? What are they? How are they different?
3. How would you rate this speech on each item on our suggested Speech Evaluation Form given in Chapter 8?
4. What are the strong points and weak points in this speech?

AN EXERCISE DESIGNED TO DEVELOP A SPEECH AND USE EVIDENCE PROPERLY

Listed below are several arguments that could be used to develop a speech on the value of a college *or* vocational education. A person could either argue for the value of a college education or take the position that people would be better served by vocational training. Please consider these possible arguments:

1. A liberal arts education provides more career opportunities.
2. College students live in their own world, isolated from normal living experiences.
3. Practically anyone who wants to go to college can do so.
4. Employers will not hire someone without a college degree.
5. People with vocational or technical training can always get some type of job.
6. Feelings of achievement and competence are promoted by mastering some employable skill.

Please decide which side of the issue, and write a thesis statement for a speech. Make that statement specify exactly what you wish the audience to believe at the end of your speech:

Thesis statement:_____

_____

_____

Select three main arguments from the list given earlier to support your thesis statement.

1._____
2._____
3._____

Now, we have listed several pieces of evidence that might be used in support of the arguments we originally listed. Select two pieces of evidence that will support the arguments *you* selected:

Evidence A: Financial aid for education has been decreased by one-half by the government since 1974.

Evidence B: Admission cuts have been planned by 68 percent of the colleges in the country.

Evidence C: To qualify for educational scholarships, students must be nationally ranked in scholastic achievement.

Evidence D: Training in a technical school or certification from a vocational school is required to qualify for 56 percent of the jobs listed by employment agencies.

Evidence E: People with college training are considered to be more qualified for a variety of jobs by employers.

Evidence F: Openings in technical and vocational schools have increased by 20 percent.

Evidence G: The majority of college students living away from home learn to become independent and how to adapt to changes in the environment.

Evidence H: Training and experience are preferred over a college education for 78 percent of the jobs not requiring a postgraduate degree.

Evidence I: Approximately 78 percent of college students indicated in a national survey that socialization is just as important as scholastic education, and possibly more important.

Please choose two pieces of evidence to support each of the three arguments you have selected. Use what you think will best support your arguments:

Argument _____: _____
      Evidence _____: _____
      Evidence _____: _____

Argument _____: _____
      Evidence _____: _____
      Evidence _____: _____

Argument _____: _____
      Evidence _____: _____
      Evidence _____: _____

Finally, we would like you to prepare a complete outline of this speech (on page 330) with an introduction, body, and conclusion. Please identify what pattern of organization you selected for the body. Why did you choose the one you did? It might be helpful to experiment with different organizational patterns.

Speech Outline

Thesis Statement:

Introduction

Body

Conclusion

Which of the following audience characteristics would be likely to change the nature of the speech you have prepared:

Unlikely __1__ __2__ __3__ __4__ __5__ Likely

Whether they:

Are Democrats or Republicans   _____
Are male or female   _____
Are in favor or opposed to vocational training   _____
Live in the North or South   _____
Are intending to go to college   _____
Are old or young or mixed   _____
Know you very well   _____
Are interested in the topic   _____
Are highly educated or not   _____
Have outdoor hobbies   _____
Are a small or large audience   _____
Have a favorite television show   _____
Are open or closed-minded   _____
Speak English   _____
Live in the city or in a rural area   _____
Are rich or poor   _____
Know much about the topic   _____

Why?

POSSIBLE SPEECH ASSIGNMENTS

1. Prepare a five-minute speech endorsing a local political candidate. The class will assemble outside (if possible) at a busy location on campus, preferably near a set of stairs so that the speaker can deliver the address from the top of the stairs. The remainder of the class and any interested bystanders will serve as the audience.
2. One class member, designated by the instructor, will deliver an extemporaneous speech on any topic of his or her choice with two minutes to prepare. Of course, the student will insure that the topic is tasteful. Prior to delivering this two-minute speech, the student will choose another class member to speak next. This procedure will continue until each student in the class has given a two-minute speech.
3. Prepare an oral presentation for delivery before a panel of interviewers. This presentation (approximately three to five minutes) should convince the panel that you could contribute some skill or expertise to their company or organization.
4. Each student will prepare a ten-minute speech that presents one side of some current

topic. Prior to delivering the speech, the student will distribute a detailed outline of the speech (choose the organizational pattern best suited to your topic) to the rest of the class.

5. Form dyads, and agree on a suitable speech topic. One member of each dyad will prepare a detailed outline for the agreed-upon topic, using two different organizational approaches. Be sure to make your outline complete and detailed enough so that the other half of your dyad can deliver a speech from your outline. The other member of each dyad will then deliver a speech from the other member's outline.

6. The instructor will place a number (a dozen or more) of miscellaneous articles into a shopping bag. The bag will be circulated through the class to one student at a time. Each student will select one object from the bag without looking and present a three-minute speech telling the class what the object reminds him or her about or what significance the object has for the human race.

7. Each class member will be given one of the following topics, which will be written on the board, and asked to give a one-minute presentation:

a. One of the worst feelings in the world is . . .
b. Most people are happy when . . .
c. I become very angry when . . .
d. The time I remember most is . . .
e. The most embarrassing situation I have ever seen was . . .
f. The trouble with the world is . . .
g. My most notable achievement is . . .
h. If I suddenly acquired unlimited wealth, I would . . .
i. What this country needs is . . .
j. The person I most admire is . . .

8. Each student will prepare a five-minute speech on a topic that is highly technical in nature. Be sure to structure the speech so that the lay audience can follow your technical presentation. After each speech, the audience members should provide feedback on whether the presentation was too technical or oversimplified.

9. Each student will select a journal article from his or her field of study and summarize the article for the class so that they will understand the intent of the author. The student should supply the instructor with a copy of the article.

10. Each class member should prepare a five- or ten-minute speech concerning a highly controversial topic of the day. Each speech should clearly identify the *issue*, all *sides* of the controversy, the speaker's *position* on the matter, and the *reasons* for this position.

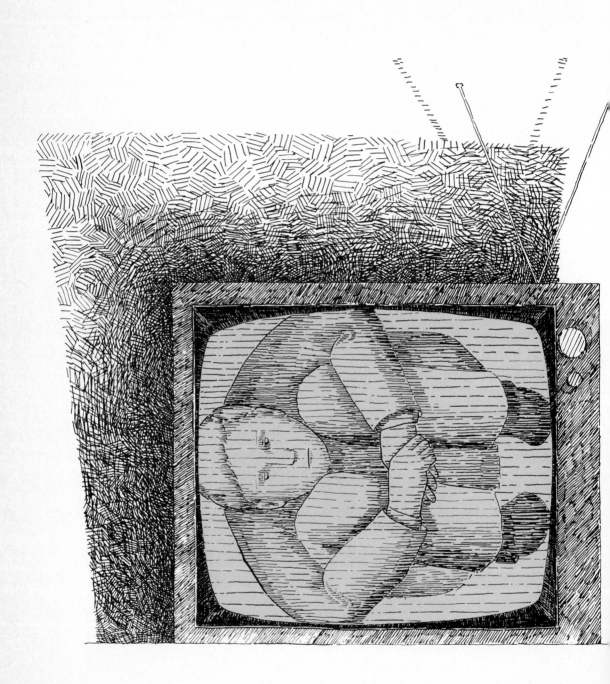

Chapter 10
MASS COMMUNICATION

During the first month of this new year, the American people bore witness to more hope, more joy, more sorrow, and more despair than they had in many years. Every man, woman, and child who could read a newspaper or view a TV set witnessed the birth and death of a nation.

The First: January 17th began as any other day. Snow was falling in New York, the desert sun was peeking over the mountains in California, and tropical breezes were blowing over Florida. But in Utah, many felt the breezes of earlier times. At 8:05 A.M. three shots shattered the silence of a decade when Gary Mark Gilmore became the first prisoner executed in the United States in a decade.

The Thirty-ninth: January 20th marked the end of nearly a century of Southern estrangement from the nation and the beginning of what many considered a new era of hope for this country. Jimmy Carter's march from Plains, Georgia, to the White House ended at 12:03 P.M. with his inauguration as the 39th President of the United States.

The type of communication we have discussed thus far in this text could not begin to accommodate the events that took place during this three-day span and the repercussions that were to follow for months and even years. The American public was showered with a barrage of information ranging from debates arguing the pros and cons of capital punishment to political commentaries discussing the virtues of peanut power. Television audiences watched as the Carter family worked and played their way from the red Georgia clay to the nation's capital, while newspaper and magazine subscribers read detailed accounts of Gary Gilmore's execution before a firing squad at Utah State Prison. Old and young alike "saw" the solar heated presidential reviewing stand and the green Naugehyde execution chair with blood covering its seat and bullet holes shattering its back.

One can appreciate the awesomeness of this type of information barrage by considering that more than 95 percent of all American homes have at least one television set and over 75 percent of American homes supplement this with one or more newspapers.[1] In addition, the average home receives six magazines on a regular basis. Even if we consider only the news content, or information like the event just described, of the media, this represents a sizable bulk of communications.

One wonders whether this mass conveyance of information—much of it repetitious, borrowing from one medium to another—does not suppress the creativity, individual diversity, and desire for self-understanding and awareness that are often the results of more personal forms of communication. To approach this problem from another angle, do these mass media serve to educate us about reality, or do they serve as a substitute for reality and for utilizing our own cognitive and interpretive abilities? Granted that we cannot be all places at once and experience all events firsthand, we must consequently acknowledge the necessity of packaged experiences via media channels. But is it not possible for mass forms of communication to facilitate at least some degree of individual participation and expression of personal experience, or must they inevitably reduce their audience to a passive and uninvolved role?

[1]See for example, A. C. Neilsen Company, *Neilsen Television '75* (Northbrook, Ill.: A. C. Neilsen Company, 1975).

Obviously, no absolute answer can be given for these questions, but there is a promising aspect to this media problem. Never before has there been a time when the media were as self-conscious about their function as they are today. People working in mass communication as well as those outside the industry have used magazines, newspapers, television, radio, and films to criticize and evaluate those very same media channels. The wealth of knowledge and opinions that has resulted from these many probes has provided insights about the nature of mass communication, its immediate and long-range function, and its actual and potential impact on our society. Our purpose in this chapter, then, is to share these insights with you in order to draw a clear distinction between mass communication and the more personal forms of communication we have discussed in earlier chapters.

The Nature of Mass Communication

In earlier chapters of this text we have focused our attention on the more personal form of interpersonal communication. We discussed variables that both facilitate and impede interpersonal communication, and we presented various theoretical approaches to the study of interpersonal communication. In short, we have characterized interpersonal communication as a sender or encoder, a message in many cases based on psychological-level data, a code in the form of some commonly accepted symbol process, a channel such as air waves or paper, a limited number of receivers, feedback or some type of re-

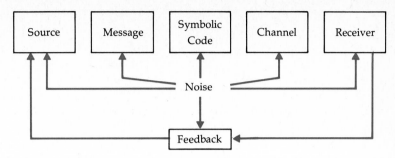

Fig. 10.1 Interpersonal communication model.

sponse to the message, and noise or some obstacles that impede the communication attempt. This conceptual model of interpersonal communication can be represented by Fig. 10.1.

Two of the most basic concepts regarding communication approaches are message flow and message storage. Message flow, or transmission, can be thought of as simply getting a message from one person to another. Variation from one communication system to another is in terms of the *speed* of transmission and the *number* and *variety* of persons to whom the message can be transmitted. Although message storage may be less critical than message flow in understanding the communication process, it helps to distinguish one communication system from another. The main elements of storage are the *ease* with which some message can be stored for future reference, the ease with which another person can *retrieve* this information, and the degree to which the message can be *accurately preserved*. These two concepts are the ones most often used in distinguishing mass communication from interpersonal communication. When a delivery system permits flow of information to large and diverse audiences, it is re-

ferred to as a mass medium to reflect the notion that the audience is massive and the message is mass-produced. The system or systems for transmitting the message may be referred to as a medium or media, respectively, because it or they lie between the source of information and the audience.

Mass communication also differs from interpersonal communication in that we receive *expanded volumes* of information. This information is also different from the type of information we receive in interpersonal communication because it is *mediated* by some person or process within the communication network. There are no guarantees that the information we receive from the mass media accurately reflect the notions originally conceived of and communicated by the information source.

The information source in mass communication is most often *far removed* from the intended audience in both time and space. This differs significantly from the spontaneity and immediacy of face-to-face communication. Moreover, the sources of mass messages need not be single individuals or even small groups. Frequently, the source of a mass communication is a

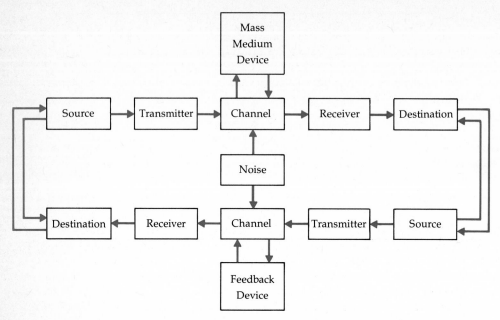

Fig. 10.2 Mass communication model.*

large group or *institution*. Even more frequently, the identity of the source is *obscured* with attributions to "a well-placed" or "official government" spokesman. In addition, many public figures read from prepared texts written by others.

Access to mass communication channels is also limited by *opinion leaders* and *gatekeepers*, who decide what the message "means" and which messages will receive access to limited media space. Although interpersonal communicators often influence others as to the "real meaning" of their words, mass communication receivers are limited to the content that *filters* through the various opinion leaders and gatekeepers.

Finally, *feedback* in mass communications differs sharply from that in interpersonal communication. The feedback is *limited, delayed,* and *indirect* compared to the feedback in face-to-face communication. This feedback often takes the form of letters to the editor or broadcast station, a public opinion poll or survey, or crowd reaction to a public address. One could hardly say that this feedback is representative of the attitudes and opinions of the larger mass audience in most cases.

These factors change mass messages and make them different from interpersonal communication messages. Though we can still apply some of the principles and concepts that are pertinent to interpersonal communication to the mass setting, we need a slightly modified conceptual model for mass communication. Although both the Lasswell and the West-

*Adapted from Melvin DeFleur's components of a general system for achieving isomorphism of meaning, in *Theories of Mass Communication,* 2d ed. (New York: David McKay, 1970), p. 92.

ley/MacLean models, which we discussed in the first chapter, are adequate for analyzing mass communication systems, the model constructed by Melvin DeFleur provides a more graphic depiction of the mass communication concepts that we just discussed.

In this representation, the source and transmitter are seen as different phases of the mass communication act performed by the originator of the message. The channel is some mass medium (radio, television, newspaper, or the like) through which the information is passed. The receiver functions as the information recipient and decoder, transforming the symbolic events of the information into a message. The human brain is the destination where the message receives some meaning through interpretation. Feedback is the response of the destination, or brain, to the source of the message. Noise is emphasized by the fact that it may interfere at any point in the mass communication process and does not have to be identified primarily with the channel or the particular medium. The gatekeeper or filtering effect is contained within the transmitter function of the process.

With this model of the functioning of the mass communication process firmly in mind, we will now examine some of the contemporary theories of mass communication. This is a tedious, but necessary, step; so please bear with us. The purpose of any theory in a given discipline is to explain and predict phenomena that occur in *that* particular discipline. Because, we are treating mass communication as a process somewhat separate from, but an extension of, interpersonal and small group communication processes, we cannot expect theories that explain and predict interpersonal

communication phenomena also to prove equally useful in the domain of mass communication. Therefore, we must employ some theoretical approaches that are specifically suited for the explanation and prediction of mass communication variables.

Theories of Mass Communication

Theories of mass communication have borrowed heavily from research in various fields such as psychology, sociology, political science, and other related social sciences. This in no way implies that mass communication theories are no more than an explication of theories from other disciplines. Rather it indicates the highly interactive nature of variables studied across disciplines. In addition, communication, with all of its classifications, is a much younger discipline than the majority of the other fields studied collectively under the general rubric of social science. The persuasive impact of certain messages, factors affecting the transmission of new innovations, and the psychological predisposition of certain group members are of equal import to scholars in many disciplines. Several specific formulations have developed from observations made in various disciplines that reflect contemporary thinking about the antecedents and consequents of mass communication.[2]

INDIVIDUAL DIFFERENCE THEORY

By the end of World War I, psychologists were intellectually prepared to abandon complex explanations for human behavior

[2]M. L. DeFleur, *Theories of Mass Communication*, 2d ed. (New York: David McKay, 1970), pp. 118–149.

based upon inherited mechanisms for more simplistic thinking. They reasoned that if nature failed to endow the individual with an automatic ability to guide his or her behavior, then he surely must acquire it from his environment. Thus, intellectuals moved away from the idea of the involuntary and inherited nature of human behavior to the concept of behavior acquired through *conditioning*. Studies of behaviorism along with the surge of classical conditioning experiments of the 1920s gave rise to the mechanistic stimulus-response theories of human behavior. Individuals were now seen as being motivated by different incentives, with the learning process taking place according to the *individual differences* of the persons involved.

The individual differences theory of mass communication is an offshoot of this type of conceptual approach. The theory is grounded in several basic assumptions, which permit explanation and prediction of the effects of mass communications. Human beings are seen to *vary* greatly in their personal psychological organization owing to differential learning. Personality variables acquired from the social milieu provide a basis for *perceiving* particular events from quite different perspectives from one individual to another. Finally, the principle of *selective attention and perception* characterizes the mass audience, rather than the notion of the mass audience as a homogeneous aggregate whose members attend uniformly to whatever message is directed their way. From a multitude of available content, each member of the audience will selectively attend to certain messages if they are related to his or her interests, consistent with prior attitudes or supportive of present values and beliefs. Moreover, responses to this message will be mediated by one's particular psychological organization.

The theory implies that mass media messages contain *stimulus* attributes that interact with specific personality characteristics of the audience, which, in turn, create differing *responses* to the communication message. Rather than being uniform among the mass audience, the effects of mass communication messages will vary from person to person because of *individual differences* in psychological structure. The popular notion of "different strokes for different folks" is clearly supported by an individual differences theory. How many times have we walked out of a movie theatre after viewing a "terrific" film like *The Godfather* or *Dirty Harry* and wondered how in the world the critics panned them? Or how could a song like "It Ain't Love But It Ain't Bad" reach the top ten in the country music charts? Or how could anyone buy a Cadillac when they could buy a Porsche for the same price? According to the individual differences theory of mass communication, people will vary in their responses to mass communications about movies, songs, and consumer products on the basis of their particular psychological structures. If you wish to explain why someone likes a particular song or predict whether someone will buy a certain type of car, you have to know the precise nature of that person's psychological organization beforehand. Obviously, the mass media institutions can rarely obtain such psychological-level data to hand-tailor messages to individuals.

SOCIAL CATEGORIES THEORY

This conceptual approach assumes that there are broad, collective aggregates in urban-industrial societies whose behavior in given situations interacts with given sets of stimuli in a similar fashion and likewise will select more or less the same communication contents. The major premise of the social categories theory is that people who have similar characteristics (for example age, sex, educational attainment, income level, religious or political affiliation, and urban-rural residence) will also have similar folkways, in spite of the heterogeneity of modern society. The assumption is that similar modes of orientation and behavior will relate them to such phenomena as mass media in similar ways. Members of a particular social category will select more or less similar communication content and will respond to it in roughly equal ways. This is equivalent to what we called making predictions based on sociological-level data.

The social categories theory is less of an explanatory conceptualization than it is a predictive or descriptive formulation. By describing the social categories that are *likely* to seek out and respond to certain types of mass communication content, the theory provides a rough prediction as to which types of mass communication are likely to be effective with what group. Knowledge of several variables distinguishing one group from another provides a generally accurate guide to the type of communication content a given individual would or would not select from available media. For instance, one could hazard a reasonably accurate guess that a middle-aged male of high intellect would probably not read a "true romance" type magazine, nor would elderly women jump at the chance for a free subscription to *Playboy*. Though members of a local Teamsters Union might endorse legalized abortions, it is highly unlikely that a group from the Older Americans Council would favor a "free morning after pill for every woman" movement.

The social categories theory, taken with the previously mentioned individual differences theory, provides an effective method for analyzing the communication act. The Lasswell model of communication, which we discussed in the first chapter, represents a distillation of these two theories and the situational variables relating to them. Though both of these theories are clearly useful to mass communication theorists, they fail to take into account patterns of interaction between and among members of the mass audience. Such an elaboration is important to the mass communication process, as the next theory suggests.

SOCIAL RELATIONSHIPS THEORY

The social relationships theory is similar to the social categories theory. In fact, the study that led to the formation of the social relationships theory was an attempt to explicate further the social categories theory. The famous Erie County Study was an elaborate design intended to analyze the impact upon voters of the mass communication campaigns of the 1940 presidential elections.[3] Contrary to the

[3]P. Lazarsfeld, B. Berelson, and H. Gaudet, *The People's Choice* (New York: Duell, Sloan and Pearce, 1944).

predictions of existing mass communication theories and the expectations of political and communication experts, when the respondents were asked to report on their recent exposures to campaign communications of all kinds, they mentioned informal political discussions more frequently than exposure to either radio or print. Approximately 10 percent more people engaged in some sort of informal exchange of ideas with other people than were exposed to campaign material directly from the mass media.[4] This unanticipated turn of events led to a recognition that *informal social relationships* will mediate the manner in which a given individual will act upon a communication message that comes to his or her attention through mass media.

The social relationships theory suggests that mass communication may occur through two distinct phases. In the first, information travels from the mass media to relatively well-informed individuals who selectively attend to communications from the media on a regular and firsthand basis. Second, it moves from these well-informed individuals, or *opinion leaders*, through interpersonal communication channels to individuals with less direct exposure to the media and who depend on "opinion leaders" for information and interpretation of that information. As would be expected, the recognition of opinion leadership has generated a plethora of research concerning the characteristics of opinion leaders and the situational context in which they are most influential. In general the research indicates that opinion leaders who are influential in the adoption process are in many respects similar to

those whom they influence.[5] In addition, opinion leadership follows a *horizontal* influence pattern in that it usually takes place between persons of similar social status. We will reserve further comment on opinion leaders and the flow of information through two phases (two-step flow) for our discussion of how mass communication works.

CULTURAL NORMS THEORY

This theoretical approach provides the basis for much criticism of the media for their purported harmful effects. The cultural norms theory postulates that the mass media, through selective presentations and emphasis of certain themes, create impressions among their audiences that common cultural norms concerning the emphasized topics are structured or defined in specific ways. For example, the overabundance of police shows on television might lead some to believe that society accepts violence. Because human behavior is in large part governed by cultural norms with respect to given topics or situations, the mass media indirectly influence that conduct. The mass media can potentially influence behavior by *reinforcing* existing patterns, *creating* new convictions, or *modifying* existing norms. In the words we used earlier, mass media are seen to create cultural-level expectations that form the basis of cultural predictions.

One can easily see that these potential sources of media influence can result in either positive or negative outcomes. Proponents of the media tend to stress the socially desirable consequences, whereas

---

[4]Ibid., p. 150.

[5]E. Rogers, *Diffusion of Innovations* (New York: The Free Press, 1962), pp. 208–247.

media critics are more inclined to accentuate the potential hazards. Whichever position is adopted, it seems unlikely that the media will change *deeply institutionalized norms*, thereby significantly altering human behavior or conduct. Though we do not reject the notion that the mass media might seriously alter socially desirable norms, we suspect that such attempts to change norms might be mediated by individual differences of the mass audience. We will take up this issue in greater detail in our discussion of the impact of mass communication in society.

The cultural norms theory, then, is one of the most controversial, least tested, and potentially most significant theory of mass communications. Imagine the positive impact on black America that the televised documentary *Roots*, which traced the history of a black family from the hold of a slave ship to American citizenship, would have if the predictions of the cultural norms theory prove to be accurate. On the other hand, think of the negative consequences that would result of increased media reliance on violence created new convictions about the expediency of violent behavior.

The four theories that we have just discussed by no means exhaust the theoretical formulations concerning the mass communication process. They are the building blocks on which some more recent and fashionable explications rest. We will present three additional theories that provide interesting and novel approaches to mass communication.

ENVIRONMENTAL THEORY

The environmental theory represents the work of Marshall McLuhan, a Canadian scholar whose radical approach to mass communication made him the fair-haired boy of the electronic media of the 1960s. His book *Understanding Media*, along with a later work, *The Medium Is the Message*, created controversy such as the broadcast media had rarely seen. The major premise of the environmental perspective, which is often overlooked, is that the media became the environment. McLuhan believes that the media not only alter the environment, but also the very messages they convey.[6] Western society, according to McLuhan, has evolved in three stages. Man's perception of the world around him was multisensory and the communication mode was oral prior to the invention of printing. The printing press thrust society into the "Gutenberg Galaxy," where literacy became essential for power and written communication became an expression of the present rather than the past. With print media, the emphasis is on visual perceptions rather than multisensory perceptions, asserts McLuhan. The emergence of electronic media, television in particular, has "retribalized" man and altered his patterns of perception and thought processes. The environmental theory of mass communication suggests that the *channel* of transmission is more important than the message content, and that mass audiences will react one way to information disseminated through print media and another way to information disseminated through electronic media.

McLuhan introduced the terms *hot media* and *cool media*, along with an endless list of nifty phrases to replace widely ac-

[6]M. McLuhan, *Understanding Media: Extension of Man* (New York: McGraw-Hill, 1964).

cepted media terms. Hot media such as print, motion pictures, radio, photography, and spectator sports are filled with detail and leave little need for the receptor to experience the message or add to their knowledge. On the other hand, cool media such as television, interpersonal communication, and telephone conversations are lacking in sensory detail and require the receptor to become more involved in the communication transaction. McLuhan has been criticized widely for his overuse of metaphors and his obvious contradictions. Nevertheless, his ideas have generated much thought and discussion about mass communications, and this, claim his proponents, is precisely the point.

PLAY THEORY

The basic assertion of the play theory of mass communication is that people's involvement in society is represented by either work or play. Work deals with productive and aspiring enterprise, and it reflects reality. Play, on the other hand, represents unproductive activity, and the only useful capacity it serves is to provide satisfaction for individuals, which will ultimately make them more productive. According to this theory, mass communication is utilized more for play or pleasure than for information or improvement.[7] At first, this seems to be an obvious contradiction of our societal image, not to mention an insult to those who consider themselves intellectual and well-read. On second thought, however, this notion does seem to be somewhat consistent with

the number of people who turn to the sports page, comics, or women's page *first* in the newspaper or with the media polls, which report low viewer participation with public service programs and documentaries.

In discussing this theory, Stephenson cites Iron Curtain countries whose media systems are employed exclusively to propagate political doctrines. Even in these systems, "fill" of entertainment kinds of information is used to keep audiences available for propaganda messages. Again, this is a much debated theory of mass communication. Regardless of the controversy generated by this approach, it is hardly likely that play theory will be rejected, at least as long as the entertainment industry has anything to say about it.

REFLECTIVE-PROJECTIVE THEORY

The reflective-projective theory also maintains that the mass media mirrors or reflects society. But it departs from the previous two theories in that it asserts that this reflective image is a distorted and ambiguous one. Society is *reflected* by the media as organized collectives, but individual members of the mass audience *project* their own view of themselves and of society into this media mirror.[8] This line of thinking views televised media as an "electronic Rorschach test" where the viewer projects his own psychological orientation into the setting depicted. Thus, the relative impact of television will

[7]W. Stephenson, *The Play Theory of Mass Communication* (Chicago: University of Chicago Press, 1967).

[8]L. Loevinger, "The Ambiguous Mirror: The Reflective-Projective Theory of Broadcasting and Mass Communications," *Journal of Broadcasting*, 12 (Spring 1968), pp. 97–116.

be determined by the moods of different individuals, at different times, and in different circumstances. The theory also asserts that we identify with people depicted in the media closer to our ideal selves than to our actual selves.

Like the other theories—or any theory for that matter—the reflective-projective theory has many critics. Many discredit this theory as a blatant attempt to justify the poor quality of television programming and add that the theory is anti-intellectual because it maintains that intellectuals are alienated by television owing to a lack of anything worthwhile to identify with. Although we might argue that this theory is more concerned with explaining reactions to televised media than supporting poor programming, we find no basis for argument with the second point.

We have reviewed theories with which mass communication in society can be examined. Some deal with certain variables associated with particular forms of media better than others. Most of these theories are clearly inadequate to cope with the mass communication process when taken alone. Together, however, they become a useful mechanism for coping with the giant communication network that has completely permeated society for the past two decades.

How Mass Communication Works

Mass communications are transmitted to large, heterogeneous audiences that is, audiences consisting of dissimilar constituents, through some mass medium. The mass media are separated into two distinct groups: the electronic or broadcast media and the print media. Common usage of the term *print media* usually refers to newspapers and magazines, whereas the term *broadcast media* usually refers to radio and television. However, these are by no means the only mass media relevant to the study of mass communication. A small sample from a potentially massive list might include books, movies, wire services, records, lectures, billboards, plays, posters, matchbooks, paintings, concerts, sculptures, and boxtops. Each type of communication situation has unique characteristics that affect the nature of the interaction that takes place within it, and each of the media differs from the others in many ways.

HOW DIFFERENT MEDIA OPERATE

The mass media differ with respect to the mode in which they operate. Some of these more important differences are outlined as follows:

1. *Speed*. News events are almost always discovered first by the nearest newspaper. This information is then passed along to the newspaper's parent wire service, which, in turn, transmits the story to the other member newspapers. Radio, however, is usually the first medium to report news events to the mass audience. Television, newspapers, and magazines, in that order, then follow with respect to the speed of transmission to the public. Speed is not an issue with the other media we discussed, for they are not concerned with reporting news events.
2. *Credibility*. Traditionally, print media have been considered to be the

most credible of the mass media. However, in recent years there is some evidence to suggest that the broadcast media are beginning to rise in perceived credibility. Many public surveys, for example, are indicating that many people believe information conveyed by television more readily than by newspapers or magazines.

3. *Detail*. The slowest media are usually the ones that provide the most depth and variety of topics. Books and films (especially documentary films) are capable of the most detail, whereas newspapers follow next in providing depth. Television rarely treats any subject with great detail, whereas radio almost never reaches past the surface.

4. *Sensory Perception*. The various forms of print media are designed primarily for the visual senses. Though both books and magazines may employ pictures, books are usually printed in black and white and could be considered the dullest of the mass media (the authors hope this one is an exception). Radio stimulates only the auditory senses. Television and films appeal to visual and auditory senses with action and color. Advertising has the potential for employing all of these sensory devices (budget permitting) and more. However, T-shirts that give off various aromas and undergarments that can be consumed are of marginal value.

5. *Permanence*. Books are perhaps the most permanent of the mass media, with magazines and newspapers following in order of endurance. Though select individuals or groups may retain advertisements, films, or tape recordings, these types of mass communication do not enjoy the same degree of permanence that other printed communications enjoy. Various art forms have endured for centuries, however, but these forms of communication are not the types we generally regard when we discuss the mass media.

TRANSMISSION OF COMMUNICATION

THE NAVY NEEDS YOU! DON'T READ AMERICAN HISTORY—MAKE IT!

So enticed a recruiting poster of 1917 when the United States entered World War I. It was only one of many posters, all part of a massive propaganda effort to mobilize the emotional energy of the nation in support of history's first global war. Newspapers, films, records, and taped radio messages—all were used in the campaign.

Such propaganda methods paralleled the then current "hypodermic needle" hypothesis accepted by most scholars. The assumption was that some stimulus (message in the mass media) would cause a direct and immediate response in a person (receiver). Communication theorists attributed to the media extensive powers to change and mobilize mass opinions, attitudes, and values. This *one-step flow* hypothesis of message transmission envisioned a society in which individuals were psychologically disconnected and isolated, therefore being unlikely to communicate face-to-face on important matters.

This one-step flow approach predominated in communication research until the 1940 Erie County Study, which we discussed in the preceding section of this chapter. An offshoot of this study was the *two-step flow* hypothesis of message transmission. This approach recognizes that ideas often flow from the media to opinion leaders, where the information is then passed to less active sections of the population. Furthermore, interpersonal communication is seen as a more important factor in shaping voter opinions than information received through the mass media.

The two-step flow hypothesis did much to humanize the concept of mass communication, redirecting toward people the major responsibility for communication flow and attitude change. At the same time, it implicitly showed the mass media to be far less powerful than people had once believed. For these and other related reasons, the approach appealed to most communication researchers, who have since studied numerous variables affecting the two-step flow. The research for the most part has concentrated on the opinion leader—who he or she is and how he or she functions.

One major elaboration of this approach is the *multistep flow* hypothesis. It suggests that message transmission is a chain reaction progressively reaching the different opinion leaders within different segments of the population.[9] When, for example, a respected member of the Senate appears on *60 Minutes*, some opinion

leaders will hear his views on strategic arms limitation or continued conflict in the Middle East. They will pass them on to family, friends, and co-workers, each of whom may be an opinion leader in another setting in addition to a passive listener in this setting. This chain reaction will result in even further dissemination and interpretation of the senator's views across social, economic, and cultural barriers.

OPINION LEADERS

A simplification of the study of opinion leaders divides people into two groups—leaders and followers. Communication interaction, of course, is much more intricate and difficult to reduce to neat categories and comprehensive formulas. But, again, certain hypotheses have tested out with consistency and some general characteristics can be described.

Some traits of the opinion leader. Opinion leaders exist in all social and economic walks of life. Their followings usually number four or five, but someone can accurately be classified as an opinion leader if he or she changes the attitude or behavior of just one other person.

Although the influence of an opinion leader is generally concentrated within the major area of his or her experience, the credibility such a leader establishes in that area may lend at least partial support to his or her authority in related fields. However, the leader's influence is likely to be sharply attenuated if he or she ventures too far beyond his or her established image. The lawyer who is asked about a recent Supreme Court decision might

[9]H. Menzel and E. Katz, "Social Relationships and Innovations in the Medical Profession: The Epidermiology of a New Drug," *Public Opinion Quarterly,* 19 (1955), pp. 337–352.

have much to say, but, when questioned on the impact of DNA research, he would probably defer to the opinion of a physician or biochemist.

Opinion leaders are typically the most conforming members of their groups, seeming to embody or personify the group interests, values, and norms. It is just this conformity and personification, in fact, that attract their following. In this position, an opinion leader not only transmits information but has the double-edged power either to encourage attitude change or inhibit it. In other words, as Westley and MacLean's model suggests, the opinion leader serves as a gatekeeper, selecting to relay from the media and his (or her) other formal information sources the information he or she considers consistent with his or her group's interests. The opinion leader is, therefore, a group interpreter and opinion maker.

Several studies have shown that opinion leaders often have more exposure to media and other sources of information than those who seek their opinions. One study of influential farmers showed that they read more farm literature, watched more television farm programs, and had more contact with agricultural scientists than the less influential farmers.[10] In another classic study it was found that women who were opinion leaders read more magazines and books than did the nonleaders and were also more apt to read material relevant to their area of leadership.[11]

Even in cases where media exposure was not significantly different for opinion leaders and opinion seekers, it was found that the seekers, nevertheless, looked to the leaders to shape the information and interpret it—that is, to give them their opinions. The broadcasting journalists who analyze news events, political speeches, and other such matters serve in this role of opinion shaper. In some cases of heavily unfavorable journalistic analysis, political and other social leaders have censured the media's attempts to shape opinions negatively; not surprisingly, bias in the other direction has not been met with the same disfavor. Research has established several other characteristics typical of opinion leaders; a summary review will suggest to some degree how opinion leadership affects mass communication and the media. Opinion leaders tend to get their information from sources other than those in their communities or locales; that is, they usually draw on more sophisticated information sources than their followers. In general, these people also belong to several large organizations and have friends and contacts in urban areas.[12] Consequently, they may have more experience in diverse social situations and broader knowledge of group and interpersonal behavior than the opinion seekers. Perhaps as a further result of their social relationships (or possibly as an explanation of their cosmopolitan background and experience), opinion leaders characteristically have higher social and economic status than opinion seekers. This status apparently carries with it the suggestion of knowledgeability, at least to those people in lower socioeconomic

[10]E. Rogers, *Diffusion of Innovations* (New York: Free Press, 1962).

[11]E. Katz and P. F. Lazarsfeld, *Personal Influence* (Glencoe, Ill.: The Free Press, 1955).

[12]H. F. Lionberger, "Some Characteristics of Farm Operators Sought as Sources of Farm Information in a Missouri County," *Rural Sociology, 19* (1953), pp. 233–243.

groups who, according to some researchers, tend to seek opinions on public affairs from those with higher status.[13] The importance of status was corroborated by other studies that showed that opinion seekers look to social peers for advice but to social superiors for information.

One implication of all these studies is that opinion leaders, especially on an interpersonal level, are in a significant position to influence the way in which media information is interpreted and responded to by opinion seekers. The relationship is a dynamic one, and opinion leaders and followers are not mutually exclusive categories. An opinion seeker in one situation may, for example, be a leader under other circumstances. Furthermore, under certain conditions, opinion seekers are directly responsive to media communication.

Opinion leaders and the media. It is known that, in times of crisis, the media serve the public directly as a source both of information and of guidance. At such times the opinion leader is bypassed, obviously because there is no need for him or her. For example, when radio stations and newspapers reported that Pearl Harbor had been bombed by the Japanese, those who heard the news did not need opinion leaders to confirm it as true. Likewise, for those who saw on television the murder of Lee Harvey Oswald or the riots of the 1968 Democratic convention, there was no need for opinion leaders to verify these realities.

Nonetheless, people will soon talk about such events; and opinion leaders, being characteristically more informed, will serve again as gatekeepers, sorting,

[13]Katz and Lazarsfeld, 1955.

interpreting, and generalizing. Thus, even if the opinion leaders are bypassed when the media information is initially being received by the audience, they are essential to the media's later impact. Thus, they have commanded a great deal of research and respect.

The role of opinion leaders as middlemen between the media and the population at large has not gone unnoticed—indeed those who plan the scope and presentation of media messages are quite sensitive to the habits and preferences of these middlemen. Perhaps one of the major concerns of the media planners is the role of opinion leaders as catalysts between the advertiser and the consumer. Media advertising, in other words, is not the only, nor necessarily the most important, variable that affects buying behavior:

. . . Communication about consumption with parents seems to be a particularly important variable intervening between exposure to commercials and actual purchase, especially among older adolescents. This finding indicates clearly that consumption behavior is a "social" process, involving overt communication with others, not simply an individual psychological process triggered by exposure to advertising.[14]

GATEKEEPERS

Gatekeepers are individuals within the media who make decisions about what is communicated, and how this is done. They are not necessarily originators of content, but they often function as creative evaluators more often than as cen-

[14]S. Ward and D. Wackman, "Family and Media Influences of Adolescent Consumer Learning," *American Behavioral Scientists,* 14 (1971), p. 423.

sors. The term was first used to describe those individuals who work within the media and control the transmission of news information through the various channels of mass communication. In time, the term was applied to all individuals who exercise some degree of information control in society—editors and publishers, reporters and authors, playwrights and critics, sportscasters and weathermen, teachers and clergymen, and even parents.

Gatekeeping involves more than just deciding what information will be transmitted to the masses. It may involve timing, repetition, prominence, withholding, display, and emphasis of certain communication messages. By exercising these types of decisions, gatekeepers wield a great deal of power and responsibility. Many believe that because mass communication controls the information and knowledge that passes to society and because gatekeepers control what is passed through the mass media, close vigilance should be kept over these gatekeepers.[15] Communication scholars believe that close examination of the gatekeeping process will provide effective methods for evaluating that which "comes through the gate," and it will force gatekeepers to examine their performance and justify their actions.[16]

Although most of us would like to believe that we receive the most relevant and pertinent information that filters through the various media channels, it is highly unlikely that we do. A classic study of the gatekeeping process reported that an editor, who freely admitted his prejudices and preferences, omitted nearly 90 percent of the wire copy received in one week from his paper.[17] When one considers the quantity of omissions that surely resulted from "preferences and prejudices" at the wire service level, the tremendous power and responsibility of the gatekeeper can be felt all too clearly.

Personal bias is not the only factor that sometimes diverts the gatekeeper from the appointed task. The news information that reaches the mass audience is determined more by the time of day it arrives at the particular media facility than by any other single factor.[18] Obviously, the closer to broadcast or press time it gets, the less likely gatekeepers are to include information that arrives "close to the wire." Other factors that influence gatekeepers in choosing certain information to the exclusion of some other information are an appraisal of information disseminated by media competitors; personal convictions of the management; editorial opinion of what the audience needs and wants; values held by professional colleagues; and personal idiosyncrasies, such as the editor who would not permit references to snakes in his paper owing to his morbid fear of the creatures.[19]

[15]G. A. Donohue, P. J. Tichenor, and C. N. Olien, "Gatekeeping: Mass Media Systems and Information Control," in *Current Perspectives in Mass Communication Research*, ed. F. G. Kline and P. J. Tichenor (London: Sage Publications, 1972), 1:41–69.

[16]W. Schramm, *Men, Messages, and Media: A Look at Human Communication* (New York: Harper and Row, 1973), p. 138.

[17]D. M. White, "The Gatekeeper, A Case Study in the Selection of News," *Journalism Quarterly*, 27 (Fall 1950), pp. 383–90.

[18]B. H. Bagdikian, "Professional Personnel and Organizational Structure in the Mass Media," in *Mass Communication Research: Major Issues and Future Directions*, ed. W. P. Davidson and F. T. Yu (New York: Praeger, 1974).

[19]B. H. Bagdikian, 1974.

We must urge the reader not to judge the gatekeeper too harshly on the basis of our discussion, however. The tremendous increase in communication technology in the past decade has forced gatekeepers into many of their decisions. There is simply too much information available for the existing pages and air waves of the media. Time, personnel, and budget considerations force gatekeepers into selection of certain information for dissemination. Gatekeepers, however, are not the only ones forced to make selections by the mass communication process.

SELECTIVITY IN EXPOSURE TO MASS COMMUNICATION

By the very functioning of the mass communication process, the audience is more or less forced to select certain messages to attend to at the exclusion of others. There is too little time in the day for most of us to attend to the mass communications that we need, let alone attending to all the mass communications that are available through the media. Individuals, then, will select certain messages that are useful to them in their everyday lives. Communication scholars have speculated as to the rationale behind these selections. Research indicates that people seem to want information that will answer a need or serve some useful purpose. Though some people view the usefulness of information as an increase in knowledge, others select certain information to escape or avoid some task or role imposed upon them by society.[20] Sometimes, however,

[20]E. Katz, "On Reopening the Question of Selectivity in Exposure to Mass Communications," *Basic Readings in Communication Theory* (New York: Harper and Row, 1973), pp. 161–174.

the belief that information is of personal irrelevance may override usefulness as a selective factor in mass media exposure. We urge the reader to review our earlier comments on the effects of all of the selectivity process.

There is some consensus, especially in mass communication, as to the motivating factors behind this audience selectivity. Central to these beliefs is the assumption that an individual's attitudes are not actually changed by the mass media because the audience will selectively tune out messages contrary to their beliefs. Individuals, then, censor intake of mass communication in order to protect personal beliefs and to defend existing behaviors. Moreover, individuals will seek out communication that supports these practices, especially when the beliefs have undergone some attack or the individual is less confident of these beliefs.[21]

We can see evidence in daily interactions, as well as support in the literature, of people seeking out others who share their political beliefs and reinforcing religious beliefs by listening to broadcasts of their own faith. While an avid Oakland Raider fan might not go out of his way to avoid watching the hated Minnesota Vikings on television, he would probably not beat his wife and dog if forced to choose between watching the Vikings and going on a Sunday picnic, as might be the case if Oakland were playing.

Selectivity, then, is a necessary process in the functioning of mass communication rather than a function of the mass communication process. In the next section we will explore some of the functions of mass communication.

[21]E. Katz, 1973.

Functions of the Mass Media

There are many ways to assess the functions of mass communication in society. Function, in a sense, implies usefulness as well as use. Some authors impose an artificial dichotomy upon this term by limiting their discussions of the functions of mass communication to either uses or usefulness. We find it more appropriate to discuss the functions of mass communication in society in terms of both the *institutional uses* and the *social usefulness* of the mass media.

INSTITUTIONAL FUNCTION

Essentially, the mass media have been charged with four major functions: to *inform* the public through surveillance of society; to *interpret* this information through commentary intended to persuade; to provide *entertainment and recreation*; and perhaps most important from an institutional perspective to *earn a profit*, which enables the media to discharge these other functions.

Information. Like the mass transit system, the mass communication system is intended to convey large numbers of items through space with maximum efficiency and minimum time loss. Many writers have referred to the media, the print media especially, as the "watchdog of the public estate." The mass media are charged with the responsibility of keeping watch over society and informing the members of that society of information that may be of concern to them.

Most people normally associate this information function with banner headlines announcing the latest national or international crisis, magazines devoting entire issues to some economic front, television stations interrupting scheduled programming to announce key political moves or natural disasters, and radio broadcasts announcing untimely deaths or routing motorists around traffic jams. There are, however, other less obvious aspects to the dissemination of information. Advertisements lead shoppers to bargains, public announcements inform interested groups of scheduled meetings and discussions, consumer reports provide comparisons of various products, interviews focus attention on the latest issues in the entertainment or political world, and statistical matter assists in buying stocks or betting on the right team.

Broadcasting is perhaps the most effective of the media for increasing immediate general knowledge of information and ideas. But though there have been attempts at in-depth television and radio coverage of certain events, specific and detailed knowledge is more available, or randomly accessible at least, in the print media. Printed matter can also be carried and referred to almost anywhere, for it does not require an energy source and does not interfere with the activities of others. Perhaps even more important is the fact that one can analyze the information and check the accuracy of the information and comprehension of it. This is an impossibility with broadcast material unless one carries a video tape recorder with one. Despite certain advantages, disadvantages, and limitations, the mass media have been rather effective disseminators of factual information in the form of hard news reports, documentaries, interviews, and investigative journalism.

Interpretation After seeking out the facts, the mass media attempt to arrange them in meaningful patterns that encourage informed interpretation. Though the information function deals primarily with facts, the interpretation function deals with both fact and opinion. The *gatekeeping* process, which we discussed earlier, is one form of interpretation—in deciding which information to disseminate and which information to delete, the gatekeeper "interprets" the relative news value of information. In this particular instance, the audience cannot judge the veracity of this interpretation because omitted information does not reach them for scrutiny.

A second type of interpretation involves the *editorial* process. Normally, the mass media segregate editorials and opinions from "news information" by placing such items on a separate editorial/opinion page or alerting the listener that the following comments "represent the express opinions of the station management only." This type of interpretation serves to clarify important issues by presenting relevant sides to current topics. Obviously, some media content attempts to sneak in opinion at every turn. We will leave you to your own devices in deciding just how much editorializing is done under the guise of factual reporting.

Finally, the mass media carry out this interpretation function by various methods selected for *presentation* of information. The documentary *Roots* carried the largest audience in media history, in addition to stirring up enormous controversy over racial issues. A frequent criticism of the program was the presentation of all blacks as good and all whites as bad. Many individuals, especially those prone to racial prejudice one way or the other, reacted harshly owing to the implications of this form of presentation. On the other hand, media presentation of events can add clarity to a confusing situation. One spectacular example of the media's ability to clarify a wild confusion of data through presentation came during the Watergate investigations, with its array of names, committees, titles, statutes, and contradictory allegations. In addition to their general news coverage, many of the media provided a periodical summary of events; gave pertinent background information regarding sophisticated electronic equipment and procedures; and devoted special programming to discussions, reviews, and interpretations as the proceedings unfolded.

Entertainment and recreation. Many people, probably too many, utilize the mass media purely for entertainment or to achieve some measure of respite from the monotony of their daily activities. Providing entertainment and aesthetic enjoyment are relatively self-explanatory functions. The print media long ago forfeited the top position in this area to films, television, and records, while generally maintaining their status as a purveyor of information and education.

Many of the media, however, entertain as they inform. It is not difficult to recognize the grain of truth to many comic strip characterizations or the stark reality underlying many situation comedies on television. Films and televised serials help us wile away our leisure hours, but they also may tell us how things were or how things are or maybe even how things could be.

One generally held belief about mass media entertainment is that it provides

Mass media entertainment provides both catharsis and stimulation. (Photograph: German Information Center)

both catharsis (a purging of the emotions) and stimulation. We can purge ourselves of unwanted aggression and stimulate our physical and emotional consciousness with equal facility by watching *Charlie's Angels* combat corruption with a combination of charm, cunning, and untethered bustlines. It goes without saying, of course, that if one relies too heavily upon the media for catharsis or stimulation, escapism (or flight from reality) will occur. Escaping from reality through the media can create an unhealthy and ineffective emotional disposition, as might be imagined.

To earn a profit. The mass media in the United States are for the most part privately owned profit-making organizations. The very continuation of mass communication in this country depends upon their earning enough profit to cover the enormous cost of media production. In this respect, earning a profit can be considered an even more basic function of the media than their intrinsic functions of disseminating, interpreting, and entertaining. In other words, there would be no mass media (other than publicly sponsored agencies) if there were no profits.

For most of the media, advertising is the

major source of income. It follows that the broadcast networks, the newspapers, and the magazines that attract the widest audiences will also attract the biggest advertisers. If a television advertiser is a manufacturer of sporting equipment, the advertiser traditionally looks for programs that reach a large percentage of the male audience. The advertiser, too, wants to make a profit from the money invested in the ability of the mass media to encourage mass consumption.

Many arguments focus on the belief that the profit motive inhibits quality production in the media. And indeed several nations—Canada, England, and Switzerland among them—have nationalized their mass communication resources in part to prevent commercial exploitation. For the American media industry, the idea of a government-operated mass communication system conflicts with the guarantees afforded by the First Amendment. As this controversy continues, both sides of the issue are being discussed by government and media spokesmen alike. This debate has caused the media to occasionally reexamine their policies in terms of profit-making needs and the public interest. One salutary effect, from our perspective, of such pressure on the media was the decision to drop cigarette advertising. Potential competition from community-operated cable television systems may be the next incentive for media to reevaluate and reorganize along the lines of public interest.

SOCIAL FUNCTIONS

The mass media also contribute to the socialization process. We can identify several social functions of the mass media—cultural transmission, control of social norms, diffusion of innovations, and agenda setting. The mass media have come to be recognized as purveyors of these goals, and society expects the media to carry out these functions.[22]

Cultural transmission. As we have stated earlier, the mass media more or less mirror society. In so doing, the media reflect the norms and values that society considers valuable and worthy of promulgation. In the normal course of disseminating information, the media transmit cues, especially to the young, that reinforce values and behaviors considered acceptable by society. For example, media coverage of the 1976 presidential campaigns focused largely on President Carter's promise to pardon all Vietnam-era draft evaders, which he did as his first official presidential duty. Debates, both pro and con, of this issue reflected society's values concerning the limits to patriotic responsibility, as well as society's notion of compassion.

The media also transmit cultural norms by interpreting the information that passes through the gates. Editorials, commentaries, and more subtle forms of media persuasion tell us how we ought to think or how we ought to respond to certain societal stimuli. When a newspaper editorial tells us that they are supporting a particular political candidate and that we should support him or her also, they are telling us that the candidate stands for cer-

[22]For an additional discussion of the social functions of the mass media see S. H. Chaffee and M. J. Petrick, *Using the Mass Media: Communication Problems in American Society* (New York: McGraw-Hill, 1975) or C. R. Wright, *Mass Communication: A Sociological Perspective*, 2d ed. (New York: Random House, 1975).

tain principles that are good for society. It makes no difference whether these principles are good or not, the point is that by endorsing the candidate, these gatekeepers tacitly imply that society embraces these very same principles.

Last but not least, cultural transmission is carried out through the various forms of entertainment presented by the media. Films and television programs teach us about family life, various occupations, the educational system, patriotism, loyalty to self and friends, and the good and the bad of our history. Though it is a much debated topic at present, the media also teach us that crime doesn't pay. We will explore this topic further at the conclusion of this chapter. The other media contribute their share to cultural transmission. The majority of records of the past decade carry some sort of social message, though it is becoming increasingly more difficult to find a comic strip that does not convey at least a modicum of cultural commentary.

Control of social norms. There are certain forms of social behavior that every society considers unacceptable. The mass media have long been looked upon as a means of controlling some of these undesirable behaviors. Much research in recent years has centered around methods for effectively controlling undesirable social behavior through mass communication. At present our society appears to be most concerned with controlling *violence, environmental pollution, sexual excesses,* and *political radicalism.*

The control of *violence* is one of the oldest social problems to plague mankind. Though many have come to depend on the media for control of violence, others have suggested that it is the mass media's proclivity for portraying violence that has caused the problem to reach epidemic proportions. One suggestion is to place a moratorium on violence depicted in the mass media, similar to the ban on cigarette advertising. This issue is not likely to be resolved for some time, for it involves First Amendment freedoms, and, besides, violence attracts large audiences, which, in turn, generate large advertising profits. We will reserve discussion of the impact of violence on society for the next section of this chapter and will concentrate here on some methods for media control of violence.

The most obvious remedy is for the news and entertainment media to prepare their messages with less reliance on violence. Television shows with themes other than detectives, police, or violence would be a refreshing and creative change. Reporting of violence is an inescapable part of information dissemination. For the most part, in our opinion, the media disseminate and interpret such events with an accompanying social message— violence is tragic and should be avoided whenever possible. Some have even suggested that the media institute a code similar to the motion picture rating code to precede mention or presentation of violence. The mass media do encourage law enforcement and adherence to societal norms; however, whether or not media portrayal of violence has a positive or negative impact on society is a question that will be debated for a long time.

During the 1960s the American public had their fill of masses of concrete, litter everywhere one looked, pollution hanging over their cities like a threatening cloud, and the alarming dissipation of natural resources. *Environmental pollution* became the nation's war cry, and the mass media picked up the gauntlet. Billboards, bumper stickers, and books like *Silent Spring* and *Quiet Crisis* warned society of the impending crisis. In the spring of 1970, Earth Day was celebrated in different ways on most campuses throughout the country. The media carried this message, and government responded with a flood of energy and environmental legislation.

The mass media have since taken on the responsibility of informing the public of energy-saving and pollution-abating steps, providing social support for those individuals and institutions that implement these suggestions and exposing similar groups and organizations that violate the environment.

Although this country probably has a legitimate desire to control *sexual excesses*, there is little, if any, consensus on what to control and how to control it. The role of the mass media in this controversy has been one of denouncing sexual excesses and then turning around and engaging in these very same sexual excesses. As you will note, we have made no attempt to define "sexual excesses," nor will we attempt to do so. This would take an effort far beyond the scope of this entire book.

Society has traditionally taken a firm stand against prostitution, the forcing of oneself upon another, exposing oneself or engaging in blatant sexual activity in public, and performing explicit acts with dogs, children, or sheep. The media have reflected this position in news reporting, films, and novels. However, no one, including the authors, is against a little sex between two (or whatever) mutually consenting adults. Most of us recognize this as a normal, human occurrence. Unfortunately, what is pleasure for some is deviancy for others. This pretty much sums up the controversy surrounding sexual excesses in society.

The mass media are firmly committed to controlling crimes of sex in society. This is obvious and needs no elaboration. The problem arises when the media carry out their entertainment function. Just how far does one go in portraying the sexual nature of men and women? Do real people say, "Gosh, Gee, Golly," or do they use profanity? Are breasts normal and healthy, whereas genitalia are abnormal and sinister? And, finally, should young children be exposed to the sexual side of life, and, if so, at what age? The answers to these and other questions will have to be answered in the courts. The mass media have no answers.

Our country has come to be recognized as a country of diverse, but conciliatory, political views. Though we welcome opposing views, we tend to reject *political radicalism*. Our political structure has institutional procedures for registering opposing views and beliefs. This institutional structure, though not perfect, has at least curbed the violence that has erupted in other systems. The mass media control political radicalism by integrating the political views of citizens, by evaluating these views, by providing a channel to advocate these views, and by informing citizens exactly how the political machinery works.

Political radicalism reached a new high in the country during the Vietnam War.

Many argued that the extensive coverage that the media afforded to these radical students further kindled their revolutionary flame. The media countered with the argument that they were simply carrying out their information function, and, besides, they did present editorials and commentaries denouncing these practices. Their critics argued that a one-page editorial or a two-minute commentary hardly balanced entire issues or broadcasts glamorizing rampaging college students. The problem is further compounded by the fact that the media have the responsibility to inform society of events such as political radicalism, in addition to their responsibility of socialization of the political process. Sometimes the two do not mix very well.

Diffusion of innovations. The matter of the comparative impact of media and interpersonal communication in effecting opinion and attitude change is related to another learning process called the adoption or innovation process. The adoption process comprises the steps that occur between diffusions of new information and the change that results from that information. What, for example, happens between the time someone hears about or becomes aware of a new candidate for public office and the day he or she votes for that candidate at the polls?

What is the adoption process? According to Everett Rogers, a noted researcher in the field, "the process by which innovations are adopted by individuals is essentially a limited example of how any type of learning takes place."[23] Learning to play

[23]E. Rogers, *Diffusion of Innovations* (New York: The Free Press, 1962).

the guitar, then, entails much the same steps as the process of switching from one brand of cigarettes to another. Essentially, there are five stages involved in this adoption process.

Before all else, one must, of course, become aware of something new, whether it is information, an idea, or a product. However, as we implied in the discussion of opinion leaders and media advertising, awareness is not an automatic result of exposure. People are inclined to perceive selectively, understand and retain that which interests them; similarly, they often remain closed even to obvious information if it does not excite their interest.

For example, let us say that you wish to buy a car but do not have (and could care less about having) an understanding of how a car functions. If, then, a television advertiser for a rotary engine car were simply to list its technical advantages over piston engines, the level of emission, the unique suspension system, and so forth, all this new information would probably be deflected from your mind by an impenetrable wall of boredom. The key to drawing your full awareness of the car's features is to sustain your interest. The advertiser, therefore, gives you the basic motivational lesson: a piston engine goes "boing, boing" (a pogo stick is used as the visual complement to make sure that you get the point), whereas the rotary engine goes "hmmmm" (a very smooth and peaceful humming sound, as though the car were powered by divine inspiration).

At this stage of interest, a person develops the motivation for seeking additional information. Perhaps he or she will talk to a few car dealers or ask for brochures. The person may check out *Consumer's Report* and gather other pertinent data that would enable him or her to proceed to the next stage in his or her decision making.

Evaluation, the third step in the adoption process, finds the individual applying the information he or she has gathered to his or her own needs and interests. Car buyers, armed with information about car costs, safety factors, and whatever else is of concern to them, attempt what Rogers calls a "mental trial." They try to determine in their minds whether, for example, a rotary engine station wagon or a foreign sports car is best suited to their needs. Before making the choice, they will find out if service for the foreign car is difficult to get and if the station wagon gets low mileage. In other words, they weigh the advantages and disadvantages of the cars before making their choice. At this point, they also turn more to friends, neighborhood auto mechanics, and others trying to find reinforcement for their own opinions in these other opinions.

In the stage before the actual purchase (or adoption), the car buyer will probably want to take each of the cars for a trial drive. This, of course, is comparable to the trial stage in the adoption process—small-scale adoption on a probationary basis, giving one last chance to reject the innovation. If the results of the trial are favorable, the individual will adopt the innovation for continued use. Or, in the case of the car buyer, if the station wagon drives better, he or she will put the license plates on the car and drive it home to his or her garage.

Communication sources in the adoption process. Which of the information sources is most important at the different adoption or innovation stages? A general conclusion, based on numerous research projects, is that media sources—impersonal, cosmopolitan, general, and informational—are most influential during the awareness stage and continue to be important during the interest stage. Personal interaction, however, is most valuable during the evaluation period. In contrast to the media channels, personal interaction is two-way, generally localized, specific, and conducive to opinion sharing. Its importance continues until the adoption is completed.

The impact of personal exchange in the later stages of adoption finds explanation in numerous formal studies. But maybe it is just as easily explained by the old saying "Birds of a feather flock together." People most often discuss ideas, values, and problems with others who share them in common. Thus when election time comes, for example, people talk over voting decisions with others they see in their everyday activities—co-workers with whom they share similar economic concerns or people of the same party with like political leanings. Such exchanges open the way for new ideas and information, and they encourage opinion sharing and evaluation. This is the point in the adoption process where opinion leaders at work or within political groups can be most persuasive.

Time required for adoption. The factors affecting the length of the adoption period are probably as numerous as the individual instance of adoption, but again the need for operating principles has led to some generalizations. For example, it is usually true that adoption occurs fastest when the innovation is simple and not a radical departure from current practices and beliefs. Another theory proposes that the time between awareness and trial is consistently longer than the time between trial and adoption. Thus it seems safe to surmise that once a person reaches the point of trying an innovation, he or she will proceed quickly to adopt or reject it.

Extensive research has measured rates of adoption among those who change first (early adopters) and those who change at slower rates (later adopters). Early adopters have been found to pass through the five stages both earlier and faster. Sometimes they are people who simply have a predisposition toward innovations of any sort. Most of us know one person who is always the first on the block to own a new item—be it a color television or a drive-it-yourself lawn mower.

More often, however, the early adopter has a special predisposition toward the innovation in question—perhaps it is an item that seems capable of satisfying a particular need or a new idea that is consonant with his or her own thinking; or perhaps it is an innovation that offers hope where there had been none before, as in the case of experimental surgical techniques for those with serious illnesses. The early adopter, therefore, becomes aware earlier of pertinent information and moves quickly into and through the interest stage, gathering what he or she needs to make an evaluation.

Interestingly enough, however, early adopters prove to take a relatively longer time to move from trial to adoption than the later adopters. The probable reason is that they are more cautious at this point, for they have few or no models to guide them. Later adopters, on the other hand, learn from the experiences of the early adopters. Consequently, they have fewer risks to take and usually move more

quickly through the last stages of adoption. Some people, of course, create a series of substages to prolong final adoption. For instance, we all know people who will wait until the millennium for color television designers to work out all the "bugs."

Early adopters and opinion leaders share several attributes. Both have wide exposure to information sources, including many beyond local sources. Both groups are also found to be more educated and to hold higher social and economic status than their followers. As the first to learn information and to accept changes, they are of great importance to the mass media. For if the media are to carry on their primary function of dispensing information effectively, they will have to understand the early adopters and opinion leaders and their power to hasten or slow down the process of change.

Agenda setting. Most individuals have a private set of beliefs that they consider to be important to them. It really does not matter if someone else does not consider these issues to be important, so long as they have some saliency or importance for the individual who holds them. Similarly, the mass media present issues that they feel are important and sometimes vital to society. This agenda, or series of issues, is likely to get extensive media coverage if the gatekeepers feel circumstances warrant it. A television station, for example, might select as the three most important issues of the day stories about the rise in crime, abortion, and the most recent strategic arms limitation negotiations. By giving this agenda prominent coverage in the news, they might influence members of the audience also to perceive these three events as the most crucial issues of the day. This type of agenda setting occurs in most of the mass media channels.

Communication researchers have determined that agenda setting most typically occurs with respect to choosing the most salient or important political issues of the day. Studies have shown that the issues that mass audiences consider to be the most salient correlate strongly with the issues presented most prominently by the media.[24] The findings suggest that television news creates more of an impact in determining the single most important issue among young voters, whereas newspapers hold other issues on the agenda for longer periods of time.

The fact that the mass media significantly influence which topical issues are considered to be the most important should come as no surprise. Without the mass media we would not even know what the issues are. If we assume that the media present the issues with the proper perspective, agenda setting will focus attention on the proper issues with the proper degree of concern. However, should the media focus attention on the wrong issues or on issues that are salient to only a select few, their function as an agent of socialization will be ill-served.

Agenda setting and the other socialization functions that we discussed are entrusted to the mass media. We must have faith in the integrity and professionalism of those who work within the media. However, we must keep a prudent eye

turned toward any possible abuses of this function. In other words, we must not blindly accept the word of the media; we must take their message and think for ourselves. Part of thinking for ourselves is determining what impact mass communication has on our society. We will examine this impact in the following section.

The Impact of Mass Communication

It is impossible to say precisely how mass communication will affect the individual. Scientific verification of the effects of the mass media on individual behavior has been difficult to achieve because the factors seem to be nearly inexhaustible. Mass media effects are seldom, if ever, simple, direct, or totally dependent upon communication messages because the personal experiences and psychological disposition of the individual constantly modify indirect media exposure. Owing to the complex nature of this process, the best we can do is attempt to analyze the impact that mass communications have on society.

As we have suggested, the effects or impact of mass communication may be approached from several perspectives. We can look at short-term or long-term effects; we can look at the effects on individuals, societies, or cultures; or we can look at the effects on attitudes or behaviors. Obviously, to make some sense out of this puzzle we need some general guidelines. Research in all areas of communication suggests that individual behavior in response to mass communication is preceded by cognition (thinking), comprehension, and attitude and value change. Walter Weiss suggests that mass commu-

[24]L. E. Mullins and M. E. McCombs, "Young Voters and the Mass Media," *American Newspaper Publishers Association Research Bulletin*, No. 5, Washington D.C., August 2, 1974, pp. 13–20.

nication media have an impact on *cognition and comprehension, attitude and value* change, and finally, *behavior* changes.[25] As this type of conceptual schema ultimately leads to behavioral change, the mass media will have some impact because a large part of the mass audience is composed of *children*, because society has come to rely on media to keep watch over the environment and forms *expectations* regarding this surveillance function, and lastly because *violence and aggression* portrayed in the media have been widely associated with violent and aggressive behavior on the part of the viewing audience.[26] We will examine the impact of mass communication in society with respect to these factors.

COGNITION AND COMPREHENSION

The selectivity process that we discussed earlier in the text plays a major role in audience cognition and comprehension. The mass audience selectively exposes themselves to certain elements of the communication message rather than attend to every word or topic. In spite of this, constant and repetitive message transmission by the media will create knowledge awareness in the audience over time.

As we stated earlier, past experiences and psychological orientation will modify an individual's exposure to the media. An individual's ability to recall a given media message will depend largely on the interaction between the message and past experiences. In other words, an individual is more likely to be aware of a message if it stimulates or reinforces some past experience or interpersonal relationship. One would probably be aware of information about a particularly heavy snowfall in Grand Rapids if one had visited there on some occasion. Similarly, the fact that an individual was planning a trip to Austria in the summer would probably alert the individual to a news story about deflation of the Austrian schilling.

The emotional reactions of a mass audience will be affected by cognition and comprehension. We are all familiar with the emotional reactions of children when they view a horror film. Prior knowledge about "how scary the movie is," the darkness of the theatre, and the child's psychological disposition will affect future exposure to such themes and to immediate cognitions about the film.

Finally, the degree to which an individual identifies with a particular topic or character in a mass communication will determine the amount of cognition and comprehension. An individual who feels some interpersonal attraction for Johnny Carson will surely attend to every word the talk show host utters, and will likewise be able to recount many of his comments to associates at the office the next day. Cognition and comprehension improve when the audience identifies with the communicator or the message.

ATTITUDE AND VALUE CHANGE

Mass communication will obviously have some effect on the attitudes and val-

[25]W. Weiss, "The Effects of the Mass Media of Communication," in *Handbook of Social Psychology*, ed. G. Lindzey and E. Aronson (Reading Mass.: Addison-Wesley, 1968), 2:77–195.

[26]D. F. Roberts, "The Nature of Communication Effects," in *The Process and Effects of Mass Communication*, ed. W. Schramm and D. F. Roberts (Urbana: University of Illinois Press, 1974), pp. 375–388.

ues that people hold. We will not discuss attitudes and attitude change in great depth here because we explore this topic extensively in Chapters 11 and 12. Mass media research indicates that the media do have an effect on values and attitudes, but the precise nature of this effect is somewhat nebulous. The vast majority of mass media studies show that the media reinforce existing attitudes and values more than they convert the audience to new ones.[27] This is not to say that the media do not convert some individuals finally to "see the light." It simply means that most of the evidence suggests the media usually reinforce attitudes rather than change them.

This reinforcement effect is not limited just to individual attitudes. As we saw in the section regarding social functions of the media, the normal attitude and behavior patterns of society are transmitted through the mass media. On the basis of this research, it seems that the mass media reinforce societal attitudes and values in the individual. In other words, the media create a kind of social conformity through the reinforcement of societal goals.

BEHAVIORAL CHANGE

A considerable amount of research has been generated in determining specific kinds of behavior change that result from exposure to the mass media. One of the most widely studied areas of behavioral change concerns *voting* behavior. Generally, the media are relatively ineffective in converting voters from one party to another. However, the mass media are effec-tive in influencing voter perception of important issues, or agenda setting.

There is also very little reason to believe that the mass media significantly alter established *family life patterns*. Regardless of media exposure to family-situation series, the American family continues to interact with more or less the same approach as always. Television perhaps alters family life somewhat in the sense that families spend more time together watching it. Many have argued that the media do alter public taste, but the best research evidence indicates that *public taste* regarding clothing styles, films, cultural events, and recreation is more influenced by interpersonal contacts.

The media do play a dominant role in changing *leisure time* patterns. As access to the media increases, so does the amount of leisure time spent with the media increase. Television is probably the biggest culprit. The Neilsen Company reports that in 1974 a typical American household had at least one television set turned on for over six hours each day.[28] When one considers that approximately 97 percent of all American households have a TV set, a great many leisure patterns are being altered around television programming. In addition, movies, music concerts, lectures, discussions, and reading also eat up leisure time. It makes one wonder what people did before the mass media became so available.

THE IMPACT ON CHILDREN

The potential effects of mass media on childhood viewers has been long recog-

[27]J. T. Klapper, *The Effects of Mass Communication* (Glencoe, Ill.: The Free Press, 1960).

[28]A. C. Neilsen, *Neilsen Television '75.*

nized. Childhood is a period when children are learning what to expect from the environment and what the environment expects from them. It is also a period in which the child is experiencing previously unstructured aspects of his or her world and is highly dependent upon others for information. Though children obtain much of this information from their parents and other nonmedia sources, society is relying more and more on the mass media to help socialize children. Of prime interest to parents, educators, and the media themselves, then, is the relative impact that the media have on children. As would be expected, most of this interest has focused on the television medium.

Research has extensively investigated this topic, and Wilbur Schramm has concluded: "For some children under some conditions, some television is harmful. For other children under the same conditions, or for the same children under other conditions, it may be beneficial. For most children, under most conditions, most television is probably neither particularly harmful or beneficial."[29] There is a great deal of evidence to suggest that children, as well as adults, learn behaviors, norms, and attitudes through film and televised presentations. Albert Bandura points out that the demonstrated efficacy of learning through symbolic modeling and the large amount of time young children spend watching television, which is a continuous form of symbolic models, provide ample reason to believe that children construct a significant part of their world image on the basis of mass-mediated information.[30]

Most of the studies examining the impact of the mass media on the maturational process in children have concluded that television has little, if any, negative effect on the health of children. Variables such as age, intelligence, social level, personality, and parental example are the most important factors in determining the impact of television on children. Children have been shown to be very selective about how much television they watch and what they watch, and they tend to reflect preferences or taste from other areas in their television preferences. Moreover, television has been shown to create little or no negative behavior patterns in normal children.

FORMING EXPECTATIONS

The American public has come to depend on the mass media for a great deal of their information about local, national, and international events. As a result, the mass audience may not question the media with the same fervor reminiscent of earlier days. Many simply accept what information is offered up and shrug their shoulders when mention is made of information that never passed through the gate. Klapper's finding that mass communication is more likely to contribute to the *status quo* than to create change stems primarily from these selection and gatekeeper processes.

---

[29]W. Schramm, J. Lyle, and E. B. Parker, *Television in the Lives of Our Children* (Stanford: Stanford University Press, 1961).

[30]A. Bandura, "Social Learning Theory of Identificatory Processes," in *Handbook of Socialization Theory and Research*, ed. D. A. Goslin (Chicago: Rand-McNally, 1969), p. 248.

As we noted earlier, selection of information for dissemination is a necessary fact of life. Gatekeepers engage in this process simply because they have to. But as previously mentioned, research indicates many subtle pressures and influences sometimes slant this selection process. The result of this, as Donald Roberts points out, is that what the media do not report may be as significant as what they report.[31] In addition, the fact that the media, especially the entertainment industries, must compete for a large share of the mass audience and the accompanying advertising revenues tends to influence transmission of information away from anything that is not likely to attract large audiences. The mass audience expects to receive all the news, although they may only be getting part of it.

The consequences or impact of this situation could result in socialization of inappropriate societal norms, dissemination of the wrong information, setting the wrong agenda, or reinforcing the wrong attitudes or values. There are still many unanswered questions in this area. A helpful start in obtaining answers to these and other questions is for both the mass media and the mass audience to recognize the problem for what it is—no more and no less.

VIOLENCE AND AGGRESSION

Violence has always been a popular condiment for spicing up mass media fare. Television, by virtue of its ubiquity, has been the prime target of the swelling apprehension about media violence, par-

[31]D. F. Roberts, 1974, p. 381.

ticularly in children. In light of this, the bulk of research investigating the impact of violence on mass media audiences has focused on television and films. Working under the assumption that adults may be capable of coping with the violence depicted in the media, much research has concerned itself primarily with the behavioral impact of violence on children in terms of immediate, short-term effects. Recent trends toward a shift in theoretical perspective are beginning to generate some investigations into the cumulative individual differences effects of violence.

Several orientations have been employed as the conceptual bases for these investigations. First, *imitation behavior* may result from the viewer's discovering new ways of approaching real-life situations. This can be unwise because the violence portrayed in the media is not real life, but fictional in many cases. A second approach is the concept of *identification*, applied to an admired character. Children are particularly susceptible to identifying with an admired character and copying his or her behavior when the occasion arises in real life. *Linkage* is a third hypothetical effect where fantasy is linked with the real world. Again, children have more difficulty in distinguishing fantasy from reality. A final theoretical approach, of obvious interest to the media, is the *catharsis hypothesis*. This notion is similar to vicarious expression in that media-oriented violence is believed to produce a natural state of catharsis such that latent aggressive impulses are satisfied by the substitute experience of viewing filmed or prerecorded violence. These four theoretical explications are the ones most often used to explain the impact of media violence on the viewer and on children in particular.[32]

There is considerable controversy within the scientific community regarding the results of behavioral research as to the impact media exposure has in triggering aggressive behavior that may lead to violence. Many findings, particularly those of Wilbur Schramm and Joseph Klapper, indicate that violence portrayed in the media is not a sufficient or crucial cause of violent behavior, whereas other researchers, namely Albert Bandura, Leonard Berkowitz, and Seymour Fesbach, suggest that under certain circumstances media violence leads to imitative aggressive behavior with other stimuli interacting with media exposure. The only consensus that was reached in this maze of contradictory findings was that media violence was generally most popular among children with deep psychological disturbances and long records of juvenile delinquency. Yet even among these groups, the evidence of violence directly traceable to television was decidedly small. Media violence came to be viewed as one very small factor among a complex pattern leading to maladjustment in children. Still, the controversy raged, and it was more or less decided by all that more investigation was needed. One such investigation is the 1972 Surgeon General's Report on Violence, which is worth a detailed examination.

[32]See, for example, S. Feshback and R. Singer, *Television and Social Learning* (Washington, D.C.: 1971); A. H. Stein and L. K. Friedrich, "Television Content and Young Children's Behavior," *Television and Social Behavior, Reports and Papers, Volume II: Television and Social Learning* (Washington, D.C.: Government Printing Office, 1971), pp. 202–317.

THE REPORT OF THE SURGEON GENERAL'S SCIENTIFIC ADVISORY COMMITTEE ON TELEVISION AND SOCIAL BEHAVIOR

The research, controversy, and concern continued into the 1970s, until in 1972 the long awaited study on violence and television initiated by Senator John Pastore's Communications Subcommittee was released by the U.S. Department of Public Health. The Surgeon General's Report on Violence, as this series of studies came to be known, produced three general findings: (1) there is a tentative and preliminary indication of a causal relationship between the viewing of violence on television and aggressive behavior, (2) an indication exists that any such causal relationship operates only for some children who are predisposed toward aggression, and (3) there is some indication that this relationship operates only in some environmental contexts.[33] Thus, the general conclusion to be drawn from this report is that individual reactions to violence, not television violence itself, largely determine the impact of media violence. This conclusion echoed much of what had been tentatively proven by earlier studies.

In response to this finding, the *New York Times* ran a headline stating: "TV Violence Held Unharmful to Youth." This and similar headlines and news bulletins only fanned the flames of debate over this topic, which had been burning for over two decades. Parents and teachers voiced the loudest complaints and charged that

[33]The Surgeon General's Scientific Advisory Committee on Television and Social Behavior, Television and Growing Up: The Impact of Televised Violence (Washington, D.C.: U.S. Government Printing Office, 1972).

violence would continue to run rampant across millions of television screens in the nation. The Surgeon General's Report was scrutinized closely, and many have criticized the research methods employed in these studies as well as apparent political considerations with respect to both selection of the researchers and subsequent conduct during the investigations.[34]

In response to this concern, the surgeon general, appearing before a Senate subcommittee, attempted to redirect popular understanding of the report. He emphasized that evidence compiled on televised violence and its relationships to undesirable social behavior was sufficiently damning to justify immediate corrective measures. No data, he explained, that deals with the variables shaping social behavior will ever be conclusive enough to satisfy all social scientists. But he added that there comes a time when the data are sufficient to justify action, and that time had come.

Probably the most significant implication to emerge from this enigma is that Congress now has more than adequate scientific justification for periodic review of what the television media are doing with regard to the violent content viewed by children. In 1973 Senator Pastore warned a group of broadcasters:

> To the extent that children's television programming is vulnerable to criticism, I assure you, ladies and gentlemen, the license renewal process will always have a climate of uncertainty about it. I hasten to add, this is not a threat on my part. It is merely a recognition that a voice more powerful than the FCC—your audience—will demand an accounting for your stewardship.[35]

Whether or not they were intended as such, these comments made over four years ago certainly sound like a threat to us. Threat or not, you be the judge of whether the mass media have heeded these words.

SUMMARY

1. The mass media are those organizationally complex systems of printed and electronic communications that make mass information readily accessible to large and distant audiences in an impersonal fashion.

2. Mass communication differs from interpersonal communication with respect to message flow, message storage, mediation by gatekeepers and opinion leaders, expanded volumes of information being transmitted, large and heterogeneous audiences, and multiple or institutional sources or originators of communication. In addition, feedback is often limited, delayed, and indirect.

3. Four traditional theories have been used to explain mass communication phenomenon: individual differences, social categories, social

[34]D. Cater and S. Strickland, *TV Violence and the Child: The Evolution and Fate of the Surgeon General's Report* (New York: Russell Sage Foundation, 1975).

[35]Quoted from remarks of Senator John Pastore at the Broadcaster's Meeting at Newport, Rhode Island, October 20, 1973.

relationships, and cultural norms. Three more contemporary theories —environmental theory, play theory, and reflective-projective theory—have emerged from these more traditional theories. All attempt to explain the antecedents and consequents of mass communication in society.

4. The various forms of mass media differ from one another with respect to speed, credibility, detail, sensory perception, and permanence. Notions of the manner in which message transmission is accomplished in the mass media has evolved through three conceptual hypotheses: the concept of society as a group of isolated individuals was the basis of the one-step flow, or hypodermic needle hypothesis; this was replaced by the two-step flow hypothesis, which regards mass communication as more indirect by virtue of the gatekeeping and opinion leader functions; finally, the multistep flow hypothesis views message transmission as a chain reaction progressively reaching different opinion leaders within different segments of the population.

5. Opinion leaders differ from followers in various ways. They tend to have influence only in their area of expertise, although some influence may transfer to related areas. Typically, the opinion leader personifies many of the group's values. Greater exposure to the media permits the opinion leader to serve as a gatekeeper, shaping and interpreting information for others. Opinion leaders tend to belong to several organizations, enjoy higher economic and social status, and be more cosmopolitan than their followers.

6. Gatekeepers are individuals within the media who make decisions about what is communicated and how. Gatekeeping may also involve timing, repetition, prominence, withholding, display, and emphasis of certain communication messages. Gatekeepers are sometimes subtly influenced by personal prejudices, the time of the day that information reaches the media facility, practices of competitors, personal convictions of the management, and editorial opinions about what the audience wants and what they need to know.

7. The major institutional functions of the mass media are to inform, interpret, provide entertainment and recreation, and earn a profit. The social functions of the mass media are cultural transmission; control of social norms such as violence, environmental pollution, sexual excesses, and political radicalism; diffusion of innovations; and agenda setting.

8. The adoption of innovations involves five stages: awareness, interest, evaluation, trial, and adoption. Impersonal, cosmopolitan, and informational sources are apparently most influential in the first two

stages, whereas interpersonal interactions are more likely to affect the later stages of adoption. Early adopters are more similar to opinion leaders in some ways: they are more widely exposed to information sources and possess higher social status than late adopters.

9. Agenda setting involves influence by the mass media in formulating the most important issues. Normally, agenda setting occurs with respect to deciding the most important political issues of the day.

10. Mass communication has some impact on cognition and comprehension, attitude and value change, and behavioral changes. In addition, the media create an impact due to the large number of young viewers. Violence and aggression are frequent media themes, and the media create certain expectations on the part of the mass audience.

11. Mass communication seems more effective in reinforcing already existing attitudes than in changing them. The selectivity process of exposure, attention, perception, and retention may explain the mass media's inability to effect major attitude change.

12. Television's image-evoking powers have made media violence a major public issue. Early research findings suggested that children react differently to different forms of violence and that observations of real violence is as harmful as observations of fictional violence. The 1972 Surgeon General's Report concluded that violence is an essential aspect of American television programming, that it has some effects on children's aggressive behavior over time, that viewers predisposed to violence will select such programming, and that individual reactions generally determine the effects of media violence.

SUGGESTED READING

Bagdikian, Ben. *The Information Machines: Their Impact on Men and the Media*. New York: Harper and Row, 1971.

Cater, Douglas, and Stephen Strickland. *TV Violence and the Child: The Evolution and Fate of the Surgeon General's Report*. New York: Russell Sage Foundation, 1975.

DeFleur, Melvin. *Theories of Mass Communication*. 2d ed. New York: David McKay Company, 1970.

Klapper, Joseph T. *The Effects of Mass Communication*. New York: The Free Press, 1960.

McLuhan, Marshall. *Understanding the Media: The Extensions of Man*. New York: McGraw-Hill, 1964.

———*The Medium Is the Message*. New York: Bantam Books, 1967.

Schramm, Wilbur. *Men, Messages, and Media: A Look at Human Communication*. New York: Harper and Row, 1973.

From the Reading

Identify the following terms.

message flow
message storage
homogeneous
heterogeneous
feedback
gatekeeper
opinion leader
horizontal influence
hot media
cool media
saliency
dissemination
diffusion
message transmission
innovations
agenda setting
cognition
catharsis

Study Questions

1. How does mass communication differ from inter-personal communication?
2. Suggest an acceptable model for viewing mass communication. How does it work? How does it differ from interpersonal models?
3. What are the four traditional theories of mass communication? How do they differ from one another?
4. Name two more contemporary mass communication theories. What elements do they contain that the older theories do not?
5. Explain McLuhan's concept of "hot" and "cool" media. Is this a useful distinction? Why?
6. List as many print media and electronic media as you can think of. What are the basic ways in which they differ from one another?
7. What are the three conceptual modes for analyzing message transmission. Which is the best?
8. What are the characteristics of opinion leaders? What are their functions?
9. What kinds of events qualify as newsworthy by the mass media?
10. What factors affect the manner in which gatekeeprs select information for dissemination?
11. How does the selectivity process affect mass communication?
12. What are the institutional functions of the mass media? Social functions?
13. How does diffusion of innovations take place? What is the adoption process? How do early adopters differ from later adopters?
14. What determines which issues are considered most salient by the mass audience? What is this process called?
15. What impact does mass communication have on cognition? Comprehension? Attitudes? Behavior?
16. What effect does media violence have on children? Give documentation for your answer.
17. How powerful are the mass media?
18. What steps would you take to improve the quality of mass communications in the United States?

EXERCISES DESIGNED TO ASSESS ATTITUDES AND BEHAVIORS TOWARD THE MASS MEDIA

1. Have each member of the class interview five people (by telephone or in person) concerning the effects which viewing violence on television *seems* to have on their family. The instructor can help in designing a suitable questionnaire. Tabulate the results for the entire class, and on the basis of this sample of approximately 200 people, discuss the impact that violence has for this sample. The class might wish to send these results to a local television station, newspaper, or the U.S. Department of Health, Education and Welfare in Washington, D.C.

2. Keep a daily log of your contacts with all forms of mass media for one week. Be sure to include the types of programs watched, types of information read, the number of hours involved with each of these, and the types of information you received from each. Itemize and compare your exposure time with each medium. Do the results surprise you?

3. Have the class divide into seven groups, and assign each group one day of the week. Have each group watch television for several hours on their assigned day and note the number of minority groups represented and analyze their roles. Have each group present their findings before the rest of the class, and discuss the role of minorities in the media.

EXERCISES DESIGNED TO INCREASE COMPETENCY IN PRODUCING MASS MEDIA MESSAGES

4. Break the class down into groups representing several of the media. Have them prepare an analysis of their potential audiences, including specific types of themes, plots and characters that would generate the largest audiences and bring the largest return on their investment through advertising.

5. Have each member of the class prepare an editorial suitable for any medium of his or her choice on a topic which he or she feels is important to society, OR have each member of the class bring in an editorial that appeared in one of the media and then suggest ways of improving this editorial.

6. Generate a list of ten commercials that are considered to be effective and a list of ten commercials that are considered relatively poor. Discuss the possible criteria that should be used to determine good from bad, effective from ineffective, and appropriate from inappropriate. Should different criteria be used for commercials when it is likely that children will be exposed to them?

EXERCISES DESIGNED TO INCREASE AWARENESS OF MASS COMMUNICATION PRINCIPLES

7. Have the class closely examine a television or motion picture film, and have them compile a list of elements that fulfill institutional and social functions. Have them do the same for a song or a record. What are the differences?

8. As mass communication studies have revealed that people are not necessarily persuaded or influenced by the media, why are vast sums spent on advertising? What justification is there for bans on cigarette and hard liquor advertising on television? Discuss with your classmates.

9. Examine the content of a daily newspaper, noting both news stories and advertisements; and identify instances where it appears that editorial or commentary has been interjected into hard news information. Examine the newspaper one more time, and speculate about where editorials or commentary might be interjected either intentionally or inadvertently. What procedures are possible for insuring that gatekeepers present only the facts?

Section 3 COMMENTS ON THE FUNCTIONS OF HUMAN COMMUNICATION

In the two previous sections of this book we have explored the nature of the communication process and the contexts in which communication occurs. In this concluding section some of the major functions of communication will be discussed. Perhaps it is best to begin with the caveat that all of the possible functions that communication serves cannot be discussed in the brief space remaining. It is important, however, to focus on a few ways that people use communication to serve several specific needs—gaining compliance, establishing social relationships, and managing conflict.

These final chapters will concentrate on the functions that occur across communication contexts. While there are surely differing strategies for persuading someone in a face-to-face interaction, small-group, public-speaking, or mediated-communication setting, there are common elements that are applicable across situations. The same can be said of communication and social relationships and of communication and conflict management. It is our hope that you will consider differing strategies for adapting the information contained in this final section to fit best the communication contexts in which you operate.

Chapter 11

PERSUASION: APPROACHES TO GAINING COMPLIANCE

It is not uncommon for a television viewer to listen to a celebrity advertise a product (aftershave or cologne, for example), to accept the celebrity's suggestion that the product will enhance one's effectiveness with the opposite sex, and subsequently to purchase the product—with little or no conscious realization of the fact that he or she has become one more statistic attesting to the power of persuasive communication. Not all successful attempts at persuasion are as easily analyzed. In this case, the viewer was probably attempting to emulate a person with status, wealth, and a publicized reputation in the field of romance; at least that is what the sponsor who paid huge sums of money to secure the endorsement assumes has happened. And not all attempts at persuasion achieve their objective with the same ease and rapidity, a frustrating fact of life for everyone from the media advertiser to the politician to the child who exasperatedly tells his or her parents, "I can't change your minds about anything!"

An unwillingness to be persuaded is not an isolated phenomenon in the communication process. Many of the same personal factors that obstruct other forms of communication similarly shape our resistance to the overt or implicit influence of others. As we mature, certain of our ideas about the nature of reality tend toward becoming absolute convictions; our affective behavior follows more or less fixed patterns; and our cognitive processes—that is, the way in which we think, analyze, and interpret—become less open to change. Thus communicators who seek to change our attitudes, emotions, and perceptual framework often must deal with rather ingrained tendencies and predispositions.

The tenacity of our past ways of thinking, feeling, and perceiving probably accounts for the fact that persuasive communication sometimes fails to be effective when most logically and directly planned and most heavily substantiated by reasons for change. A few years ago, for example, a radical activist might have made a reasonable case for the recognition of Red China. Yet many people, clinging to preconceptions about America's "enemies" and fearfully reacting to the stereotype image of the radical, would have as naturally resisted being persuaded on the basis of facts as they now have naturally accepted the present relationship between these two nations.

This example is matched by numerous other curiosities in the area of persuasive communication. Why, how, and in what ways people are persuaded to change—anything from their brand of toothpaste to their political party—is the interesting subject of several communication theories.

Defining the Persuasion Process

The various theories of persuasion radiate from some central ideas about the nature of persuasion. To understand the theories, one needs to begin with a workable definition of persuasion. A common definition says that persuasive communication is "a conscious attempt by one individual to modify the attitudes, beliefs or behaviors of another individual or group of individuals through the transmission of some message."[1] Another definition

maintains that persuasion is "the act of manipulating symbols so as to produce changes in the evaluative or approach-avoidance behavior of those who interpret the symbols."[2] That is, persuasion may simply change your opinion about pornographic bookstores, or it may change your behavior by causing you to act for or against them—for example, patronize them or picket them. Like most others, both of these definitions stress three elements in persuasion: conscious intent, message transmission, and behavioral influence.

Definitions such as these raise some problems, for they eliminate certain kinds of activity that one would tend to classify as persuasion. For example, the criterion of conscious intent eliminates a situation in which persuasion occurs without an intent to influence. A company president might unintentionally persuade junior executives to live in his or her neighborhood or join his or her country club because he or she is perceived as a success model to be emulated by them. A movie star who says he or she believes in astrology may influence millions of fans to adopt his or her position. People continually influence others inadvertently through both verbal and nonverbal communication. However, unintentional persuasion is almost impossible to study systematically. Therefore, students of persuasion are limited to the context of intentional persuasion—while acknowledging that people also exert considerable influence in unintentional and not always understandable ways.

[1] E. P. Bettinghaus, *Persuasive Communication*, 2d ed. (New York: Holt, Rinehart and Winston, Inc., 1973), p. 10.

[2] G. Cronkhite, *Persuasion: Speech and Behavioral Change* (Indianapolis: Bobbs-Merrill Company, 1969), p. 15.

In many instances, common sense provides the necessary guidelines to assess the persuasive intent of a communicator. Most people would probably agree that the company president who lives in a luxurious suburb is not necessarily exerting conscious pressure on his or her employees to do the same; in fact, such an executive might prefer to enhance his or her status by remaining the only company member who can afford to live there. On the other hand, most people would agree that a political candidate who spends millions of dollars on a campaign displays clear intent to persuade citizens to vote for him or her. In some instances, it may be difficult to discern a communicator's intent because he or she is consciously attempting to conceal it. A guest on a radio talk show may just "happen" to mention an enjoyable meal at one of a chain of taco stands—in which he or she owns a controlling interest.

A second problem raised by most definitions of persuasion centers on the nature of change necessary to so label a communicative attempt as persuasive. Has an educational television station's fund-raising effort succeeded in persuading a viewer to contribute at the point when the viewer phones in his or her pledge for fifty dollars? Would you remain convinced that persuasion had occurred if the viewer never sent in his or her fifty-dollar check? Essentially, this problem focuses on the differences between attitude and behavior. Most people assume that attitude and behavior are related; in fact, a common definition of *attitude* is "a predisposition to behave in certain ways." However, research indicates that a person's attitude and behavior are often inconsistent. The

educational television viewer may be persuaded to hold the attitude that if he or she watches public television without supporting the station financially, he or she is a parasite. But the viewer might still fail to send in a check—no matter how guilty he or she feels.

One classic study demonstrated this inconsistency between a person's attitude and behavior.[3] On the West Coast, at a time when many people held anti-Oriental attitudes, 92 percent of a group of hotel and restaurant clerks told researchers that they would not serve Chinese people. However, when a well-dressed Chinese couple arrived at the hotels and restaurants, in only one case were they refused service. Unfortunately, the attitude-behavior discrepancy also works the other way; many people express positive attitudes toward minority group members, yet behave or treat them in negative ways.

Furthermore, changed behavior does not always indicate changed attitudes. This fact is reflected in a currently popular poster that says, "Just because you have silenced a man does not mean that you have converted him." A persuader who achieves conformity without attitude change is not much of a persuader, unless he or she is merely concerned with behavior. A politician who gets votes because he or she is viewed as "the lesser of two evils" might be content with that type of victory. A persuader must decide whether he or she wants to influence behavior, attitudes, or both. In summary, persuasion can be said to be successful when the changes intended by the source of communication are realized. In any given per-

[3]R. T. LaPiere, "Attitudes vs. Actions," *Social Forces, 13* (1934), pp. 230–237.

suasion instance, there are several changes that might occur, and any one of these changes might be satisfactory to the person attempting to bring about change. It is only when we know something of the communicator's intent that we make judgments about the relative efficacy of persuasive communication.

In determining the kind of persuasion that has occurred, the communicator can only infer attitude change from behavior. We only know other people's attitudes by what they do and what they say. However, making these inferences is easier if one understands the variety of forms that change can take. Persuasive communication can lead to changes in opinions, beliefs, or values; and these changes in turn lead to changes in perception, affect, cognition, or overt action.

Opinions are verbalized evaluations of people, things, or ideas. An opinion may be favorable, neutral, or unfavorable. If you read a drama review that persuaded you to say, "I think it is impossible for American actors to perform Shakespeare well," you would have undergone an opinion change.

A *belief* is a conviction about truth or falsity. If you believe that the earth is flat and then shown pictures of the earth taken by the astronauts and if these photographs change your mind, you have undergone a change in belief. Unlike an opinion, a belief is not evaluative. For example, "Many people smoke marijuana" is a belief; "Marijuana smoking is good" is an opinion.

A *value* is similar to an opinion, but is more deeply held and more resistant to change. Values exert an enduring influence on a person's thinking and behavior. A good example of the difference between a value and an opinion was provided by a recent Supreme Court decision, which held that a man could qualify as a conscientious objector if he could demonstrate that he held value-based objections to war. In this decision the court was recognizing that values other than religious ones might exempt a man from the draft. However, the justices made it quite clear that a mere opinion against a specific war was not a basis for deferment. In short, an opinion that the war in Vietnam was immoral was legally differentiated from deeper religious, philosophical, or ethical values.

These three internal states—the holding of opinions, beliefs, and values—are the first targets of persuasive communication. Changes in these states can lead to changes in perception. For example, a change in belief may lead to a change in perception. A student who becomes convinced that a professor is discriminating against him is likely to perceive everything that happens in the classroom from this point of view. Changes in beliefs, opinions, and values can also lead to affective, or emotional, change. By appealing to emotions, persuasion can alter a person's mood, self-concept, and state of mind. Many messages try to produce affective change by inducing guilt and fear. For instance, a person who goes through a profound change in religious values may become fearful of "fire and brimstone." Sometimes affective change is the only goal of a persuader. For instance, a man may try to persuade a woman to love him. At other times, affective change is sought so that further change will result; a man may attempt to persuade a woman to love him so that she will marry him.

Cognitive change influences a person's

rational thought processes. People change their behavior partly by considering alternatives and revising their ideas to adapt to new information. A parent who wishes his or her child to give up smoking might begin by presenting factual evidence supporting the health risks associated with smoking. Cognitive change may also be desirable for its own sake. For example, a history teacher is (he or she hopes) helping the students achieve cognitive change as they move through the course. Changes in beliefs, opinions, or values can aid cognitive change, as in the case of a student who has to be convinced that a black studies course is valuable before he or she enrolls in it.

Overt action is observable behavior. Although overt action can be influenced by changes in a person's beliefs, opinions, or values, this is not always the case. For example, a person can use coercion to induce overt behavior that is unrelated to the beliefs, opinions, or values of another person. A teacher may induce students to study by threatening them with a failing grade, but the teacher may not necessarily change the students' opinion about the value of the subject matter. Of course, attitude changes are not always reflected in overt behavior. A man may be convinced that the Republican candidate would make the best governor for his or her state, but still not go to the polls on Election Day. If a person changes both his or her internal state (beliefs, opinion, or values) and his or her behavior, then optimally effective persuasion has taken place. The most enduring change of this sort occurs when a person alters his or her behavior to conform with new values. A woman who becomes convinced that feminism gives her a way to understand per-

vasive political and personal grievances and who changes her way of life and her relationships with men and other women to reflect her new values will be relatively resistant to persuasive attempts that argue counter to those values.

Fig. 11.1 summarizes the effects of persuasive communication. The persuader must decide what he or she wants to change, how to construct his or her appeal, and whether or not he or she has achieved the desired change. To a great extent, the persuader's goals determine the kind of change he or she needs to seek. One situation may warrant an attempt to change behavior; another situation may call for attitude change.

Approaches to Persuasion

There are many different approaches to understanding how one goes about changing people's opinions, beliefs, values, and/or behaviors. There are different models of persuasion that can make very different assumptions about some of the underlying psychological mechanisms that tend to make certain persuasive strategies effective while rendering other communication intended to persuade fail. These models make different assumptions about the nature of people, about how information is processed, and about how differing communication strategies ought to operate.

These different models of persuasion can be grouped for ease of understanding into three broad categories: learning theories, consistency theories, and social judgment theory. Learning theories of persuasion have been most concerned with how differing reward contingencies can be

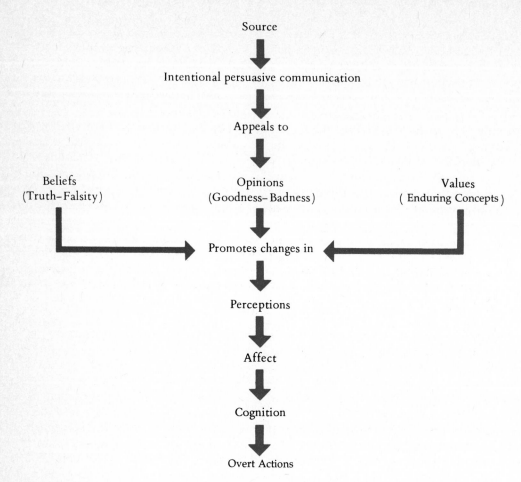

Source

↓

Intentional persuasive communication

↓

Appeals to

↓

Beliefs   Opinions   Values
(Truth–Falsity)   (Goodness–Badness)   (Enduring Concepts)

→   Promotes changes in   ←

↓

Perceptions

↓

Affect

↓

Cognition

↓

Overt Actions

Fig. 11.1 Model of persuasion.

used to shape desired behaviors. The concern of people interested in developing communication strategies from this perspective has been in creating messages that are most likely to create appropriate behavioral responses. There are a group of models of persuasion that have been labeled consistency theories. These models have in common the assumption that people change attitudes in response to a perceived inconsistency between beliefs, attitudes, and behaviors or a number of other things. When people do experience this inconsistency, there is a drive to restore consistency by changing present attitudes, beliefs, values, and/or overt behaviors. People operating from this perspective have devised communication strategies designed to make inconsistencies apparent to people in the hopes that desired changes will result from the desire to restore consistency. Social judgment theory represents a departure from the first two general classifications of persuasion. It suggests that people make judgments about any persuasive communication on the basis of how much it deviates from their present position. Too much deviation from present beliefs can result in immediate rejection of the message.

It is hoped that the reader will examine these different conceptions of persuasion in order to understand how different assumptions about the nature of people and how they process communication can lead to very different communication strategies. As will become obvious to all, these models of persuasion sometimes suggest contradictory ways of attempting to persuade people. However, there are many areas of agreement among the differing perspectives. None of these models is *right*, and none of them is totally *wrong*. All have potential use in structuring persuasive communication, and it is hoped that the reader will try to make an application of these models to differing persuasive situations to determine which, if any, might be a useful way of understanding why people change. It is highly likely that some models will be appropriate in some persuasion instances and not in others.

Learning Theories

An infant is born without any opinions, beliefs, or values. Through the socialization process, he or she learns to respond to the environment, to behave acceptably and yet in his or her own self-interest, to accept certain ideas as true or false, good, or bad. In fact, learning can be defined as the process of acquiring or changing behavior in response to individual encounters with people, events, and things.

Yet much that is said about persuasion —and about communication in general— implies that the person being persuaded already holds an opinion, belief, or value and that the communicator is simply trying to induce a switch—from Jones to Smith, from pro to anti, from Ultra-Brite to Gleem. However, in many cases the person being persuaded doesn't care any more about Jones, pro, or Ultra-Brite than he or she does about Smith, anti, or Gleem. In other words, he or she may have no feelings at all on the matter. The Esso Company spent an enormous sum of money on an advertising campaign to familiarize people with its new corporate name, Exxon. The goal was clearly factual learning rather than attitude change. In such cases, the persuader needs to be aware of general principles of learning, so that messages can be structured to be most effective.

Theories of learning center on the relationship between stimuli and responses.[4] A stimulus, in this context, is anything that occurs in the communication transaction and is perceived by the receiver; a response is what the receiver does as a result of the stimulus. For example, a speech advocating a high tariff on foreign-made televisions might be a stimulus; an attitude change in the direction of the advocated position or a vote for a bill establishing such a tariff might be the response. A speaker's choice of words and delivery

[4]See the following for further study of theories of learning: W. F. Hill, *Learning: A Survey of Psychological Interpretation* (Scranton, Pa.: Chandler Publishing Company, 1971); M. D. Smith, *Theoretical Foundations of Learning and Teaching* (Waltham, Mass.: Xerox College Publishing, 1971).

may function as stimuli. If the receiver perceives them as offensive, the response might be dislike for the speaker and resistance to his message. A pleasant spring day, the speaker's bow tie, the grinding of a garbage truck, the receiver's own emotional state, and other nonverbal or psychological factors may serve as stimuli that elicit responses.

The stimulus-response relationship can be manipulated in order to enhance learning. For instance, most learning theories assume that reinforcement is necessary to induce learning. There are two kinds of reinforcement: positive and negative. Suppose a man came to your door and asked you to allow your name to be listed in an advertisement supporting a political candidate. If the man told you that you would be listed as a "prominent" citizen along with the mayor, several movie stars, and other celebrities; that your participation would make you a patriotic person; and that you would be paid five dollars for allowing your name to be used, he would be offering you positive reinforcement or rewards. If he told you that anyone who does not allow his or her name to be used will be considered unpatriotic and furthermore might find himself or herself under investigation by the Internal Revenue Service, he would be offering negative reinforcement; that is, he would be offering you an opportunity to escape from an undesirable situation. Negative reinforcement is not the same as punishment. Negative reinforcement leaves open the door to the desired behavior; punishment takes place only after the receiver has behaved in an undesired way. If you rejected the offer to be listed in the ad and the next day found that you had been fired from your job because FBI agents had made some unsavory suggestions to your boss, that would be punishment.

Advertisers often use positive reinforcement to link products (stimuli) to increased sexuality, likability, and other supposedly desirable states in order to increase sales (desired response). They also use negative reinforcement—for example, by linking a mouthwash to escape from the supposedly undesirable state of having "bad breath." Both positive and negative reinforcers are likely to have impact on the receiver's behavior. If the communicator can demonstrate to a person the way he or she will be rewarded or will escape an undesirable state by complying with the communicator's request, behavior will probably change. However, punishment does not usually work so well. People who do not escape the undesirable state and are punished tend to withdraw from the situation. In other words, the use of punishment might be very effective in insuring that an unwanted behavior ceased; however, using punishment alone does not necessarily produce other behaviors that might be desirable.

Most learning theories also assume that the time between response and reinforcement affects the speed of learning. If you know that by signing the political advertisement you will be paid five dollars in cash on the spot, you might be more willing to sign than if you learned you would get a five-dollar tax rebate the following year. Negative reinforcement is also more effective if escape from the undesired state will be immediate. For instance, telling a young person that he or she will live to be seventy instead of sixty-eight if he or she stops smoking is not likely to be as effective as telling the person that smokers are automatically disqualified from an athletic group he or she wishes to join.

Furthermore, specific reinforcements tied to specific desired responses are more effective than vague ones. A speaker who tells you that your life will be better if you support the police is likely to be less persuasive than one who says you will not be mugged if you sign a petition to add 5,000 more policemen to the force. Therefore, learning theory suggests that a persuader design his message to state the exact behavior desired and the exact reinforcement that will result.

Because people differ in their abilities and readiness to learn, repetition can induce learning. A persuader cannot be sure that everyone has understood his or her message; repetition helps him or her reach as many receivers as possible and helps solidify the learning of those who understood the first time. Probably everyone is familiar with the kind of organization foul-up in which a manager claims to have told all his or her subordinates what was expected of them but somehow did not get through. The importance of repetition is consistent with the idea that persuasion is most successful when it is part of a campaign; that is, one-shot attempts at persuasion often do not work; follow-up communication is needed. Repetition is especially important if the receivers are people with differing backgrounds, information, and abilities. However, even people with similar capacities to handle communication differ in their willingness to respond at a given time. Within a group of receivers, some may be distracted by personal problems, noise, other messages they have recently received, and any num-

ber of additional physical and psychological factors. Repetition can help to overcome these barriers to receptivity. It can also help the persuader overcome such obstacles as selective attention, distortion, and forgetfulness. Anyone who uses repetition to persuade must be careful not to hammer away with a message that is never going to be accepted. The speaker who assumes that anyone who does not agree with him or her has simply not understood him or her is a familiar irritant. "You don't seem to get my point" can only alienate someone who has already gotten the point and rejected it.

Learning theory also indicates that simple elements are more easily learned than complex ones. For instance, in early advertisements, aspirin was advertised as a way to relieve headaches. Each company claimed that its brand did the best job. As the campaigns progressed, each company presented more complex information about its product. Language teaching proceeds in a similar way. A beginning student first learns some basic words, then strings them together into simple sentences, and finally moves on to writing paragraphs or holding conversations. Mastering simple elements strengthens the receiver's willingness to respond to more difficult material.

One of the basic assumptions of the learning model is that persuasive messages should be structured to begin on a simple level; once the receiver understands and is rewarded for complying, responses can then be made to more complex messages. Persuasion should begin on a simple level; once the receiver understands and is rewarded, he or she can respond to more complex messages.

Another assumption of most learning theories is that people generalize their responses from one situation to another. The "coattails" of a victorious political candidate, for instance, may sweep into office some more obscure members of his or her party. Institutional advertising, which popularizes the name of a company that makes many products, is also aimed at the generalization response: "If you like our company's green beans, you'll love our ketchup." It is fortunate that generalization occurs as often as it does, because it is economical. Without generalization, a persuader might have to repeat his or her message in every situation. However, learning in one situation does not always transfer to others. People may love a company's green beans but take a dislike to the shape of its ketchup bottle, and, in that case, two separate communication efforts will have to be made. One cannot assume that generalization will always occur.

Learning theory emphasizes the importance of feedback. Positive feedback can work as a form of reinforcement, rewarding the receiver and helping to insure that he or she will continue to respond in the desired way. For example, a press agent whose job is to persuade writers and reporters to do stories about his or client— say, the blue-jeans industry—may reward the authors of favorable stories with praise for their fine abilities or with "freebees"—a new pair of jeans or tickets to a rock concert. Similarly, negative feedback can facilitate learning if it is perceived as constructive. The press agent might suggest that a writer whose story on the apparel industry failed to mention blue jeans now has an excellent opportunity to sell a follow-up story that does talk about jeans. However, if negative feedback is merely critical or does not give specific suggestions for improvement, it can be perceived as punishment and have undesirable results.

Learning theory does not offer the only explanation for human change. In fact, much learning theory has been criticized for its stimulus-response model, which critics believe is a simplistic view of the nature of man. A good deal of such criticism has been focused on radical behaviorists, such as B. F. Skinner, who maintains that "attitudes" are only conditioned behavior, that a man is the sum of his conditioning—no more. According to this school of behaviorism, all social problems could be solved if people were conditioned in desirable ways. In addition to raising questions about who would control the conditioning process, this theory also raises questions about the nature of the humans species. Other theories about human change assume that people make decisions and engage in behavior that does not depend on the stimulus-response relationship. These theories deny that people merely respond to stimuli in their environment; in fact, some theories suggest that people do not always respond in the way that would bring them the best reward.

Consistency Theories

Although some learning theorists prefer to ignore variables within the receiver's mind that might interfere with the stimulus-response relationship, other persuasion theorists have focused on the mind as a "middleman" between the stimulus and the response. For example, cognitive theory sees the mind as a complex mechanism that organizes past learning and present stimuli into meaningful units. Thus, the mind is not simply being bombarded with unrelated stimuli; it is always organizing information into a pattern.

A mind operating in this fashion evaluates persuasive communication in terms of the way it fits into an organizational pattern. If the new communication fits into the pattern, the receiver's internal state remains balanced. For instance, if a man recently lost several thousand dollars because of shady and irresponsible dealings by his stockbroker and if he then hears a speech proposing stricter regulation of brokerage firms, he can fit the speaker's proposals into the pattern of his experience and feel comfortable with the conclusions. He does not need to be persuaded; his attitudes are probably already consistent with the positions being advocated by the message; that is, there is internal consistency. If the message does not conform to prior attitudes and/or presents a position opposing, or unfamiliar to, the receiver, internal inconsistency is likely to occur. For instance, if a stockbroker or an investor who had been successful in the market heard the same speech advocating stricter control, he or she might have great difficulty in resolving the speaker's proposals with prior beliefs and experiences regardless of how logical the communicator was. Strategies must be employed to persuade the receiver; one such strategy would be to maximize internal inconsistency.

Given that internal inconsistency makes people uncomfortable, it is presumed that when a person disagrees with another that is liked or respected; when one is asked to behave at odds with privately held opinions, beliefs, and values; or when attitudes are held that are incompatible, cognitive inconsistency occurs and change results. In our example, if the stockbroker respected the speaker, it might cause a great deal of inconsistency to disagree with the position being advocated. Another communication strategy might attempt to point out to the broker that the attitude of wanting to make money for clients and yet protect them from unscrupulous hucksters is incompatible unless he or she changes his or her attitudes toward stricter market controls.

Balance theories assume that people are comfort-seeking animals who will strive to reduce internal inconsistency and that they are rationalizing beings who will find ways to justify changing attitudes and/or behaviors. The goal of the communication strategist is to point out inconsistencies while simultaneously providing ways of reducing inconsistencies by accepting new positions or exhibiting alternative behaviors that are, of course, more desirable to the persuader.

The earliest balance theories dealt with relationships between two persons and some object or idea.[5] The relationships, or linkages, can be either favorable or unfavorable. When they cause internal inconsistency, one or more of the linkages can be changed to restore the balance. Fig. 11.2 shows the basic patterns of linkage in balance theory.

[5]One of the earliest attempts to elaborate on consistency notions was F. Heider, "Attitudes and Cognitive Organization," *Journal of Psychology, 21* (1946), pp. 107–112.

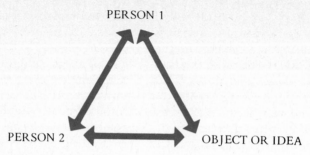

Fig. 11.2   Balance theory/linkage patterns.

Linkages between the people are favorable or unfavorable, depending upon credibility, attraction, interpersonal experience, or power relationships. Linkages between each person and the object or idea—that is, the topic of communication —can also be favorable or unfavorable, depending on each person's opinions, beliefs, and values. When the combinations of favorable-unfavorable linkages that appear in Fig. 11.3 occur, a state of balance exists and no persuasion takes place.

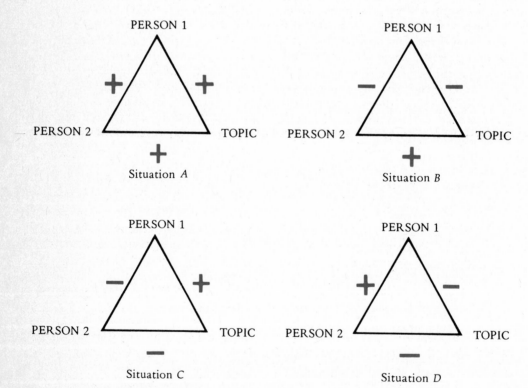

Fig. 11.3   Balance theory/balanced situations.

COMMENTS ON THE FUNCTIONS OF HUMAN COMMUNICATION

In Situation A of Fig. 11.3, Person 1 likes Person 2, is favorable toward the topic of communication, and knows that Person 2 agrees. For example, the cheated stockholder likes and agrees with the speaker advocating stricter control of brokerages. This combination of variables creates a state of balance, and persuasion is not needed. In Situation B, Person 1 is unfavorable toward both Person 2 and the topic and also knows that Person 2 disagrees. In this case, to pursue the stock market example, Person 1 might be a broker who has grown rich by questionable methods and who also dislikes the reformer's personality and politics. He or she would remain unpersuaded by Person 2, perhaps rationalizing that only a self-righteous and politically biased man would favor reforms. Again, balance remains secure. Similarly, balance is maintained in Situation C, in which Person 2 is disliked and takes an opposing position on the topic, and in situation D, in which both parties like each other and oppose the topic.

In all the balance models shown in Fig. 11.3, persuasion is not likely to occur because there is no internal inconsistency for either party—and internal inconsistency is the motive for change. Without such imbalance, the two people remain comfortable with the linkages between themselves and the issue and will seek to maintain that comfort. However, in the situations illustrated in Fig. 11.4, the link-

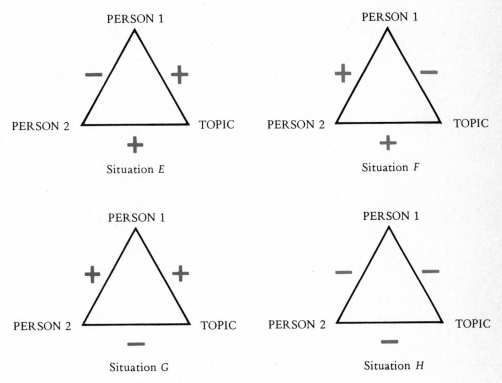

Fig. 11.4 Balance theory/unbalanced situations.

ages are unbalanced and some type of change must occur.

In Situation E of Fig. 11.4, Person 1, the cheated stockholder, dislikes the reformer but agrees with him or her on the need for reform. The stockholder will probably change his or her opinion of the speaker, because people tend to like others who agree with them. However, if the feelings of dislike are very strong, the stockholder might change his or her attitude toward the topic, deciding that someone he or she dislikes so intensely must be wrong and that the shady firm he or she bought his stocks from must have been an exception to widespread integrity in the financial world. Yet another alternative would be for the stockholder to change his perception of the reformer's position. He or she might decide that the reformer proposes only superficial changes that will not really work. Whatever the actual shift in the stockholder's position, the situation illustrated in Situation E must cause some alteration in his attitudes, because it is too uncomfortable for him or her to remain as he or she is. Situations F and G are similar in that we feel uncomfortable when someone we like favors something we oppose or opposes something we favor.

In situation H it is difficult to predict the change that will occur. We do not feel comfortable when people we dislike oppose what we oppose. We want to agree with our friends and disagree with our enemies. The receiver of persuasive communication in this situation might reevaluate the source and use the agreement as a basis of increased liking, or he (or she) might change his (or her) own opinion to disagree with the disliked source, or he (or she) might change his (or her) percep-

tion of the source by denying the honesty of the communication. For instance, if a leading conservative suddenly made a speech favoring the former Allende government in Chile, a socialist listener might decide to like the conservative, decide he himself must have been wrong about Allende's government, or decide that the conservative has some devious reason for making this statement.

There is a handy rule of thumb for determining whether or not a communication situation is balanced or unbalanced. Anytime there is an odd number of negative signs on the triangle, the linkages are unbalanced, and change must occur. When there is an even number of negative signs (or no negative signs), the linkages are balanced and change does not occur.

Several principles allow one to predict the kind of change that will occur in an unbalanced situation.[6] If there is a contradiction between a receiver's feelings toward the source of the communication and the content of the communication, the attitude toward the content is more likely to change. In other words, it is more difficult to change one's view about a person than about an idea. This fact helps explain why a highly credible source is often so successful at persuasion; people prefer to alter their opinions on the subject rather than to alter their opinions of the man's credibility. In preferring to change that way, people are altering negative linkages rather than positive ones. ("I like the man; so I'll change my dislike of his views.")

[6] W. J. McGuire, "The Current Status of Cognitive Consistency Theories," in *Cognitive Consistency: Motivational Antecedents and Behavioral Consequents*, ed. S. Feldman (New York: Academic Press, 1966), pp. 1–46.

However, if the receiver feels very negatively toward the issue, he or she will resist changing his or her attitude toward it; more likely, he or she will change his or her attitude toward the source. Thus, highly involving issues about which people are polarized are less likely to follow the negative sign-changing tendency.

Symmetry theory elaborates on the balance model and shows the way communication affects internal consistency.[7] According to symmetry theory, communication leads to more interpersonal similarity; that is, if you like another person, you desire to be similar to him or her and will, therefore, try to resolve disagreements. When you and someone you like disagree, you feel internal inconsistency and a pull toward symmetry. The strength of the pull depends on how much you like the person and how intensely you feel about the issue. The more these two factors conflict, the more pull you feel to resolve the conflict. This pull increases the likelihood that you and the other person will communicate about the issue. And as research shows, communication leads to increased similarity in views. Perhaps you and a close friend, for instance, will find ways to compromise on an issue or perhaps one of you will change his or her view after learning about the other's arguments and feelings. Symmetry theory differs from balance theory in that it suggests not only that change will occur, but also gives reasons why people end up shifting beliefs and changing behaviors. The central reason for the change is based on what we know about people's tendency to use communication as a vehicle to maintain similarity with valued others.

Congruity theory is a refinement of balance and symmetry theories.[8] It predicts mathematically both the amount and the direction of change that will occur in an unbalanced communication situation. One of the failings of balance theory is that it allows for only one change in a situation. For instance, in Situation E of Fig. 11.4, if Person 1 changes his or her opinion of Person 2, balance is restored. Congruity theory allows for more subtle changes. For example, suppose Fig. 11.5 reflects your attitudes toward the source of a communication (a respected friend) and toward his or her position (favoring amnesty for draft resisters).

Your respected friend is rated very favorably on the scale (+3), and you moderately oppose (−2) his or her statement that draft resisters should receive amnesty. According to congruity theory, you would probably change this unbalanced situation in two ways. First, you would become more favorable toward amnesty, because someone you respect is in favor of it. At the same time, you will become less favorable toward the friend, because he or she spoke for an issue you opposed. However, you will not change in an equal amount toward both source and issue; you will change most whichever attitude is least strongly held. Assuming that your attitude toward amnesty changed more than your attitude toward your friend, balance

[7]See T. M. Newcomb "An Approach to the Study of Communicative Acts," *Psychological Review, 60* (1953), pp. 393–404; "The Predictions of Interpersonal Attraction," *American Psychologist, 11* (1956), pp. 575–586.

[8]For a complete explanation of this research, see C. E. Osgood and P. H. Tannenbaum, "The Principle of Congruity in the Prediction of Attitude Change," *Psychological Review, 62* (1955), pp. 42–55.

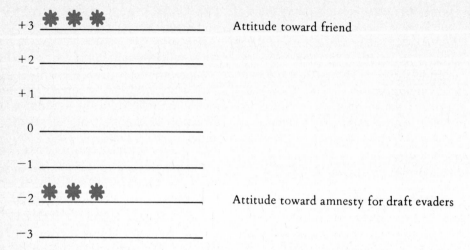

+3   Attitude toward friend

+2

+1

0

−1

−2   Attitude toward amnesty for draft evaders

−3

Fig. 11.5 Congruity theory/attitude scale.

(with both attitudes occupying the same line on the scale) would be achieved in the way shown in Fig. 11.6.

Congruity theory claims that attitudes toward both the source and the content of a message change as a result of communication. Through relatively complex mathematical formulas, congruity theory can predict the magnitude and the direction of attitude change after communication. Congruity theory is considered to be a more sophisticated representation of the process of persuasive communication in that it recognizes more of the complexities involved in bringing about desired changes. It is very useful, for it allows

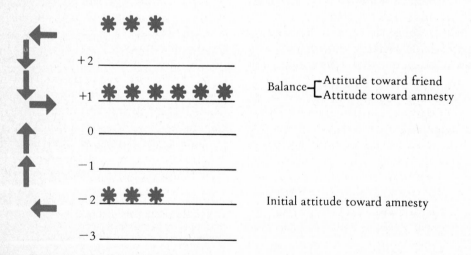

+2

+1   Balance ⎯ Attitude toward friend / Attitude toward amnesty

0

−1

−2   Initial attitude toward amnesty

−3

Fig. 11.6 Congruity theory/attitude scale.

Congruity theory claims that attitudes toward both the source and the content of a message change as a result of communication. (Photograph: American Friends Service Committee)

rather precise predictions about attitudes following persuasive communication. Perhaps a more important aspect of this model, for our purposes, is its recognition that multiple changes are likely to occur when people attempt to persuade others. It should be of interest that this model suggests that credibility will be reduced in some proportion when positions that people find unacceptable are advocated. It further posits that even though you might obtain the desired goal of persuading someone, that person will, in effect, see you differently. Furthermore, over time people can communicate in ways to restore lost esteem or credibility. This model poses an interesting question for you to consider. How important is it for you to persuade someone if it is, in fact, going to change his or her perception of you? Obviously, this varies from situation to situation, and at times it is certainly important enough for us to take certain personal risks in order to convince people of the validity of our positions. However, at other times it might not be worth either the risk or the effort it would take to restore our credibility and esteem to prior levels. At any rate, this kind of question should be considered by the potential persuader.

Another consistency theory of persuasion that deserves special attention because of the unique perspective it takes on communication and persuasion is cognitive dissonance. Like the other models discussed, the *theory of cognitive dissonance* assumes that people feel uncomfortable when they hold opinions or ideas that are psychologically inconsistent; it is further assumed that when people experience this discomfort called *cognitive dissonance*, they will be motivated to change attitudes or behaviors to reduce that inconsistency.[9] These two assumptions are not radically different from the earlier models we have discussed. However, the theory of cognitive dissonance does depart from the earlier models in that it places particular attention on the kinds of behaviors that people engage in to justify and rationalize their changes in attitudes and behaviors *after they have been persuaded to accept a new opinion or commit a behavior*. Remember that the earlier models put a great deal of emphasis on making inconsistencies apparent and then providing means to reduce those conflicts. This theory places emphasis on how people will support their new positions via a variety of communication techniques.

It is assumed that anytime people make a decision to change their attitudes or to commit some type of behavior, they will experience some amount of cognitive dissonance. For example, a person who is faced with a decision about the kind of automobile to purchase is faced with some conflict in making a choice. However, once the decision is made and a car purchased, dissonance is aroused. The person probably is somewhat unsure of whether

It is assumed that any time people make a decision to change their attitudes or to commit some type of behavior, they will experience some amount of cognitive dissonance. This is often readily apparent in making a purchase touted by a salesperson. (Photograph: Maury Englander)

he or she really made the right decision and is aware that there are positive and negative aspects about both the car purchased and the car decided against. This feeling is presumed to be dissonant, and a variety of things can be done to solve the problem. It has been found that people who purchase new automobiles tend to be more attentive to advertisements and information relating to the brand they bought. It is presumed that these people

9The original report of this theory is to be found in L. Festinger, *A Theory of Cognitive Dissonance* (Stanford, Calif.: Stanford University Press, 1957).

actively seek out information that supports their position. There is less evidence to suggest that they will seek out negative information or avoid hearing good things about the other makes of the car, but there is no doubt about their desire for supportive information about the decision they have made.

One of the most important things about this theory is the unique and interesting research that has been done to test some of its assumptions. It is also important, for it explains some human behavior that is not intuitively obvious to many of us. Perhaps reviewing some of the research is an enlightening way to demonstrate how people rationalize their behavior when it conflicts with previously held attitudes and how they move to support new attitudes that they have adopted. For example, if you were told that people had agreed to an unplesant task such as eating fried grasshoppers, it could probably be agreed that some persuasion had occurred. People were persuaded to commit a behavior at odds with their private opinions. However, what if the ultimate purpose was to persuade people to be more positive about fried grasshoppers? Would you expect people who had been persuaded to eat the grasshoppers by a high credible and well-liked source also to change their attitudes more favorably toward grasshoppers than people who had initially agreed, at the urging of a low credible or disliked source, to consume the disliked food? Most people would agree that the greatest attitude change *toward the grasshoppers* would be after agreeing to eat them when asked by the high credible source. However, research indicates that just the opposite occurs,

and dissonance theory has a very plausible explanation for these findings.[10]

Although it might be more difficult for a low credible source initially to persuade people to try the grasshoppers, once such a behavioral commitment was secured, people should experience a great deal of cognitive dissonance resulting from the discrepancy between their private opinions and their overt behaviors. They cannot reduce this dissonance by justifying the behavior on the basis of doing it because of their liking for the source because they don't like that person. The simplest way to reduce the dissonance is by changing their attitudes toward grasshoppers. They can say something like this: "They really aren't so bad after all." However, the people who initially were persuaded by a highly credible individual to try the grasshoppers were not under the same pressures to change their attitudes toward the disliked object. Although cognitive dissonance still occurs because of the inconsistency between attitudes and behaviors, there are ways that the dissonance can be reduced that do not require changing of attitudes toward the grasshoppers. The most likely outcome is for the reciever to justify the behavior by claiming that the grasshoppers were tried out of regard for the source and that anybody would do the same if asked. The receiver can comfortably continue to dislike grasshoppers given that justification.

Another example might help make the point about how people operate to reduce dissonance and support what they have

[10]P. Zimbardo, M. Weisenberg, and I. Firestone, "Changing Appetites for Eating Fried Grasshopper," in *The Cognitive Control of Motivation*, ed. P. Zimbardo (Chicago: Scott, Foresman, 1969), pp. 44–54.

been persuaded to do. Let us stress again that we are only discussing how people seek to support what they *have already been persuaded to do*. Suppose that someone persuaded you not to engage in an activity that you enjoyed. Let us further suppose that this persuasion was accompanied with a mild threat outlining the harms that would befall you if you went ahead and did the enjoyable task. Would you be likely to change your attitude toward the task itself more if the threat were mild than if the threat was severe and you were advised of the extremely harmful results of the behavior? The attitude toward the enjoyable task itself would be more likely to change if you refrained from doing it if you had been given a mild threat.[11] Most of us would probably not agree with this without further explanation; dissonance theory offers that explanation. If the consequences of doing the task were not all that bad, there would be less likelihood of justifying the behavior by pointing out that you refrained only to avoid punishment. You would have to rationalize not doing it by some other method; the easiest way to avoid the feeling of dissonance would be to claim that "you really did not like the task that much anyway and that you could either take it or leave it." People who are given threats promising extreme punishments for continuing to do the task can simply reduce the dissonance caused by discrepancies between attitudes (enjoyment in doing the task) and behavior (not doing the activity) by claiming that, under the condi-

tions, any reasonable person would not engage in the desired task. In the first case, actual attitudes toward the task have become negative, and the behavior has been extinguished. In the second instance, the behavior is extinguished, but the liking for the task has not necessarily changed. One can readily see how educational institutions and organizations of all kinds use punishment as a means of controlling behavior. Perhaps this theory further elaborates the earlier cited notions that behavior control does not always equal persuasion in the sense of changed opinions, beliefs, and values.

Any decision can potentially cause dissonance. Simply deciding on one course of action can cause you to have more favorable attitudes about the chosen alternative and more negative reactions toward what you chose not to do. Holding negative thoughts about chosen alternatives and positive thoughts about what you chose not to do is uncomfortable. One likely mode of resolution is to become even more positive about what you are doing and dismiss the negative while building up in your own mind even more reactions to that which you gave up. This is but a sampling of the research in this area. It is hoped that the use of this model of persuasion in explaining human conduct is apparent.

Dissonance can also be aroused by holding two conflicting attitudes or opinions, and the potential persuader must keep this in mind when attempting to apply this knowledge. There is a possibility that whenever you convince someone to accept your position on a given issue, it may place the person in a conflicting position because the new attitude is at odds

---

[11] E. Aronson and J. Carlsmith, "The Effect of the Severity of the Threat on the Devaluation of Forbidden Behavior," *Journal of Abnormal and Social Psychology, 66* (1963), pp. 584–588.

Latitude of Acceptance	Latitude of Noncommitment	Latitude of Rejection
1. Unconditional amnesty. 2. Amnesty when all POWs return home. 3. Amnesty if draft evaders work in some national effort for two years.	4. Amnesty if draft evaders fulfill their military commitment.	5. Make draft evaders publicly apologize. 6. Bar draft evaders from forever returning. 7. Make draft evaders serve jail sentences.

Fig. 11.7 Social judgment theory/acceptance-rejection continuum.

with positions already held. If you are aware that there will be attempts to reduce that dissonance, persuasive measures can be taken to insure that the mode of reduction will not be reversing the other person and returning to the old position after you thought you had convinced him or her. To the extent that the persuader continues to provide supportive information and views the persuasion effort as having to continue even after the initial attempt and/or commitment, success is more likely. The persuader must also constantly keep in mind that there is a difference between behavioral compliance and true commitment to a position. To the extent that people are coerced into behaving a certain way and given no choice in the matter, there is little likelihood of internal acceptance of the behavior or changes in attitudes. When the person feels responsible for his or her own actions and can provide reasons for his or her own acceptance of attitudes and behaviors, longer lasting change is likely to occur. More will be said in the next chapter about how one goes about structuring persuasive messages with these considerations in mind. The important addition that this model makes

to the family of consistency theories is its emphasis on all of the things people go through after they have been persuaded. The other models are primarily concerned with accomplishing the initial persuasion and have little to say about what happens after people accept your position or agree to do the things you ask of them.

Social Judgment Theory

Social judgment theory differs from learning theory and consistency theories in several ways.[12] First, it views attitude change as a two-stage process. In the first stage, the receiver judges the relationship of a communication to his or her own attitude. For instance, if Susan X believes that amnesty for draft resisters is a good idea and if she hears someone argue that it is tantamount to condoning treason, she will judge the communication to be widely discrepant from her view. In the second stage of attitude change, Susan X makes changes in her opinions, beliefs, or val-

[12]See C. W. Sherif, M. Sherif, and R. E. Nebergall, *Attitude and Attitude Change: The Social Judgment-Involvement Approach* (Philadelphia: W. B. Saunders, 1965).

ues. How much change she makes will depend on how much discrepancy she feels between her view and the source's view.

Social judgment theory treats attitudes as more complex than favorable-unfavorable or positive-negative reactions. It claims that attitudes are best represented by a continuum as shown in Fig. 11.7.

The receiver has his or her own position on an issue; this is called his or her *prime attitude*. In the preceding example, the receiver believes that unconditional amnesty should be granted. In addition to his or her prime attitude, he or she has a *latitude of acceptance*—a range of positions that he or she is willing to accept (1, 2, and 3). The *latitude of noncommitment* is a range of positions on which the receiver is neutral or has divided feelings (4). Finally, the range of positions that the receiver finds unacceptable (5, 6, and 7) forms the *latitude of rejection*.

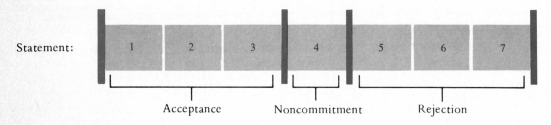

Fig. 11.8 Acceptance-rejection continuum.

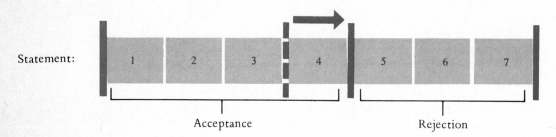

Fig. 11.9 Acceptance-rejection continuum.

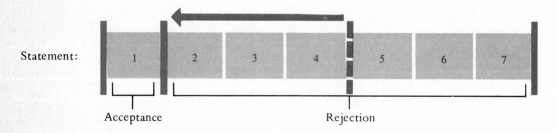

Fig. 11.10 Acceptance-rejection continuum.

COMMENTS ON THE FUNCTIONS OF HUMAN COMMUNICATION

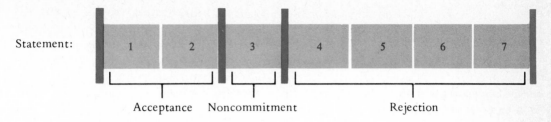

Statement:

Fig. 11.11 High ego-involved receiver.

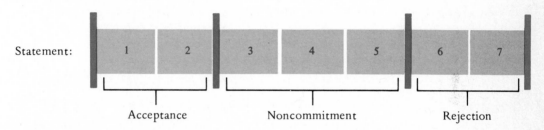

Statement:

Fig. 11.12 Low ego-involved receiver.

The receiver's attitude continuum for this example is shown in Fig. 11.8.

According to social judgment theory, a persuasive message that falls within or slightly out of the latitude of acceptance is perceived by the receiver as closer to his or her prime attitude than it really is.[13] Suppose a source argued, in a well-prepared persuasive speech, for Statement 4: "Draft evaders should be given amnesty if they fulfill their military commitment." The receiver would tend to assimilate this position into his or her own latitude of acceptance. Then his or her attitude continuum would look like Fig. 11.9. With this new continuum, Statement 5 ("Make draft evaders publicly apologize.") is now close to the latitude of acceptance and might be assimilated into it after more persuasive communication.

[13]Sherif, Sherif, and Nebergall, 1965.

On the other hand, if a source argues for a position that is in the receiver's latitude of rejection, it is seen as more discrepant than it actually is. If a source argued, for instance, that all draft resisters should be imprisoned, the receiver would contrast the source's statements with his or her own and remain unpersuaded. This contrast effect may lead in some instances to a "boomerang" effect. The receiver in the amnesty example, for instance, might be so repelled by the suggestion of imprisonment for draft resisters that he or she would shrink his or her latitude of acceptance and decide that all positions except for his or her prime attitude are unacceptable. This situation is illustrated in Fig. 11.10.

Social judgment theory also predicts the ways in which the receiver's ego-involvement affects his or her attitude change. High ego-involvement corresponds to a wide latitude of rejection; low ego-involvement corresponds to a wide latitude of noncommitment. For example, a draft resister would be highly ego-involved on the subject of amnesty. His latitudes might appear as they do in Fig. 11.11.

A person who does not even know any draft resisters and who has nothing personal at stake in the issue might have latitudes such as those shown in Fig. 11.12. (Note that ego-involvement does not affect the latitude of acceptance.)

Because an ego-involved person has a wide latitude of rejection, persuasive messages are more likely to fall into that range and be contrasted with his or her prime attitude. Thus, attitude change is difficult. A receiver who lacks ego-involvement, on the other hand, has a wide latitude of noncommitment into which persuasive messages are likely to fall. Such messages can then be assimilated into the acceptable range, and persuasion is more successful. Common sense certainly supports this conclusion that people are more reluctant to change their attitudes on issues that are directly important to them.

SUMMARY

1. Most definitions of persuasion stress three elements: conscious intent, message transmission, and behavioral influence. Although people may persuade others unintentionally, the criterion of conscious intent facilitates the formal study of persuasion. A persuasive message may lead to changes in a person's attitude (beliefs, opinions, and values), which, in turn, may lead to changes in a person's perceptions, emotions, cognition, or overt action. An opinion is a favorable, unfavorable, or neutral evaluation of a person, a thing, or an idea. A belief is a nonevaluative conviction about the truth or falsity of something. A value is a deeply held opinion that exerts influence on a person's thinking or behavior.

2. Learning theory centers on the relationship between stimuli and responses. A stimulus is anything that is perceived by the receiver; a response then is the receiver's reaction to the stimulus. According to various learning theories, the effectiveness of communication can be enhanced through the use of positive or negative reinforcement. Obviously, positive reinforcement involves rewarding people for making the appropriate or desired responses. Negative reinforcement involves threatening the receiver with an undesirable situation for making the wrong response. However, negative reinforcement is not the same as punishment. Punishment occurs *after* the receiver has responded in an undesired way; negative reinforcement provides the receiver with an opportunity to behave in the desired way. The time between the response and the reinforcement may affect the speed of learning. Specific reinforcements tied to specific desired responses are more effective than vague ones. People generalize their

responses from one situation to another. Feedback serves as positive or negative reinforcement in shaping attitudes and behaviors.

3. Three different consistency theories make similar assumptions about the persuasion process. Cognitive balance theory views the mind as a complex system that organizes past experiences and present stimuli into meaningful patterns. People tend to evaluate a persuasive message according to the way it fits into the patterns. If the message fits, the receiver's internal state remains balanced. If the message does not fit, the receiver is in a state of internal inconsistency. To establish balance, the receiver must change his or her attitude toward either the source or the message. Other things being equal, if there is a contradiction between the receiver's attitude toward the source and the message, the receiver's attitude toward the message is more likely to change. However, if the receiver feels very strongly about the topic, he or she is likely to change his or her attitude about the source. Symmetry theory modifies the balance theory by trying to explain the way communication affects internal inconsistency. Congruity theory claims that when internal inconsistency exists, attitudes toward both the source and the message change.

4. The theory of cognitive dissonance is an extension of earlier balance and consistency models of persuasion. Although this theory makes some of the same assumptions about the nature of the persuasion process, it is primarily concerned with all of the processes that people go through to rationalize or justify their behaviors after a decision or commitment has been made. There has been a considerable amount of research that suggests that dissonance does motivate people to seek reasons that will help them justify their behavior. The less justification that people have for behaving a certain way or for changing their attitudes, the more dissonance they will experience after committing the behavior. One way to reduce that dissonance is to believe even more strongly that one's new attitude is correct and that justification for change was present. When people have a great deal of justification for doing something or believing a specific way, they can go ahead and engage in the behaviors without actually changing attitudes to conform to those behaviors. They can simply claim that anybody under similar circumstances would have behaved the same way. They do not have to have conformity between beliefs and attitudes if the discrepancy can be justified.

5. Social judgment theory views attitude change as a two-step process. First the receiver judges the relationship of a communication to his or her own attitudes, and then he or she makes changes in these attitudes. According to this theory, a person's attitudes about a topic are

best represented by a continuum, ranging from the most acceptable to the most unacceptable. The position a receiver finds most acceptable is called his or her prime attitude. A receiver also has a latitude of acceptance (positions he or she finds acceptable), a latitude of noncommitment (positions about which he or she is neutral or divided, and a latitude of rejection (positions he or she finds unacceptable). A persuasive message that falls within or slightly out of the latitude of acceptance is perceived by the receiver as closer to his or her prime attitude than it really is. Thus, the receiver tends to assimilate this position into his or her latitude of acceptance. A position that falls within the receiver's latitude of rejection is seen as more discrepant than it actually is. A receiver who is very ego-involved in the topic has a wide latitude of rejection into which a persuasive message may fall, whereas a receiver who is not ego-involved has a wide range of noncommitment. Because a receiver perceives messages as more similar and more discrepant than they actually are, persuasion is likely to be more successful with the receiver who is not ego-involved than with the one who is very ego-involved.

SUGGESTED READING

Brembeck, Winston L., and William S. Howell. *Persuasion: A Means of Social Influence.* 2d ed. Englewood Cliffs, N. J.: Prentice-Hall, 1976.

Cronkhite, Gary. *Persuasion: Speech and Behavioral Change.* Indianapolis: Bobbs-Merrill, 1969.

Kiesler, Charles A.; Barry E. Collins; and Norman Miller. *Attitude Change.* New York: John Wiley and Sons, 1969.

King, Stephen W. *Communication and Social Influence.* Reading, Mass.: Addison-Wesley, 1975.

Miller, Gerald R., and Michael Burgoon. *New Techniques of Persuasion.* New York: Harper and Row, 1973.

Simons, Herbert W. *Persuasion: Understanding, Practice, and Analysis.* Reading, Mass.: Addison-Wesley, 1976.

From the Reading	Study Questions
Define the following terms. conscious intent opinion belief value	1. Why is it suggested that only intentional communication behavior is useful in the study of persuasion? 2. What is the attitude or behavior as the focus of study about? Why is it important to people interested in persuasion?

positive reinforcement
negative reinforcement
punishment
stimulus-response model
internal consistency
imbalance
symmetry theory
congruity
cognitive dissonance
justification
latitudes of acceptance, rejection, and noncommitment

3. What kinds of things are of concern to people interested in learning theory approaches to persuasion?
4. Distinguish between the use of positive reinforcement, negative reinforcement, and punishment. What are the different outcomes associated with the use of each?
5. What are the general principles or findings from learning theory that can be of use to people interested in using this approach to persuade?
6. What are the basic assumptions of balance theory? Of what is imbalance a motivator?
7. When imbalance occurs, what kinds of changes are possible? What kind are most likely to occur?
8. How does symmetry theory add to balance theory?
9. Why is congruity theory a refinement of the other consistency theories?
10. What is the primary point of departure that cognitive dissonance takes from the other consistency theories? How does it differ? How is it the same?
11. What are the assumptions that social judgment theory makes about attitude change? How does this theory relate to learning theory, the consistency theories, and cognitive dissonance? Are there similarities? Are there major differences?

Chapter 12
PERSUASION: APPLICATIONS AND MESSAGE STRATEGIES

The previous chapter discussed a sampling of the many models that have been generated to attempt to explain *why* people change their attitudes and/or behaviors. Many of these models pose interesting questions and have generated intriguing explanations for human behavior. After reading the last chapter several of our students have persuaded us that it is not enough simply to understand the underlying psychological motivations for change. They claimed that although they found the models interesting, they felt ill-equipped as potential persuaders. In fact, one of them said that he did not really know any more about communication and how to use it to persuade than he did before reading the chapter. Given this negative reinforcement, our general feelings of inconsistency and the decision that this feedback was generally close to our latitudes of acceptance, we felt it necessary to resolve the cognitive dissonance associated with our desire to do a good job and the knowledge that our readers were not being adequately served; thus, we were persuaded to make some changes in this edition.

This chapter is an attempt to acquaint the reader with some of the available research on how one goes about structuring effective persuasive messages. This synthesis represents our best understanding about what the research says, and we offer a description of what has been found to be most effective. Perhaps it is wise to elaborate briefly concerning some of our assumptions about the material included in this chapter. First, we resisted the suggestions of several of our critics to include this material in the earlier chapters on public speaking. Traditionally, some of the material in this chapter has been used in guides on how to be effective in persuading a group of people in some formal speaking situation. Although we think that many of the suggestions made in this chapter would be very useful to a speaker who wishes to persuade others, we think they have broader applicability than would be suggested if included in those earlier chapters. Frankly, we think that there are a variety of contexts in which people wish to be effective persuaders. It is important for business executives to know what kind of messages are most likely to be accepted and retained by people working for them. Anyone involved in an intimate relationship needs to know that some kinds of messages increase tension whereas others lessen it. Through practice and intelligent observation, a person can learn to communicate with messages that work.

A second issue needs to be discussed prior to our analysis of the available research. We do not think that all communication is by nature persuasive; that view is too simplistic. We are also not interested in simply training people to be manipulators. Many people find our strong emphasis on the persuasive function of communication to be somewhat irritating if not offensive, and we are willing to speak to that issue. Persuasion is a pervasive part of our daily lives, and much of our communication is suasory in nature. The suggestions we make in this chapter are likely to be useful to the would-be huckster who wishes to use the tool of communication for ends that we might personally find reprehensible. However, there is another view that we find comforting. Knowledge of how to construct

persuasive messages and how those messages are likely to affect people should also be a useful tool to help the knowledgeable person *resist persuasive claims that should not be accepted*. The power of this knowledge that would allow one to persuade is surely offset by the power to resist persuasive attempts when we understand the ways in which they are being used against us.

The Components of a Persuasive Message

We believe that one way to begin to understand how to go about constructing effective persuasive messages is by analyzing how people go about making critical decisions. If we can understand how people evaluate logical arguments, we are more likely to construct messages that will be seen as logical and increase the probability of those messages being persuasive. Toulmin has created a model of critical thinking that has great utility in persuasive discourse. He claims that arguments grow out of information (data) on a particular issue that leads to an inference or conclusion (claim). There is also a bridging statement, which he calls a warrant, that allows the data to be linked to the claim. Although Toulmin was not primarily concerned with creating persuasive messages, it is appropriate to argue that a persuasive message that facilitates this kind of critical thinking is most likely to be effective. Every persuasive message presents an idea or course of action that the communicator advocates; it then suggests reasons that listeners should agree with it. Thus, it can be argued that most persuasive messages, in their simplest form, are made up of the three components in the Toulmin model: claim, warrant, and data.[1] These elements work to reinforce each other in persuasive attempts. We shall elaborate further on these three elements.

CLAIM

A *claim* is any statement, implied or explicit, that a communicator wants his or her audience to accept or agree to. A particular claim can serve as the major point of several related arguments, or it may be used by the communicator in one part of his or her argument to support an assertion (claim) made in another part.

There are several kinds of claims that can be used in a message. In a *policy* claim, the speaker calls for a specific course of action. The statement "Heroin should be available to addicts under medical supervision," is an example of a policy claim. The speaker might make a *fact* claim: "In England, heroin is available to addicts under medical supervision." And he or she might then make a *value* claim such as the following: "The English system for treating heroin addiction is superior to that of the United States." Regardless of the kind of claim used, a single claim does not in itself provide a reason for audience acceptance of it.

WARRANT

To persuade, the communicator must support each claim with two other message parts: a warrant and data. A *warrant*

[1]S. Toulmin, *The Uses of Argument* (Cambridge, England: Cambridge University Press, 1959).

is a general belief or attitude stated in support of a claim. To be effective, a warrant must be implicitly accepted by the audience; otherwise, it remains just another claim. For example, a communicator who says, "Schools should not be racially integrated" is making a claim. He may then support his claim with the general statement "Blacks are genetically inferior to whites in mental ability." Such a statement would be a warrant. A Ku Klux Klan meeting might accept this warrant and so accept the claim. But a convention of anthropologists or black intellectuals might not believe the warrant and so would reject the claim as unwarranted. In this case, the warrant itself (that blacks are mentally inferior) becomes a claim and needs a new warrant to justify it.

Many persuasive messages fail even when the claim is acceptable to the audience because the warrant is totally rejected. For instance, suppose that a man who believes marijuana to be a dangerous drug goes to see a 1930s movie called *Reefer Madness*. It claims that marijuana is a dangerous drug, a claim he is predisposed to support; it warrants that smoking marijuana leads to mental illness and violent crime. The warrant may seem so absurdly exaggerated that the viewer rejects first it, then the claim, deciding that marijuana couldn't be as dangerous as all that. An inappropriate warrant can actually be counterpersuasive.

DATA

Data are specific beliefs stated in support of a claim. Like the warrant, the data must be accepted by the audience to be persuasive. McCroskey has suggested that there are three types of data: first-order, second-order, and third-order.[2]

First-order data are specific beliefs or knowledge shared by the communicator and his or her audience. It may be claimed, for example, that all cigarette advertising should be banned. Such a claim might be warranted by the generally accepted belief that cigarette smoking causes lung cancer. The communicator might then offer as data the information that cigarette advertising encourages smoking. The success or failure of this argument depends upon whether or not the data are first-order—that is, whether or not they are a belief or awareness of fact that the audience shares with the communicator. If they are not, the data themselves become a claim that the communicator will have to support by further argument.

Second-order data are beliefs held by the communicator, but not necessarily known or shared by his or her audience. This type of data is often called *source assertion*, for it asks the audience to accept something just because the speaker, or source, says it is so. The important message component in this case is the warrant that the speaker is a credible source. For example, a speaker might assert that consistently poor nutrition retards the mental development of children. If his or her credibility is high enough—let us say that the audience know him or her to be an established and respected member of the medical profession—the assertion itself becomes sufficient data. If the audience fully accepts the warrant (often implicit) that the speaker is a knowledgeable

[2]J. C. McCroskey, *An Introduction to Rhetorical Communication* (Englewood Cliffs, N.J.: Prentice-Hall, 1968), pp. 84–105.

source, it will probably accept the speaker's claim without the need for further documentation. In this case, the second-order data, information previously known only to the speaker, become first-order data, which the audience also accepts as part of its beliefs or knowledge, and can be used in documenting further arguments. Of course, if the audience doubts the authority of the speaker, the data are useless.

When the communicator has low credibility and the audience does not share his or her views, he or she must often use third-order data to persuade. This type of data is called *evidence*. It comes from a third party, a source outside of the communicator and the audience. Here is an example:

1. All cigarette advertising should be banned. (claim)
2. I am a truthful person. (warrant)
3. *The New York Times* said in an editorial that all cigarette advertising should be banned. (third-order data)
4. *The New York Times* is a credible source. (warrant)

As you can see, this example really consists of two separate persuasive messages. The first is:

1. *The New York Times* said in an editorial that all cigarette advertising should be banned. (claim)
2. I am a truthful person. (warrant)
3. I say that I read this editorial in *The Times*. (second-order data)

If that claim is accepted, it can be used as first-order data in a second message:

1. All cigarette advertising should be banned. (claim)
2. *The New York Times* is a credible source. (warrant)
3. *The New York Times* said in an editorial that all cigarette advertising should be banned. (now considered first-order data, because the audience accepts it)

Third-order data ask the audience to accept warrants for two separate claims. The audience must trust that the speaker is telling the truth about what he or she read in *The Times*, and it must trust *The Times*. If the communicator has low credibility or if the outside source is disliked or disbelieved by the audience, third-order data are not persuasive. Of course, no amount of credibility will persuade if the audience totally rejects the claim. For instance, an audience of Roman Catholic clergy will probably not accept a claim that abortion should be legalized, no matter how credible the speaker or data.

Although it is useful to understand these common message elements in persuasive discourse, to do so will not explain how to *construct* effective persuasive messages. So far, we have progressed only a short distance on our journey from theory to actual application of knowledge about how to gain compliance. There are several message variables that may or may not be present in any of the specific message elements that we have just discussed. The communicator must make several decisions in creating the most persuasive message possible. He or she must decide what to include in any given persuasive message, what kinds of feelings should be appealed to in the receiver, and, finally, how to organize all of these elements.

Selecting Message Appeals That Are Persuasive

Aristotle specified three basic appeals that a communicator can make in a persuasive message. A speaker can use a logical argument (*logos*), an emotional argument (*pathos*), or an argument based on credibility (*ethos*). Contemporary communication experts have attempted to distinguish between logical and emotional appeals. A logical appeal is one that presents evidence in support of the acceptance of a claim or attempts to build an argument that is logically true. An emotional appeal focuses on the consequences that will result if a person accepts or rejects the communicator's claim. According to this schema, we would probably agree that an advertisement claiming that one should buy an automobile during August because you will save a thousand dollars is appealing to our sense of logic. An advertisement that stresses the increased social status accruing to those people who buy a certain brand of automobile is an emotional appeal.

Unfortunately, not all messages are as easy to classify according to type of appeal as these two examples. Although it is clear that certain messages are more logical or more emotional than others, it is probably not very useful to view logical and emotional appeals as completely separate and distinct. First, many persuasive messages contain both emotional and logical appeals. Cold hard statistics are often included on why the status-producing automobile is also a good buy because of its continued high resale value. Other messages primarily based upon evidence and logical appeals often include emotional reasons for accepting the claims being advanced. It is probably rare in conversation to use one type of appeal exclusively in a persuasive attempt; we rely on many types of appeals in our persuasive arsenal.

There are also other problems associated with analyzing emotional and logical appeals. First, the logic or emotion of an appeal is perceived by the receiver, and those perceptions are not always identical to the perceptions of the communication source. Though one might assume that receivers would be able to differentiate between logical and emotional appeals, there is evidence to suggest that this is not always the case.[3] Research has shown that people cannot always tell whether arguments were logical or illogical. When people agree with the conclusion drawn by the communicator, they tend to claim that the argument was logical. This judgment was made whether or not the message was based on commonly accepted rules of logic. However, when people disagreed with the position being advocated, they were able to detect the faulty reasoning in the persuasive message. One would probably expect that as people became more trained in the use of logic, these results would not be the same. Bettinghaus found that students who were trained in formal logic were indeed better able to detect faulty logic than students who had not been so trained; however, even the trained students made more errors in detecting faulty logic in persuasive messages that they agreed with.[4]

Although we cannot always decide in advance what appeals will be perceived by receivers as logical or emotional, we do know that appeals to logic and/or emotion can be effective persuaders. We also know that the communicator may face situations in which logical appeals are expected. For example, many people in formal public speaker situations are expected to be appealing to the logic of their audience. When people are expecting a speaker to be logical, it is in the best interest of the speaker at least to give the appearance of being logical. Bettinghaus also found that when people used phrases such as "isn't it only logical . . ." people saw the message as more logical than emotional. There is a great deal of research to suggest that people develop expectations about the proper communication behavior of others, and, to the extent that those expectancies are not violated, the speaker can be effective.

Despite the difficulty involved in classifying different types of appeals, there are several factors that will influence the persuasiveness of a message regardless of the type of appeal used.

APPEALS BASED ON EVIDENCE

Is it important to present evidence (third-order data) to support a claim? The answer depends on the situation. Research has shown that sometimes evidence is very persuasive, whereas at other

[3]See, for example, R. C. Ruechelle, "An Experimental Study of Audience Recognition of Emotional and Intellectual Appeals in Persuasion," *Speech Monographs,* 25 (1958), p. 58; A. Lefford, "The Influence of Emotional Subject Matter on Logical Reasoning," *Journal of General Psychology,* 34 (1946), pp. 127–151.

[4]This experiment is discussed in E. P. Bettinghaus, *Persuasive Communication* (New York: Holt, Rinehart and Winston, 1968), p. 158.

times different kinds of supporting material are more effective. It is possible to extract from the research some generalizations about the usefulness of evidence.[5]

If the communicator has high credibility with his (or her) audience, he (or she) will probably not need to present evidence. For example, suppose the president's chief economic adviser claims that the nation is headed for a depression. If you believe he (or she) is a credible source, you will probably accept the statement without hearing the statistics. Citing that evidence would not make him (or her) more persuasive to you, because you already believe him (or her), the adviser's position convinces you that he (or she) is an expert in his (or her) field.

But what if the speaker has low credibility? In that case, evidence is persuasive only if the audience was previously unaware of the data. If, in the example above, the economic adviser were a man you considered untrustworthy, you would want to hear his evidence. If he gave convincing statistics that you had not known before, you might accept his claim in spite of his low credibility. But suppose you were a student of economics who had read the same statistics and drawn a different conclusion. In that case, the adviser's use of evidence would not persuade you; it might even make you resist his claim more, because you would suspect him of manipulating the facts. In general, if an audience already knows of the evidence, it

has probably made up its mind, and the communicator gains nothing by restating the evidence.

Research has also shown that evidence must be delivered clearly if it is to have maximum persuasive effect. This does not mean a speaker must use a compulsively logical and straightforward approach, for he or she may lose the audience by boring its members to death. But if there is no organic unity to the speaker's presentation, if statistics are haphazardly thrown at the audience, or if he or she mumbles words and drones away in a relentless monotone, all the evidence in the world will not help that speaker. A poor delivery will not only make evidence useless, failing to persuade the audience of the particular argument being discussed at the time; it is very possible that it will also reduce the speaker's credibility in terms of future messages he or she may present.

Apparently, a speaker runs risks in presenting evidence. It may have a neutral effect, swaying an audience neither one way nor the other; or it may actually hurt a speaker's chances of successfully conveying his or her message. What then is the ultimate value of evidence? Studies show that, whereas the immediate effect of evidence can be negligible, the long-range effects—for both high and low credible speakers—may be important. Over a period of time, audience attitudes may change slowly but decidedly if the listeners receive several doses of evidence in the messages conveyed to them. A good example is the political candidate who begins his campaign months in advance of election day. The cumulative effect of the evidence he or she presents, especially in

[5]For a detailed discussion of evidence, see J. C. McCroskey, "A Summary of Experimental Research on the Effects of Evidence in Persuasive Communication," *Quarterly Journal of Speech*, 55 (1959), pp. 169–176.

claims made against opponents, may eventually alter the attitudes of the voters. Another important effect of evidence is in making receivers more resistant to counterinfluence on the part of another potential persuader. So if we know that a person is likely to hear persuasive communication over time that argues against the claim you are proposing, it would be wise to include evidence no matter how credible you are with that individual. It seems that evidence can be remembered and used when people hear other appeals arguing on the opposite side of an issue.

There are two final points that should be made about the use of evidence. Little research is available that distinguishes between "good" and "bad" evidence. However, it is probably common sense to suggest that evidence is more likely to be perceived as good evidence when it is relevant to the claim being advanced and properly linked to that claim by an appropriate warrant. The second point to be made is that the sources of evidence also help people in making judgments about the quality of the evidence. Evidence obtained from a source low in credibility can have an adverse effect on the persuasiveness of your message, and it can also reduce your credibility. On the other hand, many times a person can increase his or her communicative effectiveness by relying on evidence and examples from other high credible sources.

APPEALS BASED ON FEAR

Many communicators try to persuade by stimulating fear in their audiences. Public health pamphlets, for example, predict a frightening future of blindness, sterility, and paralysis as the reward for sexual promiscuity (or even occasional indiscretions) unless one takes the recommended precautions. Gun-control advocates talk of unleashed violence, and their opponents talk of first steps down the road to totalitarianism. Students in a driver's education course watch a state highway department film that graphically portrays the results of reckless or negligent driving, complete with blood and bodies and intimations of one's own mortality. Because people do react strongly to fear in everyday life, much research has been done to see if fear can be used to change attitudes.

A fear appeal says that harm will befall the listener or someone important to him or her unless he or she adopts the claim of the communicator. A strong fear appeal dramatically shows this harm. A film intended to make people stop smoking that shows a close-up of a cancerous lung being removed from a corpse is an example of a high fear appeal. A moderate fear appeal states the same message less dramatically, as in the case of a film that shows people smoking, then coughing. A low fear appeal states the message in a fairly calm way—for example, a printed advertisement claiming that scientists have established a link between smoking and lung cancer. A communicator must decide which type of fear appeal will produce the change he or she wants.

Research findings on this subject are conflicting. Some studies show that a strong fear appeal is best; others show that a moderate fear appeal is best. Such confusion means that factors other than the fear appeal itself are affecting the receiver's response to the message.[6]

The credibility of the source is one influence on the audience's reaction to a fear appeal. A highly credible source is more persuasive when using a strong fear appeal. A less credible source does better with a moderate fear appeal. If a doctor tells you that you will die of heart trouble within a year if you do not stop overeating, that should provide enough incentive for you to take action. If a well-meaning friend tells you the same thing, you may not be so quickly persuaded. Therefore, a communicator who plans to persuade through fear should first attempt to establish his or her credibility in the eyes of his or her audience.

When the fear appeal threatens harm to someone important to the listener, a strong fear appeal is most effective. For instance, a claim that children undernourished on sugarcoated breakfast cereal and junk food may grow up with brain damage would be more persuasive than the claim that they grow up failing to appreciate good food. When the fear appeals threaten loved ones, the listener cannot reason that he or she is hurting only himself or herself by rejecting the claim.

A strong fear appeal with evidence is more effective than one without evidence and is stronger than any mild fear appeal, with or without evidence. In research studies, only the people who heard evidence kept their changed attitudes for longer than two weeks. Those who heard

appeals without evidence quickly returned to their original belief. Thus, an opponent of sugarcoated cereal and junk food who wants to change permanently the nutritional attitudes of mothers should make claims that he or she can support with convincing evidence. If he or she has no evidence for the brain-damage claim, he or she would do better with a mild fear appeal, citing evidence that supports the claim that bad eating habits formed in early childhood usually continue in adult life.

When people use fear appeals to point out the negative outcomes associated with not accepting the claim of the communicator, the more immediate the likely negative results, the more effective are strong fear appeals. There are probably few of us that would not respond to a fear appeal pointing out the link between smoking and lung cancer if the disease were to appear in the next month; that would be an immediate result of our refusal to give up tobacco. However, to the extent that negative outcomes are in the distant future, strong fear appeals tend to be ineffective as people dismiss the seriousness of the threat and/or refuse to attend to the fear-arousing messages. On the other hand, when there is an immediate threat, strong fear appeals can motivate people to take prompt actions.

Most of the research that we have reviewed and the examples we have advanced have been concerned with fear appeals that make threats on someone's physical well-being. There are other kinds of fear appeals that merit discussion because of their ability to motivate people to change attitudes and behaviors. The fear

[6]For a detailed discussion of fear appeals see G. R. Miller, "Studies in the Use of Fear Appeals: A Summary and Analysis," *Central States Speech Journal, 14* (1963), pp. 117–125.

of social disapproval can be a significant persuader, and little has been done to link this threat to social well-being to other kinds of fear appeals. This kind of fear appeal can be very important in the interpersonal and small-group communication arena. Few of us are without fear of disapproval by liked and respected others; we want our friends to like us and have at least some fear of their criticism. Persuasive appeals can be structured to use that fear or social disapproval as the basis for changing people's attitudes. However, as we have said earlier, very strong fear appeals based upon anxiety about social disapproval may have a backlash effect. If you threaten people who like and respect you and desire you to return those feelings with loss of your friendship unless they comply with your wishes, one possible outcome is for them to change their evaluations of you as a person. In the last chapter, we discussed in detail how imbalances between sources and attitudes topics can lead to shifts in either or both source and topic attitudes.

The final point that should be discussed is the continued use of fear appeals over time. If a communicator continually uses fear as a motivator, people are likely to dismiss his or her claims at some point in time. This kind of communicator becomes a "prophet of doom" who is known for dire predictions. People who constantly use fear as a motivator run great risks in terms of their own credibility. Also, a person who continually threatens people with social disapproval runs the same risk. Fear when used in proper proportions is no doubt an effective means of persuasion. Use of the wrong kinds of appeals or too much reliance on this tech-

nique can have outcomes that are undesirable to the potential persuader.

APPEALS BASED ON HUMOR

The use of humor to persuade is the other side of the coin from motivating people by fear. Although many speech textbooks have suggested to students that the use of humor can facilitate attitude change and improve comprehension of oral messages, the research is not so supportive of those conclusions. Although the effects of humor in persuasive discourse have not been very thoroughly investigated, there is little evidence to suggest that humor itself is persuasive or that it improves message comprehension. An early study showed that humor (puns, turns of phrase, and humorous anecdotes) did not significantly increase or decrease attitude change. Furthermore, humorous and nonhumorous messages were perceived as equally interesting and convincing by the listeners.[7] Similarly, experiments have shown that satirical humor also does not enhance the persuasiveness of a message both immediately and over a period of three weeks.[8]

There may be several explanations for the lack of findings in the research literature, and we are willing to take some editorial license and speculate on the reasons for all of this. First, many of the things

[7]P. E. Lull, "The Effectiveness of Humor in a Persuasive Speech," *Speech Monographs, 7* (1940), pp. 26–40.
[8]C. R. Gruner, "An Experimental Study of Satire as Persuasion," *Speech Monographs, 32* (1956), pp. 149–153; G. F. Pokorny and C. R. Gruner, "An Experimental Study of the Effect of Satire Used as Support in a Persuasive Speech," *Western Speech, 33* (1969), pp. 204–211.

that we find humorous tend to be spontaneous, off-the-cuff kinds of comments that may not lend themselves to the kind of research that has gone on primarily in the public speaking situation. The lack of spontaneity may have reduced the effect of humor. Furthermore, it may be very difficult to find humor that is universally perceived as funny. In our academic department recently, an anonymous publication commenting satirically on the department and people involved with it appeared. Many people perceived the publication to be extremely humorous and actually looked forward to its appearance every Wednesday. However, others (especially those who were the targets of the satire) found little humor in the document and actually asked the vice-president to order the publication to cease. All people

Although there is no solid evidence that humor affects persuasion, humor may create a sense of warmth or rapport between the communicator and the receiver. (Photograph: German Information Center)

are not equally adept at encoding humor, and a message that is seen as devoid of humor when delivered by one person may be perceived as very funny when told by another person. All of these considerations make the generating of principles about the use of humor very difficult.

Although there is no solid evidence that humor affects persuasion, humor may create a sense of warmth or rapport between the communicator and the receiver. A person who *effectively* uses humor may increase perceptions of his or her sociability. For example, people attributed much of President Kennedy's popularity to his sense of humor, which made him more attractive. It is also likely that a person who does use humor effectively will be a person whom others prefer to interact with in interpersonal and small-group communication situations. As we said in the last chapter, symmetry theory would suggest that those people who communicate more over time become more similar. Therefore, we would expect the person who is a preferred communicator to be more influential over time even if there were no effects when only one situation was considered.

Frankly, we are disappointed that we could not find more to discuss about the use of humor as a persuasive technique. Intuitively, we feel that humor does have a more important impact on communication transactions than the research literature indicates. The import of humor in persuasion is yet to be answered by researchers.

APPEALS VARYING IN LANGUAGE INTENSITY

Some of our closest friends and most respected colleagues believe that the authors of this text have obtained whatever modicum of success that they have because people have confused the intensity of their claims with the validity of their positions. People have choices to make about kinds of language that will be used in any given persuasive message, and there is evidence to suggest that those language choices will have a great effect on whether the persuasion attempt succeeds. One important language variable that influences persuasion is language intensity. Language intensity can be rated by measuring the distance between a claim and a neutral position. For example, the claim "Unions are *destroying* the newspaper industry" is certainly less neutral than saying, "Unions create *problems* in the newspaper industry." There are different ways to vary the intensity of language in a message.[9]

One way is to insert qualifiers. One kind of qualifier expresses probability. Take the statement "Recent Supreme Court decisions on the rights of accused criminals will *certainly* lead to more violent crime." This statement can be made less intense by replacing *certainly* with *perhaps*. Another kind of qualifier expresses extremity. If a presidential aide tells the press, "The president *vigorously condemns* bias in the news media," the attitude implied is obviously more intense and more threatening than if he (or she) says, "The president *frowns* upon bias in the news media."

A second way to increase intensity of language is to use metaphors, especially those with sexual or violent connotations. When a speaker claims, "The president is

[9]J. W. Bowers, "Some Correlates of Language Intensity," *Quarterly Journal of Speech*, 50 (1964), pp. 415–420.

raping the Constitution," "The recent incursion by Russia is a *molestation* of the country's territorial waters," "Public school teachers *suffocate* student creativity," or "Prejudice in the system *has brutalized* the minds of young children," he or she is going beyond a representation of the facts as they stand and attempting to persuade through the intensity of his or her images.

Whether such high-intensity language does, in fact, achieve the speaker's goal is difficult to say. One study showed that a very intense communicator seems more credible and that his messages seem clearer and more intelligent; however, the study did not indicate that such a communicator was actually more effective in persuading people to accept the positions being advocated.[10] Other research has found that messages employing low levels of language intensity are actually more persuasive than those using highly intense language. Obviously there are some intervening factors that affect how language intensity operates in persuasive messages.

One such factor that mediates the effects of language intensity is the expectations that receivers develop for what is "appropriate" communication behavior on the part of any given communicator. For example, it has been demonstrated that within this culture, different expectations about appropriate language behavior vary between male and female communicators. In a recent piece of research conducted by the first author of this book, it was found that male communicators were much more effective when they used highly intense

language than were females saying the same thing.[11] Moreover, females were very persuasive when they used language low in intensity. One *possible* explanation for these findings has to do with cultural-level stereotypes that may or may not be useful. If a culture expects males to be aggressive and demonstrate this by using forceful language, then males using highly intense language would not be violating expectations in any negative manner and would, therefore, be persuasive using language high in intensity. However, to the extent that aggressiveness in females has not been accepted, females who chose highly intense language would be negatively violating expectations and, therefore, not be as persuasive. It is also interesting to note that female receivers were the *least* persuaded by females who used highly intense language and *most* persuaded by males using language high in intensity. Though it is, no doubt, true that these kinds of stereotypes are changing, these recent results indicate that there are sex differences associated with this language variable.

Another variable that affects decisions about the level of language intensity that is most effective in persuasive discourse is the involvement of the receivers on the particular issue being discussed. Listeners who are very involved on a given topic (for example, reporters listening to an argument advocating naming of confidential sources) are especially likely to respond negatively to highly intense claims. With such audiences, a communicator will

[10]W. J. McEwen and B. S. Greenberg, "The Effects of Message Intensity on Receiver Evaluation of Source, Message and Topic," *Journal of Communication, 20* (1970), pp. 340–350.

[11]M. Burgoon and D. Stewart, "Empirical Investigations of Language Intensity: I. The Effects of Sex of Source, Receiver, and Language Intensity on Attitude Change," *Human Communication Research, 1* (1975), pp. 244–248.

effect little attitude change with highly intense language. If a topic is less crucial to the receiver, more highly intense language can be used in the persuasive attempt.

There are several possible explanations for these findings. Our discussion of the consistency models in the last chapter provides one such explanation. If people find an issue very important and hear a source advocating the opposite of what they believe, the easiest move to restore balance is to derogate the communicator. Social judgment theory offers an explanation that also tends to make a lot of sense. Selecting messages very high in intensity will obviously place the communication far from the listener's latitude of acceptance. Therefore, the claims that the communicator makes are likely to be *contrasted* with the views that the receiver privately holds. To the extent that this contrast effect operates, people will resist accepting highly intense claims. If the issue is less important, the claims are more likely to fall in the expanded latitude of noncommitment (which is large on issues of little import), and this contrasting will not occur. People can, therefore, take more extreme positions. All of these explanations taken together suggest the cautious use of extremely intense language in persuasive attempts. As most of us are aware, there is a tendency for people in discussion situations to take even more extreme positions than they really hold when there is disagreement or criticism. Moreover, many public speakers will take unusually intense positions to illustrate their support of or opposition to an issue. There are certainly pitfalls associated with this strategy.

Opinionated language is similar to intense language and has similar effects. Generally speaking, opinionated language really expresses two separate messages: the claim and the speaker's attitude toward those who agree or disagree with him or her. Opinionated language may express rejection of those who disagree, as in the statement "Only criminals with something to hide would object to being stopped and frisked by a policeman." Or it may praise those who agree with or show acceptance of the communicator—for example, "People who favor stop-and-frisk laws are responsible citizens who are willing to put up with a slight inconvenience in the interests of justice." Statements such as "Stop-and-frisk laws are good" are nonopinionated, for they merely express a claim.

Research indicates that opinionated rejections are perceived as more intense than nonopinionated statements. They can be used effectively by highly credible sources. Less credible sources, however, do better with nonopinionated language.[12] Also nonopinionated language is likely to be more persuasive with an audience that is involved in the issue being discussed. A neutral audience is more persuaded by opinionated rejections.

Because these findings are so similar to those suggesting contrast effects for highly intense language, we can offer some general conclusions. When the audience thinks the communicator is credible, more intense language can be used to support the claim. But when the communicator is unsure of his or her credibility or knows it to be low and is advocating a

[12]G. R. Miller and J. Lobe, "Opinionated Language, Open- and Closed-Mindedness and Responses to Persuasive Communications," *Journal of Communication*, 17 (1967), pp. 333–341.

COMMENTS ON THE FUNCTIONS OF HUMAN COMMUNICATION

position that is counter to beliefs that are important to the receiver, the communicator should, as a matter of strategy, choose less intense language. All of this suggests that the intuitive assumption that a passionate speaker is most persuasive needs reconsideration.

Making Strategic Decisions About What to Include in a Persuasive Message

As we have discussed them, most claims are only one side of an argument. The communicator must make a strategic decision as to whether or not it is best to cite opposing arguments. In a one-sided message, a claim is made, and the communicator attempts to support it. In a two-sided message, the same claim can be made but there is at least the acknowledgment that opposing arguments exist, with some attempt to demonstrate why the claim being advocated is superior to those in opposition. The decision to present a one-sided or two-sided message depends on several factors residing with the people with whom one is communicating.

In some cases in which an audience already agrees with the claims of a speaker, a one-sided argument will immediately increase or confirm that support.[13] In fact, if a speaker has reason to believe that his or her audience is unaware of counterarguments, he or she will probably do best deliberately to avoid these arguments. By mentioning them, the speaker might simply persuade his listeners against his or her own claim. The mayor who cites fifteen instances of alleged police corruption when the public knows only of five is at a disadvantage, no matter how well he disproves the accusations; those additional ten examples could convince people that there really is widespread police corruption.

On the other hand, if an audience is hostile, if its sympathies are unknown, or if there is any possibility that an audience is aware of opposing arguments, a speaker is best advised to present a two-sided message. Even when people are in agreement with the speaker, the more educated they are (an increasingly common situation in our society), the more likely such an audience will be persuaded by a two-sided argument.[14] Educated people are usually capable of thinking of at least a few opposing arguments for themselves and, therefore, might be suspicious of the motives or intelligence of a speaker who does not consider these same arguments.

One also has to realize that great numbers of people are exposed to conflicting arguments on issues through mass media coverage.[15] Suppose a mayor claims that there is no corruption in the city's police department. If the public has already listened to television programs highlighting instances of such corruption and read evidence cited in newspaper accounts, the mayor is going to seem foolish and incompetent—or worse. If the public believes the mayor was being dishonest in his or her message, not only will they fail

[13]C. A. Hovland, A. A. Lumsdaine, and F. D. Sheffield, *Studies in Social Psychology in World War II*, Vol. 3 (Princeton, N.J.: Princeton University Press, 1949), pp. 201–227.

[14]Ibid.

[15]For a detailed discussion of prior information and message-sidedness, see J. R. Weston, *Argumentative Message Structure and Message Sidedness and Prior Familiarity as Predictors of Source Credibility* (Ph.D. diss., Michigan State University, 1967).

to be persuaded by the mayor's immediate claim, but they might also doubt his credibility on other issues.

It would seem, therefore, that in most cases—other than outright propagandizing when the speaker is merely recycling shared beliefs for the benefit of his or her followers—it is usually better to use some form of the two-sided message. The speaker will have to use his or her discretion in deciding how much he or she should say.

Let us also *stress* that the communicator must make decisions about how discrepant the message is to be from the held beliefs of the receivers. To the extent that at least recognizing opposing arguments makes the receiver seem more informed and logical, it may also work to make the communication and the communicator seem less radical and polarized. When this happens, there is less likelihood of simply rejecting the message because it *appears* to be too discrepant from privately held beliefs.

Structuring Effective Persuasive Messages

In Chapter 9, we discussed at length some of the patterns of organization that can be used in the public speaking situation. Most of those suggestions concerned rules of logical structure, and those rules are applicable to situations other than where persuading another person or group is the goal of the communicator. We have opted to close this chapter with a section on the structuring of messages when the intent is primarily one of producing changes in attitudes and/or behavior. These sugges-

tions are also concerned with persuasion as it occurs across contexts from the interpersonal, small-group, and public speaking situations to the mass communication situation.

There is little agreement on the effects of logical structure on persuasion. Studies have shown that though severe disorganization does make a message less persuasive, moderately disorganized messages are no less persuasive than very logical ones.[16] There are several plausible explanations for this result. First, the audience may be capable of organizing information that comes to it in an "illogical" way. Marshall McLuhan, perhaps the most revolutionary communication theorist, claims that the electronic media have created an environment that forces people rapidly to recognize patterns in seemingly random information. Whereas books trained people to think in a logical, "linear" way, electronic media such as television ask us to take in vast amounts of disconnected information and do the job of ordering it ourselves. If McLuhan is right, people today are used to dealing with information that is presented in a disorganized way. They could easily understand a speaker who did not present his or her argument in a logical, step-by-step fashion.

A second explanation is that most of the research about the organization of persuasive messages was done with college students. They may be especially skilled listeners, because the college lecture is an especially good example of a disorganized message. Organization might be more im-

[16]J. C. McCroskey and R. S. Mehrley, "The Effects of Disorganization and Nonfluency on Attitude Change and Source Credibility," *Speech Monographs*, 36 (1969), pp. 13–21.

portant in communicating to a noncollege-educated audience.

A third possible explanation of these research findings focuses on the process of feedback. As we have stated, there is more opportunity for immediate feedback in the interpersonal and small-group communication situations than in the public speaking and mass communication contexts. People can disrupt the logical pattern of a communicator more easily in those situations in which immediate feedback is present. It would seem, therefore, that adherence to a strict logical structure in these situations is probably neither feasible nor necessarily desirable. There is great emphasis placed on the effective communicator's being a person who can adapt to people and situations. That adaptation may preclude use of some of the stricter organizational patterns prescribed in the formal public speaking situation.

In addition to a logical structure, a message also has a psychological structure that should be considered. What these mean is although the order of the message may not conform to any set rules of logical structure, there are strategic decisions that can be made to order the different parts of a message so that people will be more or less receptive to persuasive communication. The research and discussion that follow center on this psychological structure of messages and provide some useful generalizations that may be helpful when shaping persuasive messages.

Organizing Supporting Materials

Presenting a two-sided message always involves some decision making, for there is more than one way to organize the arguments. Suppose a speaker claims that capital punishment should be abolished. He or she might choose to plow through the opposition's arguments point for point and only then settle back to a presentation of his or her own claims. There is nothing wrong with this—except that he or she may lose the argument.

One reason is that an audience very often reacts defensively toward a speaker who begins his or her message with a strong offensive, especially if the audience happens to agree with some or all of the opposition's claims. William Shakespeare understood this psychological aspect of audience reaction very well. In *Julius Caesar*, Marc Antony faced a public whose loyalty to Caesar could be severed or reaffirmed by the "right" message. In his speech, Antony gently and unantagonistically described each of Caesar's virtues while at the same time refraining from obvious attacks against Caesar's opponents. Only later in his oration, when he sensed that audience sympathies were won, did he dare to shift the emphasis of his message from positive claims to an outright attack against Caesar's enemies.

If Shakespeare had been a professor as well as a playwright, he might have warned his students that discussing opposition arguments first may invest them with more importance than one ever intended. In other words, the very fact that a speaker gives opposition statements priority in his or her message may establish a psychological priority in the minds of audience members—even those who were previously uncommitted. As for those who already support the opposing claims, such a message structure may actually reinforce their attitudes, an unfortunate result for the speaker.

If the speaker who is trying to persuade his or her audience that capital punishment should be abolished pays any attention at all to Antony's speech and to the findings of modern research on the subject, he or she will decide that a more persuasive method would be to present his or her own claims first and subsequently discuss, and refute, the opponent's stand.[17]

The speaker could, for example, emphasize the immorality of taking human life, even in retribution; the unconstitutional nature of captial punishment; and the opinions of highly respected citizens who support his or her claim. Because an audience is often more favorably inclined toward the arguments it hears first, he or she will already have something of an advantage by the time he or she begins discussion of counterarguments.

These opposition claims might include the notion that captial punishment is the only adequate deterrent for major crimes. In that case, the speaker's refutation could be in the form of third-order data such as statistical figures relating to crime rates. But even if he or she fails to check the opposition on all points, his or her arguments will still be more persuasive if they are placed first than they would be if they are placed last.

IDENTIFYING THE SOURCE OF EVIDENCE

When citing an outside source (third-order data, or evidence), a speaker must

decide when to state the identity and qualification of the source. This depends on the source's credibility.[18] If the receiver believes the source of evidence is highly credible, he or she can be identified before or after presenting the evidence; it does not matter. However, when the source's credibility is low, it is better to cite the source after presenting the evidence. Thus, an advertising copywriter preparing a book advertisement for a new novel might proceed this way:

NORMAN MAILER SAYS: "This is the best novel I have read in 25 years!"

. . .

"A Blockbuster of a novel! Thrilling, incredibly erotic, and possibly the greatest work of fiction ever written in English!!"—*The Daily Tribune*

In fact, when the source is cited after the evidence, a highly credible source is no more persuasive than a low one. Thus, if you do not know how the audience rates a source, you should give the evidence first and then name the source. If, in the preceding example, the copywriter believed Norman Mailer had endorsed so many bad books that his credibility was low, the copywriter might decide to put Mailer's quote first, followed by his name.

Revealing Your Desire to Persuade

The question of whether it is wise to tell someone you want to change his or her mind is complex. If the members of the audience are strongly opposed to your

[17]N. Miller and D. T. Campbell, "Recency and Primacy in Persuasion as a Function of the Timing of Speeches and Measurements," *Journal of Abnormal and Social Psychology*, 59 (1959), pp. 1–9.

[18]B. S. Greenberg and G. R. Miller, "The Effects of Low-Credible Sources on Message Acceptance," *Speech Monographs*, 33 (1966), pp. 127–136.

claim, warning them in advance that you intend to persuade them is not effective.[19] A person speaking to a group of radical feminists would be ill-advised to state that he or she intended to change their minds about job discrimination against women. Let us refer once again to Marc Antony's speech. It will be remembered that he told his audience he was there "to bury Caesar, not to praise him." In reality, he was there to bury Caesar's enemies and enhance his own position. But realizing the ambivalence of the audience (and the fact that Caesar's enemies were scattered among the citizenry), he never even implied his intent to persuade.

However, if a speaker and his or her audience are known to be in strong mutual sympathy (for example, if they are friends), the speaker may be more persuasive if he or she openly admits his or her intent. If the audience obviously dislikes the speaker, the speaker will probably do better to keep quiet about his or her intent.[20] Sometimes an apparent lack of intent to persuade can become a powerful persuasive tool. When someone is led to believe he or she has accidentally overheard a message, such a person tends to be persuaded by it.[21] Political gossip columns often work this way. A government official "leaks" information to the colum-

nist, who then pretends it is a secret that has been accidentally uncovered. In such a case, our belief that the official had no intent to persuade us can lead us to accept his or her claim.

PRESENTING PROBLEMS AND SOLUTIONS

Suppose that a speaker wants to convince people that the problems of mothers on welfare can be solved by government-funded day care centers. He or she could structure his or her message in two ways. The speaker might discuss the problems of welfare mothers and then propose day-care centers as the solution. Or he or she could discuss the merits of day care centers and then explain the problems of welfare mothers.

Research indicates that the first pattern is much more effective in changing attitudes, both immediately following the message and over a period of time.[22] The problem-to-solution message is more interesting, and the solution is more understandable when presented as the answer to a specific problem or need. When the solution is presented first, people may not understand its relevance until they hear about the problem. By that time, they may have lost interest.

STATING POINTS OF AGREEMENT AND DISAGREEMENT

In most persuasive communication situations, the communicator shares some of

[19]J. Allyn and L. Festinger, "The Effectiveness of Unanticipated Persuasive Communication," *Journal of Abnormal and Social Psychology, 62* (1961), pp. 35–40.

[20]J. Mills and E. Aronson, "Opinion Change as a Function of the Communicator's Attractiveness and Desire to Influence," *Journal of Personality and Social Psychology, 1* (1965), pp. 173–177.

[21]E. Walster and L. Festinger, "The Effectiveness of Overheard Persuasive Communications," *Journal of Abnormal and Social Psychology, 65* (1962), pp. 395–402.

[22]A. R. Cohen, "Need for Cognition and Order of Communication as Determinants of Opinion Change," in *The Order of Presentation in Persuasion*, ed. C. I. Hovland (New Haven, Conn.: Yale University Press, 1957), pp. 102–120.

his or her audience's beliefs and disagrees with others. When does the communicator discuss the shared beliefs? When does he or she introduce dispute? Research shows that the best strategy is to discuss points of agreement first, then move on to disagreements.[23] In this way, the speaker captures attention and raises his or her credibility. That credibility then covers the speaker when he or she begins to disagree with the audience.

A politician telling reporters about union negotiations often uses this strategy. The politician points out that he or she also desires a higher standard of living for sanitation workers; that union members certainly deserve higher wages and more benefits for their hard work; and, finally, that he (or she) and the union leaders merely disagree on a few "minor" points, such as whether the wage increase shall be five cents or five dollars. This sort of strategy is used to persuade the public that the politician is a warmhearted fellow. However, at the actual negotiating table, one is often expected to exaggerate disagreements at the outset and then gracefully concede points one by one, as if giving up something. In such cases, however, both sides understand the implied rules of the game. The general public is not likely to be so sophisticated.

STATING YOUR CONCLUSIONS

Research shows that most audiences respond favorably to clearly stated conclusions that call for a specific course of action. A speaker who makes an explicit conclusion creates more attitude change than one who lets the audience deduce the beliefs or actions he or she favors.[24] There are some experts who say that listeners will have more lasting change of attitude if they "participate" in the communication by drawing their own conclusions. But this method is risky, for there is no assurance that the listener will arrive at the conclusion the communicator desires. Thus, in persuasive communication situations, it is always wise for the speaker to state his or her conclusions clearly and specifically.

Some Concluding Comments

In this chapter, we have considered several issues that are important to the communicator who wishes to structure effective persuasive messages. We have tried to review available research conscientiously and select the research that was carefully executed and appeared to provide valid results. We must end this with a few words of caution. The suggestions we have put forth may not work in any given situation. There may be other variables present, or we may simply not know enough to consider all of the persuasive strategies. The mark of any successful communicator is adaptation. It is our hope that you will consider and test the general suggestions we have offered from our understanding of the research; you might truly be surprised about how effective some of them can be in increasing your persuasive ability.

[23]A. R. Cohen, *Attitude Change and Social Influence* (New York: Basic Books, 1964), p. 12.

[24]G. Cronkhite, *Persuasion: Speech and Behavioral Change* (Indianapolis: Bobbs-Merrill, 1969), pp. 194–195.

SUMMARY

1. A persuasive message presents an idea or course of action that the source advocates and suggests reasons why the receiver should agree to it. Most persuasive messages are composed of three parts: claim, warrant, and data. A claim is an explicit or implicit statement that the communicator wants the receiver to accept. A warrant is a general belief stated in support of a claim. Data are specific beliefs stated in support of a claim.

2. Evidence is third-order data from a person outside the communication situation. Evidence seems to have little effect on the persuasiveness of a high credibility source, but it may increase the persuasiveness of a low credibility source if the audience was previously unaware of the data. When in doubt, a speaker should use evidence.

3. A fear appeal is a message that says to the listener that harm will befall him (or her) or someone he (or she) cares about unless he (or she) adopts the claim. The credibility of the source can influence the audience's reaction to a fear appeal. A highly credible source is more persuasive when he or she uses a strong fear appeal, whereas a less credible source does better with a moderate fear appeal. Strong fear appeals seem very effective when they threaten harm to someone important to the listener. They are most effective when used with evidence. Receivers who hear fear appeals without evidence tend to return quickly to their original beliefs. A communicator must use caution not to frighten his or her audience too much, for this may lead them to reject the threat as absurd or too unbearable to think about.

4. Research, though scant, has demonstrated that humor does not significantly increase or decrease the persuasiveness of a message. However, humor may create a sense of rapport between the source and his or her audience. Further research on the effects of humor is still needed.

5. Messages containing highly intense language are not very persuasive when the audience is very involved in the topic under discussion. If a topic is less crucial or unimportant to the receivers, highly intense language can be persuasive. Opinionated language may express rejection of those who disagree with the speaker, or it may praise those who agree with him or her. Highly credible sources can use opinionated rejections quite effectively, whereas less credible sources do better with nonopinionated language.

6. Message discrepancy refers to the distance between the views of a speaker and those of his or her audience. Research indicates that a speaker who makes his or her beliefs sound close to those of the audience will be more persuasive. A source with high credibility will

be able to depart from his or her audience's views without much loss of credibility.

7. Experimental research has provided some generalizations that are helpful when structuring a persuasive message: (a) When presenting a two-sided message, the speaker should discuss his or her arguments first. (b) When citing evidence, the speaker should consider the credibility of the source of evidence. If the source of evidence has high credibility, it is best to cite the source and then the evidence. If the source of evidence has low credibility, it is best to cite the evidence and then name the source. (c) A speaker should not forewarn the audience of his or her intent to persuade unless he or she is friendly with its members. (d) Presenting the problem first and then the solution is more persuasive than beginning with the solution and moving on to the problem. (e) A speaker who makes a specific conclusion will be more plausible than one who allows the audience to deduce the beliefs or actions he or she favors.

SUGGESTED READING

Beisecker, Thomas D., and Don W. Parson. "Characteristics of the Message," in *The Process of Social Influence*. Englewood Cliffs, N.J.: Prentice-Hall, 1972, pp. 271–370.

Miller, Gerald R. "Studies on the Use of Fear Appeals: A Summary and Analysis," *Central States Speech Journal*, 14 (1963), pp. 117–125.

Simons, Herbert W. *Persuasion: Understanding, Practice, and Analysis.* Reading, Mass.: Addison-Wesley, 1976, pp. 191–222.

From the Reading	Study Questions
Define the following terms. claim warrant data first-order data second-order data third-order data evidence fear appeal logical and emotional appeals language intensity	1. What are the three components of a persuasive message? How do they work to reinforce each other? 2. What are the difficulties involved in classifying appeals as either logical or emotional? 3. Is the use of evidence always necessary and wise? When is the use of evidence most effective? 4. Fear appeals do not always have the intended impact. How can fear be used as an effective means of persuasion? 5. Humor does not seem to be very effective in producing attitude change. Why do you suppose that is? Does this conform to your notions of the effects of humor?

opinionated rejection
statements
opinionated acceptance
statements
metaphors
qualifiers
two-sided message
message discrepancy
psychological structure

6. There are many situations in which using highly intense or emotional language might not be persuasive. When might it be effective? When might it be ineffective? What considerations should one have in mind when choosing the kinds of persuasive language one might employ?

7. What are the conditions under which you would consider using a two-sided message instead of a one-sided appeal? Why?

8. The following questions should be considered when structuring a persuasive message:

   a. When do you identify the source of evidence?
   b. Do you desire to reveal your intent to persuade to your listener?
   c. Do you present problems or solutions first in your message?
   d. Is it best to begin with points of agreement or disagreement?
   e. What is the best way to state your conclusions?

You should think about how you might answer each of the above questions.

AN EXERCISE TO ANALYZE PERSUASION ATTEMPTS CRITICALLY

The following two speeches are persuasive attempts that were obviously very important to the people who delivered them. As you read these appeals, it might be wise to keep the following questions in mind:

1. What kinds of persuasive appeals are being used in each message? Were the appeals used effectively? Why or why not?
2. What kinds of decisions concerning the structure of persuasive messages did each speaker make? Were they generally effective in structuring the messages?
3. Do the speeches differ in terms of kinds of appeals or kinds of structure?
4. How can the theories of persuasion discussed in the preceding chapter be applied to these persuasive attempts? For example, is there an attempt to create imbalances in receivers if they do not accept what the source is saying? What other kinds of things might the speakers here be manipulating in their audiences? Do the two speakers use different strategies that might be linked to different theories?
5. Which speech did you find most persuasive? List the reasons that you feel might have influenced that decision.

Radio Address of Senator Nixon: Explaining His Use of the Expense Fund

Following is the text of the radio and television address of Senator Nixon from Los Angeles on September 23, 1952:

My fellow Americans:

I come before you tonight as a candidate for the Vice Presidency and as a man whose honesty and integrity has been questioned.

Now, the usual political thing to do when charges are made against you is to either ignore them or to deny them without giving details. I believe we have had enough of that in the United States, particularly with the present Administration in Washington, D.C.

To me the office of the Vice Presidency of the United States is a great office, and I feel that the people have got to have confidence in the integrity of the men who run for that office and who might attain them.

I have a theory, too, that the best and only answer to a smear or to an honest misunderstanding of the facts is to tell the truth. And that is why I am here tonight. I want to tell you my side of the case.

I am sure that you have read the charge, and you have heard it, that I, Senator Nixon, took $18,000 from a group of my supporters.

Now, was that wrong? And let me say that it was wrong. I am saying it, incidentally, that it was wrong, not just illegal, because it isn't a question of whether it was legal or illegal, that isn't enough. The question is, was it morally wrong. I say that it was morally wrong, if any of that $18,000 went to Senator Nixon, for my personal use. I say that it was morally wrong if it was secretly given and secretly handled.

And I say that it was morally wrong if any of the contributors got special favors for the contributions that they made.

And now to answer those questions let me say this: not one cent of the $18,000 or any other money of that type ever went to me for my personal use. Every penny of it was used to pay for political expenses that I did not think should be charged to the taxpayers of the United States.

It was not a secret fund. As a matter of fact, when I was on "Meet the Press"—some of you may have seen it last Sunday—Peter Edson came up to me, after the program, and he said, "Dick, what about this fund we hear about?" and I said, "Well, there is no secret about it. Go out and see Dana Smith, who was the administrator of the fund," and I gave him his address. And I said you will find that the purpose of the fund simply was to defray political expenses that I did not feel should be charged to the Government.

And third, let me point out, and I want to make this particularly clear, that no contributor to this fund, no contributor to any of my campaigns, has ever received any consideration that he would not have received as an ordinary constituent.

I don't believe in that, and I can say that never, while I have been in the Senate of the United States, as far as the people that contributed to this fund are concerned, have I made a telephone call for them to an agency, nor have I gone down to an agency in their behalf.

And the records will show that, the records which are in the hands of the Administration.

Well, then, some of you will say, and rightly, "Well, what did you use the fund for, Senator? Why did you have to have it?"

Let me tell you in just a word how a Senate office operates. First of all, the Senator gets $15,000 a year in salary. He gets enough money to pay for one trip a year, a round trip, that is, for himself and his family, between his home and Washington, D.C., and then he gets an allowance to handle the people that work in his office to handle his mail.

And the allowance for my state of California is enough to hire 13 people. And let me say, incidentally, that this allowance is not paid to the Senator.

It is paid directly to the individuals that the Senator puts on his payroll, but all of these people and all these allowances are for strictly official business; business for example, when a constituent writes in and wants you to go down to the Veterans Administration and get some information about his GI policy—items of that type, for example. But there are other expenses which are not covered by the Government. And I think I can best discuss those expenses by asking you some questions.

Do you think that when I or any other Senator makes a political speech, has it printed, should charge the printing of that speech to the taxpayers?

Do you think, for example, when I or any other Senator makes a trip to his home state to make a purely political speech that the cost of that trip should be charged to the taxpayers?

Do you think when a Senator makes political broadcasts or political television broadcasts, radio or television, that the expense of those broadcasts should be charged to the taxpayers?

I know what your answer is; it is the same answer that audiences give me whenever I discuss this particular problem.

The answer is no. The taxpayers should not be required to finance items which are not official business but which are primarily political business.

Well, then the question arises, you say, "Well, how do you pay for these and how can you do it legally?" And there are several ways that it can be done, incidentally, and it is done legally in the United States Senate and in the Congress.

The first way is to be a rich man. I don't happen to be a rich man. So I couldn't use that.

Another way that is used is to put your wife on the pay roll. Let me say, incidentally, that my opponent, my opposite number for the Vice Presidency of the Democratic ticket, does have his wife on his pay roll and has had her on his pay roll for the past 10 years. Now just let me say this: that is his business, and I am not critical of him for doing that. You will have to pass judgment on that particular point, but I have never done that for this reason.

She is a wonderful stenographer. She used to teach stenography and she used to teach shorthand in high school. That was when I met her. And I can tell you folks that she has worked many hours nights and many hours on Saturdays and Sundays in my office, and she has done a fine job, and I am proud to say tonight that in the six years I have been in the House and in the Senate of the United States, Pat Nixon has never been on the Government pay roll.

What are the other ways that these finances can be taken care of? Some who are lawyers, and I happen to be a lawyer, continue to practice law, but I haven't been able to do that.

I am so far away from California and I have been so busy with my senatorial work that I have not engaged in any legal practice and, also, as far as law practice is concerned, it seemed to me that the relationship between an attorney and the client was so personal that you couldn't possibly represent a man as an attorney and then have an unbiased view when he presented his case to you in the event that he had one before the Government.

And so I felt that the best way to handle these necessary political expenses of getting my message to the American people and the speeches I made—the speeches that I had printed for the most part concerned this one message of exposing this Administration, the Communism in it, the corruption in it, the only way that I could do that was to accept the aid which people in my home state of California, who contributed to my campaign, and who continued to make these contributions after I was elected, were glad to make.

And let me say I am proud of the fact that not one of them has ever asked me to vote on a bill other than my own conscience would dictate. And I am proud of the fact that the taxpayers by subterfuge or otherwise, have never paid one dime for expenses which I thought were political and should not be charged to the taxpayers.

Let me say, incidentally, that some of you may say, "Well, that is all right, Senator, that is your explanation, but have you got any proof?" And I would like to tell you this evening that just an hour ago, we received an independent audit of this entire fund. I suggested to Governor Sherman Adams, who is the chief of staff of the Eisenhower campaign, that an independent audit and legal report be obtained, and I have that audit in my hand.

It is an audit made by Price Waterhouse & Co. firm, and the legal opinion by Gibson, Dunn & Crutcher, lawyers in Los Angeles, the biggest law firm, and incidentally, one of the best ones in Los Angeles.

I am proud to report to you tonight that this audit and this legal opinion is being forwarded to General Eisenhower, and I would like to read to you the opinion that was prepared by Gibson, Dunn & Crutcher, based on all the pertinent laws and statutes, together with the audit report prepared by the certified public accountants.

It is our conclusion that Senator Nixon did not obtain any financial gain from the collection and disbursement of the funds by Dana Smith; that Senator Nixon did not violate any federal or state law by reason of the operation of the fund; and that neither the portion of the fund paid by Dana Smith directly to third persons, nor the portion paid to Senator Nixon, to reimburse him for office expenses, constituted income in a sense which was either reportable or taxable as income under income *tax laws*.

(signed)
Gibson, Dunn & Crutcher
by Elmo H. Conley

That is not Nixon speaking, but that is an independent audit which was requested because I want the American people to know all the facts and I am not afraid of having independent people go in and check the facts, and that is exactly what they did.

But then I realized that there are still some who may say, and rightly so, let me say that I recognize that some will continue to smear, regardless of what the truth may be—but that there has been understandably, some honest misunderstanding on this matter, and there are some that will say, "Well, maybe you were able, Senator, to fake this thing. How can we believe what you say—after all, is there a possibility that you got some sums in cash? Is there a possibility that you might have feathered your own nest?" And so now what I am going to do—and incidentally, this is unprecedented in the history of the American politics—I am going at this time to give to this television and radio audience a complete financial history, everything I have earned, everything I have spent, everything I own, and I want you to know the facts.

I will have to start early. I was born in 1913. Our family was one of modest circumstances, and most of my early life was spent in a store, out in East Whittier. It was a grocery store, one of those family enterprises.

The only reason we were able to make it go was because my Mother and Dad had five boys, and we all worked in the store. I worked my way through college, and to a great extent, through law school. And then, in 1940, probably the best thing that ever happened to me happened. I married Pat, who is sitting over here.

We had a rather difficult time, after we were married, like so many of the young couples who might be listening to us. I practiced law. She continued to teach school.

Then, in 1942, I went into the service. Let me say that my service record was not a particularly unusual one. I went to the South Pacific. I guess I'm entitled to a couple of battle stars. I got a couple of letters of recommendation. But I was just there when the bombs were falling. And then I returned. I returned to the United States, and in 1946, I ran for the Congress. When we came out of the war, Pat and I—Pat during the war had worked as a stenographer, and in a bank, and as an economist for a Government agency—and when we came out, the total of our savings, from both my law practice, her teaching, and all the time that I was in the war, the total for that entire period was just a little less than $10,000—every cent of that, incidentally, was in Government bonds—well, that's where we start, when I go into politics.

Now, whatever I earned since I went into politics—well, here it is. I jotted it down. Let me read the note.

First of all, I have had my salary as a Congressman and as a Senator.

Second, I have received a total in this past six years of $1,600 from estates which were in my law firm at the time that I severed my connection with it. And incidentally, as I said before, I have not engaged in any legal practice, and have not accepted any fees from business that came into the firm after I went into politics.

I have made an average of approximately $1,500 a year from nonpolitical speaking engagements and lectures.

And then, fortunately, we have inherited a little money. Pat sold her interest in her father's estate for $3,000, and I inherited $1,500 from my grandfather. We lived rather modestly.

For four years we lived in an apartment in Parkfairfax, Alexandria, Virginia. The rent was $80 a month. And we saved for the time that we could buy a house. Now, that was what we took in.

What did we do with this money? What do we have today to show for it? This will surprise you, because it is so little, I suppose, as standards generally go of people in public life.

First of all, we've got a house in Washington, which cost $41,000 and on which we owe $20,000. We have a house in Whittier, California, which cost $13,000 and on which we owe $3,000. My folks are living there at the present time.

I have just $4,000 in life insurance, plus my GI policy, which I have never been able to convert, and which will run out in two years.

I have no life insurance whatever on Pat. I have life insurance on our two youngsters, Patricia and Julie.

I own a 1950 Oldsmobile car. We have our furniture. We have no stocks and bonds of any type. We have no interest of any kind, direct or indirect, in any business. Now, that is what we have. What do we owe?

Well, in addition to the mortgage, the $20,000 mortgage on the house in Washington, a $10,000 one on the house in Whittier, I owe $4,500 to the Riggs Bank, in Washington, D.C. with interest at four percent. [In his speech, Senator Nixon indicated at one point that the mortgage, the $20,000 mortgage on the house in Whittier was $3,000, at another point that it was $10,000. The latter figure is true, Nixon's secretary James Bassett told reporters later, explaining the discrepancy as "a verbal error."]

I owe $3,500 to my parents, and the interest on that loan, which I pay regularly, because it is a part of the savings they made through the years they were working so hard—I pay regularly 4 percent interest. And then I have a $500 loan, which I have on my life insurance.

Well, that's about it. That's what we have. And that's what we owe. It isn't very much. But Pat and I have the satisfaction that every dime that we have got is honestly ours.

I should say this, that Pat doesn't have a mink coat. But she does have a respectable Republican cloth coat, and I always tell her that she would look good in anything.

One other thing I probably should tell you, because if I don't they will probably be saying that about me, too. We did get something, a gift, after the election.

A man down in Texas heard Pat on the radio mention the fact that our two youngsters would like to have a dog, and believe it or not, the day before we left on this campaign trip we got a message from Union Station in Baltimore, saying they had a package for us. We went down to get it. You know what it was?

It was a little cocker spaniel dog, in a crate that he had sent all the way from Texas, black and white, spotted, and our little girl, Tricia, the six-year-old, named it Checkers.

And you know, the kids, like all kids, loved the dog, and I just want to say this, right now, that regardless of what they say about it, we are going to keep it.

It isn't easy to come before a nation wide audience and bare your life, as I have done, but I want to say some things before I conclude, that I think most of you will agree on.

Mr. Mitchell, the Chairman of the Democratic National Committee, made the statement that if a man couldn't afford to be in the United States Senate, he shouldn't run for the Senate. And I just want to make my position clear.

I don't agree with Mr. Mitchell when he says that only a rich man should serve his Government, in the United States Senate or in the Congress. I don't believe that represents the thinking of the Republican Party.

I believe that it's fine that a man like Governor Stevenson, who inherited a fortune from his father, can run for President. But I also feel that it is essential in this country of ours that a man of modest means can also run for President, because you know—remember Abraham Lincoln— you remember what he said, "God must have loved the common people, he made so many of them."

And now I'm going to suggest some courses of conduct.

First of all, you have read in the papers about other funds, now. Mr. Stevenson apparently had a couple. One of them in which a group of business people paid and helped to supplement the salaries of State employees. Here is where the money went directly into their pockets, and I think that what Mr. Stevenson should do would be to come before the American people, as I have, give the names of the people that contributed to that fund, give the names of the people who put this money into their pockets, at the same time that they were receiving money from their state government and see what favors, if any they gave out for that.

I don't condemn Mr. Stevenson for what he did, but until the facts are in there is a doubt that would be raised. And as far as Mr. Sparkman is concerned, I would suggest the same thing. He's had his wife on the pay roll. I don't condemn him for that, but I think that he should come before the American people and indicate what outside sources of income he has had. I would suggest that they come before the American people, as I have, and make a complete financial statement as to their financial history, and if they don't it will be an admission that they have something to hide.

And I think you will agree with me, because folks, remember, a man that's to be President of the United States, must have the confidence of all the people. And that's why I'm doing what I'm doing, and that is why I suggest that Mr. Stevenson and Mr. Sparkman, if they are under attack, that should be what they are doing.

Now let me say this: I know that this is not the last of the smears. In spite of my explanation tonight, other smears will be made. Others have been made in the past. And the purpose of the smears, I know, is this, to silence me, to make me let up.

Well, they just don't know who they are dealing with. I'm going to tell you this: I remember, in the dark days of the Hiss trial, some of the same columnists, some of the same radio commentators who are attacking me now and misrepresenting my position, were violently opposing me at the time I was after Alger Hiss. But I continue to fight, because I knew I was right, and I can say to this great television and radio audience that I have no apologies to the American people for my part in putting Alger Hiss where he is today. And as far as this is concerned, I intend to continue to fight.

Why do I feel so deeply? Why do I feel that in spite of the smears, the misunderstanding, the necessity for a man to come up here and bare his soul, as I have, why is it necessary for me to continue this fight? And I want to tell you why.

Because you see, I love my country. And I think my country is in danger. And I think the only man that can save America at this time is the man that's running for President, on my ticket, Dwight Eisenhower.

You say, why do I think it is in danger? And I say, look at the record. Seven years of the Truman-Acheson Administration, and what's happened? Six hundred million people lost to the Communists.

And a war in Korea in which we have lost 117,000 American casualties, and I say to all of you that a policy that results in a loss of 600,000,000 people to the Communists and a war which costs us 117,000 American casualties isn't good enough for America, and I say that those in the State Department that made the mistakes which caused that war and which resulted in those losses should be kicked out of the State Department just as fast as we can get them out of there.

And let me say that I know Mr. Stevenson won't do that, because he defends the Truman policy, and I know that Dwight Eisenhower will do that and that he will give America the Leadership that it needs.

Take the problem of corruption. You have read about the mess in Washington. Mr. Stevenson can't clean it up because he was picked by the man, Truman, under whose Administration the mess was made.

You wouldn't trust the man who made the mess to clean it up. That is Truman. And, by the same token you can't trust the man who was picked by the man who made the mess to clean it up, and this is Stevenson. And so I say, Eisenhower, who owes nothing to Truman, nothing to the big-city bosses—he is the man who can clean up the mess in Washington.

Take Communism. I say that as far as the subject is concerned the danger is great to America. In the Hiss case they got the secrets which enabled them to break the American secret State Department code.

They got secrets in the Atomic bomb case which enabled them to get the secret of the atomic bomb five years before they would have gotten it by their own devices. And I say that any man who called the Alger Hiss case a red herring isn't fit to be President of the United States.

I say that a man who, like Mr. Stevenson, has pooh-poohed and ridiculed the Communist threat in the United States—he said that they are phantoms among ourselves—he has accused us, that have attempted to expose the Communists, of looking for Communists in the Bureau of Fisheries and Wildlife. I say that a man who says that isn't qualified to be President of the United States.

And I say that the only man who can lead us into this fight to rid the Government of both those who are Communists and those who have corrupted this Government is Eisenhower, because General Eisenhower, you can be sure, recognizes the problem and knows how to handle it.

Let me say this, finally. This evening I want to read to you just briefly excerpts from a letter that I received, a letter which after all this is over, no one can take away from us. It reads as follows:

Dear Senator Nixon:

Since I am only 19 years of age, I can't vote in the presidential election, but believe me if I could you and General Eisenhower would certainly get my vote. My husband is in the Fleet Marines, in Korea. He is in the front lines. And we have a 2-months-old son he has never seen. And I feel confident that with great Americans like you and General Eisenhower in the White House, lonely Americans like myself will be united with their loved ones now in Korea. I only pray to God that you won't be too late. Enclosed is a small check to help you in your campaign. Living on $85 a month, it is all I can afford at present, but let me know what else I can do.

Folks, it is a check for $10, and it is one that I shall never cash. And just let me say this: We hear a lot about prosperity these days, but I say why can't we have prosperity built on peace, rather than a prosperity built on war? Why can't we have prosperity and an honest Government in Washington, D.C., at the same time?

But the decision, my friends, is not mine. I would do nothing that would harm the possibilities of Dwight Eisenhower to become President of the United States. And for that reason I am submitting to the Republican National Committee tonight through this television broadcast the decision which it is theirs to make. Let them decide whether my position on the ticket will help or hurt. And I am going to ask you to help them decide. Wire and write the Republican National Committee whether you think I should stay on or whether I should get off. And whatever their decision is, I will abide by it.

But just let me say this last word. Regardless of what happens, I am going to continue this fight. I am going to campaign up and down America until we drive the crooks and the Communists and those that defend them out of Washington, and remember, folks, Eisenhower is a great man. Folks, he is a great man, and a vote for Eisenhower is a vote for what is good for America.

Kennedy's Television Statement to the People of Massachusetts

Following is the text of a televised statement from the home of Joseph P. Kennedy by Senator Edward M. Kennedy, as recorded by *The New York Times*, July 26, 1969:*

My fellow citizens:

I have requested this opportunity to talk to the people of Massachusetts about the tragedy which happened last Friday evening.

This morning I entered a plea of guilty to the charge of leaving the scene of an accident. Prior to my appearance in court, it would have been improper for me to comment on these matters.

But tonight I am free to tell you what happened and to say what it means to me.

*© 1969 by The New York Times Company. Reprinted by permission.

On the weekend of July 18, I was on Martha's Vineyard Island participating with my nephew, Joe Kennedy—as for 30 years my family has participated—in the annual Edgartown Sailing Regatta.

Only reasons of health prevented my wife from accompanying me.

On Chappaquiddick Island, off Martha's Vineyard, I attended on Friday evening, July 18, a cook-out I had encouraged and helped sponsor for a devoted group of Kennedy campaign secretaries.

When I left the party, around 11:15 P.M., I was accompanied by one of these girls, Miss Mary Jo Kopechne. Mary Jo was one of the most devoted members of the staff of Senator Robert Kennedy. She worked for him for four years and was broken up over his death. For this reason, and because she was such a gentle, kind and idealistic person, all of us tried to help her feel that she still had a home with the Kennedy family.

There is no truth, no truth whatever, to the widely circulated suspicions of immoral conduct that have been leveled at my behavior and hers regarding that evening. There has never been a private relationship between us of any kind.

I know of nothing in Mary Jo's conduct on that or any other occasion, the same is true of the other girls at that party, that would lend any substance to such ugly speculation about their character.

Nor was I driving under the influence of liquor.

Little over one mile away, the car that I was driving on an unlit road went off a narrow bridge which had no guard rails and was built on a left angle to the road.

The car overturned in a deep pond and immediately filled with water. I remember thinking as the cold water rushed in around my head that I was for certain drowning.

Then water entered my lungs and I actually felt the sensation of drowning. But somehow I struggled to the surface alive. I made immediate and repeated efforts to save Mary Jo by diving into the strong and murky current but succeeded only in increasing my state of utter exhaustion and alarm.

My conduct and conversations during the next several hours to the extent that I can remember them make no sense to me at all.

Although my doctors informed me that I suffered a cerebral concussion as well as shock, I do not seek to escape responsibility for my actions by placing the blame either in the physical, emotional trauma brought on by the accident or on anyone else.

I regard as indefensible the fact that I did not report the accident to the police immediately.

Instead of looking directly for a telephone after lying exhausted in the grass for an undetermined time, I walked back to the cottage where the party was being held and requested the help of two friends, my cousin, Joseph Gargan, and Phil Markham, and directed them to return immediately to the scene with me—this was some time after midnight—in order to undertake a new effort to dive down and locate Miss Kopechne.

Their strenuous efforts, undertaken at some risk to their own lives, also proved futile.

All kinds of scrambled thoughts—all of them confused, some of them irrational, many of them which I cannot recall—and some of which I would not have seriously entertained under normal circumstances—went through my mind during this period.

They were reflected in the various inexplicable, inconsistent and inconclusive things I said and did, including such questions as whether the girl might still be alive somewhere out of that immediate area, whether some awful curse did actually hang over all the Kennedys, whether there was some justifiable reason for me to doubt what had happened and to delay my report, whether somehow the awful weight of this incredible incident might in some way pass from my shoulders.

I was overcome, I'm frank to say, by a jumble of emotions, grief, fear, doubt, exhaustion, panic, confusion and shock.

Instructing Gargan and Markham not to alarm Mary Jo's friends that night, I had them take me to the ferry crossing. The ferry having shut down for the night I suddenly jumped into the water and impulsively swam across, nearly drowning once again in the effort, and returned to my hotel about 2 A.M. and collapsed in my room.

I remember going out at one point and saying something to the room clerk.

In the morning, with my mind somewhat more lucid, I made an effort to call a family legal adviser, Burke Marshall, from a public telephone on the Chappaquiddick side of the ferry and belatedly reported the accident to the Martha's Vineyard police.

Today, as I mentioned, I felt morally obligated to plead guilty to the charge of leaving the scene of an accident. No words on my part can possibly express the terrible pain and suffering I feel over this tragic incident.

This last week has been an agonizing one for me and the members of my family, and the grief we feel over the loss of a wonderful friend will remain with us the rest of our lives.

These events, the publicity, innuendo and whispers which have surrounded them and my admission of guilt this morning—raises the question in my mind of whether my standing among the people of my state has been so impaired that I should resign my seat in the United States Senate.

If at any time the citizens of Massachusetts should lack confidence in their Senator's character or his ability, with or without justification, he could not in my opinion adequately perform his duty and should not continue in office.

The people of this state, the state which sent John Quincy Adams and Daniel Webster and Charles Summer and Henry Cabot Lodge and John Kennedy to the United States Senate, are entitled to representation in that body by men who inspire their utmost confidence.

For this reason, I would understand full well why some might think it right for me to resign. For me this will be a difficult decision to make.

It has been seven years since my first election the Senate. You and I share many memories— some of them have been glorious, some have been very sad. The opportunity to work with you and serve Massachusetts has made my life worthwhile.

And so I ask you tonight, the people of Massachusetts, to think this through with me. In facing this decision, I seek your advice and opinion. In making it, I seek your prayers. For this is a decision that I will have finally to make on my own.

It has been written a man does what he must in spite of personal consequences, in spite of obstacles and dangers and pressures, and that is the basis of all human morality.

Whatever may be the sacrifices he faces, if he follows his conscience—the loss of his friends, his fortune, his contentment, even the esteem of his fellow man—each man must decide for himself the course he will follow.

The stories of the past courage cannot supply courage itself. For this, each man must look into his own soul.

I pray that I can have the courage to make the right decision. Whatever is decided and whatever the future holds for me, I hope that I shall have, be able to put this most recent tragedy behind me and make some further contribution to our state and mankind, whether it be in public or private life.

Thank you and good night.

AN EXERCISE DESIGNED TO APPLY SOME OF THE THEORIES OF PERSUASION

As a class, decide on some issue that is of interest to you. Try to choose an issue allowing you to design a campaign to persuade people. It is important that all of you agree on what it is you want to persuade people about. Now, in smaller groups, attack the problem from different theoretical perspectives. One group can attack the problem from the point of view of balance theory; another group can choose to apply principles from learning theory. The other models we have discussed can be the focus of attention of other groups in the class.

Have each group present their persuasive attempt to the entire class. The following questions should be considered:

1. How did the theoretical perspective that people were operating from affect the kinds of persuasive messages they created?
2. Did each group truly represent the theoretical position they were assigned? Did people include things that should not work according to the model?
3. How were the overall strategies different? How were they the same?
4. Do you have any insights into which strategy was the most useful? Might different situations, topics, and so on, make the different strategies more or less useful?

AN EXERCISE DESIGNED TO ANALYZE PERSUASIVE STRATEGIES IN ADVERTISEMENTS

1. For one evening, keep a log of the kinds of commercials that are shown on television. Try to select commercials from both the major networks and from local suppliers:
   a. What kinds of appeals are being used? How effective do you think they are?
   b. What are the major differences between commercials that you think are effective and those you perceive not to be effective?
   c. What important message variables seem to be used most often in commercials?
2. What manipulative strategy might be used when a company asks people to "write in 25 words or less why you like our product." What might the purpose of such a campaign be. What theory or theories might explain why people would be more favorable toward the product after participating in such a contest? What other kinds of "hidden" persuasive strategies do you think go on in persuasive advertising?

AN EXERCISE TO ASSIST IN STRUCTURING PERSUASIVE MESSAGES

1. Select a persuasive argument that you have recently been exposed to. Can you identify the claim, warrant, and data?

2. On a topic that you feel strongly about, write a claim; then support it with warrants. Now find three different *types* of evidence to support the claim.
3. On the same issue, design a persuasive message that you think would be effective with a one-sided presentation. Now construct a two-sided message. What considerations would you use in selecting which message to present?

Chapter 13
COMMUNICATION AND THE DEVELOPMENT OF SOCIAL RELATIONSHIPS

In the previous two chapters, we have been concerned with how people communicate to influence others and bring about changes in attitudes and/or behaviors. We have been primarily concerned with how the *content* of communication can be structured and manipulated to insure that the outcome of the communication transaction is increased compliance on the part of the receiver. The focus of this chapter is somewhat different in that we are concerned with what others have labeled *relational communication*. People communicate their feelings about other people and about the communication that is occurring by many methods. Earlier we discussed the use of nonverbal communication as a system of meta-messages about what was going on in the verbal band *and* as relational communication expressing feelings about the other people involved in the communication transaction. This chapter is an attempt to investigate systematically the reasons *why* people communicate on relational levels and *how* people go about establishing social relationships and also to discuss the possible positive outcomes of communication that are effective in establishing satisfactory relationships with others.

It is probably wise to begin such a chapter by explicitly outlining some of our assumptions about this process. First, we do not believe that there really is a true dichotomy between relational communication and content communication. It is inconceivable to us that any message could be just content or just relational. Although some of our communication is more content-oriented than that of others in that we are trying simply to transmit information or convince people of the validity of our position, we still include a great number of relational cues that indicate both how we feel about our intended receivers and about the messages we are producing. The second assumption that others make that we cannot accept is that relational communication occurs in dyads but rarely occurs in any other context. Whether in the interpersonal context or in front of a functioning television camera, we are providing relational data that others will put to use. Obviously, in many interpersonal situations, we are putting much of our effort into establishing and maintaining effective relationships. We spend a great deal of our time and energy expressing feelings and sharing with others in the interpersonal arena. However, the use of communication to develop social relationships is not limited to this context; it is an important function of communication that occurs whatever the context.

We do assume that people have a need to affiliate with other people and that they desire to communicate with other people in such a way as to express their feelings toward them appropriately. There are probably several different reasons that could be advanced as to why people possess this need to affiliate, which we will discuss in detail later in this chapter. We also assume that much relational communication is done so that others may come to see us as we see ourselves or as we would like ourselves to be seen. We also believe that most people desire to be liked by other people. Communication that promotes such feelings is gratifying, and most people desire to understand better the process that leads to effective relational communication. Our last assumption is consistent with the general thrust

of this textbook. Just as people can employ strategies to produce change, make effective decisions, create better public speeches, or use the available mass media for a variety of purposes, they can also strategically use their own communication behavior to promote more effective social relationships with others.

In the next section, we discuss some of the important variables that are known to affect both how people relate to each other and the kinds of communication that will occur between them. When some of these important variables are present in any communication transaction, the probability of developing effective social relationships is markedly increased.

Factors That Promote the Establishment of Social Relationships

Liking and disliking are among the most basic factors in determining whether people will even communicate with each other and if they do communicate, what the outcomes of that interaction will be. People associate with others on the basis of those feelings, and though there is no doubt that these feelings affect communication patterns, it has been widely believed that such feelings are fundamentally irrational. Indeed, they often seem that way, as in the case of two friends who seem to have nothing in common but the fact that they "feel good" around each other.

However, people have developed methods to measure interpersonal attraction, and it is more patterned than one might first suppose. The sociometric test is one such way to test interpersonal attraction. It was devised to determine the preferences of group members for other people in the group by establishing procedures for indicating amount of liking for others. Moreover, this method allows criteria for choices of "most liked" people to be established. For example, in a company, each worker might be asked to choose people with whom he or she might like to work on a project. These choices might be unlimited in number, or the worker might be asked to pick the first three choices in order of preference, or the entire work group might be ranked from most desired to least acceptable. The criterion of preference might vary; the worker may be told to make his or her selection on the basis of work ability, which is called *task attraction;* simple *social attraction; physical attraction;* or any other basis. When the data are analyzed, one gets information about the individuals most frequently chosen and those not chosen at all, and one also gets a picture of patterns of attraction in the group. If everyone picks the same person as a first choice, it obviously indicates that this person is a key member of the group and is attractive to the others for some reason. Likewise, four or five people may all choose each other, indicating that they belong to a mutually attractive subgroup or clique.

There are other available means for the measurement of interpersonal attraction. For example, nonverbal researchers have found that eye contact, changes in the size of the pupil in the eye, and the distance between two standing persons have all been used to measure interpersonal attraction. These attempts to measure attraction have provided valuable evidence that we are attracted to people in some understandable and systematic way; liking is not *just* an irrational, affective response. However, our concern is broader than just assessing attraction when it occurs. We want to understand why people find some people attractive and, therefore, desire to continue to communicate with them and yet find other people not worth the effort communication requires. With that goal in mind, we turn our attention to some of the variables involved in the interpersonal attraction process.

REWARDS AS A DETERMINANT OF ATTRACTION

As we suggested in an earlier chapter, traditional learning theory suggests that proper applications of rewards can produce many kinds of changed behavior. It is probably obvious to all that persons generally do like others who provide rewards and come to dislike people who provide punishment and/or withhold desired rewards. These rewards can range from material inducements to social approval, but we are likely to continue communication with those people who generally provide some reward for us. However, there is much more to the relationship between reward and attraction than the commonsense notions just discussed might suggest.

To be the recipient of increased liking *or* disliking, a person need not be the one who is giving the rewards to other people. There is evidence to suggest that merely being present when a reward is provided to another person is sufficient to prompt the receiver of the reward to be more favorable toward you.[1] On the other hand, your mere presence when someone is being punished or having rewards withheld may be enough to trigger a lowering in liking for you by the person being punished. In a piece of research that cleverly tested the above assumptions, children were placed in a situation in which they were asked to play a board game independently of others in the room. If a child safely landed a rocket ship in the game, a reward was given to that child. The other children had nothing to do with the success or failure of the player, and they were not involved in providing the reward. Children who succeeded liked the other two children more than did children who failed. It is probably safe to assume that many of us have been in situations in which we generally liked people who were present in a rewarding situation even though they personally had nothing to do with making the situation more rewarding. Probably more important to this discussion of interpersonal attraction, we have likely had people respond in a liking or disliking manner to us simply because they were receiving rewards or punishments at the time. The major point is that although we can reward people and increase their liking for us or punish them and diminish their positive regard, we will also find ourselves in situations in which our attractiveness to other people will be determined by the reward and/or coercive power of others who are in control of the situation.

There may be other situational factors not associated with other people directly rewarding people with whom we would desire to develop a sensing of liking. For example, variables such as people's personal comfort can lead them to *judgments about us even if we have absolutely nothing to do with their levels of comfort.* People placed in an uncomfortably hot room rated strangers in a much more negative way than did people who were placed in a comfortably cool room.[2] Furthermore, people who perceive their discomfort to be the greatest are the most likely to rate people as unattractive.

There are factors apart from physical variables that are likely to mediate feelings of attraction. People who watch actors play positive, enthusiastic roles are more likely to rate themselves as feeling better and rate the actor as more attractive than people who watched the same actor play hostile or anxious roles. Related to these kinds of judgments is the fact that moods can be induced that alter people's perceptions of other people's attractiveness. In an interesting investigation, people were asked to watch either a movie that was funny and meant to produce positive feelings or a movie that was sad and produced depression. Following the movie, people were asked to rate a person on attractiveness and, as expected, those people who watched the movie that produced positive feelings rated the individual as more attractive.[3] In addition to positive mood states increasing the perceived

[1] B. E. Lott and A. J. Lott, "The Formation of Positive Attitudes Toward Group Members," *Journal of Abnormal and Social Psychology,* 61 (1960), pp. 297 –300.

[2] W. Griffitt and R. Veitch, "Hot and Crowded: Influence of Population Density and Temperature on Interpersonal Affective Behavior," *Journal of Personality and Social Psychology,* 17 (1971), pp. 92–98.

[3] C. Gouaux, "Induced Affective States and Interpersonal Attraction," *Journal of Personality and Social Psychology,* 20 (1971), pp. 37–43.

attractiveness of another person, they may also lessen an individual's initial negative impression toward a person. In other words, changes in moods can work to make unattractive people appear more attractive. People witnessed a person deliver an insult to others or else were themselves insulted by this person. After this insult was delivered, half of the people looked at some humorous cartoons, whereas the others did not. Those people who had been induced to change their moods by the use of humor rated the initially unattractive source as more attractive than did people who had not received the humorous intervention.[4] A hostile encounter had been altered by humor, and we have witnessed many people who play this role of tension reliever via humor very well in communication transactions.

Any event that arouses negative feelings, even if they are temporary in nature, can affect the perceived attractiveness of others present in the situation. We know of tyrants who have slain the bearers of bad news. Other kinds of evidence indicate that people are reluctant to pass on bad news because they fear that they will be disliked for doing so.[5] All of these situations point to the complexity of the relationship between rewards and liking.

We would like to suggest that it is possible to get a spiral of attraction started that can move people's perception of the attractiveness of others up or down. People who facilitate others and provide rewards

are liked; conversely, people who frustrate or block other people's goal attainment or punish them are disliked. Liking tends to produce an exception of rewards from those we like, which, in turn, encourages more frequent communication. If the rewards continue to come, the continued growth of the relationship is likely. The spiral of attraction is a positive one. If we interact with a friend and find that communication rewarding, we will probably be inclined to communicate even more with that friend; and if the more frequent communication remains positive, we will undoubtedly increase our liking for that person. As the communication with the person becomes more frequent, more expectations are developed concerning the rewarding behavior of the person. When we expect a person to deliver a certain level of reward and that level is exceeded, we increase our attraction to that person. However, if that person does not meet our expected level of reward, we can decrease our liking for him or her *even though his or her behavior could be viewed as generally rewarding.*

This level of expectancy can pose serious problems in relationship. If we expect a great deal from our friends, we can find ourselves becoming distressed when they do not provide rewards that meet those expectations. However, if their perceptions suggest that they are being rewarding, they will undoubtedly not understand how we could be upset with them. To the extent that we do not reward people *at their level of expectations,* we can expect their attraction toward us to decrease and the spiral of attraction to be negative rather than positive. It is also probably true that the closer our relationship be-

[4]D. Landy and D. Mettee, "Evaluation of an Aggressor as a Function of Exposure to Cartoon Humor," *Journal of Personality and Social Psychology,* 12 (1969), pp. 66–71.

[5]S. Rosen and A. Tesser, "On Reluctance to Communicate Undesirable Information: The MUM Effect," *Sociometry,* 33 (1970), pp. 253–263.

comes with another person, the more we expect of them. Even though we can be giving out great amounts of reward and reinforcement, it still might not be perceived as enough; obviously, in this case, a renegotiation of the relationship is in order if it is to survive.

SIMILARITY AND ATTRACTION

Although it may be true in the world of physics that opposites attract, it is generally not the case when it comes to people in social relationships. Aristotle long ago suggested that we choose those people as friends "who have come to regard the same things as good and the same things as evil."[6] There is contemporary research that clearly supports this conception of the role of similarity and attraction. Students transferring to the University of Michigan as sophomores or juniors were offered free housing for a term in exchange for their participation in filling out research questionnaires for a few hours each week. As the students came from a diverse geographical area, it was highly unlikely that any were acquainted with each other prior to the study. The initial questionnaires asked attitudes items about a variety of issues, about their fellow roommates, and about themselves. The male participants were then assigned to specific rooms; some men were assigned similar roommates whereas others were given very dissimilar partners. Over the course of the semester, the development of friendships among the participants was carefully observed.

As expected, the participants' percep-

tions of other people's attitudes, beliefs, and values tended to become more accurate over time. Because they had the opportunity to communicate on a variety of issues, it is not surprising that they could more accurately discuss the other people. In the first part of the term, the men were most attracted to their roommates or to people who lived very close to their rooms. However, these initially formed friendships did not prove to be very stable relationships. Similarity became the best predictor of who would become friends with whom. The men tended to choose as their friends those people who shared their religious views, political beliefs, class background, and so on.[7] In this and other research there has been a great deal of evidence to support the notion that attraction is in some large part based on similarity.

There are some other findings that are interesting in terms of how people perceive the similarity of others whom they find attractive. Although we have said that people become more accurate as a result of communicating with people over time, we did not say that they become totally accurate. In fact, when people are attracted to another person, there is a common perceptual distortion that occurs. People regularly judge people whom they find attractive to be more similar in attitudes and values than they actually are. In other words, we tend to judge our friends as more like us than they really are. This same tendency to overestimate the similarity of attitudes and values exists among married couples. In an interesting study of married couples, it was also found that the greater the satisfaction with the marriage,

[6]R. McKeon, ed., *Introduction to Aristotle* (New York: The Modern Library, 1947), p. 103.

[7]T. M. Newcomb, *The Acquaintance Process* (New York: Holt, Rinehart and Winston, 1961).

the greater the perceived similarity by the partners.[8]

What all of this says is that similarity can be a potent predictor of who forms satisfactory social relationships with whom. Obviously, we have more to communicate about with people who are similar to us, and as the theories discussed in Chapter 11 suggest, we tend to like people who share our attitudes, or we are in a state of inconsistency that motivates us to change attitudes and/or liking of the person. Moreover, as a result of communicating with people, we tend to become more accurate across a number of issues in judging whether they are similar or dissimilar. However, when we do become more and more attracted to someone, we judge them to be similar to us even though they may not be. In line with this, the more attractive we perceive someone to be, the more similar we also assume he or she are. It is also probably true that we tend to exaggerate differences between ourselves and those people whom we find unattractive for whatever reason. Once again we have identified a spiral effect for attraction. The more similar I perceive you to be, the more likely that I will also find you attractive; the more attractive I find you, the more similar I will perceive you to be.

PROXIMITY AND ATTRACTION

One obvious, though easily overlooked, variable that determines attraction is proximity, or nearness. Clearly, it is difficult to like someone unless you know him or her, and it is difficult to know a person with whom you do not have contact. It follows, then, that the more contact you have with a person, the more opportunity you have to develop liking, and there are good reasons to believe the greater the probability that you will actually grow to like the person. In the first edition of this book, we said that proximity had been called "the almost sufficient condition" for attraction. We also, at least implicitly, indicated agreement with that statement. Well, we have learned something in the past several years and would say at this time that though proximity is an important determinant of liking, it can also be an important agent in promoting disliking. It is obviously important in the formation of attraction.

There is a multitude of research studies to support the notion that people who are close to each other in geographical distance are more likely to become friends *or* enemies. Reinforcement theory would suggest that people who are in close proximity to each other communicate more with one another and, therefore, have more opportunity to reward or punish each other. Thus, we would expect people who communicate more to develop more intense friendships or hatreds. Another perspective predicts more positive outcomes of increased communication. Given the assumption that people are more comfortable with people who are more predictable, we can assume that the more we communicate with people, the more predictable they become to us, and, therefore, we find them more attractive because of that feeling of comfort. We shall first look at the positive effects of proximity on attraction.

Several studies have suggested that there is indeed a direct relationship be-

[8]G. Levinger and J. Breedlove, "Interpersonal Attraction and Agreement: A Study of Marriage Partners," *Journal of Personality and Social Psychology*, 3 (1966), pp. 367–372.

tween proximity and attraction. For example, students who lived together in the same residence halls or apartment buildings or who sat next to each other in classrooms tended to develop stronger friendships than with students from whom they were separated by even small distances.[9] Clerks in a department store reported being more friendly toward people who happened to work next to them than toward others who worked only several feet away.[10] There is also evidence to suggest that physical proximity is an important determinant of mate selection.[11]

In line with these findings were the results of studies of married couples living in apartment buildings in a new housing project. Friendships were found to increase in proportion to the degree of geographical proximity; couples who were next-door neighbors developed friendships with much greater frequency than did people who were separated by one or more apartments. Even more interesting in our opinion was the effect of architectural design. For example, those couples who inhabited the few apartments facing the street reported half as many friends in the apartment complex as those people residing in apartments that faced the courtyard.[12] Less prominent architectural features such as the position of stairways and mailboxes also had an effect on friendship formation; if residents lived near the stairways—and thus the major flow of traffic through the apartment complex—or if their mailboxes were clustered with those of other residents, they generally developed a greater number of friendships. It is both a bit frightening and surprising to note how the interaction patterns of people can be virtually planned by such decisions.

This can be explained by the spiral of attraction associated with communication and reward that we discussed earlier. People who are in close proximity have more opportunities to interact and more opportunity to reward others. We continue to interact with the people who reward and avoid the people who punish us *if we can*. However, sometimes people continue to interact with others who frequently punish them only because the alternative is to associate with people who punish them even more. There are many situations such as work and living arrangements in which people have no choice but to interact with people who are in close proximity.

It is usually the case that, when people are forced to be in close proximity to others, ways are found to work out amicable relationships; it is certainly in the best interest of everyone concerned. Even when there are important racial, religious, or value differences among people, overcoming of prejudices can be accomplished when proximity makes it clear that it is

[9]L. Festinger, "Group Attraction and Membership" in *Group Dynamics: Research and Theory*, ed. D. Cartwright and A. Zander (Evanston, Ill.: Row, Peterson, 1952); D. Byrne, "The Influence of Propinquity and Opportunities for Interaction on Classroom Relationships," *Human Relations*, 14 (1961), pp. 63–70.

[10]J. T. Gullahorn, "Distance and Friendship as Factors in the Gross Interaction Matrix," *Sociometry*, 15 (1952), pp. 123–134.

[11]A. M. Katz and R. Hill, "Residential Propinquity and Marital Selection: A Review of Theory, Method, and Fact," *Marriage and Family Living*, 20 (1958), pp. 27–35.

[12]L. Festinger, S. Schacter, and K. Buck, *Social Pressure in Informal Groups: A Study of Human Factors in Housing* (New York: Harper, 1950).

COMMENTS ON THE FUNCTIONS OF HUMAN COMMUNICATION

Even when there are racial, religious, or value differences among people, the overcoming of prejudices can be accomplished when proximity makes it clear that it is desirable for all involved to have satisfactory social relationships. (Photograph: Michael Weisbrot)

desirable for all involved to have satisfactory social relationships. For example, people showed less prejudice toward people of different races when they lived in integrated housing, worked together, studied together, or had been forced to interact in a variety of ways. The implications of these findings are apparent and important. Prejudice, a totally unsatisfactory social relationship, is maintained when there is no opportunity for people to share rewards and/or punishments. One way to overcome such maladaptive responses seems to be to provide more possibilities for communication.

In addition to our general preference to be optimistic about the nature of the human being, there are also good reasons to suggest that familiarity is more likely to promote affinity rather than hatred. If an individual is optimistic about the possibility of other people providing rewards, there is more likelihood that the people will also respond in a positive manner. It probably serves no purpose to assume that other people will respond negatively, for there is the danger of that feeling promoting a self-fulfilling prophecy. As the spouse of the first author often reminds him, much more can be gotten with sugar than with vinegar.

There is evidence that there is a direct relationship between familiarity and liking. People who had interacted with other members in a group several times showed more liking for the other members than did people who had communicated only a few times. It seems that mere exposure to other people can produce more positive feelings of liking. At times even though the encounters were not toally rewarding, people still tended to like other people when they had the opportunity to communicate more with them. This would be best explained by the predictability notion that we advanced in the beginning of this section. As we communicate more with others, they become predictable to us. Even though we may not like the fact that some of their communication behavior is unrewarding or even punishing, if we know more about them, we can probably explain more of their behaviors. When we have had a long history of interaction, we can probably more easily explain negative reactions by saying, "He was just in a bad mood" or "He always reacts to me that way when I am too talkative." In other words, the more we know about a person, the more we can explain

their behavior by our understanding of them and of how we affect them.

There are apparent contradictions to the direct relationship between proximity, familiarity, and liking that we must discuss. There are reasons to believe that in many cases as the distance and/or unfamiliarity between people decreases, attraction decreases. There is considerable evidence to support this hypothesis, implausible as it might seem upon first consideration. For example, police records of a major city in this country reveal that victims in a majority of robbery cases were either related to or acquainted with the thief. It was similarly found that victims of aggravated assault and homicide have lived in close proximity to the perpetrators of the crimes. In fact, almost one-third of all murders occurred within the family unit.[13]

Reconciling these contrary groups of research findings based on proximity may not be an impossible task if we understand the underlying factors involved in them. The closer people live or work together, the greater the opportunity for sharing experiences and gathering information about one another; and it is primarily through interpersonal knowledge that we develop strong sentiments. Also if people are inclined to use coercive power (see Chapter 2), they are most likely to use it on people who are close. We assume that because people will generally recognize that people need each other for a variety of personal reasons, they will utilize their knowledge of one another to promote mutually rewarding communication transactions. But we do not preclude the

[13]E. Berscheid and E. H. Walster, *Interpersonal Attraction* (Reading, Mass.: Addison-Wesley, 1969), p. 48.

fact that exploitative needs can be easily satisfied through close proximity with others.

SELF-ESTEEM, DEPENDENCE, AND ATTRACTION

Relational communication with other people constantly provides evaluative feedback to those involved in the transaction. As relationships develop, there is a tendency for people to give positive and negative feedback more willingly. In most cases, we can assume that positive feedback about one's behavior is reinforcing and should work to increase the feelings of self-concept or worth of the individual receiving the positive communication. Moreover, negative feedback should probably be viewed as a punishment that can lower people's self-esteem. How people use this kind of evaluative communication is a likely determinant of how attractive they will be to other individuals.

People who are chronically low in self-esteem may be very dependent on other people or significant groups of people; on the other hand, those who are generally high in self-esteem may be less dependent on the evaluations of others. People who are the most dependent on the evaluations of others are the most likely to shape their evaluations of the attractiveness of others on the basis of the kind of feedback they receive. It has been demonstrated that people who are low in self-esteem rate people who give them negative evaluations as very unattractive.[14] People high in self-esteem, however, rated people as equally attractive whether or not they gave positive or negative comments, although there was a general tendency to like people more when they were supportive. In general people who lack self-confidence react more strongly to positive reinforcement by showing more attraction and also react very adversely to negative feedback by disliking the source of that communication. People higher in self-esteem are *less* affected by either kind of feedback.

This raises some interesting questions. Do people low in self-esteem like others who also have low self-concepts? If a person has low self-esteem and thinks poorly of himself or herself, how will he or she react to a person who confirms that view by also being negative toward his or her worth? One could approach the first question by assuming that people low in self-esteem would not like other people similarly low in self-concept because they would tend to dislike in others what they dislike in themselves. Similarly, people high in self-esteem would be expected to prefer to interact with others who had a high sense of self-worth. The notion would be that we also like in others what we like in ourselves. The best evidence suggests that people do not respond in this expected manner. People low in self-esteem generally like people who hold similar self-concepts even if both have negative views of themselves. Moreover, people high in self-esteem prefer to interact with people who are similarly positive about themselves.[15]

[14]J. E. Dittes, "Attractiveness of Group as Function of Self-Esteem and Acceptance by Group," *Journal of Abnormal and Social Psychology, 59* (1959), pp. 77–82.

[15]W. Griffitt, "Personality Similarity and Self-Concept as Determinants of Interpersonal Attraction," *Journal of Social Psychology, 78* (1969), pp. 137–146.

The second question is whether a person who has a low opinion of himself or herself or of his or her performance will prefer someone who gives negative feedback rather than someone who gives support. It seems that people who are not pleased with their own performance do find people who frankly evaluate them negatively as more attractive than people who evaluate them as positive. When people believe they have failed, they prefer to interact with people who confirm that failure. However, people who believe they have succeeded are more attracted to people who provide positive feedback. We do not respond well to communication that points out our failures when we believe ourselves to be successful. The indication is that people prefer a congruence between their own evaluation of self and that of others; people who do provide that kind of congruent evaluative communication are seen as more attractive individuals.[16]

We would like to end this section by discussing some notions that underscore the process-orientation to communication. In any given relationship, people receive a variety of evaluations from a single person over time. Although we have continually pointed out that reinforcement theory would suggest that a recipient of totally positive communication would like the communicator more than would a recipient of uniformly negative communication, there are reasons at least to consider this conclusion. It has been argued that social approval is more valuable when given sparingly and maybe even reluctantly.[17] Praise from someone who rarely gives positive feedback should result in more positive notions of self-worth than from one who continually hands out flattering comments. A good grade from a tough professor should mean more than one from a known easy grader. Though these things may be true, it does not necessarily increase our attraction toward the person. Although the A might be very meaningful from a given professor, it might not raise our self-esteem or in any other way change our attitude that he or she was an irascible individual devoid of reasons to be liked. We believe that the research is not very supportive of the alternative spare-the-praise approach.

PHYSICAL ATTRACTION

Textbook writers being ever-vigilant of the need not to offend any segment of their potential market have given less attention to physical considerations as a determinant of attraction and, therefore, continued social interaction than this variable probably deserves. Many people resist the notion that we in this culture rely so heavily on physical attributes as the basis of our judgments of people. Simply stated, however, our perceptions of the physical attractiveness of other people are especially important predictors of subsequent communication patterns. This is especially true in the early stages of a relationship when people are making judgments on cultural- or sociological-level data. It is also probably more true in non-interpersonal situations such as the public speaking and mass media contexts where

[16]M. Deutsch and L. Solomon, "Reactions to Evaluations by Others as Influenced by Self-Evaluations," *Sociometry*, 22 (1959), pp. 93–112.

[17]G. C. Homans, *Social Behavior: Its Elementary Forms* (New York: Harcourt Brace Jovanovich, 1961).

we have less opportunity to collect psychological-level data. Whatever the context or nature of the relationship, there is ample evidence that perceptions of physical attraction are extremely important.

Physical attraction naturally varies from person to person; one man's Monroe is another man's Medusa. However, certain cultural level stereotypes do exist, and there is much research that indicates that within a society there are high levels of agreement about those characteristics that constitute physical beauty. From childhood on, one is bombarded with photographs of movie stars, fashion models, brilliant young men and women stepping out of limousines, and other standards of attractiveness. It is difficult to escape this conditioning, especially since it plays such an important role in determining attraction between members of opposite sexes. Agreements on physical attraction among people is surprisingly high and reliable. Adult males and females demonstrated great agreement in judging the physical attractiveness of eighty-four females from photographs.[18] This agreement on what constitutes beauty has been shown to exist also among different age groups. Although standards of beauty vary from culture to culture, there seems to be adequate cultural-level agreement on the nature of beauty and ugliness.

Given that we can agree on what constitutes physical attractiveness, the question of how it affects our communication behaviors is of primary concern to us. Although many of us would like to believe that we are above making judgments about the way people look, there is much evidence to suggest that we do just that. As we said, in the early stages of a communication transaction, there is limited information about the new acquaintance. There is a tendency to treat the person as "object" and evaluate him or her on the basis of looks. In study after study, people have indicated they were more attracted to physically attractive people than they were to the physically unattractive. We also tend to attribute certain personality and social characteristics to people we find physically attractive. Physically attractive people of both sexes have been judged to be more sexually responsive, kinder, stronger, more sociable, higher in character, more exciting to be around, and as having better job prospects and as more likely to have happy marriages.[19] Obviously, a lot of inferences are made from limited knowledge.

There may be sex differences that affect how important physical attraction is in developing social relationships. Surveys indicate that men consistently place more importance on physical attractiveness in making dating choices than do females. Intelligence is most often mentioned by females as the most important characteristic for dates whereas males tend to make such decisions on the basis of physical attributes. Moreover, attractive females report having more dates than do unattractive females whereas there tends to be no difference between the number of dates reported by attractive and unattractive

[18]A. A. Kopera, R. A. Maier, and J. E. Johnson, "Perception of Physical Attraction: The Influence of Group Interaction and Group Coaction on Ratings of the Attractiveness of Photographs of Women," *Proceedings of the 79th Annual Convention of the American Psychological Association*, 1971.

[19]K. Dion, E. Berscheid, and E. Walster, "What Is Beautiful Is Good," *Journal of Personality and Social Psychology*, 24 (1972), pp. 285–290.

males.[20] Many explanations might be offered for the preceding data. For one thing, it might be more socially appropriate for men to report that they desire to date only physically attractive females; it supports the image of the "macho" male. It might also be socially appropriate for females not to report that they also put a great deal of stock in the physical attributes of men. They might well be responding to decades of conditioning that suggested that such statements are not appropriate in this culture for women. Whatever the reasons, there do seem to be differences between males and females in what *they will admit to as being important* in their judgments of members of the opposite sex.

The possession of culturally defined physical attractiveness obviously has value in interpersonal relations. The physical attributes of those with whom we associate can also affect judgments of our attractiveness and social desirability. In one study a man was seated next to a very attractive or unattractive female, and people were told in one case that they were romantically linked; in the other instance, people were told that they were not associated with each other. When people believed there was no interpersonal linkage, people's impressions of the male were not different. However, when the male was romantically linked to the attractive female, he was seen as more socially desirable and more likable. The exact opposite was found when he was linked with the unattractive female.[21]

There is no doubt that physical attractiveness can be used as a source of power in social relationships. An attractive person may be the target of ingratiating communication by people who hope to gain a more intimate relationship with the beautiful person. In one instance, males were asked to rate the written essay of an unattractive and an attractive female. Half of the subjects in this experiment were given a poorly written piece whereas the other half were given a paper that was high in quality. Estimates of the quality of the essay were the highest when the woman was attractive and lowest when she was unattractive regardless of the actual quality of the writing.[22] Evidence also suggests that physically attractive people are more influential, especially when the audience is aware of the intent to persuade. People desire to give attractive people what they want, we presume. Employers are not unaware that physical attraction leads to more positive encounters with strangers, and it is not hard to understand why many employers hire the way they do to fill jobs that require dealing with the public.

It is important to remember that this reliance on physical attributes diminishes as people gather more psychological-level data about people. Although these qualities are extremely important in initial encounters, we personally take some comfort in the fact that they become less important over time. However, we do not want to diminish their importance too much, for the initial phases of any communication

[20]Ibid., pp. 286–290.

[21]H. Sigall and D. Landy, "Radiating Beauty: Effects of Having a Physically Attractive Partner on Person Perception," *Journal of Personality and Social Psychology,* 28 (1973), pp. 218–225.

[22]D. Landy and H. Sigall, "Beauty Is Talent: Task Evaluation as a Function of the Performer's Physical Attractiveness," *Journal of Personality and Social Psychology,* 29 (1974), pp. 299–304.

transaction is an important determinant of whether communication will even continue. Let us conclude by saying that an awareness of the fact that these kinds of judgments are made and that the inferences we draw from them are often error-laden might assist us in refusing to be satisfied with just cultural-level data. Even though beauty is only skin-deep, there is no reason that our communication relations must remain at that shallow depth.

PHASES OF ATTRACTION

Interpersonal attraction tends to develop along three identifiable phases.[23] In these phases of attraction, different kinds of data are used to make inferences, and the role of communication is markedly different. In the *phase of initial attraction,* we rely on cultural-level data and often tend to treat people as objects. The physical attributes of other people are often the most important variables in determining attraction. Sociological data are also used, for they are obtained as we make judgments based upon what we know about group memberships. Many of the feelings of interpersonal attraction in this phase precede communication with the others involved. Object properties such as dress, appearance, personal mannerisms, and known group affiliations shape our perceptions. As communication occurs over time, we pass from this initial phase of attraction.

In the *intermediate attraction phase,* more data are available to make sociological-

and, probably more importantly, psychological-level data judgments. The initial attraction phase is often transitory, and there are few of us who have not experienced the feelings of strong initial attraction toward another person only later to discover that we really could not tolerate him or her. Although the initial phase of attraction is based upon object properties, the second phase is based primarily on human communication. Greater emphasis is placed upon the social rewards available from the communication relationship. If other people reciprocate our attraction, we derive pleasure from the relationship. We communicate to determine similarities, and we seek to establish mutually beneficial reasons for continuing the relationships. When we do derive these satisfactions and find bases of similarity, we find more to communicate about and can become very dependent on people in the transaction. These kinds of communication encounters are dependent on continued social reinforcement and mandate considerable amounts of positive feedback. We are constantly seeking information about the other person and also desire to know just how well we are doing with them.

In *long-term attraction phases,* we develop more stable perceptions of people, and most of our inferences are based on psychological-level data. We react to the person because we know him or her. We know that, as we discover new bases of similarity, we feel more comfortable in the presence of those people. Our communication is less concerned with deriving social reinforcement, and we are probably more willing to tolerate negative feedback and idiosyncratic behavior, and we are

[23]For a more detailed discussion of the phases of attraction, see M. Burgoon, J. K. Heston, and J. C. McCroskey, *Small Group Communication: A Functional Approach* (New York: Holt, Rinehart and Winston, 1974), pp. 98–103.

less uncomfortable during periods of silence or stress. We have more understanding of both how the other people communicate and why they react in certain ways. We also probably have more understanding of our own communication behavior and are less concerned with creating certain images. However, we do not mean to indicate that in this phase attraction will always remain, regardless of how we communicate. Even in these kinds of relationships, the communicator must be willing to adapt to changes in the other and be sensitive to the kinds of properties that led to the present social relationship. One must also remember our discussion of level of expectation. There is probably a great deal expected of the participants who achieve this level of attraction. There is always the danger that expected levels of caring will not match actual behavior, and attraction even among close friends can be diminished. Understanding of the variables that determine attraction is a prerequisite for maintaining satisfactory social relationships.

POWER AND STATUS AS DETERMINANTS OF SOCIAL RELATIONSHIPS

Earlier we discussed the components of power that people can exert over other individuals. When people have the means of power, they assume different status relationships with the people with whom they communicate. Status itself is a source of power, and as power confers status, the two concepts are treated synonymously.

The status that we ascribe to people can be an important determinant of the kinds of communication behavior we will engage in with them. That status can be derived externally or internally, from outside or within the particular relationship we have with them. Sources of external power include such factors as previous success and reputation, age, socioeconomic status, education, position, and so on. A person might also gain power in a relationship with you by being highly credible, by developing your attraction toward him or her, by controlling resources, or by somehow controlling rewards and punishment. Power developed in the relationship is usually perceived as more legitimate than externally bestowed power and, therefore, is more likely to influence your relationship with the source of power. The fact that people have high status or are powerful may also be a source of attraction that might motivate a person to establish some sort of social relationship with them. It is always amusing to read about how the powerful people in politics are so sought after as social companions; it is probably less amusing to realize that many of us are also attracted to the powerful in the same way.

Power is a determinant of the kind of social relationship we will have in many ways; for it influences not only how we will communicate with those we perceive to be powerful, but it also is a potent predictor of how the people with power and high status will communicate with us. One form of dealing with the powerful is the adoption of the communication strategy of ingratiation. Ingratiation is the willing adoption of communication strategies by a person to increase his or her attractiveness in the eyes of a person who does have power. This is one of the modes of influence available to those who otherwise have no power to influence or control the nature of a given relationship. A student who attempts to use ingratiating communication to gain the favor of a professor or the shuffling and bowing of a person on the way up in a company is more understandable if one understands that this is the only way some people perceive that they may gain liking or to be influential. However, ingratiation is rarely successful if it is perceived as ingratiation. People are turned off to others who are openly seeking favor by such manipulative communication strategies. A certain amount of cleverness is mandated in concealing the intent of this form of communication from the powerful source.[24]

Ingratiation can be accomplished in several ways to better a relationship with a powerful and significant other. You can indicate your conformity with the attitudes, beliefs, and values of the high-status person. You can compliment the other, or you can spend a considerable amount of effort trying to communicate to the other person how really worthwhile you are. All of these communication strategies are accomplished to make you more likable to the powerful person because this person is somehow able to provide rewards that you consider important. We all engage in ingratiating communication to some degree, in praising a boss, attempting to develop a relationship with a friend, or in complimenting a person for doing something that we might really believe manifests extremely bad taste. It is probably true though that at some point we have to wonder if it is really worth it to have the person like us or if we want to continue trying so hard to please. Relationships that don't in some way move beyond the level of ingratiation probably will not be seen as satisfactory over time.

We also know that people who have high status or even ourselves (when we find ourselves possessing this kind of power) communicate differently with those with whom people we are involved. On the basis of an abundance of research, we can suggest ways in which status affects interaction patterns:[25]

1. High-status people have an ability to influence other people without making overt behavioral attempts to gain influence.
2. High-status people initiate more communication transactions with others than do low-status people.
3. High-status people initiate more attempts at influence and are more successful at influence; they are also more resistant to influence attempts than are low-status people.
4. People with high status tend to spend more time communicating with other people of similarly high status.
5. Low-status people tend to behave deferentially toward high-status people and are upset if ambiguity exists in how the high-status people are reacting to them.
6. There is a low level of trust exhibited by low-status people toward people of higher status.
7. When low-status people are sup-

[24]E. E. Jones, K. J. Gergen, and R. G. Jones, "Tactics of Ingratiation Among Leaders and Subordinates in a Status Hierarchy," *Psychological Monographs*, 77 (1963).

[25]B. E. Collins and H. Guetzkow, *A Social Psychology of Group Processes for Decision Making* (New York: John Wiley and Sons, Inc., 1964).

ported by their peers, they tend to be less deferential and less threatened by people with more status.

All of this suggests that we must recognize status differences as critically important in our attempts to establish satisfactory social relationships. If we are low in status, even sincere attempts to develop a relationship with someone of higher status might be perceived as ingratiation behavior. Moreover, the preceding discussion suggests that we ought to be aware of how our communication with others changes as differences in status between participants become apparent. It is through such an awareness of our communication behaviors that we can adapt to those differences and attempt to develop what we consider to be satisfactory relationships with other people even though status differences do exist.

There are also reasons to believe that as relationships develop over time and the patterns of interaction may become less based upon externally imposed status relationships and develop their own rules of conduct within that relationship, externally imposed status demands take on less import. Because the internally imposed status differentials are subject to negotiation by the parties involved, they are less likely to be looked upon as a constraint prohibiting effective communication; they are more likely to be seen as a legitimate form of behavior.

We are also not suggesting that violations of status-imposed rules of communication conduct always end in negative outcomes. One of our respected colleagues once described one of the authors of this text as a person always willing to tell a person to go straight to hell if the person deserved it without regard to whether that person was of higher status or, in fact, had means control. He further stated that this behavioral pattern was something that he found desirable and was a primary reason why a close friendship between the author and himself had developed. Obviously, this violation of rule-governed behavior paid off in this relationship. However, since we have become a bit older, the thought has crossed our mind more than once about how many people we may have denied ourselves a satisfactory relationship with simply because we did not understand or refused to comply with expected communication behaviors. There is an obvious risk involved in such behavior, and the negative outcomes associated with rule violations should be carefully considered if it is important to develop a satisfactory relationship with a significant other. There are probably some costs involved in not being your own person, too. In any case, these are the kinds of things to think about in considering this important determinant of developing social relationships.

Outcomes of Satisfactory Social Relationships

After discussing the variables that *promote* the establishment of social relationships, we may now turn our attention to some possible *outcomes* resulting from the establishment of satisfactory social relationships. In speaking of outcomes or consequences, we cannot ignore some of the underlying or antecedent conditions, which we refer to as *needs*, that cause people to engage in certain behaviors. Therefore, we can characterize the general outcome of any satisfactory social relationship as satisfying some basic need. Given any satisfactory social relationship, a specific outcome of that relationship would correspond with satisfying some *specific need.*

AFFILIATION

One of the primary consequences of satisfactory social relationships is affiliation. In fact, many people attempt social relationships solely to affiliate or satisfy a basic need to be with others. Although social scientists are in uniform agreement as to the motivating force of affiliation, the question of whether affiliation is learned or innate is still unresolved. Regardless of whether it is a learned or innate quality, the need to affiliate with others stems from several sources. First, we are all familiar with the old adages of "safety in numbers" and "misery loves company." People have been shown to express a greater need to affiliate with others when placed in a *stressful situation.* Schachter first showed this in a classic experiment in which he compared the amount of affiliation behavior that occurred under conditions of stress with the amount that occurred in the absence of stress.[26] We can witness families normally torn apart by friction and conflict that band together when confronted with some family crisis or death. Similarly, even those with more robust personalities may wish for companionship when they face a long evening alone with the night wind howling out-

side. Affiliation can also satisfy needs for protection and comfort. As we grow older, the need to affiliate for protection diminishes somewhat whereas the need to affiliate for comfort may grow stronger with the increased pressures of adulthood. Next, people will seek out others as a relief from *boredom.* Sometimes being alone with your thoughts can be pretty boring. This can be particularly true if you are a genuinely dull and unimaginative individual. People need others to provide stimulation and variety. Try to recount how many times you have planned an evening around dining with a companion. Now think back to the times when you faced an empty chair over the breakfast or dinner table. Most forms of entertainment or amusement are much more enjoyable when others are present. Psychologists have consistently shown that outside stimulation is a necessary condition for normal psychological functioning.[27]

Finally, people who are *lonely* or are experiencing *social isolation* will look to others for relief. Loneliness could be one of the most tragic aspects of any society. Loneliness can result from a number of causes such as lack of social skills, unsatisfactory social relationships, unavoidable losses or disasters, alienation with one's environment, or some internal crisis. We do not mean to imply that affiliation is the only remedy for loneliness, boredom, stress, and anxiety. Some will turn to the Bible in times of stress, others will rely on firearms and security devices for protection, and still others will alleviate boredom and loneliness through solitary activ-

[26]S. Schachter, *The Psychology of Affiliation* (Stanford: Stanford University Press, 1959).

[27]J. Zubeck, ed., *Sensory Deprivation: Fifteen Years of Research* (New York: Appleton-Century-Crofts, 1969).

People who are lonely or are experiencing social isolation will often look to others for relief. Loneliness could be one of the most tragic aspects of any society. (Photograph: Maury Englander)

ities such as reading or listening to music. We are suggesting that satisfactory social relationships may provide a natural and healthy outlet for meeting fundamental human needs.

AFFECTION

The need to be considered or held in *affection* is a second possible outcome of satisfactory social relationships. We believe, contrary to the preferences of some, that affection needs can be satisfied only with genuine feelings of warmth and love by another human being. Furthermore, we believe that each of us may display and share love and affection with several people at one time. The popular notion among social psychologists that affection can occur only between two persons at any one time[28] is somewhat disparate from ours. We draw a distinction between affection in the sense of a love relationship

[28]W. C. Shutz, *FIRO: A Three-Dimensional Theory of Interpersonal Behavior* (New York: Holt, Rinehart and Winston, 1958).

COMMENTS ON THE FUNCTIONS OF HUMAN COMMUNICATION

and affection in the sense of a need to know that someone cares about us and is concerned about our welfare. It is this latter usage of affection that represents a possible outcome of any social relationship. For example, we find no difficulty in accepting that a father can show affection for each of his five children impartially or that one person can display genuine affection and regard for numerous other individuals. Social relationships may yield concern for another's welfare, whereas the deeper, more intimate type of affection must come from love relationships. In order to satisfy the need for affection, the social relationship must include an active and reciprocal exchange. There is little likelihood for such an exchange outside of a close, personal relationship. The process of demonstrating and receiving affection requires us to share our innermost hopes, fears, and anxieties with another. In other words, another person cannot display affection for us unless they know what gives us joy, what makes us cry, and what makes us angry. Obviously, another person cannot share this knowledge with us unless the social relationship is such that we will disclose this type of information.

There is one exception to this rule. We have already discussed Sidney Jourard's notion of self-disclosure and the desire to reveal one's innermost thoughts to another with an aim toward understanding the self. We are all too familiar with the person who sits down beside us on a bus or an airplane and systematically pours his or her heart out to us. After ingesting countless intimacies involving an affair with a neighbor, a nephew with venereal disease, a daughter who is pregnant, and a husband who has taken to drink, we have this uncontrollable urge to get up and walk to our destination. Such people have violated the rules of communication and are what some psychologists refer to as overpersonal types who crave affection out of a fear that they may not be lovable. Normally, however, we do not share intimate information with another unless it is within the parameters of a close, interpersonal relationship. Moreover, most of us would not care to receive the affection of another unless it were in such a relationship.

AFFINITY

A third possible consequence of social relationships is *affinity*. The principle of affinity states that people are more inclined to like us the more they perceive us to like them. Thus, affinity is the direct result of how people perceive us. Obviously, mutual liking will not always follow perceptions of liking. Some of the people we dislike most perceive us as warm, friendly human beings. In order to understand the principle of affinity, we must also understand the ways in which people form perceptions of us. People form opinions about us on the basis of observing our object properties (age, sex, height, mode of dress, and so on), our social behaviors (manners, etiquette, verbal statements, and so on), and the way we are as individuals (morals, habits, ethics, and so on). These types of perceptions based on observation are also made in noninterpersonal relationships. When such perceptions are formulated outside of an interpersonal relationship, people are forming opinions of others based on cultural-level data or first impressions.

The dangers inherent in these methods were discussed earlier in the text.

Some communication scholars have suggested that many of all interpersonal communications exist primarily because one or more of the interactants desires to seek affinity with another. People vary in their need for affinity. Leaders, especially in the military, can generally be characterized as having a low need for affinity. Decisions must be made on the basis of goals and facts and not on the basis of whether subordinates will like them. There is a lot of truth to the saying "Command is the loneliest of posts." Others may exhibit a high need for affinity in both private relationships and business. These individuals are the yes-men of the organization and the individuals who have never learned to say "No." Most people agree that the individual who does not desire to be liked and respected by others is rare, if not atypical.

SELF-CONCEPT

A satisfactory social relationship may result in a further development of self-concept. Earlier we talked about self-concept as a predictor; now we will discuss it in terms of a possible outcome to the social relationship. When individuals are removed from others in society, they are deprived of valuable feedback that tends to reinforce appropriate behaviors and attitudes and extinguish inappropriate ones. This process of conceptualization, classifying and sorting experience into common categories, requires highly objective criteria against which to compare the self. Acceptable criteria might include the opinions of valued others, customs and practices endorsed by particular groups, or legal and moral sanctions of society. Without the benefit of social relationships, the development of an accurate self-concept can be as illusive as the proverbial butterfly. Self-concept involves five components, which we will discuss in some detail.

The first component of the self is the *material self*, which includes not only our physical body, but also the material objects we possess and care about deeply. An individual may find the damage resulting from a woman navigating her shopping cart into the side of his or her new car just as painful as some physical injury to his or her body. Although we may be attached to material objects to one degree or another, the basic anchor of our sense of self is firmly attached in the stream of sensations that relate to our bodies. When our perception of our physical self corresponds to objective reality, we are accurately reflecting what we are physically. In other words, "What you see is what you get." However, when our perceptions and reality diverge, the material self as a construct becomes clear. Many attractive women have been surprised, if not amazed, by the brazenness and persistence of some mousy guy with terminal acne who perceives his material self as similar to Robert Redford. Research has shown that individuals who have had limbs amputated may continue to feel the limb in its normal position and to experience movement in the phantom limb for many years.[29] Temporary disassociation with the physical self, or "spaciness," is a

[29]M. Simmel, "Developmental Aspects of the Body Scheme," *Child Development,* 37 (1966), pp. 83–95.

normal human experience. At one time or another, owing to physical or emotional strain, we have all experienced the sensation of watching our body talk or behave while our mental self was merely a casual observer.

The *actualized* or *psychological self* is the second component of the self. The actualized self is the private view of who you are at any given time, and it provides the standard against which you compare all other experiences. We refer to this standard for comparison as a frame of reference. The frame of reference may remain constant, or it may change with time and circumstances. For example, as a novice tennis player you may feel elated when you notch your first victory on the courts. Conversely, the club pro might have also notched a victory the same day but feel less than elated because it took him or her three sets to win. Both individuals posted victories, but different frames of reference were used in determining the actual self: promising player versus declining champion.

The next component is the *thinking* or *emotional self.* Whereas the psychological self emphasized the end result of thought and emotion, the thinking self emphasizes the actual process of thinking, imagining, and sensing. People who view themselves as highly intelligent or artistic place great value in their thought processes. In situations where people experience "anomie" or "powerlessness," they feel unprepared to cope with the logic and/or emotion of the situation. People represent themselves according to their thinking or emotional self. A casual remark will pass unnoticed by some, but others will become offended because they perceive

their thinking and emotional self as considerate and sensitive. Former football great and overall animal Dick Butkus drinks Lite beer because it's not filling, and he can't afford to get filled. He's too sensitive! Although we realize that he is neither serious nor sensitive, we can recognize that the actual process involved in thought and emotion can be as much of a determinant of the self as an actual outcome such as winning a tennis match.

The *social self* is the fourth component of self-concept. This is the part of us that others in society view. Some believe that this is the most important part of the self because it is the part offered up for the approval or rejection of others. Furthermore, the social self must frequently reflect the roles one plays. The social self of a judge is expected to coincide with the role he or she plays when sitting on the bench, whereas teachers in secondary schools are expected by students to be as stern and mean in social settings as in the classroom. As we know, this is frequently not the case. Our public and private selves influence each other, and usually the view that others have of us pretty much coincides with our view of ourselves. In fact, the two usually coincide to such an extent that we are not aware of the interplay and interaction between them. When the two do diverge, the effect can be very unsettling—as when the self-proclaimed "loner" finds out that everyone thinks him or her to be in desperate need of companionship.

A fifth aspect of self-concept is the *ideal self,* or what we would like to be. There is no need for the ideal self to be objectively worth. It simply is what you would like to be. However, the closer your ideal self is to possible reality, the least risk you run of goal frustration. For example, an adolescent girl who would like to be a glamorous and voluptuous woman can either wait for nature to take its course or, that failing, turn to silicone surgery. However, a solution is not so ready for a young man who barely grew to five feet five inches and sees his ideal self as a rugged linebacker for the Pittsburgh Steelers. Obviously, his goals or level of aspirations must be altered. We are all entitled to our daydreams as long as we recognize them as such. The ideal self can be viewed as a reflection of one's goals and expectations, regardless of whether they are stated or implicit. We would further comment that to know how a given event will affect someone, you must know his or her ideal self, or goals and expectations. We might compliment a friend on a particularly striking picture he or she had drawn and be confused or disappointed by the friend's negative reaction. Although we assume that the friend will be pleased that his or her artistic achievement has been recognized, the person's ideal self might be disappointed that the picture only took fifth place in local competition. The friend was reacting to a thwarted ideal self and not to us.

It should be obvious that a satisfactory social relationship may provide us with the opportunity of viewing these five components of the self and forming them into an integrated unit representing what we really are. Without such an opportunity we sometimes develop self-concepts ranging from "almost" to "not even close" to what we really are. Communication, then, becomes the vehicle by which we merge or attempt to merge the five components of self with reality. We communicate this self-concept to others and await

their approval or rejection in the form of feedback. Without feedback the process is one-sided and potentially deluded, but with feedback comes the opportunity for confirming what we think we are or placing ourselves in a context in which we must change our views of self.

CONFIRMATION OF SELF

Along with a satisfactory social relationship comes the potential for confirming the self. We need not remind the reader that with the possibility of confirming the self, or self-image, also comes the possibility of disconfirming the self. When we are involved in a social relationship, we will disclose information about ourselves to one degree or another. At the risk of repeating themselves, the authors will again mention that self-disclosure carries with it certain risks such as betrayal, value judgments, and rejection. We can say, then, that we potentially risk our self-image when we communicate. However, to confirm the image we have of ourself, we must run this risk. Erving Goffman, a noted sociologist, was one of the first to describe social relationships as a process through which individuals present "self" to others for acceptance or rejection.[30]

Let us assume that an individual has developed a self-concept according to the schema we suggested in the section immediately preceding this one. The individual "knows" who he or she is and "believes" who he or she is. Should the individual act out the role that best fits this self-concept—let's say it is that of an intellectual with great promise for graduate

[30]E. Goffman, *The Presentation of Self in Everyday Life* (Garden City, New York: Doubleday Anchor, 1959).

study and a bright future among scholars —or should he or she elicit the reactions of some close acquaintances "just to make sure"? If this self-concept of high intellect and great academic promise is confirmed by close intimates and indeed is accurate, no greater joy or sense of contentment could be had. However, if this self-concept were rejected, the damage to the individual's self-image could be considerable. This raises an interesting point. Is it better to seek out some type confirmation of the self and possibly risk finding out you are not who you think you are, or is it better to play it safe and avoid instances where disconfirmation is likely? The answer to this question will depend on how much you are willing to gamble, and, at the risk of sounding trite, all social relationships are a gamble.

REDUCTION OF UNCERTAINTY

Another outcome of satisfactory social relationships is reduction in the uncertainty level between the participants. Theorists have generally taken the view that we strive to make our behavior and the behavior of others predictable, and we try to develop causal structures that provide some explanation for our behavior and the behavior of others. Berger and Calabrese have developed an interesting theory concerning initial interactions between people. The central assumption of their theory is that when strangers meet, their primary concern is one of uncertainty reduction or increasing predictability about the behavior of both themselves and others in the interaction.[31] Individu-

als may be attracted to each other for reasons we discussed earlier in the chapter, but hesitant to initiate preliminary contact because they are uncertain as to how the other person will respond to their advances. Uncertainty as to the outcomes of initial encounters has probably contributed more to chronic loneliness in people than we care to think about.

It is certain that all of us can define specific types of uncertainty that are bothersome to us. Berger and Calabrese's concept of uncertainty might be useful for identifying this dimension of initial interactions. They discuss uncertainty at two distinct levels.[32] First, at the beginning phase of an interaction, there are a number of alternative ways in which each communicator might behave. Thus, one of the chores for each person is to predict the most likely alternative actions the other might employ. For example, after talking to an attractive woman for some time at a cocktail party, a man might wish to extend a dinner invitation for the coming weekend. Any normally prudent male would at least speculate as to the possible reactions of the woman. Moreover, he might attempt to predict all possible reactions and prepare satisfactory rebuttals to increase further the likelihood that she will join him for dinner. It has been suggested that this element of uncertainty in initial encounters offers the most exciting moments of social relationships. People become excited over the prospect of anticipating the outcomes of initial encounters, whereas they settle into a routine when they are certain as to the outcome.

The second sense of uncertainty involves the problem of retroactively ex-

[31]C. Berger and R. Calabrese, "Some Explorations in Initial Interaction and Beyond: Toward a Developmental Theory of Interpersonal Communication," *Human Communication Research, 1* (1975), pp. 99–112.

[32]Ibid., p. 100.

plaining the other person's behavior. Many times we are confused or uncertain as to a particular behavior of another and wonder to ouselves why that person behaved the way he or she did. We are aware that in each situation there are many possible explanations for a particular behavior. The problem here is for the individual to reduce the possible number of alternative explanations for the other person's behavior. As long as there is some element of uncertainty as to the motives of another, it is a wise strategy to remain open to plausible alternatives. Rejection of our dinner invitation might easily mean the other person is not feeling well, already has an engagement for that evening, or has pressing problems at the moment. Similarly, reluctance on the part of another to talk to us might indicate he or she is shy or nervous or simply cannot think of anything else to say.

Uncertainty, then, involves both prediction and explanation. Satisfactory social relationships afford the opportunity of reducing this uncertainty through communication. Although reduction of uncertainty can alleviate tension and create a warm climate, it can also take some of the excitement and anticipation out of a relationship. Social theorists have suggested that we engage in close, personal relationships because we desire to be certain as to where and when we will have basic needs such as love, affection, sex, and affiliation satisfied. Although this may become tedious to some, this element of certainty provides us with the stability and contentment to turn our attention to other matters such as goal and career patterns. A colleague of ours once remarked that he would be wealthy and famous had he de-

voted himself more to his work and less to finding someone to grow old with.

IMPRESSION MANAGEMENT

A satisfactory social relationship will provide a suitable outlet for engaging in impression management or creating a proper image of ourselves. Impression management theory was originally proposed as an attempt to provide an interpretation for cognitive dissonance, which we discussed in Chapter 11. The theory suggests that individuals are taught to engage in verbal rationalizations to avoid punishment or derogation for the negative consequences that could result from their behavior.[33] Such rationalizations can be interpreted as dissonance-reducing behavior, and they are necessary only when the individual can be held responsible for the consequences of his or her behavior. In other words, impression management is necessary only when the individual engages in some behavior that is freely undertaken and is known publicly.

At this point in the text, the reader should be aware that if a person follows an inconsistent pattern in his or her thoughts and actions, his or her credibility will be lowered, and his or her ability to influence others will be diminished. Credibility and influence over others can be maintained, however, *if* individuals have the opportunity of explaining or justifying seemingly inconsistent behavior. Effective social relationships provide the *opportunity* for explaining or justifying such inconsistent

[33]J. Tedeschi, B. Schlenker, and T. Banoma, "Cognitive Dissonance: Private Ratiocination or Public Spectacle?" *American Psychologist, 26* (1971), pp. 685–695.

behavior, whereas unsatisfactory social relationships thwart individuals from explaining away their behavior. In this latter case, the individual has no one to whom to explain his or her behavior and must stand behind his or her words and actions on their face value when a satisfactory explanation might be possible.

A typical example involves a graduate student who is preparing for his or her final comprehensive examinations. These examinations represent the culmination of several years of intense study, and they are likely to generate extreme anxiety in the student. A frequent reaction to this pressure is altering previously established patterns of interacting with friends and members of the academic community. In addition, irrational and insulting behavior, temporary impairment of normal body function, and inability to communicate rationally often result. The student may explain away this behavior to close acquaintances with little or no loss to his or her credibility or prestige. However, in the absence of satisfactory social relationships, the student will be judged on the basis of the irrational and unpleasant behavior. Lack of opportunity to justify this behavior could result in the student's alienating himself or herself from social and professional acquaintances, being judged as too "unstable" or "unable to cope" with the rigors of academic life, or carrying with him or her through life the stigma of being "strange."

We have discussed the factors that promote satisfactory social relationships and suggested some of the possible outcomes resulting from such relationships. We hope that you can put this information to use in deciding *when* it is likely that you

and another can establish close interpersonal bonds and *what* types of costs and rewards are possible for all concerned. Without being unduly pretentious, we will suggest *how* to establish satisfactory social relationships in the final section.

Toward Developing Social Relationships, or What Follows Hello?

We feel that we must repeat ourselves in the closing of this chapter. Although the interpersonal communication context as we have defined it is a prime arena for the development of social relationships, satisfaction of social needs and positive outcomes are obtained in a variety of communication situations. The groups we belong to can satisfy important social needs even though we are not in an interpersonal relationship with every member. Positive rapport and reinforcement by an audience, a class, or a large group can satisfy some of our basic needs to communicate effectively with others and share our feelings even though we could hardly claim to be on an interpersonal basis with anyone present. The organizations in which we work help us satisfy social needs. In most communication situations, we will be attempting to communicate in a relational manner. The following suggestions might be useful in a variety of communication situations in which something must follow *hello*.

The inclusion of the word *toward* in the section heading indicates that the development of social relationships is no easy matter. In suggesting some possible approaches to developing satisfactory social relationships, we do not mean to imply that we are necessarily good at it. Our intent is to provide some approaches that have worked for others in the hope that they might also work for you. We do recognize, however, that the way we communicate plays a vital role in this process. Communication, in one form or another, will determine whether a relationship will progress past the initial enocunter stage.

Many people are misunderstood in social relationships because their communication attempts are either lacking or inappropriate. Woody Allen characterized this situation aptly through his fictitious college professor, Sandor Needleman:

> Needleman was not an easily understood man. His reticence was mistaken for coldness, but he was capable of great compassion, and after witnessing a particularly horrible mine disaster once, he could not finish a second helping of waffles. His silence, too, put people off, but he felt speech was a flawed method of communication and he preferred to hold even his most intimate conversations with signal flags.[34]

Most of us have probably felt at one time or another that we might as well be communicating with signal flags. Although we do not recommend the use of signal flags for intimate conversations, we do agree with Needleman up to a point. Speech *can be* a flawed method of communication. It is hoped that after reading this book your speech will not be considered a flawed method of communication. In addition, we hope that you will appreciate our insistence that effective communication *must* go hand in hand with satisfactory social relationships.

[34]Woody Allen, "Remembering Needleman," *The New Republic*, July 24, 1976, p. 46.

SIMILARITY AND ATTRACTION

We strongly urge that you resist the tendency to seek out social relationships solely on the basis of physical attraction. Although we agree that physical attraction is a necessary prerequisite for many, attention to other factors is more likely to increase your chances for satisfactory social encounters. Much of the success in establishing social contacts depends greatly upon your initial *choice* of partners. A thorough analysis of the degree of similarity and attraction between you and another can be invaluable in making this choice. Why do you suppose that some people always manage to succeed in striking up acquaintances with others? The most probable explanation is that they are very careful in deciding to whom they will extend their friendship. In addition, one can notice that their self-concept is positive, probably because their rejection or failure rate is low. Choosing the "wrong" people to interact with can be disastrous because not only do you fail in your friendship overtures, but your self-concept is also weakened from repeated failure. In time your self-concept can become so negative that you communicate this to others.

Rather than reiterate the dimensions of similarity and attraction, we suggest that you review this information in the beginning of this chapter and determine the types of individuals who are most likely to respond to you and make some sort of contribution to your needs. Two approaches are possible for achieving desirable results. First, you could assess mutual interpersonal attractions and select individuals who are similar in important attributes to you. Similarity can provide mutual interests and insure harmony. A second approach is to assess interpersonal attraction but select dissimilar attributes This is the "variety is the spice of life" approach. At any rate, you should analyze interpersonal similarity and attraction carefully and choose the approach that works for you.

One final comment is in order regarding selection of potential social partners. Effective social relationships is a percentage game that *usually* begins slowly and progresses gradually. The individual who goes out with the express purpose of striking up a relationship in one night is usually ripe for much disappointment and rejection. Many of our students come to us lamenting the fact that they have scoured most of the bars and entertainment centers in town and just can't meet anyone. Some individuals are good at meeting others and quickly establishing relationships. Most of us are not. We have to proceed wisely and slowly. We could all rest easier if we accepted the fact that many desirable people will cross our paths in life, but we will never meet them or have the opportunity of establishing a social relationship with them. The one thing we can all do, however, is recognize the nature of initial encounters and be prepared whenever the situation is right for us to interact with another.

INITIAL INTERACTIONS

Many people in social settings find themselves at a loss for words after they say, "Hello" to someone. Although this could mean that they are shy, uncomfortable, or not feeling well, it could also mean that they do not understand the highly structured context of initial encounters. A recent explication of initial interactions suggests that there are three distinct phases to this process.[35] The first stage of interaction is the *entry phase*. During this phase, communication content is highly structured, with message content focusing on demographic kinds of information. This is the stage in which you alternately ask each other's name, occupation, major, hometown, and so on ad nauseam. Initially, the amount of information asked for by each interactant tends to be symmetric. If the amount of information is not symmetric, a hasty reevaluation is in order. Attention to some of the nonverbal factors we discussed earlier in the book may provide some clues as to whether the other person is bored with these trite exchanges or is not unduly impressed with your routine. If their nonverbal cues indicate that they are attracted to you, it probably doesn't matter what you talk about. At this point, you could move into the latter phase of the entry stage, where people begin to explore each other's attitudes and opinions.

The second phase of the interaction is the *personal phase*, when the interactants engage in communication about central attitudinal issues, personal problems, and basic values. This phase could begin after several minutes of interaction, but it normally does not occur until the individuals involved have interacted on several occasions. Keep in mind that when personal or intimate information is revealed too soon in a relationship, information exchange is not symmetric, and the other person

[35]Berger and Calabrese, 1975, p. 99–112.

might be tempted to "get up and walk to his or her destination."

The final phase of interaction is the *exit phase*. During this phase, decisions are made concerning the desirability of future interaction. Usually, these decisions are discussed, and plans for future interaction are made. It is usually wise to determine if the other person is willing to interact with you *generally* at some future time rather than restricting future meetings to a specific activity on a given day. With a firm commitment to interact in the future, both parties can work out the details later. Most of us at one time or another have interpreted a refusal to interact with us in a specific setting as a rejection rather than considering other possible explanations such as a prior engagement, busy work schedule, or an aversion to a suggested activity. Prior to suggesting future interaction, the prudent individual will also determine if the other interactant has some close, interpersonal ties, such as being married.

Initial encounters are obviously very important in social relationships because they will determine whether you will interact with another on a regular basis. Unfortunately, we do not have any pat formulas that, when applied, will instantly make social contacts for you. The best we can do is suggest that you employ effective communication strategies and learn what to *expect* at each state of the initial encounter. One thing is certain, however; people who expect the least are rarely disappointed.

Some communication theorists suggest that if a person is willing to exchange demographic information during the entry phase for at least four minutes, he or she is highly likely to maintain the conversation even longer.[36] This would indicate that if we can get past the first four minutes during initial encounters, we stand a good chance of developing *some type* of relationship with that person. There is also some evidence suggesting that the amount of verbal communication is directly proportional to the degree of interpersonal similarity.[37] Thus, we can make an estimate of interpersonal similarity based on the amount of information exchanged during the entry and personal stages, and we can expect others who produce a lot of communication with us to be similar in important attributes. Finally, nonverbal affiliative expressiveness has been shown to be positively related to interpersonal similarity.[38] When initial encounters are marked by high levels of eye contact, large numbers of head nods and hand gestures per unit of time, and frequent displays of pleasant facial expressions, we can expect that the other person likes us at an interpersonal level.

We hope we have provided some insights into choosing your social partners wisely and evaluating your initial encounters for possible future interactions. Satisfactory social relationships, however, require more than this. After deciding with whom you wish to interact and evaluating the potential for future interaction, the task still remains to establish a compatible

[36]L. Zunin and N. Zunin, *Contact: The First Four Minutes* (Los Angeles: Nash, 1972).

[37]M. Shaw, *Group Dynamics: The Psychology of Small Group Behavior*, 2d ed. (New York: McGraw-Hill, 1976).

[38]A. Mehrabian, "Verbal and Nonverbal Interaction of Strangers in a Waiting Situation," *Journal of Experimental Research in Personality*, 5 (1971), pp. 127–138.

COMMENTS ON THE FUNCTIONS OF HUMAN COMMUNICATION

relationship with that person. In a word, you have to develop *affinity* with that person.

DEVELOPING AFFINITY

By developing affinity, we mean that individuals should manipulate their verbal and nonverbal communications so that others will "like" them. We will not belabor the points we raised earlier concerning nonverbal cues and interpersonal similarity and attraction. Suffice it to say that others will be attracted to you on the basis of the verbal and nonverbal gestures you provide them. Your job is to provide the proper cues for the right people at the correct time.

As we stated earlier, *physical appearance* is a prime motivator in social relationships. Because social relationships often begin on the basis of first impressions, the physical image you convey to others is highly important. There is very little we can do about our physical stature, but we can control much of our physical appearance by insuring that we are dressed appropriately for the occasion, that we are clean and well groomed, and that we have maintained some semblance of fitness. Of course, it would be ridiculous to recommend a particular manner of dress or hairstyle. The important point is that your physical appearance should appeal to the object of your social interests. It is possible that two individuals who are completely polar as to physical appearance and adornment might develop a close relationship, but the chances that either will get by the first encounter are highly unlikely. Some individuals display marked preferences for a particular type of body

build. For example, males in our society seem to be fixated on copious female bustlines, whereas many females are infatuated with brawn and muscle. Very little can be done, short of instrumental conditioning, to compensate for preferences like the "boob and muscle syndromes." When dieting and exercise are inadequate in altering our body type, we simply must resign ourselves to the fact that some people just won't like the way we look.

By stressing relevant similarities, we can overcome many of the potential sources of conflict in a relationship while creating a mutually stimulating environment. As we have stated frequently in this text, people feel warmly disposed toward others who hold similar values, interests, and goals. For those who are bored with the demographic exchanges that take place during the entry phase of initial encounters, try probing the other person's attitudes and interests for possible topics of conversation during the latter phases of the encounter. In addition, by stressing relevant similarities, you are also denying the possibility of discovering strong areas of disagreement that could be fatal at the initial stage of social interaction. Very few people become attracted to another for his or her ability to start fierce and spirited discussions.

At some point in any relationship, people will make decisions concerning whether their needs will be met. One of the most effective ways of insuring a satisfactory social relationship is to *satisfy the needs* of the other person. It makes precious little difference what these needs are, for if you don't satisfy them, it is a safe bet that the person will find someone who will. During the exit phase of initial encounters, people often consider future interactions on the basis of whether certain needs will be fulfilled. Part of the rational approach to developing social relationships is to determine whether you are capable of meeting, or care to meet, the needs of the other person. If you can't, the relationship probably won't work out anyway, and the best interests of all concerned will be better served by either restricting or severing the relationship.

A spirit of *cooperation and trust* can greatly aid the development of social relationships. Affinity grows out of a climate of mutual trust and cooperation in working toward joint goals. It is difficult to conceive of a person liking another who will not cooperate in the relationship, much less liking a person whom he or she does not trust. When we are willing to forgo some of our independence by cooperating with another, we are showing our regard or affinity for that person. Likewise, we show our regard for another when we entrust him or her with many of our fragile emotions and feelings. To cite pop artist Elton John, we trust people not to ". . . Go Breaking My Heart" only when we show affinity for them. Mutual cooperation and trust do not have to result in positive outcomes. Sometimes it is simply enough that people *engage* in a cooperative effort. People will keep coming back for more as long as they believe both parties are trying. It is a case of if you don't succeed, try it again.

A final consideration in developing affinity is to engage in *self-disclosing behavior*. As we noted earlier, self-disclosure usually leads to reciprocal self-disclosure. People who are somewhat reticent to divulge personal information about themselves will usually open up more when someone reveals personal information to them. Obviously, we must be careful about the type of information we divulge. During the initial phases of a relationship, it is risky to reveal some disgusting facet of your personality. Though a person might accept the fact that you frequently pick you nose when this is disclosed later in the relationship, he or she might not be able to handle this quirk if informed of it immediately after you say, "Hello."

SUMMARY

1. People not only communicate on content levels, but also use relational cues to indicate how they feel about communication and the other participants in the communication transaction.
2. People communicate with other people because they perceive communication to be rewarding. People who provide positive reinforcements are more likely to be found attractive than those people who provide negative reinforcement or punishment.
3. Situational variables, not directly under the control of the communicator, can also affect perceived attractiveness.
4. People develop expectations about the kinds and amounts of rewards that will be forthcoming in any communication transaction. Even though others might perceive that they are being reinforcing, if they do not meet our levels of expectation, we tend to view them as less attractive.

5. There is a spiral of attraction in that the more we are attracted to a person, the more we desire to communicate with him or her; moreover, the more we communicate with a person the more attractive we find him or her.

6. Similarity is a potent predictor of interpersonal attraction. We are more attracted to those people who share our attitudes and values and tend to communicate more with them. Over time we also tend to see those people to whom we are attracted as more similar than they really are. Moreover, the more satisfied we are with a relationship, the more likely we are to see the other person as similar to us.

7. It is usually the case that when people are in close proximity, they develop more intense liking and disliking relationships. Because they interact more and have more opportunity to exchange rewards, an optimistic view would hold that increased attraction results. However, the closer people are to us, the more opportunity they have to use exploitative techniques and/or coercive power. Thus, proximity can lead to either positive or negative outcomes.

8. People low in self-esteem may be very dependent on the feedback of others. People low in this important personality variable are likely to react very favorably to people who provide positive reinforcement and are very turned off by people who provide negative feedback. People high in self-esteem are less dependent on the evaluations of others and do not react as intensely to feedback. However, when people low in self-concept believe they have failed at some task, they find people who honestly report that failure as more attractive than people who claim that they have actually succeeded.

9. Physical attraction is a very important variable, especially in the early phases of interaction. We do have culturally defined standards of physical attractiveness and tend to attribute all kinds of positive psychological and sociological characteristics to those we find physically attractive.

10. Physical attractiveness is a source of power in a relationship, and we may communicate very differently with those possessing a high degree of physical attractiveness.

11. There are three identifiable phases of attraction: initial, intermediate and long-term. The kinds and quality of communication vary markedly across these phases.

12. Status and power differences are important determinants of whether we will find others attractive. As status differentials become apparent, communication patterns change. High status people tend to interact very differently in a variety of communication contexts from the way people low in status do.

13. There are specific rule-governed behaviors that operate when people

of different status communicate. Violation of these rules often lead to the violator's being judged as less attractive. However, there are instances when violation of status rules can actually produce more attraction between participants. Externally imposed status rules probably become less important as relationships develop. As we negotiate our relationships with other people, internally imposed status differentials can be seen as very legitimate, given that we have been a part of their formation.

14. Possible outcomes of satisfactory social relationships include satisfaction of needs for affiliation, affection, and affinity and an opportunity to develop the self-concept, to confirm self-image, to reduce uncertainty, and to conduct impression management.

15. People have a strong need to be with others that can only be satisfied through social relationships. People will normally seek out others for companionship. At other times, people have shown greater needs to affiliate with others when they are in stressful situations, when they are bored, or when they are lonely or are experiencing social isolation.

16. Affection can be achieved only through social contacts with others. The human organism is incapable of providing affection and warmth for himself or herself. Affection gained from a social relationship can take one of two forms. It can be the concern that indicates another cares about us and is concerned with our welfare, or it can be the deep feelings that result from love relationships.

17. Individuals who do not wish to be liked and respected by others are rare. Affinity, or mutual liking, results from social relationships based on perceptions people form about us regarding our objective properties, our social behaviors, and our individual mannerisms. Individuals vary in their need for affinity. Traditionally, leaders have lower needs for affinity and must make decisions that may cause people not to like them.

18. A satisfactory social relationship may provide the opportunity for further developing self-concept. The five components of the self—the material self, the actualized or psychological self, the thinking or emotional self, the social self, and the ideal self—integrate into one concept of what one is. Social relationships provide feedback and objective criteria for confirming how well our self-concept merges with reality, or it places us in a context in which we must change our views of self.

19. Central to some theories is the belief that when strangers meet, their primary concern is one of reducing uncertainties about the other, or increasing predictability about the behaviors of both themselves and

others in the interaction. Uncertainty involves both prediction and explanation. One of the reasons people engage in close, personal relationships is a desire to be certain that basic needs such as love, affection, sex, and affiliation will be satisfied.

20. Impression management, or creating a proper social image of ourselves, is possible within the framework of a social relationship, because it provides the opportunity for explaining or justifying behaviors. Many times extenuating circumstances cause people to alter their behaviors, and without social relationships, they stand behind their words and actions on face value.

21. Developing satisfactory social relationships is a difficult task that requires the use of effective communication strategies. The initial choice of social partners, based on degrees of similarity and attraction, can be a potent factor in determining favorable social outcomes. Similarity and attraction should not be based solely on physical attraction.

22. The initial interaction is very important to the development of social relationships because if a favorable impression is not created at the outset, nothing much is likely to follow. The initial interaction is characterized by three highly structured stages: the entry phase, the personal phase, and the exit phase. Demographic information is usually exchanged during the entry phase, which usually terminates after approximately four minutes if one of the parties becomes disinterested. The exchange of central issues and attitudes takes place during the personal phase. Increased nonverbal affiliative behavior occurs here when one or more of the parties has some interest for the other. During the exit phase future interactions are discussed, or the relationship is terminated.

23. Active roles in developing increased affinity are one of the most effective ways to insure a satisfactory social relationship. Affinity is best achieved by stressing relevant similarities, satisfying the needs of others, mutual cooperation and trust, and self-disclosing behavior.

SUGGESTED READING   Berne, Eric. *Games People Play*. New York: Grove Press, 1964.

————. *What Do You Say After You Say Hello?* New York: Bantam, 1972.

Bercheid, Ellen, and Elaine Walster. *Interpersonal Attraction*. Reading, Mass.: Addison-Wesley, 1969.

Harris, Thomas. *I'm O.K.—You're O.K.* New York: Harper & Row, 1969.

Rossiter, Charles, Jr., and W. Barnett Pearce. *Communicating Personally:*

A Theory of Interpersonal Communication and Human Relations. Indianapolis: Bobbs-Merill, 1975.

Watzlawick, Paul; Janet Beavin; and Don Jackson. *Pragmatics of Human
Communication: A Study of Interactional Patterns*. New York: W. W.
Norton, 1967.

From the Reading	Study Questions
Define the following terms:	1. What are the three phases of interpersonal attraction? What characteristics distinguish each of these from the others?
task attraction	2. What are the different factors that promote social relationships? Are some more important than others? If so, when?
relational communication	
interpersonal attraction	3. What does reinforcement theory suggest about propinquity in social relationships?
proximity	
ingratiation	4. Explain the spiral attraction. How does it relate to rewards?
communication networks	
perceptions	5. What, if anything, distinguishes relational communication cues from other kinds of communication cues?
rule-governed behavior	
affinity	
self-concept	6. Explain how needs can be both an antecedent to and a consequence of social relationships. How do they differ in these two roles?
affiliation	
confirmation	
transaction	7. What are the possible outcomes or consequences to satisfactory social relationships? Can you think of any others?
cultural-level data	
uncertainty	
impression management	8. What components make up the self-concept? How does this process work? Explain how the perceptions of others affect the self-concept.
self-disclosure	
affection	
similarity	9. What does reduction of uncertainty have to do with initial encounters?
negotiation	
	10. What are the distinct stages of initial interactions? How is one stage distinguished from the others?
	11. Explain how impression management works. Is this strategy a common practice? Is it deceptive or unethical? Why or why not?
	12. Why is initial choice so important in social relationships?
	13. What are some specific strategies for developing satisfactory social relationships.

14. Why is affinity important in establishing social relationships? List some possible methods for developing affinity.
15. What are some possible things you can talk about after you say "Hello" to someone?

AN EXERCISE ON THE ASSESSMENT OF INTERPERSONAL ATTRACTION*

Below are some scales that have been suggested for assessing attraction between people. It might be interesting to try to determine how strangers might rate us on these items. Do the following:

1. Mark all of the items the first time through with an *A*, and judge how you would rate your *ideal self*. In other words, how would you like to be rated by a person in an initial interaction.
2. Mark the second evaluation with a *B*. Assume the stranger is of the same sex and same age. Try to think how such a person might evaluate you prior to a communication transaction.
3. The next time through the items, please mark a *C* at the place where you think a person of the same age but of the opposite sex would mark you.
4. Try any other combinations of age, background, and so on that you think might be interesting.

SOCIAL ATTRACTION

1. I think he (she) could be a friend of mine.
2. I would like to have a friendly chat with her (him).
3. It would be difficult to meet and talk with him (her).
4. We could never establish a personal friendship with her (him).
5. He (she) just wouldn't fit into my circle of friends.
6. She (he) would be pleasant to be with.
7. I feel I know her (him) personally.
8. He (she) is personally offensive to me.
9. I don't care if I ever get to meet her (him).
10. I sometimes wish I were more like him (her).

DISAGREE — — — — — AGREE

* Scale items taken from J. C. McCroskey and T. A. McCain, "The Measurement of Interpersonal Attraction," *Speech Monographs*, 41 (1974), pp. 261–266.

Physical Attraction

11. I think he (she) is quite handsome (pretty).
12. She (he) is very sexy looking.
13. I find her (him) very attractive physically.
14. I don't like the way he (she) looks.
15. He (she) is somewhat ugly.
16. She (he) wears neat clothes.
17. The clothes she (he) wears are not becoming.
18. He (she) is not very good-looking.
19. She (he) is well groomed.
20. He (she) is repulsive to me.

```
D  ___  ___  ___  ___  ___   A
I  ___  ___  ___  ___  ___   G
S                            R
A  ___  ___  ___  ___  ___   E
G  ___  ___  ___  ___  ___   E
R  ___  ___  ___  ___  ___
E  ___  ___  ___  ___  ___
E
   ___  ___  ___  ___  ___
   ___  ___  ___  ___  ___
   ___  ___  ___  ___  ___
```

Task Attraction

21. I couldn't get anything accomplished with him (her).
22. She (he) is a typical goof-off when assigned a job to do.
23. I have confidence in his (her) ability to get the job done.
24. If I wanted to get things done, I could probably depend on her (him).
25. He (she) would be a poor problem solver.
26. I think studying with her (him) would be impossible.
27. You could count on her (his) getting the job done.
28. I have the feeling he (she) is a very slow worker.
29. If we put our heads together, I think we could come up with some good ideas.
30. She (he) would be fun to work with.

Questions to Consider About This Exercise

1. Do we tend to see our ideal self as we think others will see us? How dissimilar are the *A, B,* and *C* markings? Why?
2. Are some of these easier to answer than others about how a stranger might perceive us? Which ones? Did you find it simply impossible to mark specific items?

COMMENTS ON THE FUNCTIONS OF HUMAN COMMUNICATION

3. How do you think these items would change as communication became more frequent?
4. How do you think your friends might mark you? How would you mark a very close friend?
5. Which of these items might be most important in an initial interaction? Would those items become less important as the relationship developed?
6. How would your communication behavior differ if you thought that others marked you positively on these items from the situation in which you thought they were negative.

It might be interesting to have a friend fill out these scales on you and for you, in turn, to mark the scales for a friend. Remember there might be some risk to the relationship involved; you decide if you want to do this or not.

AN EXERCISE DESIGNED TO ASSESS COMMUNICATION IN INITIAL INTER-ACTIONS

Observe or, if possible, tape-record an initial interaction between two strangers. It might be possible for one person to bring such a recording so that the entire class could analyze communication behavior. Consider the following:

1. What kinds of things did people talk about at the first of the interaction?
2. Were there identifiable phases in the communication transaction?
3. Did people use communication strategies designed to increase their attractiveness to the other person?
4. Was anything said that was likely to lead to less attraction?
5. Would you predict that these strangers would be likely to continue communicating and develop a satisfactory communication relationship? On what kinds of things would you base such a prediction?

It might be worthwhile to go to listen to someone who is giving a speech to determine if strategies were used to increase his or her attractiveness to the audience.

AN EXERCISE DESIGNED TO ASSESS THE NEEDS OUR FRIENDS SATISFY FOR US

First, write down all of the adjectives that describe someone you are close to, for example, good, aggressive, and so on. How many of these are positive? Negative? What kinds of needs are being satisfied by these traits in our friends? Now write down all of the adjectives that best describe someone with whom you do not have a satisfactory social relationship. How do the lists differ? What needs does this person block or fail to satisfy.

It might be useful to compare the lists with other members of the class. How do these lists compare with those of others in the class? Are the lists similar or dissimilar?

AN EXERCISE DESIGNED TO ASSESS THE EFFECTS OF DIFFERENT KINDS OF REINFORCEMENT

Talk to someone to whom you are not particularly close. In the first five minutes of the conversation, give only positive reinforcement (nod in agreement, give supportive verbal comments, and so on). After the first five minutes, switch and give only negative comments.

Positive Reinforcement

What I did_____   What the other person did_____
_____   _____
_____   _____
_____   _____
_____   _____
_____   _____
_____   _____

Now try the same thing with another person. However, begin with only *negative reinforcement*, and then change to *positive reinforcement*. With a third person, use some equal combinations of *positive and negative reinforcement*.

Questions to Consider

1. Were there important differences in the way people responded? Did the kinds of reinforcement affect what was being said? Which situation was most satisfying?
2. Did people develop expectations about what kind of reinforcement you might give? How do you know?
3. In which situation do you think you were perceived to be most attractive?

Chapter 14
COMMUNICATION AND CONFLICT

Conflict in one form or another seems to be an inescapable part of the human condition. It could be argued, with substantial support, that societies have advanced most when conflict has been recognized as an inevitable and even healthy aspect of human interaction and when the communication process has been valued as a means of managing that conflict. Ancient Greek and Roman civilizations recognized and valued dissent as an integral part of their societies. Our present-day legislative and judicial systems have as their origin this recognition of the inevitable nature of conflict.

Conflict can be manifested only through some sort of communication behavior. We can certainly have communication without conflict, but conflict without some type of communication is impossible. At times, conflict is readily discernable through communication, as the following anecdote shows:

> British parliamentarians Benjamin Disraeli and William Gladstone were arch political enemies who frequently bumped heads in the public arena. After a particularly heated debate on the floor of the House of Commons, Gladstone, addressing Disraeli, shouted, "Sir, you will come to your end either upon the gallows or of venereal disease." Disraeli replied rather calmly, "I should say, Mr. Gladstone, that depends on whether I embrace your principles or your mistress." On another occasion when Disraeli was called upon to define the difference between calamity and misfortune, he replied, "If Gladstone were to fall into the Thames, it would be a misfortune; but if someone dragged him out, *that* would be a calamity."

Unfortunately, some types of conflict manifested through communicative behaviors are not as easily recognized and understood as in our example. In addition, one can readily observe that there are many different kinds and intensities of conflict. The type of conflict you experience when deciding which outfit to wear to a particular social engagement is hardly the same sort of conflict you experience in deciding to give up the single life for the marriage bond or in resisting induction into the armed forces. Thus, one must differentiate between the different levels and types of conflict. Once conflict has been clearly defined, an analysis of the decisions promoting its occurrence, costs and benefits, and reduction strategies will suggest methods for the successful management of conflict.

Levels of Conflict

INTRAPERSONAL CONFLICT

Intrapersonal conflict is the first level of conflict. There are two distinct situations in which intrapersonal conflict occurs. In both of these, the manner in which a person perceives himself or herself is of prime importance because it determines most of his or her other perceptions. In the first instance, intrapersonal conflict results when an individual, on the basis of his or her own behavior or other related experiences, perceives himself or herself in a manner inconsistent with previously held notions of self-concept. During the maturational process, all of us develop highly personalized opinions regarding our true worth and identity. We are usually reluctant to express to others these personalized perceptions of ourselves and

what we think. Thus, others may not know precisely how we regard ourselves. When our notion of self-concept differs from another's perception of us, we experience intrapersonal conflict. In other words, we experience an *internal struggle* between what we think we are and what others think us to be. In psychological parlance such a situation is considered to be self-estrangement.

The term *self-estrangement* presumes that each of us has within us an inner self that consists of what we really are, what we really believe, and what we really think. To the extent that we are out of touch with our inner self, we are self-estranged.[1] The internal struggle that accompanies self-estrangement forces us to choose between behaviors consistent with our own self-image and behaviors consistent with another's opinion of how we should act or think. This element of choice suggests the second situation in which intrapersonal conflict occurs.

Everyone is familiar with the sometimes unpleasant task of choosing between several alternatives. At some point prior to reaching a final decision, we undergo some degree of internal conflict or struggle. At times, the choice is relatively easy because one tendency is much stronger than another. For example, given the choice between going to a movie and attending a social gathering, one could easily resolve the conflict on the basis of a stronger urge to relax at a movie. Some choices, however, involve serious internal conflicts, especially those choices that involve deeply held ethical values, life goals, and societal pressures. A young college

[1]C. M. Rossiter and W. Pearce, *Communicating Personally* (Indianapolis: Bobbs-Merill, 1975), p. 154.

student may be faced with the alternative of failing an examination for which he or she is ill-prepared or of cheating on the examination to have a better chance of acceptance to graduate school. The idea of cheating may be abhorrent to the student, but failure on the examination could ruin his or her chances for graduate study and subject him or her to the wrath or disappointment of his or her parents. This situation is not unlike the imbalance condition or state of inconsistency, discussed in Chapter 11, that prompts individuals to change or modify existing values, opinions, or beliefs. The type of decisions involving intrapersonal conflict will be discussed in more detail in a later section of this chapter.

INTERPERSONAL CONFLICT

Because interpersonal conflict and the three remaining levels of conflict involve two or more persons, we feel at this point it is necessary to differentiate between conflict and competition. Competition is mutual rivalry or struggle between two or more persons for the purpose of obtaining a nondivisible goal.[2] It is the means by which biogenic (produced by living organisms) or sociogenic (produced by society) needs are satisfied, and it follows some set of rules and regulations, stated or implicit. Earlier scholars and theorists have criticized competition because of the undue strain it places on interpersonal relationships. Horney insisted that competition is a problem for everyone in our so-

ciety—an "unfailing center of neurotic conflicts."[3] A more recent distinction by Deutsch suggests that the term *conflict* be used to denote incompatible activities. Whereas the term *competition* may refer to an opposition in the goals of the interdependent parties such that the probability of goal attainment for one decreases as the probability for the other increases.[4] When I win, you lose, and vice versa. Although these distinctions between competition and conflict are useful, any analysis of the structure of interpersonal conflict should focus on the degree of concordance of goals between individuals and the scarcity of resources that fosters competition between them.

The goals of two individuals in personal interactions are frequently incompatible. For example, a husband and wife may differ as to how their new home should be furnished. The husband may wish to reflect the role of a successful, young professional, whereas the wife may wish to create a very comfortable and practical surrounding for the children. The couple could be said to differ over the end result of furnishing the home. Conflict may occur even when two individuals have compatible goals. We could say that such an incompatibility represents a conflict over means, not ends. In our example of the young couple furnishing their home, both could agree as to the type of furnishings, but a fracas could ensue over whether to pay cash for the furniture or whether to assume a 15 percent finance arrangement.

---

[2]Sociologists sometimes distinguish between competition and rivalry: Rivalry implies a known competitor, whereas competition, the broader term, does not.

[3]K. Horney, *The Neurotic Personality of Our Time* (New York: W. W. Norton, 1937), p. 188.

[4]M. Deutsch, "Socially Relevant Science: Reflections on Some Studies of Interpersonal Conflict," *American Psychologist*, 24 (1969), pp. 1076–1092.

Interpersonal conflict, then, signifies a mutual opposition or aggression, always with reference to an indivisible goal or material reward. It is intermittent rather than lasting, and it may surface at any time from the docile, more stable processes of social interaction. Although interpersonal conflict most typically develops from competition, it may arise whenever one strongly motivated individual feels threatened or frustrated by another or when individuals fail to share the perceptions of others.

Several factors affect the development of conflict in interpersonal relationships. First, the degree of homophily/heterophily perceived by the interactants often determines the amount of conflict present in the relationship. As mentioned earlier in Section 1, there is a natural tendency to affiliate with those whom we perceive to share our values and ideas, whereas there is an equally strong tendency to distrust those persons who appear to be unlike ourselves. Many relationships cannot accommodate differences in attitudes, values, and interests when discovered later in the association. Our society has used these irreconcilable differences as the basis for many divorce proceedings. Second, an individual's basic personality structure may generate conflicts in interpersonal relationships. Most of us have experienced meeting someone and immediately forming a dislike for him or her on the basis of "I just don't like that person's attitude." Personality traits can create a general sense of disdain, or they can generate conflict when manifested in specific interactions. Interpersonal conflict may develop when an individual perceives another to be assuming role behavior inconsistent with the situation or in violation of previ-

ously held expectations. A classic case in point is the narrative that follows a common divorce proceeding. The young wife relates to the judge that she worked as a secretary for ten years to put her husband through college and law school. After two years of financial bliss, the husband turns into a different person and suddenly feels that his station in life calls for more than a secretary. Finally, interpersonal conflict has the potential to grow and flourish whenever two individuals communicate differing views about some topic, whether it refers to the latest Super Bowl statistics or which is the best European sportscar.

INTRAGROUP CONFLICT

Group behavior can be distinguished from other types of social behavior by the fact that its members hold membership for some particular reason and the group is patterned around a particular type of social organization. Membership in groups provides us with the opportunity to meet and interact with persons of similar values, attitudes, interests, and goals. Often, however, owing to the uniqueness of each individual, the goals of the group may be in consonance whereas the individual goals of the members may clash. When this occurs, intragroup conflict is usually the consequence. A conflict in goals, a breakdown of the communication channels, ineffectiveness of existing sanctions, normative inconsistency, and disruptions in status relationships are but a few of the possible sources of intragroup conflict, or tension and disharmony within an established group.[5] These will be discussed

[5]M. DeFleur, W. D'Antonio, and L. DeFleur, *Sociology: Man in Society* (Glenville, Illinois: Scott, Foresman and Company, 1971), p. 53.

COMMENTS ON THE FUNCTIONS OF HUMAN COMMUNICATION

separately in the paragraphs that follow.

A conflict in goals leading to individuals taking polarized opposing positions is one of the most common sources of intragroup conflict. Conflicting group goals can have devastating effects on both small aggregates of individuals and on larger institutions. A typical conflict of goals exists in practically every university in this country. Students typically feel that they deserve the full attention of their professors and that the classroom should be a place where each is an individual in his or her own right. On the other hand, university administrators feel that faculty members should divest themselves of students on occasion in order to publish and conduct research. The university professor is caught in the middle with too little time and too many students. The university community is thus reduced to intragroup conflicts between students, faculty, and administrators.

The intensity of the conflict within the group will often determine the degree to which normal communication channels are impeded. Severe or violent conflict will often lead to the complete cessation of communication within the group, as in the case of certain elements involved in the Democratic National Convention in Chicago in 1968. In less severe intragroup conflicts, communication between members will be limited such that group harmony and goals will suffer.

Whenever group members believe that existing sanctions are inadequate or will not be enforced, disruption will occur. A group that cannot control its members according to the rules of the group and society is no longer a group; it is a mob. Ineffective group control usually results in a renegotiation of group sanctions or a re-structuring of the leadership element. Conflict will persist until these elements have been renegotiated.

Members of a group may feel that the normative structure of the group conflicts with their individual principles and ethics. Conflict need not occur as long as the dissatisfied members have the option of divorcing themselves from the group. However, in many cases this is not a feasible alternative. For example, a medical practitioner may feel that his personal values have been compromised by recent lobbying by the American Medical Association. His better interests as a physician will not be served by leaving the fold of the AMA, but continuing membership will affect his moral interests. This type of normative inconsistency has resulted in some dissension within the AMA in recent years.

Excessive competition within a group may generate disruptions in the status relationships of its members. Dissatisfaction with one's status role within the group and subsequent attempts to achieve increased power and prestige will generate still further intragroup conflict. Government and business organizations are all too familiar with aspirant rank-and-file workers seeking the lofty heights of managerial status.

As one would expect, many of these sources of tension and disharmony will also affect interactions *between* groups.

INTERGROUP CONFLICT

Conflicts frequently erupt between groups when competition for scarce resources is present. Resources that would be coveted for the accomplishment of group goals are such things as prestige, material goods, power, notoriety, endorsement, and compliance with norms or standards. The most frequent source of intergroup conflict is conflicting interests. Industrial and conservation groups are finding it extremely difficult to satisfy their own self-interests in the same society, whereas, on a more global scale, the Soviet Union and Communist China find it difficult to serve their individual purposes on the same planet.

It has been long recognized that the mere existence of coalitions, neatly structured and regulated into bodies called groups, fosters conflict. The relationship between conflict and groups can be characterized as synergistic in that groups create conflict, which, in turn, creates alienation, which leads to the formation of even more groups, which creates more conflict, and so on. The United States has its origin in such a synergistic relationship. Conflict arose between British subjects over religious and political issues. The sense of alienation resulting from this intergroup conflict culminated in the formation of a new democracy in North America. A similar kind of religious and political strife resulted in differing interest groups forming independent states of the union. This arrangement has persisted to the point that we now have intergroup conflict represented at the most minute subdivisions of our society.

Mack analyzed the common fiber in intergroup conflicts. He suggested the following bases of intergroup conflict:[6]

1. Social organizations are differentiated, stratified, and held together by constraints or sanctions.

2. The exercise of power generates opposition. Often the transition from competition to conflict develops out of power pressure, in combination with violation or suspension of rules. Conflict passes from the dormant to the overt stage when rules are disregarded, or when sanctioning processes break down.
3. Differentiation, stratification, constraint, and the distribution and exercise of power develop from and also create subcultures.
4. Conflict leads to the formation of groups. Interest groups, whether political, racial, or labor, resort to conflicts to achieve their ends.
5. Conflict even further defines and maintains group boundaries and promotes their social cohesion.

An additional concept, usually reserved for discussions of small-group interactions, that could bear heavily on intergroup conflict is known as the risky shift. Simply stated, risky shift is the tendency of individuals to recommend greater risks when making decisions in groups than when alone. In other words, individuals sometimes throw caution to the wind when engaged in group decision making and take on the Walter Mitty complex.[7] Devastating consequences occur if our political leaders engage in this type of decision making. More central to our purposes here is the conflict between groups when decisions are made in this manner. For instance, members of one group may interpret decisions of another group as being highly suspect and liberal *if* such an inter-

[6]R. W. Mack, "Components of Social Conflict," *Social Problems, XII* (1965), pp. 388–397.

[7]D. G. Pruitt, "The Walter Mitty Effect in Individual and Group Risk-Taking," in *Proceedings of the 77th Annual Convention of the American Psychological Association,* 4 (1969), pp. 425–426.

COMMENTS ON THE FUNCTIONS OF HUMAN COMMUNICATION

Institutionalized conflict adheres to established rules and procedures for dissent. Perhaps the notions of protesting and going on strike best capture the essence of institutional conflict. (Photograph: American Friends Service Committee)

pretation is made outside the group on an individual basis. When seated in a body, members of the House may regard Senator Kennedy's bill for a federal shield law to be a sensible approach to insuring First Amendment rights. However, individual House members may not be willing to take the risk of giving the press so much privacy when interpreting this legislation outside of the larger group. Intergroup conflict between House and Senate supporters could result in the failure of the bill to receive confirmation. Conflict arising in institutional contexts will be discussed in the next section.

INSTITUTIONAL CONFLICT

Institutionalized conflict adheres to established rules and procedures for dissent. Perhaps the notions of protesting and going on strike best capture the essence of institutional conflict. Established methods of venting dissatisfaction are known by all and are usually followed. Whenever protests erupt into violence, as did the Kent State demonstrations against the war in Indochina, the prescribed rules and norms governing the dissent are violated, and the conflict becomes noninstitutional. Similarly, crossing a picket line constitutes an infraction of the rules, also rendering the conflict noninstitutional on the basis of its disorganized and spontaneous nature.

The 1960s could be characterized as a period of institutional conflict. College students were as well versed in the art of protest and demonstration as they were in the finer points of expository English. For the most part these demonstrations against the Indochina War followed the prescribed pattern for social unrest, and locus was the only factor distinguishing one demonstration from another. This situation clearly falls within the parameters of institutional conflict.

It should be noted that institutional conflict will not always follow the *exact* pattern denoted by the norms and sanc-

tions of the institution. Slight deviations from the norm can be found in practically all things. The degree of spontaneity and disorganization present in the conflict should be used to determine whether to classify this level of conflict institutional or noninstitutional.

We have classified conflicts involving intrapersonal, interpersonal, intragroup, and intergroup relationships and the institution as *levels* of conflict. We feel that this schema best represents conflict as it naturally occurs in the hierarchy of human interaction. The following section will present the different *types* of conflict that occur at these levels.

Types of Conflict

REAL CONFLICT

The first type of conflict that can occur at any of the five previously mentioned levels of interpersonal interaction is *real* conflict. Real conflict results when goals or

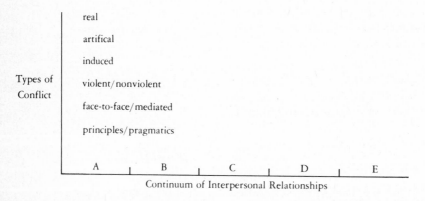

Fig. 14.1 Model of intrapersonal conflict.

behaviors are incompatible owing to a struggle for resources, *when* a zero-sum situation exists. In a zero-sum situation the gains by one person must result in losses to another, such that the gains of all persons involved equals zero. For example, if each of five people brings ten dollars to a poker game, the combined winnings and losses of all five players at the end of the game will equal zero. In other words, the poker game is a zero-sum situation because in order for one person to win a certain amount, one or more other players must lose that same amount. A real conflict will exist in interpersonal relationships when one person's winning, or meeting established goals, will result in another person's losing, or failing to meet established goals. Take, for example, the situation in which a girl receives two invitations for a date on the same evening. The two suitors would be engaged in real conflict because acceptance of one offer will have to result in rejection of the other.

ARTIFICIAL CONFLICT

The second type of conflict, *artifical* conflict, resembles real conflict except it occurs in a nonzero-sum condition. In this situation, gains by one party do not necessarily have to result in losses by another party. Compromise or cooperation can result in gains for all concerned parties. To return to our example of the two suitors competing for the attentions of the same girl, both gentlemen need not feel that they must do combat with each other. It is quite possible for each to establish a relationship with the young lady independently. This artificial conflict only becomes real conflict when the girl, or one or both of the suitors, feels that three is a crowd and one has to leave.

INDUCED CONFLICT

When an individual or group creates some conflict for purposes other than the apparent ones, it is *induced* conflict. Group leaders often will attempt to strengthen their hold on their followers by creating an "enemy" or external threat so that the group will band together in a submissive and cohesive unit to defeat this conflict or threat. Army reserve units on maneuvers frequently organize themselves into "green armies" and scurry about the countryside, giving chase to an elusive and fictitious enemy. Although the result can be humorous, the induced conflict situation does increase group cohesion and solidarity for the leaders. Most are probably familiar with the person who always seems to be in a state of crisis. If no crisis is available, he or she will create one for purposes of sympathy, attention, or the pure joy of misery.

VIOLENT VERSUS NONVIOLENT CONFLICT

The fourth type of conflict involves *violent versus nonviolent* conflict. The difference between violent and nonviolent conflict is the distinction between force and rhetoric. Whenever some conflict progresses from a verbal exchange to physical aggression, the conflict becomes violent. This distinction probably needs little further elaboration except that both can be effective methods of bringing about change. With few exceptions, most societies strongly recommend nonviolent conflict, even though many societies can trace their beginnings to violent conflict.

Communication and Conflict

FACE-TO-FACE VERSUS MEDIATED CONFLICT

The fifth type of conflict is *face-to-face versus mediated* conflict. Most conflicts arising between individuals and within small groups is face-to-face as opposed to mediated conflict. Members of larger organizations have management, labor unions, and professional groups to resolve their conflicts. Individuals and members of small groups often have immediate conflicts that have to be dealt with immediately through interpersonal communication. Therefore, the conflict is much more subjective and personal. Large organizations and institutions can retain legal counsel to settle their disputes in the impersonal and objective atmosphere of the courtroom, whereas individuals and group members can rarely be that detached from their conflict. Mediated conflict situations will also employ mass communication processes for resolution of their conflicts whenever appropriate. Interest groups will frequently take their case directly to the people through the mass media in hopes that public opinion will successfully mediate the conflict in their favor.

PRINCIPLES AND PRAGMATICS IN CONFLICT

The final type of conflict concerns *principles and pragmatics*. Every individual brings with him or her into each interpersonal and group relationship a set of values and principles. Conflict often arises when choosing the principles and values with which to operate in specific situations. For example, a group could experience considerable conflict over the principle of women participating in high government office. There could be considerable conflict over women holding high government posts; however, even if this principle were agreed to, several types of *pragmatic* conflict could occur. First, there could be considerable disagreement concerning implementation of this principle. Women might favor unabridged participation, whereas men might favor participation only by women without families or by women with little likelihood of giving birth while in office. Second, acceptance of an adherence to certain principles may generate conflict with other previously accepted principles or values. Permitting women to engage in the transient and rigorous life of high government officialdom may conflict with established principles concerning child rearing and family life. Clearly, conflict over principle and pragmatism indicates a need to recognize the overlapping nature of conflict resulting from competing sets of values. Another source of potential conflict in this area involves differing orientations. Two individuals experiencing marital discord may adopt differing orientations regarding the source of conflict. The husband may feel that the conflict does not merit becoming upset and, furthermore, says, "She will forget all about it tomorrow." On the other hand, the wife may feel that no problem is too trite to discuss and that candid and immediate discussion is the only path to marital harmony. With these two types of orientation, the probability for conflict is high.

Decisions That Promote Conflict

Involvement in and with society necessitates making all sorts of decisions. As participants in the human experience, we must choose between differing types of consumer products, ethical standards, moral philosophies, career opportunities, leisure activities, companions, and lifestyles. Although many different kinds of choices present themselves to people, we find it helpful to discuss the three major categories of choices that confront people in our society and ultimately cause the conflict.[8]

APPROACH-APPROACH

The type of decision known as approach-approach involves a choice between two conflicting alternatives, both of which have different but favorable consequences, and only one of the two may be chosen. An approach-approach conflict would be present when a voter has only two candidates to choose from on a ballot, both liked very much by the voter. Similarly, when members of a social fraternity gather to vote on whether to take prospective members on a skiing trip or to a professional football game, they place themselves in an approach-approach situation.

There are three major variables that determine the amount of conflict present in approach-approach conflicts. The first is the *value* of the alternatives. More conflict is likely to occur when the relative value of two or more alternatives is approximately equal. Moreover, conflict will be greater if the absolute values of the alternatives are high than if they are low. For example, given the choice between buying a new car and vacationing in Europe for the summer, conflict will be great owing to the high absolute value, or desirability, of both alternatives. However, the conflict

[8]R. Brown, *Social Psychology* (New York: The Free Press, 1965).

involved in deciding between the vacation in Europe and replacing the roof on your home would be less, owing to the lower absolute value of replacing a roof that looks shabby but still works. Relative values are determined by comparing available alternatives. A comparison between the new car and a vacation in Europe would yield equal relative value because both are attractive. The *probability* of occurrence of the desired outcome is the second factor affecting the amount of conflict. Conflict is greatest when the desired outcomes all have an equally likely chance of occurring. A typical situation might involve a student who has an English paper due at the end of the week and a history exam on the same day. The student recognizes the worth of both courses for his professional development and wishes to achieve a good grade in both of them. If the student has a high probability of achieving excellence in both courses, conflict will be greater when he or she is deciding whether to spend more time on the paper or for the examination than if the decision were made with an unequal chance of receiving a good grade in both courses. The third factor concerns the *number* of different alternatives available. Generally, the potential for conflict increases as the number of available alternatives increases. A large number of alternatives usually presents more conflict in group settings than in individual relationships. Two individuals can many times reconcile differences when several choices are available more readily than can a group of individuals because the available alternatives can be reduced. A husband and wife can narrow the field of all available cars to one choice each, but a group of people wishing to lease a car might only be able to narrow the field to five different choices.

Of the types of decisions affecting the amount of conflict involved in choice, the approach-approach conflict is probably the easiest to resolve. If two or more alternatives are equally desirable, the very least that can happen in choosing one over another is selection of a desirable consequence. In addition, choosing between attractive alternatives involves less potential hostility, and a method for compromise is often easier to reach. An earlier section describing modes of reducing cognitive dissonance discussed the facility of reinforcing a decision based on an approach-approach conflict.

APPROACH-AVOIDANCE

When a group or individual is faced with making one decision that carries with it intrinsic unpleasant consequences and a desirable outcome simultaneously, both are involved in an approach-avoidance conflict. The decision to accept a position with a prestigious firm at an attractive salary might carry with it the responsibility of spending many evenings and weekends away from the family working. Conflict will be present to the extent that the positive aspects and the negative aspects of the decision are equal. There are instances when refusing to "play the game" or simply making no decision is an effective response. However, this is not one of those occasions. Failure to make a decision in an approach-avoidance situation is, in fact, making one, for failure to make a decision relinquishes all positive aspects that might have been possible. Decisions concerning principles and pragmatics often involve approach-avoidance conflicts. When the positive aspects of adhering to certain principles are offset by the specific problems of making this decision, conflict must result. The award-winning movie *Serpico* is a prime example of this type of situation. The young police officer brought with him into the department a high standard of ethical and professional conduct. He was faced with the decision of maintaining his principles or succumbing to group pressures and accepting graft. Serpico stuck to his principles and became an alienated member of the New York police force. Subsequent attempts by members of the department to dissuade him from his ethical approach to law enforcement created pragmatic conflict and placed Serpico in the position of making an approach-avoidance decision based on principles and pragmatics. Much of the internal torment experienced by Serpico resulted from the fact that neither the positive nor the negative aspects of his decision outweighed each other. When an individual or group cannot reconcile the lack of equality in terms of the positive and negative consequences of a decision, the phenomenon known as *ambivalence* is likely to occur. When ambivalence is present and persists over a period of time, withdrawal from the situation is probable. After Serpico recognized the futility of his situation and nearly met his end, he became ambivalent, quit the police force, and moved to Australia.

AVOIDANCE-AVOIDANCE

When an individual or group faces the task of deciding between two alternatives, both of which carry undesirable consequences, an avoidance-avoidance situation is the result. Simply stated, it is choosing the lesser of two evils. As we pointed out in the preceding section, there are certain occasions when it is acceptable to choose none of the available alternatives. An avoidance-avoidance conflict may or may not fit this occasion. For example, a prisoner of war who must talk or be tortured faces an avoidance-avoidance conflict from which he or she cannot withdraw. He or she must choose one of the undesirable alternatives. It is sometimes possible, however, to reject both choices and withdraw from the situation, as when a husband and wife cannot decide which kind of car to purchase and resolve the conflict by not buying any car. The nature of avoidance-avoidance conflicts is such that people are rarely satisfied with any decision that comes out of this type of conflict. As a result, a job is done poorly, membership in a group is unstable, and interpersonal relationships suffer. When individuals are continuously forced to make avoidance-avoidance decisions, they usually seek new jobs, replace old friends, and make drastic changes in their life-styles. Obviously, people should strive to insure that at least one of the available options is favorable. This is easier said than done, as we shall see in the last section.

Many psychiatrists believe that the ability to handle conflicts effectively and to make rational decisions is the mark of the well-adjusted personality. The neurotic, on the other hand, may be too rigid to alter his or her goals or too lacking in self-confidence to make a decision in the first place. We are all too familiar with the nagging friend who never seems to have a handle on his or her life and always seems to make the wrong decision. He or she not only makes the wrong decisions, but also makes too many of them. The individual who changes goals or directions at every turn may have no solid core of character or values; he or she is shaped by events instead of shaping his or her life. People shape their own lives by understanding their options and choosing the best one for them.

Costs and Benefits of Conflict

In order to analyze the costs and benefits of conflict in society, one must first make some general *assumptions* concerning the nature of conflict. Our first assumption is that individuals in society are not naturally in a state of harmony, and, therefore, conflict is a natural and inevitable occurrence of the human condition. Second, an equitable solution is not always possible for resolving conflict. Some conflicts are so severe that resolution will never be possible. Third, all conflict is not detrimental to the individual and society. Fourth, conflict does not represent a breakdown in communication. Rather, it represents a distinct type of communication, and it may be the only manner in which certain values and ideals can be expressed. With these four assumptions in mind, we can now discuss the positive and negative consequences of conflict.

THE COSTS OF CONFLICT

We are all familiar with the negative consequences of conflict in interpersonal relationships. Conflict often motivates people to become *less communicative* owing to real or imagined differences. When this happens, we often withhold information, and we may even supply distorted or false information to the opposition. Marriage counselors are called upon frequently to arbitrate conflicts stemming from severe differences between sexual desires. When conflicts arise between husband and wife on the basis of an unsatisfactory sexual relationship, reticence to discuss the matter often develops on the part of one or both of the partners. When the problem becomes sufficiently magnified, the end result usually lies somewhere between the divorce court and a marriage counselor. Thus, conflict may *intensify* real or imagined differences and create the familiar case of making mountains out of molehills. Conflict may also impede *efficiency* of operation between individuals or groups. Individuals may no longer function smoothly with each other on a day-to-day basis because "something seems to be wrong with us lately." Friction also creates a climate of dissension and incompatibility in groups and often results in group goals and individual needs (the reason individuals belong to groups) being thwarted. In addition, when relationships become inefficient and less facilitating, considerable energy must be spent in resolving the conflict rather than working toward group goals or satisfying individual needs. One of the most serious consequences of conflict is the potential affect it has on a person's *self-image* or *concept.* An individual who constantly wrestles with conflict has little time left to develop skills and satisfy desires. He may develop a distorted sense of self-worth and feel inadequate before the

pressures and demands of society. Moreover, when conflict becomes severe with no solution in sight, people often assault the self-concept of others. A competing position becomes "stupid and untenable," and a failure to agree in kind and principle becomes "intolerant and pigheaded." A final drawback to conflict is that it breeds *distrust and suspicion.* Individuals cannot relate to one another on an interpersonal basis if they distrust each other, and groups cannot function cohesively if the motives of others in the group are suspect. In addition, the distrust and suspicion bred out of conflict may lead to open hostilities. We need not dwell on the armed conflicts that have occurred in recent years over religious, racial, economical, and political disagreements. We can strive toward more effective management of conflict after we understand the potentially positive aspects of this phenomenon.

THE BENEFITS OF CONFLICT

Until several years ago, scholars were in almost uniform agreement concerning the disruptive influence of conflict on society. Lewis Coser, a noted sociologist, was one of the first to support the positive value of conflict. Coser argued that conflict has socially desirable qualities because it creates associations and coalitions that bring members of society together who might otherwise have nothing to do with each other. It binds a group together and provides a safety valve that allows a release of pressure and thus promotes group autonomy. According to Coser, conflict and contradiction not only precede unity but are also operative in it at every moment of its existence. He also warns that conflict is truly nonfunctional in those social structures in which there is insufficient or no toleration of handling conflict. He suggests that the intensity of struggles that tend to tear apart a social system may result from the very *rigidity* of the structures, not from the conflict.[9] This point was clearly demonstrated during the student/police confrontations of the 1960s. The rigid structure of many police forces was unable to tolerate many of the minor disturbances in these student crusades, and the comparable rigidity of some militant activists was unable to accommodate any compromise offered by the establishment. Mutual rigidities such as these prevent the development of equilibrium, and riots result.

Thus, in explicating the positive aspects of conflict, we do not believe that all conflict should be resolved or that conflict is never warranted. Conflict is beneficial when it prompts necessary *social change.* Social change is often desirable and necessary in interpersonal relationships and among groups in society. For example, competing opinions concerning minority groups in our society may result in a more equitable system for including minorities in government, or it may cause individuals to reexamine existing values and prejudices regarding minority groups.

Sometimes the very fact that we are willing to tolerate conflict in our interpersonal relationships indicates that we *value the relationship* enough to strive toward harmony and fulfillment. When individual differences are perceived to be great

interpersonal encounters, it is easier to dissolve the relationship and search for more compatible companions than it is to maintain the relationship in spite of individual differences. In other words, a valued interpersonal relationship may be characterized by a willingness to deal with conflict.

In a similar vein, conflict can *clarify* situations and issues. When opinions concerning a specific issue are many and varied, all of the various and sundry dimensions of the issue come to light. Unless ideas are presented in the public forum and subjected to the scrutiny of many, the danger is always present that these ideas are merely a reflection of deluded and self-serving interests. As individuals in society, we cannot judge the veracity of our ideas or the appropriateness of our behavior unless we do so on the basis of objective criteria determined by the society in which we live. We need not be reminded of the injustice to humanity that occurred in Nazi Germany when the absence of conflict failed to clarify values, attitudes, and behaviors.

Conflict also tends to *evaluate* existing and operable systems of society. Foreign leaders frequently have expressed concern over whether the democratic principles representative of the United States really work. The series of events known as the Watergate Scandal tested our democratic process, found it wanting, and made the necessary adjustments. Similarly, conflict can test the strength of interpersonal bonds and determine if the relationship is worthwhile. There is no greater sense of contentment than when two people struggle, find their relationship worthy of the test, and enjoy the security of mutual con-

[9]L. Coser, *The Functions of Social Conflict* (New York: The Free Press, 1956), pp. 26–28.

cern and affection. Simons, for one, argues that cooperative communication about conflicting perspectives can actually strengthen interpersonal bonds, whereas suppression of conflict can cause irreparable damage.[10]

Advances in *scientific and technological development* can be traced to conflict and disagreement. Public disagreement can precipitate changes in the *status quo,* as did Ralph Nader's successful campaign to improve automobile safety and standards. Moreover, the confrontation between the United States and the Soviet Union for space supremacy resulted in significant advances in space exploration and also a multitude of technological innovations such as improved metals, global communications systems, and highly advanced computers.

Conflict can be used as a prime catalyst for *self-improvement.* Whether as individuals or as groups, we often settle into periods of passivity and/or unproductive activity. Sometimes challenge and conflict provide the incentive we need to engage in productive thought and activity. Even individuals whom society labels as "high achievers" sometimes fall into the abyss of complacency or attempt to live off of past accomplishments. These individuals are more than willing to defend their reputations from all challenges. Many people, however, develop patterns of resignation and acceptance of their "lot in life." Conflict can be a potent force in spurring groups and individuals to their full potential. The late Vince Lombardi created intense conflict between his players as a regular part of his coaching philosophy. With this group of athletes, some of whom were considered to be mediocre by the experts, he created a football dynasty, the likes of which the world had never seen before.

Finally, conflict can represent pure *enjoyment* for some. Remember our earlier example of the individual who is not content unless embroiled in some crisis. Some people thrive on competition and challenge. They are not happy unless they are engaged in some sort of activity that provides even a temporary escape from the mundane world. Many professional athletes cite as one of the principal reasons for choosing their profession the pure joy of conflict and combat. Dick Butkus has become legendary through his televised endorsements of the "thrill of combat you experience every Sunday afternoon when you take the field." America is infatuated with conflict and competition. Conflict is legally sanctioned through athletic competition, and competition is recognized as the only way of reaching the great American dream. We are not endorsing conflict on its own merit. Obviously, conflict can become disruptive and dangerous. Many harmless encounters with much ribbing on both sides have degenerated into harsh words and hurt feelings.

It should be obvious at this point that conflict takes many forms, occurs at many levels, and carries with it both positive and negative consequences. Because we believe that conflict is an inevitable part of the human experience, we feel that it is more appropriate to end this with a discussion of conflict management rather than conflict resolution.

[10]H. W. Simons, "Prologue," in *Perspectives on Communication in Social Conflict,* ed. Gerald R. Miller and Herbert W. Simmons (Englewood Cliffs, N.J.: Prentice-Hall, 1974), pp. 1–13.

Strategies for Managing Conflict, or What Follows <u>Go to Hell</u>?

Numerous people have offered blueprints for resolving conflict. Most of these guides are so dependent upon the situational variables present that they become useless outside of these specific contexts. We do not mean to imply, however, that all of these stratagems are without utility. Osgood has suggested a strategy called 'graduated reciprocation in tension reduction,' or GRIT, which was intended to produce a gradual reduction in international tensions [11] (but is equally applicable in interpersonal relationships). Several analyses indicate that the United States and the Soviet Union were deliberately implementing a GRIT strategy immediately following the Cuban Missile Crisis in 1963. [12] The GRIT strategy consists of a series of small, unilateral, conciliatory initiatives, which must be preceded by an announcement of the specific benevolent action to be performed. These unilateral initiatives should not be made contingent upon reciprocation by the other party (although reciprocation is invited), and deterrent power is resolutely used to discourage the adversary to interpret these conciliatory gestures as weakness. We recommend this strategy for resolving differences in interpersonal relations and will discuss it in more depth later in this section.

In reviewing the literature and scholarly publications for this chapter, we have encountered a plethora of recommendations for "reducing conflict," ranging from

[11]C. E. Osgood, *An Alternative to War or Surrender* (Urbana: University of Illinois Press, 1962).
[12]J. Tedeschi and S. Lindskold, *Social Psychology* (New York: John Wiley, 1976), p. 395.

turning the other cheek to rearranging someone's face. Clearly, there are times when we have neither the reserve nor the physical stature to do either. Successful management of conflict, as some authors suggest, does not imply that you can apply a ready-made formula and make conflict disappear. Effective management of conflict requires the same skill and diligence that effective interpersonal relationships require. Therefore, we are offering *possible* strategies for more effective management of conflict whenever it arises. We suggest that you experiment with these options and use the ones that work for you.

Conflict can manifest itself in many different ways. All too frequently it takes the form of some verbalized communication that leaves precious few options for either the speaker or the recipient. For instance, what are one's options when someone suggests you go to hell or issues some similar invective? If nothing else is certain, it should be painfully clear that we are engaged in a conflict situation. Nonetheless, even though we realize that conflict is now present, some type of counter-communication seems to be in order. Few individuals have the reserve to permit such comments to pass. Instead, we rely upon accepted rejoinders that our particular group happens to endorse, and, in so doing, we ultimately intensify the conflict. Take, for example, the world of the young, male adolescent, which is reflected through the eyes of Holden Caulfield in *Cather in the Rye*. For all the Holden Caulfields, conflict is best dealt with by looking your adversary square in the eye and stating, "Kiss my ass." Anyone worth his or her salt knows that the only acceptable response is, "Mark the spot. You're all ass." Needless to say, this approach is not too likely to ease the conflict. This type of exchange also occurs in more sophisticated circles. Winston Churchill and Lady Astor were reputed to be the bitterest of rivals who came into conflict at every turn. On one occasion, Lady Astor was alleged to have said, "Sir, were I your wife I would certainly put poison in your coffee." Churchill looked her square in the eye and replied, "Madam, were I your husband, I would drink it." Unfortunately, most of us are not as quick as Winston Churchill or as foolhardy as Holden Caulfield. Instead of searching for methods to manage this conflict, we are more prone to languishing for hours, trying to think of what we could or should have said. Although we agree that the world needs more Winston Churchills, we believe that effective management of conflict requires more skill in interpersonal communication and less reliance on snappy retorts.

The first step in effectively managing conflict is to *recognize* the type of conflict present and at which level it is operating. Artificial conflict at the intrapersonal level is clearly not the same as real conflict between groups, nor should these be dealt with in the same manner. Attempting to manage conflict when you are uncertain as to the specific type and level present is similar to accepting a blind date; you know generally what you're dealing with, but you don't know exactly what to expect.

After you recognize the nature of the conflict present, you should weigh all the pertinent factors and decide if you want to deal indirectly with the conflict. If you decide not to deal with the conflict, you can simply *tolerate* it. People vary greatly in their ability to tolerate conflict. Some can construct a wall around it and compartmentalize it from the rest of their thoughts and perceptions, whereas others become emotionally upset or feel threatened at the mere hint of conflict. The danger involved in tolerating conflict is that you no longer have any input in determining if the conflict will disappear. The initiative must come from others or with the passing of time.

The second method of indirectly dealing with conflict is *leaving the field*. People can manage conflict in this manner with one of three strategies. First, they can physically depart, as by walking out of a heated meeting, going home to mother for a few days, or turning their back on an intense confrontation. Second, they can leave the field psychologically. Couples frequently use this ploy of "silent treatment" by refusing to verbalize their feelings or by insisting that nothing is wrong when everyone involved knows better. A third method of leaving the field is changing the topic. As long as the conflict involves a particualr topic, it is wise to change the topic when tempers flare in order to avoid having the conflict become interpersonal. Leaving the field does little to resolve differences, but it may avoid aggravating the situation. In addition, this tactic requires the least amount of energy expenditure and emotional disturbance of the strategies to be discussed.

In general, studies of the effect of conflict on communication behavior indicate that under conflict conditions communication becomes polarized, defensive, restrictive, and highly controlled. Thus, *increased use of effective communication* becomes the third strategy for managing conflict. By "effective communication" we mean that the message communicated should not be *accusatory*; it should be an *accurate* representation of the source of conflict; and it should identify the *specific* attitudes, values, or behaviors in question. People cannot resolve their differences unless they make them known to others. It is indeed ironic that conflict impedes the communication that is so vital in managing the conflict. Conflict often evolves in interpersonal relationships because one or both parties become bored with the relationship. For many people, one of the most difficult feelings to communicate to another is that they are becoming boring. The situation is even more aggravated when a close, intimate relationship of many years becomes dull. A typical approach is to "find fault" with the other person at every opportunity. The conflict becomes induced and artificial with little room for constructive management of the tension. When people get on each others' nerves owing to boredom and complacency, they must communicate the real source of the friction, not criticize the other because the other's face is breaking out or some other superficial cause.

A fourth strategy for managing conflict is to *reestablish mutual trust.* As we saw earlier, conflict leads to a deterioration in interpersonal trust and the incidence of hostility. Successful management of conflict necessitates the reestablishment of the trust that was lost owing to the conflict. An adversary must trust that you are sincere, that you will uphold any agreements that are negotiated, and that your motives are genuine if an equitable solu-

tion is to be found. Trust can be established by engaging in some behavior involving compromise. If you feel that a compromise is less than you wish to settle for, you might try asking for more than you really want so that when you "give in a little" you will appear to be compromising. This is much akin to asking your parents for fifty dollars when you really only want twenty-five dollars. A final word is in order concerning trust. People who have a history of, or were caught just once, reneging on promises will have a difficult time establishing trust in others, especially if these others are aware of their past indiscretions. It is simply a matter of making your bed and lying in it.

The use of *effective persuasion* is the fifth strategy for managing conflict. We have provided what we consider to be an adequate synthesis of knowledge concerning methods of effective persuasion in Chapters 11 and 12. The techniques suggested will aid greatly in the management of conflict. Because conflicts involve differences in attitudes or behaviors, persuading someone to change his or her behaviors or attitudes will eliminate the conflict. We suggest you review these chapters with the management of conflict in mind.

Conflict management through *bargaining and negotiation* represents a sixth possible strategy. These tactics are frequently used for intergroup and institutional conflicts. Often times a neutral third party, or arbitrator, is used to permit free flow of communication and to prevent "conflicts of interest." Henry Kissinger, as secretary of state, performed this function in negotiating a settlement to the Indochina War and easing tensions in the Middle East. The GRIT strategy, which we mentioned earlier, is a form of bargaining and negotiation. In applying this strategy to interpersonal conflict, we can refer to it as "gradual reduction in interpersonal tension." Winston Churchill and Lady Astor could have resolved their differences with the GRIT strategy. The first step would have been an announcement by either of the parties of future benevolent actions. These conciliatory gestures must not be contingent on reciprocation by the other, although reciprocation is invited. Churchill, for example, could agree to refrain from making any disparaging remarks, followed by a future exchange of pleasantries, with an ultimate aim toward sitting down and discussing specific differences. Should Lady Astor interpret these gestures as a sign of weakness, deterrent power, in the form of a sharp tongue, would be forthcoming. Thus, the two could manage their conflict with a series of small, graduated gestures that would result in mutual accommodation for both. This is not an all-or-none situation, however, for the process can be stopped at any time through deterrent power. When publicly denounced as being a drunk, Winston Churchill would only respond, "That is true, Madam, but you are ugly. Very ugly. And *I* will be sober in the morning," as a form of deterrent power, indicating that his benevolent overtures should be reciprocated. The very worst that can happen is that some of the conflict will be under control.

The final strategy for managing conflict is *leveling*. When conflicts arise between people, it is possible, indeed probable, that someone is wrong. No better way exists to eliminate conflict than to admit that you are wrong. Leveling with someone that you were wrong need not be a humiliating experience; it can and should be a source of personal satisfaction and growth. Unfortunately, many people are too insecure and rigid to admit they were mistaken. What could have ended amicably with a candid admission of error too often ends in a bitter struggle. Candor in all things is usually a wise policy.

What do you say when someone tells you to go to hell? Many people make the mistake of assuming this sort of invective is always directed at a personal level. Frequently, it is not. Try to determine if there are other mitigating circumstances prompting the comment. Sometimes people are having a bad day, are under severe emotional strain, have responded without thinking, or are telling you they disagree with your ideas rather than your self-concept. Anytime you pick up the gauntlet of direct challenge, you have limited your options to either backing down or engaging in the conflict. By failing to curb their tongue, many people become engaged in conflicts not because they particularly wish to, but because they have to defend their honor. Many a barroom brawl has ensued from responding to such a directive with an equally aggressive directive. At times, the most effective approach in dealing with "Go to hell!" is simply to shrug your shoulders and place yourself above such banal interaction. You have not aggravated the conflict and precluded using some of the strategies discussed above. At other times, however, a Winston Churchill approach is undeniably appropriate, such as: "Madam, I should be glad to go to hell, or any other place, would I forever avoid your face."

SUMMARY

1. Conflict is a natural and inescapable phenomenon in the human condition. Conflict can be manifested only through some type of communication behavior. Although we can have communication without conflict, we cannot have conflict without communication. There are many different forms of conflict, some of which are more easily recognized than others.

2. Conflict manifests itself at five levels in the interpersonal hierarchy. Intrapersonal conflict represents an internal struggle between perceptions or choices. Interpersonal conflict occurs when two or more individuals compete for a scarcity of resources such as love, recognition, material goods, or affiliation. Conflict within a particular group, or intragroup conflict, is the result of group and individual goals clashing. Intergroup conflict takes place when two or more distinct groups compete for a scarcity of resources. When conflict adheres to established rules and procedures for dissent within an organization, it is institutionalized conflict.

3. There are six types of conflict that can occur at any or all levels of interpersonal interaction. Real conflict results when goals or behaviors are incompatible such that success by one interactant must result in failure for another interactant. Artificial conflict resembles real conflict except that goal attainment by one party need not result in goal frustration by another. When an individual or group creates conflict for some ulterior motive, it is induced conflict. Violent/nonviolent conflict represents the difference between force and rhetoric. In face-to-face versus mediated conflict, differences are more subjective and personal. Mediated conflict often employs a neutral third party or arbitrator to mediate the dispute. Conflict over principles involves disparate moral or ethical standards, whereas conflict over pragmatics involves the effects of implementing certain policies.

4. Participants in society are called upon to make all sorts of decisions, which ultimately result in some type of conflict. The three types of decisions that promote conflict are approach-approach (two positive but incompatible choices), approach-avoidance (an attractive choice modified by concomitant circumstances that are unpleasant), and avoidance-avoidance (two equally unattractive choices).

5. Many psychiatrists believe that the ability to handle conflict effectively and make rational choices is the mark of the well-adjusted personality. The neurotic, on the other hand, may be too rigid to alter goals when necessary or too lacking in self-confidence to make a decision in the first place.

6. All conflict is not detrimental to the individual and society. Conflict may breed suspicion and mistrust, impede normal communication,

intensify real or imagined differences, or detract from one's self-concept. On the other hand, conflict may precipitate necessary social change, serve to clarify issues, assist in evaluating existing structures of society, generate advances in science and technology, or promote self-improvement.

7. Successful management of conflict necessitates becoming cognizant of the specific type of conflict present and at which level it is operating. With this knowledge in mind, possible strategies include tolerance, leaving the field, increased use of effective communication channels, effective persuasion, bargaining or negotiation (which includes GRIT strategy), reestablishing mutual trust, and leveling.

SUGGESTED READING

Bach, George R., and Peter Wyden. *The Intimate Enemy.* New York: William Morrow, 1969.

Coser, Lewis. *Continuities in the Study of Social Conflict.* New York: Free Press, 1967.

Jandt, Fred E., ed. *Conflict Resolution Through Communication.* New York: Harper & Row, 1973.

Nye, Robert. *Conflict Among Humans.* New York: Springer Publishing Company, 1973.

Toffler, Alvin. *Future Shock.* New York: Bantam, 1970.

Miller, Gerald R., and Herbert W. Simons, eds. *Communication and Conflict.* Englewood Cliffs, N.J.: Prentice-Hall, 1974.

From the Reading

Define the following terms.

internal struggle
interpersonal conflict
opposition
aggression
intragroup conflict
intergroup conflict
competition
institutional conflict
principles

Study Questions

1. Is conflict a natural state of the human condition; or, as some authors suggest, is it a disruptive force in society? Explain.
2. What are the different levels at which conflict may occur? How can you recognize conflict at each level?
3. What effect does competition have on interpersonal and small-group behavior? Excessive competition?
4. What are some of the rules and procedures inherent in institutional conflict?
5. Explain the risky shift. Should decisions be made on this basis? Why or why not?

pragmatics
approach-approach
approach-avoidance
avoidance-avoidance
zero-sum
GRIT
conflict management

6. What are the different types of conflict? How do they differ from one another?

7. What are the three types of decisions that may promote conflict? Give examples of each type of decision.

8. What are some costs of conflict? What are the benefits of conflicts?

9. Explain the difference between reduction of conflict and management of conflict? Why is this distinction useful?

10. Can violent conflict be a valid form of social expression? Support your position.

11. What do we mean by the statement "People compete for scarce resources"? List some examples of scarce resources.

12. What are the steps involved in successfully managing conflict? Which ones are most likely to work for you?

13. Is tolerance of conflict an effective strategy for managing conflict? Why or why not?

14. Which types of conflict are the most difficult to manage?

15. What are some possible responses to "Go to Hell"? Are some replies or behaviors more appropriate than others? When?

16. What kinds of communication skills are most useful in managing conflict?

AN EXERCISE DESIGNED TO ANALYZE CONFLICT, COMPETITION, AND COMMUNICATION

Win As Much As You Can

This exercise is designed to increase understanding of conflict within and between groups. It provides an opportunity for managing both individual and group conflict in a task-completion setting. This activity requires 30 to 45 minutes and can be used appropriately with groups of eight to forty students.

Directions

The class will be divided into one or more groups, with *four* dyads per group. For eight successive rounds each dyad will simply decide whether to vote X or Y. No other decisions are required. The "Payoff" for each round will be determined on the basis of how each of the four dyads in each group votes.

Points for each round will be awarded on the following basis:

1. If each of the four dyads votes X: lose one point each.
2. If three dyads vote X and one dyad votes Y: the X votes win one point each, whereas the Y vote loses three points.
3. If two dyads vote X and two dyads vote Y: the X votes win two points each, whereas the Y votes lose two points each.
4. If one dyad votes X and three dyads vote Y: the X vote wins three points, whereas the Y votes lose one point each.
5. If each of the four dyads votes Y: win one point each.

Table 14.1 Summary of scoring

When vote is:	Scoring is:
X X X X	lose 1 pt each
X X X Y	X's win 1 pt each; Y loses 1 pt
X X Y Y	X's win 2 pts each; Y's lose 2 pts each
X Y Y Y	X wins 3 pts; Y's lose 1 pt each
Y Y Y Y	win 1 pt each

Strategy

You are to confer *only* with the other member of your dyad on each round and make a joint decision. Before rounds 4, 6, and 8, confer with the other dyads in your group for 3 minutes, and then confer only with your partner for 1 minute to discuss the group decision.

Table 14.2

			Vote				
Round	Time	Confer In	(X or Y)	Won	Lost	Net Gain	
1	1 min	dyad					
2	1 min	dyad					
3	1 min	dyad					
*4	3 mins 1 min	group dyad				Bonus: Mult. by 3	
5	1 min	dyad					
*6	3 mins 1 min	group dyad				Bonus Mult. by 5	
7	1 min	dyad					
*8	3 mins 1 min	group dyad				Bonus Mult. by 10	
			Total Points Won:				

Questions

1. What was the major source of conflict in your dyad? Group?
2. Who won the game?
3. Can there be more than one winner in this game? Why?
4. What did the different behaviors of the group suggest about managing conflict in real-life situations?
5. In what ways could your group have eliminated conflict?
6. Was this a zero-sum game? Did you assume it to be?

AN EXERCISE IN THE ASSESSMENT OF CONFLICT IN A CONVERSATION*

Dr. Richard Dodds, a physics research worker, entered the office and showed his superior, Dr. Blackman, a letter. This letter was from another research institution, offering

* Conversation taken from Abraham Zaleznik, *Human Dilemmas of Leadership* (New York: Harper & Row, 1966), pp. 52–54.

Dodds a position. Blackman read the letter.

Dodds: What do you think of that?

Blackman: I knew it was coming. He asked me if it would be all right if he sent it. I told him to go ahead, if he wanted to.

Dodds: I didn't expect it, particularly after what you said to me last time [*pause*]. I'm really quite happy here. I don't want you to get the idea that I am thinking of leaving. But I thought I should go and visit him—I think he expects it—and I wanted to let you know that just because I was thinking of going down, that didn't mean I was thinking of leaving here, unless of course, he offers me something extraordinary.

Blackman: Why are you telling me all this?

Dodds: Because I didn't want you hearing from somebody else that I was thinking of leaving here because I was going for a visit to another insititution. I really have no intention of leaving here you know, unless he offers me something really extraordinary that I can't afford to turn down. I think I'll tell him that, that I am willing to look at his laboratory, but unless there is something unusual for me, I have no intention of leaving here.

Blackman: It's up to you.

Dodds: What do you think?

Blackman: Well, what? About what? You've go to make up your mind.

Dodds: I don't consider too seriously this job. He is not offering anything really extraordinary. But I *am* interested in what he had to say, and I would like to look around his lab.

Blackman: Sooner or later you are going to have to make up your mind where you want to work.

Dodds replied sharply: That depends on the offers, doesn't it?

Blackman: No, not really; a good man always gets offers. You get a good offer and you move, and as soon as you have moved, you get other good offers. It would throw you into confusion to consider all the good offers you will receive. Isn't there a factor of how stable you want to be?

Dodds: But I'm not shopping around. I already told you that. He sent me this letter, I didn't ask him to. All I said was I think I should visit him, and to you that's shopping around.

Blackman: Well, you may choose to set aside your commitment here if he offers you something better. All I am saying is that you will still be left with the question of you've got to stay some place, and where is that going to be?

The discussion continued on how it would look if Dodds changed jobs at this point and finally Dodds said:

Dodds: Look, I came in here, and I want to be honest with you, but you go and make me feel all guilty, and I don't like that.

Blackman: You are being honest as can be.

Dodds: I didn't come in here to fight. I don't want to disturb you.

Blackman: I'm not disturbed. If you think it is best for you to go somewhere else, that is O.K. with me.

COMMENTS ON THE FUNCTIONS OF HUMAN COMMUNICATION

Again there is a lengthy exchange about what does Dodds really want and how would his leaving look to others. Finally Dodds blurts out:

Dodds: I don't understand you. I came in here to be honest with you, and you make me feel guilty. All I wanted was to show you this letter, and let you know what I was going to do. What should I have told you?

Blackman: That you had read the letter, and felt that under the circumstances it was necessary for you to pay a visit to the professor, but that you were happy here, and wanted to stay at least until you had got a job of work done.

Dodds: I can't get over it. You think there isn't a place in the world I'd rather be than here in this lab. . . .

Questions to Consider in This Exercise

1. Is conflict present? If so, what forms does it take?
2. Does there seem to be an escalation of conflict in this conversation? If so, where did it occur? What caused it?
3. What could have been done differently to avoid or manage the conflict?
4. Does this conflict seem to be healthy or unhealthy? On what basis did you decide?
5. How is the relationship between the participants likely to be altered as a result of this communication transaction?

AN EXERCISE DESIGNED TO IDENTIFY CONFLICT IN CONTEMPORARY SETTINGS

Gather newspaper or magazine accounts of some current conflict between particular interest groups or institutions. Prepare a readable account of this conflict for class discussion. Suggest some possible causes for the conflict, immediate and long-term effects, and possible strategies for effectively managing this conflict. Analyze the breakdowns in channels of communication, and suggest ways in which communication could resolve this conflict. In addition, suggest measures which could be implemented to avoid occurrence of such conflict in the future.

AN EXERCISE DESIGNED TO ASSESS INSTITUTIONALIZED CONFLICT

Divide the class into four equivalent groups. Assign each group one of the following topics: football, baseball, tennis, basketball. Have each group discuss the rules governing each of these sports and how conflict is legally sanctioned in these activities as long as the rules are not violated. Next, have each group prepare a list of rules controlling conflict in each of these activities and present these to the rest of the class.

Discuss the following questions:

1. How are infractions of the rules dealt with in each of these sports?
2. How is conflict increased by violation of institutional rules?
3. Do situations involving excessive competition constitute valid forms of conflict? When might they not?
4. How should rules governing institutional conflict be determined?
5. Does society benefit from rule-governed institutional conflict? Why or why not?
6. What are some ways we can go about changing prescribed rules governing certain types of institutional conflict?

Epilogue
COMMUNICATION IN THE THIRD 100 YEARS: CAN HUMANITY AND TECHNOLOGY COEXIST PEACEFULLY?*

Gerald R. Miller

In the morning when Mr. A. enters his office he reads his incoming mail. . . . When his secretary enters the room, she gives him a cheerful "good morning," which he acknowledges with a friendly nod of his head while he continues with his conversation on the telephone with a business associate. Later in the morning he dictates a number of letters to his secretary, then he holds a committee meeting, where he gathers the advice of his associates.—Reusch and Bateson, 1951.

After a second cup of breakfast coffee, Mr. A leaves the table and goes across the hall to his "professional room." He activates the output on his computer terminal and receives a print-out of the morning's mail. Switching to input, he dictates a number of outgoing letters. Following a quick check of the master memory of the tapedeck system for business messages, he turns on the closed-circuit television network and participates in a teleconference with the rest of the company's board of directors.—Author Uncertain, 20??

In the 1950s and 1960s, casual perusal of a textbook or an essay about communication often revealed a scenario akin to the one sketched by Reusch and Bateson. Such vignettes exemplified the fact that people communicate with each other in many *ways* and stressed the sheer *frequency* of daily communicative contacts. Typically, they concluded with a pronouncement that the average American spends 70–75 percent of his or her waking hours communicating verbally, a statistic calculated to impress the reader with the importance of this fundamental human process.

The second scenario is imaginatively

*From *Centennial Review*, 21 (1977), pp. 176–193. Reprinted by permission.

excerpted from a hypothetical text or essay of the twenty-first century. Like its ancestral counterpart, it alerts the reader to the pervasiveness and significance of communication. But, in addition, it signals a fundamental change in the relationships of people; the friendly secretary's "Good morning" and the face-to-face contact of a business meeting have become quaint anachronisms of a bygone era, replaced by the technological wonders of mediated communication systems. Moreover, the environment envisioned by this vignette requires no fanciful excursion into the realm of science fiction, because, for the most part, the technology presently exists to create such a social milieu. Indeed, someone more skilled in soothsaying and futurism than myself could undoubtedly extend the scenario to the outer limits of our imaginations.

The tension and interplay between humanity—or, more specifically, human communicators—and technology—or, more precisely, mediated communication systems—provide the central focus for my remarks in this essay. Tempting as it is to speculate about the scientific communicative marvels of the next century or to paint a Utopian vision of the ideal communicative universe of tomorrow, I shall refrain, out of both a sense of uncertainty and humility. Instead, I shall undertake the much more modest (yet I would contend relatively important) task of analyzing several dimensions of one of the most critical, perplexing communication problems we face in the third 100 years: *the problem of achieving a harmonious, healthy coexistence between the system of human communicators and the technological systems of mediated communication.*

Conflict between these two spheres is virtually ensured by the fact that communication is a goal-directed activity. To state it differently, we communicate purposively, whether the purpose lies in the preservation and coordination of an entire society or in the individual's validation of self-concept through mutual human recognition with others. Because it is trivially true that all modes and forms of communication do not serve the same ends, trade-offs in the realization of objectives are inevitable. The trick, then, is to maintain some sort of reasonable balance between realization of the many objectives served by communication and, ultimately, the myriad of human needs satisfied by communication. Advances in communication technology pose the challenge of striking a balance between the individual, self-identity needs served by interpersonal communication and the collective, community needs satisfied by systems of mediated communication.

As the preceding point may seem abstruse, I will illustrate it by recourse to some contemporary examples, several of which will be discussed in greater detail later in this essay. One indicator of possible imbalance between today's human and technological systems can be seen in the current wide interest in sensitivity and encounter groups, communication experiences that ostensibly serve to authenticate the individual and sharpen his or her ability to relate meaningfully to others. Obviously, many societal forces have given rise to this movement; still, one factor often pointed to is the increasing depersonalization of communication, the tendency to rely upon mediated rather than interpersonal messages. As people construct communication barriers that isolate them from others—or, alternatively, as society imposes such barriers upon them—a heightened sense of alienation results, and the individual feels increasingly divorced from human contact. The distinguished contemporary psychologist Carl Rogers captures the dynamics of this process, offering the following explanation for the growth of the encounter movement:

> What accounts for the quick spread of groups? I believe the soil out of which this demand grows has two elements. The first is the increasing dehumanization of our culture, where the person does not count—only his IBM card or Social Security number. This impersonal quality runs through all the institutions in our land. The second element is that we are sufficiently affluent to pay attention to our psychological wants. As long as I am concerned over next month's rent, I am not very sharply aware of my loneliness. . . .
>
> But what is the psychological need that draws people into encounter groups? I believe it is a hunger for something the person does not find in his work environment, in his church, certainly not in his school or college, and sadly enough, not even in modern family life. It is a hunger for relationships which are close and real; in which feelings and emotions can be spontaneously expressed without first being carefully censored or bottled up; where deep experiences —disappointments and joys—can be shared; where new ways of behaving can be risked and tried out; where, in a word, he approaches the state where all is known and all accepted, and thus further growth becomes possible.[1]

Whether or not one believes that encounter groups afford a solution to these human concerns, the fact is inescapable that the concerns exist. And central to my ar-

[1] Carl R. Rogers, *Carl Rogers on Encounter Groups* (New York: Harper & Row, 1970), pp. 10–11.

gument is the expectation that as further refinements and advances in our ability to employ communication technology occur, these human concerns will be felt even more deeply.

Consider a second contemporary case in point, the so-called information explosion. Certainly, information is a primary ingredient of communication: we exchange information to improve the quality of decision making, and to the extent that it fosters better decisions, information is, indeed, power. Moreover, our vast expansion of the storehouse of information that can be brought to bear on decision making is partially attributable to advances in communication technology; one of the reasons information has grown by quantum leaps can be found in our increased ability to store and to retrieve it.

At first glance, this surplus of informational riches may seem to provide an unmixed social blessing. But what of the individual, schooled in the value of rational economic and political decision making? Given this informational glut along with the complexity of the economic and political problems that must be faced, how can he or she hope to marshal the resources needed for intelligent decision making? Currently, there are indications that many persons despair of trying; they are simply overwhelmed by the enormity of the situation. Unfortunately, their feelings of futility are often reinforced by the institutional leadership, who assures them that an attitude of unquestioning assent can be substituted for an act of informed participation. But as recent events have graphically illustrated, the leadership is not only fallible but also subject to despotic enticements—power corrupts no less in the realm of information than in any other human sphere. Thus society is confronted with a widening credibility gap, a general air of public cynicism, and a sharply accentuated sense of powerlessness on the part of the average citizen. For, in a sense, the citizen is between the proverbial rock and a hard place; on the one hand, the informational demands for effective participation in the political system seem mind-boggling; on the other, faith in the credibility of the political leadership appears naïve and doomed to betrayal.

No census of contemporary symptoms would be complete without a journey into the electronic world of the mass media. In the past several decades, countless research dollars and innumerable hours of intellectual effort and creativity have been devoted to assessing the behavioral impact of violent and pornographic media content.[2] I will not tarry here, for, regardless of the results of these studies, such writers as Marshall McLuhan have alerted us to the fact that media affect us in much more fundamental, pervasive ways.[3] "Come outside and watch the moon's eclipse with me, son," entreated a father in Florida recently. "I can't," the boy replied, "I'm watching it on TV."

This anecdote points to one of the most troublesome areas of possible current imbalance between the human and technological systems. Phrased in interrogative form, it can be stated as follows: how are human beings affected when there is a wholesale substitution of mediated events for direct experiences? Although social commentators may whimsically or caustically label the television set the "glass tit," Harry Harlow's research with primate surrogate mothers speaks forcefully to their limitations.[4] When mediated communication systems replace face-to-face contact with others, there is bound to be a decline in the satisfaction of certain individual needs, for much of our humanity is acquired by direct experiences with other persons and with our environments as a whole. Just as the mechanical theory of heat was never intended to replace the warmth and glow of a fireplace on a cold winter's night, the mass media were never meant to satisfy all basic human needs.

By now the thrust of my argument should be clear. Even in today's society, there is a danger that the balance between the system of human communicators and the systems of mediated communication technology has been upset. As our capacity for technological application grows, the chasm between the two systems will probably widen. Unless we anticipate this widening gulf and plan systematically to minimize its harmful effects, the consequences are likely to be, at best, detrimental and, at worst, catastrophic for both us and our heirs. Thus my earlier contention bears repeating: achievement of a harmonious, healthy coexistence between the system of human communicators and the technological systems of mediated communication constitutes one of the most critical, perplexing communication problems that must be faced in the third 100 years.

[2]See, for example, Seymour Feshbach and Robert Singer, *Television and Aggression.* (San Francisco: Jossey-Bass, 1971); also *Report of the Commission on Obscenity and Pornography* (New York: Bantam Books, 1970).

[3]Marshall McLuhan, *Understanding Media: The Extensions of Man* (New York: McGraw-Hill, 1964).

[4]See, for example, Harry F. Harlow, "Love in Infant Monkeys," *Scientific American*, 200 (June 1959), pp. 68–74; also Harry F. Harlow and Robert R. Zimmerman, "Affectional Responses in the Infant Monkey," *Science*, 130 (August 1959), pp. 421–432.

The remainder of this essay examines three dimensions of this problem. First, as some may feel the easiest solution is a moratorium on technological development, I will explain why I believe further technological expansion is all but inevitable. Second, I will identify some of the potential harmful effects that may result from an increased imbalance between the two systems, particularly as they relate to our inability to satisfy certain basic human needs. Finally, I will sketch some very general proposals for alleviating the problem, fully realizing that the many possible alternative strategies cannot be adequately explored in this short essay.

The Inevitable Growth of Communication Technology

There is an ancient anecdote about the man who, when asked why he was a mountain climber, answered that he climbed mountains because they were there.[5] This anecdote captures one of the reasons why the growth of communication technology is all but inevitable. *In communication, as in most other areas, technology is self-perpetuating.* If technology produces a commercial airliner that will travel 700 miles an hour, it seeks to develop one that will travel twice that speed. If the present technology permits the storage of 100,000 words on a three-by-five-inch microfiche card, new technology is immediately sought that will make it possible to increase the number of words to 200,000; reduce the size of the card to one and one-half by three inches; or, ideally, to do both. In other words, technological advancement is seen by some as an end in itself rather than a means toward other ends.

It is precisely this "technology for technology's sake" mentality that causes some humanistic writers to berate the technological enterprise. Actually, *if we assume that other factors are carefully weighed,* the mentality has a great deal to commend it, for it ensures continued creative efforts aimed at improving humanity's technological tools. The rub, of course, is that other factors are not always carefully weighed: some advocates of the supersonic airliner appeared oblivious to such troublesome considerations as noise pollution, stratospheric contamination, and the existing primitive state of the technology for moving passengers the 10 or 15 miles from the airport to a downtown hotel—to mention but a few.[6] Thus, as I have consistently implied, the self-perpetuating nature of technology often causes it to operate *in vacuo,* to push forward the technological frontiers with little thought about the harmful consequences or byproducts that may result.

Illustrations of this potential shortcoming abound in communication technology. For instance, while writing this essay, I have frequently found myself wondering how many of this volume's contributors would have tackled the task if

---

[5]Actually, the anecdote relates closely to the psychological notions of Alfred Adler concerning the innate need to strive for superiority. Once one technological mountain is climbed, another replaces it—the mountain range is potentially infinite.

[6]To mention the primitive state of the technology for moving passengers from airports to urban centers underscores the issue of *priorities.* What is the point of transporting people from New York to Chicago in one hour if it takes them two hours to get from O'Hare Airport to the Loop? In other words, solutions to certain technological problems logically precede solutions to others.

they had reason to believe that the finished product might be a microfiche card that could be carried in a vest pocket or a coin purse. After all, for the author (and, for that matter, the inveterate reader and collector), books have a familiar and pleasurable substance; one might say they have highly meaningful mass. Furthermore, books have a potential for tickling our aesthetic appreciation that is not shared by a microfiche card; the covers, typography, and art work of some books ensure their human value quite apart from the substance of their contents.

And finally, to be perfectly frank, there is a sense of ego-satisfaction associated with contributing to a book that cannot be matched, at least under present circumstances, by adding to the contents of a microfiche card. I cannot imagine that I would derive the same enjoyment from handing my friends or colleagues a microfiche card as I would from handing them a copy of this volume.

On the surface, the preceding example may seem relatively trivial, but I think it underscores an important point. Books communicate in many ways; they serve numerous purposes besides conveying information. No less of a hardheaded behaviorist than B. F. Skinner has told us that behavior is a function of its consequences.[7] My example suggests many positive contingencies that are linked with the reinforcer "book" but are not linked with the reinforcer "microfiche card." If this is so, should the latter largely replace the former as the major consequence of the behavior we label "writ-

[7]See B. F. Skinner, *Beyond Freedom and Dignity* (New York: Knopf, 1971); also B. F. Skinner, *About Behaviorism* (New York: Knopf, 1974).

ing," a sharp reduction in that behavior would be anticipated, at least until other contingencies of reinforcement came to be associated with microfiche cards.

This same radical behavioristic paradigm can be applied to other areas where technological advancement impacts human communicative endeavors, and, in most cases, the paradigm implies that the immediate consequence would be a reduction in these endeavors. But no matter how much we lament its potential motivational hazards, the Skinnerian dictum also provides telling evidence for the inevitability of continued technological growth in communication. For technological achievement is also accompanied by numerous contingencies of reinforcement: a societal and personal consequence of technological accomplishment is reward for the technologist. To be sure, opponents of this state of affairs may themselves succumb to the lure of technology and call for a reengineered society that divorces positive reinforcement from technological achievement. But, at present, such a call is likely to be little more than a cry in the wilderness; the self-perpetuating features of technology are too firmly embedded in our society to be dislodged in the short run.

Still, if self-perpetuation were the only reason for the continued growth of communication technology, the game of social reengineering might eventually be worth the candle, even if short-term outcomes proved minimal. Such is not the case; however, there is a more defensible, rational reason why communication technology will continue to expand. Mediated systems of communication are much more than expensive tinker toys for the amusement of the technologically astute. Inherent in the development of these systems is the potential for ameliorating certain difficult social problems and for satisfying certain pressing social and personal needs, and this promise of a better tomorrow also augers for the inevitability of continued technological growth.

To make this claim is not, of course, to say anything new or profound, but rather to reassert a basic tenet of our technologically oriented society. Nevertheless, the tenet has validity. A currently popular television commercial for one of the giants of the communication industry pictures a member of a monastic order toiling over the hand-lettering of a church document. Upon his presentation of the finished product to the abbot, his skill and industry are rewarded by a request for another 1,000 copies. Fortunately, the somewhat worldly monk numbers among his friends a person who has access to a copying machine. When the monk returns a short time later with the additional copies, the abbot, after perusing the documents briefly, gazes skyward and exclaims with great feeling, "It's a miracle!"—a miracle, naturally, wrought by the marvels of communication technology.

Even the modest contribution of communication technology to the solution of human problems would not be without its hazards *if* it were contended that the only useful way monks have to occupy their time is copying church documents. Given the implausibility of such a contention, however, one is hard-pressed to argue that there is anything ennobling or personally gratifying about the drudgery of hand-copying a document 1,000 times. Better the monk should get about the business of communing with the Almighty, saving souls, or other important spiritual undertakings.

This example is neither startling nor controversial: first, because the benefits are obvious; and, second, because the necessary communication technology is commonplace. But reflect again on the hypothetical scenario of Mr. A. in his professional room, the vignette that commenced this essay. This scenario envisions the eventual obsolescence (or, at least, the marked decline in importance) of a concept common to the educational confines of Michigan State University, the industrial setting of General Motors, and the governmental environs of the Pentagon: the concept of people assembling for work in centralized geographic locations. The potential social benefits of such a profound change in working habits are easily enunciated, for the daily pilgrimage to campus and business district exacts a heavy toll in environmental pollution, urban congestion, and energy drain—each of which is part of the inventory of pressing social problems that confront us in the third 100 years. Thus there are strong grounds for contending that the development of systems of mediated communication that would permit people to conduct their business at home could contribute mightily to curing or, at a minimum, arresting some of the apparent ills that afflict the society. Furthermore, the example is only one of countless possible applications of mediated systems. And the admitted promise of these systems virtually ensures continued experimentation, development, and ultimately, technological growth.

As I have already indicated, however, it

is easier and more enticing to speculate on the gains that may accrue from the heightened hegemony of mediated communication systems than it is to anticipate potential losses. For one thing, the credit side of the ledger is more easily calculated: the expertise exists to formulate equations specifying the reduction in pollution and the saving in energy resources that would result from various levels of reduction in automobile traffic. But where are the equations specifying how much and what kind of personal loss will occur from reduced face-to-face contact with a friendly secretary or a congenial colleague? Or, for that matter, where are the data pertaining to possible changes in patterns or outcomes of family communication that may result from increased propinquity of family members? Though behavioral scientists could make some educated guesses, these guesses would lack the precision and specificity that are possible when calculating the impact of certain variables on pollution levels. Still, if the potentially harmful effects of an escalating imbalance between the human and mediated communication systems are to be anticipated and countered, educated guesses are both necessary and infinitely better than nothing. Consequently, I will now turn my attention to this guessing game.

The Debit Side of the Ledger: Possible Harmful Effects of Increased Technology

Recently, while in San Francisco attending the national convention of a scholarly association, I was seated at a table in the bar with several colleagues from various parts of the United States. During the course of the evening, the conversation turned to the cost and inconvenience involved in attending the convention. Someone then suggested it would be possible to have the convention without any of the conventioneers leaving their homes. For the next hour, we shared the task of constructing such a scenario: we imagined a closed circuit television system linking all the major university communities throughout the country with coordination accomplished by means of a central control system. Each convention participant could turn on the set in his or her home and phase into the particular program of interest. Moreover, we agreed there would be no problem devising a system that would permit each participant to converse with other individuals or with small groups of people. Once we warmed to the discussion, we envisioned all manner of mediated communication legerdemain.

Nor was it difficult to imagine a number of social and economic benefits that might result from such a change in convention relationships. Think of the energy savings that would accrue from the reduction in travel! Furthermore, once the system became operational, a substantial monetary saving could be realized by the conventioneers and their university employers. And because this particular convention is typically held in late December, a mediated event would eliminate the strained family relations caused by a member of the household packing up and heading for the convention the day after Christmas.

For a time, the idea seemed promising. Suddenly, however, someone asked who among us would enjoy participating in such a convention. Not a person responded affirmatively; in fact, quite the opposite. There was consensus that our impromptu innovation would detract mightily from the value and enjoyment of the convention. Upon reflection, we realized that both our anticipation of attending the convention and the benefits realized from attendance were inextricably bound up in the assumption of face-to-face communication. All year long we had engaged in mediated communication with our colleagues: we wrote to them and talked with them on the phone about professional assignments; we read about each other's accomplishments in the association's news letter; we exchanged research reports and read each other's journal articles; in some cases, we even swapped videotaped lectures for use in our classes. Now we desired the opportunity to reminisce about graduate school days over dinner, to share information about common acquaintances, to brainstorm about ideas as yet insufficiently honed to provide the substance for published papers, and to observe again the mannerisms and idiosyncrasies that contributed to our unique mental pictures of one another. In addition, though we had examined their vitae and read their research, we wanted to *talk to* people whom we were considering as potential colleagues, for we truly believed that we could learn more about these persons (or at least, more about some aspects of them) in a 30-minute conversation than we could in many hours of reading their credentials. In short, we viewed the convention as an opportunity to satisfy personal and professional needs that could not be met through the most elaborate systems of mediated communication.

In itself, of course, our convention fantasy is of little import. As a microcosmic view of a larger problem, however, it assumes considerable significance. To be fully healthy and human, people require interpersonal contact; as I have already indicated, certain needs can only be satisfied by face-to-face relationships. Even when seeking to feather her corporate nest by means of persuasive advertising, Ma Bell remains honest and realistic enough to claim only that "long distance is *the next best thing* to being there." Given the inherent limitations of mediated communication, whenever an opportunity for personal contact is eliminated or drastically reduced because of the substitution of mediated systems, the opportunity to satisfy certain individual needs is lessened.

It would be presumptuous to proclaim that such a wholesale substitution of mediated for direct communication is bound to occur, for I have no hard evidence to support that contention. Still, certain social trends and examples portend this possibility. Medical examinations used to be conducted by doctors; increasingly they are carried out by computers. Certainly, I do not question that computers can process large amounts of physical data more effectively than a single human mind, no matter how well-trained; nor do I even challenge the anticipated rejoinder that a conscientious physician will augment the computer's analysis with a face-to-face explanation and diagnosis for the patient. Nevertheless, the information storage and processing capabilities of the computer have removed the doctor as an indispensable element of the diagnostic communicative process. With the heightened patient load resulting from our burgeoning population, it becomes easier to rationalize decreased personal contact with patients; after all, existing technology could be used to provide a print-out diagnosis for patients, particularly those with no unusual symptoms. And even if every patient has the benefit of an after-the-fact conversation with the physician, what about the questions and anxieties that arise during the examination itself? Will the opportunities for immediate feedback that exist when the doctor performs the examination be retained in a computerized diagnostic system? It is certainly no indictment of the medical profession to entertain some skepticism about the answer to this latter question.

Similarly, some of my research dealing with the effects of using video tape in the courtroom reflects the trend toward greater reliance on mediated communication in the legal system, for without increased acceptance of the idea, the studies would probably not have been conducted.[8] Once again, numerous potential social and legal benefits can be enumerated: video tape makes it possible to try a greater number of cases, thereby reducing backlog and relieving crowded dockets; it permits deletion of inadmissible testimony before jurors are exposed to it, thus assuring that verdicts will not be tainted by legally unacceptable material; and it allows expert witnesses to record testimony at their convenience, thus enhancing the likelihood that jurors will have the benefit of knowledgeable opinions and skilled insights.

At the same time, however, added reliance on video tape reduces personal contact between trial participants; what was formerly a drama of direct confrontation could conceivably become a series of taped depositions, a cut-and-paste celluloid montage. Perhaps the benefits alluded to earlier more than justify such a fundamental change in courtroom communication. On the other hand, there is cause to worry about the possible long-term effects of more extensive use of mediated courtroom communication on people's attitudes about the legal system. Trials serve the important social function of providing a sanctioned, accepted method for peaceful resolution of conflict. Some legal scholars and social scientists have argued persuasively that the dignity and majesty of the court rely heavily on the sense of psychological immediacy that accompanies direct confrontation of the contesting parties. In other words, satisfaction of the individual's desire for equitable proceedings—the feeling that "justice has been done"—may hinge on eyeball-to-eyeball encounters between trial participants. To the extent that this is true (and it must be granted that the jury is still out because of a paucity of data on the issue), the benefits of using video tape in trial proceedings may be more than offset by individual and collective loss of confidence in the legal system.

[8]See, for example, Gerald R. Miller, "The Effects of Videotaped Trial Materials on Juror Response," in *Psychology and the Law: Research Frontiers*, ed. Gordon Bermant (Lexington, Mass.: D.C. Heath, in press); Gerald R. Miller, "Jurors' Responses to Videotaped Trial Materials: Some Recent Findings," *Personality and Social Psychology Bulletin*, 1 (Fall 1975), pp. 561–569; and Gerald R. Miller, David C. Bender, F. Joseph Boster, B. Thomas Florence, Norman E. Fontes, John E. Hocking, and Henry E. Nicholson, "The Effects of Videotape Testimony in Jury Trials," *Brigham Young University Law Review*, 1 (1975, No. 2), pp. 331–373.

Thus far, I have speculated about some possible negative effects of greater use of mediated communication systems in areas of our lives where we have formerly relied primarily on interpersonal communication. When we scrutinize an established mediated communication system such as the mass media, other potential dangers are readily identifiable. *By their very nature, the mass media cater to cultural and sociological stereotypes; they largely sacrifice the many uniquenesses and idiosyncrasies of individuals at the altar of shared cultural norms and commonly held role prescriptions.* Such a communication strategy is dictated by the large, heterogeneous audience the media seek to attract and to persuade. To use a mundane, marketplace example, large deodorant sales depend upon appeals to shared expectations concerning the importance of social acceptability and social approval—smelling "nice" (or, more accurately, radiating the uniformly antiseptic order created by a deodorant) is championed as an ultimate cultural triumph, with no consideration of the possibility that some people may actually prefer the infinite variety of our many natural body chemistries. Of course, because individuality has always been a strongly held value in our society, media messages sometimes seek to pander to it. Thus viewers are assured that a particular perfume or cologne "interacts with normal body chemistry" to produce a unique scent for each wearer—a logically pernicious, if somewhat amusing, attempt to curry conformity through appeals to individuality.

Again, though the specific examples may seem relatively harmless or unimportant, the general problem that they underscore is not. As people spend more time consuming media messages, their habitual thinking patterns become increasingly stereotypic. Other persons are viewed as caricatures, undifferentiated one- or two-dimensional silhouettes of humanity. As a result, the task of relating to other people *as individuals* may become evermore difficult, and relationships may fixate at the cultural or sociological level. Each of us needs to be recognized as a unique individual, and each of us desires to share a few highly meaningful, intimate relationships with other persons. The closeness of such relationships largely depends on the quality of information participants are capable of sharing. If they find it difficult or impossible to transcend cultural and sociological similarities and to discover the unique traits and qualities that stamp them as individuals, anomie, alienation, and relational dissatisfaction are the almost certain consequences.[9]

Thus the most calamitous possible effect of increased reliance on mediated communication lies in people's diminished ability to function and relate as individuals, and even more important, in their subsequent failure to satisfy basic human needs that are served by interpersonal contact. To say this in no way demeans the important gains that can be realized by improved and expanded communication technology; rather, it underscores the necessity of maintaining a balanced perspective between the social benefits to

[9]The importance of moving beyond the cultural and sociological levels of a relationship is explored more extensively in Gerald R. Miller and Mark Steinberg, *Between People: A New Analysis of Interpersonal Communication* (Palo Alto, Calif.: Science Research Associates, 1975).

be reaped from advances in mediated communication systems and the individual rewards gained from face-to-face encounters. Given the pressing collective problems of the larger social community, how can such a communicative balance be achieved in the third 100 years? My excursion into America's third century ends with some truncated, tentative thoughts concerning this question.

Some Thoughts on Balancing the Scales Between Human Communicators and Mediated Systems

In order to maintain a healthy, harmonious future balance between human communicators and mediated communication systems, we must make attempts to anticipate potentially harmful consequences of wider reliance on communication technology and to estimate the extent of their psychological severity. Admittedly, this essay is short on facts; although I am certain that some individual needs suffer from heightened dependence on mediated communication, the precise kinds of damage, as well as the extent of harm, are unknown to me. My ignorance certainly is not the fault of the technologists; it results from a lack of relevant research—or, at least, clearly informative, relevant research—on the part of communication scientists, psychologists, and sociologists. To be sure, there is no shortage of speculative commentary about the problem, as witness this essay itself. But speculation is a poor substitute for systematic research, and one hopes that the third 100 years will witness an upswing in scientific inquiry aimed at shedding light on critical social problems such as the one addressed in this essay.

If the detrimental consequences of expanded use of communication technology can be anticipated, existing social institutions can be modified or new institutions created to eliminate or, at least, minimize harmful social fallout. Consider, for instance, my earlier remarks concerning the information explosion. Most thoughtful observers realize that the phenomenal growth of information has rendered obsolete a model of education predicated on a view of the student as an *information storer*. Not only is it impossible for today's students to store all the information they will need to conduct their professional and personal affairs intelligently, but advances in computer technology have also yielded instruments for storing information that are far more efficient than the human mind. What is needed, then, is an educational model that views the student as *information processor and retriever:* learning experiences should be designed to acquaint students with the techniques to be used in retrieving information and with the skills required to process information intelligently. Although some encouraging steps have been made in this direction, I suspect that many teachers continue to view the educational process as an exercise in storing isolated bits of information about the content area—bits of information not only inadequate for the disciplinary task but almost certain to become obsolete within a matter of years or even months.

In a similar vein, reductions in opportunities for interpersonal contact occasioned by wider use of mediated communication in particular institutional settings must be offset by the creation of added opportunities for human communion in other settings. If our hypothetical Mr. A no longer engages in face-to-face interaction with his business colleagues, he must find ways to satisfy interpersonal needs in leisure clubs, political organizations, church groups, or other similar endeavors. The real danger lies in the possibility that all these avenues will be increasingly closed to him, that communication encounters will become more highly automated in all walks of life. Should this happen, the human consequences of our growing technological sophistication are likely to be devastating.

Obviously, achievement of a harmonious communicative balance between human and mediated systems is a formidable task, one that will tax both our human ingenuity and our physical and economic resources in the coming decades. But as I have tried to indicate, it is not a task we can shirk, because the stakes for humanity are high. Robert Altman's recent film commentary on American society, *Nashville,* begins with a venerable country and Western singing star proclaiming tunefully, "We must be doing something right, to last 200 years." If society can maintain a healthy balance between the system of human communicators and the technological systems of mediated communication, it will be doing something right in the third 100 years, and the chances for our communicative survival in 2076 will be considerably enhanced.

Acknowledgments

For the materials copyrighted by authors, publishers, and agents, the authors of this book wish to acknowledge the following:

David K. Berlo, "The SMCR Model," in *The Process of Communication: an Introduction to Theory and Practice*, copyright © 1960 by Holt, Rinehart and Winston. Reprinted by permission of Holt, Rinehart and Winston. D. C. Bryant and Karl R. Wallace, *Fundamentals of Public Speaking*, 5th ed. (Englewood Cliffs, N.J., Prentice-Hall, 1976), pp. 445–446. Michael Burgoon, Judee K. Heston, and James McCroskey, *Small Group Communication: A Functional Approach*, p. 147, copyright © 1974 by Holt, Rinehart and Winston. Reprinted by permission of Holt, Rinehart and Winston. J. K. Burgoon, "The Unwillingness to Communicate Scale: Development and Validation," *Communication Monographs*, 43 (1976), pp. 60–69, and J. K. Burgoon and M. Burgoon, "Unwillingness to Communicate, Anomia-Alienation, and Communication Apprehension as Predictors of Small Group Communication," *Journal of Psychology*, 88 (1974), pp. 31–38. Richard Christie and Florence L. Geis, "An exercise to analyze willingness to manipulate," in *Studies in Machiavellianism*, Academic Press, New York. Melvin DeFleur and Sandra Ball-Rokeach, *Theories of Mass Communication*, 3d ed., p. 127, copyright © 1966, 1970, 1975 by Longman, Inc. Previously published by David McKay Co., Inc. Reprinted by permission of Longman, Inc. Roderick P. Hart, Gustav W. Friedrich, and William D. Brooks, *Public Communication*, p. 25, copyright © 1975 by Roderick P. Hart, Gustav W. Friedrich, and William D. Brooks. Reprinted by permission of Harper & Row, Publishers, Inc. Senator Edward M. Kennedy's Television Statement to the People of Massachusetts, July 26, 1969, © 1969 by The New York Times Company. Reprinted by permission. Karen R. Krupar, adapted from *Communication Games*, with permission from Macmillan Publishing Co., Inc., copyright © 1953 by The Free Press, a Division of Macmillan Publishing Co., Inc. J. C. McCroskey, "Measures of Communication-Bound Anxiety," *Speech Monographs*, 37 (1970), p. 277. J. C. McCroskey, "Personal Report of Communication Anxiety," *Speech Monographs*, 37 (1970), p. 277. J. C. McCroskey and D. W. Wright, "The Development of an Instrument for Measuring Interaction Behavior in Small Groups," *Speech Monographs*, 38 (1971), pp. 335–340. J. C. McCroskey and T. A. McCain, "The Measurement of Interpersonal Attraction," *Speech Monographs*, 41 (1974), pp. 261–266. James Michener, "Keeping Up," in *Parade Magazine*, November 21, 1971. Gerald R. Miller, "Communication in the Third 100 Years," *Centennial Review*, 1977, Vol. 21, pp. 176–193. C. E. Shannon and W. Weaver, "The Shannon and Weaver Model," Fig. 2, p. 26, of Michael Burgoon, *Approaching Speech/Communication*, 1st ed., copyright © 1974 by Holt, Rinehart and Winston, adapted from *The Mathematical Theory of Communication*, p. 98. University of Illinois Press, 1949. B. H. Westley and Malcolm S. MacLean, Jr., "A Conceptual Model for Communication Research," 34, *Journalism Quarterly*, 1957, pp. 31–38.

Index

Abstract symbols, 96, 120
Abstracting, 112
Accentuation
    nonverbal codes, 148
Accommodation, 66
Adoption process, 358
Advertising, 354
Affection, 460, 474
Affective nature, 10
Affiliate, 442
Affiliation, 459
Affinity, 461, 474
    developing, 471
Africans, 148
Age
    demographic analysis, 67
Agenda
    small group, 243
Agenda setting, 360, 369
Aggression, 486
    mass media, 362, 365
Aggressiveness and hostility
    personality analysis, 74, 87
Allness, 111, 121
American Indians, 98, 134
Americans, 130, 134, 135, 142, 148
Androgyny, 69
Anticlimactic organization, 306
Anxiety
    personality analysis, 75, 87
    public speaking, 275
Appearance: *see* Physical appearance
Approach-approach, 493, 503
Approach-avoidance, 494, 503
Appropriateness, 177
    self-disclosure, 205
Arabs, 130
Aristotle, 19, 27, 35, 409, 446
Artifacts, 144, 152, 159
Artificial conflict, 491, 503

Artificial dichotomies, 115, 121
Assembly effect bonus, 228
Assessment of agreement, 194
Attention, Selective: *see* Selective attention
    and perception
Attitude and value change, 362
Attitudes, 379, 398; *see also* Prior attitudes
Attitudinal message, 151
Attraction, 443
    dependence, 451
    nonverbal codes, 150
    phases, 455
    proximity, 447
    self-esteem, 451
    similarity, 446, 468
    social, 443
Audience, 19
    mass communication, 345, 362
    public speaking, 271, 272, 275
    topic relevance, 289
Audience analysis, 66, 67, 87, 275, 287, 296
Audience response, Observable: *see*
    Observable audience response
Authoritarian leader, 255, 257
Avoidance-avoidance, 494, 503
Awareness, 16, 17

Backtrack Programming, 245
Balance theories, 387, 401
Bales's Interaction Process Analysis, 235
Bargaining, 501
Behavior
    defensive, 86, 249
    goal-directed, 18
    kinesics, 136
    negative, 115
    nonverbal, 147, 148, 157
    patterns, 5
    purposive, 18
    self-disclosing, 472

Behavioral change, 362, 363, 365, 379
Behaviorism, 340
Being understood, 196, 197, 198, 209
Belief, 380, 400
Belief approach, 195
Berlo's SMCR model, 21, 27
Blindering, 110, 121
Blockers, 249
Body movements, 154, 156; *see also* Gesture;
    Kinesics
Brevity, 310
Broadcast media, 345, 352
Bypassing, 118, 121

Catharsis, 354
Catharsis hypothesis, 365
Cause-effect organization, 301
Centrality, 233
Channels, 21, 23, 232, 233
Character, 35, 38, 55
Charisma, 30
Childhood, 8
Children
    mass media, 362, 363
Chronemics, 134, 158
Chronic syndrome, 75
Claim, 406, 407, 425
Climactic organization, 306
Clothing, 141
    self-presentation, 153, 154, 157
    violations, 157
Coactive people, 193, 209
Codes
    nonverbal, 130, 158, 159
    symbolic, 21, 26
    voice, 144
Coercive power, 50, 56
Cognition and comprehension
    mass media, 362
Cognitive dissonance, 394, 401
Communication apprehension, 280
Communication breakdown, 6
Communication networks, 233
Communication problems, 4
Communication process, 8, 13, 26
Communication technology, 511, 514, 515

Comparison-contrast organization, 304
Competence, 35, 36, 55
Competition, 485
Complementary relationships, 199, 210
Composure, 39, 55
Comprehension, 77
Conclusions, 424
Conditioning, 340
    social, 117
Confirmation of self, 464
Conflict, 483, 512
Conflict management, 499, 504
Conformity, 250, 252
Congruity theory, 391, 401
Consistency theories, 382, 386, 401
Consummatory purpose, 12
Contagion, 273
Content approach, 194
Contradiction
    nonverbal codes, 149
    conversational speech, 309
Cool media, 343
Cosmetics, 141
Courtship, 150
Credibility, 34, 151, 345
    source, 41, 55, 425
Crowds, 133
Cultural and ethnic background: *see* Ethnic
    and cultural background
Cultural norms theory, 342
Cultural transmission, 355
Culture-level data, 177, 208, 461
Culture-specific displays, 148

Data, 406, 407, 425
Decision making: *see* Problem solving and
    decision making
Decoders, 22
Decoding, 23
Deductive organization, 300
Defensive behavior, 86, 249
Delivery
    public speaking, 83, 88, 294, 314
Demographic analysis of an audience, 67, 87;
    see also Audience analysis
Dependence, 451

Dialects, 151
Diffused point pattern, 135
Diffusion of innovations, 358
Diplomatic leader, 255
Direct perspective, 194, 209
Discussion, 247
Displaced point pattern, 135
Disposition, 294
Distrust and suspicion, 496
Dogmatism, 72
Dress: *see* Clothing
Duration
   chronemics, 135
Dyadic communication, 188, 190
Dynamogenic effect, 226

Economic and social background, 70
Editorial process, 353
Elaboration
   nonverbal codes, 149
Emblems, 148
Emergent leader, 253
Emotional appeals, 409, 410
Emotions, 10, 26, 109
   nonverbal, 147
   see also Pathos
Empathy 47, 56
Emphasis
   public speaking, 312
Enacted roles, 184
Encoder, 22
Encoding, 22
Encounter groups, 512
Entertainment
   mass media, 353, 356
Environment, 152
   manipulating others, 155
   public communication, 272
Environmental pollution, 357
Environmental theory, 343
Ethnic and cultural background
   kinesics, 139
   proxemics, 132
Ethnic and racial factors: *see* Racial and ethnic
   factors
Ethos, 35, 299, 409

Evidence, 408, 426
   appeals, 410
   identifying source, 422
Expectancy, Level of: *see* Level of expectancy
Expectations, 364
Experience, 102, 104
Experience factor, Limited: *see* Limited
   experience factor
Expert power, 51, 56
Exposure, Selective: *see* Selective exposure
External locus of control, 182, 209
Extroversion, 40, 55
Eye contact, 151
   public speaking, 316, 318

Face-to-face versus mediated conflict, 497, 503
Facial expression, 154, 156
   public speaking, 316, 318
Fact claim, 407
Fact hunting, 81
Failure to be understood, 17
Family-life patterns, 363
Fear appeals, 412, 425
Feedback, 9
   communicating with another, 192, 209
   mass communication, 338
   negative, 83, 86, 386, 451
   persuasion, 421
   public communication, 271, 274
   receiver variables, 81, 83, 87
   Westley-MacLean model, 23
Filtering system, 24, 25
First-order data, 408
Fluency, 144
Formal time, 134
Free feedback, 83
Frozen evaluation, 113
Furniture and furnishings, 145, 152

Gatekeeping, 24, 27, 338, 349, 353, 365, 368
   small groups, 254
Gender: *see* Sex differences
General American dialect, 151
Generalizations, 66
Gestures
   nonverbal codes, 11, 147, 151, 156
   public speaking, 316, 318

Goal-directed behavior, 18
Graduated reciprocation in tension reduction (GRIT), 499
Group achievement theory, 230
Group behavior, 486
Group cohesiveness, 227
Group identity, 247
Group norms, 226
Group personality, 226
Group structure, 248
Group-think, 252, 259

Haptics, 141, 157, 158
Hearing, 77
Heterophily, 43, 56
Hidden agenda, 249
Hierarchical organization, 302
Homophily, 43, 56
Hopi Indians, 98, 134
Horizontal influence, 342
Hostility: *see* Aggressiveness and hostility
Hot media, 343
Humor
    appeals, 414, 425
    public speaking, 313

Identification, 365
    public speaking, 299
Imitation behavior, 365
Impression management, 202, 466, 475
Individual difference theory, 339
Individual differences, 104
Induced conflict, 491, 503
Infants, 8
Inference, 107, 120
Inflammatory language, 79
Informal time, 135
Information
    mass media, 352
Information-centered model, 20
Information explosion, 513
Ingratiation, 457
Inhibiting factors, 95
Initial credibility: *see* Source credibility
Initial interactions, 469
Innovations, 368

Institutional conflict, 489
Institutional function, 352
Instrumental nature, 11, 26
Intelligence
    demographic analysis, 71
Intensional orientations, 109, 121
Intent, 13, 14, 16, 18, 26
Interaction Behavior Measure, 236
Interaction process, 224, 235
Interaction Process Analysis, 235
Intergroup conflict, 487
Internal inconsistency, 387
Internal locus of control, 184
Internal struggle, 484
Interpersonal attraction, 442
Interpersonal communication, 175, 336
Interpersonal conflict, 485, 503
Interpersonal trust, 84, 88
Interpretation
    mass communication, 353
    word, 119
Intragroup conflict, 486
Intrapersonal conflict, 484, 503
Introversion, 41
Invention
    public speaking, 294

Justification, 401

Kinesic norms, 137
Kinesics, 136, 152, 158
Knowing, Levels of: *see* Levels of knowing
Knowledge of reality, 111

Labeling, 113
Laissez-faire leader, 256
Language, 96, 97, 120; *see also* Dialects
Language intensity
    appeals, 416, 425
Lasswell model, 341
Latin Americans, 132, 134
Latitude of acceptance, 398, 402
Latitude of noncommitment, 398, 402
Latitude of rejection, 398, 402
Leadership, 248, 253
Learning process, 154

Learning theories of persuasion, 381, 383, 400
Leisure time, 363
Legitimate power, 52, 56
Level of expectancy, 445
Levels of knowing, 181, 186
Limited experience factor, 98
Linkage, 365
Listening ability, 77, 87
Logic, Improper, 251
Logic appeals, 409, 410
Logos, 299, 409

Mach, 76, 87
Machiavellianism, 76, 87
Manipulation, 12, 155
Meaning, 10, 26, 118
Memory: *see* Retention
Mass communication, 335
Mediated conflict, 497, 503
Memory
    public speaking, 294
Message, 21, 22
    attitudinal, 151
Message elements
    chronemics, 135
    kinesics, 137
Message flow, 337
Message storage, 337
Message strategies, 405
Metamessages
    nonverbal, 148, 159
Meta-metaperspective, 196
Metaperspective, 195, 209
Metaphors, 416
Mixed-level relationships, 181
Models of communication, 18, 27
Monroe's motivated sequence, 305
Motive bases, 49
Multistep flow, 347
Mutual trust, 50

Negative behavior, 115
Negative feedback, 83, 86, 386, 451
Negative reinforcement, 384, 400
Negative sanctions, 50, 56
Negotiated roles, 183, 186, 209

Negotiation, 501
Noise, 21, 103
Nonfluencies, 78
Nonverbal behavior, 16, 147, 148, 157
Nonverbal communication, 129
Norms
    group, 226
    social, 356
    violations, 157
Note taking, 80

Objects of orientation, 24
Observable audience response, 274
Observation, 107, 120
One-sided message, 419
One-step flow, 346
Opinion leaders, 338, 342, 347, 368
Opinionated language, 418, 425
Opinions, 380, 400
Opposition, 486
Optimal heterophily, 45, 56
Originality, 312
Outlining, 306

Paralanguage, 143, 158
    self-presentation, 153, 154, 155
Parallel relationship, 201
Parallel structure
    public speaking, 311
Pathos, 299, 409
Perceived competence, 36, 37
Perceived composure, 39
Perceived privacy, 190, 209
Perception, 98, 120
    affinity, 461
    sensory, 346
    see also Selective perception
Perceptual phenomenon, 35; *see also*
        Perception
Personal attraction, 132
Personal space, 131
    courting, 151
Personality analysis, 72, 87
Personalization
    public speaking, 313

Persuasion, 377
    applications and message strategies, 405
    small group, 240
Physical appearance, 140, 153, 156, 157
Physical attraction, 443, 453, 468, 473; *see also*
        Attraction
Pitch (voice), 144
    public speaking, 315
Play theory, 344
Pointing, 110, 121
Polarization, 115, 121
Policy claim, 407
Political radicalism, 357
Pollution, Environmental: *see* Environmental
        pollution
Positive reinforcement, 384, 400
Posture, 156
Power, 48, 56, 473
Pragmatics, 492
Predictions, 66, 176, 208
Preening behavior, 150
Prescribed role, 182, 209
Prime attitude, 398
Principles and pragmatics, 492, 503
Print media, 345
Prior attitudes
    personality analysis, 75, 87
Problem solving and decision making, 241
Process organization
    public speaking, 303
Profit-making media, 354
Proxemics, 130, 158
Proximity
    attraction, 447, 473
Psychological dispositions, 98
Psychological-level data, 180, 208
Psychological noise, 21
Public communication, 269; *see also* Mass
        communication
Public speaking
    evaluating, 287
    planning, 287
    preparing and delivering, 293
Punishment, 384, 400
Purposive behavior, 18
Pyramidal organization, 306

Qualifiers, 416
Quasi-courtship, 150

Race
    kinesics, 137
    proxemics, 131
Racial and ethnic factors
    demographic analysis, 71
Real conflict, 490, 503
Reality, Knowledge of: *see* Knowledge of
        reality
Realization or failure of realization, 195
Receiver, 9, 22, 65, 86, 120
Receiver-oriented definitions, 14, 16, 26
Receiver variables, 65
Reciprocity, 206
Recreation: *see* Entertainment
Redundancy
    nonverbal codes, 148
    public speaking, 310
Referent power, 51, 56
Reflective-projective theory, 344
Reflective thinking, 242, 258
Reflective thinking organization, 305
Reinforcement, 363, 384, 400
Relational communication, 441
Relational messages, 149
Retention, 77; *see also* Selective retention
Reward power, 49, 56
Rewards, 443
Risks
    inference-observation dilemma, 108, 120
    self-disclosure, 207
Risky shift, 228, 252
Roles
    enacted, 184
    interpersonal communication, 182, 208
    negotiated, 183, 186, 209
    prescribed, 182, 209
    sex, 69
    small group, 247
    women's, 114

Second-order data, 408
Selective attention and perception, 101, 340
Selective exposure, 100

Selective perception, 103, 120, 340
Selective retention, 105
Selectivity, 100, 111, 120
  mass communication, 351
Self-concept, 462, 474
  trust, 85
Self-disclosure, 202, 207, 210, 246
  risks, 207
Self-disclosing behavior, 472
Self-esteem, 451, 473
  personality analysis, 73, 87
Self-estrangement, 484
Self-image, 496
Self-improvement, 498
Self-presentation, 153, 159
Sensory perception, 346; see also Perception
Sequencing, 135
Sex
  demographic analysis, 68
Sex differences
  kinesics, 137
  nonverbal codes, 147
  physical attraction, 453
  proxemics, 131
Sex roles
  demographic analysis, 69
Sexual excesses
  mass media, 357
Short-term sensory storage, 101
Similarity and attraction, 468, 473
Small-group communication, 223
Small-group structure, 231
SMCR model: see Berlo's SMCR model
Social and economic background, 70
Social attraction, 443
Social categories, 341
Social class, 139
Social comparison theory, 229
Social conditioning, 117
Social exchange theory, 230
Social facilitation, 226
Social functions, 355
Social isolation, 459
Social judgment theory, 382, 397, 401
Social norms, Control of, 356
Social relationships, 441

small group, 239
Social relationships theory, 341
Sociability, 40, 55
Sociological-level data, 178, 208, 341
Sociometric theory, 230
Source, 9, 21, 337
Source assertion, 408
Source credibility (initial), 41, 55, 56, 425
  see also Credibility
Source-oriented definitions, 14, 15, 26
Source variables, 33
Spatial organization
  public speaking, 302
Speaker characteristics, 79
Speaker suitability, 288
Speech, 96
  rate of, 81, 144, 156, 315
  volume, 315
Stage fright, 276
Status, 456, 473
  proxemics, 131
Stereotypes, 70, 178
  kinesics, 137
  small group, 250
Stimuli and responses, 383, 400
Structure-function organization
  public speaking, 304
Structuring interaction, 152
Style
  public speaking, 294, 298, 309, 318
Substitution, 149
Suspicion: see Distrust and suspicion
Symbolic codes, 21, 26
Symbolic displays, 146
Symbols, 11, 26, 96, 118, 120
Symmetrical relationships, 198, 209
Symmetry theory, 391, 401
Syntality, 229
Systematic desensitization, 284

Task attraction, 443
Task orientation, 255
Taste, Public, 363
Technical time, 134
Technology: see Communication technology
Terminal credibility, 42, 56

Territoriality, 130
Therapy groups, 245
Thinking, 98; *see also* Reflective thinking
Third-order data, 409, 425
Time, 135
Timing, 135
Topic choice
  public speaking, 288
Touching: *see* Haptics
Transactional credibility, 42, 56
Transactional nature, 9, 26, 65
True dichotomy, 115, 121
Trust: *see* Interpersonal trust; Mutual trust
Two-sided message, 419, 421
Two-step flow, 347

Unbalanced situation, 390
Uncertainty, 465, 478
Understanding, 118, 195, 196, 197, 198, 209
Universal displays, 147

Valence, 206
Value, 380, 400
Value claim, 407, 425
Variables
  inhibiting, 96
  receiver, 65
  source, 33

Variety
  public speaking, 312
Verbal complements, 148
Violations of norms, 157
Violence
  control, 356
  mass media, 362, 365, 369
Violent versus nonviolent conflict, 491, 503
Visual audience condition, 83
Vividness
  public speaking, 310
Vocal characteristics, 144
Vocal patterns, 144
Vocal cues
  self-presentation, 153
Vocal segregates, 144
Voice, 143, 156, 315, 318
  intensity, 144
  quality, 144, 315
  see also Speech

Warrant, 406, 407, 425
Westley-MacLean model, 23, 27
Whorf-Sapir hypothesis, 98, 120
Women's roles, 114
Word usage, 118
Words, 96, 118

Zero feedback condition, 83
Zero-sum situation, 491